OXFORD WORLD'S CLASSICS

PYGMALION, HEARTBREAK HOUSE, AND SAINT JOAN

GEORGE BERNARD SHAW was ~~~~~~~~~~~~~~~
of Ireland's well-established P~~~~~~~~~~~~
alcoholism and business ineptit~~~~~~~~~~~~
decline, and Shaw left school at ~~~~~~~~~~~
office. In 1876, he moved to Lo~~~~~~~~~~~~~
tures, joined political and cultu~~~~~~~~~~~~
furthered his learning in the Reading Room of the British ~~~~~~
In 1884, he became a member of the newly founded Fabian Society,
which was devoted to political reform along socialist principles, and
remained one of their leading pamphleteers and campaigners for
much of his life. Starting in the mid-1880s, Shaw worked variously as
a book, music, art, and theatre reviewer, and this cultural criticism
formed the basis of his important studies *The Quintessence of Ibsenism*
(1891) and *The Perfect Wagnerite* (1898). He began playwrighting in
earnest in the early 1890s, with *Widowers' Houses* (1892), but his
early plays were largely unperformed as they did not conform with
the commercial theatre's demands for musicals, farces, and melodramas. Shaw finally found success in New York in 1898 with *The
Devil's Disciple* (1897). With the windfall from the production, he
retired from journalism and married Irish heiress Charlotte Payne-
Townshend. In the new century, Shaw embarked on forging a theatre
of the future, transforming the problem and discussion play into
a theatre of ideas with *Man and Superman* (1903), *John Bull's Other
Island*, and *Major Barbara* (1905). The popular writer of *Fanny's
First Play* (1911) and *Pygmalion* (1912) became a pariah following his
condemnation of jingoistic patriotism at the outset of the First
World War. His comeback was slow but he achieved worldwide
acclaim as the writer of *Saint Joan* (1923) and was awarded the 1925
Nobel Prize for Literature. He continued to write plays, including
The Apple Cart (1928) and *Geneva* (1936), but his output dropped off
significantly in the 1940s. Shaw died at his home in Ayot St Lawrence
in 1950.

BRAD KENT is Professor of British and Irish Literatures at
Université Laval in Quebec City, Canada. His publications include
The Selected Essays of Sean O'Faolain (McGill-Queen's University
Press, 2016) and *George Bernard Shaw in Context* (Cambridge
University Press, 2015). He is general editor of the Oxford World's
Classics series of Bernard Shaw's writings.

OXFORD WORLD'S CLASSICS

*For over 100 years Oxford World's Classics have brought
readers closer to the world's great literature. Now with over 700
titles—from the 4,000-year-old myths of Mesopotamia to the
twentieth century's greatest novels—the series makes available
lesser-known as well as celebrated writing.*

*The pocket-sized hardbacks of the early years contained
introductions by Virginia Woolf, T. S. Eliot, Graham Greene,
and other literary figures which enriched the experience of reading.
Today the series is recognized for its fine scholarship and
reliability in texts that span world literature, drama and poetry,
religion, philosophy and politics. Each edition includes perceptive
commentary and essential background information to meet the
changing needs of readers.*

OXFORD WORLD'S CLASSICS

GEORGE BERNARD SHAW

Pygmalion,
Heartbreak House,
and *Saint Joan*

Edited with an Introduction and Notes by
BRAD KENT

OXFORD
UNIVERSITY PRESS

OXFORD

UNIVERSITY PRESS

Great Clarendon Street, Oxford, OX2 6DP,
United Kingdom

Oxford University Press is a department of the University of Oxford.
It furthers the University's objective of excellence in research, scholarship,
and education by publishing worldwide. Oxford is a registered trade mark of
Oxford University Press in the UK and in certain other countries

Editorial material © Brad Kent 2021

The moral rights of the author have been asserted

First published as an Oxford World's Classics paperback 2021

Impression: 1

British Library Cataloguing in Publication Data

Data available

ISBN 978-0-19-879328-1

Printed and bound in Great Britain by
Clays Ltd, Elcograf S.p.A.

ACKNOWLEDGEMENTS

I HAVE benefited from the support of several people in assembling this edition. Marianne Paquin helpfully tracked down scores of sources. Similarly, the staff and archivists at Université Laval's library, the British Library, the Victoria & Albert Theatre and Performance Archives, and the University of Texas at Austin's Harry Ransom Center have facilitated my research in countless ways. I have benefited enormously from collaborating with Sos Eltis, David Kornhaber, Liz Miller, Jim Moran, Larry Switzky, and Matt Yde—my fellow editors in the Oxford World's Classics' Shaw series, wonderfully gifted scholars, and kind people all. Leonard Conolly, Nicky Grene, Gustavo Rodríguez Martín, and Michel Pharand have been generous with their friendship, expertise, advice, and criticism. At Oxford University Press, Luciana O'Flaherty and Kizzy Taylor-Richelieu have provided guidance at every stage of the series' development. And, as always, I am grateful to Anne, Ryan, and Zoé for all of the love and the laughs.

CONTENTS

INTRODUCTION

By the time *Pygmalion* opened in London on 11 April 1914, Shaw was the best-known personality in England. The play's success in the West End and across the globe solidified his reputation as the world's greatest living playwright. Within a matter of months, though, he fell from those heights, becoming public enemy number one for his criticism of British jingoism at the outset of the First World War. Prime Minister Herbert Henry Asquith told people that Shaw ought to be shot, many of the colleagues whom Shaw had supported and aided over the years turned their backs on him, and his plays thereafter were rarely performed. Yet just as the Church canonized the former heretic Joan of Arc in 1920, Shaw's play about her led to his own apotheosis and redemption: *Saint Joan* stormed stages, garnered some of the strongest reviews of his career, and led to his public adoration. His play *Mrs Warren's Profession*, which the British censorship had banned for over three decades, was suddenly granted a licence for a public performance, causing Shaw to remark that he was 'in the very odor of sanctity after St Joan'.[1] Producers, consumed with a Shaw 'monomania',[2] now flooded him with requests to perform his works, and he was awarded the 1925 Nobel Prize for Literature. The plays in this volume are the fruits of these three distinct personal contexts, representing two pinnacles separated by a traumatic nadir. Although highly critical of melodramas, even Shaw would admit that audiences always love a good comeback story.

They also love the self-made man's tale of rags to riches. Born in Dublin on 26 July 1856 to a family in economic and social decline, Shaw was raised in genteel poverty. Having left school at the age of 15, he clerked for a land agency until he fled his native Ireland for London on 1 April 1876. As he later commented, 'London was the literary centre for the English language, and for such artistic culture as the realm of the English language (in which I proposed to be king) could afford.'[3] Once settled, he adopted a highly disciplined routine of intellectual betterment, spending his days in the Reading Room of the British Museum where in five years he churned out five novels, four of

---

[1] Letter of 20 August 1924, in *CL* iii. 883.
[2] Letter of 21 January 1925, in *CL* iii. 901.
[3] Bernard Shaw, *Immaturity* (London: Constable, 1931), pp. xxxiv–xxxv.

which appeared episodically in socialist periodicals. The autodidactic
Shaw read widely and voraciously, attended public debates on all manner of social, political, economic, and cultural topics, and became
a member of a number of literary associations. In 1884, he joined the
newly founded Fabian Society, an organization dedicated to popular-
izing socialist objectives, and quickly became its most recognizable
proponent.

If in *Pygmalion* Higgins is the Pygmalion-creator and Eliza is his
Galatea-creation, then we might best understand Shaw as Pygmalion
to his own Galatea. Upon receiving a reader's ticket for the British
Museum, he immediately consulted books on etiquette, including
Manners and Tone of Good Society, or Solecisms to be Avoided, by
A Member of the Aristocracy.[4] However, his rise was slow and he only
completed his first play, *Widowers' Houses*, at the age of 36. He wrote
another nine plays in the last decade of the nineteenth century, but they
were largely unperformed, failing to find favour with the commercial
theatres and instead depending upon the nascent independent theatre
movement for smaller-scale productions with limited runs for a coterie
audience. He was able to survive those first few years in London thanks
to his mother, who fed and lodged him. However, with friends vouch-
ing for his abilities, Shaw embarked on a career in journalism in the
1880s and was variously employed as a music and art critic, a book
reviewer, and eventually a theatre critic. Despite this rather modest
beginning, Shaw candidly confessed to a friend, 'My goal is to incarnate the Zeitgeist.'[5]

Through his memberships in various cultural associations throughout the 1890s, most notably the Independent Theatre Society and its
successor, the Stage Society, Shaw formed allegiances with a number of
other avant-gardist individuals who sought to forge drama for a new
age. One of them, Harley Granville Barker, was perhaps the most tal-
ented actor of his generation. Together with theatre manager
J. E. Vedrenne, in 1904 Barker gave the New Drama its first English
home when they signed a lease for London's Court Theatre. Over the
three years that followed, they staged the best of classical and contemporary European drama. And at the heart of it all was Bernard Shaw: of
the Court's 988 performances, 701—an astounding 71 per cent—were

[4] Dan H. Laurence, 'Shaw, Books, and Libraries', *Papers of the Bibliographical Society
of America*, 69 (1975), 465–79, at 466.
[5] Letter of 31 August 1889, in *CL* i. 221.

Shaw's plays, including several world premieres.[6] Politicians, amongst
them Prime Minister Arthur Balfour, several members of his Cabinet,
and leaders of the Opposition, repeatedly flocked to the Court to see
how Shaw treated such pressing social issues as poverty and the Irish
question. His popularity was cemented when King Edward VII, attending a Royal Command Performance of Shaw's *John Bull's Other Island*
on 11 March 1905, laughed so hard that he broke his chair. With the
help of the Court's gifted ensemble of actors, Shaw became the most
notable playwright of his generation. After a little over a decade, the
zeitgeist had come round to him.

Shaw's Style and Technique

Just as the contexts surrounding the three plays in this volume are
decidedly dissimilar, so too are the plays themselves. Indeed, Shaw
works in three distinct modes: the problem-play comedy of *Pygmalion*,
the modernist experimentation of *Heartbreak House*, and the history of
Saint Joan. Yet the well-known adjective 'Shavian' indicates anything
that is typical of him, and despite their apparent generic and tonal differences, each of these plays illustrates the inimitable Shaw style.

Shaw was somewhat dismissive about cultivating style in the sense of
fashioned prose. Nearing his eightieth year, he claimed: 'I have never
aimed at style in my life: style is a sort of melody that comes into my
sentences by itself.'[7] This notion of melody is central to any discussion
of Shaw's style and the leitmotifs of his characters' linguistic patterns.
He regularly referred to the cast in musical terms: this actor was a bass,
that one a tenor, this one a soprano, that one an alto. His mother was
a gifted mezzo-soprano who taught singing lessons, and Shaw himself
was a gifted amateur pianist; thus it was perhaps inevitable that music
had a significant effect on how he heard spoken language. In 1942,
referring to Shaw as 'probably the best music critic who ever lived', the
poet W. H. Auden remarked that 'his writing has an effect nearer to that
of music than the work of any of the so-called pure writers'.[8] Likewise,
Lewis Casson, a leading British actor and director, claimed that 'His

[6] For accounts of the Court Theatre, see Desmond McCarthy, *The Court Theatre*
(London: A. H. Bullen, 1907) and Dennis Kennedy, *Granville Barker and The Dream of
Theatre* (Cambridge: Cambridge University Press, 1985).

[7] Shaw, 'Preface', *Immaturity*, p. xxxix.

[8] W. H. Auden, 'The Fabian Figaro', *The Commonweal*, 23 October 1942; repr. in
W. H. Auden: Prose, ii. *1939–1948*, ed. Edward Mendelson (Princeton: Princeton
University Press, 2002), 158–61, at 161.

combined technical training in music and public speaking enabled him always to analyse how effects were got, and to pass on the knowledge of how as well as why. It was the same training that enabled him in his writing instinctively to arrange his thought and his words so that when spoken with their full intent and meaning they produce good music in melody, rhythm, and phrasing; and surely that is the test of good prose.'[9] Casson's wife, the actor Sybil Thorndike, who played the lead role in the first London production of *Saint Joan*, recalled that Shaw 'knew the exact tune of every line he wrote. It was like a musical score.'[10]

However, Shaw's style has proven difficult to pin down, to the point that some critics have claimed that he does not have one.[11] Yet so recognizable was his style that when he anonymously submitted *Pygmalion* to the British censor of plays, the reader immediately detected its authorship: 'It is understood that this is by Bernard Shaw and on internal evidence no one else could have written it.'[12] Other commentators have concluded that his plays have one overarching trait: they are decidedly undramatic. William Archer, Shaw's long-time friend and colleague who also happened to be one of the most perceptive drama critics of the day, admitted that any assessment of Shaw's technique was a challenge for many people:

Perhaps the most difficult task that criticism can attempt is a valuation of Mr Bernard Shaw as a dramatist. Some people simplify the task by denying that he is a dramatist at all, and considering him purely as a merchant of ideas. They regard his plays as mere extensions or illustrations of his prefaces. But this is an altogether too high-handed method of getting out of the difficulty.[13]

---

[9] Sir Lewis Casson, 'G.B.S. at Rehearsal', in Raymond Mander and Joe Mitchenson (eds), *Theatrical Companion to Shaw: A Pictorial Record of the First Performances of the Plays of George Bernard Shaw* (London: Rockcliff, 1954), 16–18, at 17.

[10] Elizabeth Sprigge, *Sybil Thorndike Casson* (London: Gollancz, 1971), 67.

[11] See e.g. Jonathan Goldman, 'Celebrity', in Brad Kent (ed.), *George Bernard Shaw in Context* (Cambridge: Cambridge University Press, 2015), 255–64.

[12] G. S. Street, Reader's report on *Pygmalion*, 23 February 1914 (LC P).

[13] William Archer, *The Old Drama and the New: An Essay in Re-Evaluation* (London: William Heinemann, 1923), 341–2. His biographer and fellow Irishman St John Ervine also noted this tendency, suggesting that such was the general opinion with which genius was met: 'Mr Shaw was told that his plays were "not plays" when he first set himself to assault the English stage. Even now, when his renown is world-wide, gentlemen arise and assert with all the pomposity of arid professors that he is "not a dramatist." They would have said the same of Shakespeare had they been contemporary with him, nor could Sophocles have hoped, had they lived in his time, to escape from their censure.' See St John Ervine, *How to Write a Play* (London: George Allen & Unwin, 1928), 96.

Eric Bentley provides a more capacious and perceptive catalogue of Shaw's qualities: 'the endlessly witty and eloquent talk, the wideness of reference in the dialogue, the incredible liveliness of the characters, the swift tempo, the sudden and unexpected reverses (especially anti-climaxes), in a phrase, the unusual energy coupled with the unusual intellect'.[14] These are many of the hallmarks of Shaw's style, the iconoclastic combination of which informs our understanding of what it means to be 'Shavian'.

Rather than simply parroting the charge that Shaw is undramatic, it is more useful to understand that the definition of drama was founded on conventions, which, as Shaw insisted, needed to be radically over-turned. In the 1890s, drama was informed by action. Action, however, was narrowly conceived as physical action and intrigue. For Shaw, this notion was encapsulated in the rigid structure of the so-called well-made play. Shaw considered well-made plays—popularized by Eugène Scribe and Victorien Sardou—too constructed and artificial, and vilified them as 'Sardoodledom'.[15] He insisted that he was 'furi-ously opposed' to 'the method and principles' of such contemporaries as Arthur Wing Pinero, Henry Arthur Jones, and Oscar Wilde: 'They were all for "constructed" plays, the technique of construction being that made fashionable by Scribe in Paris, and the sanction claimed for it no less than that of Aristotle.'[16] He therefore had to fight not only what was currently fashionable, but also the conventions and rigid generic boundaries in place since the advent of Western theatre in ancient Greece.

As theatre critic for the *Saturday Review* from 1895 to 1898, Shaw's articles were, he admitted, 'a siege laid to the theatre of the XIXth Century by an author who had to cut his own way into it at the point of the pen, and throw some of its defenders into the moat'.[17] Taken as a whole, 'they contain something like a body of doctrine, because when I criticized I really did know definitely what I wanted'.[18] As the com-mercial theatres would not make room for the type of plays he wrote and wished to see, Shaw criticized the fashionable drama, exposing its

[14] Eric Bentley, *Bernard Shaw* (1947; New York: Limelight Editions, 1985), 80.

[15] Bernard Shaw, 'Sardoodledom', *Our Theatre in the Nineties*, i (London: Constable, 1932), 133–40.

[16] Bernard Shaw, 'My Way with a Play', *London Observer*, 29 September 1946; repr. in Bernard Shaw, *Shaw on Theater*, ed. E. J. West (New York: Hill and Wang, 1958), 267–73, at 268.

[17] Bernard Shaw, *Our Theatre in the Nineties*, vol. i, p. v.

[18] Bernard Shaw, *Our Theatre in the Nineties*, vol. i, p. vi.

mechanical constructions, lack of intelligence, and support of conservative values. 'Stage life', he lamented, 'is artificially simple and well
understood by the masses; but it is very stale; its feeling is conventional; it is totally unsuggestive of thought because all its conclusions
are foregone; and it is constantly in conflict with the real knowledge
which the separate members of the audience derive from their own
daily occupations.'[19]

As opposed to constructedness and emphasis on outward action,
Shaw instead recognized that drama was first derived from the conflict
of ideas and the conflicts within individuals. He found evidence for this
in the plays of Henrik Ibsen, who for Shaw was a revolutionary writer
because he proffered a new dramatic structure. After Ibsen, Shaw
declared, the 'new technical factor in the art of popular stage-play making' of 'every considerable playwright' is

the discussion. Formerly you had in what was called a well-made play an
exposition in the first act, a situation in the second, and unravelling in the
third. Now you have exposition, situation, and discussion; and the discussion is the test of the playwright. The critics protest in vain. They declare
that discussions are not dramatic, and that art should not be didactic.
Neither the playwrights nor the public take the smallest notice of them.[20]

The discussion, however, is not didactic from the point of view of
Shaw merely creating straw men that are done away with one by one to
allow his socialist ideals to prevail. Unlike the unilinear writing found
in the essays he wrote as a public intellectual or the arguments of his
prefaces, Shaw's plays are multilinear.[21] Yet all too often critics have
confused the public man with the artist, seeing the discussion in his
plays as mere extensions of his polemics because they engage with
many of the social and political issues he dealt with in his journalism
and Fabian Society pamphlets. In these accounts, Shaw's characters,
despite their vastly different opinions, are denigrated as lifeless puppets that merely spout Shaw's views. Instead, Shaw works through the
issues, testing them via characters who hold a variety of positions and
at times change their perspectives. He thereby invites his audiences and

[19] Bernard Shaw, 'A Dramatic Realist to His Critics', *New Review* 11 (July 1894); repr.
in Bernard Shaw, *Shaw on Theater*, 18–41, at 20.

[20] J. L. Wisenthal, *Shaw and Ibsen: Bernard Shaw's The Quintessence of Ibsenism and
Related Writings* (Toronto: University of Toronto Press, 1979), 210. Shaw published the
revised edition in 1913, the year *Pygmalion* was first staged.

[21] For more on this point, see the introduction to Arnold J. Silver, *Bernard Shaw: The
Darker Side* (Stanford, CA: Stanford University Press, 1982).

readers to do the same. This is also the point of his inconclusive endings, which tend to subvert or undermine expectations: the audience's
dissatisfaction with the lack of resolution incites reflection and further
discussion.

Shaw noted of his characters:

They are all right from their several points of view; and their points of view
are, for the dramatic moment, mine also. This may puzzle the people who
believe that there is such a thing as an absolutely right point of view, usually
their own. It may seem to them that nobody who doubts this can be in
a state of grace. However that may be, it is certainly true that nobody who
agrees with them can possibly be a dramatist, or indeed anything else that
turns upon a knowledge of mankind. Hence it has been pointed out that
Shakespear had no conscience. Neither have I, in that sense.[22]

Even T. S. Eliot, who was otherwise adversarial in his opinion of Shaw,
esteemed this ability in a review of *Saint Joan*: 'No one can grasp more
firmly an idea which he does not maintain, or expound it with more
cogency, than Mr Shaw. He manipulates every idea so brilliantly that he
blinds us when we attempt to look for the ideas with which he works.'[23]
No one viewpoint is entirely true, and thus each character has their
limitations. The result is a more encompassing vision of the world,
one that frustrates people who expect consistency in personality and
finality in plot.[24] Recognizing this equivocal trait in his plays, critics
have referred to it in both derogatory and admiring terms as Shavian
paradox.[25]

A Shaw play generally has three characters—though on occasion
more—who represent different viewpoints. In a rhetorical sense, these
represent thesis, antithesis, and synthesis, with the third character
undergoing a conversion. In these instances, the drama lies in the inner
struggle that is provoked by and manifested in the outer conflict of
ideas. The drama of ideas is therefore simultaneously performed on the
outer and inner planes of the characters. With the melodrama and conservative morality of most well-made plays, outer action is necessary

[22] George Bernard Shaw, *Man and Superman, John Bull's Other Island, and Major Barbara*, ed. Brad Kent (Oxford: OUP, 2021).

[23] T. S. Eliot, *The Criterion* (October 1924), 4; repr. in T. F. Evans (ed.), *Shaw: The Critical Heritage* (London: Routledge & Kegan Paul, 1976), 293–4, at 294.

[24] The outstanding work on this feature of Shaw's writing is J. L. Wisenthal, *The Marriage of Contraries: Bernard Shaw's Middle Plays* (Cambridge, MA: Harvard University Press, 1974).

[25] For an example of the latter, see Margery M. Morgan, *The Shavian Playground: Exploration of the Art of Bernard Shaw* (London: Methuen, 1972), 4.

because the values of the characters are fixed: villains and heroes have always been and always will be villains and heroes. In effect, their representative white and black hats are not interchangeable and no one dons grey headwear. The advent of the omnipresent anti-hero in more contemporary literature has in many ways its origins in Shaw's drama.

This is further evidence that changes in form and content tend to stem from one another. Shaw's oeuvre engaged with genres that had long traditions in the theatre, including romantic comedy, the history play, farce, and melodrama.[26] Yet he always challenged their tenets. Shaw's romantic comedy, for example, is not terribly romantic, and in his plays it is often the woman who chases the man rather than the other way around. Similarly, in Shaw's melodrama the sheriff or pastor is conflicted, while the supposedly cussed and amoral rogue does good in the end—but for no recognizably altruistic or ethical reason. Hesione illustrates this in *Heartbreak House* when she tells Ellie: 'People dont have their virtues and vices in sets: they have them anyhow: all mixed' (p. 166). By incarnating such internal conflicts on stage, Shaw allows his audience to realize their own contradictions and uncertainties as valid and not as signs of weakness and failure to enforce rigid moral codes. In this way, people who subject themselves to new experiences and points of view become open to conversion and growth along the same lines as Shaw's characters.

Pygmalion

Shaw was a notably quick writer of plays. He began *Pygmalion* on 7 March 1912 and completed it on 10 June. However, this short compositional period masks the fact that he often allowed his ideas to gestate for some time before finally putting pen to paper. In a letter written fifteen years earlier, Shaw said that he would like to write a play involving 'a west end gentleman' and a 'rapscallionly flower girl', 'an east end dona' who would wear 'an apron and three orange and red ostrich feathers'.[27]

The story, however, has a much older pedigree. Shaw borrowed it in part from Ovid's *Metamorphoses*, which recounts the story of Pygmalion.[28] According to myth, the goddess Venus was so enraged at

---

[26] The best study on this subject remains Martin Meisel, *Shaw and the Nineteenth-Century Theater* (Princeton: Princeton University Press, 1963).

[27] Letter of 8 September 1897, in *CL* i. 803.

[28] See Ovid, *Metamorphoses*, trans. A. D. Melville (Oxford: Oxford University Press, 1987), 232–4.

the perversion of her veneration rites that she transformed the profligate priestesses into prostitutes. The sculptor Pygmalion watched their wickedness and was so horrified that he became celibate, then carved a female statue of such beauty that he fell in love with it. Honouring Venus on her feast day, he asked her to bring his work to life. Because of Pygmalion's faith and good practices, she breathed life into Galatea and, nine months later, a child was born. It is the ultimate patriarchal wish-fulfilment: the ideal virginal beauty object becomes the passionate possession of its male creator.

Critics have recognized other literary forebears. The many references made to Milton, for example, suggest that, like the great poet, Henry Higgins is a rewriter of Genesis.[29] Perhaps logically, then, given the influence of Milton on Mary Shelley, parallels have likewise been found with Victor Frankenstein and his monster.[30] There are also resonances of Cinderella and her makeover that leads to the climax of a grand ball scene.[31] Several people pointed out to Shaw that his story resembles chapter 87 of Tobias Smollett's *Peregrine Pickle* (1751), titled 'Peregrine sets out for the Garrison, and meets with a Nymph of the Road, whom he takes into Keeping and metamorphoses into a fine Lady'. But Shaw, having never read the novel and was thus unaware of the episode, protested: 'The experiment of two writers of fiction treating the same subject and producing the same series of incidents—the same result practically—shews that the human imagination runs in the same grooves, and that this is the explanation of almost all the alleged plagiarisms.'[32] Scholars are therefore forewarned from being too assertive in declaring influences, while rigorous comparative work, whether arising from whimsy or Shavian references, has led to greater understanding of the play's dynamics and politics.

Aware of *Pygmalion*'s potential for tremendous success, Shaw took great care with it. In the past, he felt that London reviewers had negatively impacted his ability to mount successful productions of his plays abroad, with managers unwilling to take their chances on a work that had been savaged as undramatic. Yet Shaw was a favourite of Germanic audiences, and so when Siegfried Trebitsch, Shaw's

---

[29] John A. Bertolini, *The Playwrighting Self of Bernard Shaw* (Carbondale, IL: Southern Illinois University Press, 1991), 100–1.

[30] See e.g. A. M. Gibbs, *The Art and the Mind of Shaw: Essays in Criticism* (New York: St Martin's Press, 1983), 171–2.

[31] Many examples exist, but for the most extended such treatment, see Charles A. Berst, *Pygmalion: Shaw's Spin on Myth and Cinderella* (New York: Twayne, 1995).

[32] Letter from Blanche Patch, on behalf of Shaw, 27 May 1925, in *CL* iii. 912.

Austrian translator, suggested that he premiere *Pygmalion* at Vienna's iconic Burgtheater, Shaw agreed.[33] It duly opened there on 16 October 1913.

After its rapturous success in Vienna, Shaw began rehearsing the play at His Majesty's Theatre. Located in London's West End, the 1,720-seat theatre was built for the famous actor-manager Herbert Beerbohm Tree.[34] Shaw had always exercised casting decisions and directed his own works, but in opting for His Majesty's Theatre, he accepted that Tree would play a major role. Tree petitioned for Doolittle, but Shaw demurred, believing that Tree could hold his own as Higgins. For Eliza, Shaw chose Mrs Patrick Campbell, who had long been one of London's leading actors. She celebrated her forty-ninth birthday only days before *Pygmalion* opened, when she was asked to convince an audience that she was a flower girl more than thirty years her junior. In 1913, after reading both *Androcles and the Lion* and *Pygmalion* to friends, Shaw reflected: 'I believe I was slightly mad last year.'[35] Little did he suspect that the first London production of *Pygmalion* would take him to the brink of losing his sanity.

Shaw first read the play to Mrs Pat shortly after he completed it. She flirtatiously thanked him 'for thinking I could play your pretty slut. I wonder if I could please you.'[36] He responded to her: 'I must have my Liza and no other Liza. There is no other Liza and can be no other Liza.'[37] However, the wooing began in earnest in February 1913, Shaw lamenting, 'It seems to me that all the poets have been in love with you; for they seem to have said everything; and my words that would praise thee are impotent things.'[38] By the time Mrs Pat finally signed on to play Eliza the following year, Shaw was completely smitten. Yet his rationale for casting her went beyond his mawkish crush. As he had told Trebitsch, '*Pygmalion* is essentially a star play; unless you have an actress of extraordinary qualifications and popularity, failure is

[33] Letter of 29 January 1913, in *Bernard Shaw's Letters to Siegfried Trebitsch*, ed. Samuel A. Weiss (Stanford, CA: Stanford University Press, 1986), 163. It was then known as the Hofburg Theater.

[34] For the theatre's seating capacity at the time of the play's premiere, see John Parker (ed.), *Who's Who in the Theatre: A Biographical Record of the Contemporary Stage* (London: Isaac Pitman & Sons, 1914), 869.

[35] Letter of 10 April 1913, in *Bernard Shaw's Letters to Granville Barker*, ed. C. B. Purdom (London: Phoenix House, 1956), 190.

[36] Letter of 27 June 1912, in *Bernard Shaw and Mrs Patrick Campbell: Their Correspondence*, ed. Alan Dent (London: V. Gollancz, 1952), 19.

[37] Letter of 5 July 1912, in *CL* iii. 97.

[38] Letter of 7 February 1913, in *CL* iii. 149.

certain.'[39] When they began rehearsals, no one was bigger than Mrs Pat, who was able to leverage her popularity into a lucrative contract for a £130 weekly salary, plus 2.5 per cent of the receipts with an eight-week guarantee.[40]

In casting Tree and Mrs Pat as the leads, Shaw had signed on to direct a couple of 'histrionic monsters'.[41] In Shaw's world, the ideal production was a collaboration between artists, but failing competent actors, he resorted to authorial dictatorship. In this case, neither Tree nor Mrs Pat understood what he wanted and at times they merely ignored his instructions. They often arrived not having learned their lines, with Tree, much to Shaw's horror, always prepared to improvise. 'As far as I could discover,' Shaw later recalled, 'the notion that a play could succeed without any further help from the actor than a simple impersonation of his part never occurred to Tree. The author, whether Shakespear or Shaw, was a lame dog to be helped over the stile by the ingenuity and inventiveness of the actor-producer.'[42] The conflict of egos made the production a trial for all three. Tree found Shaw's direction difficult to take, while Mrs Pat on more than one occasion refused to act until Shaw had left the theatre. Shaw got his revenge, however, at one point calling to her from the stalls: 'Good God: you are forty years too old for Eliza; sit still and it's not so noticeable!'[43] Meanwhile, she purposely infuriated Tree and the two of them spent days at a time refusing to speak to one another. Subjected to their obstinacy and petulance, Shaw took to writing them lengthy letters filled with advice. Vexed with this approach, Tree fumed: 'I will not go so far as to say that all people who write letters of more than eight pages are mad, but it is a curious fact that all madmen write letters of more than eight pages.'[44]

Despite the backstage acrimony, the play received plenty of positive advance publicity. In addition to reporting its success on the Continent, the London press produced puff pieces featuring the stars and the world's most recognizable playwright. Ticket sales were further driven by a whisper campaign about the play's shocking use of an expletive.

[39] Letter of 29 January 1913, in *Bernard Shaw's Letters to Siegfried Trebitsch*, ed. Weiss, 164.

[40] Margot Peters, *Mrs Pat: The Life of Mrs Patrick Campbell* (New York: Knopf, 1984), 336.

[41] Hesketh Pearson, *Beerbohm Tree: His Life and Laughter* (New York: Harper & Brothers, 1956), 179.

[42] Bernard Shaw, *Pen Portraits and Reviews* (London: Constable, 1932), 267.

[43] Peters, *Mrs Pat*, 337.   [44] Pearson, *Beerbohm Tree*, 180.

One paper fuelled the fire by sponsoring a contest to guess the naughty word that Eliza was rumoured to say.

With profanity and strong language now rather commonplace in the theatre, it is rather difficult to imagine that someone saying 'bloody' on stage could cause a sensation. The reader's report for the censor rationally suggested that in this case it was innocuous: 'The word is not used in anger, of course, and the incident is merely funny. I think it would be a mistake to be particular about it, but since the word has been forbidden in other plays—in a different sort of connection, however—I mention it.'[45] Tree was not convinced and asked Shaw to substitute it for 'ruddy'.[46] He was right that it would cause ripples, as the theatre world was forever altered after Eliza's resounding 'Not bloody likely' (p. 57). At the London premiere, the stage manager timed the delirium that followed the line at 'an unparalleled minute and a quarter'.[47] Shaw felt that this 'nearly wrecked' the performance, as the audience 'laughed themselves into such utter abandonment and disorder that it was really doubtful for some time whether they could recover themselves and let the play go on'.[48]

Press coverage included accounts by scholars and intellectuals discussing the origins of the word 'bloody'. The Oxford Union and Eton Debating Society argued over its use on the stage, the former seeing it as having 'a liberating influence on the English language' and the latter as contributing to 'the debasement and vulgarization of the commercial theatre'.[49] Shaw defended it as being 'in common use as an expletive by four-fifths of the English nation, including educated persons'.[50] It is actually Higgins who uses the word most often, but this is kept offstage from the audience. Early on, Mrs Pearce upbraids him for swearing:

I dont mind your damning and blasting, and what the devil and where the devil and who the devil . . . but there is a certain word I must ask you not to use. The girl used it herself when she began to enjoy the bath. It begins with the same letter as bath. *She* knows no better: she learnt it at her mother's knee. But she must not hear it from *your* lips. . . . Only this morning,

[45] G. S. Street, Reader's report on *Pygmalion*, 23 February 1914, in LC P.

[46] Letter of 12 April 1914, in *CL* iii. 226–7.

[47] Peters, *Mrs Pat*, 341.   [48] Letter of 12 April 1914, in *CL* iii. 227.

[49] Michael Holroyd, *Bernard Shaw*, ii. *1898–1918: The Pursuit of Power* (London: Penguin, 1991), 340.

[50] Bernard Shaw, 'G.B.S., Eliza and the Critics', *Daily News*, 17 April 1914; repr. in Bernard Shaw, *Collected Plays with Their Prefaces*, ed. Dan H. Laurence, iv (London: Bodley Head, 1970), 801–2.

sir, you applied it to your boots, to the butter, and to the brown bread. (p. 35)

At this point, the audience has a good idea of what to expect. In this way, Shaw infuses his play with the same suspense and expectation as the press had.

Pygmalion ran for 118 performances at His Majesty's Theatre, grossing a lucrative £2,000 per week. Shaw used his royalties to help his old Fabian colleagues Beatrice and Sidney Webb finance the *New Statesman*, a leading socialist paper.[51] Mrs Pat took the play on a successful tour of the United States in 1914 and 1915, and revived it again in 1920. While it played to full houses on the world's stages, it achieved another level of triumph when it was made into a movie in 1938. German and Dutch companies had previously filmed it in 1935 and 1937, but Shaw personally adapted the 1938 script from his play. The screen version was massively successful, and there was a certain irony in the fact that it was directed by Anthony Asquith, whose father, the prime minister, had wished Shaw shot only two decades earlier. Shaw won the Oscar for best adapted screenplay, but there was little reason for him to celebrate as his script had been unknowingly changed against his wishes. Most notably, the film closes with Eliza returning to Higgins.[52]

From the time of those first rehearsals with Tree and Mrs Pat, Shaw found himself at odds with others in how to interpret *Pygmalion*. While the press and the public enjoyed what they saw at His Majesty's Theatre, Shaw said he 'writhed in hell'. While Mrs Pat had capably acted, Tree was abominable:

I had particularly coached him at the last rehearsal in the concluding lines, making him occupy himself affectionately with his mother, & throw Eliza the commission to buy the ham &c. over his shoulder. The last thing I saw as I left the house was Higgins shoving his mother rudely out of his way and wooing Eliza with appeals to buy a ham for his lonely home like a bereaved Romeo.[53]

[51] Beatrice Webb considered the fortunes of the *New Statesman* as dependent on Shaw's play. With *Pygmalion*'s success, she reported him as 'making piles of money—which is fortunate for the *New Statesman*'. See her journal entry on 23 April 1914, in *The Diary of Beatrice Webb*, iii. *1905–1924*, ed. Norman and Jeanne MacKenzie (London: Virago Press, 1984), 201.

[52] For Shaw's relations with the cinema and his film scripts, see *The Collected Screenplays of Bernard Shaw*, ed. Bernard F. Dukore (Athens, GA: University of Georgia Press, 1980).

[53] Letter of 12 April 1914, in CL iii. 227–8.

Despite having vowed not to watch the play ever again, Shaw returned for the one hundredth performance. Unfortunately, Tree had further improvised, and now, just before the final curtain, he alluded even more directly to a romance with Eliza by throwing a bouquet of flowers at her.[54] Shaw considered this 'a stroke of comic business so outrageously irrelevant that I solemnly cursed the whole enterprise, and bade the delinquents farewell for ever'.[55] Yet this problem went beyond Tree and Mrs Pat. Years later, Shaw confessed to William Archer: 'I have never been able to stop the silly and vulgar gag with which Eliza in Pygmalion, both here and abroad, gets the last word and implies that she is going to marry Pygmalion.'[56]

What vexed Shaw most is that he thought it was evident that they would not marry. Higgins treats Eliza as her own father might, threatening her with violence when she fails to be pliant to his wishes. When Pickering wonders whether Higgins has honourable intentions, Higgins takes offence: 'You see, she'll be a pupil; and teaching would be impossible unless pupils were sacred. Ive taught scores of American millionairesses how to speak English: the best looking women in the world. I'm seasoned. They might as well be blocks of wood. *I* might as well be a block of wood' (p. 34). While revising the play, Shaw deleted an early exchange at Mrs Higgins's at-home wherein Higgins reveals 'We were a lot of brothers with just one little sister at the tail end of the family. We spoilt her like anything.'[57] Higgins treats Eliza similarly, lavishing food, dresses, and jewels on her and thereby suggesting he sees her as a sibling of sorts. A further obstacle to romance is Higgins's mother-fixation. Incapable of having a romantic relationship with a young, vibrant woman like Eliza, he remains stuck at the Oedipal stage of development, of which his narcissism, bullying, and boorishness are direct manifestations.[58]

Shaw's difficulty derives in part from the title he gave his play, as *Pygmalion* implies that Higgins falls in love with and marries Eliza. In subtitling it 'A Romance', he further led his audience to expect this outcome. Yet Shaw was fond of encouraging expectations only to

[54] Pearson, *Beerbohm Tree*, 182.

[55] Bernard Shaw, *Pen Portraits and Reviews*, 273.

[56] Letter of 19 April 1919, in *Bernard Shaw and William Archer*, ed. Thomas Postlewait (Toronto: University of Toronto Press, 2017), 341.

[57] P Type, 59–60.

[58] For a perceptive and nuanced psychoanalytic reading of Higgins, see David Plant, 'A Look at Narcissism through Professor Higgins in *Pygmalion*', *British Journal of Psychotherapy*, 28/1 (2012), 50–65.

subvert them. There is romance in the play, but the romance is the social transformation that Eliza undergoes.[59] Shaw was attracted by this transformative element of the Pygmalion–Galatea myth, not by the marriage–birth with which it ends. Eliza's romantic rise is paralleled by that of her father, and Shaw perhaps creates some misdirection by having Doolittle marry, leading his audience to suppose that the same fate awaits Eliza. It does, but not with the leading man.

Shaw also sows confusion when, at the end of Act IV, Eliza takes a ring off and yells at Higgins: 'This ring isnt the jeweller's: it's the one you bought me in Brighton. I dont want it now' (p. 75). A series of questions arise: What were they doing at a seaside resort? What motivated Higgins to buy Eliza the ring? And how much did it cost? There is no other mention of the ring or of the mysterious trip. Only one critic has examined this important moment to any extent, suggesting that in flinging the ring at Higgins, Eliza symbolically ends their partnership.[60] That Higgins purchased this ring—as opposed to the jewels he rented for Eliza's garden party appearance—suggests that there is something genuinely personal about it. Though it might be innocent, the ring's ambiguity invites a decidedly more 'romantic' interpretation, especially as it could be understood to signal an impending marriage.

However, it is essential for Eliza that she not develop a romantic relationship with Higgins. As Shaw insists at the end of the sequel, 'Galatea never does quite like Pygmalion: his relation to her is too godlike to be altogether agreeable' (p. 109). When Mrs Pat revived the role in 1920, Shaw told her: 'When Eliza emancipates herself—when Galatea comes to life—she must not relapse. She must retain her pride and triumph to the end.'[61] She is not an object to be won by the hero. If the transformation is the most important aspect of the myth, then she must become a fully realized and confident young woman who makes choices for herself and lives on her own terms.

Frustrated by *Pygmalion*'s ongoing romantic interpretations, Shaw added a prose sequel for the play's publication in 1916.[62] However, the

[59] For more on this, see ch. 8, 'Pygmalion: A Potboiler as Art', in Charles A. Berst, *Bernard Shaw and the Art of Drama* (Urbana, IL: University of Illinois Press, 1973), 196–220; and Timothy G. Vesonder, 'Eliza's Choice: Transformation Myth and the Ending of *Pygmalion*', in Rodelle Weintraub (ed.), *Fabian Feminist: Bernard Shaw and Woman* (University Park: Pennsylvania State University Press, 1977), 39–45, at 44.

[60] Bertolini, *The Playwrighting Self of Bernard Shaw*, 104.

[61] Letter of 5 February 1920, in *CL* iii. 155.

[62] Letter of 19 December 1915, in *CL* iii. 335.

critical consensus is that in doing so he marred his work.[63] Until the
1941 edition, Eliza's last line in the play, when Higgins says he needs
her to get some things for him, is the simple 'Buy them yourself.' With
this rejoinder, spoken disdainfully and followed by her sweeping out of
the room, she is the unwomanly woman that Shaw had praised in
Ibsen's work, the sort who rebels against conformity and abandons the
man to his illusion of domestic bliss and authority.[64] In the sequel,
Shaw shows how Eliza's story continues after the play ends, including
her marriage and business with Freddy, to prevent people from thinking that Eliza and Higgins would eventually become a couple. In so
doing, he robs Eliza of her assertiveness. Moreover, she becomes
beholden to the financial largess of Pickering and Higgins while tending a store named for her husband.[65]

Instead of radically breaking away from marriage, many of Shaw's
female characters tend to reinvent or reform it.[66] In Eliza's case, it is
questionable if she even does this. If Shaw had not included the
sequel, audiences would be left to imagine the possibility that she followed through on her threat to Higgins to teach phonetics for a living,
making good on her extraordinary talent for language.[67] Though he is
at first offended by her rebellion, Higgins is quickly delighted by her
demonstration of independence: 'By George, Eliza, I said I'd make
a woman of you; and I have. I like you like this. . . . Five minutes ago you
were like a millstone round my neck. Now youre a tower of strength:

[63] For arguments in favour of the original ending, see Derek McGovern, 'From Stage
Play to Hybrid: Shaw's Three Editions of *Pygmalion*', *SHAW* 31 (2011), 9–30; Gibbs,
The Art and the Mind of Shaw, 168–76; and Silver, *Bernard Shaw*, 179–276.

[64] Wisenthal, *Shaw and Ibsen*, 124–31.

[65] For a feminist critique of the play and the sequel, see J. Ellen Gainor, *Shaw's
Daughters: Dramatic and Narrative Constructions of Gender* (Ann Arbor: University of
Michigan Press, 1991), 225–39. For a more positive assessment of Shaw's bona fides by
second-wave feminist scholars, see Barbara Bellow Watson, *A Shavian Guide to the
Intelligent Woman* (London: Chatto & Windus, 1964) and Sonja Lorichs, *The Unwomanly
Woman in Bernard Shaw's Drama and Her Social and Political Background* (Uppsala: Acta
Universitatis Upsaliensis, 1973). For more equivocal scholarship, see Philip Graham,
'Bernard Shaw's Neglected Role in English Feminism, 1880–1914', *Journal of Gender
Studies*, 23/2 (2014), 167–83; and the various contributions to D. A. Hadfield and Jean
Reynolds (eds), *Shaw and Feminisms: On Stage and Off* (Gainesville, FL: University
Press of Florida, 2013).

[66] On this point, see D. A. Hadfield, 'Feminism', in Kent (ed.), *George Bernard Shaw
in Context*, 215–21.

[67] Maurice Valency is even more damning in his consideration of the sequel: 'From
every point of view the proposed resolution is unsatisfactory.' Valency, *The Cart and
the Trumpet: The Plays of George Bernard Shaw* (New York: Oxford University Press,
1973), 316.

a consort battleship' (p. 98). He encourages Galatea's independent streak, while Shaw, by attempting to control his own creation, in the end renders Eliza less independent.[68] Yet he never did win out: both stage productions and film versions tend to ignore his advice and the sequel's intention, ending instead with Eliza's return to a visibly distraught Higgins. The Alan Jay Lerner and Frederick Loewe musical adaptation *My Fair Lady*, which was wildly successful on stage with Julie Andrews as Eliza and on film with Audrey Hepburn taking over the role, and Rex Harrison as Higgins in both, opted for the same conclusion as Asquith's film.[69]

In addition to complaining about the play's romanticization, Shaw opined 'that all the political and social questions have been swept from the public mind by Eliza's expletive. Triviality can go no further.'[70] This explains his insistence on the play's didacticism. *Pygmalion* is a problem play, a drama that uses a social question as the source of its conflict, with Shaw taking aim at the class-speech matrix that impedes people from advancing in life.[71] For Shaw, like Higgins, phonetics offered a way for people to cross otherwise rigid class boundaries. In a speech he gave at the War Against Poverty Demonstration organized by the Independent Labour Party at London's Royal Albert Hall in October 1912, Shaw said that 'there is nothing in the world I hate more than a poor man. . . . I want to cure poverty as an abominable disease and as a very horrible crime.'[72] He did not blame the poor for their situation: Eliza, for example, is hard-working and dreams of one day owning her own shop. Rather, Shaw considered that all of society was implicated in perpetrating the crime of poverty by creating unfair conditions. This was, in part, why he helped such a large number of his

[68] Based on their research, management scientists have suggested that Eliza would not be successful as a mentor even in the twenty-first century because of the prevailing male culture. See Len Karakowsky, Nadia DeGama, and Kenneth McBey, 'Deconstructing Higgins: Gender Bias in the Pygmalion Phenomenon', *Gender in Management: An International Journal*, 32/1 (2017), 2–18.

[69] For criticism of the 1938 film, see Gainor, *Shaw's Daughters*, 238. For criticism of *My Fair Lady*, see Paul Bauschatz, 'The Uneasy Evolution of *My Fair Lady* from *Pygmalion*', *SHAW* 18 (1998), 181–98; and Derek McGovern, 'Shavian Elements in the *My Fair Lady* Film', *SHAW* 33 (2013), 160–75.

[70] Letter of 19 April 1914, in *CL* iii. 229.

[71] For a discussion of this genre, see Bernard Shaw, 'The Problem Play: A Symposium', *The Humanitarian* (May 1895); repr. in *The Drama Observed*, i, ed. Bernard F. Dukore (University Park: Pennsylvania State University Press, 1993), 324–9.

[72] Bernard Shaw, 'The Crime of Poverty', *Labour Leader*, 17 October 1912; repr. in Bernard Shaw, *Platform and Pulpit*, ed. Dan H. Laurence (London: Rupert Hart-Davis, 1962), 93–6, at 94.

friends by financing their children's education, referring to this assistance as his own 'Pygmalion experiments'.[73]

Like Shaw, Higgins is able to be Pygmalion because he is wealthy. A good deal of Higgins's authority comes from his superior social and financial position in addition to his expertise. He signals this on more than one occasion when he noisily rustles coins in his pocket. In the opening scene, when he is discovered taking notes, it is the poorer people who are afraid and suspicious. Eliza is pliant when she arrives at Wimpole Street because Higgins has the ability to facilitate her transformation, but she is also overawed by his wealth. The discrepancy between the poverty of her flat and the relative luxury of Higgins's lab indicates that she has stepped into a significantly higher stratosphere. Higgins's maid Mrs Pearce emphasizes this difference, calling Eliza a 'slut' and remarking on her filth.

Yet Eliza is timid, indeed almost afraid, not only because of her 'lower' status, but because of the potential threat that Higgins represents. On seven occasions, she insists: 'I'm a good girl.' She does so because a young woman of her class, brought to such a wealthy place, would tend to be a prostitute. This accounts for the concern that both Pickering and Mrs Pearce express about Eliza's status in the house: neither of them wants to be a party to immorality or crime. Even Higgins recognizes this, offering Eliza half of a chocolate after eating the first half himself to show that he has not drugged it and does not wish to take advantage of her. Shortly after this scene, her own father offers to sell her for money. For so many destitute London girls of Eliza's day, prostitution was considered a natural career or a temporary job to make ends meet.[74]

As Higgins notes, phonetics has the power to remake people and he considers Eliza worthless not because of her background, but because of how she speaks. In an age of upstarts, people seek to hide their origins and become something else, to realize their dreams of a better life. In this way, Eliza's transformation is not only of her own time, an era marked by greater movement between social classes thanks to increasing democratization, workers' rights, and public education; it is also of the twenty-first century, when reality shows subject rough-edged ingénues to a more worldly jury of professionals and celebrities to be

[73] Letter of 13 October 1945, in *CL* iv. 754.

[74] For the most thorough treatment of this subject in relation to the play, see ch. 2, 'Bernard Shaw's Defensive Laughter', in Celia Marshik, *British Modernism and Censorship* (Cambridge: Cambridge University Press, 2006), 46–87.

made over into slick stars. The difference between Shaw's play and these reality shows is that while Higgins targets the form, that is, the sounds of the words and how they are produced, Pickering focuses on the content, that is, both the meanings of the words and the inner self. This complementary relationship makes Eliza's transformation something more than a superficial improvement in her pronunciation of vowels and consonants and the addition of a new dress, jewellery, and hairstyle, instead tapping into and giving voice to her humanity.

Despite his bluster and insensitivity, Higgins reveals himself to be a humanist at heart. When Eliza suggests that she would like to take a taxi to Tottenham Court Road to show off to her friends, Higgins chastises her for being a snob. Notwithstanding his bet with Pickering and his periodic bragging about his students' accomplishments, teaching phonetics is not about Higgins's ego; it is, rather, a noble profession, he says, 'filling up the deepest gulf that separates class from class and soul from soul' (p. 61). When Eliza upbraids him for treating her badly even after she becomes a lady, Higgins notes that he treats all people impetuously. He confides to her: 'The great secret, Eliza, is not having bad manners or good manners or any other particular sort of manners, but having the same manner for all human souls: in short, behaving as if you were in Heaven, where there are no third-class carriages, and one soul is as good as another' (p. 92). Importantly, he becomes most eloquent in this scene. Just as Eliza undergoes a transformation, she provokes Higgins into revealing his own humanity and undergoing a transformation of sorts himself. In Shaw's world, Galatea is a creator, too.

Heartbreak House

Shaw once said, 'I am not an explicable phenomenon; neither is *Heartbreak House*.'[75] Yet a great deal has been written to explain them both. As Shaw makes clear in his preface, the context of the First World War is essential for understanding the play and how his career experienced a significant change in fortune. Even before Britain entered the conflict on 4 August 1914, Shaw had been critical of the inevitability of the war and the press's braying jingoism.[76] Because of the public's

[75] Archibald Henderson, *George Bernard Shaw: Man of the Century* (New York: Appleton-Century-Crofts, 1956), 626.

[76] For a treatment of these writings, see Nelson O'Ceallaigh Ritschel, *Bernard Shaw, W. T. Stead, and the New Journalism: Whitechapel, Parnell, Titanic, and the Great War* (London: Palgrave Macmillan, 2017), 153–60.

limited sophistication, he charged that the authorities deemed it necessary to present the war to the average person 'as a crude melodrama in which his country is the hero and the enemy the villain'.[77] Shaw thus cast his war journalism in the same light as his theatre criticism: both attacked the artificially simplistic visions of life that only served to support the status quo.

The *New Statesman* published Shaw's *Common Sense about the War* as an eighty-page supplement on 14 November 1914; it sold 75,000 copies.[78] In the main, he argued that German and British societies were equally imperialistic and warmongering, an unorthodox view that was widely condemned. Some decried the pamphlet as yet another perverse example of Shaw's tendency to seek publicity through provocation.[79] Several of his colleagues, amongst them Arnold Bennett and H. G. Wells, denounced his views. Essayist Robert Lynd said that from that moment, the conflict 'was spoken of and written about as a war between Allies on the one hand, and, on the other, Germany, Austria, Turkey, and Bernard Shaw'.[80] Shaw's infamy was such that people would leave as soon as he made an appearance at a public event.[81] Despite rising to the heights of popularity with *Pygmalion* only a matter of months earlier, he was now the country's great pariah.

The war further affected Shaw by changing the country's theatre culture. As he notes in his preface, soldiers on leave swamped London. These young men tended to be unworldly and sought to escape the grim reality of the battlefield with light enlightenment.[82] Managers loved that whatever nonsense they staged played to full houses. The result was that the renaissance of British drama that had occurred over the course of the previous twenty-five years more or less faded away.[83]

[77] From ch. 12 of *What I Really Wrote about the War*, first published in the *New York American* between January and March 1919; repr. in J. L. Wisenthal and Daniel O'Leary (eds), *What Shaw Really Wrote about the War* (Gainesville, FL: University Press of Florida, 2006), 248.

[78] Archibald Henderson, *Table-Talk of G.B.S.: Conversations of Things in General between George Bernard Shaw and his Biographer* (New York: Harper, 1925), 125.

[79] For a discussion of this topic, see Stanley Weintraub, *Journey to Heartbreak: The Crucible Years of Bernard Shaw, 1914–1918* (New York: Weybright and Talley, 1971), 59–66.

[80] Bernard Shaw, *Sixteen Self Sketches* (London: Constable, 1949), 118.

[81] St John Ervine, *Bernard Shaw: His Life, Work and Friends* (London: Constable, 1956), 464.

[82] Recent research supports his viewpoint. See e.g. Andrew Maunder (ed.), *British Theatre and the Great War, 1914–1919* (London: Palgrave Macmillan, 2015).

[83] This was a view promoted in the more left-wing, intellectual press. See *The Nation*, 27 September 1919, p. 770.

Shaw's own output reflects this downturn: *Heartbreak House* is the only full-length play that he wrote during the war and, despite finishing it in 1917, he did not publish it until 1919; and it was first produced in 1920 in New York and in 1921 in London. In the meantime, he wrote several one-act plays, most of them topical comedies. Yet Shaw had difficulty getting even these staged: *O'Flaherty, V.C.*, for example, was first performed in 1917, two years after its composition, by soldiers on the Western Front.

As the war years proved to be a trial for Shaw, it is understandable that, of all of his plays, the composition of *Heartbreak House* would be among the longest and most difficult of his career. It took him more than a year to write it, from 4 March 1916 to 26 May 1917.[84] By mid-May 1916, Shaw moaned that 'I, who once wrote plays *d'un seul trait*, am creeping through a new one (to prevent myself crying) at odd moments, two or three speeches at a time ... and I have hardly come to the beginning of the first scene yet'.[85] He made some progress when he was invited by the Webbs to stay with them from 6 to 20 June in the Sussex countryside. Here the Shaws spent two weeks with not only the Webbs, but also Virginia and Leonard Woolf, the latter a prominent member of the Fabian Society.[86] The cultured discussions in an English manor house influenced the writing and the sexual politics of the play, which replicate something of a Bloomsbury group dynamic. Years later, Shaw admitted to Virginia Woolf: 'There is a play of mine called Heartbreak House which I always connect with you because I conceived it in that house somewhere in Sussex where I first met you and, of course, fell in love with you.'[87] Her response was likewise playful:

Your letter reduced me to two days silence from sheer pleasure. . . . As for falling in love, it was not, let me confess, one-sided. . . . Indeed you have acted a lover's part in my life for the past thirty years; and though I daresay it's not much to boast of, I should have been a worser woman without Bernard Shaw. . . . Heartbreak House, by the way, is my favourite of all your works.[88]

---

[84] Shaw wrote 'The End' on 12 May, but finished his stage directions on 26 May. Stanley Weintraub and Anne Wright, 'Introduction', in Bernard Shaw, *Heartbreak House: A Facsimile of the Revised Typescript* (New York: Garland Publishing, 1981), p. ix.

[85] Letter of 14 May 1916, in *Bernard Shaw and Mrs Patrick Campbell*, ed. Dent, 186.

[86] Leonard Woolf authored the Fabian Society's report on the creation of a League of Nations to prevent future wars; the American president Woodrow Wilson considered it a 'seminal' essay on the subject. Stanley Weintraub, *Journey to Heartbreak*, 97.

[87] Letter of 10 May 1940, in *CL* iv. 557.

[88] Letter of 15 May 1940, in *CL* iv. 557–8.

Although England was not attacked by land, recent technological developments led to air raids. Planes now duelled in the skies and Germany turned Zeppelins into bombers. In October 1916, Shaw watched a Zeppelin float across the sky and pass directly over his Hertfordshire house, but as it turned and headed Londonwards, it was shot down. As he recounted to the Webbs:

What is hardly credible, but true, is that the sound of the Zepp's engines was so fine, and its voyage through the stars so enchanting, that I positively caught myself hoping next night that there would be another raid. I grieve to add that after seeing the Zepp fall like a burning newspaper, with its human contents roasting for some minutes (it was frightfully slow) I went to bed and was comfortably asleep in ten minutes. One is so pleased at having seen the show that the destruction of a dozen people or so in hideous terror and torment does not count. 'I didnt half cheer, I tell you' said a damsel at the wreck. Pretty lot of animals we are![89]

This is precisely the exhilarating nihilism on which the play ends.

Shaw had now found his *deus ex machina* conclusion, yet he was still struggling to write. Then, at the outset of 1917, Douglas Haig, the British commander-in-chief, invited him to the Western Front. Given Shaw's hostility to the war, this was a rather audacious request, but it was part of a strategy to co-opt writers to support the war effort as public opinion flagged. Shaw recorded his visit in a series of articles in the *Daily Chronicle* from 5 to 8 March 1917. Like his characters who hear Beethoven in the hovering Zeppelin, he noted a German attack in distinctly musical terms:

There was no Belgian carillon, but plenty of German music: an imposing orchestration in which all the instruments were instruments of percussion. I cannot say I disliked it: the big drum always excites me. . . . Boom! whizzzzzz!!! Boom! whizzzzzz!!! Boom! whizzzzzz!!!—all *fortissimo diminuendo*; then, *crescendo molto subito*, Whizzzzzz-bangclatter![90]

On leaving Ypres, which was devastated by fighting, he 'found the world suddenly duller. From this I infer that Ypres and its orchestra had been rather exciting, though I had not noticed it at the time.'[91]

In addition to the war, Shaw was inspired by friends like the Woolfs. Sydney Olivier, another of his Fabian colleagues, was governor of

[89] Letter of 5 October 1916, in *CL* iii. 426.
[90] Bernard Shaw, 'Joy Riding at the Front', in Wisenthal and O'Leary (eds), *What Shaw Really Wrote about the War*, 196.
[91] Bernard Shaw, 'Joy Riding at the Front', 197.

Jamaica, just as Ariadne's husband is a colonial administrator. Similar to Shotover, Olivier was rather more progressive than Hastings in his regard of native populations and he had daughters whom the poet Rupert Brooke had alternately wooed.[92] The play's initial title, *Lena's Father*, indicates further personal connections. The actor Lena Ashwell, who had starred in *Misalliance* (1910), was born on her family's ship, which was moored on the River Tyne. Her father, Captain Pocock, lived in the captain's quarters, built a greenhouse onboard for his wife, and maintained a drawing room that overlooked the stern's gallery.[93] Pocock was eccentric in many of his habits, and when he was dying in Lausanne, Switzerland, he demanded to have his Eucharist served with cheese. While on vacation with Shaw in Biarritz, Ashwell remembered that 'he delighted in the stories which I told him about Father, saying he must have that character for a play. When afterwards he read me "Heartbreak House" he told me that the old sea captain was my father.'[94] That Shaw first heard these stories in October 1913 perhaps explains his claim in the preface that he had begun the play before the war broke out.

However, the play's most commented-upon influence is not personal, but literary: 'the Russian manner' that Shaw signals in the subtitle.[95] While at work on *Heartbreak House*, Shaw told Wells that 'The Russians are beyond all comparison the most fascinating people in the world. . . . Everything we write in England seems sawdust after Tchekov and the rest of them.'[96] Shaw had urged an English production of Chekhov's *The Cherry Orchard*, 'scornfully' attacked the audience's negative response when the Stage Society produced it in May 1911, and attended the English premieres of Chekhov's *The Seagull* in March 1912 and *Uncle Vanya* in May 1914.[97] He name-checks Tolstoy's *The Fruits of the Enlightenment* in his preface, but it is the Chekhovian

[92] For more on this and Shaw's play as a riposte to Brooke's hyper-patriotic war poetry, see Ronald Bryden, 'The Roads to *Heartbreak House*', in Christopher Innes (ed.), *The Cambridge Companion to George Bernard Shaw* (Cambridge: Cambridge University Press, 1998), 185–8.

[93] Lena Ashwell, *Myself a Player* (London: M. Joseph, 1936), 13–15.

[94] Ashwell, *Myself a Player*, 66.

[95] For an original reading of the Russian influence on the play, see Miriam Handley, 'Chekhov Translated: Shaw's Use of Sounds Effects in *Heartbreak House*', *Modern Drama*, 42/4 (Winter 1999), 565–78. For an overview of some of the most important influences, see A. M. Gibbs, '*Heartbreak House*: Chamber of Echoes', *SHAW* 13 (1993), 113–32.

[96] Letter of 7 December 1916, in *CL* iii. 439.

[97] Christopher Innes, *A Sourcebook on Naturalist Theatre* (London: Routledge, 2000), 232.

elegiac mood that dominates his play. The plays are not traditional but rather modern elegies in that they refuse to console, both indifferent to and delighting in death and destruction.[98] Like Chekhov and Tolstoy, Shaw saw one epoch ending and another beginning and was not too terribly distraught about it, hoping that something more positive would emerge from the ashes of an aristocratic civilization.

The other major literary influence on the play is Shakespeare's *King Lear*.[99] In Shaw's puppet play *Shakes versus Shav* (1949), Shakespeare asks, 'Where is thy Hamlet? Couldst thou write King Lear?' Shaw's response: 'Aye, with his daughters all complete. Couldst thou have written Heartbreak House? Behold my Lear.'[100] Shaw even lifted his title from Shakespeare, for when Lear collapses and dies at the end, Kent commands: 'Break, heart; I prithee, break!'[101] This link is less obvious than Ellie's references to *Othello*, whose eponymous character is, like Shotover, a naval leader who has interracial relations and weds a young woman. However, Shotover is similar to Lear in resisting the tempest and for his intensely complex relationships with his daughters. These men face death bravely, and both plays have a cataclysmic element that speaks directly to Shaw's time. In his preface, Shaw borrows Shakespeare's image of man as an angry ape and his compatriot Jonathan Swift's misanthropic depiction of humans as yahoos in *Gulliver's Travels*, and he alludes to the Trojan War through the names of several of his characters. Humans have wrought the end of their own civilization, perhaps leading to the emergence of a new figure. It would not, however, be the Shavian Superman birthed by the Life Force and Creative Evolution, but something rather more ambiguous. Hector interprets a noise in the sky as 'Heaven's threatening growl of disgust at us useless futile creatures. . . . Either out of that darkness some new creation will come to supplant us as we have supplanted the animals, or the heavens will fall in thunder and destroy us' (p. 226). This line has its correlative in *King Lear* when Albany curses Goneril and Regan for deposing their father, a situation he decries as 'barbarous' and

---

[98] For an excellent study of the modern elegy in poetry, see Jahan Ramazani, *Poetry of Mourning: The Modern Elegy from Hardy to Heaney* (Chicago: University of Chicago Press, 1994).

[99] For sample studies on this influence, see Stanley Weintraub, '*Heartbreak House*: Shaw's *Lear*', *Modern Drama*, 15/3 (Fall 1972), 255–65; Sonya Freeman Loftis, 'Shakespeare, Shotover, Surrogation: "Blaming the Bard" in *Heartbreak House*', *SHAW* 29 (2009), 50–65; and Brett Gamboa, '*King Lear*, *Heartbreak House*, and the Dynamics of Inertia', *SHAW* 35/1 (2015), 86–106.

[100] George Bernard Shaw, *Playlets*, ed. James Moran (Oxford: OUP, 2021).

[101] Shakespeare, *King Lear*, V. iii. 378.

'degenerate' while wondering whether the heavens will intervene as humankind preys 'on itself | Like monsters of the deep.'[102]

Given this dark vision, *Heartbreak House* could not have been successfully produced during the war. Shaw understood that society was traumatized and could not yet subject itself to introspection. With that in mind, in 1919, almost 20,000 copies of the play were published on both sides of the Atlantic.[103] Publishing also served to increase his income at a time when his works were not being produced. By the onset of 1920, Shaw had spent two years selling stocks to survive and even the book's sales were not enough to improve his finances.[104]

His fortunes began to change when Lawrence Langner, the manager of the New York Theatre Guild, approached Shaw about producing his play. Convinced by St John Ervine that Langner could be trusted, given his recent success with Ervine's *John Ferguson*, Shaw offered Langner the world premiere of *Heartbreak House*. It opened at the Garrick Theatre on 10 November 1920 and was a hit, running for 125 performances over five months. Impressed with the quality of the production, Shaw gave the Theatre Guild the world premieres of five more plays, calling the company 'the salvation of the drama in New York'.[105] He now had every right to believe that public opinion had turned, that his plays could be popular again, and that London was ready for the taking.

He gave the London production to the Belfast-born James B. Fagan, a capable producer of the new drama who was already working on a revival of *John Bull's Other Island* at the Court Theatre. As a new full-length Shaw play had not opened in London since *Pygmalion*, there was considerable buzz over *Heartbreak House*. Leading actors, including Lillah McCarthy, Mrs Pat, and Lena Ashwell, tripped over themselves to play Ellie.[106] Shaw rejected them all, having written the part for Ellen O'Malley, who had already appeared in several of his plays, beginning with Nora in the Court's original production of *John Bull's Other Island* in 1904.[107] He wanted Ellie to have an Irish accent, believing that this would effectively demarcate her as an outsider to the

---

[102] Shakespeare, *King Lear*, IV. ii. 54 and 60–1.

[103] The exact number is 19,429 copies. Dan H. Laurence, *Bernard Shaw: A Bibliography* (Oxford: Clarendon Press, 1983), i. 138–9.

[104] Letter of 12 January 1920, in *CL* iii. 654.

[105] Henderson, *Table-Talk of G.B.S.*, 59.

[106] Margot Peters, *Bernard Shaw and the Actresses* (Garden City, NY: Doubleday, 1980), 400.

[107] Letters of 20 and 23 October 1928, in *CL* iii. 741–2.

house's inhabitants.[108] With a successful run in New York, and his theatre, director, and cast in place, the stars seemed aligned for Shaw's return to greatness.

However, when it opened at the Court on 18 October 1921, the production was an unmitigated disaster. There were considerable technical difficulties that led to scene-changes taking an inordinately long time. This was the death knell for a play that ran for over three and a half hours, lacked traditional action, and thus was already making considerable demands on the audience's attention. In savaging the play, critics evinced fatigue and perplexity. There were a few, though, who were more divided in their sympathies. Writing in the *Saturday Review*, James Agate said, 'As an entertainment pure and simple it is dull and incoherent—even for Shaw,' but 'I found it quite exhilarating and deeply moving, and it therefore ranks for me among the great testaments.'[109] Desmond MacCarthy lamented 'Shaw's indifference to Art, or that side of it which deals with methods and form', yet called it 'the queerest and subtlest' of Shaw's plays and suggested that were he to cut it further, it would be 'a masterpiece'.[110] In an incredible example of professional courtesy, James Douglas, the editor of the *Sunday Express*, asked his colleagues to give the play a second chance, deeming *Heartbreak House* worthy of the opportunity. Many returned, and Shaw was invited on stage to debate with his critics; he then told the audience that whether or not they liked the play, 'Three hundred years hence you will come to see it again.'[111] Despite its future greatness, the production lost money and Fagan incurred massive debts, including over £7,600 to Shaw. Even though he was in financial straits himself, Shaw said that Fagan could pay at his convenience, effectively wiping the debt clean.[112]

As a full-length work, *Heartbreak House* sits somewhat awkwardly in the chronology of Shaw's oeuvre, nestled between the broad social comedy of *Pygmalion* and the sprawling five-play science fiction *Back to Methuselah*. It should rather be considered as the last of a trilogy of discussion plays that Shaw began a decade earlier with *Getting Married* (1908) and *Misalliance*. Respectively, the subtitles of these predecessors

---

[108] Letter of 28 October 1928, in *CL* iii. 744.

[109] James Agate, *Saturday Review*, 21 October 1921; repr. in Evans (ed.), *Shaw: The Critical Heritage*, 250–3, at 252 and 253.

[110] Desmond MacCarthy, *New Statesman*, 29 October 1921, p. 103; repr. in Evans (ed.), *Shaw: The Critical Heritage*, 257–8, at 257.

[111] Beverly Baxter gives an account of this performance in A. M. Gibbs (ed.), *Shaw: Interviews and Recollections* (London: Palgrave Macmillan, 1990), 299.

[112] Letter of 22 June 1922, in *CL* iii. 776.

are 'A Disquisitory Play' (originally 'A Conversation') and 'A Debate in One Sitting'. With these works, Shaw took the discussion that he had found in Ibsen's plays and, instead of keeping it for the end, built his entire plays around it. This became a new, Shavian form: the disquisitory play. A discussion play on steroids, the disquisitory play does not prioritize discussion over action and resolution, but completely elides incident and closure. There is no plot; some critics have tried to discern one in *Heartbreak House*, but the best they have done is to suggest Ellie's educational journey from innocent girl to materialist conniver to cynical existentialist. While Shaw himself railed against the tendency to define drama according to rigid Aristotelian technique, the irony is that his disquisitory plays tend to conform to the classical unities, unfolding in one place in under twenty-four hours.

Not all were pleased with this experimentation. William Archer, for one, complained that since *Man and Superman*, Shaw had tended 'to drop all pretence at dramatic structure, to renounce everything resembling story or situation, and to make his plays consist of what may be called more or less emotionalised discussions'.[113] This set off an epistolary debate between the old friends. Shaw responded: 'My plays and their acts and their characters happily exist for their own sake, and not for that of any peg or plot or scenario; and if you don't like them you can lump them.'[114] Archer commented that a traditional play was like a cat with a backbone, while his friend posited a 'Tcheko-Shavian cat' that was really a jellyfish, claiming that the former definition was only the product of old-fashioned thinking.[115] Shaw rebuffed this interpretation: 'The alternatives are not a cat and a jellyfish, but a clockwork cat and a live cat. The clockwork cat is very ingenious and very amusing (for five minutes); but the organisation of the live cat beats the construction of the mechanical one all to nothing; and it amuses you not for an age but for all time.'[116] Shaw's discursive plays were organic and alive, while the Scribean well-made play was artificial and lacked the vitalism that Shaw held so dear. *Heartbreak House* was the logical outcome of this dramaturgical viewpoint.

His modernist experimentation with form is signalled in the play's subtitle: *A Fantasia*. This is a distinctly Shavian genre. In the world of

[113] William Archer, *The Old Drama and the New: An Essay in Re-Evaluation* (London: William Heinemann, 1923), 352–3.

[114] Letter of 19 June 1923, in *Bernard Shaw and William Archer*, ed. Postlewait, 384.

[115] Letter of 20 June 1923, in *Bernard Shaw and William Archer*, ed. Postlewait, 387.

[116] Letter of 22 June 1923, in *Bernard Shaw and William Archer*, ed. Postlewait, 391.

music, it is an episodic composition with improvisational qualities.[117] The play breaks from conventional techniques and forms, and Shaw identified this in one of its working titles, 'The House in the Clouds'. As Shaw said to Georges Pitoëff as he prepared the Paris premiere, the house is an 'espèce de palais enchanté', a kind of enchanted palace.[118] Like something hovering in the ether, there is a sense that the play is unmoored from earthly reality and has the shape and character of a dream. The words 'dream' and 'sleep' appear in the play twenty-two and forty-seven times respectively, and Ellie hypnotizes Boss Mangan.[119] The play opens with Ellie falling asleep and Hector and Hesione's family name is Hushabye, hinting at a lullaby, a song used to hush children to sleep. When not catching some shut-eye, the characters act as though they are in dreams, constantly coming and going with the chaos extending to the disjointed conversations. Moreover, there are several fantastic dreamlike coincidences: Hector has been wooing Ellie, who happens to be an acquaintance of his wife; the burglar turns out to be Nurse Guinness's husband, Captain Shotover's pirate, and, as the typescript reveals, Mazzini Dunn's cousin; and at this moment, Ariadne chances to return home for the first time in decades. People walk around in pyjamas and Hector, with no notice from the others, suddenly appears in an Arab's robes. All of this occurs at night, the time of dreams and fancy.[120]

Taken as a whole, these qualities mark the play as expressionistic, with *Heartbreak House* structured by the same sense of reverie as August Strindberg's *A Dream Play* (1901) and George Grosz's *Methuselam* (1922).[121] There are also commonalities in the violent sexual politics of Shaw's play and the works of Strindberg and the German expressionists. Expressionism as a mode arose out of trauma, in Strindberg's case his descent into madness and in the case of Shaw and so many of the Germans the psychological wounds of the First World War. Moreover, the nihilism in Shaw's play has a distinctly expressionist tone, the polar opposite of the meliorism and hope in the Life Force that infuses his plays before the war. In fact, there is no sign of the Life

---

[117] 'Fantasia', in Michael and Joyce Kennedy and Tim Rutherford-Johnson (eds), *The Oxford Dictionary of Music* (6th edn, Oxford: Oxford University Press, 2013).

[118] Letter of 16 November 1927, in *CL* iv. 77.

[119] The word count includes variants such as 'dreaming' and 'asleep'.

[120] For one of the better readings of the play's dream resonances, see ch. 12, 'Heartbreak House: Shaw's Dream Play', in Morgan, *The Shavian Playground*, 200–20.

[121] For a sustained reading of the play as expressionistic, see ch. 9, '*Heartbreak House*: Shavian Expressionism', in Berst, *Bernard Shaw and the Art of Drama*, 221–58.

Force in *Heartbreak House*. Ellie 'marries' the elderly, drunken Shotover, there are no men of her generation because they are off dying in Flanders, and the play ends with a death wish. With this more apocalyptic outlook, Shaw was close to not only the expressionists, but also the broader body of modernists that emerged following the conflict, as evidenced in Yeats's 'The Second Coming', T. S. Eliot's *The Waste Land*, and D. H. Lawrence's *Women in Love*.[122]

The rich allusiveness of *Heartbreak House*, including the nods to Shakespeare and the Russians, further indicates its modernism. People living in a boat might have been inspired by Lena Ashwell's father, but Shaw aligned this quirky lifestyle with a rich literary tradition that has broader implications. Shaw signals this to his readers at the outset of his preface: 'HEARTBREAK HOUSE is not merely the name of the play. . . . It is cultured, leisured Europe before the war' (p. 113). At one point, Hector wonders what will become of 'this ship that we are all in? This soul's prison we call England?' (p. 240). The image of the ship of state has a long history, beginning with Plato who, in the *Republic*, notes that a good captain, like the leader of a state, 'must give his attention to the time of the year, the seasons, the sky, the winds, the stars, and all that pertains to his art if he is to be a true ruler of a ship'.[123] Ellie evokes a more contemporary allusion in referring to Shotover as 'O Captain, my captain'. Here she not only breathlessly admires him, but cites the title of a Walt Whitman poem that recounts a ship arriving safely in port with the captain dead, which is itself an allegory of the United States surviving the Civil War despite the death of its president, Abraham Lincoln.

For Shaw and Shotover, the crisis of the war was brought about by an absence of capable captains in control of the ships of state. Shotover declaims that England is caught in a maelstrom while led by a man who 'is in his bunk, drinking bottled ditch-water; and the crew is gambling in the forecastle'. The ship will inevitably 'strike and sink and split'. His moral: 'Navigation. Learn it and live; or leave it and be damned' (p. 240). Without competence and care, society will merely float aimlessly and eventually be smashed to smithereens on the rocks. Shaw adopted this imagery throughout his career. In *Man and Superman*, Don Juan

---

[122] For such comparisons, see Anne Wright, *Literature of Crisis, 1910–1922: Howard's End, Heartbreak House, Women in Love, and The Waste Land* (London: Macmillan, 1984); Gibbs, *The Art and the Mind of Shaw*, 178; and Nicholas Grene, *Bernard Shaw: A Critical View* (London: Palgrave, 1984), 131.

[123] Plato, *Republic*, 488d.

says, 'To be in hell is to drift: to be in heaven is to steer.'[124] And Shaw titled his 1932 play dealing with the social crisis of the Depression *On the Rocks*. For Shaw, it is the supposed best that society has to offer who have failed to recognize the perils and navigate accordingly, thereby leading to the First World War and the destruction of civilization.

Even Boss Mangan, who at first appears to be a competent individual, is unmasked as a fraud. Referred to as a Napoleon of Industry, he evokes Undershot, the representative Captain of Industry that Thomas Carlyle depicts in *Past and Present* (1843) and whose name served as a model for Shaw's own captain. Examining the horrors wrought by the Industrial Revolution, Carlyle describes Undershot as a selfish hoarder of money, ruthlessly exploiting his workers and thereby leading to the demise of a formerly harmonious society through an inevitably bloody revolution. He compares Undershot not only to the 'uncivilized' natives of North America to highlight his lack of refinement and humanity, but to buccaneers. While critics at first saw the introduction of Shaw's burglar-pirate as a digressive flaw in his stagecraft, they have come to believe that it is essential for consolidating this link between the Captains of Industry and pirate-thieves who care for nothing but their own well-being.[125] Given Shaw's socialism, this condemnation of heartless capitalists and incompetent political leaders reveals how he was able to find some meaning in the wild and messy dream world of *Heartbreak House* that he had such difficulty coming to grips with while composing it.

Saint Joan

In the preface to *Saint Joan*, Shaw says of his titular heroine that there were two opinions of her: 'One was that she was miraculous: the other that she was unbearable' (p. 248). He could have been talking about himself. Both Shaw and Joan were boundlessly energetic visionaries who understood that their purpose was to shape the world by instigating positive progress. Their certainty and assertiveness often led to them being insufferable, though Shaw was blessed with a better capacity to placate and avoid humiliating his opponents than was Joan, who

---

[124] George Bernard Shaw, *Man and Superman, John Bull's Other Island, and Major Barbara*, ed. Brad Kent (Oxford: OUP, 2021).

[125] In two essays written more than three decades apart, Frederick P. W. McDowell proffers himself as an example of this critical about face. See McDowell, 'Technique, Symbol, and Theme in *Heartbreak House*', *PMLA* 68/3 (June 1953), 335–56; and McDowell, 'Apocalypse and After: Recent Interpretations of *Heartbreak House*', *Independent Shavian*, 25 (1987), 3–15.

could bluster with the frustrating self-righteousness of an adolescent. Coming out of the war years and beginning his own upward trajectory in the public's esteem, Shaw identified with Joan as a force of nature whose reputation had suffered fickle fortunes. In writing the play when he did, he effectively aligned their rehabilitations and canonizations.

While *Saint Joan* is tied to Shaw's post-war context, as with his other plays, he had considered the idea for some time. One possible dating of its origins comes from the Court days, when Gilbert Murray, who was reading French historian Jules Michelet's *Jeanne d'Arc* (1853), suggested to Shaw 'that a closely historical account of that trial or the trial of Mary Queen of Scots would make an effective play of quite a new kind'.[126] Shaw had seen Tom Taylor's popular melodrama *Joan of Arc* as a boy in Dublin and Percy Mackaye's *Jeanne d'Arc* in May 1907, and as a music critic he attended recitals of Franz Liszt's *Jeanne d'Arc au bûcher* (Joan of Arc at the Stake) and Moritz Moszkowski's *Johanna D'Arc*.[127] A list of such dubious quality reveals that there was an opening for a great playwright to tackle one of history's most compelling stories. Shaw first admitted an interest in doing so in a letter he wrote while travelling in France in 1913:

I shall do a Joan play some day, beginning with the sweeping up of the cinders and orange peel *after* her martyrdom, and going on with Joan's arrival in heaven. I should have God about to damn the English for their share in her betrayal and Joan producing an end of burnt stick in arrest of Judgment. 'What's that? Is it one of the faggots?' says God. 'No,' says Joan 'it's what is left of the two sticks a common English soldier tied together and gave me as I went to the stake; for they wouldn't even give me a crucifix; and you cannot damn the common people of England, represented by that soldier, because a poor cowardly riff raff of barons and bishops were too futile to resist the devil.'[128]

It appears that William Archer was responsible for finally prodding Shaw to begin his Joan play. As he had done so often in the past, Archer voiced his frustration that Shaw had an immense talent that he constantly undermined with his humour—deflating and jesting when taking things through to their serious conclusion would be more to the

---

[126] *New Statesman and Nation*, 16 August 1947; repr. in Gibbs (ed.), *Shaw: Interviews and Recollections*, 144–5.

[127] Brian Tyson, *The Story of Shaw's Saint Joan* (Montreal: McGill-Queen's University Press, 1982), 26; Michael Holroyd, *Bernard Shaw*, iii. *1918–1950: The Lure of Fantasy* (London: Penguin, 1993), 72.

[128] Letter of 8 September 1913, in *CL* iii. 201–2.

point—and that he foregrounded his philosophic dialectic at the expense of constructed action. As a result, Archer claimed, Shaw had yet to write a world-class play of historical importance. He implored Shaw:

Do your own smelting: let us for once, or twice, or thrice, have the gold without slag; working it into whatever artistic form you please. Say, for instance, a great play, realistic or symbolic, that should go to every city in the world, & shake the souls of people instead of their midriffs. Or a sober analysis of the situation, exact in statement, moderate in invective, silent upon your pet aversions where they are not indispensable to the argument. Vivacious but not undignified, brilliant but not freakish. A book to be translated into every civilized language & read from Tangier to Tokyo.[129]

Since completing his five-play cycle *Back to Methuselah* in 1920, Shaw had been at a loss for inspiration. His wife Charlotte, who had long admired Joan, bought as many books on the saint as she could find and began leaving them around the house. As though suddenly struck by the muses, Shaw one day excitedly announced to her: 'I have a wonderful idea for a new play! It's to be about Saint Joan!'[130]

Shaw understood that the best way forward was to track down the historical record. He went directly to the source, reading T. Douglas Murray's 1902 English translation of Jules Quicherat's five-volume transcription of the 1431 trial and 1456 rehabilitation. Consulting Murray, one is struck by the number of instances in which Shaw openly plagiarizes some of Joan's responses to her interrogators. He was in awe of Joan, admiring her energy, her defiance, her worldly wisdom beyond her years and station in life, and her clarity of thought that bordered on inspired genius. While he was immersing himself in the research in late 1922, he attended a revival of Percy Bysshe Shelley's horror-incest play, *The Cenci*. Watching Sybil Thorndike in the role of Beatrice as she stood on trial for the murder of her villainous father and defiantly pled her innocence, Shaw turned to Charlotte: 'I have found my Joan!'[131]

---

[129] Letter of 22 June 1921, in *Bernard Shaw and William Archer*, ed. Postlewait, 359–60.

[130] Lawrence Langner, *G.B.S and the Lunatic; Reminiscences of the Long, Lively and Affectionate Friendship between George Bernard Shaw and the Author* (New York: Atheneum, 1963), 57.

[131] Sheridan Morley, *Sybil Thorndike: A Life in the Theatre* (London: Weidenfeld & Nicolson, 1977), 68. Other models for Joan include T. E. Lawrence, also known as Lawrence of Arabia, who became a surrogate son of the Shaws during the writing of the play, and the Fabian summer school host Mary Hankinson, who was athletic and puritan. On the former, see Stanley Weintraub, *Private Shaw and Public Shaw: A Dual Portrait of Lawrence of Arabia and G.B.S.* (New York: G. Braziller, 1963), 47–55. On the latter, see Shaw's inscription of her copy of the play: 'To Mary Hankinson, the only woman I know who does not believe she was the model for Joan and also the only woman who actually was', *CL* iii. 554.

As Joan was canonized on 16 May 1920, Shaw feared that renewed interest in the saint would give rise to a host of competitors. He accordingly warned others away from her story, including John Drinkwater, John Masefield, and Laurence Binyon, who had been rumoured to be writing a Joan play.[132] Beginning composition in Malvern on 29 April 1923, Shaw completed it a few months later in Parknasilla, Co. Kerry, Ireland, on 24 August. The Irish playwright Lady Augusta Gregory, who spent a great deal of time with Shaw that May, recalled him reading the scene in which Joan arrives on the banks of the River Loire. She suggested that he have the boy sneeze to indicate that the wind had changed directions in the French forces' favour, which Shaw promptly added.[133] Yet he was unimpressed with the play's opening three scenes. 'This thing is so horribly ridiculous to me', he declared, 'that I am utterly incapable of judging it.'[134] After reading them to Sybil Thorndike, he dismissed them as 'flapdoodle. Now the real play starts.'[135]

The real play, as he called the next three scenes and the epilogue, was meant to be a riposte to other Joan stories. Shaw began with the biggest of them all: Shakespeare. Starting with *Caesar and Cleopatra* (1898), Shaw had written a number of plays that were meant to improve upon the Bard's works. Although Shakespeare did not write a Joan play, she features in *Henry VI, Part I* where she is depicted as a prostitute, a witch, and an agent of the Devil. Shaw referred to this portrait as 'not more authentic than the descriptions in the London papers of George Washington in 1780, of Napoleon in 1803, of the German Crown Prince in 1915, or of Lenin in 1917. It ends in mere scurrility' (p. 263). If the scurrility of Shakespeare's Joan stems from his blind patriotism, then that of Voltaire's arises from his anticlericalism. Voltaire's massive twenty-one-canto *La Pucelle* is part Rabelaisian extravagance and part fantasy, featuring a couple of monks attempting to rape a sleeping Joan, Joan falling in love with Dunois and stripping herself naked before him, and the Devil incarnating Joan's donkey to seduce her into bestiality. It is also blatantly ahistorical, ending with Joan riding off into the sunset with Dunois and featuring sex scenes with Agnès Sorel, Charles VII's mistress who would have been only 7 years old at the time of Joan's battles. In that 1913 letter in which he stated his intention to write a Joan play, Shaw noted: 'English literature must be saved (by an

---

[132] Entry on 20 May 1923, in Lady Gregory, *Lady Gregory's Journals, 1916–1930*, ed. Lennox Robinson (London: Putnam & Company, 1946), 212–13.

[133] Entry on 23 May 1923, in Lady Gregory, *Lady Gregory's Journals*, 215.

[134] Letter of 31 May 1923, in *CL* iii. 827.

[135] Elizabeth Sprigge, *Sybil Thorndike Casson* (London: Gollancz, 1971), 155.

Irishman, as usual) from the disgrace of having nothing to show concerning Joan except the piffling libel in Henry VI, which reminds me that one of my scenes will be Voltaire and Shakespear running down bye streets in heaven to avoid meeting Joan.'[136]

In addition to Shakespeare and Voltaire, Shaw desired to correct the heroic depiction of Joan in contemporary melodrama. The first and most flagrant of these was the German Romantic playwright Friedrich von Schiller's _The Maid of Orleans_ (1801). Schiller began the Romantic tradition in depicting Joan as a beautiful woman. His Joan kills people in battle, rejects marriage proposals from both Dunois and La Hire, interacts with a knight sent from Hell, falls in love with an English soldier, escapes from the English, and, incredibly, dies on the battlefield. Succeeding melodramas, like those by Taylor and MacKaye, and even Mark Twain's 1896 novel _Personal Recollections of Joan of Arc_, keep closer to the historical record, but they too insist on Joan's beauty and the depiction of her accusers and executioners as heartless villains intent only on her destruction and their own power. Shaw insisted that Joan was tried fairly and, therefore, 'There are no villains in the piece' (p. 284). This perspective stemmed from his commitment to history and to drama of a seriously artistic and politically complex nature.

In actuality, Shaw's first three 'flapdoodle' scenes are romance, showing the rise of Joan from a peasant girl to her gaining acceptance at the French court and leading troops to victory. However, they are a decidedly 'anti-romance romance', as Joan is not the beauty of romanticized accounts and has decidedly rough manners.[137] As the succeeding three scenes entail Joan's downfall, the play then becomes a classic tragedy. It ends with the return and canonization of Joan in the epilogue, a sense of renewal in her changing fortunes that points towards comedy. Thus, _Saint Joan_, despite its reliance on the historical record, is further evidence of Shaw's artistic innovation. It is a hybrid with a dual tripartite structure: the typically Shavian exposition–situation–discussion and the Shavian genre mash-up romance–tragedy–comedy.[138]

On 28 December 1923, Lawrence Langner produced the world premiere of _Saint Joan_ at New York's Garrick Theatre. Starring the unheralded Winifred Lenihan, the play ran for 214 performances before touring across the country.[139] In London, it was co-directed by

---

[136] Letter of 8 September 1913, in _CL_ iii. 202.

[137] Grene, _Bernard Shaw: A Critical View_, 134.

[138] A number of critics have commented on this latter structure of the play. The first to do so was Eric Bentley, _Bernard Shaw_, 118.

[139] Langner, _G.B.S and the Lunatic_, 77.

Shaw and Lewis Casson and was likewise a hit with English audiences, with a run of 244 performances at the New Theatre beginning on 24 March 1924. It then toured the provinces before returning to London's Regent's Park Open Air Theatre for another 321 performances.[140] The popularity of the productions did not come at the expense of artistic compromise. Rejecting the lavish decor of melodrama, Shaw continued his aesthetic evolution by opting for a pared-down, modernist stage design. He told Langner to draw upon the work of Gordon Craig and Lee Simonson, the new generation of innovative scenographers on either side of the Atlantic: 'The scenes in Joan can all be reduced to extreme simplicity. A single pillar of the Gordon Craig sort will make the cathedral. All the Loire needs is a horizon and a few of Simonson's lanterns. The trial scene is as easy as the cathedral.'[141]

The critics were more laudatory than they had been in years. Writing in *The Times*, A. B. Walkley called the play 'one of Mr. Shaw's finest achievements'.[142] Desmond MacCarthy declared that *Saint Joan* 'is immensely serious and extremely entertaining; it is a magnificent effort of intellectual energy and full of pathos and sympathy; it is long but it never flags; it is deep, and I am by no means sure that I have got, or that I am going to get, to the bottom of it; it is a play it would be disgraceful to treat inadequately.'[143] Shaw was most enthused by Luigi Pirandello's review, which he considered the 'great press feature of the production'.[144] *Saint Joan*, the Italian playwright claimed, 'is a work of poetry from beginning to end'. It

represents in marvellous fashion what, among so many elements of negation, is the positive element, indeed the fundamental underpinning, in the character, thought and art of this great writer—an outspoken Puritanism, which brooks no go-betweens and no mediations between man and God; a vigorous and independent vital energy, that frees itself restlessly and with joyous scorn from all the stupid and burdensome shackles of habit, routine and tradition, to conquer for itself a natural law more consonant with the poet's own being, and therefore more rational and more sound.

Pirandello knew Shaw well, concluding that 'Joan, like Shaw, cannot exist without a life that is free and fruitful. When she tears up her

[140] Morley, *Sybil Thorndike*, 82.

[141] Letter of 16 October 1923, in BL Add. MS 50539.

[142] A. B. Walkley, *The Times*, 27 March 1924, p. 12.

[143] Desmond MacCarthy, '*Saint Joan*: The Theme and the Drama', *New Statesman*, 5 and 12 April 1924; repr. in Stanley Weintraub (ed.), *Saint Joan: Fifty Years After* (Baton Rouge, LA: Louisiana State University Press, 1973), 31–8, at 31.

[144] Letter of 1 February 1924, in BL Add. MS 50539.

recantation in the face of her deaf and blind accusers, she exemplifies the basic germ of Shaw's art, which is the germ also of his spiritual life.'[145]

From the stages of the anglophone world, *Saint Joan* went on to conquer other parts of the globe. Beginning on 14 October 1924, it had a successful run of 146 performances at Berlin's Deutsches Theater under the direction of Max Reinhardt. Working as a stagehand on the production, a young Bertolt Brecht was later inspired to write a highly appreciative article on Shaw as well as his own Joan play, *Saint Joan of the Stockyards*, which also owes an enormous debt to Shaw's *Major Barbara*.[146] Paris represented another substantial success in a production directed by Georges Pitoëff and starring his wife Ludmilla, who, much to Shaw's horror but to the delight of the French public, played Joan as a melodramatic, pious heroine.[147] Beatrice Webb noted of Shaw that his 'prestige since the publication of *St Joan* has bounded upwards, everywhere he is treated as a "great man" '.[148]

Shaw's subtitle for *Saint Joan* was *A Chronicle Play*, meaning an episodic account of her life. It is, more properly, a history play, a genre that has its origins in the works of Shakespeare. Generally, the history play tends to two forms: a romantic drama that is set in a historical period or a drama (such as Shaw's) wherein the playwright imagines himself a historian.[149] The latter type of history plays are about a particular period, but as they are written through the lens of another context, they carry the biases of the playwright's present. At least implicitly, they raise a series of questions: Where were we then and where are we now? Have we progressed, regressed, or remained static? If change has occurred, what is the nature of this change and how might it have come about? If change has yet to occur, what might we do to avoid stagnation or the endlessly cyclical nature of history?

---

[145] Luigi Pirandello, 'Bernard Shaw's *Saint Joan*', *Times Sunday Magazine*, 3 January 1924, pp. 7–12; repr. in Weintraub (ed.), *Saint Joan: Fifty Years After*, 23–8, at 27–8.

[146] Bertolt Brecht, 'Three Cheers for Shaw', in *Brecht on Theatre: The Development of an Aesthetic*, trans. John Willett (London: Methuen, 1964), 10–13. The original version, 'Ovation für Shaw', was published in the *Berliner Börsen-Courier* on 25 July 1926, the day before Shaw's seventieth birthday.

[147] For accounts of the Pitoëff production, see Daniel C. Gerould, '*Saint Joan* in Paris', *Shaw Review*, 7/1 (January 1964), 11–23; and Michel Pharand, *Bernard Shaw and the French* (Gainesville, FL: University Press of Florida, 2000), 157–69.

[148] Entry on 19 March 1925; Beatrice Webb, *The Diary of Beatrice Webb*, iv. *1924–1943*, ed. Norman and Jeanne MacKenzie (London: Virago Press, 1985), 48.

[149] Matthew K. Wikander, 'Reinventing the History Play: *Caesar and Cleopatra*, *Saint Joan*, "*In Good King Charles's Golden Days*," ', in Innes (ed.), *The Cambridge Companion to George Bernard Shaw*, 195–217, at 195.

Saint Joan comprises a complex layering of times: that of our collective past depicted in the play (1429–31 and 1456); that of Shaw's present, which is embodied in Shaw's preface, the play itself, and the emissary in the epilogue who announces Joan's canonization (1920–3); and our present, whenever it is that we read or watch the play. One of the major differences between *Saint Joan* and Shakespeare's history plays is that Shaw's epilogue juxtaposes these various times, thereby enacting a decoding of history. Shaw highlights this in his preface: 'the question raised by Joan's burning is a burning question still, though the penalties involved are not so sensational. That is why I am probing it. If it were only an historical curiosity I would not waste my readers' time and my own on it for five minutes' (p. 275). Unfortunately, as he laments in his preface to *Heartbreak House*, 'we learn from history that men never learn anything from history' (p. 141). Shaw's role as he saw it was to teach those unlearned lessons.

Yet the demands of the drama are much different from those of a historical study. Aware of this, Shaw provided the audience of the first London production with an explanation. *Saint Joan*, he said, 'does not depart from ascertainable historical truth in any essential particular; but historical facts cannot be put on the stage exactly as they occurred, because they will not fit into its limits of time and space'.[150] As examples, he pointed out that Joan went thrice to Vaucouleurs before she won over the captain, whereas in his play she goes only once; the miracle of the laying hens replaced Joan's advance news of the Battle of Herrings because such detail would have been boring; and her visit to the court at Chinon was likewise compressed. So, too, were her examination, recantation, relapse, and execution, which took place over months. Shaw's artistry is rather evident in how he adapted the historical record. While he maintained most of the facts and some verbatim quotes, he had to make the trial scene more poetic. He admitted that he magnified 'Cauchon, Warwick & The Inquisitor considerably to make the situation intelligible. There is no reason to believe that any of them was capable of expounding it as they do in the play. I had to wash their hands and clear their heads a bit; but I see no evidence that they were false to their own lights.'[151] Moreover, in his history plays, Shaw abandons the physical conflicts and pictorial realism of melodrama and spectacle. There is no battle or sword-fight, no pageantry of the

---

[150] Bernard Shaw, programme note to *Saint Joan*; repr. in Mander and Mitchenson, *Theatrical Companion to Shaw*, 207–8, at 207.

[151] Letter of 7 June 1924, in *CL* iii. 877.

coronation, and no glorious death scene for Joan at the stake. Instead, Shaw emphasizes the clash of ideas over action, seeing history as a process and a drama built upon the conflict of opposing ways of interpreting the world. In so doing, he ushered in the modern history play.

Furthermore, Shaw overhauls the language of the genre. Before him, such works tended to adopt an elevated pseudo-poetic diction, whereas his characters speak in a direct and contemporary prose. The result is that the audience considers the play from its own perspective. Shaw enhances this jarring of the audience's sensibilities through his repeated anachronisms. Characters in feudal times recognize and label the concepts of nationalism and Protestantism, and they reveal a hypermodern self-awareness of the future significance of their actions. This is in many ways what Brecht had in mind when he developed his concept of alienating or distancing the audience from the action, drawing them outside the world of the play and back to their lived reality.

Saint Joan presents the audience with three examples of Joan's heresies, the first being her nationalism. As Shaw's creative addition to history, de Stogumber represents the warmongering patriotism of a colonial power that seeks to expand its borders and control far-flung dominions, the very mentality that justified the British Empire and the bellicose nationalism that led to the First World War. Just as Joan wants France for the French, de Stogumber ties himself to the soil of his land. Shaw further links Joan to nationalists by discussing her in the preface in relation to Roger Casement, who was executed for running guns to Ireland on board a German submarine to assist with the anti-colonial 1916 Easter Rising. For Shaw, Joan represents the beginnings of a shift from medieval feudalism, with its emphasis on local relations and adherence to aristocratic lords, towards modern nationalism, with its emphasis on broader loyalties to an imagined community rendered coherent by the institutions of a complex state. Such a shift threatened the local powers of her day, which explains the aristocratic Warwick's desire to see her destroyed.

Joan's second threat to the authorities is her proto-Protestantism. Shaw uses the term 'Protestantism' not in its narrow contemporary meaning of Protestant Christianity, but in the sense of a broader religious protest similar to the Old Testament prophets, Jesus, and Muhammad.[152] 'All religions begin with a revolt against morality,' Shaw wrote some time before composing the play, 'and perish when

---

[152] On this point, see Anthony S. Abbott, *Shaw and Christianity* (New York: Seabury Press, 1965), 165.

morality conquers them and stamps out such words as grace and sin, substituting for them morality and immorality.'[153] Throughout his oeuvre, Shaw identifies himself as deeply immoral, that is, as one who differs from current morality. Morality expressed in cultural, religious, social, or political terms is merely the conglomeration of the dominant or accepted norms and mores; immorality is therefore not inherently evil, but authorities cast it as such because it challenges them.[154] While the Catholic Church required its adherents to conform to its doctrine, Joan listened to her voices and insisted that she was in direct communion with God. As Warwick says, 'It is the protest of the individual soul against the interference of priest or peer between the private man and his God. I should call it Protestantism if I had to find a name for it' (p. 337).

In both the play and the transcript of the trial, Joan is also condemned for dressing as a man. In many respects, the one heresy stems from the other, with her voices commanding her to don men's clothes. It might be tempting to see Joan as desexualized merely to satisfy a puritan streak in Shaw himself or in an author who advertises himself as feminist while unable to consider that a woman could be both feminine and a warrior.[155] Having read Anatole France's biography of Joan, Shaw was struck by the fact that the Frenchman 'was completely disabled as to Joan herself by a simple disbelief in the existence of *ability* (in the manly sense) in women'.[156] He does not mean here ability in the manly sense as he sees it, but as society sees it, writing that Joan's 'success was a genuine success of ability of the kind supposed to be exclusively masculine'.[157] Lady Rhondda, a prominent suffragist, noted Shaw's recognition of this ability in his depiction of Joan: 'Here is a man who can understand that a woman can be attractive as a person without being concerned with sex; and, more than that, one who can be interested in a woman who is not sexually interesting—here in fact is a man whose concern with people of either sex lies in the fact that they are human beings. Oh, marvel!'[158] For Shaw and many others of his

---

[153] Wisenthal, *Shaw and Ibsen*, 198.

[154] For more on this, see Brad Kent, 'Censorship and Immorality: Bernard Shaw's *The Devil's Disciple*', *Modern Drama* 54/4 (Winter 2011), 511–33.

[155] The latter charge is more typical of those who are critical of too facilely accepting Shaw's tendency to depict strong female characters as evidence of his feminist bona fides. See e.g. Gainor, *Shaw's Daughters*, 136–48.

[156] Letter of 1 May 1924, in *CL* iii. 876.

[157] Letter of 5 January 1924, in *CL* iii. 858.

[158] Lady Rhondda, *Time and Tide*, 11 April 1930.

time, Joan represented militant suffragist feminism. He discusses Sylvia Pankhurst in the preface and, in a BBC address marking the five hundredth anniversary of Joan's burning, he told listeners: 'If you read Miss Pankhurst, you will understand a great deal more about the psychology of Joan, and her position at the trial, than you will by reading the historical accounts, which are very dry.'[159]

In Joan, these three heresies—nationalism, Protestantism, and feminism—condemn her in the eyes of the conservative authorities and thereby raise her in Shaw's esteem. As he argues in the preface, society must be more tolerant and allow for such heretics and immorality. Linking Joan to Socrates, Christ, Giordano Bruno, Galileo, Napoleon, Edith Cavell, Casement, and Pankhurst, Shaw makes the case that heretics are progressive visionaries without whom society would stagnate and fall to ruin. In this sense, Joan is Shaw's incarnation of the Life Force willing a new and better world into being.

While their heresies made controversial figures of Shaw and Joan, the most debated part of the play has consistently been the epilogue. When it was first performed, leading critics considered it 'an artistic error', lacking 'dramatic effectiveness', and even 'wholly unnecessary'.[160] Yet one outlier at the time recognized that it was central to the play's effect:

It is as though Shaw were to step out into the audience and shake the fat fellow in the front row whom the play has worked up into such a glow of sympathy, such a flutter of easy pity—shake him and whisper in his ear: 'If you had been in Rouen that day are you sure you would not have voted with the Bishop of Beauvais and run with the witch-burning mob to see the torch applied!'[161]

In a programme note to the audience, Shaw said that without the epilogue, 'the play would be only a sensational tale of a girl who was burnt, leaving the spectators plunged in horror, despairing of humanity. The true tale of Saint Joan is a tale with a glorious ending; and any play that did not make this clear would be an insult to her memory.'[162]

---

[159] Bernard Shaw, 'Saint Joan: A Radio Talk', *The Listener*, 3 June 1931; repr. in Shaw, *Platform and Pulpit*, ed. Laurence, 208–16, at 215.

[160] Respectively, from A. B. Walkley, *The Times*, 27 March 1924; *The Stage*, 10 January 1924; and James Agate, *Sunday Times*, 30 March 1924; all repr. in Evans (ed.), *Shaw: The Critical Heritage*, 277–90.

[161] Alexander Woolcott, *New York Herald*, 29 December 1923; repr. in Evans (ed.), *Shaw: The Critical Heritage*, 275–7, at 277.

[162] Bernard Shaw, programme note to *Saint Joan*; repr. in Mander and Mitchenson, *Theatrical Companion to Shaw*, 207–8, at 207.

Academic critics have long embraced Shaw's view.[163] Joan returns to
France in 1456, but she intermingles with a harbinger of the modern
age, too. The motley cast comments directly on the meaning of her
story and its relation to society. In so doing, they shatter the historical
illusion in a manner that further predicts Brecht's methods. Working in
conjunction with the anachronisms, the epilogue confronts the audience with its modernity. Warwick concludes the play in 1431 by wondering if they have indeed heard the end of Joan, which is a merely
ironic moment. In contradistinction, the epilogue set in 1456 raises
questions that remain unanswered. When de Stogumber admits that he
had not been saved by depictions of Christ's sufferings, but that he was
by Joan's, Cauchon asks: 'Must then a Christ perish in torment in every
age to save those that have no imagination?' (p. 385). The play ends on
a series of even more direct questions: 'O God that madest this beautiful earth, when will it be ready to receive Thy saints? How long, O Lord,
how long?' (p. 391). Importantly, Joan is alone on stage, in effect directing her question to the audience, who in turn must cultivate society to
be more tolerant and accepting of saints and visionary geniuses—like
Joan, as well as Shaw.

It is somewhat paradoxical that Shaw's aesthetic and political modernity can be gleaned through a play about a medieval saint. Yet all
three of the plays in this volume, separately and collectively, demon-
strate how Shaw was a major innovator of the theatre, challenging
received ideas and introducing avant-garde dramaturgical methods.

---

[163] For some of the more thoughtful defences of the epilogue, see Warren Sylvester
Smith, *Bishop of Everywhere: Bernard Shaw and the Life Force* (University Park:
Pennsylvania State University Press, 1982), 128–9; Grene, *Bernard Shaw: A Critical
View*, 148; Stephen Watt, 'Shaw's *Saint Joan* and the Modern History Play', *Comparative
Drama*, 19/1 (1985), 58–86, at 75–7; Bertolini, *The Playwrighting Self of Bernard Shaw*,
130; and Jean Chothia, *English Drama of the Early Modern Period, 1890–1940* (London:
Longman, 1996), 159.

NOTE ON THE TEXT

THE copy-texts for the plays are from Constable's *Androcles and the Lion, Overruled, Pygmalion* (1941); *Heartbreak House, Great Catherine, Playlets of the War* (1931); and *Saint Joan: A Chronicle, and The Apple Cart: A Political Extravaganza* (1933). These are the standard editions and the last authoritative versions that Shaw published in his lifetime. Two other sources were consulted in the production of the definitive texts: *The Bodley Head Bernard Shaw: Collected Plays with Their Prefaces*, volumes iv, v, and vi (1970), and the editions of Shaw's plays published by Penguin (2000–1); Dan H. Laurence edited both of these series. These later editions were helpful in confirming a few errors that I found in Shaw's work, which I have silently corrected.

The annotations indicate revisions that Shaw made to his plays over the years, using former published editions, proofs, and typescripts. Constable published earlier editions of *Pygmalion* (1916, 1931, and 1939), *Heartbreak House* (1919), and *Saint Joan* (1924). For *Pygmalion*, I have also consulted the 1913 proofs of the Constable edition (British Library, Add. MS 50629), the bound copy Shaw submitted to the Lord Chamberlain's Office in February 1914 (British Library, Add. MS 66056 F), the play's typescript (Harry Ransom Center, Bernard Shaw Collection, Box 24, Folder 5), an insert for that typescript (Harry Ransom Center, Bernard Shaw Collection, Box 24, Folder 6), and the typescript of the preface and sequel (Harry Ransom Center, Bernard Shaw Collection, Box 25, Folder 4), all of which include Shaw's manuscript emendations. For *Heartbreak House*, I consulted a facsimile of the first typescript that was published by Garland in 1981 as well as the original in the British Library (Add. MS 59901). For *Saint Joan*, I have consulted the typed transcript (British Library, Add. MS 50633), the copy Shaw submitted to the Lord Chamberlain in 1924 (British Library, Add. MS 66385 A), Shaw's research notes (British Library, Add. MS 63182), proofs of the 1924 Constable edition (Harry Ransom Center, Bernard Shaw Collection, Box 27, Folders 1–2), and a 1934 scenario that Shaw wrote (Harry Ransom Center, Bernard Shaw Collection, Box 27, Folder 4). Shaw also kept rehearsal notes for the productions of the plays that he oversaw (British Library, Add. MS 50644); these enlighten how Shaw further imagined his script being transformed on the stage. I have indicated discrepancies between the various versions where I feel that they add something to our understanding of the plays and Shaw's changing vision.

Shaw had some idiosyncrasies in terms of punctuation and spelling that I have maintained, so some explanation is warranted in the event that readers believe typographical errors have crept into the text. He considered the apostrophe unsightly and thus refrained from using it in contractions except for in cases where it would cause some confusion, such as *he'll, it's, we're*. However, at times, he employed apostrophes in the transcripts; when these documents are cited, apostrophes are kept as they appear in the original. Although he was an Irishman living in London, Shaw preferred the American form of dropping the 'u' in words ending in *-our*, such as *honor*. Despite these apparent modernizations, he also held fast to some archaic spellings, notably preferring *shew* to *show*. Moreover, Shaw spelled some names, like Tchekov, differently than how they are written today, but in keeping with how they appeared in his time, whereas others, notably Shakespear, are spelled according to his own preference. At times, I have standardized his spelling to remain consistent across the volume when the same word appears in more than one way in the original, such as 'flower girl' and 'flower-girl'.

Lastly, Shaw signified emphasis in dialogue by spacing his words and, at times, using a slightly larger font, so that *has* appeared as h a s. However, this manner of emphasizing words is particularly difficult to detect in some of the editions. To facilitate reading and to minimize the risk of missing these directions, I have changed all emphases to italics.

SELECT BIBLIOGRAPHY

Autobiographical Writing and Letters

Shaw, Bernard, *Bernard Shaw: An Autobiography 1856–1950*, ed. Stanley Weintraub, 2 vols (New York: Max Reinhardt, 1970).

Shaw, Bernard, *Bernard Shaw and Mrs. Patrick Campbell: Their Correspondence*, ed. Alan Dent (London: Victor Gollancz, 1952).

Shaw, Bernard, *Bernard Shaw: Collected Letters*, ed. Dan H. Laurence, 4 vols (London: Max Reinhardt, 1965–88).

Shaw, Bernard, *Bernard Shaw's Letters to Siegfried Trebitsch*, ed. Samuel A. Weiss (Stanford, CA: Stanford University Press, 1986).

Shaw, Bernard, *Selected Correspondence of Bernard Shaw*, ed. L. W. Conolly and J. Percy Smith, 9 vols (Toronto: University of Toronto Press, 1995–2017).

Shaw, Bernard, *Sixteen Self Sketches* (London: Constable, 1949).

Biography

Ervine, St John, *Bernard Shaw: His Life, Work and Friends* (London: Constable, 1956).

Gibbs, A. M., *Bernard Shaw: A Life* (Gainesville, FL: University Press of Florida, 2005).

Holroyd, Michael, *Bernard Shaw*, 4 vols (London: Penguin, 1990–3).

Weintraub, Stanley, *Journey to Heartbreak: The Crucible Years of Bernard Shaw 1914–1918* (New York: Weybright and Talley, 1971).

Reference Works

Gibbs, A. M., *Shaw: A Chronology* (London: Palgrave Macmillan, 2001).

Laurence, Dan H., *Bernard Shaw: A Bibliography*. 2 vols (Oxford: Clarendon Press, 1983).

Wearing, J. P., Adams, Elsie B., and Haberman, Donald C. (eds), *G. B. Shaw: An Annotated Bibliography of Writings About Him*, 3 vols (DeKalb, IL: Northern Illinois University Press, 1986).

General Studies

Berst, Charles A., *Bernard Shaw and the Art of Drama* (Urbana, IL: University of Illinois Press, 1973).

Bertolini, John A., *The Playwrighting Self of Bernard Shaw* (Carbondale, IL: Southern Illinois University Press, 1991).

Dukore, Bernard F., *Shaw's Theater* (Gainesville, FL: University Press of Florida, 2000).

Grene, Nicholas, *Shaw: A Critical View* (London: Palgrave, 1984).

Innes, Christopher (ed.), *The Cambridge Companion to George Bernard Shaw* (Cambridge: Cambridge University Press, 1998).

Select Bibliography

Kent, Brad (ed.), *George Bernard Shaw in Context* (Cambridge: Cambridge University Press, 2015).

Morgan, Margery M., *The Shavian Playground: An Exploration of the Art of George Bernard Shaw* (London: Methuen, 1972).

Wisenthal, J. L., *The Marriage of Contraries: Bernard Shaw's Middle Plays* (Cambridge, MA: Harvard University Press, 1974).

Criticism on Pygmalion

Bauschatz, Paul, 'The Uneasy Evolution of *My Fair Lady* from *Pygmalion*', *SHAW* 18 (1998), 181–98.

Berst, Charles A., *Pygmalion: Shaw's Spin on Myth and Cinderella* (New York: Twayne, 1995).

Buckley, Jennifer, 'Talking Machines: Shaw, Phonography, and *Pygmalion*', *SHAW* 35/1 (2015), 21–45.

Karakowsky, Len, DeGama, Nadia, and McBey, Kenneth, 'Deconstructing Higgins: Gender Bias in the Pygmalion Phenomenon', *Gender in Management: An International Journal*, 32/1 (2017), 2–18.

McGovern, Derek, 'From Stage Play to Hybrid: Shaw's Three Editions of *Pygmalion*', *SHAW* 31 (2011), 9–30.

Marshik, Celia, 'Parodying the £5 Virgin: Bernard Shaw and the Playing of *Pygmalion*', *Yale Journal of Criticism*, 13/2 (2000), 321–41.

Plant, David, 'A Look at Narcissism through Professor Higgins in *Pygmalion*', *British Journal of Psychotherapy*, 28/1 (2012), 50–65.

Reynolds, Jean, *Pygmalion's Word Play: The Postmodern Shaw* (Gainesville: University Press of Florida, 1999).

Reynolds, Jean, 'Shaw's *Pygmalion*: The Play's the Thing', *SHAW* 36/2 (2016), 238–55.

Criticism on Heartbreak House

Gamboa, Brett, '*King Lear, Heartbreak House*, and the Dynamics of Inertia', *SHAW* 35/1 (2015), 86–106.

Gibbs, A. M., '*Heartbreak House*: Chamber of Echoes', *SHAW* 13 (1993), 113–32.

Harding, Desmond, 'Bearing Witness: *Heartbreak House* and the Poetics of Trauma', *SHAW* 26 (2006), 6–26.

Leary, D. J., 'Shaw's Blakean Vision: A Dialectic Approach to *Heartbreak House*', *Modern Drama*, 15/1 (1972), 89–103.

Nathan, Rhoda, 'The "Daimons" of *Heartbreak House*', *Modern Drama*, 21/3 (1978), 253–65.

Stockholder, Fred E., 'A Schopenhauerian Reading of *Heartbreak House*', *Shaw Review*, 19/1 (1976), 22–43.

Vogt, Sally Peters, '*Heartbreak House*: Shaw's Ship of Fools', *Modern Drama*, 21/3 (1978), 267–86.

Woodfield, James, 'Ellie in Wonderland: Dream and Madness in *Heartbreak House*', *English Studies in Canada*, 11/3 (1985), 334–45.

Wright, Anne, *Literature of Crisis, 1910–1922: Howard's End, Heartbreak House, Women in Love, and The Waste Land* (London: Macmillan, 1984).

Criticism on Saint Joan

Boas, Frederick S., 'Joan of Arc in Shakespeare, Schiller, and Shaw', *Shakespeare Quarterly*, 2/1 (1951), 35–45.

Cuomo, Glenn R., '"Saint Joan before the Cannibals": George Bernard Shaw in the Third Reich', *German Studies Review*, 16/3 (1993), 435–61.

Hill, Holly, *Playing Joan: Actresses on the Challenge of Shaw's Saint Joan: Twenty-Six Interviews* (New York: Theatre Communications Group, 1987).

Kent, Brad, 'Towards a Progressive Ethics of Shamelessness: Heresy and Affect in Bernard Shaw's *Saint Joan*', *Modern Drama*, 63/3 (2020), 289–310.

Kiberd, Declan, 'Saint Joan—Fabian Feminist, Protestant Mystic', in *Inventing Ireland: The Literature of the Modern Nation* (Cambridge, MA: Harvard University Press, 1996), 428–37.

Moran, James, 'Meditations in Time of Civil War: *Back to Methuselah* and *Saint Joan* in Production, 1919–1924', *SHAW* 30 (2010), 147–60.

Solomon, Stanley J., '*Saint Joan* as Epic Tragedy', *Modern Drama*, 6/4 (1963), 437–49.

Tyson, Brian, *The Story of Shaw's Saint Joan* (Montreal: McGill-Queen's University Press, 1982).

Watt, Stephen, 'Shaw's *Saint Joan* and the Modern History Play', *Comparative Drama*, 19/1 (1985), 58–86.

Weintraub, Stanley (ed.), *Saint Joan: Fifty Years After* (Baton Rouge, LA: Louisiana State University Press, 1973).

Further Reading in Oxford World's Classics

Shaw, George Bernard, *Arms and the Man, The Devil's Disciple, and Caesar and Cleopatra*, ed. Lawrence Switzky.

Shaw, George Bernard, *The Apple Cart, Too True to Be Good, On the Rocks, and The Millionairess*, ed. Matthew Yde.

Shaw, George Bernard, *Major Cultural Essays*, ed. David Kornhaber.

Shaw, George Bernard, *Man and Superman, John Bull's Other Island, and Major Barbara*, ed. Brad Kent.

Shaw, George Bernard, *Mrs Warren's Profession, Candida, and You Never Can Tell*, ed. Sos Eltis.

Shaw, George Bernard, *Playlets*, ed. James Moran.

Shaw, George Bernard, *Major Political Writings*, ed. Elizabeth Miller.

A CHRONOLOGY OF
GEORGE BERNARD SHAW

Plays and novels are listed according to the dates on which their composition was completed. The parenthetical information provides the date and place of the play's first performance, not including specially arranged copyright performances, as well as the subtitle in some instances; in the case of novels, the date on which each was first published as a book—as opposed to serialized in a journal—is indicated. Other major writings are listed according to their date of publication.

1856 Born in Dublin on 26 July.

1871 Leaves school for good in October; begins work as an office boy for a Dublin land agent in November.

1873 Promoted to cashier in February.

1876 Leaves job with Dublin land agent in March; moves to London on 1 April.

1878 *Passion Play* (unfinished).

1879 *Immaturity* (1930).

1880 *The Irrational Knot* (1905).

1882 *Love Among the Artists* (1900).

1883 *Cashel Byron's Profession* (1886); *An Unsocial Socialist* (1887).

1884 The Fabian Society is founded on 4 January; GBS attends his first meeting on 16 May and formally joins on 5 September; publishes his first pamphlet for them, 'A Manifesto', in October.

1886 Begins as art critic for *The World*, a position he will keep until January 1890.

1889 Begins as music critic for *The Star* under the pseudonym 'Corno di Bassetto' in February; *Fabian Essays in Socialism*.

1890 Resigns as music critic for *The Star* and begins as music critic for *The World* in May under the name G.B.S.

1891 *The Quintessence of Ibsenism*.

1892 *Widowers' Houses* (9 December 1892, Royalty Theatre, London).

1893 *The Philanderer: A Topical Comedy* (20 February 1905, Cripplegate Institute, London); *Mrs Warren's Profession* (5 January 1902, New Lyric Club, London).

1894   *Arms and the Man: An Anti-Romantic Comedy* (21 April 1894, Avenue
          Theatre, London); *Candida: A Mystery* (30 July 1897, Her Majesty's
          Theatre, Aberdeen); writes last article for *The World* in August.

1895   Begins as theatre critic at the *Saturday Review* in January; *The Man
          of Destiny: A Fictitious Paragraph of History* (1 July 1897, Grand
          Theatre, Croydon).

1896   *You Never Can Tell: A Comedy* (26 November 1899, Royalty Theatre,
          London).

1897   *The Devil's Disciple: A Melodrama* (1 October 1897, Harmanus
          Bleecker Hall, Albany, NY); elected as a member of the Vestry of the
          Parish of St Pancras, 18 May 1897.

1898   Resigns as theatre critic at the *Saturday Review* in May; marries
          Charlotte Frances Payne-Townshend at the Registry Office,
          Henrietta Street, Covent Garden, on 1 June; *The Perfect Wagnerite*;
          Caesar and Cleopatra: A History (1 May 1901, Anna Morgan Studios
          for Art and Expression at the Fine Arts Building, Chicago).

1899   *Captain Brassbound's Conversion: An Adventure* (16 December 1900,
          Strand Theatre, London).

1900   Re-elected for a second (and final) three-year term as a member of
          the St Pancras Borough Council (reconfigured since the prior
          election of 1897); *Fabianism and the Empire*.

1901   *The Admirable Bashville: or, Constancy Unrewarded* (14 December
          1902, Pharos Club, London).

1903   *Man and Superman: A Comedy and a Philosophy* (21 May 1905, Court
          Theatre, London, though without Act III; *Don Juan in Hell* is first
          performed on 4 June 1907, Court Theatre, London; the entire play is
          first performed on 11 June 1915, Lyceum Theatre, Edinburgh).

1904   *How He Lied to Her Husband* (26 September 1904, Berkeley Lyceum,
          New York); *John Bull's Other Island* (1 November 1904, Court
          Theatre, London).

1905   *Passion, Poison, and Petrifaction: or the Fatal Gazogene* (A Brief
          Tragedy for Barns and Booths) (14 July 1905, Theatrical Garden
          Party, Regent's Park, London); *Major Barbara* (A Discussion) (28
          November 1905, Court Theatre, London).

1906   *The Doctor's Dilemma: A Tragedy* (20 November 1906, Court
          Theatre, London).

1908   *The Sanity of Art* (First published as 'A Degenerate's View of
          Nordau', in *Liberty* (New York), 27 July 1895); *Getting Married:
          A Disquisitory Play* (12 May 1908, Haymarket Theatre, London).

1923 *Saint Joan: A Chronicle Play in Six Scenes and an Epilogue* (28 December 1923, Garrick Theatre, New York).

1926 *Translations and Tomfooleries*; the Swedish Academy announces that Shaw has won the 1925 Nobel Prize for Literature, 12 November.

1927 Accepts the Nobel Prize in February.

1928 *The Intelligent Woman's Guide to Socialism and Capitalism*; *The Apple Cart: A Political Extravaganza* (14 June 1929, Teatr Polski, Warsaw).

1931 *Music in London 1890–94: Criticisms contributed Week by Week to the World*; *Our Theatres in the Nineties*; *Too True To Be Good: A Political Extravaganza* (29 February 1932, Colonial Theatre, Boston, MA).

1932 *The Adventures of the Black Girl in Her Search for God.*

1933 *Village Wooing: A Comedietta for Two Voices* (16 April 1934, Little Theatre, Dallas, TX); *On the Rocks: A Political Comedy* (25 November 1933, Winter Garden Theatre, London).

1934 *The Simpleton of the Unexpected Isles: A Vision of Judgment* (18 February 1935, Guild Theatre, New York); *The Six of Calais: A Medieval War Story* (17 July 1934, Open Air Theatre, Regent's Park, London).

1935 *The Millionairess* (A Jonsonian Comedy) (4 January 1936, Akademie Theater, Vienna).

1936 *Geneva: Another Political Extravaganza* (25 July 1938, Teatr Polski, Warsaw).

1937 *Cymbeline Refinished: A Variation on Shakespear's Ending* (16 November 1937, Embassy Theatre, London).

1939 Wins the Academy Award for the best screenplay for the cinematic adaptation of *Pygmalion*; '*In Good King Charles's Golden Days*': *A True History that Never Happened* (12 August 1939, Festival Theatre, Malvern); outbreak of the Second World War: Britain and France declare war on Germany on 3 September.

1944 *Everybody's Political What's What.*

1945 Second World War ends.

1947 *Buoyant Billions: A Comedy of No Manners* (21 October 1948, Schauspielhaus, Zurich, Switzerland).

1949 *Sixteen Self Sketches*; *Shakes Versus Shav: A Puppet Play* (9 August 1949, Lyttelton Hall, Malvern).

1950 *Farfetched Fables* (6 September 1950, Watergate Theatre, London). Dies in Ayot St Lawrence on 2 November.

ABBREVIATIONS

CL	*Bernard Shaw: Collected Letters*, ed. Dan H. Lawrence, 4 vols:
	vol. i. *1874–1897* (London: Max Reinhardt; New York: Dodd, Mead, 1965);
	vol. ii. *1898–1910* (London: Max Reinhardt; New York: Dodd, Mead, 1972);
	vol. iii. *1911–1925* (London and New York: Penguin Viking Group, 1985);
	vol. iv. *1926–1950* (London and New York: Penguin Viking Group, 1988)
CON P 1913	British Library, Add. MS 50629; proofs for the 1913 Constable edition of *Pygmalion*, with Shaw's emendations
CON P 1916	1916 edition of *Pygmalion*, published by Constable with *Androcles and the Lion* and *Overruled*
CON P 1931	1931 edition of *Pygmalion*, published by Constable with *Androcles and the Lion* and *Overruled*
CON P 1939	1939 edition of *Pygmalion*, published by Constable with *Androcles and the Lion* and *Overruled*
HH Type	British Library, Add. MS 59901: revised Typescript of *Heartbreak House*
LC P	British Library, Add. MS 66056 F: bound copy of *Pygmalion* and George S. Street's Reader's Report for the Lord Chamberlain, dated 23 February 1914; also includes a Reader's comment on the revised 1941 edition when it was submitted for performance
LCP SJ	British Library, LCP Corr 1924/5376: *Saint Joan*: the Lord Chamberlain's Reader's Report, by George S. Street, for *Saint Joan*, 28 February 1924
Murray	T. Douglas Murray (ed.), *Jeanne D'Arc, Maid of Orleans, Deliverer of France: Being the Story of her Life, her Achievements, and her Death, as attested on Oath and Set forth in the Original Documents* (New York: McClure, Phillips, 1902)
P Type	Harry Ransom Center, Bernard Shaw Collection, Box 24, Folder 5: typescript of *Pygmalion* with Shaw's manuscript emendations

P Type Ins	Harry Ransom Center, Bernard Shaw Collection, Box 24, Folder 6: typescript insert for *Pygmalion* with Shaw's manuscript emendations
P Pre/Ep	Harry Ransom Center, Bernard Shaw Collection, Box 25, Folder 4: typescript for the Preface and Epilogue to *Pygmalion* with Shaw's manuscript emendations
RN HH 1921	British Library, Add. MS 50644: Shaw's rehearsal notes for the Court Theatre production of *Heartbreak House*, 22, 23, 26, 27, 28, 29, and 30 September 1921
RN P 1920	British Library, Add. MS 50644: Shaw's rehearsal notes for a production of *Pygmalion*, 22 January and 9 February 1920
RN P 1936	British Library, Add. MS 50644: Shaw's rehearsal notes made at Birmingham on 15 July 1936, in preparation for a production of *Pygmalion* at the Malvern Festival
RN SJ 1924	British Library, Add. MS 50644: Shaw's rehearsal notes for *Saint Joan* in London, with Sybil Thorndike as Joan, 3, 5, 8, 10, 11, 12, 13, 15, 17, 18, 19, 20, and 24 March 1924
RN SJ 1936	British Library, Add. MS 50644: Shaw's rehearsal notes made at Birmingham on 13 July 1936, in preparation for a production of *Saint Joan* at the Malvern Festival
RN SJ n.d.	Harry Ransom Center, Bernard Shaw Collection, Box 27, Folder 3: Shaw's undated rehearsal notes for a production of *Saint Joan*
SHAW	*SHAW: The Annual of Bernard Shaw Studies* (1981 to 2014); *SHAW: The Journal of Bernard Shaw Studies* (2015–)
SJ Folio	British Library, Add. MS 50633, fos. 1–28: typed transcript of the original shorthand draft of *Saint Joan*
SJ LC	British Library, Add. MS 66385 A *Saint Joan*: the Lord Chamberlain's bound copy of *Saint Joan*, an unpublished proof of the 1924 Constable edition
SJ Notes	British Library, Add. MS 63182, fos. 1–6: Shaw's research notes for *Saint Joan*
SJ Proof	Harry Ransom Center, Bernard Shaw Collection, Box 27, Folder 1: Rough Proof of *Saint Joan* for the 1924 Constable Edition
SJ Proof 2	Harry Ransom Center, Bernard Shaw Collection, Box 27, Folder 2: Rough Proof of *Saint Joan* for the 1924 Constable Edition

SJ Proof 3 Harry Ransom Center, Bernard Shaw Collection, Box 27,
            Folder 2: Rough Proof of *Saint Joan* for the 1924 Constable
            Edition
SJ Scenario Harry Ransom Center, Bernard Shaw Collection, Box 27,
            Folder 4: Holograph scenario for *Saint Joan*, 1934

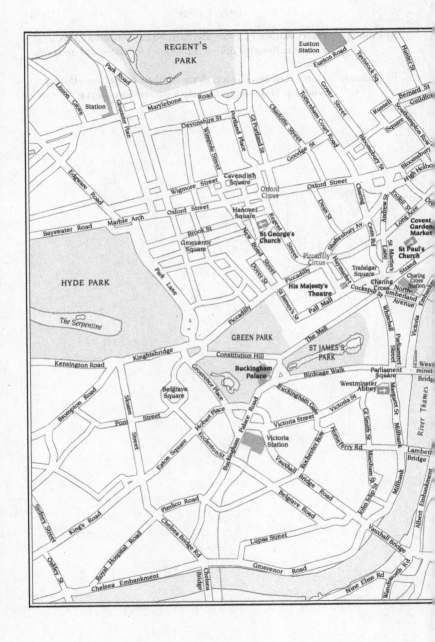

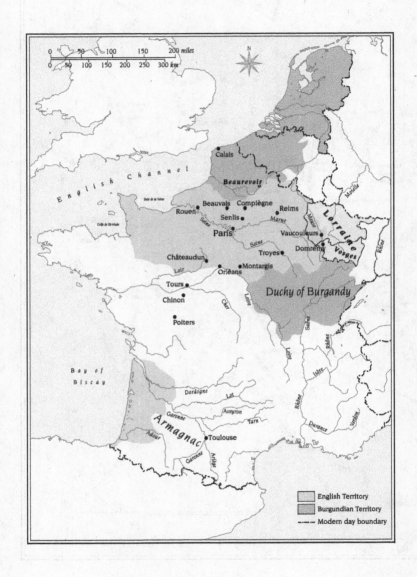

Calais

Beaurevoir

Beauvais Compiègne
Rouen Reims
Senlis Marne
Paris
Vaucouleurs
Troyes Domrémy
Châteaudun Vosges
Montargis
Orléans
Tours
Chinon
Poiters

Duchy of Burgandy

Bay of
Biscay

Armagnac
Toulouse

English Channel

Lorraine

Seine

Loire

Cher

Dordogne Lot
Garonne Aveyron
Tarn
Garonne Ariège
Adour

Rhône

Isère

Durance

Moselle

Meuse

Saône

Verdon

0 50 100 150 200 *miles*
0 50 100 150 200 250 300 *km*

N

English Territory
Burgundian Territory
------- Modern day boundary

PYGMALION

A Romance in Five Acts

NOTE FOR TECHNICIANS.* A complete representation of the play as printed for the first time in this edition is technically possible only on the cinema screen or on stages furnished with exceptionally elaborate machinery. For ordinary theatrical use the scenes separated by rows of asterisks are to be omitted.

In the dialogue an e upside down* indicates the indefinite vowel, sometimes called obscure or neutral, for which, though it is one of the commonest sounds in English speech, our wretched alphabet has no letter.

PREFACE TO PYGMALION
A PROFESSOR OF PHONETICS

As will be seen later on, Pygmalion needs, not a preface, but a sequel, which I have supplied in its due place.

The English have no respect for their language, and will not teach their children to speak it. They cannot spell it because they have nothing to spell it with but an old foreign alphabet of which only the consonants—and not all of them—have any agreed speech value. Consequently no man can teach himself what it should sound like from reading it; and it is impossible for an Englishman to open his mouth without making some other Englishman despise him. Most European languages are now accessible in black and white to foreigners: English and French are not thus accessible even to Englishmen and Frenchmen.* The reformer we need most today is an energetic phonetic enthusiast: that is why I have made such a one the hero of a popular play.

There have been heroes of that kind crying in the wilderness for many years past. When I became interested in the subject towards the end of the eighteen-seventies, the illustrious Alexander Melville Bell, the inventor of Visible Speech, had emigrated to Canada, where his son invented the telephone;* but Alexander J. Ellis* was still a London patriarch, with an impressive head always covered by a velvet skull cap, for which he would apologize to public meetings in a very courtly manner. He and Tito Pagliardini,* another phonetic veteran, were men whom it was impossible to dislike. Henry Sweet,* then a young man, lacked their sweetness of character: he was about as conciliatory to conventional mortals as Ibsen* or Samuel Butler.* His great ability as a phonetician (he was, I think, the best of them all at his job) would have entitled him to high official recognition, and perhaps enabled him to popularize his subject, but for his Satanic contempt for all academic dignitaries and persons in general who thought more of Greek than of phonetics. Once, in the days when the Imperial Institute rose in South Kensington,* and Joseph Chamberlain was booming the Empire,* I induced the editor of a leading monthly review to commission an article from Sweet on the imperial importance of his subject. When it arrived, it contained nothing but a savagely derisive attack on a professor of language and literature whose chair Sweet regarded as proper to a phonetic expert only. The article, being libellous, had to be returned as impossible; and I had to renounce my dream of dragging its author into the limelight. When I met him afterwards, for the first time for many years, I found to my astonishment that he, who had been a quite tolerably presentable young man, had actually managed by sheer scorn to alter his personal appearance until he had become a sort of walking repudiation of Oxford and all its traditions. It must have been largely in his own despite that he was squeezed into something called a Readership of phonetics there. The future of phonetics rests probably with his pupils, who all swore by him; but nothing could bring the man himself into any sort of compliance with the university to which he nevertheless clung by divine right in an intensely Oxonian way. I daresay his papers, if he has left any, include some satires that may be published without too destructive results fifty years hence. He was, I believe, not in the least an illnatured man: very much the opposite, I should say; but he would not suffer fools gladly; and to him all scholars who were not rabid phoneticians were fools.

Those who knew him will recognize in my third act the allusion to the Current Shorthand in which he used to write postcards. It may be acquired from a four and sixpenny manual published by the Clarendon Press.* The postcards which Mrs Higgins describes* are such as I have received from Sweet. I would decipher a sound which a cockney would represent by *zerr*, and a Frenchman by *seu*, and then write demanding with some heat what on earth it meant. Sweet, with boundless contempt for my stupidity, would reply that it not only meant but obviously was the word Result, as no other word containing that sound, and capable of making sense with the context, existed in any language spoken on earth. That less expert mortals should require fuller indications was beyond Sweet's patience. Therefore, though the whole point of his Current Shorthand is that it can express every sound in the language perfectly, vowels as well as consonants, and that your hand has to make no stroke except the easy and current ones with which you write m, n, and u, l, p, and q, scribbling them at whatever angle comes easiest to you, his unfortunate determination to make this remarkable and quite legible script serve also as a shorthand reduced it in his own practice to the most inscrutable of cryptograms. His true objective was the provision of a full, accurate, legible script for our language; but he was led past that by his contempt for the popular Pitman system of shorthand,* which he called the Pitfall system. The triumph of Pitman was a triumph of business organization: there was a weekly paper to persuade you to learn Pitman: there were cheap textbooks and exercise books and transcripts of speeches for you to copy, and schools where experienced teachers coached you up to the necessary proficiency.

Sweet could not organize his market in that fashion. He might as well have been the Sybil who tore up the leaves of prophecy that nobody would attend to.* The four and sixpenny manual, mostly in his litho-graphed handwriting, that was never vulgarly advertized, may perhaps some day be taken up by a syndicate and pushed upon the public as The Times* pushed the Encyclopædia Britannica;* but until then it will certainly not prevail against Pitman. I have bought three copies of it during my lifetime; and I am informed by the publishers that its clois-tered existence is still a steady and healthy one. I actually learned the system two several times; and yet the shorthand in which I am writing these lines is Pitman's. And the reason is, that my secretary cannot transcribe Sweet, having been perforce taught in the schools of Pitman. In America I could use the commercially organized Gregg shorthand,* which has taken a hint from Sweet by making its letters writable (cur-rent, Sweet would have called them) instead of having to be geometric-ally drawn like Pitman's; but all these systems, including Sweet's, are spoilt by making them available for verbatim reporting, in which com-plete and exact spelling and word division are impossible. A complete and exact phonetic script is neither practicable nor necessary for ordin-ary use; but if we enlarge our alphabet to the Russian size, and make our spelling as phonetic as Spanish, the advance will be prodigious.*

Pygmalion Higgins is not a portrait of Sweet, to whom the adventure of Eliza Doolittle would have been impossible; still, as will be seen, there are touches of Sweet in the play. With Higgins's physique and temperament Sweet might have set the Thames on fire. As it was, he impressed himself professionally on Europe to an extent that made his comparative personal obscurity, and the failure of Oxford to do justice to his eminence, a puzzle to foreign specialists in his subject. I do not blame Oxford, because I think Oxford is quite right in demanding a certain social amenity from its nurslings (heaven knows it is not exor-bitant in its requirements!); for although I well know how hard it is for a man of genius with a seriously underrated subject to maintain serene and kindly relations with the men who underrate it, and who keep all the best places for less important subjects which they profess without originality and sometimes without much capacity for them, still, if he overwhelms them with wrath and disdain, he cannot expect them to heap honors on him.

Of the later generations of phoneticians I know little. Among them towered Robert Bridges, to whom perhaps Higgins may owe his Miltonic sympathies,* though here again I must disclaim all portrait-ure. But if the play makes the public aware that there are such people as phoneticians, and that they are among the most important people in England at present, it will serve its turn.

I wish to boast that Pygmalion has been an extremely successful play, both on stage and screen, all over Europe and North America as well as at home. It is so intensely and deliberately didactic, and its subject is esteemed so dry, that I delight in throwing it at the heads of the wise-acres who repeat the parrot cry that art should never be didactic. It goes to prove my contention that great art can never be anything else.

Finally, and for the encouragement of people troubled with accents that cut them off from all high employment, I may add that the change wrought by Professor Higgins in the flower girl is neither impossible nor uncommon. The modern concierge's daughter who fulfils her ambition by playing the Queen of Spain in Ruy Blas* at the Théâtre Français* is only one of many thousands of men and women who have sloughed off their native dialects and acquired a new tongue. Our West End shop assistants and domestic servants are bi-lingual. But the thing has to be done scientifically, or the last state of the aspirant may be worse than the first. An honest slum dialect is more tolerable than the attempts of phonetically untaught persons to imitate the plutocracy. Ambitious flower girls who read this play must not imagine that they can pass themselves off as fine ladies by untutored imitation. They must learn their alphabet over again, and different, from a phonetic expert. Imitation will only make them ridiculous.

PYGMALION

ACT I

London at 11.15 p.m. Torrents of heavy summer rain. Cab whistles blowing frantically in all directions. Pedestrians running for shelter into the portico of St Paul's church (not Wren's cathedral but Inigo Jones's church in Covent Garden vegetable market),* among them a lady and her daughter in evening dress. All are peering out gloomily at the rain, except one man with his back turned to the rest, wholly preoccupied with a notebook in which he is writing.

The church clock strikes the first quarter.*

THE DAUGHTER [*in the space between the central pillars, close to the one on her left*] I'm getting chilled to the bone. What can Freddy be doing all this time? He's been gone twenty minutes.

THE MOTHER [*on her daughter's right*] Not so long. But he ought to have got us a cab by this.

A BYSTANDER [*on the lady's right*] He wont get no cab not until half-past eleven, missus, when they come back after dropping their theatre fares.

THE MOTHER. But we must have a cab. We cant stand here until half-past eleven. It's too bad.*

THE BYSTANDER. Well, it aint my fault, missus.

THE DAUGHTER. If Freddy had a bit of gumption, he would have got one at the theatre door.

THE MOTHER. What could he have done, poor boy?

THE DAUGHTER. Other people got cabs. Why couldnt he?

Freddy rushes in out of the rain from the Southampton Street side, and comes between them closing a dripping umbrella. He is a young man of twenty,* in evening dress, very wet round the ankles.

THE DAUGHTER. Well, havnt you got a cab?

FREDDY. Theres not one to be had for love or money.

THE MOTHER. Oh, Freddy, there must be one. You cant have tried.

THE DAUGHTER. It's too tiresome. Do you expect us to go and get one ourselves?

FREDDY. I tell you theyre all engaged. The rain was so sudden: nobody was prepared; and everybody had to take a cab. Ive been to Charing Cross one way and nearly to Ludgate Circus the other; and they were all engaged.

THE MOTHER. Did you try Trafalgar Square?

FREDDY. There wasnt one at Trafalgar Square.*

THE DAUGHTER. Did you try?

FREDDY. I tried as far as Charing Cross Station. Did you expect me to walk to Hammersmith?*

THE DAUGHTER. You havnt tried at all.

THE MOTHER. You really are very helpless, Freddy. Go again; and dont come back until you have found a cab.

FREDDY. I shall simply get soaked for nothing.

THE DAUGHTER. And what about us? Are we to stay here all night in this draught, with next to nothing on? You selfish pig—

FREDDY. Oh, very well: I'll go, I'll go. [*He opens his umbrella and dashes off Strandwards,* but comes into collision with a flower girl* who is hurrying in for shelter, knocking her basket out of her hands. A blinding flash of lightning, followed instantly by a rattling peal of thunder, orchestrates the incident*].

THE FLOWER GIRL. Nah then, Freddy: look wh' y' gowin, deah.

FREDDY. Sorry [*he rushes off*].

THE FLOWER GIRL [*picking up her scattered flowers and replacing them in the basket*] Theres menners f' yer! Tə-oo banches o voylets trod into the mad.* [*She sits down on the plinth of the column, sorting her flowers, on the lady's right. She is not at all a romantic* figure. She is perhaps eighteen, perhaps twenty, hardly older. She wears a little sailor hat of black straw that has long been exposed to the dust and soot of London and has seldom if ever been brushed. Her hair needs washing rather badly: its mousy color can hardly be natural. She wears a shoddy black coat that reaches nearly to her knees and is shaped to her waist.*

She has a brown skirt with a coarse apron. Her boots are much the worse for wear. She is no doubt as clean as she can afford to be; but compared to the ladies she is very dirty. Her features are no worse than theirs; but their condition leaves something to be desired; and she needs the services of a dentist].

THE MOTHER. How do you know that my son's name is Freddy, pray?

THE FLOWER GIRL. Ow, eez yə-ooa san, is e? Wal, fewd dan y' də-ooty bawmz a mather should, eed now bettern to spawl a pore gel's flahrzn than ran awy athaht pyin. Will ye-oo py me f'them?* [*Here, with apologies, this desperate attempt to represent her dialect without a phonetic alphabet must be abandoned as unintelligible outside London*].

THE DAUGHTER. Do nothing of the sort, mother. The idea!

THE MOTHER. Please allow me, Clara. Have you any pennies?

THE DAUGHTER. No. Ive nothing smaller than sixpence.

THE FLOWER GIRL [*hopefully*] I can give you change for a tanner,* kind lady.

THE MOTHER [*to Clara*] Give it to me. [*Clara parts reluctantly*]. Now [*to the girl*]. This is for your flowers.

THE FLOWER GIRL. Thank you kindly, lady.

THE DAUGHTER. Make her give you the change. These things are only a penny a bunch.

THE MOTHER. Do hold your tongue, Clara. [*To the girl*] You can keep the change.

THE FLOWER GIRL. Oh, thank you, lady.

THE MOTHER. Now tell me how you know that young gentleman's name.

THE FLOWER GIRL. I didnt.

THE MOTHER. I heard you call him by it. Dont try to deceive me.

THE FLOWER GIRL [*protesting*] Who's trying to deceive you? I called him Freddy or Charlie same as you might yourself if you was talking to a stranger and wished to be pleasant.

THE DAUGHTER. Sixpence thrown away! Really, mamma, you might have spared Freddy that. [*She retreats in disgust behind the pillar*].

An elderly gentleman of the amiable military type rushes into the shelter, and closes a dripping umbrella. He is in the same plight as Freddy, very wet about the ankles. He is in evening dress, with a light overcoat. He takes the place left vacant by the daughter.

THE GENTLEMAN. Phew!

THE MOTHER [*to the gentleman*] Oh, sir, is there any sign of its stopping?

THE GENTLEMAN. I'm afraid not. It started worse than ever about two minutes ago [*he goes to the plinth beside the flower girl; puts up his foot on it; and stoops to turn down his trouser ends*].

THE MOTHER. Oh dear! [*She retires sadly and joins her daughter*].

THE FLOWER GIRL [*taking advantage of the military gentleman's proximity to establish friendly relations with him*] If it's worse, it's a sign it's nearly over. So cheer up, Captain; and buy a flower off a poor girl.*

THE GENTLEMAN. I'm sorry. I havnt any change.

THE FLOWER GIRL. I can give you change, Captain.

THE GENTLEMAN. For a sovereign?* Ive nothing less.

THE FLOWER GIRL. Garn! Oh do buy a flower off me, Captain. I can change half-a-crown. Take this for tuppence.*

THE GENTLEMAN. Now dont be troublesome: theres a good girl. [*Trying his pockets*] I really havnt any change—Stop: heres three hapence,* if thats any use to you [*he retreats to the other pillar*].

THE FLOWER GIRL [*disappointed, but thinking three halfpence better than nothing*] Thank you, sir.

THE BYSTANDER [*to the girl*] You be careful: give him a flower for it. Theres a bloke* here behind taking down every blessed word youre saying. [*All turn to the man who is taking notes*].

THE FLOWER GIRL [*springing up terrified*] I aint done nothing wrong by speaking to the gentleman. Ive a right to sell flowers if I keep off the kerb. [*Hysterically**] I'm a respectable girl: so help me, I never spoke to him except to ask him to buy a flower off me.

General hubbub, mostly sympathetic to the flower girl, but deprecating her excessive sensibility. Cries of Dont start hollerin. Who's hurting you? Nobody's going to touch you. Whats the good of fussing? Steady on. Easy easy, etc., *come from the elderly staid spectators, who pat* her comfortingly. Less patient ones bid her shut her head, or ask her roughly what is wrong with her. A remoter group, not knowing what the matter is, crowd in and increase the noise with question and answer: Whats the row? What-she-do? Where is he? A tec* taking her down. What! him? Yes: him over there: Took money off the gentleman, etc.

THE FLOWER GIRL [*breaking through them* to the gentleman, crying wildly] Oh, sir, dont let him charge me. You dunno what it means to me. Theyll take away my character and drive me on the streets for speaking to gentlemen. They—

THE NOTE TAKER [*coming forward on her right, the rest crowding after him*] There! there! there! there! who's hurting you, you silly girl? What do you take me for?

THE BYSTANDER. It's aw rawt: e's a genleman: look at his bə-oots.* [*Explaining to the note taker*] She thought you was a copper's nark, sir.

THE NOTE TAKER [*with quick interest*] Whats a copper's nark?

THE BYSTANDER [*inapt at definition*] It's a—well, it's a copper's nark, as you might say. What else would you call it? A sort of informer.

THE FLOWER GIRL [*still hysterical*] I take my Bible oath I never said a word—

THE NOTE TAKER [*overbearing but good-humored*] Oh, shut up, shut up. Do I look like a policeman?

THE FLOWER GIRL [*far from reassured*] Then what did you take down my words for? How do I know whether you took me down right? You just shew me what youve wrote about me. [*The note taker opens his book and holds it steadily under her nose, though the pressure of the mob trying to read it over his shoulders would upset a weaker man*]. Whats that? That aint proper writing. I cant read that.

THE NOTE TAKER. I can. [*Reads, reproducing her pronunciation exactly*] 'Cheer ap, Keptin; n' baw ya flahr orf a pore gel.'

THE FLOWER GIRL [*much distressed**] It's because I called him Captain. I meant no harm. [*To the gentleman*] Oh, sir, dont let him lay a charge agen* me for a word like that. You—

THE GENTLEMAN. Charge! I make no charge. [*To the note taker*] Really, sir, if you are a detective, you need not begin protecting me against molestation by young women until I ask you. Anybody could see that the girl meant no harm.

THE BYSTANDERS GENERALLY [*demonstrating against police espionage*]
Course they could. What business is it of yours? You mind your own
affairs. He wants promotion, he does. Taking down people's words!
Girl never said a word to him. What harm if she did? Nice thing
a girl cant shelter from the rain without being insulted, etc., etc.,
etc.* [*She is conducted by the more sympathetic demonstrators back to
her plinth, where she resumes her seat and struggles with her emotion*].

THE BYSTANDER. He aint a tec. He's a blooming busybody: thats what
he is. I tell you, look at his bə–oots.

THE NOTE TAKER [*turning on him genially*] And how are all your
people down at Selsey?*

THE BYSTANDER [*suspiciously*] Who told you my people come from
Selsey?

THE NOTE TAKER. Never you mind. They did. [*To the girl*] How do
you come to be up so far east? You were born in Lisson Grove.*

THE FLOWER GIRL [*appalled*] Oh, what harm is there in my leaving
Lisson Grove? It wasnt fit for a pig to live in; and I had to pay four-
and-six* a week. [*In tears*] Oh, boo—hoo—oo—

THE NOTE TAKER. Live where you like; but stop that noise.

THE GENTLEMAN [*to the girl*] Come, come! he cant touch you: you
have a right to live where you please.

A SARCASTIC BYSTANDER [*thrusting himself between the note taker and
the gentleman*] Park Lane,* for instance. I'd like to go into the Housing
Question* with you, I would.

THE FLOWER GIRL [*subsiding into a brooding melancholy over her basket, and talking very low-spiritedly to herself*] I'm a good girl, I am.

THE SARCASTIC BYSTANDER [*not attending to her*] Do you know
where *I* come from?

THE NOTE TAKER [*promptly*] Hoxton.*

Titterings. Popular interest in the note taker's performance increases.

THE SARCASTIC ONE [*amazed*] Well, who said I didnt? Bly me!* you
know everything, you do.

THE FLOWER GIRL [*still nursing her sense of injury*] Aint no call to
meddle with me, he aint.

THE BYSTANDER [*to her*] Of course he aint. Dont you stand it from him. [*To the note taker*] See here: what call have you to know about people what never offered to meddle with you?*

THE FLOWER GIRL. Let him say what he likes. I dont want to have no truck with him.*

THE BYSTANDER. You take us for dirt under your feet, dont you? Catch you taking liberties with a gentleman!

THE SARCASTIC BYSTANDER. Yes: tell him where he come from if you want to go fortune-telling.

THE NOTE TAKER. Cheltenham, Harrow, Cambridge,* and India.

THE GENTLEMAN. Quite right.

Great laughter. Reaction in the note taker's favor. Exclamations of He knows all about it. Told him proper. Hear him tell the toff* where he come from? *etc.*

THE GENTLEMAN. May I ask, sir, do you do this for your living at a music hall?

THE NOTE TAKER. Ive thought of that. Perhaps I shall some day.

The rain has stopped; and the persons on the outside of the crowd begin to drop off.

THE FLOWER GIRL [*resenting the reaction*] He's no gentleman, he aint, to interfere with a poor girl.

THE DAUGHTER [*out of patience, pushing her way rudely to the front and displacing the gentleman, who politely retires to the other side of the pillar*] What on earth is Freddy doing? I shall get pneumownia if I stay in this draught any longer.

THE NOTE TAKER [*to himself, hastily making a note of her pronunciation of 'monia'*] Earlscourt.*

THE DAUGHTER [*violently*] Will you please keep your impertinent remarks to yourself.

THE NOTE TAKER. Did I say that out loud? I didnt mean to. I beg your pardon. Your mother's Epsom,* unmistakeably.

THE MOTHER [*advancing between her daughter and the note taker*] How very curious! I was brought up in Largelady Park, near Epsom.

THE NOTE TAKER [*uproariously amused*] Ha! ha! What a devil of a name! Excuse me. [*To the daughter*] You want a cab, do you?

THE DAUGHTER. Dont dare speak to me.

THE MOTHER. Oh please, please, Clara. [*Her daughter repudiates her with an angry shrug and retires haughtily*]. We should be so grateful to you, sir, if you found us a cab. [*The note taker produces a whistle*]. Oh, thank you. [*She joins her daughter*].

The note taker blows a piercing blast.

THE SARCASTIC BYSTANDER. There! I knowed he was a plain-clothes copper.*

THE BYSTANDER. That aint a police whistle: thats a sporting whistle.

THE FLOWER GIRL [*still preoccupied with her wounded feelings*] He's no right to take away my character. My character is the same to me as any lady's.

THE NOTE TAKER. I dont know whether youve noticed it; but the rain stopped about two minutes ago.

THE BYSTANDER. So it has. Why didnt you say so before? and us losing our time listening to your silliness! [*He walks off towards the Strand*].

THE SARCASTIC BYSTANDER. I can tell where you come from. You come from Anwell. Go back there.

THE NOTE TAKER [*helpfully*] Hanwell.*

THE SARCASTIC BYSTANDER [*affecting great distinction of speech*] Thenk you, teacher. Haw haw! So long [*he touches his hat with mock respect and strolls off*].

THE FLOWER GIRL. Frightening people like that! How would he like it himself?

THE MOTHER. It's quite fine now, Clara. We can walk to a motor bus. Come. [*She gathers her skirts above her ankles and hurries off towards the Strand*].

THE DAUGHTER. But the cab—[*her mother is out of hearing*]. Oh, how tiresome! [*She follows angrily*].

All the rest have gone except the note taker, the gentleman, and the flower girl, who sits arranging her basket, and still pitying herself in murmurs.

THE FLOWER GIRL. Poor girl! Hard enough for her to live without being worrited and chivied.*

THE GENTLEMAN [*returning to his former place on the note taker's left*] How do you do it, if I may ask?

THE NOTE TAKER. Simply phonetics. The science of speech.* Thats my profession: also my hobby. Happy is the man who can make a living by his hobby! *You* can spot an Irishman or a Yorkshireman by his brogue.* *I* can place any man within six miles. I can place him within two miles in London. Sometimes within two streets.*

THE FLOWER GIRL. Ought to be ashamed of himself, unmanly coward!

THE GENTLEMAN. But is there a living in that?

THE NOTE TAKER. Oh yes. Quite a fat one. This is an age of upstarts. Men begin in Kentish Town* with £80 a year, and end in Park Lane with a hundred thousand. They want to drop Kentish Town; but they give themselves away every time they open their mouths. Now I can teach them—

THE FLOWER GIRL. Let him mind his own business and leave a poor girl—

THE NOTE TAKER [*explosively*] Woman: cease this detestable boohooing instantly; or else seek the shelter of some other place of worship.

THE FLOWER GIRL [*with feeble defiance**] Ive a right to be here if I like, same as you.

THE NOTE TAKER. A woman who utters such depressing and disgusting sounds has no right to be anywhere—no right to live. Remember that you are a human being with a soul and the divine gift of articulate speech: that your native language is the language of Shakespear and Milton and The Bible; and dont sit there crooning like a bilious pigeon.

THE FLOWER GIRL [*quite overwhelmed, looking up at him in mingled wonder and deprecation without daring to raise* her head*] Ah-ah-ah-ow-ow-ow-oo!

THE NOTE TAKER [*whipping out his book*] Heavens! what a sound! [*He writes; then holds out the book and reads, reproducing her vowels exactly*] Ah-ah-ah-ow-ow-ow-oo!

THE FLOWER GIRL [*tickled by the performance, and laughing in spite of herself*] Garn!*

THE NOTE TAKER. You see this creature with her kerbstone English: the English that will keep her in the gutter to the end of her days. Well, sir, in three months I could pass that girl off as a duchess at an ambassador's garden party.* I could even get her a place as lady's maid or shop assistant, which requires better English.

THE FLOWER GIRL. What's that you say?

THE NOTE TAKER. Yes, you squashed cabbage leaf, you disgrace to the noble architecture of these columns, you incarnate insult to the English language: I could pass you off as the Queen of Sheba.* [*To the Gentleman*] Can you believe that?

THE GENTLEMAN. Of course I can. I am myself a student of Indian dialects; and—

THE NOTE TAKER [*eagerly*] Are you? Do you know Colonel Pickering,* the author of Spoken Sanscrit?

THE GENTLEMAN. I *am* Colonel Pickering. Who are you?

THE NOTE TAKER. Henry Higgins,* author of Higgins's Universal Alphabet.

PICKERING [*with enthusiasm*] I came from India to meet you.

HIGGINS. I was going to India to meet you.

PICKERING. Where do you live?

HIGGINS. 27A Wimpole Street. Come and see me tomorrow.

PICKERING. I'm at the Carlton.* Come with me now and lets have a jaw over some supper.

HIGGINS. Right you are.

THE FLOWER GIRL [*to Pickering, as he passes her*] Buy a flower, kind gentleman. I'm short for my lodging.

PICKERING. I really havnt any change. I'm sorry [*he goes away*].

HIGGINS [*shocked at the girl's mendacity*] Liar. You said you could change half-a-crown.*

THE FLOWER GIRL [*rising in desperation*] You ought to be stuffed with nails, you ought. [*Flinging the basket at his feet*] Take the whole blooming basket for sixpence.

The church clock strikes the second quarter.

HIGGINS [*hearing in it the voice of God, rebuking him for his Pharisaic want of charity* to the poor girl*] A reminder. [*He raises his hat solemnly; then throws a handful of money into the basket and follows Pickering*].

THE FLOWER GIRL [*picking up a half-crown*] Ah-ow-ooh! [*Picking up a couple of florins**] Aaah-ow-ooh! [*Picking up several coins*] Aaaaaah-ow-ooh! [*Picking up a half-sovereign*] Aaaaaaaaaaaah-ow-ooh!!!

FREDDY [*springing out of a taxicab*] Got one at last. Hallo! [*To the girl*] Where are the two ladies that were here?

THE FLOWER GIRL. They walked to the bus when the rain stopped.

FREDDY. And left me with a cab on my hands! Damnation!

THE FLOWER GIRL [*with grandeur*] Never mind, young man. I'm going home in a taxi. [*She sails off to the cab. The driver puts his hand behind him and holds the door firmly shut against her. Quite understanding his mistrust, she shews him her handful of money*]. A taxi fare aint no object to me, Charlie. [*He grins and opens the door*]. Here. What about the basket?

THE TAXIMAN. Give it here. Tuppence extra.

LIZA. No: I dont want nobody to see it. [*She crushes it into the cab and gets in, continuing the conversation through the window*] Goodbye, Freddy.

FREDDY [*dazedly raising his hat*] Goodbye.

TAXIMAN. Where to?

LIZA. Bucknam Pellis [Buckingham Palace].

TAXIMAN. What d'ye mean—Bucknam Pellis?

LIZA. Dont you know where it is? In the Green Park, where the King lives. Goodbye, Freddy. Dont let me keep you standing there. Goodbye.

FREDDY. Goodbye. [*He goes*].

TAXIMAN. Here? Whats this about Bucknam Pellis? What business have you at Bucknam Pellis?

LIZA. Of course I havnt none. But I wasnt going to let him know that. You drive me home.

TAXIMAN. And wheres home?

LIZA. Angel Court, Drury Lane,* next Meiklejohn's oil shop.

TAXIMAN. That sounds more like it, Judy. [*He drives off*].

＊　＊　＊　＊　＊　＊

Let us follow the taxi to the entrance to Angel Court, a narrow little archway between two shops, one of them Meiklejohn's oil shop. When it stops there, Eliza gets out, dragging her basket with her.

LIZA. How much?

TAXIMAN [*indicating the taximeter*] Cant you read? A shilling.

LIZA. A shilling for two minutes!!

TAXIMAN. Two minutes or ten: it's all the same.

LIZA. Well, I dont call it right.

TAXIMAN. Ever been in a taxi before?

LIZA [*with dignity*] Hundreds and thousands of times, young man.

TAXIMAN [*laughing at her*] Good for you, Judy. Keep the shilling, darling, with best love from all at home. Good luck! [*He drives off*].

LIZA [*humiliated*] Impidence!*

She picks up the basket and trudges up the alley with it to her lodging: a small room with very old wall paper hanging loose in the damp places. A broken pane in the window is mended with paper. A portrait of a popular actor and a fashion plate of ladies' dresses, all wildly beyond poor Eliza's means, both torn from newspapers, are pinned up on the wall. A birdcage hangs in the window; but its tenant died long ago: it remains as a memorial only.

These are the only visible luxuries: the rest is the irreducible minimum of poverty's needs: a wretched bed heaped with all sorts of coverings that have any warmth in them, a draped packing case with a basin and jug on it and a little looking glass over it, a chair and table, the refuse of some suburban kitchen, and an American alarum clock on the shelf above the unused fireplace: the whole lighted with a gas lamp with a penny in the slot meter. Rent: four shillings a week.

Here Eliza, chronically weary, but too excited to go to bed, sits, counting her new riches and dreaming and planning what to do with them, until the gas goes out, when she enjoys for the first time the sensation of being able to put in another penny without grudging it. This prodigal mood does not extinguish her gnawing sense of the need for economy sufficiently to prevent her from calculating that she can dream and plan in bed more cheaply and warmly than sitting up without a fire. So she takes off her shawl and skirt and adds them to the miscellaneous bedclothes. Then she kicks off her shoes and gets into bed without any further change.

ACT II

Next day at 11 a.m. Higgins's laboratory in Wimpole Street. It is a room
on the first floor, looking on the street, and was meant for the drawing room.
The double doors are in the middle of the back wall; and persons entering
find in the corner to their right two tall file cabinets at right angles to one
another against the walls. In this corner stands a flat writing-table, on
which are a phonograph, a laryngoscope, a row of tiny organ pipes with
a bellows,* a set of lamp chimneys for singing flames with burners attached
to a gas plug in the wall by an indiarubber tube, several tuning-forks of
different sizes, a life-size image of half a human head, shewing in section
the vocal organs, and a box containing a supply of wax cylinders for the
phonograph.*

*Further down the room, on the same side, is a fireplace, with a comfort-
able leather-covered easy-chair at the side of the hearth nearest the door,
and a coal-scuttle. There is a clock on the mantelpiece. Between the fireplace
and the phonograph table is a stand for newspapers.*

*On the other side of the central door, to the left of the visitor, is a cabinet
of shallow drawers. On it is a telephone and the telephone directory. The
corner beyond, and most of the side wall, is occupied by a grand piano, with
the keyboard at the end furthest from the door, and a bench for the player
extending the full length of the keyboard. On the piano is a dessert dish
heaped with fruit and sweets, mostly chocolates.**

*The middle of the room is clear. Besides the easy-chair, the piano bench,
and two chairs at the phonograph table, there is one stray chair. It stands
near the fireplace. On the walls, engravings: mostly Piranesis and mezzotint
portraits.* No paintings.*

*Pickering is seated at the table, putting down some cards and a tuning-
fork which he has been using. Higgins is standing up near him, closing two or
three file drawers which are hanging out. He appears in the morning light as
a robust, vital, appetizing sort of man of forty or thereabouts, dressed in
a professional-looking black frock-coat* with a white linen collar and black
silk tie. He is of the energetic, scientific type, heartily, even violently interested in everything that can be studied as a scientific subject, and careless
about himself and other people, including their feelings. He is, in fact, but for
his years and size, rather like a very impetuous baby 'taking notice' eagerly
and loudly, and requiring almost as much watching to keep him out of unin-
tended mischief. His manner varies from genial bullying when he is in a good
humor to stormy petulance when anything goes wrong; but he is so entirely
frank and void of malice that he remains likeable even in his least reasonable moments.**

HIGGINS [*as he shuts the last drawer*] Well, I think thats the whole show.

PICKERING. It's really amazing. I havnt taken half of it in, you know.

HIGGINS. Would you like to go over any of it again?

PICKERING [*rising and coming to the fireplace, where he plants himself with his back to the fire*] No, thank you: not now. I'm quite done up for this morning.

HIGGINS [*following him, and standing beside him on his left*] Tired of listening to sounds?

PICKERING. Yes. It's a fearful strain. I rather fancied myself because I can pronounce twenty-four distinct vowel sounds; but your hundred and thirty beat me. I cant hear a bit of difference between most of them.

HIGGINS [*chuckling, and going over to the piano to eat sweets*] Oh, that comes with practice. You hear no difference at first; but you keep on listening, and presently you find theyre all as different as A from B. [*Mrs Pearce looks in: she is Higgins's housekeeper*]. Whats the matter?

MRS PEARCE [*hesitating, evidently perplexed*] A young woman asks to see you, sir.

HIGGINS. A young woman! What does she want?

MRS PEARCE. Well, sir, she says youll be glad to see her when you know what she's come about. She's quite a common girl, sir. Very common indeed. I should have sent her away, only I thought perhaps you wanted her to talk into your machines. I hope Ive not done wrong; but really you see such queer people sometimes—youll excuse me, I'm sure, sir—

HIGGINS. Oh, thats all right, Mrs Pearce. Has she an interesting accent?

MRS PEARCE. Oh, something dreadful, sir, really. I dont know how you can take an interest in it.

HIGGINS [*to Pickering*] Lets have her up. Shew her up, Mrs Pearce [*he rushes across to his working table and picks out a cylinder to use on the phonograph*].

MRS PEARCE [*only half resigned to it*] Very well, sir. It's for you to say.* [*She goes downstairs*].

HIGGINS. This is rather a bit of luck. I'll shew you how I make records. We'll set her talking; and I'll take it down first in Bell's Visible Speech; then in broad Romic;* and then we'll get her on the phonograph so that you can turn her on as often as you like with the written transcript before you.

MRS PEARCE [*returning*] This is the young woman, sir.

The flower girl enters in state. She has a hat with three ostrich feathers, orange, sky-blue, and red. She has a nearly clean apron, and the shoddy coat has been tidied a little. The pathos of this deplorable figure, with its innocent vanity and consequential air, touches Pickering, who has already straightened himself in the presence of Mrs Pearce. But as to Higgins, the only distinction he makes between men and women is that when he is neither bullying nor exclaiming to the heavens against some feather-weight cross, he coaxes women as a child coaxes its nurse when it wants to get anything out of her.

HIGGINS [*brusquely, recognizing her with unconcealed disappointment, and at once, babylike, making an intolerable grievance of it*] Why, this is the girl I jotted down last night. She's no use: Ive got all the records I want of the Lisson Grove lingo; and I'm not going to waste another cylinder on it. [*To the girl*] Be off with you: I dont want you.

THE FLOWER GIRL. Dont you be so saucy.* You aint heard what I come for yet. [*To Mrs Pearce, who is waiting at the door for further instructions*] Did you tell him I come in a taxi?

MRS PEARCE. Nonsense, girl! what do you think a gentleman like Mr Higgins cares what you came in?

THE FLOWER GIRL. Oh, we *are* proud! He aint above giving lessons, not him: I heard him say so. Well, I aint come here to ask for any compliment; and if my money's not good enough I can go elsewhere.

HIGGINS. Good enough for what?

THE FLOWER GIRL. Good enough for yə-oo. Now you know, dont you? I'm come to have lessons, I am. And to pay for em tə-oo: make no mistake.

HIGGINS [*stupent**] Well!!! [*Recovering his breath with a gasp*] What do you expect me to say to you?

THE FLOWER GIRL. Well, if you was a gentleman, you might ask me to sit down, I think. Dont I tell you I'm bringing you business?*

HIGGINS. Pickering: shall we ask this baggage to sit down, or shall we throw her out of the window?

THE FLOWER GIRL [*running away in terror to the piano, where she turns at bay*] Ah-ah-oh-ow-ow-ow-oo! [*Wounded and whimpering*] I wont be called a baggage when Ive offered to pay like any lady.

Motionless, the two men stare at her from the other side of the room, amazed.

PICKERING [*gently*] But what is it you want?

THE FLOWER GIRL. I want to be a lady in a flower shop stead of sellin at the corner of Tottenham Court Road.* But they wont take me unless I can talk more genteel. He said he could teach me. Well, here I am ready to pay him—not asking any favor—and he treats me zif* I was dirt.

MRS PEARCE. How can you be such a foolish ignorant girl as to think you could afford to pay Mr Higgins?

THE FLOWER GIRL. Why shouldnt I? I know what lessons cost as well as you do; and I'm ready to pay.

HIGGINS. How much?

THE FLOWER GIRL [*coming back to him, triumphant*] Now youre talking! I thought youd come off it when you saw a chance of getting back a bit of what you chucked at me last night. [*Confidentially*] Youd had a drop in, hadnt you?*

HIGGINS [*peremptorily**] Sit down.

THE FLOWER GIRL. Oh, if youre going to make a compliment of it—

HIGGINS [*thundering at her*] Sit down.

MRS PEARCE [*severely*] Sit down, girl. Do as youre told.

THE FLOWER GIRL. Ah-ah-ah-ow-ow-oo! [*She stands, half rebellious, half bewildered*].

PICKERING [*very courteous*] Wont you sit down? [*He places the stray chair near the hearthrug between himself and Higgins*].

LIZA [*coyly*] Dont mind if I do. [*She sits down. Pickering returns to the hearthrug*].

HIGGINS. Whats your name?

THE FLOWER GIRL. Liza Doolittle.

HIGGINS [*declaiming gravely*]

> Eliza, Elizabeth, Betsy and Bess,
> They went to the woods to get a bird's nes':

PICKERING. They found a nest with four eggs in it:

HIGGINS. They took one apiece, and left three in it.

They laugh heartily at their own fun.

LIZA. Oh, dont be silly.

MRS PEARCE [*placing herself behind Eliza's chair*] You mustnt speak to the gentleman like that.

LIZA. Well, why wont he speak sensible to me?

HIGGINS. Come back to business. How much do you propose to pay me for the lessons?

LIZA. Oh, I know whats right. A lady friend of mine gets French lessons for eighteenpence an hour from a real French gentleman. Well, you wouldnt have the face to ask me the same for teaching me my own language as you would for French; so I wont give more than a shilling. Take it or leave it.*

HIGGINS [*walking up and down the room, rattling his keys and his cash in his pockets*] You know, Pickering, if you consider a shilling, not as a simple shilling, but as a percentage of this girl's income, it works out as fully equivalent to sixty or seventy guineas* from a millionaire.

PICKERING. How so?

HIGGINS. Figure it out. A millionaire has about £150 a day. She earns about half-a-crown.

LIZA [*haughtily*] Who told you I only—

HIGGINS [*continuing*] She offers me two-fifths of her day's income for a lesson. Two-fifths of a millionaire's income for a day would be somewhere about £60. It's handsome. By George, it's enormous! it's the biggest offer I ever had.

LIZA [*rising, terrified*] Sixty pounds! What are you talking about? I never offered you sixty pounds. Where would I get—

HIGGINS. Hold your tongue.

LIZA [*weeping*] But I aint got sixty pounds. Oh—

MRS PEARCE. Dont cry, you silly girl. Sit down.* Nobody is going to touch your money.

HIGGINS. Somebody is going to touch *you*, with a broomstick, if you dont stop snivelling. Sit down.

LIZA [*obeying slowly*] Ah-ah-ah-ow-oo-o! One would think you was my father.

HIGGINS. If I decide to teach you, I'll be worse than two fathers to you. Here! [*He offers her his silk handkerchief*]

LIZA. Whats this for?

HIGGINS. To wipe your eyes. To wipe any part of your face that feels moist. Remember: thats your handkerchief; and thats your sleeve. Dont mistake the one for the other if you wish to become a lady in a shop.

Liza, utterly bewildered, stares helplessly at him.

MRS PEARCE. It's no use talking to her like that, Mr Higgins: she doesnt understand you. Besides, youre quite wrong: she doesnt do it that way at all [*she takes the handkerchief*].

LIZA [*snatching it*] Here! You give me that handkerchief. He gev it to me, not to you.

PICKERING [*laughing*] He did. I think it must be regarded as her property, Mrs Pearce.

MRS PEARCE [*resigning herself*] Serve you right, Mr Higgins.

PICKERING. Higgins: I'm interested. What about the ambassador's garden party?* I'll say youre the greatest teacher alive if you make that good. I'll bet you all the expenses of the experiment you cant do it. And I'll pay for the lessons.

LIZA. Oh, you are real good. Thank you, Captain.

HIGGINS [*tempted, looking at her*] It's almost irresistible. She's so deliciously low—so horribly dirty—*

LIZA [*protesting extremely*] Ah-ah-ah-ah-ow-ow-oo-oo!!! I aint dirty: I washed my face and hands afore I come, I did.*

PICKERING. Youre certainly not going to turn her head with flattery, Higgins.

MRS PEARCE [*uneasy*] Oh, dont say that, sir: theres more ways than one of turning a girl's head; and nobody can do it better than Mr Higgins, though he may not always mean it. I do hope, sir, you wont encourage him to do anything foolish.

HIGGINS [*becoming excited as the idea grows on him*] What is life but a series of inspired follies?* The difficulty is to find them to do. Never lose a chance: it doesnt come every day. I shall make a duchess of this draggletailed guttersnipe.

LIZA [*strongly deprecating this view of her*] Ah-ah-ah-ow-ow-oo!

HIGGINS [*carried away*] Yes: in six months—in three if she has a good ear and a quick tongue—I'll take her anywhere and pass her off as anything. We'll start today: now! this moment! Take her away and clean her, Mrs Pearce. Monkey Brand,* if it wont come off any other way. Is there a good fire in the kitchen?

MRS PEARCE [*protesting*] Yes; but—

HIGGINS [*storming on*] Take all her clothes off and burn them.* Ring up Whiteley* or somebody for new ones. Wrap her up in brown paper til they come.

LIZA. Youre no gentleman, youre not, to talk of such things. I'm a good girl, I am; and I know what the like of you are, I do.

HIGGINS. We want none of your Lisson Grove prudery here, young woman. Youve got to learn to behave like a duchess. Take her away, Mrs Pearce. If she gives you any trouble, wallop her.

LIZA [*springing up and running between Pickering and Mrs Pearce for protection*] No! I'll call the police, I will.

MRS PEARCE. But Ive no place to put her.

HIGGINS. Put her in the dustbin.

LIZA. Ah-ah-ah-ow-ow-oo!

PICKERING. Oh come, Higgins! be reasonable.

MRS PEARCE [*resolutely*] You *must* be reasonable, Mr Higgins: really you must. You cant walk over everybody like this.

Higgins, thus scolded, subsides. The hurricane is succeeded by a zephyr of amiable surprise.

HIGGINS [*with professional exquisiteness of modulation*] I walk over everybody!* My dear Mrs Pearce, my dear Pickering, I never had the slightest intention of walking over anyone. All I propose is that we should be kind to this poor girl. We must help her to prepare and fit herself for her new station in life. If I did not express myself clearly it was because I did not wish to hurt her delicacy, or yours.

Liza, reassured, steals back to her chair.

MRS PEARCE [*to Pickering*] Well, did you ever hear anything like that, sir?

PICKERING [*laughing heartily*] Never, Mrs Pearce: never.

HIGGINS [*patiently*] Whats the matter?

MRS PEARCE. Well, the matter is, sir, that you cant take a girl up like that as if you were picking up a pebble on the beach.

HIGGINS. Why not?

MRS PEARCE. Why not! But you dont know anything about her. What about her parents? She may be married.

LIZA. Garn!

HIGGINS. There! As the girl very properly says, Garn! Married indeed!* Dont you know that a woman of that class looks a worn out drudge of fifty a year after she's married?

LIZA. Whood marry *me*?

HIGGINS [*suddenly resorting to the most thrillingly beautiful low tones in his best elocutionary style*] By George, Eliza, the streets will be strewn with the bodies of men shooting themselves for your sake before Ive done with you.

MRS PEARCE. Nonsense, sir. You mustnt talk like that to her.

LIZA [*rising and squaring herself determinedly*] I'm going away. He's off his chump, he is. I dont want no balmies* teaching me.

HIGGINS [*wounded in his tenderest point by her insensibility to his elocution*] Oh, indeed! I'm mad, am I? Very well, Mrs Pearce: you neednt order the new clothes for her. Throw her out.

LIZA [*whimpering*] Nah-ow. You got no right to touch me.

MRS PEARCE. You see now what comes of being saucy.* [*Indicating the door*] This way, please.

LIZA [*almost in tears*] I didnt want no clothes. I wouldnt have taken them [*she throws away the handkerchief*]. I can buy my own clothes.

HIGGINS [*deftly retrieving the handkerchief and intercepting her on her reluctant way to the door*] Youre an ungrateful wicked girl. This is my return for offering to take you out of the gutter and dress you beautifully and make a lady of you.

MRS PEARCE. Stop, Mr Higgins. I wont allow it. It's you that are wicked. Go home to your parents, girl; and tell them to take better care of you.

LIZA. I aint got no parents. They told me I was big enough to earn my own living and turned me out.

MRS PEARCE. Wheres your mother?

LIZA. I aint got no mother.* Her that turned me out was my sixth stepmother. But I done without them. And I'm a good girl, I am.

HIGGINS. Very well, then, what on earth is all this fuss about? The girl doesnt belong to anybody—is no use to anybody but me. [*He goes to Mrs Pearce and begins coaxing*]. You can adopt her, Mrs Pearce: I'm sure a daughter would be a great amusement to you. Now dont make any more fuss. Take her downstairs; and—

MRS PEARCE. But whats to become of her? Is she to be paid anything? Do be sensible, sir.

HIGGINS. Oh, pay her whatever is necessary: put it down in the house-keeping book. [*Impatiently*] What on earth will she want with money? She'll have her food and her clothes. She'll only drink if you give her money.

LIZA [*turning on him*] Oh you are a brute.* It's a lie: nobody ever saw the sign of liquor on me. [*To Pickering*] Oh, sir: youre a gentleman: dont let him speak to me like that.*

PICKERING [*in good-humored remonstrance*] Does it occur to you, Higgins, that the girl has some feelings?

HIGGINS [*looking critically at her*] Oh no, I dont think so. Not any feelings that we need bother about. [*Cheerily*] Have you, Eliza?

LIZA. I got my feelings same as anyone else.

HIGGINS [*to Pickering, reflectively*] You see the difficulty?

PICKERING. Eh? What difficulty?

HIGGINS. To get her to talk grammar. The mere pronunciation is easy enough.

LIZA. I dont want to talk grammar. I want to talk like a lady in a flower shop.*

MRS PEARCE. Will you please keep to the point, Mr Higgins. I want to know on what terms the girl is to be here. Is she to have any wages? And what is to become of her when youve finished your teaching? You must look ahead a little.

HIGGINS [*impatiently*] Whats to become of her if I leave her in the gutter? Tell me that, Mrs Pearce.

MRS PEARCE. Thats her own business, not yours, Mr Higgins.

HIGGINS. Well, when Ive done with her, we can throw her back into the gutter; and then it will be her own business again; so thats all right.

LIZA. Oh, youve no feeling heart in you: you dont care for nothing but yourself. [*She rises and takes the floor resolutely*]. Here! Ive had enough of this. I'm going [*making for the door*]. You ought to be ashamed of yourself, you ought.

HIGGINS [*snatching a chocolate cream from the piano, his eyes suddenly beginning to twinkle with mischief*] Have some chocolates, Eliza.*

LIZA [*halting, tempted*] How do I know what might be in them? Ive heard of girls being drugged by the like of you.

Higgins whips out his penknife; cuts a chocolate in two; puts one half into his mouth and bolts it; and offers her the other half.

HIGGINS. Pledge of good faith, Eliza. I eat one half: you eat the other. [*Liza opens her mouth to retort: he pops the half chocolate into it*]. You shall have boxes of them, barrels of them, every day. You shall live on them. Eh?

LIZA [*who has disposed of the chocolate after being nearly choked by it*] I wouldnt have ate it, only I'm too ladylike to take it out of my mouth.

HIGGINS. Listen, Eliza. I think you said you came in a taxi.

LIZA. Well, what if I did? Ive as good a right to take a taxi as anyone else.

HIGGINS. You have, Eliza; and in future you shall have as many taxis as you want. You shall go up and down and round the town in a taxi every day. Think of that, Eliza.

MRS PEARCE. Mr Higgins: youre tempting the girl. It's not right. She should think of the future.

HIGGINS. At her age! Nonsense! Time enough to think of the future when you havnt any future to think of. No, Eliza: do as this lady does: think of other people's futures; but never think of your own. Think of chocolates, and taxis, and gold, and diamonds.

LIZA. No: I dont want no gold and no diamonds. I'm a good girl, I am. [*She sits down again, with an attempt at dignity*].

HIGGINS. You shall remain so, Eliza, under the care of Mrs Pearce. And you shall marry an officer in the Guards, with a beautiful moustache: the son of a marquis, who will disinherit him for marrying you, but will relent when he sees your beauty and goodness—

PICKERING. Excuse me, Higgins; but I really must interfere. Mrs Pearce is quite right. If this girl is to put herself in your hands for six months for an experiment in teaching, she must understand thoroughly what she's doing.

HIGGINS. How can she? She's incapable of understanding anything. Besides, do any of us understand what we are doing? If we did, would we ever do it?

PICKERING. Very clever, Higgins; but not to the present point. [*To Eliza*] Miss Doolittle—

LIZA [*overwhelmed*] Ah-ah-ow-oo!

HIGGINS. There! Thats all youll get out of Eliza. Ah-ah-ow-oo! No use explaining. As a military man you ought to know that. Give her her orders: thats enough for her. Eliza: you are to live here for the next six months, learning how to speak beautifully, like a lady in a florist's shop. If youre good and do whatever youre told, you shall sleep in a proper bedroom, and have lots to eat, and money to buy chocolates and take rides in taxis. If youre naughty and idle you will sleep in the back kitchen among the black beetles, and be walloped by Mrs Pearce with a broomstick. At the end of six months you shall go to Buckingham Palace in a carriage, beautifully dressed. If the King finds out youre not a lady, you will be taken by the police to the Tower of London, where your head will be cut off as a warning to other presumptuous flower girls.* If you are not found out, you shall have a present of seven-and-sixpence to start life with as a lady in a shop. If you refuse this offer you will be a most ungrateful wicked girl; and the angels will weep for you. [*To Pickering*] Now are you satisfied, Pickering? [*To Mrs Pearce*] Can I put it more plainly and fairly, Mrs Pearce?

MRS PEARCE [*patiently*] I think youd better let me speak to the girl properly in private. I dont know that I can take charge of her or consent to the arrangement at all. Of course I know you dont mean her any harm; but when you get what you call interested in people's accents, you never think or care what may happen to them or you. Come with me, Eliza.

HIGGINS. Thats all right. Thank you, Mrs Pearce. Bundle her off to the bathroom.

LIZA [*rising reluctantly and suspiciously*] Youre a great bully, you are. I wont stay here if I dont like. I wont let nobody wallop me. I never asked to go to Bucknam Palace, I didnt. I was never in trouble with the police, not me. I'm a good girl—

MRS PEARCE. Dont answer back, girl. You dont understand the gentleman. Come with me. [*She leads the way to the door, and holds it open for Eliza*].

LIZA [*as she goes out*] Well, what I say is right. I wont go near the King, not if I'm going to have my head cut off. If I'd known what I was letting myself in for, I wouldnt have come here. I always been a good girl; and I never offered to say a word to him; and I dont owe him nothing; and I dont care; and I wont be put upon; and I have my feelings the same as anyone else—

*Mrs Pearce shuts the door; and Eliza's plaints are no longer audible.**

* * * * * *

Eliza is taken upstairs to the third floor greatly to her surprise; for she expected to be taken down to the scullery.* There Mrs Pearce opens a door and takes her into a spare bedroom.

MRS PEARCE. I will have to put you here. This will be your bedroom.

LIZA. O-h, I couldnt sleep here, missus. It's too good for the likes of me. I should be afraid to touch anything. I aint a duchess yet, you know.

MRS PEARCE. You have got to make yourself as clean as the room: then you wont be afraid of it. And you must call me Mrs Pearce, not missus. [*She throws open the door of the dressingroom, now modernized as a bathroom*].

LIZA. Gawd! whats this? Is this where you wash clothes? Funny sort of copper* I call it.

MRS PEARCE. It is not a copper. This is where we wash ourselves, Eliza, and where I am going to wash you.

LIZA. You expect me to get into that and wet myself all over! Not me. I should catch my death. I knew a woman did it every Saturday night; and she died of it.

MRS PEARCE. Mr Higgins has the gentlemen's bathroom downstairs; and he has a bath every morning, in cold water.

LIZA. Ugh! He's made of iron, that man.

MRS PEARCE. If you are to sit with him and the Colonel and be taught you will have to do the same. They wont like the smell of you if you dont. But you can have the water as hot as you like. There are two taps: hot and cold.

LIZA [*weeping*] I couldnt. I dursnt. It's not natural: it would kill me. Ive never had a bath in my life: not what youd call a proper one.

MRS PEARCE. Well, dont you want to be clean and sweet and decent, like a lady? You know you cant be a nice girl inside if youre a dirty slut* outside.

LIZA. Boohoo!!!!

MRS PEARCE. Now stop crying and go back into your room and take off all your clothes. Then wrap yourself in this [*taking down a gown from its peg and handing it to her*] and come back to me. I will get the bath ready.

LIZA [*all tears*] I cant. I wont. I'm not used to it. Ive never took off all my clothes before. It's not right: it's not decent.

MRS PEARCE. Nonsense, child. Dont you take off all your clothes every night when you go to bed?

LIZA [*amazed*] No. Why should I? I should catch my death. Of course I take off my skirt.

MRS PEARCE. Do you mean that you sleep in the underclothes you wear in the daytime?

LIZA. What else have I to sleep in?

MRS PEARCE. You will never do that again as long as you live here. I will get you a proper nightdress.

LIZA. Do you mean change into cold things and lie awake shivering half the night? You want to kill me, you do.

MRS PEARCE. I want to change you from a frowzy slut to a clean respectable girl fit to sit with the gentlemen in the study. Are you going to trust me and do what I tell you or be thrown out and sent back to your flower basket?

LIZA. But you dont know what the cold is to me. You dont know how I dread it.

MRS PEARCE. Your bed wont be cold here: I will put a hot water bottle in it. [*Pushing her into the bedroom*] Off with you and undress.

LIZA. Oh, if only I'd a known what a dreadful thing it is to be clean I'd never have come. I didnt know when I was well off. I—[*Mrs Pearce pushes her through the door, but leaves it partly open lest her prisoner should take to flight*].

Mrs Pearce puts on a pair of white rubber sleeves, and fills the bath, mixing hot and cold, and testing the result with the bath thermometer. She perfumes it with a handful of bath salts and adds a palmful of mustard. She then takes a formidable looking long handled scrubbing brush and soaps it profusely with a ball of scented soap.

Eliza comes back with nothing on but the bath gown huddled tightly round her, a piteous spectacle of abject terror.

MRS PEARCE. Now come along. Take that thing off.

LIZA. Oh I couldnt, Mrs Pearce: I reely couldnt. I never done such a thing.

MRS PEARCE. Nonsense. Here: step in and tell me whether it's hot enough for you.

LIZA. Ah-oo! Ah-oo! It's too hot.

MRS PEARCE [*deftly snatching the gown away and throwing Eliza down on her back*] It wont hurt you. [*She sets to work with the scrubbing brush*].

Eliza's screams are heartrending.

* * * * * *

Meanwhile the Colonel has been having it out with Higgins about Eliza. Pickering has come from the hearth to the chair and seated himself astride of it with his arms on the back to cross-examine him.

PICKERING. Excuse the straight question, Higgins. Are you a man of good character where women are concerned?

HIGGINS [*moodily*] Have you ever met a man of good character where women are concerned?

PICKERING. Yes: very frequently.

HIGGINS [*dogmatically, lifting himself on his hands to the level of the piano, and sitting on it with a bounce*] Well, I havnt. I find that the moment I let a woman make friends with me, she becomes jealous, exacting, suspicious, and a damned nuisance. I find that the moment I let myself make friends with a woman, I become selfish and tyrannical. Women upset everything. When you let them into your life, you find that the woman is driving at one thing and youre driving at another.

PICKERING. At what, for example?

HIGGINS [*coming off the piano restlessly*] Oh, Lord knows! I suppose the woman wants to live her own life; and the man wants to live his; and each tries to drag the other on to the wrong track. One wants to go north and the other south; and the result is that both have to go east, though they both hate the east wind. [*He sits down on the bench at the keyboard*]. So here I am, a confirmed old bachelor, and likely to remain so.

PICKERING [*rising and standing over him gravely*] Come, Higgins! You know what I mean. If I'm to be in this business I shall feel responsible for that girl. I hope it's understood that no advantage is to be taken of her position.

HIGGINS. What! That thing! Sacred, I assure you. [*Rising to explain*] You see, she'll be a pupil; and teaching would be impossible unless pupils were sacred. Ive taught scores of American millionairesses how to speak English: the best looking women in the world. I'm seasoned. They might as well be blocks of wood. *I* might as well be a block of wood. It's—

Mrs Pearce opens the door. She has Eliza's hat in her hand. Pickering retires to the easy-chair at the hearth and sits down.

HIGGINS [*eagerly*] Well, Mrs Pearce: is it all right?

MRS PEARCE [*at the door*] I just wish to trouble you with a word, if I may, Mr Higgins.

HIGGINS. Yes, certainly. Come in. [*She comes forward*]. Dont burn that, Mrs Pearce. I'll keep it as a curiosity. [*He takes the hat*].

MRS PEARCE. Handle it carefully, sir, please. I had to promise her not to burn it; but I had better put it in the oven for a while.

HIGGINS [*putting it down hastily on the piano*] Oh! thank you. Well, what have you to say to me?

PICKERING. Am I in the way?

MRS PEARCE. Not at all, sir.* Mr Higgins: will you please be very particular what you say before the girl?

HIGGINS [*sternly*] Of course. I'm always particular about what I say. Why do you say this to me?

MRS PEARCE [*unmoved*] No, sir: youre not at all particular when youve mislaid anything or when you get a little impatient. Now it doesnt matter before me: I'm used to it. But you really must not swear before the girl.

HIGGINS [*indignantly*] *I* swear! [*Most emphatically*] I never swear. I detest the habit. What the devil do you mean?

MRS PEARCE [*stolidly*] Thats what I mean, sir. You swear a great deal too much. I dont mind your damning and blasting, and what the devil and where the devil and who the devil—

HIGGINS. Mrs Pearce: this language from your lips! Really!

MRS PEARCE [*not to be put off*]—but there is a certain word I must ask you not to use. The girl used it herself when she began to enjoy the bath. It begins with the same letter as bath. *She* knows no better: * she learnt it at her mother's knee. But she must not hear it from *your* lips.

HIGGINS [*loftily*] I cannot charge myself with having ever uttered it, Mrs Pearce. [*She looks at him steadfastly. He adds, hiding an uneasy conscience with a judicial air*] Except perhaps in a moment of extreme and justifiable excitement.

MRS PEARCE. Only this morning, sir, you applied it to your boots, to the butter, and to the brown bread.

HIGGINS. Oh, that! Mere alliteration, Mrs Pearce, natural to a poet.

MRS PEARCE. Well, sir, whatever you choose to call it, I beg you not to let the girl hear you repeat it.

HIGGINS. Oh, very well, very well. Is that all?

MRS PEARCE. No, sir. We shall have to be very particular with this girl as to personal cleanliness.

HIGGINS. Certainly. Quite right. Most important.

MRS PEARCE. I mean not to be slovenly about her dress or untidy in leaving things about.

HIGGINS [*going to her solemnly*] Just so. I intended to call your attention to that. [*He passes on to Pickering, who is enjoying the conversation immensely*]. It is these little things that matter, Pickering. Take care of the pence and the pounds will take care of themselves is as true of personal habits as of money. [*He comes to anchor on the hearthrug, with the air of a man in an unassailable position*].

MRS PEARCE. Yes, sir. Then might I ask you not to come down to breakfast in your dressing-gown, or at any rate not to use it as a napkin to the extent you do, sir. And if you would be so good as not to eat everything off the same plate, and to remember not to put the porridge saucepan out of your hand on the clean tablecloth, it would be a better example to the girl. You know you nearly choked yourself with a fishbone in the jam only last week.

HIGGINS [*routed from the hearthrug and drifting back to the piano*] I may do these things sometimes in absence of mind; but surely I dont do them habitually. [*Angrily*] By the way: my dressing-gown smells most damnably of benzine.*

MRS PEARCE. No doubt it does, Mr Higgins. But if you will wipe your fingers—

HIGGINS [*yelling*] Oh very well, very well: I'll wipe them in my hair in future.

MRS PEARCE. I hope youre not offended, Mr Higgins.

HIGGINS [*shocked at finding himself thought capable of an unamiable sentiment*] Not at all, not at all. Youre quite right, Mrs Pearce: I shall be particularly careful before the girl. Is that all?

MRS PEARCE. No, sir. Might she use some of those Japanese dresses you brought from abroad? I really cant put her back into her old things.

HIGGINS. Certainly. Anything you like. Is *that* all?

MRS PEARCE. Thank you, sir. Thats all. [*She goes out*].

HIGGINS. You know, Pickering, that woman has the most extraordinary ideas about me. Here I am, a shy, diffident sort of man. Ive never
been able to feel really grown-up and tremendous, like other chaps.
And yet she's firmly persuaded that I'm an arbitrary overbearing boss-
ing kind of person. I cant account for it.

Mrs Pearce returns.

MRS PEARCE. If you please, sir, the trouble's beginning already. Theres
a dustman* downstairs, Alfred Doolittle, wants to see you. He says
you have his daughter here.

PICKERING [*rising*] Phew! I say!

HIGGINS [*promptly*] Send the blackguard* up.

MRS PEARCE. Oh, very well, sir. [*She goes out*].

PICKERING. He may not be a blackguard, Higgins.

HIGGINS. Nonsense. Of course he's a blackguard.

PICKERING. Whether he is or not, I'm afraid we shall have some
trouble with him.

HIGGINS [*confidently*] Oh no: I think not. If theres any trouble he
shall have it with me, not I with him.* And we are sure to get something interesting out of him.

PICKERING. About the girl?

HIGGINS. No. I mean his dialect.

PICKERING. Oh!

MRS PEARCE [*at the door*] Doolittle, sir. [*She admits Doolittle and
retires*].

*Alfred Doolittle is an elderly but vigorous dustman, clad in the costume of
his profession, including a hat with a back brim covering his neck and shoulders. He has well marked and rather interesting features, and seems equally
free from fear and conscience. He has a remarkably expressive voice, the
result of a habit of giving vent to his feelings without reserve. His present
pose is that of wounded honor and stern resolution.*

DOOLITTLE [*at the door, uncertain which of the two gentlemen is his man*]
Professor Iggins?

HIGGINS. Here. Good morning. Sit down.

DOOLITTLE. Morning, Governor. [*He sits down magisterially*] I come about a very serious matter, Governor.

HIGGINS [*to Pickering*] Brought up in Hounslow.* Mother Welsh, I should think. [*Doolittle opens his mouth, amazed. Higgins continues*] What do you want, Doolittle?

DOOLITTLE [*menacingly**] I want my daughter: thats what I want. See?

HIGGINS. Of course you do. Youre her father, arnt you? You dont suppose anyone else wants her, do you? I'm glad to see you have some spark of family feeling left.* She's upstairs. Take her away at once.

DOOLITTLE [*rising, fearfully taken aback*] What!

HIGGINS. Take her away. Do you suppose I'm going to keep your daughter for you?

DOOLITTLE [*remonstrating*] Now, now, look here, Governor. Is this reasonable?* Is it fairity* to take advantage of a man like this? The girl belongs to me. You got her. Where do I come in? [*He sits down again*].

HIGGINS. Your daughter had the audacity to come to my house and ask me to teach her how to speak properly so that she could get a place in a flower shop. This gentleman and my housekeeper have been here all the time. [*Bullying him*] How dare you come here and attempt to blackmail me? You sent her here on purpose.

DOOLITTLE [*protesting*] No, Governor.

HIGGINS. You must have. How else could you possibly know that she is here?

DOOLITTLE. Dont take a man up like that, Governor.

HIGGINS. The police shall take you up. This is a plant—a plot to extort money by threats. I shall telephone for the police [*he goes resolutely to the telephone and opens the directory*].

DOOLITTLE. Have I asked you for a brass farthing?* I leave it to the gentleman here: have I said a word about money?

HIGGINS [*throwing the book aside and marching down on Doolittle with a poser**] What else did you come for?

DOOLITTLE [*sweetly*] Well, what would a man come for?* Be human, Governor.

HIGGINS [*disarmed*] Alfred: did you put her up to it?

DOOLITTLE. So help me, Governor, I never did. I take my Bible oath I aint seen the girl these two months past.

HIGGINS. Then how did you know she was here?

DOOLITTLE ['*most musical, most melancholy*'*] I'll tell you, Governor, if youll only let me get a word in. I'm willing to tell you. I'm wanting to tell you. I'm waiting to tell you.*

HIGGINS. Pickering: this chap has a certain natural gift of rhetoric. Observe the rhythm of his native woodnotes wild.* 'I'm willing to tell you: I'm wanting to tell you: I'm waiting to tell you.' Sentimental rhetoric! thats the Welsh strain in him. It also accounts for his mendacity and dishonesty.

PICKERING. Oh, please,* Higgins: I'm west country myself. [*To Doolittle*] How did you know the girl was here if you didnt send her?

DOOLITTLE. It was like this, Governor. The girl took a boy in the taxi to give him a jaunt. Son of her landlady, he is. He hung about on the chance of her giving him another ride home. Well, she sent him back for her luggage when she heard you was willing for her to stop here. I met the boy at the corner of Long Acre and Endell Street.*

HIGGINS. Public house.* Yes?

DOOLITTLE. The poor man's club, Governor: why shouldnt I?

PICKERING. Do let him tell his story, Higgins.

DOOLITTLE. He told me what was up. And I ask you, what was my feelings and my duty as a father? I says to the boy, 'You bring me the luggage,' I says—

PICKERING. Why didnt you go for it yourself?

DOOLITTLE. Landlady wouldnt have trusted me with it, Governor. She's that kind of woman: you know. I had to give the boy a penny afore he trusted me with it, the little swine. I brought it to her just to oblige you like, and make myself agreeable. Thats all.

HIGGINS. How much luggage?

DOOLITTLE. Musical instrument, Governor. A few pictures, a trifle of jewelry, and a bird-cage. She said she didnt want no clothes. What was I to think from that, Governor? I ask you as a parent what was I to think?

HIGGINS.   So you came to rescue her from worse than death, eh?

DOOLITTLE [*appreciatively: relieved at being so well understood*] Just so, Governor. Thats right.

PICKERING.   But why did you bring her luggage if you intended to take her away?

DOOLITTLE.   Have I said a word about taking her away? Have I now?

HIGGINS [*determinedly*] Youre going to take her away, double quick. [*He crosses to the hearth and rings the bell*].

DOOLITTLE [*rising*] No, Governor. Dont say that. I'm not the man to stand in my girl's light. Heres a career opening for her, as you might say; and—

Mrs Pearce opens the door and awaits orders.

HIGGINS.   Mrs Pearce: this is Eliza's father. He has come to take her away. Give her to him. [*He goes back to the piano, with an air of washing his hands of the whole affair*].

DOOLITTLE.   No. This is a misunderstanding. Listen here—

MRS PEARCE.   He cant take her away, Mr Higgins: how can he? You told me to burn her clothes.

DOOLITTLE.   Thats right. I cant carry the girl through the streets like a blooming monkey, can I? I put it to you.

HIGGINS.   You have put it to me that you want your daughter. Take your daughter. If she has no clothes go out and buy her some.

DOOLITTLE [*desperate*] Wheres the clothes she come in? Did I burn them or did your missus here?

MRS PEARCE.   I am the housekeeper, if you please. I have sent for some clothes for your girl. When they come you can take her away. You can wait in the kitchen. This way, please.

Doolittle, much troubled, accompanies her to the door; then hesitates; finally turns confidentially to Higgins.

DOOLITTLE.   Listen here, Governor. You and me is men of the world, aint we?

HIGGINS.   Oh! Men of the world, are we? Youd better go, Mrs Pearce.

MRS PEARCE.   I think so, indeed, sir. [*She goes, with dignity*].*

PICKERING. The floor is yours, Mr Doolittle.

DOOLITTLE [*to Pickering*] I thank you, Governor. [*To Higgins, who takes refuge on the piano bench, a little overwhelmed by the proximity of his visitor; for Doolittle has a professional flavor of dust about him*]. Well, the truth is, Ive taken a sort of fancy to you, Governor; and if you want the girl, I'm not so set on having her back home again but what I might be open to an arrangement. Regarded in the light of a young woman, she's a fine handsome girl. As a daughter she's not worth her keep; and so I tell you straight. All I ask is my rights as a father; and youre the last man alive to expect me to let her go for nothing; for I can see youre one of the straight sort, Governor. Well, whats a five-pound note to you? and whats Eliza to me? [*He turns to his chair and sits down judicially*].

PICKERING. I think you ought to know, Doolittle, that Mr Higgins's intentions are entirely honorable.

DOOLITTLE. Course they are, Governor. If I thought they wasn't, I'd ask fifty.

HIGGINS [*revolted*] Do you mean to say* that you would sell your daughter for £50?

DOOLITTLE. Not in a general way I wouldnt; but to oblige a gentleman like you I'd do a good deal, I do assure you.

PICKERING. Have you no morals, man?*

DOOLITTLE [*unabashed*] Cant afford them, Governor. Neither could you if you was as poor as me. Not that I mean any harm, you know. But if Liza is going to have a bit out of this, why not me too?

HIGGINS [*troubled*] I dont know what to do, Pickering. There can be no question that as a matter of morals it's a positive crime to give this chap a farthing. And yet I feel a sort of rough justice in his claim.

DOOLITTLE. Thats it, Governor. Thats all I say. A father's heart, as it were.

PICKERING. Well, I know the feeling; but really it seems hardly right—

DOOLITTLE. Dont say that, Governor. Dont look at it that way. What am I, Governors both? I ask you, what *am* I? I'm one of the undeserving poor: thats what I am. Think of what that means to a man. It means that he's up agen middle class morality all the time. If theres

anything going, and I put in for a bit of it, it's always the same story:
'Youre undeserving; so you cant have it.' But my needs is as great as
the most deserving widow's that ever got money out of six different
charities in one week for the death of the same husband. I dont need
less than a deserving man: I need more. I dont eat less hearty than
him; and I drink a lot more. I want a bit of amusement, cause I'm
a thinking man. I want cheerfulness and a song and a band when
I feel low. Well, they charge me just the same for everything as they
charge the deserving. What is middle class morality?* Just an excuse
for never giving me anything. Therefore, I ask you, as two gentlemen, not to play that game on me. I'm playing straight with you.
I aint pretending to be deserving. I'm undeserving; and I mean to go
on being undeserving. I like it; and thats the truth. Will you take
advantage of a man's nature to do him out of the price of his own
daughter what he's brought up and fed and clothed by the sweat of
his brow until she's growed big enough to be interesting to you two
gentlemen? Is five pounds unreasonable? I put it to you; and I leave
it to you.

HIGGINS [*rising, and going over to Pickering*] Pickering: if we were to
take this man in hand for three months, he could choose between
a seat in the Cabinet and a popular pulpit in Wales.

PICKERING. What do you say to that, Doolittle?

DOOLITTLE. Not me, Governor, thank you kindly. Ive heard all the
preachers and all the prime ministers—for I'm a thinking man and
game for politics or religion or social reform same as all the other
amusements—and I tell you it's a dog's life any way you look at it.
Undeserving poverty is my line. Taking one station in society with
another, it's—it's—well, it's the only one that has any ginger in it, to
my taste.

HIGGINS. I suppose we must give him a fiver.

PICKERING. He'll make a bad use of it, I'm afraid.

DOOLITTLE. Not me, Governor, so help me I wont. Dont you be
afraid that I'll save it and spare it and live idle on it. There wont be
a penny of it left by Monday: I'll have to go to work same as if I'd
never had it. It wont pauperize me, you bet. Just one good spree for
myself and the missus, giving pleasure to ourselves and employment
to others, and satisfaction to you to think it's not been throwed away.
You couldnt spend it better.

HIGGINS [*taking out his pocket book and coming between Doolittle and the piano*] This is irresistible. Lets give him ten. [*He offers two notes to the dustman*].

DOOLITTLE. No, Governor. She wouldnt have the heart to spend ten; and perhaps I shouldnt neither. Ten pounds is a lot of money: it makes a man feel prudent like;* and then goodbye to happiness. You give me what I ask you, Governor: not a penny more, and not a penny less.

PICKERING. Why dont you marry that missus of yours? I rather draw the line at encouraging that sort of immorality.

DOOLITTLE. Tell her so, Governor: tell her so. *I*'m willing. It's me that suffers by it. Ive no hold on her. I got to be agreeable to her. I got to give her presents. I got to buy her clothes something sinful. I'm a slave to that woman, Governor, just because I'm not her lawful husband. And she knows it too. Catch her marrying me! Take my advice, Governor: marry Eliza while she's young and dont know no better. If you dont youll be sorry for it after. If you do, *she'll* be sorry for it after; but better her than you, because youre a man, and she's only a woman and dont know how to be happy anyhow.

HIGGINS. Pickering: if we listen to this man another minute, we shall have no convictions left. [*To Doolittle*] Five pounds I think you said.

DOOLITTLE. Thank you kindly, Governor.

HIGGINS. Youre sure you wont take ten?

DOOLITTLE. Not now. Another time, Governor.

HIGGINS [*handing him a five-pound note*] Here you are.

DOOLITTLE. Thank you, Governor. Good morning. [*He hurries to the door, anxious to get away with his booty. When he opens it he is confronted with a dainty and exquisitely clean young Japanese lady in a simple blue cotton kimono printed cunningly with small white jasmine blossoms. Mrs Pearce is with her. He gets out of her way deferentially and apologizes*]. Beg pardon, miss.

THE JAPANESE LADY. Garn! Dont you know your own daughter?

DOOLITTLE		Bly me! it's Eliza!
HIGGINS	*exclaiming simul- taneously*	Whats that? This!
PICKERING		By Jove!

LIZA. Dont I look silly?

HIGGINS. Silly?

MRS PEARCE [*at the door*] Now, Mr Higgins, please dont say anything to make the girl conceited* about herself.

HIGGINS [*conscientiously*] Oh! Quite right, Mrs Pearce. [*To Eliza*] Yes: damned silly.

MRS PEARCE. Please, sir.

HIGGINS [*correcting himself*] I mean extremely silly.

LIZA. I should look all right with my hat on. [*She takes up her hat; puts it on; and walks across the room to the fireplace with a fashionable air*].

HIGGINS. A new fashion, by George! And it ought to look horrible!

DOOLITTLE [*with fatherly pride*] Well, I never thought she'd clean up as good looking as that, Governor. She's a credit to me, aint she?

LIZA. I tell you, it's easy to clean up here. Hot and cold water on tap, just as much as you like, there is. Woolly towels, there is; and a towel horse* so hot, it burns your fingers. Soft brushes to scrub yourself, and a wooden bowl of soap smelling like primroses. Now I know why ladies is so clean. Washing's a treat for them. Wish they could see what it is for the like of me!

HIGGINS. I'm glad the bathroom met with your approval.

LIZA. It didnt: not all of it; and I dont care who hears me say it. Mrs Pearce knows.

HIGGINS. What was wrong, Mrs Pearce?

MRS PEARCE [*blandly*] Oh, nothing, sir. It doesnt matter.

LIZA. I had a good mind to break it. I didnt know which way to look. But I hung a towel over it, I did.

HIGGINS. Over what?

MRS PEARCE. Over the looking-glass, sir.

HIGGINS. Doolittle: you have brought your daughter up too strictly.

DOOLITTLE. Me!* I never brought her up at all, except to give her a lick of a strap* now and again. Dont put it on me, Governor. She aint accustomed to it, you see: thats all. But she'll soon pick up your free-and-easy ways.

LIZA. I'm a good girl, I am; and I wont pick up no free-and-easy ways.

HIGGINS. Eliza: if you say again that youre a good girl, your father shall take you home.

LIZA. Not him. You dont know my father. All he come here for was to touch you for some money to get drunk on.

DOOLITTLE. Well, what else would I want money for? To put into the plate in church, I suppose. [*She puts out her tongue at him. He is so incensed by this that Pickering presently finds it necessary to step between them*]. Dont you give me none of your lip; and dont let me hear you giving this gentleman any of it neither, or youll hear from me about it. See?

HIGGINS. Have you any further advice to give her before you go, Doolittle? Your blessing, for instance.*

DOOLITTLE. No, Governor: I aint such a mug as to put up my children to all I know myself. Hard enough to hold them in without that. If you want Eliza's mind improved, Governor, you do it yourself with a strap. So long, gentlemen. [*He turns to go*].

HIGGINS [*impressively*] Stop. Youll come regularly to see your daughter. It's your duty, you know. My brother is a clergyman; and he could help you in your talks with her.

DOOLITTLE [*evasively*] Certainly, I'll come, Governor. Not just this week, because I have a job at a distance. But later on you may depend on me. Afternoon, gentlemen. Afternoon, maam. [*He touches his hat to Mrs Pearce, who disdains the salutation and goes out. He winks at Higgins, thinking him probably a fellow-sufferer from Mrs Pearce's difficult disposition, and follows her*].

LIZA. Dont you believe the old liar. He'd as soon you set a bulldog on him as a clergyman. You wont see him again in a hurry.

HIGGINS. I dont want to, Eliza. Do you?

LIZA. Not me. I dont want never to see him again, I dont. He's a disgrace to me, he is, collecting dust, instead of working at his trade.

PICKERING. What is his trade, Eliza?

LIZA. Talking money out of other people's pockets into his own. His proper trade's a navvy;* and he works at it sometimes too—for exercise—and earns good money at it. Aint you going to call me Miss Doolittle any more?

PICKERING. I beg your pardon, Miss Doolittle. It was a slip of the tongue.

LIZA. Oh, I dont mind; only it sounded so genteel. I *should* just like to take a taxi to the corner of Tottenham Court Road and get out there and tell it to wait for me, just to put the girls in their place a bit. I wouldnt speak to them, you know.

PICKERING. Better wait til we get you something really fashionable.

HIGGINS. Besides, you shouldnt cut your old friends now that you have risen in the world. Thats what we call snobbery.

LIZA. You dont call the like of them my friends now, I should hope. Theyve took it out of me often enough with their ridicule when they had the chance; and now I mean to get a bit of my own back. But if I'm to have fashionable clothes, I'll wait. I should like to have some. Mrs Pearce says youre going to give me some to wear in bed at night different to what I wear in the daytime; but it do seem a waste of money when you could get something to shew. Besides, I never could fancy changing into cold things on a winter night.

MRS PEARCE [*coming back*] Now, Eliza. The new things have come for you to try on.

LIZA. Ah-ow-oo-ooh! [*She rushes out*].

MRS PEARCE [*following her*] Oh, dont rush about like that, girl. [*She shuts the door behind her*].

HIGGINS. Pickering: we have taken on a stiff job.

PICKERING [*with conviction*] Higgins: we have.*

* * * * * *

There seems to be some curiosity as to what Higgins's lessons to Eliza were like. Well, here is a sample: the first one.

Picture Eliza, in her new clothes, and feeling her inside put out of step by a lunch, dinner, and breakfast of a kind to which it is unaccustomed, seated with Higgins and the Colonel in the study, feeling like a hospital out-patient at a first encounter with the doctors.

Higgins, constitutionally unable to sit still, discomposes her still more by striding restlessly about. But for the reassuring presence and quietude of her friend the Colonel she would run for her life, even back to Drury Lane.

HIGGINS. Say your alphabet.

LIZA. I know my alphabet. Do you think I know nothing? I dont need to be taught like a child.

HIGGINS [*thundering*] Say your alphabet.

PICKERING. Say it, Miss Doolittle. You will understand presently. Do what he tells you; and let him teach you in his own way.

LIZA. Oh well, if you put it like that—Ahyee, bəyee, cəyee, dəyee—

HIGGINS [*with the roar of a wounded lion*] Stop. Listen to this, Pickering. This is what we pay for as elementary education. This unfortunate animal has been locked up for nine years in school at our expense* to teach her to speak and read the language of Shakespear and Milton. And the result is Ahyee, Bə-yee, Cə-yee, Də-yee. [*To Eliza*] Say A, B, C, D.

LIZA [*almost in tears*] But I'm sayin it. Ahyee, Bəyee, Cə-yee—

HIGGINS. Stop. Say a cup of tea.

LIZA. A cappətə-ee.

HIGGINS. Put your tongue forward until it squeezes against the top of your lower teeth. Now say cup.

LIZA. C-c-c—I cant. C-Cup.

PICKERING. Good. Splendid, Miss Doolittle.

HIGGINS. By Jupiter, she's done it at the first shot. Pickering: we shall make a duchess of her. [*To Eliza*] Now do you think you could possibly say tea? Not tə-yee, mind: if you ever say bə-yee cə-yee də-yee again you shall be dragged round the room three times by the hair of your head. [*Fortissimo**] T, T, T, T.

LIZA [*weeping*] I cant hear no difference cep* that it sounds more genteel-like when you say it.

HIGGINS. Well, if you can hear that difference, what the devil are you crying for? Pickering: give her a chocolate.

PICKERING. No, no. Never mind crying a little, Miss Doolittle: you are doing very well; and the lessons wont hurt. I promise you I wont let him drag you round the room by your hair.

HIGGINS. Be off with you to Mrs Pearce and tell her about it. Think about it. Try to do it by yourself: and keep your tongue well forward in your mouth instead of trying to roll it up and swallow it. Another lesson at half-past four this afternoon. Away with you.

Eliza, still sobbing, rushes from the room.

And that is the sort of ordeal poor Eliza has to go through for months before we meet her again on her first appearance in London society of the professional class.

ACT III

It is Mrs Higgins's at-home day. Nobody has yet arrived. Her drawing room, in a flat on Chelsea Embankment,* has three windows looking on the river; and the ceiling is not so lofty as it would be in an older house of the same pretension. The windows are open, giving access to a balcony with flowers in pots. If you stand with your face to the windows, you have the fireplace on your left and the door in the right-hand wall close to the corner nearest the windows.

Mrs Higgins was brought up on Morris and Burne Jones;* and her room, which is very unlike her son's room in Wimpole Street, is not crowded with furniture and little tables and nicknacks. In the middle of the room there is a big ottoman; and this, with the carpet, the Morris wall-papers, and the Morris chintz window curtains and brocade covers of the ottoman and its cushions, supply all the ornament, and are much too handsome to be hidden by odds and ends of useless things. A few good oil-paintings from the exhibitions in the Grosvenor Gallery* thirty years ago (the Burne Jones, not the Whistler* side of them) are on the walls. The only landscape is a Cecil Lawson on the scale of a Rubens.* There is a portrait of Mrs Higgins as she was when she defied fashion in her youth in one of the beautiful Rossettian costumes* which, when caricatured by people who did not understand, led to the absurdities of popular estheticism in the eighteen-seventies.

In the corner diagonally opposite the door Mrs Higgins, now over sixty and long past taking the trouble to dress out of the fashion, sits writing at an elegantly simple writing-table with a bell button within reach of her hand. There is a Chippendale chair* further back in the room between her and the window nearest her side. At the other side of the room, further forward, is an Elizabethan chair roughly carved in the taste of Inigo Jones.* On the same side a piano in a decorated case. The corner between the fireplace and the window is occupied by a divan cushioned in Morris chintz.

It is between four and five in the afternoon.

The door is opened violently; and Higgins enters with his hat on.

MRS HIGGINS [*dismayed*] Henry! [*Scolding him*] What are you doing here today? It is my at-home day: you promised not to come. [*As he bends to kiss her, she takes his hat off, and presents it to him*].

HIGGINS. Oh bother! [*He throws the hat down on the table*].

MRS HIGGINS. Go home at once.

HIGGINS [*kissing her*] I know, mother. I came on purpose.

MRS HIGGINS. But you mustnt. I'm serious, Henry. You offend all my friends: they stop coming whenever they meet you.*

HIGGINS. Nonsense! I know I have no small talk; but people dont mind. [*He sits on the settee*].

MRS HIGGINS. Oh! dont they? Small talk indeed! What about your large talk?* Really, dear, you mustnt stay.

HIGGINS. I must.* Ive a job for you. A phonetic job.

MRS HIGGINS. No use, dear. I'm sorry; but I cant get round your vowels; and though I like to get pretty postcards in your patent short-hand, I always have to read the copies in ordinary writing you so thoughtfully send me.

HIGGINS. Well, this isnt a phonetic job.

MRS HIGGINS. You said it was.

HIGGINS. Not your part of it. Ive picked up a girl.

MRS HIGGINS. Does that mean that some girl has picked you up?

HIGGINS. Not at all. I dont mean a love affair.

MRS HIGGINS. What a pity!

HIGGINS. Why?

MRS HIGGINS. Well, you never fall in love with anyone under forty-five. When will you discover that there are some rather nice-looking young women about?

HIGGINS. Oh, I cant be bothered with young women. My idea of a lovable woman is somebody as like you as possible. I shall never get into the way of seriously liking young women: some habits lie too deep to be changed. [*Rising abruptly and walking about, jingling his money and his keys in his trouser pockets*] Besides, theyre all idiots.

MRS HIGGINS. Do you know what you would do if you really loved me, Henry?

HIGGINS. Oh bother! What? Marry, I suppose.

MRS HIGGINS. No. Stop fidgeting and take your hands out of your pockets. [*With a gesture of despair, he obeys and sits down again*]. Thats a good boy. Now tell me about the girl.

HIGGINS. She's coming to see you.

MRS HIGGINS. I dont remember asking her.

HIGGINS. You didnt. *I* asked her. If youd known her you wouldnt have asked her.

MRS HIGGINS. Indeed! Why?

HIGGINS. Well, it's like this. She's a common flower girl. I picked her off the kerbstone.

MRS HIGGINS. And invited her to my at–home!

HIGGINS [*rising and coming to her to coax her*] Oh, thatll be all right. Ive taught her to speak properly; and she has strict orders as to her behavior. She's to keep to two subjects: the weather and everybody's health—Fine day and How do you do, you know—and not to let herself go on things in general. That will be safe.

MRS HIGGINS. Safe! To talk about our health! about our insides! perhaps about our outsides! How could you be so silly, Henry?

HIGGINS [*impatiently*] Well, she must talk about something.* [*He controls himself and sits down again*]. Oh, she'll be all right: dont you fuss. Pickering is in it with me. Ive a sort of bet on that I'll pass her off as a duchess in six months. I started on her some months ago; and she's getting on like a house on fire. I shall win my bet. She has a quick ear; and she's been easier to teach than my middle-class pupils because she's had to learn a complete new language. She talks English almost as you talk French.

MRS HIGGINS. Thats satisfactory, at all events.

HIGGINS. Well, it is and it isnt.

MRS HIGGINS. What does that mean?

HIGGINS. You see, Ive got her pronunciation all right; but you have to consider not only *how* a girl pronounces, but *what* she pronounces; and that's where—

They are interrupted by the parlormaid, announcing guests.

THE PARLORMAID. Mrs and Miss Eynsford Hill. [*She withdraws*].

HIGGINS. Oh Lord! [*He rises; snatches his hat from the table; and makes for the door; but before he reaches it his mother introduces him*].

Mrs and Miss Eynsford Hill are the mother and daughter who sheltered from the rain in Covent Garden. The mother is well bred, quiet, and has the habitual anxiety of straitened means. The daughter has acquired a gay air of being very much at home in society: the bravado of genteel poverty.

MRS EYNSFORD HILL [*to Mrs Higgins*] How do you do? [*They shake hands*].

MISS EYNSFORD HILL. How d'you do? [*She shakes*].

MRS HIGGINS [*introducing*] My son Henry.

MRS EYNSFORD HILL. Your celebrated son! I have so longed to meet you, Professor Higgins.

HIGGINS [*glumly, making no movement in her direction*] Delighted. [*He backs against the piano and bows brusquely*].

MISS EYNSFORD HILL [*going to him with confident familiarity*] How do you do?

HIGGINS [*staring at her*] Ive seen you before somewhere.* I havnt the ghost of a notion where; but Ive heard your voice. [*Drearily*] It doesnt matter. Youd better sit down.

MRS HIGGINS. I'm sorry to say that my celebrated son has no manners. You mustnt mind him.

MISS EYNSFORD HILL [*gaily*] I dont. [*She sits in the Elizabethan chair*].

MRS EYNSFORD HILL [*a little bewildered*] Not at all. [*She sits on the ottoman between her daughter and Mrs Higgins, who has turned her chair away from the writing-table*].

HIGGINS. Oh, have I been rude? I didnt mean to be.

He goes to the central window, through which, with his back to the company, he contemplates the river and the flowers in Battersea Park on the opposite bank as if they were a frozen desert.
The parlormaid returns, ushering in Pickering.

THE PARLORMAID. Colonel Pickering. [*She withdraws*].

PICKERING. How do you do, Mrs Higgins?

MRS HIGGINS. So glad youve come. Do you know Mrs Eynsford Hill—Miss Eynsford Hill? [*Exchange of bows. The Colonel brings the Chippendale chair a little forward between Mrs Hill and Mrs Higgins, and sits down*].

PICKERING. Has Henry told you what weve come for?

HIGGINS [*over his shoulder*] We were interrupted: damn it!

MRS HIGGINS. Oh Henry, Henry, really!

MRS EYNSFORD HILL [*half rising*] Are we in the way?

MRS HIGGINS [*rising and making her sit down again*] No, no. You couldnt have come more fortunately: we want you to meet a friend of ours.

HIGGINS [*turning hopefully*] Yes, by George! We want two or three people. Youll do as well as anybody else.*

The parlormaid returns, ushering Freddy.

THE PARLORMAID. Mr Eynsford Hill.

HIGGINS [*almost audibly, past endurance*] God of Heaven! another of them.

FREDDY [*shaking hands with Mrs Higgins*] Ahdedo?*

MRS HIGGINS. Very good of you to come. [*Introducing*] Colonel Pickering.

FREDDY [*bowing*] Ahdedo?

MRS HIGGINS. I dont think you know my son, Professor Higgins.

FREDDY [*going to Higgins*] Ahdedo?

HIGGINS [*looking at him much as if he were a pickpocket*] I'll take my oath Ive met you before somewhere. Where was it?

FREDDY. I dont think so.

HIGGINS [*resignedly*] It dont matter, anyhow. Sit down.

He shakes Freddy's hand, and almost slings him on to the ottoman with his face to the windows; then comes round to the other side of it.

HIGGINS. Well, here we are, anyhow! [*He sits down on the ottoman next Mrs Eynsford Hill, on her left*]. And now, what the devil are we going to talk about until Eliza comes?

MRS HIGGINS. Henry: you are the life and soul of the Royal Society's soirées;* but really youre rather trying on more commonplace occasions.

HIGGINS. Am I? Very sorry. [*Beaming suddenly*] I suppose I am, you know. [*Uproariously*] Ha, ha!

MISS EYNSFORD HILL [*who considers Higgins quite eligible matrimonially*] I sympathize. *I* havnt any small talk. If people would only be frank and say what they really think!

HIGGINS [*relapsing into gloom*] Lord forbid!

MRS EYNSFORD HILL [*taking up her daughter's cue*] But why?

HIGGINS. What they think they ought to think is bad enough, Lord knows; but what they really think would break up the whole show. Do you suppose it would be really agreeable if I were to come out now with what *I* really think?

MISS EYNSFORD HILL [*gaily*] Is it so very cynical?

HIGGINS. Cynical! Who the dickens said it was cynical? I mean it wouldnt be decent.

MRS EYNSFORD HILL [*seriously*] Oh! I'm sure you dont mean that, Mr Higgins.

HIGGINS. You see, we're all savages, more or less. We're supposed to be civilized and cultured—to know all about poetry and philosophy and art and science, and so on; but how many of us know even the meanings of these names? [*To Miss Hill*] What do *you* know of poetry? [*To Mrs Hill*] What do *you* know of science? [*Indicating Freddy*] What does *he* know of art or science or anything else? What the devil do you imagine I know of philosophy?

MRS HIGGINS [*warningly*] Or of manners, Henry?*

THE PARLORMAID [*opening the door*] Miss Doolittle. [*She withdraws*].

HIGGINS [*rising hastily and running to Mrs Higgins*] Here she is, mother. [*He stands on tiptoe and makes signs over his mother's head to Eliza to indicate to her which lady is her hostess*].

Eliza, who is exquisitely dressed, produces an impression of such remarkable distinction and beauty as she enters that they all rise, quite fluttered. Guided by Higgins's signals, she comes to Mrs Higgins with studied grace.

LIZA [*speaking with pedantic correctness of pronunciation and great beauty of tone*] How do you do, Mrs Higgins? [*She gasps slightly in making sure of the H in Higgins, but is quite successful*]. Mr Higgins told me I might come.

MRS HIGGINS [*cordially*] Quite right: I'm very glad indeed to see you.

PICKERING. How do you do, Miss Doolittle?

LIZA [*shaking hands with him*] Colonel Pickering, is it not?

MRS EYNSFORD HILL. I feel sure we have met before, Miss Doolittle. I remember your eyes.

LIZA. How do you do? [*She sits down on the ottoman gracefully in the place just left vacant by Higgins*].

MRS EYNSFORD HILL [*introducing*] My daughter Clara.

LIZA. How do you do?

CLARA [*impulsively*] How do you do? [*She sits down on the ottoman beside Eliza, devouring her with her eyes*].

FREDDY [*coming to their side of the ottoman*] Ive certainly had the pleasure.

MRS EYNSFORD HILL [*introducing*] My son Freddy.

LIZA. How do you do?

Freddy bows and sits down in the Elizabethan chair, infatuated.

HIGGINS [*suddenly*] By George, yes: it all comes back to me! [*They stare at him*]. Covent Garden! [*Lamentably*] What a damned thing!

MRS HIGGINS. Henry, please! [*He is about to sit on the edge of the table*] Dont sit on my writing-table: youll break it.

HIGGINS [*sulkily*] Sorry.

He goes to the divan, stumbling into the fender and over the fire-irons on his way; extricating himself with muttered imprecations; and finishing his disastrous journey by throwing himself so impatiently on the divan that he almost breaks it. Mrs Higgins looks at him, but controls herself and says nothing.

A long and painful pause ensues.

MRS HIGGINS [*at last, conversationally*] Will it rain, do you think?

LIZA. The shallow depression in the west of these islands is likely to move slowly in an easterly direction. There are no indications of any great change in the barometrical situation.*

FREDDY. Ha! ha! how awfully funny!

LIZA. What is wrong with that, young man? I bet I got it right.

FREDDY. Killing!

MRS EYNSFORD HILL. I'm sure I hope it wont turn cold. Theres so much influenza about. It runs right through our whole family regularly every spring.

LIZA [*darkly*] My aunt died of influenza: so they said.

MRS EYNSFORD HILL [*clicks her tongue sympathetically*]!!!

LIZA [*in the same tragic tone*] But it's my belief they done the old woman in.

MRS HIGGINS [*puzzled*] Done her in?

LIZA. Y-e-e-e-es, Lord love you! Why should she die of influenza?* She come through diphtheria right enough the year before. I saw her with my own eyes. Fairly blue with it, she was. They all thought she was dead; but my father he kept ladling gin down her throat til she came to so sudden that she bit the bowl off the spoon.

MRS EYNSFORD HILL [*startled*] Dear me!

LIZA [*piling up the indictment*] What call would a woman with that strength in her have to die of influenza? What become of her new straw hat that should have come to me? Somebody pinched it;* and what I say is, them as pinched it done her in.

MRS EYNSFORD HILL. What does doing her in mean?

HIGGINS [*hastily*] Oh, thats the new small talk. To do a person in means to kill them.

MRS EYNSFORD HILL [*to Eliza, horrified*] You surely dont believe that your aunt was killed?

LIZA. Do I not! Them she lived with would have killed her for a hatpin, let alone a hat.

MRS EYNSFORD HILL. But it cant have been right for your father to pour spirits down her throat like that. It might have killed her.

LIZA. Not her. Gin was mother's milk to her. Besides,* he'd poured so much down his own throat that he knew the good of it.

MRS EYNSFORD HILL. Do you mean that he drank?

LIZA. Drank! My word! Something chronic.

MRS EYNSFORD HILL. How dreadful for you!

LIZA. Not a bit. It never did him no harm what I could see. But then he did not keep it up regular. [*Cheerfully*] On the burst, as you might say, from time to time. And always more agreeable when he had a drop in. When he was out of work, my mother used to give him fourpence and tell him to go out and not come back until he'd drunk himself cheerful and loving-like. Theres lots of women has to make their husbands drunk to make them fit to live with. [*Now quite at her ease*] You see, it's like this. If a man has a bit of a conscience, it always takes him when he's sober; and then it makes him low-spirited. A drop of booze just takes that off and makes him happy. [*To Freddy, who is in convulsions of suppressed laughter*] Here! what are you sniggering at?

FREDDY. The new small talk. You do it so awfully well.

LIZA. If I was doing it proper, what was you laughing at? [*To Higgins*] Have I said anything I oughtnt?

MRS HIGGINS [*interposing*] Not at all, Miss Doolittle.

LIZA. Well, thats a mercy, anyhow. [*Expansively*] What I always say is—

HIGGINS [*rising and looking at his watch*] Ahem!

LIZA [*looking round at him; taking the hint; and rising*] Well: I must go. [*They all rise. Freddy goes to the door*]. So pleased to have met you. Goodbye. [*She shakes hands with Mrs Higgins*].

MRS HIGGINS. Goodbye.

LIZA. Goodbye, Colonel Pickering.

PICKERING. Goodbye, Miss Doolittle. [*They shake hands*].

LIZA [*nodding to the others*] Goodbye, all.

FREDDY [*opening the door for her*] Are you walking across the Park, Miss Doolittle? If so—

LIZA [*with perfectly elegant diction*] Walk! Not bloody likely.* [*Sensation**]. I am going in a taxi. [*She goes out*].

Pickering gasps and sits down. Freddy goes out on the balcony to catch another glimpse of Eliza.

MRS EYNSFORD HILL [*suffering from shock*] Well, I really cant get used to the new ways.

CLARA [*throwing herself discontentedly into the Elizabethan chair*] Oh, it's all right, mamma, quite right. People will think we never go anywhere or see anybody if you are so old-fashioned.

MRS EYNSFORD HILL. I daresay I am very old-fashioned; but I do hope you wont begin using that expression, Clara. I have got accustomed to hear you talking about men as rotters, and calling everything filthy and beastly; though I do think it horrible and unladylike. But this last is really too much. Dont you think so, Colonel Pickering?

PICKERING. Dont ask me. Ive been away in India for several years; and manners have changed so much that I sometimes dont know whether I'm at a respectable dinner-table or in a ship's forecastle.

CLARA. It's all a matter of habit. Theres no right or wrong in it. Nobody means anything by it. And it's so quaint, and gives such a smart emphasis to things that are not in themselves very witty. I find the new small talk delightful and quite innocent.

MRS EYNSFORD HILL [*rising*]. Well, after that, I think it's time for us to go.

Pickering and Higgins rise.

CLARA [*rising*] Oh yes: we have three at-homes to go to still. Goodbye, Mrs Higgins. Goodbye, Colonel Pickering. Goodbye, Professor Higgins.

HIGGINS [*coming grimly at her from the divan, and accompanying her to the door*] Goodbye. Be sure you try on that small talk at the three at-homes. Dont be nervous about it. Pitch it in strong.

CLARA [*all smiles*] I will. Goodbye. Such nonsense, all this early Victorian prudery!

HIGGINS [*tempting her*] Such damned nonsense!

CLARA. Such bloody nonsense!

MRS EYNSFORD HILL [*convulsively*] Clara!

CLARA. Ha! ha! [*She goes out radiant, conscious of being thoroughly up to date, and is heard descending the stairs in a stream of silvery laughter*].

FREDDY [*to the heavens at large*] Well, I ask you—[*He gives it up, and comes to Mrs Higgins*]. Goodbye.

MRS HIGGINS [*shaking hands*] Goodbye. Would you like to meet Miss Doolittle again?

FREDDY [*eagerly*] Yes, I should, most awfully.

MRS HIGGINS. Well, you know my days.

FREDDY. Yes. Thanks awfully. Goodbye. [*He goes out*].

MRS EYNSFORD HILL. Goodbye, Mr Higgins.

HIGGINS. Goodbye. Goodbye.

MRS EYNSFORD HILL [*to Pickering*] It's no use. I shall never be able to bring myself to use that word.

PICKERING. Dont. It's not compulsory, you know. Youll get on quite well without it.

MRS EYNSFORD HILL. Only, Clara is so down on me if I am not positively reeking with the latest slang. Goodbye.

PICKERING. Goodbye [*They shake hands*].

MRS EYNSFORD HILL [*to Mrs Higgins*] You mustnt mind Clara. [*Pickering, catching from her lowered tone that this is not meant for him to hear, discreetly joins Higgins at the window*]. We're so poor! and she gets so few parties, poor child! She doesnt quite know. [*Mrs Higgins, seeing that her eyes are moist, takes her hand sympathetically and goes with her to the door*]. But the boy is nice. Dont you think so?

MRS HIGGINS. Oh, quite nice. I shall always be delighted to see him.

MRS EYNSFORD HILL. Thank you, dear. Goodbye. [*She goes out*].

HIGGINS [*eagerly*] Well? Is Eliza presentable [*he swoops on his mother and drags her to the ottoman, where she sits down in Eliza's place with her son on her left*]?

Pickering returns to his chair on her right.

MRS HIGGINS. You silly boy, of course she's not presentable. She's a triumph of your art and of her dressmaker's; but if you suppose for a moment that she doesnt give herself away in every sentence she utters, you must be perfectly cracked about her.

PICKERING. But dont you think something might be done? I mean something to eliminate the sanguinary element from her conversation.

MRS HIGGINS. Not as long as she is in Henry's hands.

HIGGINS [*aggrieved*] Do you mean that *my* language is improper?

MRS HIGGINS. No, dearest: it would be quite proper—say on a canal barge; but it would not be proper for her at a garden party.

HIGGINS [*deeply injured*] Well I must say——

PICKERING [*interrupting him*] Come, Higgins: you must learn to know yourself. I havnt heard such language as yours since we used to review the volunteers in Hyde Park* twenty years ago.

HIGGINS [*sulkily*] Oh, well, if *you* say so, I suppose I dont always talk like a bishop.*

MRS HIGGINS [*quieting Henry with a touch*] Colonel Pickering: will you tell me what is the exact state of things in Wimpole Street?

PICKERING [*cheerfully: as if this completely changed the subject*] Well, I have come to live there with Henry. We work together at my Indian Dialects; and we think it more convenient——

MRS HIGGINS. Quite so. I know all about that: it's an excellent arrangement. But where does this girl live?

HIGGINS. With us, of course. Where *should* she live?

MRS HIGGINS. But on what terms? Is she a servant? If not, what is she?

PICKERING [*slowly*] I think I know what you mean, Mrs Higgins.

HIGGINS. Well, dash me if *I* do! Ive had to work at the girl every day for months to get her to her present pitch. Besides, she's useful. She knows where my things are, and remembers my appointments and so forth.

MRS HIGGINS. How does your housekeeper get on with her?

HIGGINS. Mrs Pearce? Oh, she's jolly glad to get so much taken off her hands; for before Eliza came, *she* used to have to find things and remind me of my appointments. But she's got some silly bee in her bonnet about Eliza. She keeps saying 'You dont *think*, sir': doesnt she, Pick?

PICKERING. Yes: thats the formula. 'You dont *think*, sir.' Thats the end of every conversation about Eliza.

HIGGINS. As if I ever stop thinking about the girl and her confounded vowels and consonants. I'm worn out, thinking about her, and watching her lips and her teeth and her tongue, not to mention her soul, which is the quaintest of the lot.

MRS HIGGINS. You certainly are a pretty pair of babies, playing with your live doll.

HIGGINS. Playing! The hardest job I ever tackled: make no mistake about that, mother. But you have no idea how frightfully interesting it is to take a human being and change her into a quite different human being by creating a new speech for her. It's filling up the deepest gulf that separates class from class and soul from soul.

PICKERING [*drawing his chair closer to Mrs Higgins and bending over to her eagerly*] Yes: it's enormously interesting. I assure you, Mrs Higgins, we take Eliza very seriously. Every week—every day almost—there is some new change. [*Closer again*] We keep records of every stage—dozens of gramophone disks and photographs—

HIGGINS [*assailing her at the other ear*] Yes, by George: it's the most absorbing experiment I ever tackled. She regularly fills our lives up: doesnt she, Pick?

PICKERING. We're always talking Eliza.

HIGGINS. Teaching Eliza.

PICKERING. Dressing Eliza.

MRS HIGGINS. What!

HIGGINS. Inventing new Elizas.

HIGGINS.	[*speaking together*]	You know, she has the most extraordinary quickness of ear:
PICKERING.		I assure you, my dear Mrs Higgins, that girl
HIGGINS.		just like a parrot. Ive tried her with every
PICKERING.		is a genius. She can play the piano quite beautifully.
HIGGINS.		possible sort of sound that a human being can make—
PICKERING.		We have taken her to classical concerts and to music
HIGGINS.		Continental dialects, African dialects, Hottentot
PICKERING.		halls; and it's all the same to her: she plays everything
HIGGINS.		clicks,* things it took me years to get hold of; and
PICKERING.		she hears right off when she comes home, whether it's

HIGGINS.	she picks them up like a shot, right away, as if she had
PICKERING.	Beethoven and Brahms or Lehar and Lionel Monckton;*
HIGGINS.	been at it all her life.
PICKERING.	though six months ago, she'd never as much as touched a piano—

MRS HIGGINS [*putting her fingers in her ears, as they are by this time shouting one another down with an intolerable noise*] Sh-sh-sh—sh! [*They stop*].

PICKERING. I beg your pardon. [*He draws his chair back apologetically*].

HIGGINS. Sorry. When Pickering starts shouting nobody can get a word in edgeways.

MRS HIGGINS. Be quiet, Henry. Colonel Pickering: dont you realize that when Eliza walked into Wimpole Street, something walked in with her?*

PICKERING. Her father did. But Henry soon got rid of him.

MRS HIGGINS. It would have been more to the point if her mother had. But as her mother didnt something else did.

PICKERING. But what?

MRS HIGGINS [*unconsciously dating herself by the word*] A problem.

PICKERING. Oh, I see. The problem of how to pass her off as a lady.

HIGGINS. I'll solve that problem. Ive half solved it already.

MRS HIGGINS. No, you two infinitely stupid male creatures: the problem of what is to be done with her afterwards.

HIGGINS. I dont see anything in that. She can go her own way, with all the advantages I have given her.

MRS HIGGINS. The advantages of that poor woman who was here just now! The manners and habits that disqualify a fine lady from earning her own living without giving her a fine lady's income! Is that what you mean?

PICKERING [*indulgently, being rather bored*] Oh, that will be all right, Mrs Higgins. [*He rises to go*].

HIGGINS [*rising also*] We'll find her some light employment.

PICKERING. She's happy enough. Dont you worry about her. Goodbye. [*He shakes hands as if he were consoling a frightened child, and makes for the door*].

HIGGINS. Anyhow, theres no good bothering now. The thing's done. Goodbye, mother. [*He kisses her, and follows Pickering*].

PICKERING [*turning for a final consolation*] There are plenty of openings. We'll do whats right. Goodbye.

HIGGINS [*to Pickering as they go out together*] Lets take her to the Shakespear exhibition at Earlscourt.*

PICKERING. Yes: lets. Her remarks will be delicious.

HIGGINS. She'll mimic all the people for us when we get home.

PICKERING. Ripping. [*Both are heard laughing as they go downstairs*].

MRS HIGGINS [*rises with an impatient bounce, and returns to her work at the writing-table. She sweeps a litter of disarranged papers out of her way; snatches a sheet of paper from her stationery case; and tries resolutely to write. At the third line she gives it up; flings down her pen; grips the table angrily and exclaims*] Oh, men! men!! men!!!*

*   *   *   *   *   *

Clearly Eliza will not pass as a duchess yet; and Higgins's bet remains unwon. But the six months are not yet exhausted; and just in time Eliza does actually pass as a princess. For a glimpse of how she did it imagine an Embassy in London one summer evening after dark. The hall door has an awning and a carpet across the sidewalk to the kerb, because a grand reception is in progress. A small crowd is lined up to see the guests arrive.

A Rolls-Royce car drives up. Pickering in evening dress, with medals and orders, alights, and hands out Eliza, in opera cloak, evening dress, diamonds, fan, flowers and all accessories. Higgins follows. The car drives off; and the three go up the steps and into the house, the door opening for them as they approach.

Inside the house they find themselves in a spacious hall from which the grand staircase rises. On the left are the arrangements for the gentlemen's cloaks. The male guests are depositing their hats and wraps there.

On the right is a door leading to the ladies' cloakroom. Ladies are going in cloaked and coming out in splendor. Pickering whispers to Eliza and points out the ladies' room. She goes into it. Higgins and Pickering take off their overcoats and take tickets for them from the attendant.

One of the guests, occupied in the same way, has his back turned. Having taken his ticket, he turns round and reveals himself as an important looking young man with an astonishingly hairy face. He has an enormous moustache, flowing out into luxuriant whiskers. Waves of hair cluster on his brow. His hair is cropped closely at the back, and glows with oil. Otherwise he is very smart. He wears several worthless orders. He is evidently a foreigner, guessable as a whiskered Pandour from Hungary;* but in spite of the ferocity of his moustache he is amiable and genially voluble.

Recognizing Higgins, he flings his arms wide apart and approaches him enthusiastically.

WHISKERS. Maestro, maestro [*he embraces Higgins and kisses him on both cheeks*]. You remember me?

HIGGINS. No I dont. Who the devil are you?

WHISKERS. I am your pupil: your first pupil, your best and greatest pupil. I am little Nepommuck, the marvellous boy. I have made your name famous throughout Europe. You teach me phonetic. You cannot forget ME.

HIGGINS. Why dont you shave?

NEPOMMUCK. I have not your imposing appearance, your chin, your brow. Nobody notice me when I shave. Now I am famous: they call me Hairy Faced Dick.

HIGGINS. And what are you doing here among all these swells?

NEPOMMUCK. I am interpreter. I speak 32 languages. I am indispensable at these international parties. You are great cockney specialist: you place a man anywhere in London the moment he open his mouth. I place any man in Europe.

A footman hurries down the grand staircase and comes to Nepommuck.

FOOTMAN. You are wanted upstairs. Her Excellency cannot understand the Greek gentleman.

NEPOMMUCK. Thank you, yes, immediately.

The footman goes and is lost in the crowd.

NEPOMMUCK [*to Higgins*] This Greek diplomatist pretends he cannot speak nor understand English. He cannot deceive me. He is the son of a Clerkenwell* watchmaker. He speaks English so villainously that he dare not utter a word of it without betraying his origin. I help him to pretend; but I make him pay through the nose. I make them all pay. Ha ha! [*He hurries upstairs*].

PICKERING. Is this fellow really an expert? Can he find out Eliza and blackmail her?

HIGGINS. We shall see. If he finds her out I lose my bet.

Eliza comes from the cloakroom and joins them.

PICKERING. Well, Eliza, now for it. Are you ready?

LIZA. Are you nervous, Colonel?

PICKERING. Frightfully. I feel exactly as I felt before my first battle. It's the first time that frightens.

LIZA. It is not the first time for me, Colonel. I have done this fifty times—hundreds of times—in my little piggery in Angel Court in my day-dreams. I am in a dream now. Promise me not to let Professor Higgins wake me; for if he does I shall forget everything and talk as I used to in Drury Lane.

PICKERING. Not a word, Higgins. [*To Eliza*] Now, ready?

LIZA. Ready.

PICKERING. Go.

They mount the stairs, Higgins last. Pickering whispers to the footman on the first landing.

FIRST LANDING FOOTMAN. Miss Doolittle, Colonel Pickering, Professor Higgins.

SECOND LANDING FOOTMAN. Miss Doolittle, Colonel Pickering, Professor Higgins.

At the top of the staircase the Ambassador and his wife, with Nepommuck at her elbow, are receiving.

HOSTESS [*taking Eliza's hand*] How d'ye do?

HOST [*same play*] How d'ye do? How d'ye do, Pickering?

LIZA [*with a beautiful gravity that awes her hostess*] How do you do? [*She passes on to the drawing room*].

HOSTESS. Is that your adopted daughter, Colonel Pickering? She will make a sensation.

PICKERING. Most kind of you to invite her for me. [*He passes on*].

HOSTESS [*to Nepommuck*] Find out all about her.

NEPOMMUCK [*bowing*] Excellency—[*he goes into the crowd*].

HOST. How d'ye do, Higgins? You have a rival here tonight. He introduced himself as your pupil. Is he any good?

HIGGINS. He can learn a language in a fortnight—knows dozens of them. A sure mark of a fool. As a phonetician, no good whatever.

HOSTESS. How d'ye do, Professor?

HIGGINS. How do you do? Fearful bore for you this sort of thing. Forgive my part in it. [*He passes on*].

In the drawing room and its suite of salons the reception is in full swing. Eliza passes through. She is so intent on her ordeal that she walks like a somnambulist* in a desert instead of a débutante* in a fashionable crowd. They stop talking to look at her, admiring her dress, her jewels, and her strangely attractive self. Some of the younger ones at the back stand on their chairs to see.

The Host and Hostess come in from the staircase and mingle with their guests. Higgins, gloomy and contemptuous of the whole business, comes into the group where they are chatting.

HOSTESS. Ah, here is Professor Higgins: he will tell us. Tell us all about the wonderful young lady, Professor.

HIGGINS [*almost morosely*] What wonderful young lady?

HOSTESS. You know very well. They tell me there has been nothing like her in London since people stood on their chairs to look at Mrs Langtry.*

Nepommuck joins the group, full of news.

HOSTESS. Ah, here you are at last, Nepommuck. Have you found out all about the Doolittle lady?

NEPOMMUCK. I have found out all about her. She is a fraud.

HOSTESS. A fraud! Oh no.

NEPOMMUCK. YES, yes. She cannot deceive me. Her name cannot be Doolittle.

HIGGINS. Why?

NEPOMMUCK. Because Doolittle is an English name. And she is not English.

HOSTESS. Oh, nonsense! She speaks English perfectly.

NEPOMMUCK. Too perfectly. Can you shew me any English woman who speaks English as it should be spoken? Only foreigners who have been taught to speak it speak it well.

HOSTESS. Certainly she terrified me by the way she said How d'ye do. I had a schoolmistress who talked like that; and I was mortally afraid of her. But if she is not English what is she?

NEPOMMUCK. Hungarian.

ALL THE REST. Hungarian!

NEPOMMUCK. Hungarian. And of royal blood. I am Hungarian. My blood is royal.

HIGGINS. Did you speak to her in Hungarian?

NEPOMMUCK. I did. She was very clever. She said 'Please speak to me in English: I do not understand French.' French! She pretend not to know the difference between Hungarian and French. Impossible: she knows both.

HIGGINS. And the blood royal? How did you find that out?

NEPOMMUCK. Instinct, maestro, instinct. Only the Magyar races* can produce that air of the divine right, those resolute eyes. She is a princess.

HOST. What do you say, Professor?

HIGGINS. I say an ordinary London girl out of the gutter and taught to speak by an expert. I place her in Drury Lane.

NEPOMMUCK. Ha ha ha! Oh, maestro, maestro, you are mad on the subject of cockney dialects. The London gutter is the whole world for you.

HIGGINS [*to the Hostess*] What does your Excellency say?

HOSTESS. Oh, of course I agree with Nepommuck. She must be a princess at least.

HOST. Not necessarily legitimate, of course. Morganatic* perhaps. But that is undoubtedly her class.

HIGGINS. I stick to my opinion.

HOSTESS. Oh, you are incorrigible.

The group breaks up, leaving Higgins isolated. Pickering joins him.

PICKERING. Where is Eliza? We must keep an eye on her.

Eliza joins them.

LIZA. I dont think I can bear much more. The people all stare so at me. An old lady has just told me that I speak exactly like Queen Victoria. I am sorry if I have lost your bet. I have done my best; but nothing can make me the same as these people.

PICKERING. You have not lost it, my dear. You have won it ten times over.

HIGGINS. Let us get out of this. I have had enough of chattering to these fools.

PICKERING. Eliza is tired; and I am hungry. Let us clear out and have supper somewhere.

ACT IV

The Wimpole Street laboratory. Midnight. Nobody in the room. The clock on the mantelpiece strikes twelve. The fire is not alight: it is a summer night. Presently Higgins and Pickering are heard on the stairs.

HIGGINS [*calling down to Pickering*] I say, Pick: lock up, will you? I shant be going out again.

PICKERING. Right. Can Mrs Pearce go to bed? We dont want anything more, do we?

HIGGINS. Lord, no!

Eliza opens the door and is seen on the lighted landing in all the finery in which she has just won Higgins's bet for him.* She comes to the hearth, and switches on the electric lights there. She is tired: her pallor contrasts strongly with her dark eyes and hair; and her expression is almost tragic. She takes off her cloak; puts her fan and gloves on the piano; and sits down on the bench, brooding and silent. Higgins, in evening dress, with overcoat and hat, comes in, carrying a smoking jacket which he has picked up downstairs. He takes off the hat and overcoat; throws them carelessly on the newspaper stand; disposes of his coat in the same way; puts on the smoking jacket; and throws himself wearily into the easy-chair at the hearth. Pickering, similarly attired, comes in. He also takes off his hat and overcoat, and is about to throw them on Higgins's when he hesitates.

PICKERING. I say: Mrs Pearce will row if we leave these things lying about in the drawing room.

HIGGINS. Oh, chuck them over the bannisters into the hall. She'll find them there in the morning and put them away all right. She'll think we were drunk.

PICKERING. We are, slightly. Are there any letters?

HIGGINS. I didnt look. [*Pickering takes the overcoats and hats and goes downstairs. Higgins begins half singing half yawning an air from La Fanciulla del Golden West.* Suddenly he stops and exclaims*] I wonder where the devil my slippers are!

Eliza looks at him darkly; then rises suddenly and leaves the room. Higgins yawns again, and resumes his song. Pickering returns, with the contents of the letter-box in his hand.

PICKERING. Only circulars, and this coroneted billet-doux* for you. [*He throws the circulars into the fender, and posts himself on the hearthrug, with his back to the grate*].

HIGGINS [*glancing at the billet-doux*] Money-lender. [*He throws the letter after the circulars*].

Eliza returns with a pair of large down-at-heel slippers. She places them on the carpet before Higgins, and sits as before without a word.

HIGGINS [*yawning again*] Oh Lord! What an evening! What a crew! What a silly tomfoolery! [*He raises his shoe to unlace it, and catches sight of the slippers. He stops unlacing and looks at them as if they had appeared there of their own accord*]. Oh! theyre there, are they?

PICKERING [*stretching himself*] Well, I feel a bit tired. It's been a long day. The garden party, a dinner party, and the reception! Rather too much of a good thing. But youve won your bet, Higgins. Eliza did the trick, and something to spare, eh?

HIGGINS [*fervently*] Thank God it's over!

Eliza flinches violently; but they take no notice of her; and she recovers herself and sits stonily as before.

PICKERING. Were you nervous at the garden party? *I* was. Eliza didnt seem a bit nervous.

HIGGINS. Oh, *she* wasnt nervous. I knew she'd be all right. No: it's the strain of putting the job through all these months that has told on me. It was interesting enough at first, while we were at the phonetics; but after that I got deadly sick of it. If I hadnt backed myself to do it I should have chucked the whole thing up two months ago. It was a silly notion: the whole thing has been a bore.

PICKERING. Oh come! the garden party was frightfully exciting. My heart began beating like anything.

HIGGINS. Yes, for the first three minutes. But when I saw we were going to win hands down, I felt like a bear in a cage, hanging about doing nothing. The dinner was worse: sitting gorging there for over an hour, with nobody but a damned fool of a fashionable woman to talk to! I tell you, Pickering, never again for me. No more artificial duchesses. The whole thing has been simple purgatory.

PICKERING. Youve never been broken in properly to the social routine. [*Strolling over to the piano*] I rather enjoy dipping into it occasionally myself: it makes me feel young again. Anyhow, it was a great success: an immense success. I was quite frightened once or twice because Eliza was doing it so well. You see, lots of the real people cant do it at all: theyre such fools that they think style comes by nature to people in their position; and so they never learn. Theres always something professional* about doing a thing superlatively well.

HIGGINS. Yes: thats what drives me mad: the silly people dont know their own silly business. [*Rising*] However, it's over and done with; and now I can go to bed at last without dreading tomorrow.

Eliza's beauty becomes murderous.

PICKERING. I think I shall turn in too. Still, it's been a great occasion: a triumph for you. Goodnight. [*He goes*].

HIGGINS [*following him*] Goodnight. [*Over his shoulder, at the door*] Put out the lights, Eliza; and tell Mrs Pearce not to make coffee for me in the morning: I'll take tea. [*He goes out*].

Eliza tries to control herself and feel indifferent as she rises and walks across to the hearth to switch off the lights. By the time she gets there she is on the point of screaming. She sits down in Higgins's chair and holds on hard to the arms. Finally she gives way and flings herself furiously on the floor, raging.

HIGGINS [*in despairing wrath outside*] What the devil have I done with my slippers? [*He appears at the door*].

LIZA [*snatching up the slippers, and hurling them at him one after the other with all her force*] There are your slippers. And there. Take your slippers; and may you never have a day's luck with them!*

HIGGINS [*astounded*] What on earth—! [*He comes to her*]. Whats the matter? Get up. [*He pulls her up*]. Anything wrong?

LIZA [*breathless*] Nothing wrong—with *you*. Ive won your bet for you, havnt I? Thats enough for you. *I* dont matter, I suppose.

HIGGINS. *You* won my bet! You! Presumptuous insect! *I* won it. What did you throw those slippers at me for?

LIZA. Because I wanted to smash your face. I'd like to kill you, you selfish brute. Why didnt you leave me where you picked me out of—in the gutter? You thank God it's all over, and that now you can throw me back again there, do you? [*She crisps* her fingers frantically*].

HIGGINS [*looking at her in cool wonder*] The creature is nervous, after all.

LIZA [*gives a suffocated scream of fury, and instinctively darts her nails at his face*]!!

HIGGINS [*catching her wrists*] Ah! would you? Claws in, you cat. How dare you shew your temper to me? Sit down and be quiet. [*He throws her roughly into the easy-chair*].

LIZA [*crushed by superior strength and weight*] Whats to become of me? Whats to become of me?

HIGGINS. How the devil do I know whats to become of you? What does it matter what becomes of you?

LIZA. You dont care. I know you dont care. You wouldnt care if I was dead. I'm nothing to you—not so much as them slippers.

HIGGINS [*thundering*] *Those* slippers.

LIZA [*with bitter submission*] Those slippers. I didnt think it made any difference now.

A pause. Eliza hopeless and crushed. Higgins a little uneasy.

HIGGINS [*in his loftiest manner*] Why have you begun going on like this? May I ask whether you complain of your treatment here?

LIZA. No.

HIGGINS. Has anybody behaved badly to you? Colonel Pickering? Mrs Pearce? Any of the servants?

LIZA. No.

HIGGINS. I presume you dont pretend that *I* have treated you badly?

LIZA. No.

HIGGINS. I am glad to hear it. [*He moderates his tone*]. Perhaps youre tired after the strain of the day. Will you have a glass of champagne? [*He moves towards the door*].

LIZA. No. [*Recollecting her manners*] Thank you.

HIGGINS [*good-humored again*] This has been coming on you for some days. I suppose it was natural for you to be anxious about the garden party. But thats all over now. [*He pats her kindly on the shoulder. She writhes*]. Theres nothing more to worry about.

LIZA. No. Nothing more for *you* to worry about. [*She suddenly rises and gets away from him by going to the piano bench, where she sits and hides her face*]. Oh God! I wish I was dead.

HIGGINS [*staring after her in sincere surprise*] Why? In heaven's name, why? [*Reasonably, going to her*] Listen to me, Eliza. All this irritation is purely subjective.

LIZA. I dont understand. I'm too ignorant.

HIGGINS. It's only imagination. Low spirits and nothing else. Nobody's hurting you. Nothing's wrong. You go to bed like a good girl and sleep it off. Have a little cry and say your prayers: that will make you comfortable.

LIZA. I heard *your* prayers. 'Thank God it's all over!'

HIGGINS [*impatiently*] Well, *dont* you thank God it's all over? Now you are free and can do what you like.

LIZA [*pulling herself together in desperation*] What am I fit for? What have you left me fit for? Where am I to go? What am I to do? Whats to become of me?

HIGGINS [*enlightened, but not at all impressed*] Oh, *thats* whats worrying you, is it? [*He thrusts his hands into his pockets, and walks about in his usual manner, rattling the contents of his pockets, as if condescending to a trivial subject out of pure kindness*]. I shouldnt bother about it if I were you. I should imagine you wont have much difficulty in settling yourself somewhere or other, though I hadnt quite realized that you were going away. [*She looks quickly at him: he does not look at her, but examines the dessert stand on the piano and decides that he will eat an apple*]. You might marry, you know. [*He bites a large piece out of the apple and munches it noisily*]. You see, Eliza, all men are not confirmed old bachelors like me and the Colonel. Most men are the marrying sort (poor devils!); and youre not bad-looking: it's quite a pleasure to look at you sometimes—not now, of course, because youre crying and looking as ugly as the very devil; but when youre all right and quite yourself, youre what I should call attractive. That is, to the people in the marrying line, you understand. You go to bed and have a good nice rest; and then get up and look at yourself in the glass; and you wont feel so cheap.

Eliza again looks at him, speechless, and does not stir.
The look is quite lost on him: he eats his apple with a dreamy expression of happiness, as it is quite a good one.

HIGGINS [*a genial afterthought occurring to him*] I daresay my mother could find some chap or other who would do very well.

LIZA. We were above that at the corner of Tottenham Court Road.

HIGGINS [*waking up*] What do you mean?

LIZA. I sold flowers. I didnt sell myself. Now youve made a lady of me I'm not fit to sell anything else. I wish youd left me where you found me.

HIGGINS [*slinging the core of the apple decisively into the grate*] Tosh, Eliza. Dont you insult human relations by dragging all this cant about buying and selling into it. You neednt marry the fellow if you dont like him.

LIZA. What else am I to do?

HIGGINS. Oh, lots of things. What about your old idea of a florist's shop? Pickering could set you up in one: he has lots of money. [*Chuckling*] He'll have to pay for all those togs you have been wearing today; and that, with the hire of the jewellery, will make a big hole in two hundred pounds. Why, six months ago you would have thought it the millennium to have a flower shop of your own. Come! youll be all right. I must clear off to bed: I'm devilish sleepy. By the way, I came down for something: I forget what it was.

LIZA. Your slippers.

HIGGINS. Oh yes, of course. You shied* them at me. [*He picks them up, and is going out when she rises and speaks to him*].

LIZA. Before you go, sir—

HIGGINS [*dropping the slippers in his surprise at her calling him Sir*] Eh?

LIZA. Do my clothes belong to me or to Colonel Pickering?

HIGGINS [*coming back into the room as if her question were the very climax of unreason*] What the devil use would they be to Pickering?

LIZA. He might want them for the next girl you pick up to experiment on.

HIGGINS [*shocked and hurt*] Is *that* the way you feel towards us?

LIZA. I dont want to hear anything more about that. All I want to know is whether anything belongs to me. My own clothes were burnt.

HIGGINS. But what does it matter? Why need you start bothering about that in the middle of the night?

LIZA. I want to know what I may take away with me. I dont want to be accused of stealing.

HIGGINS [*now deeply wounded*] Stealing! You shouldnt have said that, Eliza. That shews a want of feeling.

LIZA. I'm sorry. I'm only a common ignorant girl; and in my station I have to be careful. There cant be any feelings between the like of you and the like of me. Please will you tell me what belongs to me and what doesnt?

HIGGINS [*very sulky*] You may take the whole damned houseful if you like. Except the jewels. Theyre hired. Will that satisfy you? [*He turns on his heel and is about to go in extreme dudgeon*].

LIZA [*drinking in his emotion like nectar, and nagging him to provoke a further supply*] Stop, please. [*She takes off her jewels*]. Will you take these to your room and keep them safe? I dont want to run the risk of their being missing.

HIGGINS [*furious*] Hand them over. [*She puts them into his hands*]. If these belonged to me instead of to the jeweller, I'd ram them down your ungrateful throat. [*He perfunctorily* thrusts them into his pockets, unconsciously decorating himself with the protruding ends of the chains*].

LIZA [*taking a ring off*] This ring isnt the jeweller's: it's the one you bought me in Brighton.* I dont want it now. [*Higgins dashes the ring violently into the fireplace, and turns on her so threateningly that she crouches over the piano with her hands over her face, and exclaims*] Dont you hit me.

HIGGINS. Hit you! You infamous creature, how dare you accuse me of such a thing? It is you who have hit me. You have wounded me to the heart.*

LIZA [*thrilling with hidden joy*] I'm glad. Ive got a little of my own back, anyhow.

HIGGINS [*with dignity, in his finest professional style*] You have caused me to lose my temper: a thing that has hardly ever happened to me before. I prefer to say nothing more tonight. I am going to bed.

LIZA [*pertly*] Youd better leave a note for Mrs Pearce about the coffee; for she wont be told by me.

HIGGINS [*formally*] Damn Mrs Pearce; and damn the coffee; and damn you; and [*wildly*] damn my own folly in having lavished my hard-earned knowledge and the treasure of my regard and intimacy on a heartless guttersnipe. [*He goes out with impressive decorum, and spoils it by slamming the door savagely*].*

Eliza goes down on her knees on the hearthrug to look for the ring. When she finds it she considers for a moment what to do with it. Finally she flings it down on the dessert stand and goes upstairs in a tearing rage.

*   *   *   *   *   *

The furniture of Eliza's room has been increased by a big wardrobe and a sumptuous dressing-table. She comes in and switches on the electric light. She goes to the wardrobe; opens it; and pulls out a walking dress, a hat, and a pair of shoes, which she throws on the bed. She takes off her evening dress and shoes; then takes a padded hanger from the wardrobe; adjusts it carefully in the evening dress; and hangs it in the wardrobe, which she shuts with a slam. She puts on her walking shoes, her walking dress, and hat. She takes her wrist watch from the dressing-table and fastens it on. She pulls on her gloves; takes her vanity bag; and looks into it to see that her purse is there before hanging it on her wrist. She makes for the door. Every movement expresses her furious resolution.

She takes a last look at herself in the glass.

She suddenly puts out her tongue at herself; then leaves the room, switching off the electric light at the door.

Meanwhile, in the street outside, Freddy Eynsford Hill, lovelorn, is gazing up at the second floor, in which one of the windows is still lighted.

The light goes out.

FREDDY. Goodnight, darling, darling, darling.

Eliza comes out, giving the door a considerable bang behind her.

LIZA. Whatever are you doing here?

FREDDY. Nothing. I spend most of my nights here. It's the only place where I'm happy. Dont laugh at me, Miss Doolittle.

LIZA. Dont you call me Miss Doolittle, do you hear? Liza's good enough for me. [*She breaks down and grabs him by the shoulders*] Freddy: you dont think I'm a heartless guttersnipe, do you?

FREDDY. Oh no, no, darling: how can you imagine such a thing? You are the loveliest, dearest—

He loses all self-control and smothers her with kisses. She, hungry for comfort, responds. They stand there in one another's arms.
An elderly police constable arrives.

CONSTABLE [*scandalized*] Now then! Now then!! Now then!!!

They release one another hastily.

FREDDY. Sorry, constable. Weve only just become engaged.

They run away.

The constable shakes his head, reflecting on his own courtship and on the vanity of human hopes. He moves off in the opposite direction with slow professional steps.

The flight of the lovers takes them to Cavendish Square.* There they halt to consider their next move.

LIZA [*out of breath*] He didnt half give me a fright, that copper. But you answered him proper.

FREDDY. I hope I havnt taken you out of your way. Where were you going?

LIZA. To the river.

FREDDY. What for?

LIZA. To make a hole in it.

FREDDY [*horrified*] Eliza, darling. What do you mean? What's the matter?

LIZA. Never mind. It doesnt matter now. Theres nobody in the world now but you and me, is there?

FREDDY. Not a soul.

They indulge in another embrace, and are again surprised by a much younger constable.

SECOND CONSTABLE. Now then, you two! What's this? Where do you think you are? Move along here, double quick.

FREDDY. As you say, sir, double quick.

They run away again, and are in Hanover Square* before they stop for another conference.

FREDDY. I had no idea the police were so devilishly prudish.

LIZA. It's their business to hunt girls off the streets.

FREDDY. We must go somewhere. We cant wander about the streets all night.

LIZA. Cant we? I think it'd be lovely to wander about for ever.

FREDDY. Oh, darling.

They embrace again, oblivious of the arrival of a crawling taxi. It stops.

TAXIMAN. Can I drive you and the lady anywhere, sir?

They start asunder.

LIZA. Oh, Freddy, a taxi. The very thing.

FREDDY. But, damn it, Ive no money.

LIZA. I have plenty. The Colonel thinks you should never go out without ten pounds in your pocket. Listen. We'll drive about all night; and in the morning I'll call on old Mrs Higgins and ask her what I ought to do. I'll tell you all about it in the cab. And the police wont touch us there.

FREDDY. Righto! Ripping. [*To the Taximan*] Wimbledon Common.* [*They drive off*].

ACT V

Mrs Higgins's drawing room. She is at her writing-table as before. The parlormaid comes in.

THE PARLORMAID [*at the door*] Mr Henry, maam, is downstairs with Colonel Pickering.

MRS HIGGINS. Well, shew them up.

THE PARLORMAID. Theyre using the telephone, maam. Telephoning to the police, I think.

MRS HIGGINS. What!

THE PARLORMAID [*coming further in and lowering her voice*] Mr Henry is in a state, maam. I thought I'd better tell you.

MRS HIGGINS. If you had told me that Mr Henry was not in a state it would have been more surprising. Tell them to come up when theyve finished with the police. I suppose he's lost something.

THE PARLORMAID. Yes, maam [*going*].

MRS HIGGINS. Go upstairs and tell Miss Doolittle that Mr Henry and the Colonel are here. Ask her not to come down til I send for her.*

THE PARLORMAID. Yes, maam.

Higgins bursts in. He is, as the parlormaid has said, in a state.

HIGGINS. Look here, mother: heres a confounded thing!

MRS HIGGINS. Yes, dear. Good morning. [*He checks his impatience and kisses her, whilst the parlormaid goes out*]. What is it?

HIGGINS. Eliza's bolted.

MRS HIGGINS [*calmly continuing her writing*] You must have frightened her.

HIGGINS. Frightened her! nonsense! She was left last night, as usual, to turn out the lights and all that; and instead of going to bed she changed her clothes and went right off: her bed wasnt slept in. She came in a cab for her things before seven this morning; and that fool Mrs Pearce let her have them without telling me a word about it. What am I to do?*

MRS HIGGINS. Do without, I'm afraid, Henry. The girl has a perfect right to leave if she chooses.

HIGGINS [*wandering distractedly across the room*] But I cant find anything. I dont know what appointments Ive got. I'm—[*Pickering comes in. Mrs Higgins puts down her pen and turns away from the writing-table*].

PICKERING [*shaking hands*] Good morning, Mrs Higgins. Has Henry told you? [*He sits down on the ottoman*].

HIGGINS. What does that ass of an inspector say? Have you offered a reward?

MRS HIGGINS [*rising in indignant amazement*] You dont mean to say you have set the police after Eliza.

HIGGINS. Of course. What are the police for? What else could we do? [*He sits in the Elizabethan chair*].

PICKERING. The inspector made a lot of difficulties. I really think he suspected us of some improper purpose.

MRS HIGGINS. Well, of course he did. What right have you to go to the police and give the girl's name as if she were a thief, or a lost umbrella, or something? Really! [*She sits down again, deeply vexed*].

HIGGINS. But we want to find her.

PICKERING. We cant let her go like this, you know, Mrs Higgins. What were we to do?

MRS HIGGINS. You have no more sense, either of you, than two children. Why—

The parlormaid comes in and breaks off the conversation.

THE PARLORMAID. Mr Henry: a gentleman wants to see you very particular. He's been sent on from Wimpole Street.

HIGGINS. Oh, bother! I cant see anyone now. Who is it?

THE PARLORMAID. A Mr Doolittle, sir.

PICKERING. Doolittle! Do you mean the dustman?

THE PARLORMAID. Dustman! Oh no, sir: a gentleman.

HIGGINS [*springing up excitedly*] By George, Pick, it's some relative of hers that she's gone to. Somebody we know nothing about. [*To the parlormaid*] Send him up, quick.

THE PARLORMAID. Yes, sir. [*She goes*].

HIGGINS [*eagerly, going to his mother*] Genteel relatives! now we shall hear something. [*He sits down in the Chippendale chair*].

MRS HIGGINS. Do you know any of her people?

PICKERING. Only her father: the fellow we told you about.

THE PARLORMAID [*announcing*] Mr Doolittle. [*She withdraws*].

Doolittle enters. He is resplendently dressed as for a fashionable wedding, and might, in fact, be the bridegroom. A flower in his buttonhole, a dazzling silk hat, and patent leather shoes complete the effect. He is too concerned with the business he has come on to notice Mrs Higgins. He walks straight to Higgins, and accosts him with vehement reproach.*

DOOLITTLE [*indicating his own person*] See here! Do you see this? You done this.

HIGGINS. Done what, man?

DOOLITTLE. This, I tell you. Look at it. Look at this hat. Look at this coat.

PICKERING. Has Eliza been buying you clothes?

DOOLITTLE. Eliza! not she. Why would she buy me clothes?*

MRS HIGGINS. Good morning, Mr Doolittle. Wont you sit down?

DOOLITTLE [*taken aback as he becomes conscious that he has forgotten his hostess*] Asking your pardon, maam. [*He approaches her and shakes her proffered hand*]. Thank you. [*He sits down on the ottoman, on Pickering's right*]. I am that full of what has happened to me that I cant think of anything else.

HIGGINS. What the dickens has happened to you?

DOOLITTLE. I shouldnt mind if it had only *happened* to me: anything might happen to anybody and nobody to blame but Providence, as you might say. But this is something that *you* done to me: yes, *you*, Enry Iggins.

HIGGINS. Have you found Eliza?

DOOLITTLE. Have you lost her?

HIGGINS. Yes.

DOOLITTLE. You have all the luck, you have. I aint found her; but she'll find me quick enough now after what you done to me.

MRS HIGGINS. But what has my son done to you, Mr Doolittle?

DOOLITTLE. Done to me! Ruined me. Destroyed my happiness. Tied me up and delivered me into the hands of middle class morality.

HIGGINS [*rising intolerantly and standing over Doolittle*] Youre raving. Youre drunk. Youre mad. I gave you five pounds. After that I had two conversations with you, at half-a-crown an hour. Ive never seen you since.

DOOLITTLE. Oh! Drunk am I? Mad am I? Tell me this. Did you or did you not write a letter to an old blighter in America that was giving five millions to found Moral Reform Societies* all over the world, and that wanted you to invent a universal language for him?

HIGGINS. What! Ezra D. Wannafeller!* He's dead. [*He sits down again carelessly*].

DOOLITTLE. Yes: he's dead; and I'm done for. Now did you or did you not write a letter to him to say that the most original moralist at present in England, to the best of your knowledge, was Alfred Doolittle, a common dustman?

HIGGINS. Oh, after your first visit I remember making some silly joke of the kind.

DOOLITTLE. Ah! you may well call it a silly joke. It put the lid on me right enough. Just give him the chance he wanted to shew that Americans is not like us: that they reckonize and respect merit in every class of life, however humble. Them words is in his blooming will, in which, Henry Higgins, thanks to your silly joking, he leaves me a share in his Pre-digested Cheese Trust worth three thousand a year* on condition that I lecture for his Wannafeller Moral Reform World League as often as they ask me up to six times a year.

HIGGINS. The devil he does! Whew! [*Brightening suddenly*] What a lark!

PICKERING. A safe thing for you, Doolittle. They wont ask you twice.

DOOLITTLE. It aint the lecturing I mind. I'll lecture them blue in the face, I will, and not turn a hair. It's making a gentleman of me that I object to. Who asked him to make a gentleman of me? I was happy.

I was free. I touched pretty nigh everybody for money when I wanted it, same as I touched you, Enry Iggins. Now I am worrited; tied neck and heels; and everybody touches me for money. It's a fine thing for you, says my solicitor. Is it? says I. You mean it's a good thing for you, I says. When I was a poor man and had a solicitor once when they found a pram in the dust cart, he got me off, and got shut of me and got me shut of him as quick as he could. Same with the doctors: used to shove me out of the hospital before I could hardly stand on my legs, and nothing to pay. Now they finds out that I'm not a healthy man and cant live unless they looks after me twice a day. In the house I'm not let do a hand's turn for myself: somebody else must do it and touch me for it. A year ago I hadnt a relative in the world except two or three that wouldnt speak to me. Now Ive fifty, and not a decent week's wages among the lot of them. I have to live for others and not for myself: thats middle class morality. *You* talk of losing Eliza. Dont you be anxious: I bet she's on my doorstep by this: she that could support herself easy by selling flowers if I wasnt respectable. And the next one to touch me will be you, Enry Iggins. I'll have to learn to speak middle class language from you, instead of speaking proper English. Thats where *youll* come in; and I daresay thats what you done it for.

MRS HIGGINS. But, my dear Mr Doolittle, you need not suffer all this if you are really in earnest. Nobody can force you to accept this bequest. You can repudiate it. Isnt that so, Colonel Pickering?

PICKERING. I believe so.

DOOLITTLE [*softening his manner in deference to her sex*] Thats the tragedy of it, maam. It's easy to say chuck it; but I havnt the nerve. Which of us has? We're all intimidated. Intimidated, maam: thats what we are. What is there for me if I chuck it but the workhouse in my old age? I have to dye my hair already to keep my job as a dustman. If I was one of the deserving poor, and had put by a bit, I could chuck it; but then why should I, acause the deserving poor might as well be millionaires for all the happiness they ever has. They dont know what happiness is. But I, as one of the undeserving poor, have nothing between me and the pauper's uniform but this here blasted three thousand a year that shoves me into the middle class. (Excuse the expression, maam; youd use it yourself if you had my provocation.) Theyve got you every way you turn: it's a choice between the Skilly of the workhouse and the Char Bydis* of the middle class; and I havnt the nerve for the workhouse. Intimidated: thats what I am.

Broke. Bought up. Happier men than me* will call for my dust, and touch me for their tip; and I'll look on helpless, and envy them. And thats what your son has brought me to. [*He is overcome by emotion*].

MRS HIGGINS. Well, I'm very glad youre not going to do anything foolish, Mr Doolittle. For this solves the problem of Eliza's future. You can provide for her now.

DOOLITTLE [*with melancholy resignation*] Yes, maam: I'm expected to provide for everyone now, out of three thousand a year.

HIGGINS [*jumping up*] Nonsense! he cant provide for her. He shant provide for her. She doesnt belong to him. I paid him five pounds for her. Doolittle: either youre an honest man or a rogue.

DOOLITTLE [*tolerantly*] A little of both, Henry, like the rest of us: a little of both.

HIGGINS. Well, you took that money for the girl; and you have no right to take her as well.

MRS HIGGINS. Henry: dont be absurd. If you want to know where Eliza is, she is upstairs.

HIGGINS [*amazed*] Upstairs!!! Then I shall jolly soon fetch her downstairs. [*He makes resolutely for the door*].

MRS HIGGINS [*rising and following him*] Be quiet, Henry. Sit down.

HIGGINS. I—

MRS HIGGINS. Sit down, dear; and listen to me.

HIGGINS Oh very well, very well, very well. [*He throws himself ungraciously on the ottoman, with his face towards the windows*]. But I think you might have told us this half an hour ago.

MRS HIGGINS. Eliza came to me this morning.* She told me of the brutal way you two treated her.

HIGGINS [*bounding up again*] What!

PICKERING [*rising also*] My dear Mrs Higgins, she's been telling you stories. We didnt treat her brutally. We hardly said a word to her; and we parted on particularly good terms. [*Turning on Higgins*] Higgins: did you bully her after I went to bed?

HIGGINS. Just the other way about. She threw my slippers in my face. She behaved in the most outrageous way. I never gave her the slightest provocation. The slippers came bang into my face the moment I entered the room—before I had uttered a word. And used perfectly awful language.

PICKERING [*astonished*] But why? What did we do to her?*

MRS HIGGINS. I think I know pretty well what you did. The girl is naturally rather affectionate, I think. Isnt she, Mr Doolittle?

DOOLITTLE. Very tender-hearted, maam. Takes after me.

MRS HIGGINS. Just so. She had become attached to you both. She worked very hard for you, Henry. I dont think you quite realize what anything in the nature of brain work means to a girl of her class.* Well, it seems that when the great day of trial came, and she did this wonderful thing for you without making a single mistake, you two sat there and never said a word to her, but talked together of how glad you were that it was all over and how you had been bored with the whole thing.* And then you were surprised because she threw your slippers at you! *I* should have thrown the fire-irons at you.

HIGGINS. We said nothing except that we were tired and wanted to go to bed. Did we, Pick?

PICKERING [*shrugging his shoulders*] That was all.

MRS HIGGINS [*ironically*] Quite sure?

PICKERING. Absolutely. Really, that was all.

MRS HIGGINS. You didnt thank her, or pet her, or admire her, or tell her how splendid she'd been.

HIGGINS [*impatiently*] But she knew all about that. We didnt make speeches to her, if thats what you mean.

PICKERING [*conscience stricken*] Perhaps we were a little inconsiderate. Is she very angry?

MRS HIGGINS [*returning to her place at the writing-table*] Well, I'm afraid she wont go back to Wimpole Street,* especially now that Mr Doolittle is able to keep up the position you have thrust on her; but she says she is quite willing to meet you on friendly terms and to let bygones be bygones.

HIGGINS [*furious*] Is she, by George? Ho!

MRS HIGGINS. If you promise to behave yourself, Henry, I'll ask her to come down.* If not, go home; for you have taken up quite enough of my time.

HIGGINS. Oh, all right. Very well. Pick: you behave yourself. Let us put on our best Sunday manners for this creature that we picked out of the mud. [*He flings himself sulkily into the Elizabethan chair*].

DOOLITTLE [*remonstrating*] Now, now, Enry Iggins! Have some consideration for my feelings as a middle class man.

MRS HIGGINS. Remember your promise, Henry. [*She presses the bell-button on the writing-table*]. Mr Doolittle: will you be so good as to step out on the balcony for a moment. I dont want Eliza to have the shock of your news until she has made it up with these two gentlemen. Would you mind?

DOOLITTLE. As you wish, lady. Anything to help Henry to keep her off my hands. [*He disappears through the window*].

The parlormaid answers the bell. Pickering sits down in Doolittle's place.

MRS HIGGINS. Ask Miss Doolittle to come down, please.

THE PARLORMAID. Yes, maam. [*She goes out*].

MRS HIGGINS. Now, Henry: be good.

HIGGINS. I am behaving myself perfectly.

PICKERING. He is doing his best, Mrs Higgins.*

A pause. Higgins throws back his head; stretches out his legs; and begins to whistle.

MRS HIGGINS. Henry, dearest, you dont look at all nice in that attitude.

HIGGINS [*pulling himself together*] I was not trying to look nice, mother.

MRS HIGGINS. It doesnt matter, dear. I only wanted to make you speak.

HIGGINS. Why?

MRS HIGGINS. Because you cant speak and whistle at the same time.

Higgins groans. Another very trying pause.

HIGGINS [*springing up, out of patience*] Where the devil is that girl? Are we to wait here all day?

Eliza enters, sunny, self-possessed, and giving a staggeringly convincing exhibition of ease of manner. She carries a little work-basket, and is very much at home. Pickering is too much taken aback to rise.

LIZA. How do you do, Professor Higgins? Are you quite well?

HIGGINS [*choking*] Am I—[*He can say no more*].

LIZA. But of course you are: you are never ill. So glad to see you again, Colonel Pickering. [*He rises hastily; and they shake hands*]. Quite chilly this morning, isnt it? [*She sits down on his left. He sits beside her*].

HIGGINS. Dont you dare try this game on me. I taught it to you; and it doesnt take me in. Get up and come home; and dont be a fool.

Eliza takes a piece of needlework from her basket, and begins to stitch at it, without taking the least notice of this outburst.

MRS HIGGINS. Very nicely put, indeed, Henry. No woman could resist such an invitation.

HIGGINS. You let her alone, mother. Let her speak for herself. You will jolly soon see whether she has an idea that I havnt put into her head or a word that I havnt put into her mouth. I tell you I have created this thing out of the squashed cabbage leaves of Covent Garden; and now she pretends to play the fine lady with me.

MRS HIGGINS [*placidly*] Yes, dear; but youll sit down, wont you?

Higgins sits down again, savagely.

LIZA [*to Pickering, taking no apparent notice of Higgins, and working away deftly*] Will *you* drop me altogether now that the experiment is over, Colonel Pickering?

PICKERING. Oh dont. You mustnt think of it as an experiment. It shocks me, somehow.

LIZA. Oh, I'm only a squashed cabbage leaf—

PICKERING [*impulsively*] No.

LIZA [*continuing quietly*]—but I owe so much to you that I should be very unhappy if you forgot me.

PICKERING. It's very kind of you to say so, Miss Doolittle.*

LIZA. It's not because you paid for my dresses. I know you are generous to everybody with money. But it was from you that I learnt really nice manners; and that is what makes one a lady, isnt it? You see it was so very difficult for me with the example of Professor Higgins always before me. I was brought up to be just like him,* unable to control myself, and using bad language on the slightest provocation. And I should never have known that ladies and gentlemen didnt behave like that if you hadnt been there.

HIGGINS. Well!!

PICKERING. Oh, thats only his way, you know. He doesnt mean it.

LIZA. Oh, *I* didnt mean it either, when I was a flower girl. It was only my way. But you see I did it;* and thats what makes the difference after all.

PICKERING. No doubt. Still, he taught you to speak; and I couldnt have done that, you know.

LIZA [*trivially*] Of course: that is his profession.

HIGGINS. Damnation!

LIZA [*continuing*] It was just like learning to dance in the fashionable way: there was nothing more than that in it. But do you know what began my real education?

PICKERING. What?

LIZA [*stopping her work for a moment*] Your calling me Miss Doolittle that day when I first came to Wimpole Street. That was the beginning of self-respect for me. [*She resumes her stitching*]. And there were a hundred little things you never noticed, because they came naturally to you. Things about standing up and taking off your hat and opening doors—

PICKERING. Oh, that was nothing.

LIZA. Yes: things that shewed you thought and felt about me as if I were something better than a scullery-maid; though of course I know you would have been just the same to a scullery-maid if she had been let into the drawing room. *You* never took off your boots in the dining room when I was there.

PICKERING. You mustnt mind that. Higgins takes off his boots all over the place.

LIZA. I know. I am not blaming him. It is his way, isnt it? But it made *such* a difference to me that you didnt do it. You see, really and truly, apart from the things anyone can pick up (the dressing and the proper way of speaking, and so on), the difference between a lady and a flower girl is not how she behaves, but how she's treated. I shall always be a flower girl to Professor Higgins, because he always treats me as a flower girl, and always will; but I know I can be a lady to you, because you always treat me as a lady, and always will.

MRS HIGGINS. Please dont grind your teeth, Henry.*

PICKERING. Well, this is really very nice of you, Miss Doolittle.

LIZA. I should like you to call me Eliza, now, if you would.

PICKERING. Thank you. Eliza, of course.

LIZA. And I should like Professor Higgins to call me Miss Doolittle.

HIGGINS. I'll see you damned first.

MRS HIGGINS. Henry! Henry!

PICKERING [*laughing*] Why dont you slang back at him? Dont stand it. It would do him a lot of good.

LIZA. I cant. I could have done it once; but now I cant go back to it.* You told me, you know, that when a child is brought to a foreign country, it picks up the language in a few weeks, and forgets its own. Well, I am a child in your country. I have forgotten my own language, and can speak nothing but yours. Thats the real break-off with the corner of Tottenham Court Road. Leaving Wimpole Street finishes it.

PICKERING [*much alarmed*] Oh! but youre coming back to Wimpole Street, arnt you? Youll forgive Higgins?

HIGGINS [*rising*] Forgive! Will she, by George! Let her go. Let her find out how she can get on without us. She will relapse into the gutter in three weeks without me at her elbow.

Doolittle appears at the centre window. With a look of dignified reproach at Higgins, he comes slowly and silently to his daughter, who, with her back to the window, is unconscious of his approach.

PICKERING. He's incorrigible, Eliza. You wont relapse, will you?

LIZA. No: not now. Never again. I have learnt my lesson. I dont believe I could utter one of the old sounds if I tried. [*Doolittle touches her on her left shoulder. She drops her work, losing her self-possession utterly at the spectacle of her father's splendor*] A-a-a-a-a-ah-ow-ooh!

HIGGINS [*with a crow of triumph*] Aha! Just so. A-a-a-a-ahowooh! A-a-a-a-ahowooh! A-a-a-a-ahowooh! Victory! Victory! [*He throws himself on the divan, folding his arms, and spraddling* arrogantly*].

DOOLITTLE. Can you blame the girl? Dont look at me like that, Eliza. It aint my fault. Ive come into some money.

LIZA. You must have touched a millionaire this time, dad.

DOOLITTLE. I have. But I'm dressed something special today. I'm going to St George's, Hanover Square.* Your stepmother is going to marry me.

LIZA [*angrily*] Youre going to let yourself down to marry that low common woman!

PICKERING [*quietly*] He ought to, Eliza. [*To Doolittle*] Why has she changed her mind?

DOOLITTLE [*sadly*] Intimidated, Governor. Intimidated. Middle class morality claims its victim. Wont you put on your hat, Liza, and come and see me turned off?

LIZA. If the Colonel says I must, I—I'll [*almost sobbing*] I'll demean myself. And get insulted for my pains, like enough.

DOOLITTLE. Dont be afraid: she never comes to words with anyone now, poor woman! respectability has broke all the spirit out of her.

PICKERING [*squeezing Eliza's elbow gently*] Be kind to them, Eliza. Make the best of it.

LIZA [*forcing a little smile for him through her vexation*] Oh well, just to shew theres no ill feeling. I'll be back in a moment. [*She goes out*].

DOOLITTLE [*sitting down beside Pickering*] I feel uncommon nervous about the ceremony, Colonel. I wish youd come and see me through it.

PICKERING. But youve been through it before, man. You were married to Eliza's mother.

DOOLITTLE. Who told you that, Colonel?

PICKERING. Well, nobody told me. But I concluded—naturally—

DOOLITTLE. No: that aint the natural way, Colonel: it's only the middle class way. My way was always the undeserving way. But dont say nothing to Eliza. She dont know: I always had a delicacy about telling her.

PICKERING. Quite right. We'll leave it so, if you dont mind.

DOOLITTLE. And youll come to the church, Colonel, and put me through straight?

PICKERING. With pleasure. As far as a bachelor can.*

MRS HIGGINS. May I come, Mr Doolittle? I should be very sorry to miss your wedding.

DOOLITTLE. I should indeed be honored by your condescension, maam; and my poor old woman would take it as a tremenjous* compliment. She's been very low, thinking of the happy days that are no more.

MRS HIGGINS [*rising*] I'll order the carriage and get ready. [*The men rise, except Higgins*]. I shant be more than fifteen minutes. [*As she goes to the door Eliza comes in, hatted and buttoning her gloves*]. I'm going to the church to see your father married, Eliza. You had better come in the brougham* with me. Colonel Pickering can go on with the bridegroom.

Mrs Higgins goes out. Eliza comes to the middle of the room between the centre window and the ottoman. Pickering joins her.

DOOLITTLE. Bridegroom! What a word! It makes a man realize his position, somehow. [*He takes up his hat and goes towards the door*].

PICKERING. Before I go, Eliza, do forgive Higgins and come back to us.

LIZA. I dont think dad* would allow me. Would you, dad?

DOOLITTLE [*sad but magnanimous*] They played you off very cunning, Eliza, them two sportsmen. If it had been only one of them, you could have nailed him. But you see, there was two; and one of them chaperoned the other, as you might say. [*To Pickering*] It was artful of you, Colonel; but I bear no malice: I should have done the same myself. I been the victim of one woman after another all my life; and I dont grudge you two getting the better of Eliza. I shant interfere. It's time for us to go, Colonel. So long, Henry. See you in St George's, Eliza. [*He goes out*].

PICKERING [*coaxing*] Do stay with us, Eliza. [*He follows Doolittle*].

Eliza goes out on the balcony to avoid being alone with Higgins. He rises and joins her there. She immediately comes back into the room and makes for the door; but he goes along the balcony quickly and gets his back to the door before she reaches it.

HIGGINS. Well, Eliza, youve had a bit of your own back, as you call it. Have you had enough? and are you going to be reasonable? Or do you want any more?

LIZA. You want me back only to pick up your slippers and put up with your tempers and fetch and carry for you.

HIGGINS. I havnt said I wanted you back at all.

LIZA. Oh, indeed. Then what are we talking about?

HIGGINS. About you, not about me. If you come back I shall treat you just as I have always treated you. I cant change my nature; and I dont intend to change my manners. My manners are exactly the same as Colonel Pickering's.

LIZA. Thats not true. He treats a flower girl as if she was a duchess.

HIGGINS. And I treat a duchess as if she was a flower girl.

LIZA. I see. [*She turns away composedly, and sits on the ottoman, facing the window*]. The same to everybody.

HIGGINS. Just so.

LIZA. Like father.

HIGGINS [*grinning, a little taken down*] Without accepting the comparison at all points, Eliza, it's quite true that your father is not a snob, and that he will be quite at home in any station of life to which his eccentric destiny may call him. [*Seriously*] The great secret, Eliza, is not having bad manners or good manners or any other particular sort of manners, but having the same manner for all human souls: in short, behaving as if you were in Heaven, where there are no third-class carriages, and one soul is as good as another.

LIZA. Amen. You are a born preacher.*

HIGGINS [*irritated*] The question is not whether I treat you rudely, but whether you ever heard me treat anyone else better.

LIZA [*with sudden sincerity*] I dont care how you treat me. I dont mind your swearing at me. I shouldnt mind a black eye: Ive had one before this. But [*standing up and facing him*] I wont be passed over.

HIGGINS. Then get out of my way; for I wont stop for you. You talk about me as if I were a motor bus.

LIZA. So you are a motor bus: all bounce and go, and no consideration for anyone.* But I can do without you: dont think I cant.

HIGGINS. I know you can. I told you you could.

LIZA [*wounded, getting away from him to the other side of the ottoman with her face to the hearth*] I know you did, you brute. You wanted to get rid of me.

HIGGINS. Liar.

LIZA. Thank you. [*She sits down with dignity*].

HIGGINS. You never asked yourself, I suppose, whether *I* could do without you.

LIZA [*earnestly*] Dont you try to get round me. Youll *have* to do without me.

HIGGINS [*arrogant*] I can do without anybody. I have my own soul: my own spark of divine fire. But [*with sudden humility*] I shall miss you, Eliza. [*He sits down near her on the ottoman*]. I have learnt something from your idiotic notions: I confess that humbly and gratefully. And I have grown accustomed to your voice and appearance. I like them, rather.

LIZA. Well, you have both of them on your gramophone and in your book of photographs. When you feel lonely without me, you can turn the machine on. It's got no feelings to hurt.

HIGGINS. I cant turn your soul on. Leave me those feelings; and you can take away the voice and the face. They are not you.

LIZA. Oh, you *are* a devil. You can twist the heart in a girl as easy as some could twist her arms to hurt her. Mrs Pearce warned me. Time and again she has wanted to leave you; and you always got round her at the last minute. And you dont care a bit for her. And you dont care a bit for me.

HIGGINS. I care for life, for humanity; and you are a part of it that has come my way and been built into my house. What more can you or anyone ask?

LIZA. I wont care for anybody that doesnt care for me.

HIGGINS. Commercial principles, Eliza. Like [*reproducing her Covent Garden pronunciation with professional exactness*] s'yollin voylets [selling violets],* isnt it?

LIZA. Dont sneer at me. It's mean to sneer at me.

HIGGINS. I have never sneered in my life. Sneering doesnt become either the human face or the human soul. I am expressing my right-eous contempt for Commercialism. I dont and wont trade in affection.* You call me a brute because you couldnt buy a claim on me by fetching my slippers and finding my spectacles. You were a fool: I think a woman fetching a man's slippers is a disgusting sight: did I ever fetch *your* slippers? I think a good deal more of you for throwing them in my face. No use slaving for me and then saying you want to be cared for: who cares for a slave? If you come back, come back for the sake of good fellowship; for youll get nothing else. Youve had a thousand times as much out of me as I have out of you; and if you dare to set up your little dog's tricks of fetching and carrying slippers against my creation of a Duchess Eliza, I'll slam the door in your silly face.

LIZA. What did you do it for if you didnt care for me?

HIGGINS [*heartily*] Why, because it was my job.

LIZA. You never thought of the trouble it would make for me.*

HIGGINS. Would the world ever have been made if its maker had been afraid of making trouble? Making life means making trouble. Theres only one way of escaping trouble; and thats killing things. Cowards, you notice, are always shrieking to have troublesome people killed.

LIZA. I'm no preacher: I dont notice things like that. I notice that you dont notice me.

HIGGINS [*jumping up and walking about intolerantly*] Eliza: youre an idiot. I waste the treasures of my Miltonic mind by spreading them before you. Once for all, understand that I go my way and do my work without caring twopence what happens to either of us. I am not intimidated, like your father and your stepmother. So you can come back or go to the devil: which you please.

LIZA. What am I to come back for?

HIGGINS [*bouncing up on his knees on the ottoman and leaning over it to her*] For the fun of it. Thats why I took you on.

LIZA [*with averted face*] And you may throw me out tomorrow if I dont do everything you want me to?

HIGGINS. Yes; and you may walk out tomorrow if I dont do everything *you* want me to.

LIZA. And live with my stepmother?

HIGGINS. Yes, or sell flowers.

LIZA. Oh! if I only *could* go back to my flower basket! I should be independent of both you and father and all the world! Why did you take my independence from me? Why did I give it up? I'm a slave now, for all my fine clothes.

HIGGINS. Not a bit. I'll adopt you as my daughter and settle money on you if you like. Or would you rather marry Pickering?

LIZA [*looking fiercely round at him*] I wouldnt marry *you* if you asked me; and youre nearer my age than what he is.

HIGGINS [*gently*] Than he is: not 'than what he is.'

LIZA [*losing her temper and rising*] I'll talk as I like. Youre not my teacher now.

HIGGINS [*reflectively*] I dont suppose Pickering would, though. He's as confirmed an old bachelor as I am.

LIZA. Thats not what I want; and dont you think it. Ive always had chaps enough wanting me that way. Freddy Hill writes to me twice and three times a day, sheets and sheets.

HIGGINS [*disagreeably surprised*] Damn his impudence! [*He recoils and finds himself sitting on his heels*].

LIZA. He has a right to if he likes, poor lad. And he does love me.

HIGGINS [*getting off the ottoman*] You have no right to encourage him.

LIZA. Every girl has a right to be loved.

HIGGINS. What! By fools like that?

LIZA. Freddy's not a fool. And if he's weak and poor and wants me, may be he'd make me happier than my betters that bully me and dont want me.

HIGGINS. Can he *make* anything of you? Thats the point.

LIZA. Perhaps I could make something of him. But I never thought of us making anything of one another; and you never think of anything else. I only want to be natural.

HIGGINS. In short, you want me to be as infatuated about you as Freddy? Is that it?

LIZA. No I dont. Thats not the sort of feeling I want from you. And
dont you be too sure of yourself or of me. I could have been a bad girl
if I'd liked. Ive seen more of some things than you, for all your learning. Girls like me can drag gentlemen down to make love to them
easy enough. And they wish each other dead the next minute.

HIGGINS. Of course they do. Then what in thunder are we quarrelling
about?

LIZA [*much troubled*] I want a little kindness. I know I'm a common
ignorant girl, and you a book-learned gentleman; but I'm not dirt
under your feet. What I done [*correcting herself*] what I did was not
for the dresses and the taxis: I did it because we were pleasant
together and I come—came—to care for you; not to want you to
make love to me, and not forgetting the difference between us, but
more friendly like.

HIGGINS. Well, of course. Thats just how I feel. And how Pickering
feels. Eliza: youre a fool.

LIZA. Thats not a proper answer to give me [*she sinks on the chair at
the writing-table in tears*].

HIGGINS. It's all youll get until you stop being a common idiot. If
youre going to be a lady, youll have to give up feeling neglected if the
men you know dont spend half their time snivelling over you and the
other half giving you black eyes. If you cant stand the coldness of my
sort of life, and the strain of it, go back to the gutter. Work til youre
more a brute than a human being; and then cuddle and squabble and
drink til you fall asleep. Oh, it's a fine life, the life of the gutter. It's
real: it's warm: it's violent: you can feel it through the thickest skin:
you can taste it and smell it without any training or any work. Not
like Science and Literature and Classical Music and Philosophy and
Art. You find me cold, unfeeling, selfish, dont you? Very well: be off
with you to the sort of people you like. Marry some sentimental hog
or other with lots of money, and a thick pair of lips to kiss you with
and a thick pair of boots to kick you with. If you cant appreciate what
youve got, youd better get what you can appreciate.

LIZA [*desperate*] Oh, you *are* a cruel tyrant. I cant talk to you: you turn
everything against me: I'm always in the wrong. But you know very
well all the time that youre nothing but a bully. You know I cant go
back to the gutter, as you call it, and that I have no real friends in the
world but you and the Colonel. You know well I couldnt bear to live

with a low common man after you two; and it's wicked and cruel of you to insult me by pretending I could. You think I must go back to Wimpole Street because I have nowhere else to go but father's. But dont you be too sure that you have me under your feet to be trampled on and talked down. I'll marry Freddy, I will, as soon as I'm able to support him.

HIGGINS [*thunderstruck*] Freddy!!! that young fool! That poor devil who couldnt get a job as an errand boy even if he had the guts to try for it! Woman: do you not understand that I have made you a consort for a king?

LIZA. Freddy loves me: that makes him king enough for me. I dont want him to work: he wasnt brought up to it as I was. I'll go and be a teacher.*

HIGGINS. Whatll you teach, in heaven's name?

LIZA. What you taught me. I'll teach phonetics.

HIGGINS. Ha! ha! ha!

LIZA. I'll offer myself as an assistant to that hairyfaced Hungarian.*

HIGGINS [*rising in a fury*] What! That impostor! that humbug! that toadying ignoramus! Teach him my methods! my discoveries! You take one step in his direction and I'll wring your neck. [*He lays hands on her*]. Do you hear?

LIZA [*defiantly non-resistant*] Wring away. What do I care? I knew youd strike me some day. [*He lets her go, stamping with rage at having forgotten himself, and recoils so hastily that he stumbles back into his seat on the ottoman*]. Aha! Now I know how to deal with you. What a fool I was not to think of it before! You cant take away the knowledge you gave me. You said I had a finer ear than you. And I can be civil and kind to people, which is more than you can. Aha! [*Purposely dropping her aitches to annoy him*] Thats done you, Enry Iggins,* it az. Now I dont care *that* [*snapping her fingers*] for your bullying and your big talk. I'll advertize it in the papers that your duchess is only a flower girl that you taught, and that she'll teach anybody to be a duchess just the same in six months for a thousand guineas. Oh, when I think of myself crawling under your feet and being trampled on and called names, when all the time I had only to lift up my finger to be as good as you, I could just kick myself.

HIGGINS [*wondering at her*] You damned impudent slut, you! But it's better than snivelling; better than fetching slippers and finding spectacles, isnt it? [*Rising*] By George, Eliza, I said I'd make a woman of you; and I have. I like you like this.*

LIZA. Yes: you turn round and make up to me now that I'm not afraid of you, and can do without you.

HIGGINS. Of course I do, you little fool. Five minutes ago you were like a millstone round my neck. Now youre a tower of strength: a consort battleship. You and I and Pickering will be three old bachelors together instead of only two men and a silly girl.

Mrs Higgins returns, dressed for the wedding. Eliza instantly becomes cool and elegant.

MRS HIGGINS. The carriage is waiting, Eliza. Are you ready?

LIZA. Quite. Is the Professor coming?

MRS HIGGINS. Certainly not. He cant behave himself in church. He makes remarks out loud all the time on the clergyman's pronunciation.

LIZA. Then I shall not see you again, Professor. Goodbye. [*She goes to the door*].

MRS HIGGINS [*coming to Higgins*] Goodbye, dear.

HIGGINS. Goodbye, mother. [*He is about to kiss her, when he recollects something*]. Oh, by the way, Eliza, order a ham and a Stilton cheese, will you? And buy me a pair of reindeer gloves, number eights, and a tie to match that new suit of mine.* You can choose the color. [*His cheerful, careless, vigorous voice shews that he is incorrigible*].*

LIZA [*disdainfully*] Number eights are too small for you if you want them lined with lamb's wool. You have three new ties that you have forgotten in the drawer of your washstand. Colonel Pickering prefers double Gloucester to Stilton; and you dont notice the difference. I telephoned Mrs Pearce this morning not to forget the ham. What you are to do without me I cannot imagine. [*She sweeps out*].

MRS HIGGINS. I'm afraid youve spoilt that girl, Henry. I should be uneasy about you and her if she were less fond of Colonel Pickering.

HIGGINS. Pickering! Nonsense: she's going to marry Freddy. Ha ha! Freddy! Freddy!! Ha ha ha ha ha!!!!! [*He roars with laughter as the play ends*].

*   *   *   *   *   *

The rest of the story need not be shewn in action, and indeed, would hardly need telling if our imaginations were not so enfeebled by their lazy dependence on the ready-mades and reach-me-downs of the rag-shop in which Romance keeps its stock of 'happy endings' to misfit all stories. Now, the history of Eliza Doolittle, though called a romance because the transfiguration it records seems exceedingly improbable, is common enough. Such transfigurations have been achieved by hundreds of resolutely ambitious young women since Nell Gwynne* set them the example by playing queens and fascinating kings in the theatre in which she began by selling oranges. Nevertheless, people in all directions have assumed, for no other reason than that she became the heroine of a romance, that she must have married the hero of it. This is unbearable, not only because her little drama, if acted on such a thoughtless assumption, must be spoiled, but because the true sequel is patent to anyone with a sense of human nature in general, and of feminine instinct in particular.*

Eliza, in telling Higgins she would not marry him if he asked her, was not coquetting: she was announcing a well-considered decision. When a bachelor interests, and dominates, and teaches, and becomes important to a spinster, as Higgins with Eliza, she always, if she has character enough to be capable of it, considers very seriously indeed whether she will play for becoming that bachelor's wife, especially if he is so little interested in marriage that a determined and devoted woman might capture him if she set herself resolutely to do it. Her decision will depend a good deal on whether she is really free to choose; and that, again, will depend on her age and income. If she is at the end of her youth, and has no security for her livelihood, she will marry him because she must marry anybody who will provide for her. But at Eliza's age a good-looking girl does not feel that pressure: she feels free to pick and choose. She is therefore guided by her instinct in the matter. Eliza's instinct tells her not to marry Higgins. It does not tell her to give him up. It is not in the slightest doubt as to his remaining one of the strongest personal interests in her life. It would be very sorely strained if there was another woman likely to supplant her with him. But as she feels sure of him on that last point, she has no doubt at all as to her course, and would not have any, even if the difference of twenty years in age, which seems so great to youth, did not exist between them.*

As our own instincts are not appealed to by her conclusion, let us see whether we cannot discover some reason in it. When Higgins excused his indifference to young women on the ground that they had an irresistible rival in his mother, he gave the clue to his inveterate old-bachelordom.

The case is uncommon only to the extent that remarkable mothers are uncommon. If an imaginative boy has a sufficiently rich mother who has intelligence,* personal grace, dignity of character without harshness, and a cultivated sense of the best art of her time to enable her to make her house beautiful, she sets a standard for him against which very few women can struggle, besides effecting for him a disengagement of his affections, his sense of beauty, and his idealism from his specifically sexual impulses. This makes him a standing puzzle to the huge number of uncultivated people who have been brought up in tasteless homes by commonplace or disagreeable parents, and to whom, consequently, literature, painting, sculpture, music, and affectionate personal relations come as modes of sex if they come at all. The word passion means nothing else to them; and that Higgins could have a passion for phonetics and idealize his mother instead of Eliza, would seem to them absurd and unnatural. Nevertheless, when we look round and see that hardly anyone is too ugly or disagreeable to find a wife or a husband if he or she wants one, whilst many old maids and bachelors are above the average in quality and culture, we cannot help suspecting that the disentanglement of sex from the associations with which it is so commonly confused, a disentanglement which persons of genius achieve by sheer intellectual analysis, is sometimes produced or aided by parental fascination.

Now, though Eliza was incapable of thus explaining to herself Higgins's formidable powers of resistance to the charm that prostrated Freddy at the first glance, she was instinctively aware that she could never obtain a complete grip of him, or come between him and his mother (the first necessity of the married woman). To put it shortly, she knew that for some mysterious reason he had not the makings of a married man in him, according to her conception of a husband as one to whom she would be his nearest and fondest and warmest interest. Even had there been no mother-rival, she would still have refused to accept an interest in herself that was secondary to philosophic interests. Had Mrs Higgins died, there would still have been Milton and the Universal Alphabet. Landor's remark that to those who have the greatest power of loving, love is a secondary affair, would not have recommended Landor* to Eliza. Put that along with her resentment of Higgins's domineering superiority, and her mistrust of his coaxing cleverness in getting round her and evading her wrath when he had gone too far with his impetuous bullying, and you will see that Eliza's instinct had good grounds for warning her not to marry her Pygmalion.

And now, whom did Eliza marry? For if Higgins was a predestinate old bachelor, she was most certainly not a predestinate old maid. Well, that can be told very shortly to those who have not guessed it from the indications she has herself given them.

Almost immediately after Eliza is stung into proclaiming her considered determination not to marry Higgins, she mentions the fact that young Mr Frederick Eynsford Hill is pouring out his love for her daily through the post. Now Freddy is young, practically twenty years younger than Higgins: he is a gentleman (or, as Eliza would qualify him, a toff), and speaks like one. He is nicely dressed, is treated by the Colonel as an equal, loves her unaffectedly, and is not her master, nor ever likely to dominate her in spite of his advantage of social standing. Eliza has no use for the foolish romantic tradition that all women love to be mastered, if not actually bullied and beaten. 'When you go to women' says Nietzsche 'take your whip with you.'* Sensible despots have never confined that precaution to women: they have taken their whips with them when they have dealt with men, and been slavishly idealized by the men over whom they have flourished the whip much more than by women. No doubt there are slavish women as well as slavish men; and women, like men, admire those that are stronger than themselves. But to admire a strong person and to live under that strong person's thumb are two different things. The weak may not be admired and hero-worshipped; but they are by no means disliked or shunned; and they never seem to have the least difficulty in marrying people who are too good for them. They may fail in emergencies; but life is not one long emergency: it is mostly a string of situations for which no exceptional strength is needed, and with which even rather weak people can cope if they have a stronger partner to help them out. Accordingly, it is a truth everywhere in evidence that strong people, masculine or feminine, not only do not marry stronger people, but do not shew any preference for them in selecting their friends. When a lion meets another with a louder roar 'the first lion thinks the last a bore.'* The man or woman who feels strong enough for two, seeks for every other quality in a partner than strength.

The converse is also true. Weak people want to marry strong people who do not frighten them too much; and this often leads them to make the mistake we describe metaphorically as 'biting off more than they can chew.' They want too much for too little; and when the bargain is unreasonable beyond all bearing, the union becomes impossible: it ends in the weaker party being either discarded or borne as a cross, which is worse. People who are not only weak, but silly or obtuse as well, are often in these difficulties.

This being the state of human affairs, what is Eliza fairly sure to do when she is placed between Freddy and Higgins? Will she look forward to a lifetime of fetching Higgins's slippers or to a lifetime of Freddy fetching hers? There can be no doubt about the answer. Unless Freddy is biologically repulsive to her, and Higgins biologically attractive to a degree that overwhelms all her other instincts, she will, if she marries either of them, marry Freddy.

And that is just what Eliza did.

Complications ensued; but they were economic, not romantic. Freddy had no money and no occupation. His mother's jointure, a last relic of the opulence of Largelady Park, had enabled her to struggle along in Earlscourt with an air of gentility, but not to procure any serious secondary education for her children, much less give the boy a profession. A clerkship at thirty shillings a week was beneath Freddy's dignity, and extremely distasteful to him besides. His prospects consisted of a hope that if he kept up appearances somebody would do something for him. The something appeared vaguely to his imagination as a private secretaryship or a sinecure* of some sort. To his mother it perhaps appeared as a marriage to some lady of means who could not resist her boy's niceness. Fancy her feelings when he married a flower girl who had become disclassed under extraordinary circumstances which were now notorious!

It is true that Eliza's situation did not seem wholly ineligible. Her father, though formerly a dustman, and now fantastically disclassed, had become extremely popular in the smartest society by a social talent which triumphed over every prejudice and every disadvantage. Rejected by the middle class, which he loathed, he had shot up at once into the highest circles by his wit, his dustmanship (which he carried like a banner), and his Nietzschean transcendence of good and evil.* At intimate ducal dinners he sat on the right hand of the Duchess; and in country houses he smoked in the pantry and was made much of by the butler when he was not feeding in the dining room and being consulted by cabinet ministers. But he found it almost as hard to do all this on four thousand a year* as Mrs Eynsford Hill to live in Earlscourt on an income so pitiably smaller that I have not the heart to disclose its exact figure. He absolutely refused to add the last straw to his burden by contributing to Eliza's support.

Thus Freddy and Eliza, now Mr and Mrs Eynsford Hill, would have spent a penniless honeymoon but for a wedding present of £500 from the Colonel to Eliza. It lasted a long time because Freddy did not know how to spend money, never having had any to spend, and Eliza, socially trained by a pair of old bachelors, wore her clothes as long as they held together and looked pretty, without the least regard to their being many months out of fashion. Still, £500 will not last two young people for ever; and they both knew, and Eliza felt as well, that they must shift* for themselves in the end. She could quarter herself on Wimpole Street because it had come to be her home; but she was quite aware that she ought not to quarter Freddy there, and that it would not be good for his character if she did.

Not that the Wimpole Street bachelors objected. When she consulted them, Higgins declined to be bothered about her housing problem when that solution was so simple. Eliza's desire to have Freddy in the house with her seemed of no more importance than if she had wanted an extra piece of bedroom furniture. Pleas as to Freddy's character, and the moral obligation on him to earn his own living, were lost on Higgins. He denied that Freddy had any character, and declared that if he tried to do any useful work some competent person would have the trouble of undoing it: a procedure involving a net loss to the community, and great unhappiness to Freddy himself, who was obviously intended by Nature for such light work as amusing Eliza, which, Higgins declared, was a much more useful and honorable occupation than working in the city.* When Eliza referred again to her project of teaching phonetics, Higgins abated not a jot of his violent opposition to it. He said she was not within ten years of being qualified to meddle with his pet subject; and as it was evident that the Colonel agreed with him, she felt she could not go against them in this grave matter, and that she had no right, without Higgins's consent, to exploit the knowledge he had given her; for his knowledge seemed to her as much his private property as his watch: Eliza was no communist. Besides, she was superstitiously devoted to them both, more entirely and frankly after her marriage than before it.

It was the Colonel who finally solved the problem, which had cost him much perplexed cogitation. He one day asked Eliza, rather shyly, whether she had quite given up her notion of keeping a flower shop. She replied that she had thought of it, but had put it out of her head, because the Colonel had said, that day at Mrs Higgins's, that it would never do. The Colonel confessed that when he said that, he had not quite recovered from the dazzling impression of the day before. They broke the matter to Higgins that evening. The sole comment vouchsafed* by him very nearly led to a serious quarrel with Eliza. It was to the effect that she would have in Freddy an ideal errand boy.

Freddy himself was next sounded on the subject. He said he had been thinking of a shop himself; though it had presented itself to his pennilessness as a small place in which Eliza should sell tobacco at one counter whilst he sold newspapers at the opposite one. But he agreed that it would be extraordinarily jolly to go early every morning with Eliza to Covent Garden and buy flowers on the scene of their first meeting: a sentiment which earned him many kisses from his wife. He added that he had always been afraid to propose anything of the sort, because Clara would make an awful row about a step that must damage her matrimonial chances, and his mother could not be expected to like it after clinging for so many years to that step of the social ladder on which retail trade is impossible.

This difficulty was removed by an event highly unexpected by Freddy's mother. Clara, in the course of her incursions into those artistic circles which were the highest within her reach, discovered that her conversational qualifications were expected to include a grounding in the novels of Mr H. G. Wells.* She borrowed them in various directions so energetically that she swallowed them all within two months. The result was a conversion of a kind quite common today. A modern Acts of the Apostles* would fill fifty whole Bibles if anyone were capable of writing it.

Poor Clara, who appeared to Higgins and his mother as a disagreeable and ridiculous person, and to her own mother as in some inexplicable way a social failure, had never seen herself in either light; for, though to some extent ridiculed and mimicked in West Kensington like everybody else there, she was accepted as a rational and normal—or shall we say inevitable?—sort of human being. At worst they called her The Pusher; but to them no more than to herself had it ever occurred that she was pushing the air, and pushing it in a wrong direction. Still, she was not happy. She was growing desperate. Her one asset, the fact that her mother was what the Epsom greengrocer called a carriage lady, had no exchange value, apparently. It had prevented her from getting educated, because the only education she could have afforded was education with the Earlscourt greengrocer's daughter. It had led her to seek the society of her mother's class; and that class simply would not have her, because she was much poorer than the greengrocer, and, far from being able to afford a maid, could not afford even a housemaid, and had to scrape along at home with an illiberally treated general servant. Under such circumstances nothing could give her an air of being a genuine product of Largelady Park. And yet its tradition made her regard a marriage with anyone within her reach as an unbearable humiliation. Commercial people and professional people in a small way were odious to her. She ran after painters and novelists; but she did not charm them; and her bold attempts to pick up and practise artistic and literary talk irritated them. She was, in short, an utter failure, an ignorant, incompetent, pretentious, unwelcome, penniless, useless little snob; and though she did not admit these disqualifications (for nobody ever faces unpleasant truths of this kind until the possibility of a way out dawns on them) she felt their effects too keenly to be satisfied with her position.

Clara had a startling eyeopener when, on being suddenly wakened to enthusiasm by a girl of her own age who dazzled her and produced in her a gushing desire to take her for a model, and gain her friendship, she discovered that this exquisite apparition had graduated from the gutter in a few months time. It shook her so violently, that when Mr H. G. Wells lifted her on the point of his puissant pen, and placed her at the angle of view from which the life she was leading and the society to which she clung appeared in its true relation to real human needs and worthy social structure, he effected a conversion and a conviction of sin comparable to the most sensational feats of General Booth or Gypsy Smith.* Clara's snobbery went bang. Life suddenly began to move with her. Without knowing how or why, she began to make friends and enemies. Some of the acquaintances to whom she had been a tedious or indifferent or ridiculous affliction, dropped her: others became cordial. To her amazement she found that some 'quite nice' people were saturated with Wells, and that this accessibility to ideas was the secret of their niceness. People she had thought deeply religious, and had tried to conciliate on that tack with disastrous results, suddenly took an interest in her, and revealed a hostility to conventional religion which she had never conceived possible except among the most desperate characters. They made her read Galsworthy;* and Galsworthy exposed the vanity of Largelady Park and finished her. It exasperated her to think that the dungeon in which she had languished for so many unhappy years had been unlocked all the time, and that the impulses she had so carefully struggled with and stifled for the sake of keeping well with society, were precisely those by which alone she could have come into any sort of sincere human contact. In the radiance of these discoveries, and the tumult of their reaction, she made a fool of herself as freely and conspicuously as when she so rashly adopted Eliza's expletive in Mrs Higgins's drawing room; for the new-born Wellsian had to find her bearings almost as ridiculously as a baby; but nobody hates a baby for its ineptitudes, or thinks the worse of it for trying to eat the matches; and Clara lost no friends by her follies. They laughed at her to her face this time; and she had to defend herself and fight it out as best she could.

When Freddy paid a visit to Earlscourt (which he never did when he could possibly help it) to make the desolating announcement that he and his Eliza were thinking of blackening the Largelady scutcheon* by opening a shop, he found the little household already convulsed by a prior announcement from Clara that she also was going to work in an old furniture shop in Dover Street,* which had been started by a fellow Wellsian. This appointment Clara owed, after all, to her old social accomplishment of Push. She had made up her mind that, cost what it might, she would see Mr Wells in the flesh; and she had achieved her end at a garden party. She had better luck than so rash an enterprise deserved. Mr Wells came up to her expectations. Age had not withered him, nor could custom stale his infinite variety in half an hour.* His pleasant neatness and compactness, his small hands and feet, his teeming ready brain, his unaffected accessibility, and a certain fine apprehensiveness which stamped him as susceptible from his topmost hair to his tipmost toe, proved irresistible. Clara talked of nothing else for weeks and weeks afterwards. And as she happened to talk to the lady of the furniture shop, and that lady also desired above all things to know Mr Wells and sell pretty things to him, she offered Clara a job on the chance of achieving that end through her.

And so it came about that Eliza's luck held, and the expected opposition to the flower shop melted away. The shop is in the arcade of a railway station not very far from the Victoria and Albert Museum;* and if you live in that neighborhood you may go there any day and buy a buttonhole from Eliza.

Now here is a last opportunity for romance. Would you not like to be assured that the shop was an immense success, thanks to Eliza's charms and her early business experience in Covent Garden? Alas! the truth is the truth: the shop did not pay for a long time, simply because Eliza and her Freddy did not know how to keep it. True, Eliza had not to begin at the very beginning: she knew the names and prices of the cheaper flowers; and her elation was unbounded when she found that Freddy, like all youths educated at cheap, pretentious, and thoroughly inefficient schools, knew a little Latin. It was very little, but enough to make him appear to her a Porson or Bentley,* and to put him at his ease with botanical nomenclature. Unfortunately he knew nothing else; and Eliza, though she could count money up to eighteen shillings or so, and had acquired a certain familiarity with the language of Milton from her struggles to qualify herself for winning Higgins's bet, could not write out a bill without utterly disgracing the establishment. Freddy's power of stating in Latin that Balbus built a wall and that Gaul was divided into three parts* did not carry with it the slightest knowledge of accounts or business: Colonel Pickering had to explain to him what a cheque book and a bank account meant. And the pair were by no means easily teachable. Freddy backed up Eliza in her obstinate refusal to believe that they could save money by engaging a bookkeeper with some knowledge of the business. How, they argued, could you possibly save money by going to extra expense when you already could not make both ends meet? But the Colonel, after making the ends meet over and over again, at last gently insisted; and Eliza, humbled to the dust by having to beg from him so often, and stung by the uproarious derision of Higgins, to whom the notion of Freddy succeeding at anything was a joke that never palled, grasped the fact that business, like phonetics, has to be learned.

On the piteous spectacle of the pair spending their evenings in short-hand schools and polytechnic classes, learning bookkeeping and typewriting with incipient junior clerks, male and female, from the elementary schools, let me not dwell. There were even classes at the London School of Economics,* and a humble personal appeal to the director of that institution to recommend a course bearing on the flower business. He, being a humorist, explained to them the method of the celebrated Dickensian essay on Chinese Metaphysics by the gentleman who read an article on China and an article on Metaphysics and combined the information.* He suggested that they should combine the London School with Kew Gardens.* Eliza, to whom the procedure of the Dickensian gentleman seemed perfectly correct (as in fact it was) and not in the least funny (which was only her ignorance), took the advice with entire gravity. But the effort that cost her the deepest humiliation was a request to Higgins, whose pet artistic fancy, next to Milton's verse, was calligraphy, and who himself wrote a most beautiful Italian hand, that he would teach her to write. He declared that she was congenitally incapable of forming a single letter worthy of the least of Milton's words; but she persisted; and again he suddenly threw himself into the task of teaching her with a combination of stormy intensity, concentrated patience, and occasional bursts of interesting disquisition on the beauty and nobility, the august mission and destiny, of human handwriting. Eliza ended by acquiring an extremely uncommercial script which was a positive extension of her personal beauty, and spending three times as much on stationery as anyone else because certain qualities and shapes of paper became indispensable to her. She could not even address an envelope in the usual way because it made the margins all wrong.

Their commercial schooldays were a period of disgrace and despair for the young couple. They seemed to be learning nothing about flower shops. At last they gave it up as hopeless, and shook the dust of the shorthand schools, and the polytechnics, and the London School of Economics from their feet for ever. Besides, the business was in some mysterious way beginning to take care of itself. They had somehow forgotten their objections to employing other people. They came to the conclusion that their own way was the best, and that they had really a remarkable talent for business. The Colonel, who had been compelled for some years to keep a sufficient sum on current account at his bankers to make up their deficits, found that the provision was unnecessary: the young people were prospering. It is true that there was not quite fair play between them and their competitors in trade. Their week-ends in the country cost them nothing, and saved them the price of their Sunday dinners; for the motor car was the Colonel's; and he and Higgins paid the hotel bills. Mr F. Hill, florist and greengrocer (they soon discovered that there was money in asparagus; and asparagus led to other vegetables), had an air which stamped the business as classy; and in private life he was still Frederick Eynsford Hill, Esquire.* Not that there was any swank* about him: nobody but Eliza knew that he had been christened Frederick Challoner. Eliza herself swanked like anything.

That is all. That is how it has turned out. It is astonishing how much Eliza still manages to meddle in the housekeeping at Wimpole Street in spite of the shop and her own family. And it is notable that though she never nags her husband, and frankly loves the Colonel as if she were his favorite daughter, she has never got out of the habit of nagging Higgins that was established on the fatal night when she won his bet for him. She snaps his head off on the faintest provocation, or on none. He no longer dares to tease her by assuming an abysmal inferiority of Freddy's mind to his own. He storms and bullies and derides; but she stands up to him so ruthlessly that the Colonel has to ask her from time to time to be kinder to Higgins; and it is the only request of his that brings a mulish expression into her face. Nothing but some emergency or calamity great enough to break down all likes and dislikes, and throw them both back on their common humanity—and may they be spared any such trial!—will ever alter this. She knows that Higgins does not need her, just as her father did not need her. The very scrupulousness with which he told her that day that he had become used to having her there, and dependent on her for all sorts of little services, and that he should miss her if she went away (it would never have occurred to Freddy or the Colonel to say anything of the sort) deepens her inner certainty that she is 'no more to him than them slippers'; yet she has a sense, too, that his indifference is deeper than the infatuation of commoner souls. She is immensely interested in him. She has even secret mischievous moments in which she wishes she could get him alone, on a desert island, away from all ties and with nobody else in the world to consider, and just drag him off his pedestal and see him making love like any common man. We all have private imaginations of that sort. But when it comes to business, to the life that she really leads as distinguished from the life of dreams and fancies, she likes Freddy and she likes the Colonel; and she does not like Higgins and Mr Doolittle. Galatea never does quite like Pygmalion: his relation to her is too godlike to be altogether agreeable.

THE END

HEARTBREAK HOUSE

A Fantasia* in the Russian Manner on English Themes

HEARTBREAK HOUSE
AND HORSEBACK HALL

Where Heartbreak House Stands

HEARTBREAK HOUSE is not merely the name of the play which follows this preface. It is cultured, leisured Europe before the war. When the play was begun not a shot had been fired; and only the professional diplomatists and the very few amateurs whose hobby is foreign policy even knew that the guns were loaded. A Russian playwright, Tchekov,* had produced four fascinating dramatic studies of Heartbreak House, of which three, The Cherry Orchard, Uncle Vanya, and The Seagull, had been performed in England. Tolstoy, in his Fruits of Enlightenment,* had shewn us through it in his most ferociously contemptuous manner. Tolstoy did not waste any sympathy on it: it was to him the house in which Europe was stifling its soul; and he knew that our utter enervation and futilization in that overheated drawing-room atmosphere was delivering the world over to the control of ignorant and soulless cunning and energy, with the frightful consequences which have now overtaken it. Tolstoy was no pessimist: he was not disposed to leave the house standing if he could bring it down about the ears of its pretty and amiable voluptuaries; and he wielded the pickaxe with a will. He treated the case of the inmates as one of opium poisoning, to be dealt with by seizing the patients roughly and exercising them violently until they were broad awake. Tchekov, more of a fatalist, had no faith in these charming people extricating themselves. They would, he thought, be sold up and sent adrift by the bailiffs; therefore he had no scruple in exploiting and even flattering their charm.

The Inhabitants

Tchekov's plays, being less lucrative than swings and roundabouts, got no further in England, where theatres are only ordinary commercial affairs, than a couple of performances by the Stage Society.* We stared and said, 'How Russian!' They did not strike me in that way. Just as Ibsen's intensely Norwegian plays exactly fitted every middle and professional class suburb in Europe, these intensely Russian plays fitted all the country houses in Europe in which the pleasures of music, art, literature, and the theatre had supplanted hunting, shooting, fishing, flirting, eating, and drinking. The same nice people, the same utter futility. The nice people could read; some of them could write; and they were the only repositories of culture who had social opportunities of contact with our politicians, administrators, and newspaper proprietors, or any chance of sharing or influencing their activities. But they shrank from that contact. They hated politics. They did not wish to realize Utopia for the common people: they wished to realize their favorite fictions and poems in their own lives; and, when they could, they lived without scruple on incomes which they did nothing to earn. The women in their girlhood made themselves look like variety theatre stars, and settled down later into the types of beauty imagined by the previous generation of painters. They took the only part of our society in which there was leisure for high culture, and made it an economic, political, and, as far as practicable, a moral vacuum; and as Nature, abhorring the vacuum, immediately filled it up with sex and with all sorts of refined pleasures, it was a very delightful place at its best for moments of relaxation. In other moments it was disastrous. For prime ministers and their like, it was a veritable Capua.*

Horseback Hall

But where were our front benchers to nest if not here? The alternative to Heartbreak House was Horseback Hall, consisting of a prison for horses with an annex for the ladies and gentlemen who rode them, hunted them, talked about them, bought them and sold them, and gave nine-tenths of their lives to them, dividing the other tenth between charity, churchgoing (as a substitute for religion), and conservative electioneering (as a substitute for politics). It is true that the two establishments got mixed at the edges. Exiles from the library, the music room, and the picture gallery would be found languishing among the stables, miserably discontented; and hardy horsewomen who slept at the first chord of Schumann* were born, horribly misplaced, into the garden of Klingsor;* but sometimes one came upon horsebreakers and heartbreakers who could make the best of both worlds. As a rule, however, the two were apart and knew little of one another; so the prime minister folk had to choose between barbarism and Capua. And of the two atmospheres it is hard to say which was the more fatal to statesmanship.

Revolution on the Shelf

Heartbreak House was quite familiar with revolutionary ideas on paper. It aimed at being advanced and freethinking, and hardly ever went to church or kept the Sabbath* except by a little extra fun at week-ends. When you spent a Friday to Tuesday in it you found on the shelf in your bedroom not only the books of poets and novelists, but of revolutionary biologists and even economists. Without at least a few plays by myself and Mr Granville Barker,* and a few stories by Mr H. G. Wells, Mr Arnold Bennett,* and Mr John Galsworthy, the house would have been out of the movement. You would find Blake among the poets, and beside him Bergson, Butler, Scott Haldane, the poems of Meredith and Thomas Hardy,* and, generally speaking, all the literary implements for forming the mind of the perfect modern Socialist and Creative Evolutionist. It was a curious experience to spend Sunday in dipping into these books, and on Monday morning to read in the daily paper that the country had just been brought to the verge of anarchy because a new Home Secretary* or chief of police, without an idea in his head that his great-grandmother might not have had to apologize for, had refused to 'recognize' some powerful Trade Union, just as a gondola might refuse to recognize a 20,000-ton liner.*

In short, power and culture were in separate compartments. The barbarians were not only literally in the saddle, but on the front bench in the House of Commons, with nobody to correct their incredible ignorance of modern thought and political science but upstarts from the counting-house, who had spent their lives furnishing their pockets instead of their minds. Both, however, were practised in dealing with money and with men, as far as acquiring the one and exploiting the other went; and although this is as undesirable an expertness as that of the medieval robber baron, it qualifies men to keep an estate or a business going in its old routine without necessarily understanding it, just as Bond Street* tradesmen and domestic servants keep fashionable society going without any instruction in sociology.

The Cherry Orchard

The Heartbreak people neither could nor would do anything of the sort. With their heads as full of the Anticipations of Mr H. G. Wells as the heads of our actual rulers were empty even of the anticipations of Erasmus or Sir Thomas More,* they refused the drudgery of politics, and would have made a very poor job of it if they had changed their minds. Not that they would have been allowed to meddle anyhow, as only through the accident of being a hereditary peer can anyone in these days of Votes for Everybody* get into parliament if handicapped by a serious modern cultural equipment; but if they had, their habit of living in a vacuum would have left them helpless and ineffective in public affairs. Even in private life they were often helpless wasters of their inheritance, like the people in Tchekov's Cherry Orchard. Even those who lived within their incomes were really kept going by their solicitors and agents, being unable to manage an estate or run a business without continual prompting from those who have to learn how to do such things or starve.

From what is called Democracy no corrective to this state of things could be hoped. It is said that every people has the Government it deserves. It is more to the point that every Government has the electorate it deserves; for the orators of the front bench can edify or debauch an ignorant electorate at will. Thus our democracy moves in a vicious circle of reciprocal worthiness and unworthiness.

Nature's Long Credits

Nature's way of dealing with unhealthy conditions is unfortunately not one that compels us to conduct a solvent hygiene on a cash basis. She demoralizes us with long credits and reckless overdrafts, and then pulls us up cruelly with catastrophic bankruptcies. Take, for example, common domestic sanitation. A whole city generation may neglect it utterly and scandalously, if not with absolute impunity, yet without any evil consequences that anyone thinks of tracing to it. In a hospital two generations of medical students may tolerate dirt and carelessness, and then go out into general practice to spread the doctrine that fresh air is a fad, and sanitation an imposture set up to make profits for plumbers. Then suddenly Nature takes her revenge. She strikes at the city with a pestilence and at the hospital with an epidemic of hospital gangrene, slaughtering right and left until the innocent young have paid for the guilty old, and the account is balanced. And then she goes to sleep again and gives another period of credit, with the same result.

This is what has just happened in our political hygiene. Political science has been as recklessly neglected by Governments and electorates during my lifetime as sanitary science was in the days of Charles the Second.* In international relations diplomacy has been a boyishly lawless affair of family intrigues, commercial and territorial brigandage, torpors of pseudo-goodnature produced by laziness, and spasms of ferocious activity produced by terror. But in these islands we muddled through. Nature gave us a longer credit than she gave to France or Germany or Russia. To British centenarians who died in their beds in

1914, any dread of having to hide underground in London from the shells of an enemy* seemed more remote and fantastic than a dread of the appearance of a colony of cobras and rattlesnakes in Kensington Gardens.* In the prophetic works of Charles Dickens we were warned against many evils which have since come to pass; but of the evil of being slaughtered by a foreign foe on our own doorsteps there was no shadow. Nature gave us a very long credit; and we abused it to the utmost. But when she struck at last she struck with a vengeance. For four years she smote our firstborn and heaped on us plagues of which Egypt never dreamed.* They were all as preventible as the great Plague of London,* and came solely because they had not been prevented. They were not undone by winning the war. The earth is still bursting with the dead bodies of the victors.

The Wicked Half Century

It is difficult to say whether indifference and neglect are worse than false doctrine; but Heartbreak House and Horseback Hall unfortunately suffered from both. For half a century before the war civilization had been going to the devil very precipitately under the influence of a pseudo-science as disastrous as the blackest Calvinism.* Calvinism taught that as we are predestinately saved or damned, nothing that we do can alter our destiny. Still, as Calvinism gave the individual no clue as to whether he had drawn a lucky number or an unlucky one, it left him a fairly strong interest in encouraging his hopes of salvation and allaying his fear of damnation by behaving as one of the elect might be expected to behave rather than as one of the reprobate. But in the middle of the XIX century naturalists and physicists assured the world, in the name of Science, that salvation and damnation are all nonsense, and that predestination is the central truth of religion, inasmuch as human beings are produced by their environment, their sins and good deeds being only a series of chemical and mechanical reactions over which they have no control. Such figments as mind, choice, purpose, conscience, will, and so forth, are, they taught, mere illusions, produced because they are useful in the continual struggle of the human machine to maintain its environment in a favorable condition, a process incidentally involving the ruthless destruction or subjection of its competitors for the supply (assumed to be limited) of subsistence available. We taught Prussia* this religion; and Prussia bettered our instruction so effectively that we presently found ourselves confronted with the necessity of destroying Prussia to prevent Prussia destroying us. And that has just ended in each destroying the other to an extent doubtfully reparable in our time.

It may be asked how so imbecile and dangerous a creed ever came to be accepted by intelligent beings. I will answer that question more fully in my next volume of plays,* which will be entirely devoted to the subject. For the present I will only say that there were better reasons than the obvious one that such sham science as this opened a scientific career to very stupid men, and all the other careers to shameless rascals, provided they were industrious enough. It is true that this motive operated very powerfully; but when the new departure in scientific doctrine which is associated with the name of the great naturalist Charles Darwin* began, it was not only a reaction against a barbarous pseudo-evangelical teleology intolerably obstructive to all scientific progress, but was accompanied, as it happened, by discoveries of extraordinary interest in physics, chemistry, and that lifeless method of evolution which its investigators called Natural Selection. Howbeit, there was only one result possible in the ethical sphere, and that was the banishment of conscience from human affairs, or, as Samuel Butler vehemently put it, 'of mind from the universe.'*

Hypochondria

Now Heartbreak House, with Butler and Bergson and Scott Haldane alongside Blake and the other major poets on its shelves (to say nothing of Wagner and the tone poets), was not so completely blinded by the doltish materialism of the laboratories as the uncultured world outside. But being an idle house it was a hypochondriacal house, always running after cures. It would stop eating meat, not on valid Shelleyan grounds,* but in order to get rid of a bogey called Uric Acid;* and it would actually let you pull all its teeth out to exorcize another demon named Pyorrhea.* It was superstitious, and addicted to table-rapping, materialization séances, clairvoyance, palmistry, crystal-gazing and the like to such an extent that it may be doubted whether ever before in the history of the world did soothsayers, astrologers, and unregistered therapeutic specialists of all sorts flourish as they did during this half century of the drift to the abyss.* The registered doctors and surgeons were hard put to it to compete with the unregistered. They were not clever enough to appeal to the imagination and sociability of the Heartbreakers by the arts of the actor, the orator, the poet, the winning conversationalist. They had to fall back coarsely on the terror of infection and death. They prescribed inoculations and operations. Whatever part of a human being could be cut out without necessarily killing him they cut out; and he often died (unnecessarily of course) in consequence. From such trifles as uvulas and tonsils they went on to ovaries and appendices until at last no one's inside was safe. They explained that the human intestine was too long, and that nothing could make a child of Adam* healthy except short circuiting the pylorus by cutting a length out of the lower intestine and fastening it directly to the stomach. As their mechanist theory taught them that medicine was the business of the chemist's laboratory, and surgery of the carpenter's shop, and also that Science (by which they meant their practices) was so important that no consideration for the interests of any individual creature, whether frog or philosopher, much less the vulgar commonplaces of sentimental ethics, could weigh for a moment against the remotest off-chance of an addition to the body of scientific knowledge, they operated and vivisected and inoculated and lied on a stupendous scale, clamoring for and actually acquiring such legal powers over the bodies of their fellow-citizens as neither king, pope, nor parliament dare ever have claimed. The Inquisition* itself was a Liberal institution compared to the General Medical Council.*

Those Who do not Know how to Live must Make a Merit of Dying

Heartbreak House was far too lazy and shallow to extricate itself from this palace of evil enchantment. It rhapsodized about love; but it believed in cruelty. It was afraid of the cruel people; and it saw that cruelty was at least effective. Cruelty did things that made money, whereas Love did nothing but prove the soundness of Larochefoucauld's saying that very few people would fall in love if they had never read about it.* Heartbreak House, in short, did not know how to live, at which point all that was left to it was the boast that at least it knew how to die: a melancholy accomplishment which the outbreak of war presently gave it practically unlimited opportunities of displaying. Thus were the firstborn of Heartbreak House smitten; and the young, the innocent, the hopeful expiated the folly and worthlessness of their elders.

War Delirium

Only those who have lived through a first-rate war, not in the field, but at home, and kept their heads, can possibly understand the bitterness of Shakespear and Swift,* who both went through this experience. The horror of Peer Gynt* in the madhouse, when the lunatics, exalted by illusions of splendid talent and visions of a dawning millennium, crowned him as their emperor, was tame in comparison. I do not know whether anyone really kept his head completely except those who had to keep it because they had to conduct the war at first hand. I should not have kept my own (as far as I did keep it) if I had not at once understood that as a scribe and speaker I too was under the most serious public obligation to keep my grip on realities; but this did not save me from a considerable degree of hyperaesthesia.* There were of course some happy people to whom the war meant nothing: all political and general matters lying outside their little circle of interest. But the ordinary war-conscious civilian went mad, the main symptom being a conviction that the whole order of nature had been reversed. All foods, he felt, must now be adulterated. All schools must be closed. No advertisements must be sent to the newspapers, of which new editions must appear and be bought up every ten minutes. Travelling must be stopped, or, that being impossible, greatly hindered. All pretences about fine art and culture and the like must be flung off as an intolerable affectation; and the picture galleries and museums and schools at once occupied by war workers. The British Museum* itself was saved only by a hairsbreadth. The sincerity of all this, and of much more which would not be believed if I chronicled it, may be established by one conclusive instance of the general craziness. Men were seized with the illusion that they could win the war by giving away money. And they not only subscribed millions to Funds of all sorts with no discoverable object, and to ridiculous voluntary organizations for doing what was plainly the business of the civil and military authorities, but actually handed out money to any thief in the street who had the presence of mind to pretend that he (or she) was 'collecting' it for the annihilation of the enemy. Swindlers were emboldened to take offices; label themselves Anti-Enemy Leagues; and simply pocket the money that was heaped on them. Attractively dressed young women found that they had nothing to do but parade the streets, collecting-box in hand, and live gloriously on the profits. Many months elapsed before, as a first sign of returning sanity, the police swept an Anti-Enemy secretary into prison *pour encourager les autres*, and the passionate penny collecting of the Flag Days was brought under some sort of regulation.*

Madness in Court

The demoralization did not spare the Law Courts. Soldiers were acquitted, even on fully proved indictments for wilful murder, until at last the judges and magistrates had to announce that what was called the Unwritten Law, which meant simply that a soldier could do what he liked with impunity in civil life, was not the law of the land, and that a Victoria Cross* did not carry with it a perpetual plenary indulgence. Unfortunately the insanity of the juries and magistrates did not always manifest itself in indulgence. No person unlucky enough to be charged with any sort of conduct, however reasonable and salutary, that did not smack of war delirium had the slightest chance of acquittal. There were in the country, too, a certain number of people who had conscientious objections to war as criminal or unchristian. The Act of Parliament introducing Compulsory Military Service* thoughtlessly exempted these persons, merely requiring them to prove the genuineness of their convictions. Those who did so were very ill-advised from the point of view of their own personal interest; for they were persecuted with savage logicality in spite of the law; whilst those who made no pretence of having any objection to war at all, and had not only had military training in Officers' Training Corps,* but had proclaimed on public occasions that they were perfectly ready to engage in civil war on behalf of their political opinions, were allowed the benefit of the Act on the ground that they did not approve of this particular war. For the Christians there was no mercy. In cases where the evidence as to their being killed by ill treatment was so unequivocal that the verdict would certainly have been one of wilful murder had the prejudice of the coroner's jury been on the other side, their tormentors were gratuitously declared to be blameless. There was only one virtue, pugnacity: only one vice, pacifism. That is an essential condition of war; but the Government had not the courage to legislate accordingly; and its law was set aside for Lynch law.*

The climax of legal lawlessness was reached in France. The greatest Socialist statesman in Europe, Jaurès,* was shot and killed by a gentleman who resented his efforts to avert the war. M. Clemenceau* was shot by another gentleman of less popular opinions, and happily came off no worse than having to spend a precautionary couple of days in bed. The slayer of Jaurès was recklessly acquitted: the would-be slayer of M. Clemenceau was carefully found guilty. There is no reason to doubt that the same thing would have happened in England if the war had begun with a successful attempt to assassinate Keir Hardie, and ended with an unsuccessful one to assassinate Mr Lloyd George.*

The Long Arm of War

The pestilence which is the usual accompaniment of war was called influenza.* Whether it was really a war pestilence or not was made doubtful by the fact that it did its worst in places remote from the battle-fields, notably on the west coast of North America and in India. But the moral pestilence, which was unquestionably a war pestilence, reproduced this phenomenon. One would have supposed that the war fever would have raged most furiously in the countries actually under fire, and that the others would be more reasonable. Belgium and Flanders, where over large districts literally not one stone was left upon another as the opposed armies drove each other back and forward over it after terrific preliminary bombardments, might have been pardoned for relieving their feelings more emphatically than by shrugging their shoulders and saying 'C'est la guerre.'* England, inviolate for so many centuries that the swoop of war on her homesteads had long ceased to be more credible than a return of the Flood,* could hardly be expected to keep her temper sweet when she knew at last what it was to hide in cellars and underground railway stations, or lie quaking in bed, whilst bombs crashed, houses crumbled, and aircraft guns distributed shrapnel on friend and foe alike until certain shop windows in London, formerly full of fashionable hats, were filled with steel helmets. Slain and mutilated women and children, and burnt and wrecked dwellings, excuse a good deal of violent language, and produce a wrath on which many suns go down before it is appeased. Yet it was in the United States of America, where nobody slept the worse for the war, that the war fever went beyond all sense and reason. In European Courts there was vindictive illegality: in American Courts there was raving lunacy. It is not for me to chronicle the extravagances of an Ally: let some candid American do that. I can only say that to us sitting in our gardens in England, with the guns in France making themselves felt by a throb in the air as unmistakeable as an audible sound, or with tightening hearts studying the phases of the moon in London in their bearing on the chances whether our houses would be standing or ourselves alive next morning, the newspaper accounts of the sentences American Courts were passing on young girls and old men alike for the expression of opinions which were being uttered amid thundering applause before huge audiences in England, and the more private records of the methods by which the American War Loans* were raised, were so amazing that they would put the guns and the possibilities of a raid clean out of our heads for the moment.

The Rabid Watchdogs of Liberty

Not content with these rancorous abuses of the existing law, the war maniacs made a frantic rush to abolish all constitutional guarantees of liberty and well-being. The ordinary law was superseded by Acts under which newspapers were seized and their printing machinery destroyed by simple police raids *à la Russe*,* and persons arrested and shot without any pretence of trial by jury or publicity of procedure or evidence. Though it was urgently necessary that production should be increased by the most scientific organization and economy of labor, and though no fact was better established than that excessive duration and intensity of toil reduces production heavily instead of increasing it, the factory laws were suspended, and men and women recklessly overworked until the loss of their efficiency became too glaring to be ignored. Remonstrances and warnings were met either with an accusation of pro-Germanism or the formula, 'Remember that we are at war now.' I have said that men assumed that war had reversed the order of nature, and that all was lost unless we did the exact opposite of everything we had found necessary and beneficial in peace. But the truth was worse than that. The war did not change men's minds in any such impossible way. What really happened was that the impact of physical death and destruction, the one reality that every fool can understand, tore off the masks of education, art, science, and religion from our ignorance and barbarism, and left us glorying grotesquely in the licence suddenly accorded to our vilest passions and most abject terrors. Ever since Thucydides* wrote his history, it has been on record that when the angel of death sounds his trumpet the pretences of civilization are blown from men's heads into the mud like hats in a gust of wind. But when this scripture was fulfilled among us, the shock was not the less appalling because a few students of Greek history were not surprised by it. Indeed these students threw themselves into the orgy as shamelessly as the illiterate. The Christian priest joining in the war dance without even throwing off his cassock first, and the respectable school governor expelling the German professor with insult and bodily violence, and declaring that no English child should ever again be taught the language of Luther and Goethe,* were kept in countenance by the most impudent repudiations of every decency of civilization and every lesson of political experience on the part of the very persons who, as university professors, historians, philosophers, and men of science, were the accredited custodians of culture. It was crudely natural, and perhaps necessary for recruiting purposes, that German militarism and German dynastic ambition should be painted by journalists and recruiters in black and red as European dangers (as in fact they are), leaving it to be inferred that our own militarism and our own political constitution are millennially democratic (which they certainly are not);

but when it came to frantic denunciations of German chemistry, German biology, German poetry, German music, German literature, German philosophy, and even German engineering, as malignant abominations standing towards British and French chemistry and so forth in the relation of heaven to hell, it was clear that the utterers of such barbarous ravings had never really understood or cared for the arts and sciences they professed and were profaning, and were only the appallingly degenerate descendants of the men of the seventeenth and eighteenth centuries who, recognizing no national frontiers in the great realm of the human mind, kept the European comity of that realm loftily and even ostentatiously above the rancors of the battle-field. Tearing the Garter from the Kaiser's* leg, striking the German dukes from the roll of our peerage, changing the King's illustrious and historically appropriate surname for that of a traditionless locality,* was not a very dignified business; but the erasure of German names from the British rolls of science and learning was a confession that in England the little respect paid to science and learning is only an affectation which hides a savage contempt for both. One felt that the figure of St George and the Dragon* on our coinage should be replaced by that of the soldier driving his spear through Archimedes.* But by that time there was no coinage: only paper money in which ten shillings called itself a pound as confidently as the people who were disgracing their country called themselves patriots.

The Sufferings of the Sane

The mental distress of living amid the obscene din of all these carmagnoles* and corobberies was not the only burden that lay on sane people during the war. There was also the emotional strain, complicated by the offended economic sense, produced by the casualty lists. The stupid, the selfish, the narrow-minded, the callous and unimaginative were spared a great deal. 'Blood and destruction shall be so in use that mothers shall but smile when they behold their infants quartered by the hands of war,'* was a Shakespearean prophecy that very nearly came true; for when nearly every house had a slaughtered son to mourn, we should all have gone quite out of our senses if we had taken our own and our friends' bereavements at their peace value. It became necessary to give them a false value; to proclaim the young life worthily and gloriously sacrificed to redeem the liberty of mankind, instead of to expiate the heedlessness and folly of their fathers, and expiate it in vain. We had even to assume that the parents and not the children had made the sacrifice, until at last the comic papers were driven to satirize fat old men, sitting comfortably in club chairs, and boasting of the sons they had 'given' to their country.

No one grudged these anodynes to acute personal grief; but they only embittered those who knew that the young men were having their teeth set on edge because their parents had eaten sour political grapes. Then think of the young men themselves! Many of them had no illusions about the policy that led to the war: they went clear-sighted to a horribly repugnant duty. Men essentially gentle and essentially wise, with really valuable work in hand, laid it down voluntarily and spent months forming fours* in the barrack yard, and stabbing sacks of straw in the public eye, so that they might go out to kill and maim men as gentle as themselves. These men, who were perhaps, as a class, our most efficient soldiers (Frederick Keeling,* for example), were not duped for a moment by the hypocritical melodrama that consoled and stimulated the others. They left their creative work to drudge at destruction, exactly as they would have left it to take their turn at the pumps in a sinking ship. They did not, like some of the conscientious objectors, hold back because the ship had been neglected by its officers and scuttled by its wreckers. The ship had to be saved, even if Newton* had to leave his fluxions and Michael Angelo* his marbles to save it; so they threw away the tools of their beneficent and ennobling trades, and took up the bloodstained bayonet and the murderous bomb, forcing themselves to pervert their divine instinct for perfect artistic execution to the effective handling of these diabolical things, and their economic faculty for organization to the contriving of ruin and slaughter. For it gave an ironic edge to their tragedy that the very talents they were forced to prostitute made the prostitution not only effective, but even interesting; so that some of them were rapidly promoted, and found themselves actually becoming artists in war, with a growing relish for it, like Napoleon* and all the other scourges of mankind, in spite of themselves. For many of them there was not even this consolation. They 'stuck it,' and hated it, to the end.

Evil in the Throne of Good

This distress of the gentle was so acute that those who shared it in civil life, without having to shed blood with their own hands, or witness destruction with their own eyes, hardly care to obtrude their own woes. Nevertheless, even when sitting at home in safety, it was not easy for those who had to write and speak about the war to throw away their highest conscience, and deliberately work to a standard of inevitable evil instead of to the ideal of life more abundant. I can answer for at least one person who found the change from the wisdom of Jesus and St Francis* to the morals of Richard III* and the madness of Don Quixote* extremely irksome. But that change had to be made; and we are all the worse for it, except those for whom it was not really a change at all, but only a relief from hypocrisy.

Think, too, of those who, though they had neither to write nor to fight, and had no children of their own to lose, yet knew the inestimable loss to the world of four years of the life of a generation wasted on destruction. Hardly one of the epoch-making works of the human mind might not have been aborted or destroyed by taking their authors away from their natural work for four critical years. Not only were Shakespears and Platos* being killed outright; but many of the best harvests of the survivors had to be sown in the barren soil of the trenches. And this was no mere British consideration. To the truly civilized man, to the good European, the slaughter of the German youth was as disastrous as the slaughter of the English. Fools exulted in 'German losses.' They were our losses as well. Imagine exulting in the death of Beethoven because Bill Sikes* dealt him his death blow!

*Straining at the Gnat and Swallowing the Camel**

But most people could not comprehend these sorrows. There was a frivolous exultation in death for its own sake, which was at bottom an inability to realize that the deaths were real deaths and not stage ones. Again and again, when an air raider dropped a bomb which tore a child and its mother limb from limb, the people who saw it, though they had been reading with great cheerfulness of thousands of such happenings day after day in their newspapers, suddenly burst into furious imprecations on 'the Huns'* as murderers, and shrieked for savage and satisfying vengeance. At such moments it became clear that the deaths they had not seen meant no more to them than the mimic deaths of the cinema screen. Sometimes it was not necessary that death should be actually witnessed: it had only to take place under circumstances of sufficient novelty and proximity to bring it home almost as sensationally and effectively as if it had been actually visible.

For example, in the spring of 1915 there was an appalling slaughter of our young soldiers at Neuve Chapelle and at the Gallipoli landing.* I will not go so far as to say that our civilians were delighted to have such exciting news to read at breakfast. But I cannot pretend that

I noticed either in the papers, or in general intercourse, any feeling beyond the usual one that the cinema show at the front was going splendidly, and that our boys were the bravest of the brave. Suddenly there came the news that an Atlantic liner, the Lusitania,* had been torpedoed, and that several well-known first class passengers, including a famous theatrical manager and the author of a popular farce, had been drowned, among others. The others included Sir Hugh Lane;* but as he had only laid the country under great obligations in the sphere of the fine arts, no great stress was laid on that loss.

Immediately an amazing frenzy swept through the country. Men who up to that time had kept their heads now lost them utterly. 'Killing saloon passengers! What next?' was the essence of the whole agitation; but it is far too trivial a phrase to convey the faintest notion of the rage which possessed us. To me, with my mind full of the hideous cost of Neuve Chapelle, Ypres,* and the Gallipoli landing, the fuss about the Lusitania seemed almost a heartless impertinence, though I was well acquainted personally with the three best-known victims,* and understood, better perhaps than most people, the misfortune of the death of Lane. I even found a grim satisfaction, very intelligible to all soldiers, in the fact that the civilians who found the war such splendid British sport should get a sharp taste of what it was to the actual combatants. I expressed my impatience very freely, and found that my very straightforward and natural feeling in the matter was received as a monstrous and heartless paradox. When I asked those who gaped at me whether they had anything to say about the holocaust of Festubert,* they gaped wider than before, having totally forgotten it, or rather, having never realized it. They were not heartless any more than I was; but the big catastrophe was too big for them to grasp, and the little one had been just the right size for them. I was not surprised. Have I not seen a public body for just the same reason pass a vote for £30,000 without a word, and then spend three special meetings, prolonged into the night, over an item of seven shillings for refreshments?

Little Minds and Big Battles

Nobody will be able to understand the vagaries of public feeling during the war unless they bear constantly in mind that the war in its entire magnitude did not exist for the average civilian. He could not conceive even a battle, much less a campaign. To the suburbs the war was nothing but a suburban squabble. To the miner and navvy it was only a series of bayonet fights between German champions and English ones. The enormity of it was quite beyond most of us. Its episodes had to be reduced to the dimensions of a railway accident or a shipwreck before it could produce any effect on our minds at all. To us the ridiculous bombardments of Scarborough and Ramsgate* were colossal tragedies, and the battle of Jutland* a mere ballad. The words 'after thorough artillery preparation' in the news from the front meant nothing to us; but when our seaside trippers learned that an elderly gentleman at breakfast in a week-end marine hotel had been interrupted by a bomb dropping into his egg-cup, their wrath and horror knew no bounds. They declared that this would put a new spirit into the army, and had no suspicion that the soldiers in the trenches roared with laughter over it for days, and told each other that it would do the blighters at home good to have a taste of what the army was up against. Sometimes the smallness of view was pathetic. A man would work at home regardless of the call 'to make the world safe for democracy.' His brother would be killed at the front. Immediately he would throw up his work and take up the war as a family blood feud against the Germans. Sometimes it was comic. A wounded man, entitled to his discharge, would return to the trenches with a grim determination to find the Hun who had wounded him and pay him out for it.

It is impossible to estimate what proportion of us, in khaki* or out of it, grasped the war and its political antecedents as a whole in the light of any philosophy of history or knowledge of what war is. I doubt whether it was as high as our proportion of higher mathematicians. But there can be no doubt that it was prodigiously outnumbered by the comparatively ignorant and childish. Remember that these people had to be stimulated to make the sacrifices demanded by the war, and that this could not be done by appeals to a knowledge which they did not possess, and a comprehension of which they were incapable. When the armistice at last set me free to tell the truth about the war at the following general election,* a soldier said to a candidate whom I was supporting 'If I had known all that in 1914, they would never have got me into khaki.' And that, of course, was precisely why it had been necessary to stuff him with a romance that any diplomatist would have laughed at. Thus the natural confusion of ignorance was increased by a deliberately propagated confusion of nursery bogey stories and melodramatic nonsense, which at last overreached itself and made it impossible to stop the war before we had not only achieved the triumph of vanquishing the German army and thereby overthrowing its militarist monarchy, but made the very serious mistake of ruining the centre of Europe, a thing that no sane European State could afford to do.

The Dumb Capables and the Noisy Incapables

Confronted with this picture of insensate delusion and folly, the critical reader will immediately counterplead that England all this time was conducting a war which involved the organization of several millions of fighting men and of the workers who were supplying them with provisions, munitions, and transport, and that this could not have been done by a mob of hysterical ranters. This is fortunately true. To pass from the newspaper offices and political platforms and club fenders and suburban drawing-rooms to the Army and the munition factories was to pass from Bedlam* to the busiest and sanest of workaday worlds. It was to rediscover England, and find solid ground for the faith of those who still believed in her. But a necessary condition of this efficiency was that those who were efficient should give all their time to their business and leave the rabble raving to its hearts' content. Indeed the raving was useful to the efficient, because, as it was always wide of the mark, it often distracted attention very conveniently from operations that would have been defeated or hindered by publicity. A precept which I endeavored vainly to popularize early in the war, 'If you have anything to do go and do it: if not, for heaven's sake get out of the way,' was only half carried out. Certainly the capable people went and did it; but the incapables would by no means get out of the way: they fussed and bawled and were only prevented from getting very seriously into the way by the blessed fact that they never knew where the way was. Thus whilst all the efficiency of England was silent and invisible, all its imbecility was deafening the heavens with its clamor and blotting out the sun with its dust. It was also unfortunately intimidating the Government by its blusterings into using the irresistible powers of the State to intimidate the sensible people, thus enabling a despicable minority of would-be lynchers to set up a reign of terror which could at any time have been broken by a single stern word from a responsible minister. But our ministers had not that sort of courage: neither Heartbreak House nor Horseback Hall had bred it, much less the suburbs. When matters at last came to the looting of shops by criminals under patriotic pretexts, it was the police force and not the Government that put its foot down. There was even one deplorable moment, during the submarine scare,* in which the Government yielded to a childish cry for the maltreatment of naval prisoners of war, and, to our great disgrace, was forced by the enemy to behave itself.* And yet behind all this public blundering and misconduct and futile mischief, the effective England was carrying on with the most formidable capacity and activity. The ostensible England was making the empire sick with its incontinences, its ignorances, its ferocities, its panics, and its endless and intolerable blarings of Allied national anthems in season and out. The esoteric England was proceeding irresistibly to the conquest of Europe.

The Practical Business Men

From the beginning the useless people set up a shriek for 'practical business men.' By this they meant men who had become rich by placing their personal interests before those of the country, and measuring the success of every activity by the pecuniary profit it brought to them and to those on whom they depended for their supplies of capital. The pitiable failure of some conspicuous samples from the first batch we tried of these poor devils helped to give the whole public side of the war an air of monstrous and hopeless farce. They proved not only that they were useless for public work, but that in a well-ordered nation they would never have been allowed to control private enterprise.

How the Fools Shouted the Wise Men Down

Thus, like a fertile country flooded with mud, England shewed no sign of her greatness in the days when she was putting forth all her strength to save herself from the worst consequences of her littleness. Most of the men of action, occupied to the last hour of their time with urgent practical work, had to leave to idler people, or to professional rhetoricians, the presentation of the war to the reason and imagination of the country and the world in speeches, poems, manifestos, picture posters, and newspaper articles. I have had the privilege of hearing some of our ablest commanders talking about their work; and I have shared the common lot of reading the accounts of that work given to the world by the newspapers. No two experiences could be more different. But in the end the talkers obtained a dangerous ascendancy over the rank and file of the men of action; for though the great men of action are always inveterate talkers and often very clever writers, and therefore cannot have their minds formed for them by others, the average man of action, like the average fighter with the bayonet, can give no account of himself in words even to himself, and is apt to pick up and accept what he reads about himself and other people in the papers, except when the writer is rash enough to commit himself on technical points. It was not uncommon during the war to hear a soldier, or a civilian engaged on war work, describing events within his own experience that reduced to utter absurdity the ravings and maunderings of his daily paper, and yet echo the opinions of that paper like a parrot. Thus, to escape from the prevailing confusion and folly, it was not enough to seek the company of the ordinary man of action: one had to get into contact with the master spirits. This was a privilege which only a handful of people could enjoy. For the unprivileged citizen there was no escape. To him the whole country seemed mad, futile, silly, incompetent, with no hope of victory except the hope that the enemy might be just as mad. Only by very resolute reflection and reasoning could he reassure himself that if there was nothing more solid beneath these appalling appearances the war could not possibly have gone on for a single day without a total breakdown of its organization.

The Mad Election

Happy were the fools and the thoughtless men of action in those days. The worst of it was that the fools were very strongly represented in parliament, as fools not only elect fools, but can persuade men of action to elect them too. The election that immediately followed the armistice was perhaps the maddest that has ever taken place. Soldiers who had done voluntary and heroic service in the field were defeated by persons who had apparently never run a risk or spent a farthing that they could avoid, and who even had in the course of the election to apologize publicly for bawling Pacifist or Pro-German at their opponent. Party leaders seek such followers, who can always be depended on to walk tamely into the lobby at the party whip's orders, provided the leader will make their seats safe for them by the process which was called, in derisive reference to the war rationing system, 'giving them the coupon.'* Other incidents were so grotesque that I cannot mention them without enabling the reader to identify the parties, which would not be fair, as they were no more to blame than thousands of others who must necessarily be nameless. The general result was patently absurd; and the electorate, disgusted at its own work, instantly recoiled to the opposite extreme, and cast out all the coupon candidates at the earliest bye-elections by equally silly majorities. But the mischief of the general election could not be undone; and the Government had not only to pretend to abuse its European victory as it had promised, but actually to do it by starving the enemies who had thrown down their arms.* It had, in short, won the election by pledging itself to be thriftlessly wicked, cruel, and vindictive; and it did not find it as easy to escape from this pledge as it had from nobler ones. The end, as I write, is not yet; but it is clear that this thoughtless savagery will recoil on the heads of the Allies so severely that we shall be forced by the sternest necessity to take up our share of healing the Europe we have wounded almost to death instead of attempting to complete her destruction.

The Yahoo and the Angry Ape*

Contemplating this picture of a state of mankind so recent that no denial of its truth is possible, one understands Shakespear comparing Man to an angry ape, Swift describing him as a Yahoo rebuked by the superior virtue of the horse, and Wellington* declaring that the British can behave themselves neither in victory nor defeat. Yet none of the three had seen war as we have seen it. Shakespear blamed great men, saying that 'Could great men thunder as Jove himself does Jove would ne'er be quiet; for every pelting petty officer would use his heaven for thunder: nothing but thunder.'* What would Shakespear have said if he had seen something far more destructive than thunder in the hand of every village laborer, and found on the Messines Ridge* the craters of the nineteen volcanoes that were let loose there at the touch of a finger that might have been a child's finger without the result being a whit less ruinous? Shakespear may have seen a Stratford* cottage struck by one of Jove's thunderbolts, and have helped to extinguish the lighted thatch and clear away the bits of the broken chimney. What would he have said if he had seen Ypres as it is now, or returned to Stratford, as French peasants are returning to their homes today, to find the old familiar signpost inscribed 'To Stratford, 1 mile,' and at the end of the mile nothing but some holes in the ground and a fragment of a broken churn here and there? Would not the spectacle of the angry ape endowed with powers of destruction that Jove never pretended to, have beggared even his command of words?

And yet, what is there to say except that war puts a strain on human nature that breaks down the better half of it, and makes the worse half a diabolical virtue? Better for us if it broke it down altogether; for then the warlike way out of our difficulties would be barred to us, and we should take greater care not to get into them. In truth, it is, as Byron said, 'not difficult to die,'* and enormously difficult to live: that explains why, at bottom, peace is not only better than war, but infinitely more arduous. Did any hero of the war face the glorious risk of death more bravely than the traitor Bolo* faced the ignominious certainty of it? Bolo taught us all how to die: can we say that he taught us all how to live? Hardly a week passes now without some soldier who braved death in the field so recklessly that he was decorated or specially commended for it, being haled before our magistrates for having failed to resist the paltriest temptations of peace, with no better excuse than the old one that 'a man must live.'* Strange that one who, sooner than do honest work, will sell his honor for a bottle of wine, a visit to the theatre, and an hour with a strange woman, all obtained by passing a worthless cheque, could yet stake his life on the most desperate chances of the battle-field! Does it not seem as if, after all, the glory of death were cheaper than the glory of life? If it is not easier to attain, why do so many more men attain it? At all events it is clear that the kingdom of the Prince of Peace* has not yet become the kingdom of this world. His attempts at invasion have been resisted far more fiercely than the Kaiser's. Successful as that resistance has been, it has piled up a sort of National Debt that is not the less oppressive because we have no figures for it and do not intend to pay it. A blockade that cuts off 'the grace of our Lord'* is in the long run less bearable than the blockades which merely cut off raw materials; and against that blockade our Armada* is impotent. In the blockader's house, he has assured us, there are many mansions; but I am afraid they do not include either Heartbreak House or Horseback Hall.

*Plague on Both your Houses!**

Meanwhile the Bolshevist* picks and petards are at work on the foundations of both buildings; and though the Bolshevists may be buried in the ruins, their deaths will not save the edifices. Unfortunately they can be built again. Like Doubting Castle, they have been demolished many times by successive Greathearts, and rebuilt by Simple, Sloth, and Presumption, by Feeble Mind and Much Afraid, and by all the jurymen of Vanity Fair.* Another generation of 'secondary education' at our ancient public schools* and the cheaper institutions that ape them will be quite sufficient to keep the two going until the next war.

For the instruction of that generation I leave these pages as a record of what civilian life was during the war: a matter on which history is usually silent. Fortunately it was a very short war. It is true that the people who thought it could not last more than six months were very signally refuted by the event. As Sir Douglas Haig* has pointed out, its Waterloos* lasted months instead of hours. But there would have been nothing surprising in its lasting thirty years. If it had not been for the fact that the blockade achieved the amazing feat of starving out Europe, which it could not possibly have done had Europe been properly organized for war, or even for peace, the war would have lasted until the belligerents were so tired of it that they could no longer be compelled to compel themselves to go on with it. Considering its magnitude, the war of 1914–18 will certainly be classed as the shortest in history. The end came so suddenly that the combatants literally stumbled over it; and yet it came a full year later than it should have come if the belligerents had not been far too afraid of one another to face the situation sensibly. Germany, having failed to provide for the war she began, failed again to surrender before she was dangerously exhausted. Her opponents, equally improvident, went as much too close to bankruptcy as Germany to starvation. It was a bluff at which both were bluffed. And, with the usual irony of war, it remains doubtful whether Germany and Russia, the defeated, will not be the gainers; for the victors are already busy fastening on themselves the chains they have struck from the limbs of the vanquished.

How the Theatre Fared

Let us now contract our view rather violently from the European theatre of war to the theatre in which the fights are sham fights, and the slain, rising the moment the curtain has fallen, go comfortably home to supper after washing off their rosepink wounds. It is nearly twenty years since I was last obliged to introduce a play in the form of a book for lack of an opportunity of presenting it in its proper mode by a performance in a theatre. The war has thrown me back on this expedient. Heartbreak House has not yet reached the stage.* I have withheld it because the war has completely upset the economic conditions which formerly enabled serious drama to pay its way in London. The change is not in the theatres nor in the management of them, nor in the authors and actors, but in the audiences. For four years the London theatres were crowded every night with thousands of soldiers on leave from the front. These soldiers were not seasoned London playgoers. A childish experience of my own gave me a clue to their condition. When I was a small boy I was taken to the opera. I did not then know what an opera was, though I could whistle a good deal of opera music. I had seen in my mother's album photographs of all the great opera singers, mostly in evening dress. In the theatre I found myself before a gilded balcony filled with persons in evening dress whom I took to be the opera singers. I picked out one massive dark lady as Alboni,* and wondered how soon she would stand up and sing. I was puzzled by the fact that I was made to sit with my back to the singers instead of facing them. When the curtain went up, my astonishment and delight were unbounded.

The Soldier at the Theatre Front

In 1915 I saw in the theatres men in khaki in just the same predicament. To everyone who had my clue to their state of mind it was evident that they had never been in a theatre before and did not know what it was. At one of our great variety theatres I sat beside a young officer, not at all a rough specimen, who, even when the curtain rose and enlightened him as to the place where he had to look for his entertainment, found the dramatic part of it utterly incomprehensible. He did not know how to play his part of the game. He could understand the people on the stage singing and dancing and performing gymnastic feats. He not only understood but intensely enjoyed an artist who imitated cocks crowing and pigs squeaking. But the people who pretended that they were somebody else, and that the painted picture behind them was real, bewildered him. In his presence I realized how very sophisticated the natural man has to become before the conventions of the theatre can be easily acceptable, or the purpose of the drama obvious to him.

Well, from the moment when the routine of leave for our soldiers was established, such novices, accompanied by damsels (called flappers*) often as innocent as themselves, crowded the theatres to the doors. It was hardly possible at first to find stuff crude enough to nurse them on. The best music-hall comedians ransacked their memories for the oldest quips and the most childish antics to avoid carrying the military spectators out of their depth. I believe that this was a mistake as far as the novices were concerned. Shakespear, or the dramatized histories of George Barnwell, Maria Martin, or the Demon Barber of Fleet Street,* would probably have been quite popular with them. But the novices were only a minority after all. The cultivated soldier, who in time of peace would look at nothing theatrical except the most advanced post-Ibsen plays in the most artistic settings, found himself, to his own astonishment, thirsting for silly jokes, dances, and brainlessly sensuous exhibitions of pretty girls. The author of some of the most grimly serious plays of our time told me that after enduring the trenches for months without a glimpse of the female of his species, it gave him an entirely innocent but delightful pleasure merely to see a flapper. The reaction from the battle-field produced a condition of hyperaesthesia in which all the theatrical values were altered. Trivial things gained intensity and stale things novelty. The actor, instead of having to coax his audiences out of the boredom which had driven them to the theatre in an ill humor to seek some sort of distraction, had only to exploit the bliss of smiling men who were no longer under fire and under military discipline, but actually clean and comfortable and in a mood to be pleased with anything and everything that a bevy of pretty girls and a funny man, or even a bevy of girls pretending to be pretty and a man pretending to be funny, could do for them.

Then could be seen every night in the theatres old-fashioned farcical comedies, in which a bedroom, with four doors on each side and a practicable window in the middle, was understood to resemble exactly the bedroom in the flats beneath and above, all three inhabited by couples consumed with jealousy. When these people came home drunk at night; mistook their neighbor's flats for their own; and in due course got into the wrong beds, it was not only the novices who found the resulting complications and scandals exquisitely ingenious and amusing, nor their equally verdant flappers who could not help squealing in a manner that astonished the oldest performers when the gentleman who had just come in drunk through the window pretended to undress, and allowed glimpses of his naked person to be descried from time to time. Men who had just read the news that Charles Wyndham* was dying, and were thereby sadly reminded of Pink Dominos* and the torrent of farcical comedies that followed it in his heyday until every trick of that trade had become so stale that the laughter they provoked turned to loathing: these veterans also, when they returned from the field, were as much pleased by what they knew to be stale and foolish as the novices by what they thought fresh and clever.

Commerce in the Theatre

Wellington said that an army moves on its belly.* So does a London theatre. Before a man acts he must eat. Before he performs plays he must pay rent. In London we have no theatres for the welfare of the people: they are all for the sole purpose of producing the utmost obtainable rent for the proprietor. If the twin flats and twin beds produce a guinea more than Shakespear, out goes Shakespear, and in come the twin flats and the twin beds. If the brainless bevy of pretty girls and the funny man outbid Mozart,* out goes Mozart.

Unser* Shakespear

Before the war an effort was made to remedy this by establishing a national theatre in celebration of the tercentenary of the death of Shakespear.* A committee was formed; and all sorts of illustrious and influential persons lent their names to a grand appeal to our national culture. My play, The Dark Lady of The Sonnets,* was one of the incidents of that appeal. After some years of effort the result was a single handsome subscription from a German gentleman.* Like the celebrated swearer in the anecdote when the cart containing all his household goods lost its tailboard at the top of the hill and let its contents roll in ruin to the bottom, I can only say, 'I cannot do justice to this situation,' and let it pass without another word.

The Higher Drama put out of Action

The effect of the war on the London theatres may now be imagined. The beds and the bevies drove every higher form of art out of it. Rents went up to an unprecedented figure. At the same time prices doubled everywhere except at the theatre pay-boxes, and raised the expenses of management to such a degree that unless the houses were quite full every night, profit was impossible. Even bare solvency could not be attained without a very wide popularity. Now what had made serious drama possible to a limited extent before the war was that a play could pay its way even if the theatre were only half full until Saturday and three-quarters full then. A manager who was an enthusiast and a desperately hard worker, with an occasional grant-in-aid from an artistically disposed millionaire, and a due proportion of those rare and happy accidents by which plays of the higher sort turn out to be potboilers as well, could hold out for some years, by which time a relay might arrive in the person of another enthusiast. Thus and not otherwise occurred that remarkable revival of the British drama at the beginning of the century which made my own career as a playwright possible in England. In America I had already established myself, not as part of the ordinary theatre system, but in association with the exceptional genius of Richard Mansfield.* In Germany and Austria I had no difficulty: the system of publicly aided theatres there, Court and Municipal, kept drama of the kind I dealt in alive; so that I was indebted to the Emperor of Austria for magnificent productions of my works at a time when the sole official attention paid me by the British Court was the announcement to the English-speaking world that certain plays of mine were unfit for public performance, a substantial set-off against this being that the British Court, in the course of its private playgoing, paid no regard to the bad character given me by the chief officer of its household.*

Howbeit, the fact that my plays effected a lodgment on the London stage, and were presently followed by the plays of Granville Barker,

Gilbert Murray, John Masefield, St John Hankin, Laurence Housman, Arnold Bennett, John Galsworthy, John Drinkwater,* and others which would in the XIX century have stood rather less chance of production at a London theatre than the Dialogues of Plato, not to mention revivals of the ancient Athenian drama, and a restoration to the stage of Shakespear's plays as he wrote them,* was made economically possible solely by a supply of theatres which could hold nearly twice as much money as it cost to rent and maintain them. In such theatres work appealing to a relatively small class of cultivated persons, and therefore attracting only from half to three-quarters as many spectators as the more popular pastimes, could nevertheless keep going in the hands of young adventurers who were doing it for its own sake, and had not yet been forced by advancing age and responsibilities to consider the commercial value of their time and energy too closely. The war struck this foundation away in the manner I have just described. The expenses of running the cheapest West End theatres rose to a sum which exceeded by twenty-five per cent the utmost that the higher drama can, as an ascertained matter of fact, be depended on to draw. Thus the higher drama, which has never really been a commercially sound speculation, now became an impossible one. Accordingly, attempts are being made to provide a refuge for it in suburban theatres in London and repertory theatres in the provinces. But at the moment when the army has at last disgorged the survivors of the gallant band of dramatic pioneers whom it swallowed, they find that the economic conditions which formerly made their work no worse than precarious now put it out of the question altogether, as far as the West End of London is concerned.

Church and Theatre

I do not suppose many people care particularly. We are not brought up to care; and a sense of the national importance of the theatre is not born in mankind: the natural man, like so many of the soldiers at the beginning of the war, does not know what a theatre is. But please note that all these soldiers who did not know what a theatre was, knew what a church was. And they had been taught to respect churches. Nobody had ever warned them against a church as a place where frivolous women paraded in their best clothes; where stories of improper females like Potiphar's wife,* and erotic poetry like the Song of Songs,* were read aloud; where the sensuous and sentimental music of Schubert, Mendelssohn, Gounod, and Brahms* was more popular than severe music by greater composers; where the prettiest sort of pretty pictures of pretty saints assailed the imagination and senses through stained-glass windows; and where sculpture and architecture came to the help of painting. Nobody ever reminded them that these things had sometimes produced such developments of erotic idolatry that men who were not only enthusiastic amateurs of literature, painting, and music, but famous practitioners of them, had actually exulted when mobs and even regular troops under express command had mutilated church statues, smashed church windows, wrecked church organs, and torn up the sheets from which the church music was read and sung. When they saw broken statues in churches, they were told that this was the work of wicked godless rioters, instead of, as it was, the work partly of zealots bent on driving the world, the flesh, and the devil out of the temple, and partly of insurgent men who had become intolerably poor because the temple had become a den of thieves. But all the sins and perversions that were so carefully hidden from them in the history of the Church were laid on the shoulders of the Theatre: that stuffy, uncomfortable place of penance in which we suffer so much inconvenience on the slenderest chance of gaining a scrap of food for our starving souls. When the Germans bombed the Cathedral of Rheims* the world rang with the horror of the sacrilege. When they bombed the Little Theatre in the Adelphi,* and narrowly missed bombing two writers of plays who lived within a few yards of it, the fact was not even mentioned in the papers. In point of appeal to the senses no theatre ever built could touch the fane* at Rheims: no actress could rival its Virgin in beauty, nor any operatic tenor look otherwise than a fool beside its David. Its picture glass was glorious even to those who had seen the glass of Chartres.* It was wonderful in its very grotesques: who would look at the Blondin Donkey* after seeing its leviathans? In spite of the Adam-Adelphian decoration on which Miss Kingston* had lavished so much taste and care, the Little Theatre was in comparison with Rheims the gloomiest of little conventicles: indeed the cathedral must, from the Puritan point of view, have debauched a million voluptuaries for every one whom the Little Theatre had sent home thoughtful to a chaste bed after Mr Chesterton's Magic or Brieux's *Les Avariés.** Perhaps that is the real reason why the Church is lauded and the Theatre reviled. Whether or no, the fact remains that the lady to whose public spirit and sense of the national value of the theatre I owed the first regular public performance of a play of mine had to conceal her action as if it had been a crime, whereas if she had given the money to the Church she would have worn a halo for it. And I admit, as I have always done, that this state of things may have been a very sensible one. I have asked Londoners again and again why they pay half a guinea to go to a theatre when they can go to St Paul's or Westminster Abbey* for nothing. Their only possible reply is that they want to see something new and possibly something wicked; but the theatres mostly disappoint both hopes. If ever a revolution makes me Dictator, I shall establish a heavy charge for admission to our churches. But everyone who pays at the church door shall receive a ticket entitling him or her to free admission to one performance at any theatre he or she prefers. Thus shall the sensuous charms of the church service be made to subsidize the sterner virtue of the drama.

The Next Phase

The present situation will not last. Although the newspaper I read at breakfast this morning before writing these words contains a calculation that no less than twenty-three wars are at present being waged to confirm the peace, England is no longer in khaki; and a violent reaction is setting in against the crude theatrical fare of the four terrible years. Soon the rents of theatres will once more be fixed on the assumption that they cannot always be full, nor even on the average half full week in and week out. Prices will change. The higher drama will be at no greater disadvantage than it was before the war; and it may benefit, first, by the fact that many of us have been torn from the fools' paradise in which the theatre formerly traded, and thrust upon the sternest real-ities and necessities until we have lost both faith in and patience with the theatrical pretences that had no root either in reality or necessity; second, by the startling change made by the war in the distribution of income. It seems only the other day that a millionaire was a man with £50,000 a year. Today, when he has paid his income tax and super tax,* and insured his life for the amount of his death duties,* he is lucky if his net income is £10,000, though his nominal property remains the same. And this is the result of a Budget which is called 'a respite for the rich.' At the other end of the scale millions of persons have had regular incomes for the first time in their lives; and their men have been regu-larly clothed, fed, lodged, and taught to make up their minds that cer-tain things have to be done, also for the first time in their lives. Hundreds of thousands of women have been taken out of their domestic cages and tasted both discipline and independence. The thoughtless and snob-bish middle classes have been pulled up short by the very unpleasant experience of being ruined to an unprecedented extent. We have all had a tremendous jolt; and although the widespread notion that the shock of the war would automatically make a new heaven and a new earth, and that the dog would never go back to his vomit nor the sow to her wallowing in the mire, is already seen to be a delusion, yet we are far more conscious of our condition than we were, and far less disposed to submit to it. Revolution, lately only a sensational chapter in history or a demagogic claptrap, is now a possibility so imminent that hardly by trying to suppress it in other countries by arms and defamation, and calling the process anti-Bolshevism, can our Government stave it off at home.

Perhaps the most tragic figure of the day is the American President* who was once a historian. In those days it became his task to tell us how, after that great war in America which was more clearly than any other war of our time a war for an idea, the conquerors, confronted with a heroic task of reconstruction, turned recreant, and spent fifteen years in abusing their victory under cover of pretending to accomplish the task they were doing what they could to make impossible. Alas! Hegel was right when he said that we learn from history that men never learn anything from history.* With what anguish of mind the President sees that we, the new conquerors, forgetting everything we professed to fight for, are sitting down with watering mouths to a good square meal of ten years revenge upon and humiliation of our prostrate foe, can only be guessed by those who know, as he does, how hopeless is remonstrance, and how happy Lincoln* was in perishing from the earth before his inspired messages became scraps of paper. He knows well that from the Peace Conference will come, in spite of his utmost, no edict on which he will be able, like Lincoln, to invoke 'the considerate judgment of mankind, and the gracious favor of Almighty God.'* He led his people to destroy the militarism of Zabern;* and the army they rescued is busy in Cologne imprisoning every German who does not salute a British officer; whilst the Government at home, asked whether it approves, replies that it does not propose even to discontinue this Zabernism when the Peace is concluded, but in effect looks forward to making Germans salute British officers until the end of the world. That is what war makes of men and women. It will wear off; and the worst it threatens is already proving impracticable; but before the humble and contrite heart ceases to be despised, the President and I, being of the same age, will be dotards. In the meantime there is, for him, another history to write; for me, another comedy to stage. Perhaps, after all, that is what wars are for, and what historians and playwrights are for. If men will not learn until their lessons are written in blood, why, blood they must have, their own for preference.

The Ephemeral Thrones and the Eternal Theatre

To the theatre it will not matter. Whatever Bastilles* fall, the theatre will stand. Apostolic Hapsburg* has collapsed; All Highest Hohenzollern* languishes in Holland, threatened with trial on a capital charge of fighting for his country against England; Imperial Romanoff,* said to have perished miserably by a more summary method of murder, is perhaps alive or perhaps dead: nobody cares more than if he had been a peasant; the lord of Hellas* is level with his lackeys in republican Switzerland; Prime Ministers and Commanders-in-Chief have passed from a brief glory as Solons* and Caesars into failure and obscurity as closely on one another's heels as the descendants of Banquo;* but Euripides and Aristophanes,* Shakespear and Molière, Goethe and Ibsen remain fixed in their everlasting seats.

How War Muzzles the Dramatic Poet

As for myself, why, it may be asked, did I not write two plays about the war instead of two pamphlets* on it? The answer is significant. You cannot make war on war and on your neighbor at the same time. War cannot bear the terrible castigation of comedy, the ruthless light of laughter that glares on the stage. When men are heroically dying for their country, it is not the time to shew their lovers and wives and fathers and mothers how they are being sacrificed to the blunders of boobies, the cupidity of capitalists, the ambition of conquerors, the electioneering of demagogues, the Pharisaism* of patriots, the lusts and lies and rancors and bloodthirsts that love war because it opens their prison doors, and sets them in the thrones of power and popularity. For unless these things are mercilessly exposed they will hide under the mantle of the ideals on the stage just as they do in real life.

And though there may be better things to reveal, it may not, and indeed cannot, be militarily expedient to reveal them whilst the issue is still in the balance. Truth telling is not compatible with the defence of the realm. We are just now reading the revelations of our generals and admirals, unmuzzled at last by the armistice. During the war, General A, in his moving despatches from the field, told how General B had covered himself with deathless glory in such and such a battle. He now tells us that General B came within an ace of losing us the war by disobeying his orders on that occasion, and fighting instead of running away as he ought to have done. An excellent subject for comedy now that the war is over, no doubt; but if General A had let this out at the time, what would have been the effect on General B's soldiers? And had the stage made known what the Prime Minister and the Secretary of State for War who overruled General A thought of him, and what he thought of them, as now revealed in raging controversy, what would have been the effect on the nation? That is why comedy, though sorely tempted, had to be loyally silent; for the art of the dramatic poet knows no patriotism; recognizes no obligation but truth to natural history; cares not whether Germany or England perish; is ready to cry with Brynhild, 'Lass' uns verderben, lachend zu grunde geh'n'* sooner than deceive or be deceived; and thus becomes in time of war a greater military danger than poison, steel, or trinitrotoluene.* That is why I had to withhold Heartbreak House from the footlights during the war; for the Germans might on any night have turned the last act from play into earnest, and even then might not have waited for their cues.

June 1919

HEARTBREAK HOUSE

ACT I

The hilly country in the middle of the north edge of Sussex, looking very pleasant on a fine evening at the end of September, is seen through the windows of a room which has been built so as to resemble the after part of an old-fashioned high-pooped ship with a stern gallery;* for the windows are ship built with heavy timbering, and run right across the room as continuously as the stability of the wall allows. A row of lockers under the windows provides an unupholstered window-seat interrupted by twin glass doors, respectively halfway between the stern post and the sides. Another door strains the illusion a little by being apparently in the ship's port side,* and yet leading, not to the open sea, but to the entrance hall of the house. Between this door and the stern gallery are bookshelves. There are electric light switches beside the door leading to the hall and the glass doors in the stern gallery. Against the starboard wall is a carpenter's bench. The vice has a board in its jaws; and the floor is littered with shavings, overflowing from a waste-paper basket. A couple of planes and a centrebit are on the bench. In the same wall, between the bench and the windows, is a narrow doorway with a half door, above which a glimpse of the room beyond shews that it is a shelved pantry with bottles and kitchen crockery.*

On the starboard side, but close to the middle, is a plain oak drawing-table with drawing-board, T-square, straightedges, set squares, mathematical instruments, saucers of water color, a tumbler of discolored water, Indian ink,* pencils, and brushes on it. The drawing-board is set so that the draughtsman's chair has the window on its left hand. On the floor at the end of the table, on his right, is a ship's fire bucket.* On the port side of the room, near the bookshelves, is a sofa with its back to the windows. It is a sturdy mahogany* article, oddly upholstered in sailcloth, including the bolster, with a couple of blankets hanging over the back. Between the sofa and the drawing-table is a big wicker chair, with broad arms and a low sloping back, with its back to the light. A small but stout table of teak,* with a round top and gate legs, stands against the port wall between the door and the bookcase. It is the only article in the room that suggests (not at all convincingly) a woman's hand in the furnishing. The uncarpeted floor of narrow boards is caulked and holystoned* like a deck.*

The garden to which the glass doors lead dips to the south before the land-scape rises again to the hills. Emerging from the hollow is the cupola* of an observatory. Between the observatory and the house is a flagstaff on a little esplanade, with a hammock on the east side and a long garden seat on the west.

A young lady, gloved and hatted, with a dust coat on, is sitting in the window-seat with her body twisted to enable her to look out at the view. One hand props her chin: the other hangs down with a volume of the Temple Shakespear* in it, and her finger stuck in the page she has been reading.

A clock strikes six.

The young lady turns and looks at her watch. She rises with an air of one who waits and is almost at the end of her patience. She is a pretty girl, slender, fair, and intelligent looking, nicely but not expensively dressed, evidently not a smart idler.

With a sigh of weary resignation she comes to the draughtsman's chair; sits down; and begins to read Shakespear. Presently the book sinks to her lap; her eyes close; and she dozes into a slumber.

An elderly womanservant comes in from the hall with three unopened bottles of rum on a tray. She passes through and disappears in the pantry without noticing the young lady. She places the bottles on the shelf and fills her tray with empty bottles. As she returns with these, the young lady lets her book drop, awakening herself, and startling the womanservant so that she all but lets the tray fall.*

THE WOMANSERVANT. God bless us! [*The young lady picks up the book and places it on the table*]. Sorry to wake you, miss, I'm sure; but you are a stranger to me. What might you be waiting here for now?

THE YOUNG LADY. Waiting for somebody to shew some signs of knowing that I have been invited here.

THE WOMANSERVANT. Oh, youre invited, are you? And has nobody come? Dear! dear!

THE YOUNG LADY. A wild-looking old gentleman came and looked in at the window; and I heard him calling out 'Nurse: there is a young and attractive female waiting in the poop. Go and see what she wants.' Are you the nurse?

THE WOMANSERVANT. Yes, miss: I'm Nurse Guinness. That was old Captain Shotover, Mrs Hushabye's father. I heard him roaring;* but I thought it was for something else. I suppose it was Mrs Hushabye that invited you, ducky?*

THE YOUNG LADY. I understood her to do so. But really I think I'd better go.

NURSE GUINNESS. Oh, dont think of such a thing, miss. If Mrs Hushabye has forgotten all about it, it will be a pleasant surprise for her to see you, wont it?

THE YOUNG LADY. It has been a very unpleasant surprise to me to find that nobody expects me.

NURSE GUINNESS. Youll get used to it, miss: this house is full of surprises for them that dont know our ways.

CAPTAIN SHOTOVER [*looking in from the hall suddenly: an ancient but still hardy man with an immense white beard, in a reefer jacket* with a whistle hanging from his neck*] Nurse: there is a hold-all and a handbag on the front steps for everybody to fall over. Also a tennis racquet. Who the devil left them there?

THE YOUNG LADY. They are mine, I'm afraid.*

THE CAPTAIN [*advancing to the drawing-table*] Nurse: who is this misguided and unfortunate young lady?

NURSE GUINNESS. She says Miss Hessy invited her, sir.

THE CAPTAIN. And had she no friend, no parents, to warn her against my daughter's invitations? This is a pretty sort of house, by heavens! A young and attractive lady is invited here. Her luggage is left on the steps for hours; and she herself is deposited in the poop and abandoned, tired and starving. This is our hospitality. These are our manners. No room ready. No hot water. No welcoming hostess. Our visitor is to sleep in the toolshed, and to wash in the duckpond.

NURSE GUINNESS. Now it's all right, Captain: I'll get the lady some tea; and her room shall be ready before she has finished it. [*To the young lady*] Take off your hat, ducky; and make yourself at home [*she goes to the door leading to the hall*].

THE CAPTAIN [*as she passes him*] Ducky! Do you suppose, woman, that because this young lady has been insulted and neglected, you have the right to address her as you address my wretched children, whom you have brought up in ignorance of the commonest decencies of social intercourse?

NURSE GUINNESS. Never mind him, doty. [*Quite unconcerned, she goes out into the hall on her way to the kitchen*].

THE CAPTAIN. Madam: will you favor me with your name? [*He sits down in the big wicker chair*].

THE YOUNG LADY. My name is Ellie Dunn.*

THE CAPTAIN. Dunn! I had a boatswain whose name was Dunn. He was originally a pirate in China. He set up as a ship's chandler with stores which I have every reason to believe he stole from me. No doubt he became rich. Are you his daughter?

ELLIE [*indignant*] No: certainly not.* I am proud to be able to say that though my father has not been a successful man, nobody has ever had one word to say against him. I think my father is the best man I have ever known.

THE CAPTAIN. He must be greatly changed. Has he attained the seventh degree of concentration?*

ELLIE. I dont understand.

THE CAPTAIN. But how could he, with a daughter? I, madam, have two daughters. One of them is Hesione Hushabye,* who invited you here. I keep this house: she upsets it. I desire to attain the seventh degree of concentration: she invites visitors and leaves me to entertain them. [*Nurse Guinness returns with the tea-tray, which she places on the teak table*]. I have a second daughter who is, thank God, in a remote part of the Empire with her numskull of a husband.* As a child she thought the figure-head* of my ship, the Dauntless, the most beautiful thing on earth. He resembled it. He had the same expression: wooden yet enterprising. She married him, and will never set foot in this house again.

NURSE GUINNESS [*carrying the table, with the tea-things on it, to Ellie's side*] Indeed you never were more mistaken. She is in England this very moment. You have been told three times this week that she is coming home for a year for her health. And very glad you should be to see your own daughter again after all these years.

THE CAPTAIN. I am not glad. The natural term of the affection of the human animal for its offspring is six years. My daughter Ariadne was born when I was forty-six.* I am now eighty-eight.* If she comes, I am not at home. If she wants anything, let her take it. If she asks for me, let her be informed that I am extremely old, and have totally forgotten her.

NURSE GUINNESS. Thats no talk to offer to a young lady. Here, ducky, have some tea; and dont listen to him [*she pours out a cup of tea*].

THE CAPTAIN [*rising wrathfully*] Now before high heaven they have given this innocent child Indian tea: the stuff they tan their own leather insides with. [*He seizes the cup and the tea-pot and empties both into the leathern* bucket*].

ELLIE [*almost in tears*] Oh, please! I am so tired. I should have been glad of anything.

NURSE GUINNESS. Oh, what a thing to do! The poor lamb is ready to drop.

THE CAPTAIN. You shall have some of my tea. Do not touch that fly-blown cake: nobody eats it here except the dogs.* [*He disappears into the pantry*].

NURSE GUINNESS. Theres a man for you! They say he sold himself to the devil in Zanzibar* before he was a captain; and the older he grows the more I believe them.*

A WOMAN'S VOICE [*in the hall*] Is anyone at home? Hesione! Nurse! Papa! Do come, somebody; and take in my luggage.

Thumping heard, as of an umbrella, on the wainscot.

NURSE GUINNESS. My gracious! It's Miss Addie, Lady Utterword, Mrs Hushabye's sister: the one I told the Captain about. [*Calling*] Coming, Miss, coming.

She carries the table back to its place by the door, and is hurrying out when she is intercepted by Lady Utterword, who bursts in much flustered. Lady Utterword, a blonde, is very handsome, very well dressed, and so precipitate in speech and action that the first impression (erroneous) is one of comic silliness.

LADY UTTERWORD. Oh, is that you, Nurse? How are you? You dont look a day older. Is nobody at home? Where is Hesione? Doesnt she expect me? Where are the servants? Whose luggage is that on the steps? Where's Papa? Is everybody asleep? [*Seeing Ellie*] Oh! I beg your pardon. I suppose you are one of my nieces. [*Approaching her with outstretched arms*] Come and kiss your aunt, darling.

ELLIE. I'm only a visitor. It is my luggage on the steps.

NURSE GUINNESS. I'll go get you some fresh tea, ducky. [*She takes up the tray*].

ELLIE. But the old gentleman said he would make some himself.

NURSE GUINNESS. Bless you! he's forgotten what he went for already. His mind wanders from one thing to another.

LADY UTTERWORD. Papa, I suppose?

NURSE GUINNESS. Yes, Miss.

LADY UTTERWORD [*vehemently*] Dont be silly, nurse. Dont call me Miss.

NURSE GUINNESS [*placidly*] No, lovey [*she goes out with the tea-tray*].

LADY UTTERWORD [*sitting down with a flounce on the sofa*] I know what you must feel. Oh, this house, this house! I come back to it after twenty-three years; and it is just the same: the luggage lying on the steps, the servants spoilt and impossible, nobody at home to receive anybody, no regular meals, nobody ever hungry because they are always gnawing bread and butter or munching apples, and, what is worse, the same disorder in ideas, in talk, in feeling. When I was a child I was used to it: I had never known anything better, though I was unhappy, and longed all the time—oh, how I longed!—to be respectable, to be a lady, to live as others did, not to have to think of everything for myself. I married at nineteen to escape from it. My husband is Sir Hastings* Utterword, who has been governor of all the crown colonies in succession. I have always been the mistress of Government House.* I have been so happy: I had forgotten that people could live like this. I wanted to see my father, my sister, my nephews and nieces (one ought to, you know), and I was looking forward to it. And now the state of the house! the way I'm received! the casual impudence of that woman Guinness, our old nurse! really Hesione might at least have been here: *some* preparation might have been made for me. You must excuse my going on in this way; but I am really very much hurt and annoyed and disillusioned: and if I had realized it was to be like this, I wouldnt have come. I have a great mind to go away without another word [*she is on the point of weeping*].

ELLIE [*also very miserable*] Nobody has been here to receive me either. I thought I ought to go away too. But how can I, Lady Utterword? My luggage is on the steps; and the station fly has gone.

The Captain emerges from the pantry with a tray of Chinese lacquer* and a very fine tea-set on it. He rests it provisionally on the end of the table; snatches away the drawing-board, which he stands on the floor *against the table legs; and puts the tray in the space thus cleared. Ellie pours out a cup greedily.*

THE CAPTAIN. Your tea, young lady. What! another lady! I must fetch another cup [*he makes for the pantry*].

LADY UTTERWORD [*rising from the sofa, suffused with emotion*] Papa! Dont you know me? I'm your daughter.

THE CAPTAIN. Nonsense! my daughter's upstairs asleep. [*He vanishes through the half door*].

*Lady Utterword retires to the window to conceal her tears.**

ELLIE [*going to her with the cup*] Dont be so distressed. Have this cup of tea. He is very old and very strange: he has been just like that to me. I know how dreadful it must be: my own father is all the world to me. Oh, I'm sure he didnt mean it.

The Captain returns with another cup.

THE CAPTAIN. Now we are complete. [*He places it on the tray*].

LADY UTTERWORD [*hysterically*] Papa: you cant have forgotten me. I am Ariadne.* I'm little Paddy Patkins.* Wont you kiss me? [*She goes to him and throws her arms round his neck*].

THE CAPTAIN [*woodenly enduring her embrace*] How can you be Ariadne? You are a middle-aged woman: well preserved, madam, but no longer young.

LADY UTTERWORD. But think of all the years and years I have been away, Papa. I have had to grow old, like other people.

THE CAPTAIN [*disengaging himself*] You should grow out of kissing strange men: they may be striving to attain the seventh degree of concentration.

LADY UTTERWORD. But I'm your daughter. You havnt seen me for years.

THE CAPTAIN. So much the worse!* When our relatives are at home, we have to think of all their good points or it would be impossible to endure them. But when they are away, we console ourselves for their absence by dwelling on their vices. That is how I have come to think my absent daughter Ariadne a perfect fiend; so do not try to ingratiate yourself here by impersonating her* [*he walks firmly away to the other side of the room*].

LADY UTTERWORD. Ingratiating myself indeed! [*With dignity*] Very well, papa. [*She sits down at the drawing-table and pours out tea for herself*].

THE CAPTAIN. I am neglecting my social duties. You remember Dunn? Billy Dunn?

LADY UTTERWORD. Do you mean that villainous sailor who robbed you?

THE CAPTAIN [*introducing Ellie*] His daughter. [*He sits down on the sofa*].

ELLIE [*protesting*] No—*

Nurse Guinness returns with fresh tea.

THE CAPTAIN. Take that hogwash* away. Do you hear?

NURSE. Youve actually remembered about the tea! [*To Ellie*] O, miss, he didnt forget you after all! You *have* made an impression.

THE CAPTAIN [*gloomily*] Youth! beauty! novelty! They are badly wanted in this house. I am excessively old. Hesione is only moderately young. Her children are not youthful.

LADY UTTERWORD. How can children be expected to be youthful in this house? Almost before we could speak we were filled with notions that might have been all very well for pagan philosophers of fifty, but were certainly quite unfit for respectable people of any age.

NURSE. You were always for respectability, Miss Addy.

LADY UTTERWORD. Nurse: will you please* remember that I am Lady Utterword, and not Miss Addy, nor lovey, nor darling, nor doty? Do you hear?

NURSE. Yes, ducky: all right. I'll tell them all they must call you my lady. [*She takes her tray out with undisturbed placidity*].

LADY UTTERWORD. What comfort? what sense is there in having servants with no manners?

ELLIE [*rising and coming to the table to put down her empty cup*] Lady Utterword: do you think Mrs Hushabye really expects me?

LADY UTTERWORD. Oh, dont ask me.* You can see for yourself that Ive just arrived; her only sister, after twenty-three years absence! and it seems that *I* am not expected.

THE CAPTAIN. What does it matter whether the young lady is expected or not? She is welcome. There are beds: there is food. I'll find a room for her myself [*he makes for the door*].

ELLIE [*following him to stop him*] Oh please—[*he goes out*]. Lady Utterword: I dont know what to do. Your father persists in believing that my father is some sailor who robbed him.

LADY UTTERWORD. You had better pretend not to notice it. My father is a very clever man; but he always forgot things; and now that he is old, of course he is worse.* And I must warn you that it is sometimes very hard to feel quite sure that he really forgets.

Mrs Hushabye bursts into the room tempestuously, and embraces Ellie. She is a couple of years older than Lady Utterword, and even better looking. She has magnificent black hair, eyes like the fishpools of Heshbon, and a nobly modelled neck, short at the back and low between her shoulders in front. Unlike her sister she is uncorseted and dressed anyhow in a rich robe of black pile that shews off her white skin and statuesque contour.*

MRS HUSHABYE. Ellie, my darling, my pettikins [*kissing her*]: how long have you been here? Ive been at home all the time: I was putting flowers and things in your room; and when I just sat down for a moment to try how comfortable the armchair was I went off to sleep. Papa woke me and told me you were here. Fancy your finding no one, and being neglected and abandoned. [*Kissing her again*]. My poor love! [*She deposits Ellie on the sofa. Meanwhile Ariadne has left the table and come over to claim her share of attention*]. Oh! youve brought someone with you. Introduce me.

LADY UTTERWORD. Hesione: is it possible that *you* dont know me?

MRS HUSHABYE [*conventionally*] Of course I remember your face quite well. Where have we met?

LADY UTTERWORD. Didnt Papa tell you I was here? Oh! this is really too much. [*She throws herself sulkily into the big chair*].

MRS HUSHABYE. Papa!

LADY UTTERWORD. Yes: Papa. *Our* papa, you unfeeling wretch. [*Rising angrily*] I'll go straight to a hotel.

MRS HUSHABYE [*seizing her by the shoulders*] My goodness gracious goodness, you dont mean to say that youre Addy!

LADY UTTERWORD. I certainly am Addy; and I dont think I can be so changed that you would not have recognized me if you had any real affection for me. And papa didnt think me even worth mentioning!

MRS HUSHABYE. What a lark! Sit down [*she pushes her back into the chair instead of kissing her, and posts herself behind it*]. You *do* look a swell. Youre much handsomer than you used to be. Youve made the acquaintance of Ellie, of course. She is going to marry a perfect hog of a millionaire for the sake of her father, who is as poor as a church mouse;* and you must help me to stop her.

ELLIE. Oh *please*, Hesione.

MRS HUSHABYE. My pettikins, the man's coming here today with your father to begin persecuting you;* and everybody will see the state of the case in ten minutes; so whats the use of making a secret of it?

ELLIE. He is not a hog, Hesione. You dont know how wonderfully good he was to my father, and how deeply grateful I am to him.

MRS HUSHABYE [*to Lady Utterword*]* Her father is a very remarkable man, Addy. His name is Mazzini Dunn. Mazzini was a celebrity of some kind who knew Ellie's grandparents. They were both poets, like the Brownings;* and when her father came into the world Mazzini* said 'Another soldier born for freedom!' So they christened him Mazzini; and he has been fighting for freedom in his quiet way ever since. Thats why he is so poor.

ELLIE. I am proud of his poverty.

MRS HUSHABYE. Of course you are, pettikins. Why not leave him in it, and marry someone you love?

LADY UTTERWORD [*rising suddenly and explosively*] Hesione: are you going to kiss me or are you not?

MRS HUSHABYE. What do you want to be kissed for?

LADY UTTERWORD. I *dont* want to be kissed; but I do want you to behave properly and decently. We are sisters. We have been separated for twenty-three years. You *ought* to kiss me.

MRS HUSHABYE. Tomorrow morning, dear, before you make up. I hate the smell of powder.

LADY UTTERWORD. Oh! you unfeeling—[*she is interrupted by the return of the captain*].

THE CAPTAIN [*to Ellie*] Your room is ready. [*Ellie rises*]. The sheets were damp; but I have changed them [*he makes for the garden door on the port side*].

LADY UTTERWORD. Oh! What about my sheets?*

THE CAPTAIN [*halting at the door*] Take my advice: air them; or take them off and sleep in blankets.* You shall sleep in Ariadne's old room.

LADY UTTERWORD. Indeed I shall do nothing of the sort. That little hole! I am entitled to the best spare room.

THE CAPTAIN [*continuing unmoved*] She married a numskull. She told me she would marry anyone to get away from home.

LADY UTTERWORD. You are pretending not to know me on purpose. I will leave the house.

Mazzini Dunn enters from the hall. He is a little elderly man with bulging credulous eyes and earnest manners. He is dressed in a blue serge jacket suit with an unbuttoned mackintosh over it, and carries a soft black hat of clerical cut.*

ELLIE. At last! Captain Shotover: here is my father.

THE CAPTAIN. This! Nonsense! not a bit like him [*he goes away through the garden, shutting the door sharply behind him*].

LADY UTTERWORD. I will not be ignored and pretended to be somebody else. I will have it out with papa now, this instant. [*To Mazzini*] Excuse me. [*She follows the Captain out, making a hasty bow to Mazzini, who returns it*].

MRS HUSHABYE [*hospitably, shaking hands*] How good of you to come, Mr Dunn! You dont mind papa, do you? He is as mad as a hatter,* you know, but quite harmless, and extremely clever. You will have some delightful talks with him.

MAZZINI. I hope so. [*To Ellie*] So here you are, Ellie, dear. [*He draws her arm affectionately through his*]. I must thank you, Mrs Hushabye, for your kindness to my daughter. I'm afraid she would have had no holiday if you had not invited her.

MRS HUSHABYE. Not at all. Very nice of her to come and attract young people to the house for us.

MAZZINI [*smiling*] I'm afraid Ellie is not interested in young men, Mrs Hushabye. Her taste is on the graver, solider side.

MRS HUSHABYE [*with a sudden rather hard brightness in her manner*] Wont you take off your overcoat, Mr Dunn? You will find a cupboard for coats and hats and things in the corner of the hall.

MAZZINI [*hastily releasing Ellie*] Yes—thank you—I had better—[*he goes out*].

MRS HUSHABYE [*emphatically*] The old brute!

ELLIE. Who?

MRS HUSHABYE. Who! Him. He. It [*pointing after Mazzini*]. 'Graver, solider tastes,' indeed!

ELLIE [*aghast*] You dont mean that you were speaking like that of my father!

MRS HUSHABYE. I was. You know I was.

ELLIE [*with dignity*] I will leave your house at once. [*She turns to the door*].

MRS HUSHABYE. If you attempt it, I'll tell your father why.

ELLIE [*turning again*] Oh! How can you treat a visitor like this, Mrs Hushabye?

MRS HUSHABYE. I thought you were going to call me Hesione.

ELLIE. Certainly not now?

MRS HUSHABYE. Very well: I'll tell your father.

ELLIE [*distressed*] Oh!

MRS HUSHABYE. If you turn a hair—if you take his part against me and against your own heart for a moment, I'll give that born soldier of freedom a piece of my mind that will stand him on his selfish old head for a week.

ELLIE. Hesione! My father selfish! How little you know—

She is interrupted by Mazzini, who returns, excited and perspiring.

MAZZINI. Ellie: Mangan* has come: I thought youd like to know. Excuse me, Mrs Hushabye: the strange old gentleman—

MRS HUSHABYE. Papa. Quite so.

MAZZINI. Oh, I beg your pardon: of course: I was a little confused by his manner. He is making Mangan help him with something in the garden; and he wants me too—

A powerful whistle is heard.

THE CAPTAIN'S VOICE. Bosun ahoy!* [*the whistle is repeated*].

MAZZINI [*flustered*] Oh dear! I believe he is whistling for me. [*He hurries out*].

MRS HUSHABYE. Now *my* father is a wonderful man if you like.

ELLIE. Hesione: listen to me. You dont understand. My father and Mr Mangan were boys together. Mr Ma—

MRS HUSHABYE. I dont care what they were: we must sit down if you are going to begin as far back as that [*She snatches at Ellie's waist, and makes her sit down on the sofa beside her*]. Now, pettikins: tell me all about Mr Mangan. They call him Boss Mangan, dont they? He is a Napoleon of industry and disgustingly rich, isnt he? Why isnt your father rich?

ELLIE. My poor father should never have been in business. His parents were poets; and they gave him the noblest ideas; but they could not afford to give him a profession.

MRS HUSHABYE. Fancy your grandparents, with their eyes in fine frenzy rolling!* And so your poor father had to go into business. Hasnt he succeeded in it?

ELLIE. He always used to say he could succeed if he only had some capital. He fought his way along, to keep a roof over our heads and bring us up well; but it was always a struggle: always the same difficulty of not having capital enough. I dont know how to describe it to you.

MRS HUSHABYE. Poor Ellie! I know. Pulling the devil by the tail.*

ELLIE [*hurt*] Oh no. Not like that. It was at least dignified.

MRS HUSHABYE. That made it all the harder, didnt it? *I* shouldnt have pulled the devil by the tail with dignity. I should have pulled hard—[*between her teeth*] hard. Well? Go on.

ELLIE. At last it seemed that all our troubles were at an end. Mr Mangan did an extraordinarily noble thing out of pure friendship for my father and respect for his character. He asked him how much capital he wanted, and gave it to him. I dont mean that he lent it to him, or that he invested it in his business. He just simply made him a present of it. Wasnt that splendid of him?

MRS HUSHABYE. On condition that you married him?

ELLIE. Oh no, no, no. This was when I was a child. He had never even seen me: he never came to our house. It was absolutely disinterested. Pure generosity.

MRS HUSHABYE. Oh! I beg the gentleman's pardon. Well, what became of the money?

ELLIE. We all got new clothes and moved into another house. And I went to another school for two years.

MRS HUSHABYE. Only two years?

ELLIE. That was all; for at the end of two years my father was utterly ruined.

MRS HUSHABYE. How?

ELLIE. I dont know. I never could understand. But it was dreadful. When we were poor my father had never been in debt. But when he launched out into business on a large scale, he had to incur liabilities.* When the business went into liquidation he owed more money than Mr Mangan had given him.

MRS HUSHABYE. Bit off more than he could chew, I suppose.

ELLIE. I think you are a little unfeeling about it.

MRS HUSHABYE. My pettikins: you mustnt mind my way of talking. I was quite as sensitive and particular as you once; but I have picked up so much slang from the children that I am really hardly presentable. I suppose your father had no head for business, and made a mess of it.

ELLIE. Oh, that just shews how entirely you are mistaken about him. The business turned out a great success. It now pays forty-four per cent after deducting the excess profits tax.

MRS HUSHABYE. Then why arnt you rolling in money?

ELLIE. I dont know. It seems very unfair to me. You see, my father was made bankrupt. It nearly broke his heart, because he had persuaded several of his friends to put money into the business. He was sure it would succeed; and events proved that he was quite right. But they all lost their money. It was dreadful. I dont know what we should have done but for Mr Mangan.

MRS HUSHABYE. What! Did the Boss come to the rescue again, after all his money being thrown away?

ELLIE. He did indeed, and never uttered a reproach to my father. He bought what was left of the business—the buildings and the machinery and things—from the official trustee for enough money to enable my father to pay six and eightpence in the pound and get his discharge. Everyone pitied papa so much, and saw so plainly that he was an honorable man, that they let him off at six-and-eightpence instead of ten shillings. Then Mr Mangan started a company to take up the business, and made my father a manager in it to save us from starvation; for I wasnt earning anything then.

MRS HUSHABYE. Quite a romance. And when did the Boss develop the tender passion?

ELLIE. Oh, that was years after, quite lately. He took the chair one night at a sort of people's concert. I was singing there. As an amateur, you know: half a guinea for expenses and three songs with three encores. He was so pleased with my singing that he asked might he walk home with me. I never saw anyone so taken aback as he was when I took him home and introduced him to my father: his own manager. It was then that my father told me how nobly he had behaved. Of course it was considered a great chance for me, as he is so rich. And—and—we drifted into a sort of understanding— I suppose I should call it an engagement—[*she is distressed and cannot go on*].

MRS HUSHABYE [*rising and marching about*] You may have drifted into it; but you will bounce out of it, my pettikins, if I am to have anything to do with it.

ELLIE [*hopelessly*] No: it's no use. I am bound in honor and gratitude. I will go through with it.

MRS HUSHABYE [*behind the sofa, scolding down at her*] You know, of course, that it's not honorable or grateful to marry a man you dont love. Do you love this Mangan man?

ELLIE. Yes. At least—

MRS HUSHABYE. I dont want to know about 'the least': I want to know the worst. Girls of your age fall in love with all sorts of impossible people, especially old people.

ELLIE. I like Mr Mangan very much; and I shall always be—

MRS HUSHABYE [*impatiently completing the sentence and prancing away intolerantly to starboard*]—grateful to him for his kindness to dear father.* I know. Anybody else?

ELLIE. What do you mean?

MRS HUSHABYE. Anybody else? Are you in love with anybody else?

ELLIE. Of course not.

MRS HUSHABYE. Humph! [*The book on the drawing-table catches her eye. She picks it up, and evidently finds the title very unexpected. She looks at Ellie, and asks, quaintly*]. Quite sure youre not in love with an actor?

ELLIE. No, no. Why? What put such a thing into your head?

MRS HUSHABYE. This is yours, isnt it? Why else should you be reading Othello?*

ELLIE. My father taught me to love Shakespear.

MRS HUSHABYE [*flinging the book down on the table*] Really! your father does seem to be about the limit.

ELLIE [*naïvely*] Do you never read Shakespear, Hesione? That seems to me so extraordinary. I like Othello.

MRS HUSHABYE. Do you indeed? He was jealous, wasnt he?

ELLIE. Oh, not that. I think all the part about jealousy is horrible. But dont you think it must have been a wonderful experience for Desdemona, brought up so quietly at home, to meet a man who had been out in the world doing all sorts of brave things and having terrible adventures, and yet finding something in her that made him love to sit and talk with her and tell her about them?

MRS HUSHABYE. Thats your idea of romance, is it?

ELLIE. Not romance, exactly. It might really happen.

Ellie's eyes shew that she is not arguing, but in a daydream. Mrs Hushabye, watching her inquisitively, goes deliberately back to the sofa and resumes her seat beside her.

MRS HUSHABYE. Ellie darling: have you noticed that some of those stories that Othello told Desdemona couldnt have happened?*

ELLIE. Oh no. Shakespear thought they could have happened.

MRS HUSHABYE. Hm! Desdemona thought they could have happened. But they didnt.

ELLIE. Why do you look so enigmatic about it? You are such a sphinx: I never know what you mean.

MRS HUSHABYE. Desdemona would have found him out if she had lived, you know. I wonder was that why he strangled her!

ELLIE. Othello was not telling lies.

MRS HUSHABYE. How do you know?

ELLIE. Shakespear would have said if he was. Hesione: there are men who have done wonderful things: men like Othello, only, of course, white, and very handsome, and—

MRS HUSHABYE. Ah! Now we're coming to it. Tell me all about him. I knew there must be somebody, or youd never have been so miserable about Mangan: youd have thought it quite a lark to marry him.

ELLIE [*blushing vividly*] Hesione: you are dreadful. But I dont want to make a secret of it, though of course I dont tell everybody. Besides, I dont know him.

MRS HUSHABYE. Dont know him! What does that mean?

ELLIE. Well, of course I know him to speak to.

MRS HUSHABYE. But you want to know him ever so much more intimately, eh?

ELLIE. No no: I know him quite—almost intimately.

MRS HUSHABYE. You dont know him; and you know him almost intimately. How lucid!

ELLIE. I mean that he does not call on us. I—I got into conversation with him by chance at a concert.

MRS HUSHABYE. You seem to have rather a gay time at your concerts, Ellie.

ELLIE. Not at all: we talk to everyone in the green-room* waiting for our turns. I thought he was one of the artists: he looked so splendid.

But he was only one of the committee. I happened to tell him that I was copying a picture at the National Gallery.* I make a little money that way. I cant paint much; but as it's always the same picture I can do it pretty quickly and get two or three pounds for it. It happened that he came to the National Gallery one day.

MRS HUSHABYE. One student's day. Paid sixpence to stumble about through a crowd of easels, when he might have come in next day for nothing and found the floor clear! Quite by accident?

ELLIE [*triumphantly*] No. On purpose. He liked talking to me. He knows lots of the most splendid people. Fashionable women who are all in love with him. But he ran away from them to see me at the National Gallery and persuade me to come with him for a drive round Richmond Park* in a taxi.

MRS HUSHABYE. My pettikins, you have been going it.* It's wonderful what you good girls can do without anyone saying a word.

ELLIE. I am not in society, Hesione. If I didnt make acquaintances in that way I shouldnt have any at all.

MRS HUSHABYE. Well, no harm if you know how to take care of yourself. May I ask his name?

ELLIE [*slowly and musically*] Marcus Darnley.*

MRS HUSHABYE [*echoing the music*] Marcus Darnley! What a splendid name!

ELLIE. Oh, I'm so glad you think so. I think so too; but I was afraid it was only a silly fancy of my own.

MRS HUSHABYE. Hm! Is he one of the Aberdeen Darnleys?

ELLIE. Nobody knows. Just fancy! He was found in an antique chest—*

MRS HUSHABYE. A what?

ELLIE. An antique chest, one summer morning in a rose garden, after a night of the most terrible thunderstorm.

MRS HUSHABYE. What on earth was he doing in the chest? Did he get into it because he was afraid of the lightning?

ELLIE. Oh no, no: he was a baby. The name Marcus Darnley was embroidered on his babyclothes. And five hundred pounds in gold.

MRS HUSHABYE [*looking hard at her*] Ellie!

ELLIE. The garden of the Viscount—

MRS HUSHABYE. —de Rougemont?*

ELLIE [*innocently*] No: de Larochejaquelin.* A French family. A vicomte. His life has been one long romance. A tiger—

MRS HUSHABYE. Slain by his own hand?

ELLIE. Oh no: nothing vulgar like that. He saved the life of the tiger from a hunting party: one of King Edward's hunting parties in India.* The King was furious: that was why he never had his military services properly recognized. But he doesnt care. He is a Socialist and despises rank, and has been in three revolutions fighting on the barricades.

MRS HUSHABYE. How can you sit there telling me such lies? You, Ellie, of all people! And I thought you were a perfectly simple, straightforward, good girl.

ELLIE [*rising, dignified but very angry*] Do you mean to say you dont believe me?

MRS HUSHABYE. Of course I dont believe you. Youre inventing every word of it. Do you take me for a fool?

Ellie stares at her. Her candor is so obvious that Mrs Hushabye is puzzled.

ELLIE. Goodbye, Hesione. I'm very sorry. I see now that it sounds very improbable as I tell it. But I cant stay if you think that way about me.

MRS HUSHABYE [*catching her dress*] You shant go. I couldnt be so mistaken: I know too well what liars are like. Somebody has really told you all this.

ELLIE [*flushing*] Hesione: dont say that you dont believe *him*. I couldnt bear that.

MRS HUSHABYE [*soothing her*] Of course I believe him, dearest. But you should have broken it to me by degrees. [*Drawing her back to her seat*] Now tell me all about him. Are you in love with him?

ELLIE. Oh no. I'm not so foolish. I dont fall in love with people. I'm not so silly as you think.

MRS HUSHABYE. I see. Only something to think about—to give some interest and pleasure to life.

ELLIE. Just so. Thats all, really.

MRS HUSHABYE. It makes the hours go fast, doesnt it?* No tedious waiting to go to sleep at nights and wondering whether you will have a bad night. How delightful it makes waking up in the morning! How much better than the happiest dream! All life transfigured! No more wishing one had an interesting book to read, because life is so much happier than any book! No desire but to be alone and not to have to talk to anyone: to be alone and just think about it.

ELLIE [*embracing her*] Hesione: you are a witch. How do you know? Oh, you are the most sympathetic woman in the world.

MRS HUSHABYE [*caressing her*] Pettikins, my pettikins: how I envy you! and how I pity you!

ELLIE. Pity me! Oh, why?

A very handsome man of fifty, with mousquetaire moustaches, wearing a rather dandified* curly brimmed hat, and carrying an elaborate walking-stick, comes into the room from the hall, and stops short at sight of the women on the sofa.*

ELLIE [*seeing him and rising in glad surprise*] Oh! Hesione: this is Mr Marcus Darnley.

MRS HUSHABYE [*rising*] What a lark! He is my husband.

ELLIE. But how——[*she stops suddenly; then turns pale and sways*].

MRS HUSHABYE [*catching her and sitting down with her on the sofa*] Steady, my pettikins.

THE MAN [*with a mixture of confusion and effrontery, depositing his hat and stick on the teak table*] My real name, Miss Dunn, is Hector* Hushabye. I leave you to judge whether that is a name any sensitive man would care to confess to. I never use it when I can possibly help it. I have been away for nearly a month; and I had no idea you knew my wife, or that you were coming here. I am none the less delighted to find you in our little house.

ELLIE [*in great distress*] I dont know what to do. Please, may I speak to papa? Do leave me. I cant bear it.

MRS HUSHABYE. Be off, Hector.

HECTOR. I——

MRS HUSHABYE. Quick, quick. Get out.

HECTOR. If you think it better—[*he goes out, taking his hat with him but leaving the stick on the table*].

MRS HUSHABYE [*laying Ellie down at the end of the sofa*] Now, pettikins, he is gone. Theres nobody but me. You can let yourself go. Dont try to control yourself. Have a good cry.

ELLIE [*raising her head*] Damn!

MRS HUSHABYE. Splendid! Oh, what a relief! I thought you were going to be broken-hearted. Never mind me. Damn him again.

ELLIE. I am not damning him: I am damning myself for being such a fool. [*Rising*] How could I let myself be taken in so? [*She begins prowling to and fro, her bloom gone, looking curiously older and harder*].

MRS HUSHABYE [*cheerfully*] Why not, pettikins? Very few young women can resist Hector. I couldnt when I was your age. He is really rather splendid, you know.

ELLIE [*turning on her*] Splendid! Yes: splendid *looking*, of course. But how can you love a liar?

MRS HUSHABYE. I dont know. But you can, fortunately. Otherwise there wouldnt be much love in the world.

ELLIE. But to lie like that! To be a boaster! a coward!

MRS HUSHABYE [*rising in alarm*] Pettikins: none of that, if you please. If you hint the slightest doubt of Hector's courage, he will go straight off and do the most horribly dangerous things to convince himself that he isnt a coward. He has a dreadful trick of getting out of one third-floor window and coming in at another, just to test his nerve. He has a whole drawerful of Albert Medals for saving people's lives.*

ELLIE. He never told me that.

MRS HUSHABYE. He never boasts of anything he really did: he cant bear it; and it makes him shy if anyone else does. All his stories are made-up stories.

ELLIE [*coming to her*] Do you mean that he is really brave, and really has adventures, and yet tells lies about things that he never did and that never happened?

MRS HUSHABYE. Yes, pettikins, I do. People dont have their virtues and vices in sets: they have them anyhow: all mixed.

ELLIE [*staring at her thoughtfully*] Theres something odd about this house, Hesione, and even about you. I dont know why I'm talking to you so calmly. I have a horrible fear that my heart is broken, but that heartbreak is not like what I thought it must be.

MRS HUSHABYE [*fondling her*] It's only life educating you, pettikins. How do you feel about Boss Mangan now?

ELLIE [*disengaging herself with an expression of distaste*] Oh, how can you remind me of him, Hesione?

MRS HUSHABYE. Sorry, dear. I think I hear Hector coming back. You dont mind now, do you, dear?

ELLIE. Not in the least. I am quite cured.

Mazzini Dunn and Hector come in from the hall.

HECTOR [*as he opens the door and allows Mazzini to pass in*] One second more, and she would have been a dead woman!

MAZZINI. Dear! dear! what an escape! Ellie, my love: Mr Hushabye has just been telling me the most extraordinary—

ELLIE. Yes: Ive heard it [*She crosses to the other side of the room*].

HECTOR [*following her*] Not this one: I'll tell it to you after dinner. I think youll like it. The truth is, I made it up for you, and was looking forward to the pleasure of telling it to you. But in a moment of impatience at being turned out of the room, I threw it away on your father.

ELLIE [*turning at bay with her back to the carpenter's bench, scornfully self-possessed*] It was not thrown away. He believes it. I should not have believed it.*

MAZZINI [*benevolently*] Ellie is very naughty, Mr Hushabye. Of course she does not really think that. [*He goes to the bookshelves, and inspects the titles of the volumes*].

Boss Mangan comes in from the hall, followed by the Captain. Mangan, carefully frock-coated as for church or for a directors' meeting, is about fiftyfive, with a careworn, mistrustful expression, standing a little on an entirely imaginary dignity, with a dull complexion, straight, lustreless hair, and features so entirely commonplace that it is impossible to describe them.

CAPTAIN SHOTOVER [*to Mrs Hushabye, introducing the newcomer*] Says his name is Mangan. Not ablebodied.

MRS HUSHABYE [*graciously*] How do you do, Mr Mangan?

MANGAN [*shaking hands*] Very pleased.

CAPTAIN SHOTOVER. Dunn's lost his muscle, but recovered his nerve. Men seldom do after three attacks of delirium tremens* [*he goes into the pantry*].

MRS HUSHABYE. I congratulate you, Mr Dunn.*

MAZZINI [*dazed*] I am a lifelong teetotaler.*

MRS HUSHABYE. You will find it far less trouble to let papa have his own way than try to explain.

MAZZINI. But three attacks of delirium tremens, really!

MRS HUSHABYE [*to Mangan*] Do you know my husband, Mr Mangan [*she indicates Hector*].

MANGAN [*going to Hector, who meets him with outstretched hand*] Very pleased. [*Turning to Ellie*] I hope, Miss Ellie, you have not found the journey down too fatiguing. [*They shake hands*].

MRS HUSHABYE. Hector: shew Mr Dunn his room.

HECTOR. Certainly. Come along, Mr Dunn. [*He takes Mazzini out*].

ELLIE. You havnt shewn me my room yet, Hesione.

MRS HUSHABYE. How stupid of me! Come along. Make yourself quite at home, Mr Mangan. Papa will entertain you. [*She calls to the Captain in the pantry*] Papa: come and explain the house to Mr Mangan.

She goes out with Ellie. The Captain comes from the pantry.

CAPTAIN SHOTOVER. Youre going to marry Dunn's daughter. Dont. Youre too old.

MANGAN [*staggered*] Well! Thats fairly blunt, Captain.

CAPTAIN SHOTOVER. It's true.

MANGAN. She doesnt think so.

CAPTAIN SHOTOVER. She does.

MANGAN. Older men than I have—

CAPTAIN SHOTOVER [*finishing the sentence for him*]—made fools of themselves. That, also, is true.

MANGAN [*asserting himself*] I dont see that this is any business of yours.

CAPTAIN SHOTOVER. It is everybody's business. The stars in their courses are shaken when such things happen.

MANGAN. I'm going to marry her all the same.

CAPTAIN SHOTOVER. How do you know?

MANGAN [*playing the strong man*] I intend to. I mean to. See? I never made up my mind to do a thing yet that I didnt bring it off. Thats the sort of man I am; and there will be a better understanding between us when you make up your mind to that, Captain.

CAPTAIN SHOTOVER. You frequent picture palaces.

MANGAN. Perhaps I do. Who told you?

CAPTAIN SHOTOVER. Talk like a man, not like a movy.* You mean that you make a hundred thousand a year.

MANGAN. I dont boast. But when I meet a man that makes a hundred thousand a year, I take off my hat to that man, and stretch out my hand to him and call him brother.

CAPTAIN SHOTOVER. Then you also make a hundred thousand a year, hey?

MANGAN. No. I cant say that. Fifty thousand, perhaps.

CAPTAIN SHOTOVER. His half brother only [*he turns away from Mangan with his usual abruptness, and collects the empty tea-cups on the Chinese tray*].*

MANGAN [*irritated*] See here, Captain Shotover. I dont quite understand my position here. I came here on your daughter's invitation. Am I in her house or in yours?

CAPTAIN SHOTOVER. You are beneath the dome of heaven, in the house of God. What is true within these walls is true outside them. Go out on the seas; climb the mountains; wander through the valleys. She is still too young.

MANGAN [*weakening*] But I'm very little over fifty.

CAPTAIN SHOTOVER. You are still less under sixty. Boss Mangan: you will not marry the pirate's child [*he carries the tray away into the pantry*].

MANGAN [*following him to the half door*] What pirate's child? What are you talking about?

CAPTAIN SHOTOVER [*in the pantry*] Ellie Dunn. You will not marry her.

MANGAN. Who will stop me?

CAPTAIN SHOTOVER [*emerging*] My daughter [*he makes for the door leading to the hall*].

MANGAN [*following him*] Mrs Hushabye! Do you mean to say she brought me down here to break it off?

CAPTAIN SHOTOVER [*stopping and turning on him*] I know nothing more than I have seen in her eye. She *will* break it off. Take my advice: marry a West Indian* negress: they make excellent wives. I was married to one myself for two years.

MANGAN. Well, I *am* damned!

CAPTAIN SHOTOVER. I thought so.* I was, too, for many years. The negress redeemed me.

MANGAN [*feebly*] This is queer. I ought to walk out of this house.

CAPTAIN SHOTOVER. Why?

MANGAN. Well, many men would be offended by your style of talking.

CAPTAIN SHOTOVER. Nonsense! It's the other sort of talking that makes quarrels. Nobody ever quarrels with me.

A gentleman, whose firstrate tailoring and frictionless manners proclaim the wellbred West Ender, comes in from the hall. He has an engaging air of being young and unmarried, but on close inspection is found to be at least over forty.*

THE GENTLEMAN. Excuse my intruding in this fashion; but there is no knocker on the door; and the bell does not seem to ring.

CAPTAIN SHOTOVER. Why should there be a knocker? Why should the bell ring? The door is open.

THE GENTLEMAN. Precisely. So I ventured to come in.

CAPTAIN SHOTOVER. Quite right. I will see about a room for you [*he makes for the door*].

THE GENTLEMAN [*stopping him*] But I'm afraid you dont know who I am.

CAPTAIN SHOTOVER. Do you suppose that at my age I make distinctions between one fellow-creature and another? [*He goes out. Mangan and the newcomer stare at one another*].

MANGAN. Strange character, Captain Shotover, sir.

THE GENTLEMAN. Very.

CAPTAIN SHOTOVER [*shouting outside*] Hesione: another person has arrived and wants a room. Man about town, well dressed, fifty.

THE GENTLEMAN. Fancy Hesione's feelings! May I ask are you a member of the family?

MANGAN. No.

THE GENTLEMAN. I am. At least a connexion.

Mrs Hushabye comes back.

MRS HUSHABYE. How do you do? How good of you to come!

THE GENTLEMAN. I am very glad indeed to make your acquaintance, Hesione. [*Instead of taking her hand he kisses her. At the same moment the Captain appears in the doorway*]. You will excuse my kissing your daughter, Captain, when I tell you that—

CAPTAIN SHOTOVER. Stuff! Everyone kisses my daughter. Kiss her as much as you like [*he makes for the pantry*].

THE GENTLEMAN. Thank you. One moment, Captain. [*The Captain halts and turns. The gentleman goes to him affably*]. Do you happen to remember—but probably you dont, as it occurred many years ago—that your younger daughter married a numskull.

CAPTAIN SHOTOVER. Yes. She said she'd marry anybody to get away from this house. I should not have recognized you: your head is no longer like a walnut. Your aspect is softened. You have been boiled in bread and milk for years and years, like other married men. Poor devil! [*He disappears into the pantry*].

MRS HUSHABYE [*going past Mangan to the gentleman and scrutinizing him*] I dont believe you are Hastings Utterword.

THE GENTLEMAN. I am not.

MRS HUSHABYE. Then what business had you to kiss me?

THE GENTLEMAN. I thought I would like to. The fact is, I am Randall Utterword, the unworthy younger brother of Hastings. I was abroad diplomatizing when he was married.

LADY UTTERWORD [*dashing in*] Hesione: where is the key of the wardrobe in my room? My diamonds are in my dressing-bag: I must lock it up—[*recognizing the stranger with a shock*] Randall: how dare you? [*She marches at him past Mrs Hushabye, who retreats and joins Mangan near the sofa*].

RANDALL. How dare I what? I am not doing anything.

LADY UTTERWORD. Who told you I was here?

RANDALL. Hastings. You had just left when I called on you at Claridge's;* so I followed you down here. You are looking extremely well.

LADY UTTERWORD. Dont presume to tell me so.

MRS HUSHABYE. What is wrong with Mr Randall, Addy?

LADY UTTERWORD [*recollecting herself*] Oh, nothing. But he has no right to come bothering you and papa without being invited [*she goes to the window-seat and sits down, turning away from them ill-humoredly and looking into the garden, where Hector and Ellie are now seen strolling together*].

MRS HUSHABYE. I think you have not met Mr Mangan, Addy.

LADY UTTERWORD [*turning her head and nodding coldly to Mangan*] I beg your pardon. Randall: you have flustered me so: I made a perfect fool of myself.

MRS HUSHABYE. Lady Utterword. My sister. My *younger* sister.

MANGAN [*bowing*] Pleased to meet you, Lady Utterword.*

LADY UTTERWORD [*with marked interest*] Who is that gentleman walking in the garden with Miss Dunn?

MRS HUSHABYE. I dont know. She quarrelled mortally with my husband only ten minutes ago; and I didn't know anyone else had come. It must be a visitor. [*She goes to the window to look*]. Oh, it *is* Hector. Theyve made it up.

LADY UTTERWORD. Your husband! That handsome man?

MRS HUSHABYE. Well, why shouldnt my husband be a handsome man?

RANDALL [*joining them at the window*] One's husband never is, Ariadne [*he sits by Lady Utterword, on her right*].

MRS HUSHABYE. One's sister's husband always is, Mr Randall.

LADY UTTERWORD. Dont be vulgar, Randall.* And you, Hesione, are just as bad.

Ellie and Hector come in from the garden by the starboard door. Randall rises. Ellie retires into the corner near the pantry. Hector comes forward; and Lady Utterword rises looking her very best.

MRS HUSHABYE. Hector: this is Addy.

HECTOR [*apparently surprised*] Not this lady.

LADY UTTERWORD [*smiling*] Why not?

HECTOR [*looking at her with a piercing glance of deep but respectful admiration, his moustache bristling*] I thought—[*pulling himself together*] I beg your pardon, Lady Utterword. I am extremely glad to welcome you at last under our roof [*he offers his hand with grave courtesy*].

MRS HUSHABYE. She wants to be kissed, Hector.

LADY UTTERWORD. Hesione! [*but she still smiles*].

MRS HUSHABYE. Call her Addy; and kiss her like a good brother-in-law; and have done with it. [*She leaves them to themselves*].

HECTOR. Behave yourself, Hesione. Lady Utterword is entitled not only to hospitality but to civilization.

LADY UTTERWORD [*gratefully*] Thank you, Hector. [*They shake hands cordially*].

Mazzini Dunn is seen crossing the garden from starboard to port.

CAPTAIN SHOTOVER [*coming from the pantry and addressing Ellie*] Your father has washed himself.

ELLIE [*quite self-possessed*] He often does, Captain Shotover.

CAPTAIN SHOTOVER. A strange conversion! I saw him through the pantry window.

Mazzini Dunn enters through the port window door, newly washed and brushed, and stops, smiling benevolently, between Mangan and Mrs Hushabye.

MRS HUSHABYE [*introducing*] Mr Mazzini Dunn, Lady Ut—oh, I forgot: youve met. [*Indicating Ellie*] Miss Dunn.

MAZZINI [*walking across the room to take Ellie's hand, and beaming at his own naughty irony*] I have met Miss Dunn also. She is my daughter. [*He draws her arm through his caressingly*].

MRS HUSHABYE. Of course: how stupid! Mr Utterword, my sister's—er—

RANDALL [*shaking hands agreeably*] Her brother-in-law, Mr Dunn. How do you do?

MRS HUSHABYE. This is my husband.

HECTOR. We have met, dear. Dont introduce us any more. [*He moves away to the big chair, and adds*] Wont you sit down, Lady Utterword? [*She does so very graciously*].

MRS HUSHABYE. Sorry. I hate it: it's like making people shew their tickets.

MAZZINI [*sententiously*] How little it tells us, after all! The great question is, not who we are, but what we are.

CAPTAIN SHOTOVER. Ha! What are you?

MAZZINI [*taken aback*] What am I?

CAPTAIN SHOTOVER. A thief, a pirate, and a murderer.

MAZZINI. I assure you you are mistaken.

CAPTAIN SHOTOVER. An adventurous life; but what does it end in? Respectability. A ladylike daughter. The language and appearance of a city missionary. Let it be a warning to all of you [*he goes out through the garden*].

DUNN. I hope nobody here believes that I am a thief, a pirate, or a murderer. Mrs Hushabye: will you excuse me a moment? I must really go and explain. [*He follows the Captain*].

MRS HUSHABYE [*as he goes*] It's no use. Youd really better—[*but Dunn has vanished*]. We had better all go out and look for some tea. We never have regular tea; but you can always get some when you want: the servants keep it stewing all day. The kitchen veranda is the best place to ask. May I shew you? [*She goes to the starboard door*].

RANDALL [*going with her*] Thank you, I dont think I'll take any tea this afternoon. But if you will shew me the garden—?

MRS HUSHABYE. Theres nothing to see in the garden except papa's observatory, and a gravel pit with a cave where he keeps dynamite and things of that sort.* However, it's pleasanter out of doors; so come along.

RANDALL. Dynamite! Isnt that rather risky?

MRS HUSHABYE. Well, we dont sit in the gravel pit when theres a thunderstorm.

LADY UTTERWORD. Thats something new. What is the dynamite for?

HECTOR. To blow up the human race if it goes too far. He is trying to discover a psychic ray that will explode all the explosives at the will of a Mahatma.*

ELLIE. The Captain's tea is delicious, Mr Utterword.

MRS HUSHABYE [*stopping in the doorway*] Do you mean to say that youve had some of my father's tea? that you got round him before you were ten minutes in the house?

ELLIE. I did.

MRS HUSHABYE. You little devil! [*She goes out with Randall*].

MANGAN. Wont you come, Miss Ellie?

ELLIE. I'm too tired. I'll take a book up to my room and rest a little. [*She goes to the bookshelf*].

MANGAN. Right. You cant do better. But I'm disappointed. [*He follows Randall and Mrs Hushabye*].

Ellie, Hector, and Lady Utterword are left. Hector is close to Lady Utterword. They look at Ellie, waiting for her to go.

ELLIE [*looking at the title of a book*] Do you like stories of adventure, Lady Utterword?

LADY UTTERWORD [*patronizingly*] Of course, dear.

ELLIE. Then I'll leave you to Mr Hushabye. [*She goes out through the hall*].

HECTOR. That girl is mad about tales of adventure. The lies I have to tell her!

LADY UTTERWORD [*not interested in Ellie*] When you saw me what did you mean by saying that you thought, and then stopping short? What did you think?

HECTOR [*folding his arms and looking down at her magnetically*] May I tell you?

LADY UTTERWORD. Of course.

HECTOR. It will not sound very civil. I was on the point of saying 'I thought you were a plain woman.'

LADY UTTERWORD. Oh for shame, Hector! What right had you to notice whether I am plain or not?

HECTOR. Listen to me, Ariadne. Until today I have seen only photographs of you; and no photograph can give the strange fascination of the daughters of that supernatural old man. There is some damnable quality in them that destroys men's moral sense, and carries them beyond honor and dishonor. You know that, dont you?

LADY UTTERWORD. Perhaps I do, Hector. But let me warn you once for all that I am a rigidly conventional woman. You may think because I'm a Shotover that I'm a Bohemian, because we are all so horribly Bohemian. But I'm not. I hate and loathe Bohemianism. No child brought up in a strict Puritan household ever suffered from Puritanism as I suffered from our Bohemianism.*

HECTOR. Our children are like that. They spend their holidays in the houses of their respectable schoolfellows.

LADY UTTERWORD. I shall invite them for Christmas.

HECTOR. Their absence leaves us both without our natural chaperons.

LADY UTTERWORD. Children are certainly very inconvenient sometimes. But intelligent people can always manage, unless they are Bohemians.

HECTOR. You are no Bohemian; but you are no Puritan either: your attraction is alive and powerful. What sort of woman do you count yourself?

LADY UTTERWORD. I am a woman of the world, Hector; and I can assure you that if you will only take the trouble always to do the perfectly correct thing, and to say the perfectly correct thing, you can do just what you like. An ill-conducted, careless woman gets simply no chance. An ill-conducted, careless man is never allowed within arms length of any woman worth knowing.

HECTOR. I see. You are neither a Bohemian woman nor a Puritan woman. You are a dangerous woman.

LADY UTTERWORD. On the contrary, I am a safe woman.

HECTOR. You are a most accursedly attractive woman. Mind: I am not making love to you. I do not like being attracted. But you had better know how I feel if you are going to stay here.

LADY UTTERWORD. You are an exceedingly clever lady-killer, Hector. And terribly handsome. I am quite a good player, myself, at that game. Is it quite understood that we are only playing?

HECTOR. Quite. I am deliberately playing the fool,* out of sheer worthlessness.*

LADY UTTERWORD [*rising brightly*] Well, you are my brother-in-law. Hesione asked you to kiss me. [*He seizes her in his arms, and kisses her strenuously*]. Oh! that was a little more than play, brother-in-law. [*She pushes him suddenly away*]. You shall not do that again.

HECTOR. In effect, you got your claws deeper into me than I intended.

MRS HUSHABYE [*coming in from the garden*] Dont let me disturb you: I only want a cap to put on daddiest. The sun is setting; and he'll catch cold [*she makes for the door leading to the hall*].

LADY UTTERWORD. Your husband is quite charming, darling.* He has actually condescended to kiss me at last. I shall go into the garden: it's cooler now [*she goes out by the port door*].

MRS HUSHABYE. Take care, dear child. I dont believe any man can kiss Addy without falling in love with her. [*She goes into the hall*].

HECTOR [*striking himself on the chest*] Fool! Goat!

Mrs Hushabye comes back with the Captain's cap.

HECTOR. Your sister is an extremely enterprising old girl. Wheres Miss Dunn!

MRS HUSHABYE. Mangan says she has gone up to her room for a nap. Addy wont let you talk to Ellie: she has marked you for her own.

HECTOR. She has the diabolical family fascination. I began making love to her automatically. What am I to do? I cant fall in love; and I cant hurt a woman's feelings by telling her so when she falls in love with me. And as women are always falling in love with my moustache I get landed in all sorts of tedious and terrifying flirtations in which I'm not a bit in earnest.

MRS HUSHABYE. Oh, neither is Addy. She has never been in love in her life, though she has always been trying to fall in head over ears. She is worse than you, because you had one real go at least, with me.

HECTOR. That was a confounded madness. I cant believe that such an amazing experience is common. It has left its mark on me. I believe that is why I have never been able to repeat it.

MRS HUSHABYE [*laughing and caressing his arm*] We were frightfully in love with one another, Hector. It was such an enchanting dream that I have never been able to grudge it to you* or anyone else since. I have invited all sorts of pretty women to the house on the chance of giving you another turn. But it has never come off.

HECTOR. I dont know that I want it to come off. It was damned dangerous. You fascinated me; but I loved you; so it was heaven. This sister of yours fascinates me; but I hate her; so it is hell. I shall kill her if she persists.

MRS HUSHABYE. Nothing will kill Addy: she is as strong as a horse. [*Releasing him*] Now *I* am going off to fascinate somebody.

HECTOR. The Foreign Office toff? Randall?

MRS HUSHABYE. Goodness gracious, no! Why should I fascinate him?

HECTOR. I presume you dont mean the bloated capitalist, Mangan?

MRS HUSHABYE. Hm! I think he had better be fascinated by me than by Ellie. [*She is going into the garden when the Captain comes in from it with some sticks in his hand*].* What have you got there, daddiest?

CAPTAIN SHOTOVER. Dynamite.

MRS HUSHABYE. Youve been to the gravel pit. Dont drop it about the house: theres a dear. [*She goes into the garden, where the evening light is now very red*].

HECTOR. Listen, O sage. How long dare you concentrate on a feeling without risking having it fixed in your consciousness all the rest of your life?

CAPTAIN SHOTOVER. Ninety minutes. An hour and a half. [*He goes into the pantry*].

Hector, left alone, contracts his brows, and falls into a daydream. He does not move for some time. Then he folds his arms. Then, throwing his hands behind him, and gripping one with the other, he strides tragically once to and fro. Suddenly he snatches his walking-stick from the teak table, and draws it; for it is a sword-stick. He fights a desperate duel with an imaginary antagonist, and after many vicissitudes runs him through the body up to the hilt. He sheathes his sword and throws it on the sofa, falling into another reverie as he does so. He looks straight into the eyes of an imaginary woman; seizes her by the arms; and says in a deep and thrilling tone 'Do you love me!'* The Captain comes out of the pantry at this moment; and Hector, caught with his arms stretched out and his fists clenched, has to account for his attitude by going through a series of gymnastic exercises.

CAPTAIN SHOTOVER. That sort of strength is no good. You will never be as strong as a gorilla.

HECTOR. What is the dynamite for?

CAPTAIN SHOTOVER. To kill fellows like Mangan.

HECTOR. No use. They will always be able to buy more dynamite than you.

CAPTAIN SHOTOVER. I will make a dynamite that he cannot explode.

HECTOR. And that you can, eh?

CAPTAIN SHOTOVER. Yes: when I have attained the seventh degree of concentration.

HECTOR. Whats the use of that? You never do attain it.

CAPTAIN SHOTOVER. What then is to be done? Are we to be kept for ever in the mud by these hogs to whom the universe is nothing but a machine for greasing their bristles and filling their snouts?*

HECTOR. Are Mangan's bristles worse than Randall's lovelocks?*

CAPTAIN SHOTOVER. We must win powers of life and death over them both. I refuse to die until I have invented the means.

HECTOR. Who are we that we should judge them?

CAPTAIN SHOTOVER. What are they that they should judge us? Yet they do, unhesitatingly. There is enmity between our seed and their seed. They know it and act on it, strangling our souls. They believe in themselves. When we believe in ourselves, we shall kill them.

HECTOR. It is the same seed. You forget that your pirate has a very nice daughter. Mangan's son may be a Plato: Randall's a Shelley. What was my father?

CAPTAIN SHOTOVER. The damndest scoundrel I ever met. [*He replaces the drawing-board; sits down at the table; and begins to mix a wash of color*].

HECTOR. Precisely. Well, dare you kill his innocent grandchildren?

CAPTAIN SHOTOVER. They are mine also.*

HECTOR. Just so. We are members one of another. [*He throws himself carelessly on the sofa*]. I tell you I have often thought of this killing of human vermin.* Many men have thought of it. Decent men are like Daniel in the lion's den: their survival is a miracle; and they do not always survive. We live among the Mangans and Randalls and Billie Dunns as they, poor devils, live among the disease germs and the doctors and the lawyers and the parsons and the restaurant chefs and the tradesmen and the servants and all the rest of the parasites and blackmailers.* What are our terrors to theirs? Give me the power to kill them; and I'll spare them in sheer—

CAPTAIN SHOTOVER [*cutting in sharply*] Fellow feeling?

HECTOR. No. I should kill myself if I believed that. I must believe that my spark, small as it is, is divine, and that the red light over their door is hell fire. I should spare them in simple magnanimous pity.

CAPTAIN SHOTOVER. You cant spare them until you have the power to kill them. At present they have the power to kill you. There are millions of blacks over the water for them to train and let loose on us. Theyre going to do it. Theyre doing it already.

HECTOR. They are too stupid to use their power.

CAPTAIN SHOTOVER [*throwing down his brush and coming to the end of the sofa*] Do not deceive yourself: they do use it. We kill the better half of ourselves every day to propitiate them. The knowledge that these people are there to render all our aspirations barren prevents us having the aspirations. And when we are tempted to seek their destruction they bring forth demons to delude us, disguised as pretty daughters, and singers and poets and the like, for whose sake we spare them.

HECTOR [*sitting up and leaning towards him*] May not Hesione be such a demon, brought forth by you lest I should slay you?

CAPTAIN SHOTOVER. That is possible. She has used you up, and left you nothing but dreams, as some women do.

HECTOR. Vampire women, demon women.

CAPTAIN SHOTOVER. Men think the world well lost for them, and lose it accordingly. Who are the men that do things? The husbands of the shrew and of the drunkard, the men with the thorn in the flesh. [*Walking distractedly away towards the pantry*] I must think these things out. [*Turning suddenly*] But I go on with the dynamite none the less.* I will discover a ray mightier than any X-ray: a mind ray that will explode the ammunition in the belt of my adversary before he can point his gun at me. And I must hurry. I am old: I have no time to waste in talk [*he is about to go into the pantry, and Hector is making for the hall, when Hesione comes back*].

MRS HUSHABYE. Daddiest: you and Hector must come and help me to entertain all these people. What on earth were you shouting about?

HECTOR [*stopping in the act of turning the doorhandle*] He is madder than usual.

MRS HUSHABYE. We all are.

HECTOR. I must change* [*he resumes his door opening*].

MRS HUSHABYE. Stop, stop. Come back, both of you. Come back. [*They return, reluctantly*]. Money is running short.

HECTOR. Money! Where are my April dividends?

MRS HUSHABYE. Where is the snow that fell last year?

CAPTAIN SHOTOVER. Where is all the money you had for that patent lifeboat I invented?

MRS HUSHABYE. Five hundred pounds; and I have made it last since Easter!

CAPTAIN SHOTOVER. Since Easter! Barely four months! Monstrous extravagance! I could live for seven years on £500.

MRS HUSHABYE. Not keeping open house as we do here, daddiest.

CAPTAIN SHOTOVER. Only £500 for that lifeboat! I got twelve thousand for the invention before that.

MRS HUSHABYE. Yes, dear; but that was for the ship with the magnetic keel that sucked up submarines. Living at the rate we do, you cannot afford life-saving inventions. Cant you think of something that will murder half Europe at one bang?

CAPTAIN SHOTOVER. No. I am ageing fast. My mind does not dwell on slaughter as it did when I was a boy. Why doesnt your husband invent something? He does nothing but tell lies to women.

HECTOR. Well, that is a form of invention, is it not? However, you are right: I ought to support my wife.

MRS HUSHABYE. Indeed you shall do nothing of the sort: I should never see you from breakfast to dinner. I want my husband.

HECTOR [*bitterly*] I might as well be your lapdog.

MRS HUSHABYE. Do you want to be my breadwinner, like the other poor husbands?

HECTOR. No, by thunder! What a damned creature a husband is anyhow!

MRS HUSHABYE [*to the Captain*] What about that harpoon cannon?

CAPTAIN SHOTOVER. No use. It kills whales, not men.

MRS HUSHABYE. Why not? You fire the harpoon out of a cannon. It sticks in the enemy's general; you wind him in; and there you are.

HECTOR. You are your father's daughter, Hesione.

CAPTAIN SHOTOVER. There is something in it. Not to wind in generals: they are not dangerous. But one could fire a grapnel and wind in a machine gun or even a tank. I will think it out.

MRS HUSHABYE [*squeezing the Captain's arm affectionately*] Saved! You *are* a darling, daddiest. Now we must go back to these dreadful people and entertain them.

CAPTAIN SHOTOVER. They have had no dinner. Dont forget that.

HECTOR.   Neither have I. And it is dark: it must be all hours.

MRS HUSHABYE.   Oh, Guinness will produce some sort of dinner for them. The servants always take jolly good care that there is food in the house.*

CAPTAIN SHOTOVER [*raising a strange wail in the darkness*] What a house! What a daughter!

MRS HUSHABYE [*raving*] What a father!

HECTOR [*following suit*] What a husband!

CAPTAIN SHOTOVER.   Is there no thunder in heaven?

HECTOR.   Is there no beauty, no bravery, on earth?

MRS HUSHABYE.   What do men want? They have their food, their firesides, their clothes mended, and our love at the end of the day. Why are they not satisfied? Why do they envy us the pain with which we bring them into the world, and make strange dangers and torments for themselves to be even with us?

CAPTAIN SHOTOVER [*weirdly chanting*]
I built a house for my daughters, and opened the doors thereof,
That men might come for their choosing, and their betters spring from their love;
But one of them married a numskull;

HECTOR [*taking up the rhythm*]
                                        The other a liar wed;

MRS HUSHABYE [*completing the stanza*]
And now must she lie beside him, even as she made her bed.

LADY UTTERWORD [*calling from the garden*] Hesione! Hesione! Where are you?

HECTOR.   The cat is on the tiles.

MRS HUSHABYE.   Coming, darling, coming [*she goes quickly into the garden*].

The Captain goes back to his place at the table.

HECTOR [*going into the hall*] Shall I turn up the lights for you?

CAPTAIN SHOTOVER.   No. Give me deeper darkness. Money is not made in the light.*

ACT II

The same room, with the lights turned up and the curtains drawn. Ellie comes in, followed by Mangan. Both are dressed for dinner. She strolls to the drawing-table. He comes between the table and the wicker chair.

MANGAN. What a dinner! I dont call it a dinner: I call it a meal.

ELLIE. I am accustomed to meals, Mr Mangan, and very lucky to get them. Besides, the captain cooked some macaroni for me.

MANGAN [*shuddering liverishly*] Too rich: I cant eat such things. I suppose it's because I have to work so much with my brain. Thats the worst of being a man of business: you are always thinking, thinking, thinking. By the way, now that we are alone, may I take the opportunity to come to a little understanding with you?

ELLIE [*settling into the draughtsman's seat*] Certainly. I should like to.

MANGAN [*taken aback*] Should you? That surprises me; for I thought I noticed this afternoon that you avoided me all you could. Not for the first time either.

ELLIE. I was very tired and upset. I wasn't used to the ways of this extraordinary house. Please forgive me.

MANGAN. Oh, thats all right: I dont mind. But Captain Shotover has been talking to me about you. You and me, you know.

ELLIE [*interested*] The Captain! What did he say?*

MANGAN. Well, he noticed the difference between our ages.

ELLIE. He notices everything.*

MANGAN. You dont mind, then?

ELLIE. Of course I know quite well that our engagement—

MANGAN. Oh! you call it an engagement.

ELLIE. Well, isnt it?

MANGAN. Oh, yes, yes: no doubt it is if you hold to it. This is the first time youve used the word; and I didnt quite know where we stood: thats all. [*He sits down in the wicker chair; and resigns himself to allow her to lead the conversation*]. You were saying—?

ELLIE. Was I? I forget.* Tell me. Do you like this part of the country? I heard you ask Mr Hushabye at dinner whether there are any nice houses to let down here.

MANGAN. I like the place. The air suits me.* I shouldnt be surprised if I settled down here.

ELLIE. Nothing would please me better. The air suits me too. And I want to be near Hesione.

MANGAN [*with growing uneasiness*] The air may suit us; but the question is, should we suit one another? Have you thought about that?

ELLIE. Mr Mangan: we must be sensible, mustnt we? It's no use pretending that we are Romeo and Juliet. But we can get on very well together if we choose to make the best of it. Your kindness of heart will make it easy for me.

MANGAN [*leaning forward, with the beginning of something like deliberate unpleasantness in his voice*] Kindness of heart, eh? I ruined your father, didnt I?

ELLIE. Oh, not intentionally.

MANGAN. Yes I did.* Ruined him on purpose.

ELLIE. On purpose!

MANGAN. Not out of ill-nature, you know. And youll admit that I kept a job for him when I had finished with him. But business is business; and I ruined him as a matter of business.

ELLIE. I dont understand how that can be. Are you trying to make me feel that I need not be grateful to you, so that I may choose freely?

MANGAN [*rising aggressively*] No. I mean what I say.

ELLIE. But how could it possibly do you any good to ruin my father? The money he lost was yours.

MANGAN [*with a sour laugh*] Was mine! It *is* mine, Miss Ellie, and all the money the other fellows lost too. [*He shoves his hands into his pockets and shews his teeth*]. I just smoked them out like a hive of bees. What do you say to that? A bit of a shock, eh?

ELLIE. It would have been, this morning. Now! you cant think how little it matters. But it's quite interesting. Only, you must explain it to me. I dont understand it. [*Propping her elbows on the drawing-board and her chin on her hands, she composes herself to listen with a combination of conscious curiosity with unconscious contempt which provokes him to more and more unpleasantness, and an attempt at patronage of her ignorance*].

MANGAN. Of course you dont understand: what do you know about business? You just listen and learn. Your father's business was a new business; and I dont start new businesses: I let other fellows start them. They put all their money and their friends' money into starting them. They wear out their souls and bodies trying to make a success of them. Theyre what you call enthusiasts. But the first dead lift of the thing is too much for them; and they havnt enough financial experience. In a year or so they have either to let the whole show go bust, or sell out to a new lot of fellows for a few deferred ordinary shares: that is, if theyre lucky enough to get anything at all. As likely as not the very same thing happens to the new lot. They put in more money and a couple of years more work; and then perhaps *they* have to sell out to a third lot. If it's really a big thing the third lot will have to sell out too, and leave *their* work and *their* money behind them. And thats where the real business man comes in: where I come in. But I'm cleverer than some: I dont mind dropping a little money to start the process. I took your father's measure. I saw that he had a sound idea, and that he would work himself silly for it if he got the chance. I saw that he was a child in business, and was dead certain to outrun his expenses and be in too great a hurry to wait for his market. I knew that the surest way to ruin a man who doesnt know how to handle money is to give him some. I explained my idea to some friends in the city, and they found the money; for I take no risks in ideas,* even when theyre my own. Your father and the friends that ventured their money with him were no more to me than a heap of squeezed lemons. Youve been wasting your gratitude: my kind heart is all rot. I'm sick of it. When I see your father beaming at me with his moist, grateful eyes, regularly wallowing in gratitude, I sometimes feel I must tell him the truth or burst. What stops me is that I know he wouldnt believe me. He'd think it was my modesty, as you did just now. He'd think anything rather than the truth, which is that he's a blamed fool, and I am a man that knows how to take care of himself. [*He throws himself back into the big chair with large self-approval*]. Now what do you think of me, Miss Ellie?

ELLIE [*dropping her hands*] How strange! that my mother, who knew nothing at all about business, should have been quite right about you! She always said—not before papa, of course, but to us children—that you were just that sort of man.

MANGAN [*sitting up, much hurt*] Oh! did she? And yet she'd have let you marry me.

ELLIE. Well, you see, Mr Mangan, my mother married a very good man—for whatever you may think of my father as a man of business, he is the soul of goodness—and she is not at all keen on my doing the same.

MANGAN. Anyhow, you dont want to marry me now, do you?

ELLIE [*very calmly*] Oh, I think so. Why not?

MANGAN [*rising aghast*] Why not!

ELLIE. I dont see why we shouldnt get on very well together.

MANGAN. Well, but look here, you know—[*he stops, quite at a loss*].

ELLIE [*patiently*] Well?

MANGAN. Well, I thought you were rather particular about people's characters.

ELLIE. If we women were particular about men's characters, we should never get married at all, Mr Mangan.

MANGAN. A child like you talking of 'we women'! What next! Youre not in earnest?

ELLIE. Yes I am. Arnt you?

MANGAN. You mean to hold me to it?

ELLIE. Do you wish to back out of it?

MANGAN. Oh no. Not exactly back out of it.

ELLIE. Well?

He has nothing to say. With a long whispered whistle, he drops into the wicker chair and stares before him like a beggared gambler. But a cunning look soon comes into his face. He leans over towards her on his right elbow, and speaks in a low steady voice.

MANGAN. Suppose I told you I was in love with another woman!

ELLIE [*echoing him*] Suppose I told you I was in love with another man!

MANGAN [*bouncing angrily out of his chair*] I'm not joking.

ELLIE. Who told you *I* was?

MANGAN. I tell you I'm serious. Youre too young to be serious; but youll have to believe me. I want to be near your friend Mrs Hushabye. I'm in love with her. Now the murder's out.

ELLIE. I want to be near your friend Mr Hushabye. I'm in love with him. [*She rises and adds with a frank air*] Now we are in one another's confidence, we shall be real friends. Thank you for telling me.

MANGAN [*almost beside himself*] Do you think I'll be made a convenience of like this?

ELLIE. Come, Mr Mangan! you made a business convenience of my father. Well, a woman's business is marriage. Why shouldnt I make a domestic convenience of you?

MANGAN. Because I dont choose, see? Because I'm not a silly gull like your father. Thats why.

ELLIE [*with serene contempt*] You are not good enough to clean my father's boots, Mr Mangan; and I am paying you a great compliment in condescending to make a convenience of you, as you call it. Of course you are free to throw over our engagement if you like; but, if you do, youll never enter Hesione's house again: I will take care of that.

MANGAN [*gasping*] You little devil, youve done me. [*On the point of collapsing into the big chair again he recovers himself*]. Wait a bit, though: youre not so cute as you think. You cant beat Boss Mangan as easy as that. Suppose I go straight to Mrs Hushabye and tell her that youre in love with her husband.

ELLIE. She knows it.

MANGAN. You told her!!!

ELLIE. She told me.

MANGAN [*clutching at his bursting temples*] Oh, this is a crazy house. Or else I'm going clean off my chump. Is she making a swop with you—she to have your husband and you to have hers?

ELLIE. Well, you dont want us both, do you?

MANGAN [*throwing himself into the chair distractedly*] My brain wont stand it. My head's going to split. Help! Help me to hold it. Quick: hold it: squeeze it. Save me. [*Ellie comes behind his chair; clasps his head hard for a moment; then begins to draw her hands from his forehead back to his ears*]. Thank you. [*Drowsily*] Thats very refreshing. [*Waking a little*] Dont you hypnotize me, though. Ive seen men made fools of by hypnotism.*

ELLIE. [*steadily*] Be quiet. Ive seen men made fools of without hypnotism.

MANGAN [*humbly*] You dont dislike touching me, I hope. You never touched me before, I noticed.

ELLIE. Not since you fell in love naturally with a grown-up nice woman, who will never expect you to make love to her. And I will never expect him to make love to me.

MANGAN. He may, though.

ELLIE [*making her passes rhythmically*] Hush. Go to sleep. Do you hear? You are to go to sleep, go to sleep, go to sleep; be quiet, deeply deeply quiet; sleep, sleep, sleep, sleep, sleep.

He falls asleep. Ellie steals away; turns the light out; and goes into the garden.

Nurse Guinness opens the door and is seen in the light which comes in from the hall.

GUINNESS [*speaking to someone outside*] Mr Mangan's not here, ducky: theres no one here. It's all dark.

MRS HUSHABYE [*without*] Try the garden. Mr Dunn and I will be in my boudoir. Shew him the way.

GUINNESS. Yes, ducky. [*She makes for the garden door in the dark; stumbles over the sleeping Mangan; and screams*] Ahoo! Oh Lord, sir! I beg your pardon, I'm sure: I didnt see you in the dark. Who is it? [*She goes back to the door and turns on the light*]. Oh, Mr Mangan, sir, I hope I havnt hurt you plumping into your lap like that. [*Coming to him*] I was looking for you, sir. Mrs Hushabye says will you please—[*noticing that he remains quite insensible*] Oh, my good Lord, I hope I havnt killed him. Sir! Mr Mangan! Sir! [*She shakes him; and he is rolling inertly off the chair on the floor when she holds him up and props him against the cushion*]. Miss Hessy! Miss Hessy! Quick, doty darling. Miss Hessy! [*Mrs Hushabye comes in from the hall, followed by Mazzini Dunn*]. Oh, Miss Hessy, Ive been and killed him.

Mazzini runs round the back of the chair to Mangan's right hand, and sees that the nurse's words are apparently only too true.

MAZZINI. What tempted you to commit such a crime, woman?

MRS HUSHABYE [*trying not to laugh*] Do you mean you did it on purpose?

GUINNESS. Now is it likely I'd kill any man on purpose. I fell over him in the dark; and I'm a pretty tidy weight. He never spoke nor moved until I shook him; and then he would have dropped dead on the floor. Isnt it tiresome?

MRS HUSHABYE [*going past the nurse to Mangan's side, and inspecting him less credulously than Mazzini*] Nonsense! he is not dead: he is only asleep. I can see him breathing.

GUINNESS. But why wont he wake?

MAZZINI [*speaking very politely into Mangan's ear*] Mangan! My dear Mangan! [*he blows into Mangan's ear*].

MRS HUSHABYE. Thats no good [*she shakes him vigorously*]. Mr Mangan: wake up. Do you hear? [*He begins to roll over*]. Oh! Nurse, nurse: he's falling: help me.

Nurse Guinness rushes to the rescue. With Mazzini's assistance, Mangan is propped safely up again.

GUINNESS [*behind the chair; bending over to test the case with her nose*] Would he be drunk, do you think, pet?

MRS HUSHABYE. Had he any of papa's rum?

MAZZINI. It cant be that: he is most abstemious. I am afraid he drank too much formerly, and has to drink too little now. You know, Mrs Hushabye, I really think he has been hypnotized.

GUINNESS. Hip no what, sir?

MAZZINI. One evening at home, after we had seen a hypnotizing performance, the children began playing at it; and Ellie stroked my head. I assure you I went off dead asleep; and they had to send for a professional to wake me up after I had slept eighteen hours. They had to carry me upstairs; and as the poor children were not very strong, they let me slip; and I rolled right down the whole flight and never woke up. [*Mrs Hushabye splutters*]. Oh, you may laugh, Mrs Hushabye; but I might have been killed.

MRS HUSHABYE. I couldnt have helped laughing even if you had been, Mr Dunn. So Ellie has hypnotized him. What fun!

MAZZINI. Oh no, no, no. It was such a terrible lesson to her: nothing would induce her to try such a thing again.

MRS HUSHABYE. Then who did it? *I* didnt.

MAZZINI. I thought perhaps the Captain might have done it unintentionally. He is so fearfully magnetic: I feel vibrations whenever he comes close to me.

GUINNESS. The Captain will get him out of it anyhow, sir: I'll back him for that. I'll go fetch him [*she makes for the pantry*].

MRS HUSHABYE. Wait a bit. [*To Mazzini*] You say he is all right for eighteen hours?

MAZZINI. Well, *I* was asleep for eighteen hours.

MRS HUSHABYE. Were you any the worse for it?

MAZZINI. I dont quite remember. They had poured brandy down my throat, you see; and—

MRS HUSHABYE. Quite. Anyhow, you survived. Nurse, darling: go and ask Miss Dunn to come to us here. Say I want to speak to her particularly. You will find her with Mr Hushabye probably.

GUINNESS. I think not, ducky: Miss Addy is with him. But I'll find her and send her to you. [*She goes out into the garden*].

MRS HUSHABYE [*calling Mazzini's attention to the figure on the chair*] Now, Mr Dunn, look. Just look. Look hard.* Do you still intend to sacrifice your daughter to that thing?

MAZZINI [*troubled*] You have completely upset me, Mrs Hushabye, by all you have said to me. That anyone could imagine that I—*I*, a consecrated soldier of freedom, if I may say so—could sacrifice Ellie to anybody or anyone, or that I should ever have dreamed of forcing her inclinations in any way, is a most painful blow to my—well, I suppose you would say to my good opinion of myself.

MRS HUSHABYE [*rather stolidly*] Sorry.

MAZZINI [*looking forlornly at the body*] What is your objection to poor Mangan, Mrs Hushabye? He looks all right to me. But then I am so accustomed to him.

MRS HUSHABYE. Have you no heart? Have you no sense? Look at the brute! Think of poor weak innocent Ellie in the clutches of this slavedriver, who spends his life making thousands of rough violent workmen bend to his will and sweat for him: a man accustomed to have great masses of iron beaten into shape for him by steam-hammers! to fight with women and girls over a halfpenny* an hour ruthlessly! a captain of industry,* I think you call him, dont you? Are you going to fling your delicate, sweet, helpless child into such a beast's claws just because he will keep her in an expensive house and make her wear diamonds to shew how rich he is?

MAZZINI [*staring at her in wide-eyed amazement*] Bless you, dear Mrs Hushabye, what romantic ideas of business you have! Poor dear Mangan isnt a bit like that.

MRS HUSHABYE [*scornfully*] Poor dear Mangan indeed!

MAZZINI. But he doesnt know anything about machinery. He never goes near the men: he couldnt manage them: he is afraid of them. I never can get him to take the least interest in the works: he hardly knows more about them than you do. People are cruelly unjust to Mangan: they think he is all rugged strength just because his manners are bad.

MRS HUSHABYE. Do you mean to tell me he isnt strong enough to crush poor little Ellie?

MAZZINI. Of course it's very hard to say how any marriage will turn out; but speaking for myself, I should say that he wont have a dog's chance* against Ellie. You know, Ellie has remarkable strength of character. I think it is because I taught her to like Shakespear when she was very young.

MRS HUSHABYE [*contemptuously*] Shakespear! The next thing you will tell me is that you could have made a great deal more money than Mangan. [*She retires to the sofa, and sits down at the port end of it in the worst of humors*].

MAZZINI [*following her and taking the other end*] No: I'm no good at making money. I dont care enough for it, somehow. I'm not ambitious! that must be it. Mangan is wonderful about money: he thinks of nothing else. He is so dreadfully afraid of being poor. I am always thinking of other things: even at the works I think of the things we are doing and not of what they cost. And the worst of it is, poor Mangan doesnt know what to do with his money when he gets it. He is such a baby that he doesnt know even what to eat and drink: he has ruined his liver eating and drinking the wrong things; and now he can hardly eat at all. Ellie will diet him splendidly. You will be surprised when you come to know him better: he is really the most helpless of mortals.* You get quite a protective feeling towards him.

MRS HUSHABYE. Then who manages his business, pray?

MAZZINI. I do. And of course other people like me.

MRS HUSHABYE. Footling people, you mean.

MAZZINI. I suppose youd think us so.

MRS HUSHABYE. And pray why dont you do without him if youre all so much cleverer?*

MAZZINI. Oh, we couldnt: we should ruin the business in a year. I've tried; and I know. We should spend too much on everything. We should improve the quality of the goods and make them too dear. We should be sentimental about the hard cases among the workpeople. But Mangan keeps us in order. He is down on us about every extra halfpenny. We could never do without him. You see, he will sit up all night thinking of how to save sixpence. Wont Ellie make him jump, though, when she takes his house in hand!

MRS HUSHABYE. Then the creature is a fraud even as a captain of industry!

MAZZINI. I am afraid all the captains of industry are what *you* call frauds, Mrs Hushabye. Of course there are some manufacturers who really do understand their own works; but they dont make as high a rate of profit as Mangan does. I assure you Mangan is quite a good fellow in his way. He means well.

MRS HUSHABYE. He doesnt look well. He is not in his first youth, is he?

MAZZINI. After all, no husband is in his first youth for very long, Mrs Hushabye. And men cant afford to marry in their first youth nowadays.

MRS HUSHABYE. Now if *I* said that, it would sound witty. Why cant *you* say it wittily?* What on earth is the matter with you? Why dont you inspire everybody with confidence? with respect?

MAZZINI [*humbly*] I think that what is the matter with me is that I am poor. You dont know what that means at home. Mind: I dont say they have ever complained. Theyve all been wonderful: theyve been proud of my poverty. Theyve even joked about it quite often. But my wife has had a very poor time of it. She has been quite resigned—

MRS HUSHABYE [*shuddering involuntarily*]!!

MAZZINI. There! You see, Mrs Hushabye. I dont want Ellie to live on resignation.

MRS HUSHABYE. Do you want her to have to resign herself to living with a man she doesnt love?

MAZZINI [*wistfully*] Are you sure that would be worse than living with a man she did love, if he was a footling person?

MRS HUSHABYE [*relaxing her contemptuous attitude, quite interested in Mazzini now*] You know, I really think you must love Ellie very much; for you become quite clever when you talk about her.

MAZZINI. I didnt know I was so very stupid on other subjects.

MRS HUSHABYE. You are, sometimes.

MAZZINI [*turning his head away; for his eyes are wet*] I have learnt a good deal about myself from you, Mrs Hushabye; and I'm afraid I shall not be the happier for your plain speaking. But if you thought I needed it to make me think of Ellie's happiness you were very much mistaken.

MRS HUSHABYE [*leaning towards him kindly*] Have I been a beast?

MAZZINI [*pulling himself together*] It doesnt matter about me, Mrs Hushabye. I think you like Ellie; and that is enough for me.

MRS HUSHABYE. I'm beginning to like you a little. I perfectly loathed you at first. I thought you the most odious, self-satisfied, boresome elderly prig I ever met.

MAZZINI [*resigned, and now quite cheerful*] I daresay I am all that. I never have been a favorite with gorgeous women like you. They always frighten me.

MRS HUSHABYE [*pleased*] Am I a gorgeous woman, Mazzini? I shall fall in love with you presently.

MAZZINI [*with placid gallantry*] No you wont, Hesione. But you would be quite safe. Would you believe it that quite a lot of women have flirted with me because I am quite safe? But they get tired of me for the same reason.

MRS HUSHABYE [*mischievously*] Take care. You may not be so safe as you think.

MAZZINI. Oh yes, quite safe. You see, I have been in love really: the sort of love that only happens once. [*Softly*] Thats why Ellie is such a lovely girl.

MRS HUSHABYE. Well, really, you *are* coming out. Are you quite sure you wont let me tempt you into a second grand passion?

MAZZINI. Quite. It wouldnt be natural. The fact is, you dont strike on my box, Mrs Hushabye; and I certainly dont strike on yours.

MRS HUSHABYE. I see. Your marriage was a safety match.

MAZZINI. What a very witty application of the expression I used! I should never have thought of it.

Ellie comes in from the garden, looking anything but happy.

MRS HUSHABYE [*rising*] Oh! here is Ellie at last. [*She goes behind the sofa*].

ELLIE [*on the threshold of the starboard door*] Guinness said you wanted me: you and papa.

MRS HUSHABYE. You have kept us waiting so long that it almost came to—well, never mind. Your father is a very wonderful man [*she ruffles his hair affectionately*]: the only one I ever met who could resist me when I made myself really agreeable. [*She comes to the big chair, on Mangan's left*]. Come here. I have something to shew you.* [*Ellie strolls listlessly to the other side of the chair*]. Look.

ELLIE [*contemplating Mangan without interest*] I know. He is only asleep. We had a talk after dinner; and he fell asleep in the middle of it.

MRS HUSHABYE. You did it, Ellie. You put him asleep.

MAZZINI [*rising quickly and coming to the back of the chair*] Oh, I hope not. Did you, Ellie?

ELLIE [*wearily*] He asked me to.

MAZZINI. But it's dangerous. You know what happened to me.

ELLIE [*utterly indifferent*] Oh, I daresay I can wake him. If not, somebody else can.

MRS HUSHABYE. It doesnt matter, anyhow, because I have at last persuaded your father that you dont want to marry him.

ELLIE [*suddenly coming out of her listlessness, much vexed*] But why did you do that, Hesione? I do want to marry him. I fully intend to marry him.

MAZZINI. Are you quite sure, Ellie? Mrs Hushabye has made me feel that I may have been thoughtless and selfish about it.

ELLIE [*very clearly and steadily*] Papa. When Mrs Hushabye takes it on herself to explain to you what I think or dont think, shut your ears tight; and shut your eyes too. Hesione knows nothing about me: she hasnt the least notion of the sort of person I am, and never will. I promise you I wont do anything I dont want to do and mean to do for my own sake.*

MAZZINI. You are quite, quite sure?

ELLIE. Quite, quite sure. Now you must go away and leave me to talk to Mrs Hushabye.

MAZZINI. But I should like to hear. Shall I be in the way?

ELLIE [*inexorable*] I had rather talk to her alone.

MAZZINI [*affectionately*] Oh, well, I know what a nuisance parents are, dear. I will be good and go. [*He goes to the garden door*]. By the way, do you remember the address of that professional who woke me up? Dont you think I had better telegraph* to him.

MRS HUSHABYE [*moving towards the sofa*] It's too late to telegraph tonight.

MAZZINI. I suppose so. I do hope he'll wake up in the course of the night. [*He goes out into the garden*].

ELLIE [*turning vigorously on Hesione the moment her father is out of the room*] Hesione: what the devil do you mean by making mischief with my father about Mangan?

MRS HUSHABYE [*promptly losing her temper*] Dont you dare speak to me like that, you little minx. Remember that you are in my house.

ELLIE. Stuff! Why dont you mind your own business? What is it to you whether I choose to marry Mangan or not?

MRS HUSHABYE. Do you suppose you can bully me, you miserable little matrimonial adventurer?

ELLIE. Every woman who hasnt any money is a matrimonial adventurer. It's easy for you to talk: you have never known what it is to want money; and you can pick up men as if they were daisies. I am poor and respectable—

MRS HUSHABYE [*interrupting*] Ho! respectable! How did you pick up Mangan? How did you pick up my husband? You have the audacity to tell me that I am a—a—a—

ELLIE. A siren.* So you are. You were born to lead men by the nose: if you werent, Marcus would have waited for me, perhaps.

MRS HUSHABYE [*suddenly melting and half laughing*] Oh, my poor Ellie, my pettikins, my unhappy darling! I am so sorry about Hector. But what can I do? It's not my fault: I'd give him to you if I could.

ELLIE. I dont blame you for that.

MRS HUSHABYE. What a brute I was to quarrel with you and call you names! Do kiss me and say youre not angry with me.

ELLIE [*fiercely*] Oh, dont slop and gush and be sentimental. Dont you see that unless I can be hard—as hard as nails—I shall go mad. I dont care a damn about your calling me names: do you think a woman in my situation can feel a few hard words?*

MRS HUSHABYE. Poor little woman! Poor little situation!

ELLIE. I suppose you think youre being sympathetic. You are just foolish and stupid and selfish.* You see me getting a smasher* right in the face that kills a whole part of my life: the best part that can never come again; and you think you can help me over it by a little coaxing and kissing. When I want all the strength I can get to lean on: something iron, something stony, I dont care how cruel it is, you go all mushy and want to slobber over me. I'm not angry; I'm not unfriendly; but for God's sake do pull yourself together; and dont think that because youre on velvet and always have been, women who are in hell can take it as easily as you.

MRS HUSHABYE [*shrugging her shoulders*] Very well. [*She sits down on the sofa in her old place*]. But I warn you that when I am neither coaxing and kissing nor laughing, I am just wondering how much longer I can stand living in this cruel, damnable world.* You object to the siren: well, I drop the siren. You want to rest your wounded bosom against a grindstone.* Well [*folding her arms*], here is the grindstone.

ELLIE [*sitting down beside her, appeased*] Thats better: you really have the trick of falling in with everyone's mood; but you dont understand, because you are not the sort of woman for whom there is only one man and only one chance.

MRS HUSHABYE. I certainly dont understand how your marrying that object [*indicating Mangan*] will console you for not being able to marry Hector.

ELLIE. Perhaps you dont understand why I was quite a nice girl this morning, and am now neither a girl nor particularly nice.

MRS HUSHABYE. Oh yes I do. It's because you have made up your mind to do something despicable and wicked.*

ELLIE. I dont think so, Hesione. I must make the best of my ruined house.

MRS HUSHABYE. Pooh! Youll get over it. Your house isnt ruined.

ELLIE. Of course I shall get over it. You dont suppose I'm going to sit down and die of a broken heart, I hope, or be an old maid living on a pittance from the Sick and Indigent Room-keepers' Association.* But my heart is broken,* all the same. What I mean by that is that I know that what has happened to me with Marcus will not happen to me ever again. In the world for me there is Marcus and a lot of other men of whom one is just the same as another. Well, if I cant have love, thats no reason why I should have poverty. If Mangan has nothing else, he has money.

MRS HUSHABYE. And are there no *young* men with money?

ELLIE. Not within my reach. Besides, a young man would have the right to expect love from me, and would perhaps leave me when he found I could not give it to him. Rich young men can get rid of their wives, you know, pretty cheaply. But this object, as you call him, can expect nothing more from me than I am prepared to give him.

MRS HUSHABYE. He will be your owner, remember. If he buys you, he will make the bargain pay him and not you. Ask your father.

ELLIE [*rising and strolling to the chair to contemplate their subject*] You need not trouble on that score, Hesione. I have more to give Boss Mangan than he has to give me: it is I who am buying him, and at a pretty good price too, I think. Women are better at that sort of bargain than men. I have taken the Boss's measure;* and ten Boss Mangans shall not prevent me doing far more as I please as his wife than I have ever been able to do as a poor girl. [*Stooping to the recumbent figure*] Shall they, Boss? I think not. [*She passes on to the drawing-table, and leans against the end of it, facing the windows*]. I shall not have to spend most of my time wondering how long my gloves will last, anyhow.

MRS HUSHABYE [*rising superbly*] Ellie: you are a wicked sordid little beast. And to think that I actually condescended to fascinate that creature there to save you from him! Well, let me tell you this: if you make this disgusting match, you will never see Hector again if I can help it.

ELLIE [*unmoved*] I nailed Mangan by telling him that if he did not marry me he should never see you again [*she lifts herself on her wrists and seats herself on the end of the table*].

MRS HUSHABYE [*recoiling*] Oh!

ELLIE. So you see I am not unprepared for your playing that trump against me. Well, you just try it: thats all. I should have made a man of Marcus, not a household pet.

MRS HUSHABYE [*flaming*] You dare!

ELLIE [*looking almost dangerous*] Set him thinking about me if *you* dare.

MRS HUSHABYE. Well, of all the impudent little fiends I ever met! Hector* says there is a certain point at which the only answer you can give to a man who breaks all the rules is to knock him down. What would you say if I were to box your ears?

ELLIE [*calmly*] I should pull your hair.

MRS HUSHABYE [*mischievously*] That wouldnt hurt me. Perhaps it comes off at night.

ELLIE [*so taken aback that she drops off the table and runs to her*] Oh, you dont mean to say, Hesione, that your beautiful black hair is false?

MRS HUSHABYE [*patting it*] Dont tell Hector. He believes in it.

ELLIE [*groaning*] Oh! Even the hair that ensnared him false! Everything false!

MRS HUSHABYE. Pull it and try. Other women can snare men in their hair; but I can swing a baby on mine.* Aha! you cant do that, Goldylocks.

ELLIE [*heartbroken*] No. You have stolen my babies.

MRS HUSHABYE. Pettikins: dont make me cry. You know, what you said about my making a household pet of him is a little true. Perhaps he ought to have waited for you. Would any other woman on earth forgive you?

ELLIE. Oh, what right had you to take him all for yourself! [*Pulling herself together*] There! You couldnt help it:* neither of us could help it. He couldnt help it. No: dont say anything more: I cant bear it. Let us wake the object. [*She begins stroking Mangan's head, reversing the movement with which she put him to sleep*]. Wake up, do you hear? You are to wake up at once. Wake up, wake up, wake—

MANGAN [*bouncing out of the chair in a fury and turning on them*] Wake up! So you think Ive been asleep, do you? [*He kicks the chair violently back out of his way, and gets between them*]. You throw me into a trance so that I cant move hand or foot—I might have been buried alive! it's a mercy I wasnt—and then you think I was only asleep. If youd let me drop the two times you rolled me about, my nose would have been flattened for life against the floor. But Ive found you all out, anyhow. I know the sort of people I'm among now. Ive heard every word youve said, you and your precious father, and [*to Mrs Hushabye*] you too. So I'm an object, am I? I'm a thing, am I? I'm a fool that hasnt sense enough to feed myself properly, am I? I'm afraid of the men that would starve if it werent for the wages I give them, am I? I'm nothing but a disgusting old skinflint* to be made a convenience of by designing women and fool managers of my works, am I? I'm—

MRS HUSHABYE [*with the most elegant aplomb*] Sh-sh-sh-sh-sh! Mr Mangan: you are bound in honor to obliterate from your mind all you heard while you were pretending to be asleep. It was not meant for you to hear.

MANGAN. Pretending to be asleep! Do you think if I was only pretending that I'd have sprawled there helpless, and listened to such unfairness, such lies, such injustice and plotting and backbiting and slandering of me, if I could have up and told you what I thought of you! I wonder I didnt burst.

MRS HUSHABYE [*sweetly*] You dreamt it all, Mr Mangan. We were only saying how beautifully peaceful you looked in your sleep. That was all, wasnt it, Ellie? Believe me, Mr Mangan, all those unpleasant things came into your mind in the last half second before you woke. Ellie rubbed your hair the wrong way; and the disagreeable sensation suggested a disagreeable dream.

MANGAN [*doggedly*] I believe in dreams.

MRS HUSHABYE. So do I. But they go by contraries, dont they?

MANGAN [*depths of emotion suddenly welling up in him*] I shant forget,* to my dying day, that when you gave me the glad eye that time in the garden, you were making a fool of me. That was a dirty low mean thing to do. You had no right to let me come near you if I disgusted you. It isnt my fault if I'm old and havnt a moustache like a bronze candlestick as your husband has. There are things no decent woman would do to a man—like a man hitting a woman in the breast.

Hesione, utterly shamed, sits down on the sofa and covers her face with her hands. Mangan sits down also on his chair and begins to cry like a child. Ellie stares at them. Mrs Hushabye, at the distressing sound he makes, takes down her hands and looks at him. She rises and runs to him.

MRS HUSHABYE. Dont cry: I cant bear it. Have I broken your heart? I didnt know you had one. How could I?

MANGAN. I'm a man aint I?

MRS HUSHABYE [*half coaxing, half rallying, altogether tenderly*] Oh no: not what I call a man. Only a Boss: just that and nothing else. What business has a Boss with a heart?

MANGAN. Then youre not a bit sorry for what you did, nor ashamed?

MRS HUSHABYE. I was ashamed for the first time in my life when you said that about hitting a woman in the breast, and I found out what I'd done. My very bones blushed red. Youve had your revenge, Boss. Arnt you satisfied?

MANGAN. Serve you right! Do you hear? Serve you right! Youre just cruel. Cruel.

MRS HUSHABYE. Yes: cruelty would be delicious if one could only find some sort of cruelty that didnt really hurt. By the way [*sitting down beside him on the arm of the chair*], whats your name? It's not really Boss, is it?

MANGAN [*shortly*] If you want to know, my name's Alfred.

MRS HUSHABYE [*springing up*] Alfred!! Ellie: he was christened after Tennyson!!!*

MANGAN [*rising*] I was christened after my uncle, and never had a penny from him, damn him! What of it?

MRS HUSHABYE. It comes to me suddenly that you are a real person:* that you had a mother, like anyone else. [*Putting her hands on his shoulders and surveying him*] Little Alf!

MANGAN. Well, you have a nerve.

MRS HUSHABYE. And you have a heart, Alfy, a whimpering little heart, but a real one. [*Releasing him suddenly*] Now run and make it up with Ellie. She has had time to think what to say to you, which is more than I had [*she goes out quickly into the garden by the port door*].

MANGAN. That woman has a pair of hands that go right through you.

ELLIE. Still in love with her, in spite of all we said about you?

MANGAN. Are all women like you two? Do they never think of anything about a man except what they can get out of him? *You* werent even thinking that about me. You were only thinking whether your gloves would last.

ELLIE. I shall not have to think about that when we are married.

MANGAN. And you think I am going to marry you after what I heard there!

ELLIE. You heard nothing from me that I did not tell you before.

MANGAN. Perhaps you think I cant do without you.

ELLIE. I think you would feel lonely without us all now, after coming to know us so well.

MANGAN [*with something like a yell of despair*] Am I never to have the last word?

CAPTAIN SHOTOVER [*appearing at the starboard garden door*] There is a soul in torment here. What is the matter?

MANGAN. This girl doesnt want to spend her life wondering how long her gloves will last.

CAPTAIN SHOTOVER [*passing through*] Dont wear any. I never do [*he goes into the pantry*].

LADY UTTERWORD [*appearing at the port garden door, in a handsome dinner dress*] Is anything the matter?

ELLIE. This gentleman wants to know is he never to have the last word?

LADY UTTERWORD [*coming forward to the sofa*] I should let him have it, my dear. The important thing is not to have the last word, but to have your own way.

MANGAN. She wants both.

LADY UTTERWORD. She wont get them, Mr Mangan. Providence* always has the last word.

MANGAN [*desperately*] Now *you* are going to come religion over me. In this house a man's mind might as well be a football. I'm going. [*He makes for the hall, but is stopped by a hail from the Captain, who has just emerged from his pantry*].

CAPTAIN SHOTOVER. Whither away, Boss Mangan?

MANGAN. To hell out of this house: let that be enough for you and all here.

CAPTAIN SHOTOVER. You were welcome to come: you are free to go. The wide earth, the high seas, the spacious skies are waiting for you outside.

LADY UTTERWORD. But your things, Mr Mangan. Your bags, your comb and brushes, your pyjamas—

HECTOR [*who has just appeared in the port doorway in a handsome Arab costume**] Why should the escaping slave take his chains with him?

MANGAN. Thats right, Hushabye. Keep the pyjamas, my lady; and much good may they do you.

HECTOR [*advancing to Lady Utterword's left hand*] Let us all go out into the night and leave everything behind us.

MANGAN. You stay where you are, the lot of you. I want no company, especially female company.

ELLIE. Let him go. He is unhappy here. He is angry with us.

CAPTAIN SHOTOVER. Go, Boss Mangan; and when you have found the land where there is happiness and where there are no women, send me its latitude and longitude;* and I will join you there.

LADY UTTERWORD. You will certainly not be comfortable without your luggage, Mr Mangan.

ELLIE [*impatient*] Go, go: why dont you go? It is a heavenly night: you can sleep on the heath.* Take my waterproof* to lie on: it is hanging up in the hall.

HECTOR. Breakfast at nine, unless you prefer to breakfast with the Captain at six.

ELLIE. Good night, Alfred.*

HECTOR. Alfred! [*He runs back to the door and calls into the garden*] Randall: Mangan's Christian name is Alfred.

RANDALL [*appearing in the starboard doorway in evening dress*] Then Hesione wins her bet.

Mrs Hushabye appears in the port doorway. She throws her left arm round Hector's neck; draws him with her to the back of the sofa; and throws her right arm round Lady Utterword's neck.

MRS HUSHABYE. They wouldnt believe me, Alf.

They contemplate him.

MANGAN. Is there any more of you coming in to look at me, as if I was the latest thing in a menagerie.*

MRS HUSHABYE. You *are* the latest thing in this menagerie.

Before Mangan can retort, a fall of furniture is heard from upstairs; then a pistol shot, and a yell of pain. The staring group breaks up in consternation.

MAZZINI'S VOICE [*from above*] Help! A burglar! Help!

HECTOR [*his eyes blazing*] A burglar!!!

MRS HUSHABYE. No, Hector: youll be shot [*but it is too late: he has dashed out past Mangan, who hastily moves towards the bookshelves out of his way*].

CAPTAIN SHOTOVER [*blowing his whistle*] All hands aloft! [*He strides out after Hector*].

LADY UTTERWORD. My diamonds! [*She follows the Captain*].

RANDALL [*rushing after her*] No, Ariadne. Let me.

ELLIE. Oh, is papa shot? [*she runs out*].

MRS HUSHABYE. Are you frightened, Alf?

MANGAN. No. It aint my house, thank God.

MRS HUSHABYE. If they catch a burglar, shall we have to go into court as witnesses, and be asked all sorts of questions about our private lives?

MANGAN. You wont be believed if you tell the truth.*

Mazzini, terribly upset, with a duelling pistol in his hand, comes from the hall, and makes his way to the drawing-table.

MAZZINI. Oh, my dear Mrs Hushabye, I might have killed him [*He throws the pistol on the table and staggers round to the chair*]. I hope you wont believe I really intended to.

Hector comes in, marching an old and villainous looking man before him by the collar. He plants him in the middle of the room and releases him.
Ellie follows, and immediately runs across to the back of her father's chair, and pats his shoulders.

RANDALL [*entering with a poker*] Keep your eye on this door, Mangan. I'll look after the other [*he goes to the starboard door and stands on guard there*].

Lady Utterword comes in after Randall, and goes between Mrs Hushabye and Mangan.
Nurse Guinness brings up the rear, and waits near the door, on Mangan's left.

MRS HUSHABYE. What has happened?

MAZZINI. Your housekeeper told me there was somebody upstairs, and gave me a pistol that Mr Hushabye had been practising with. I thought it would frighten him; but it went off at a touch.

THE BURGLAR. Yes, and took the skin off my ear. Precious near took the top off my head. Why dont you have a proper revolver instead of a thing like that, that goes off if you as much as blow on it?

HECTOR. One of my duelling pistols. Sorry.

MAZZINI. He put his hands up and said it was a fair cop.*

THE BURGLAR. So it was. Send for the police.

HECTOR. No, by thunder! It was not a fair cop. We were four to one.

MRS HUSHABYE. What will they do to him?

THE BURGLAR. Ten years. Beginning with solitary.* Ten years off my life. I shant serve it all: I'm too old. It will see me out.

LADY UTTERWORD. You should have thought of that before you stole my diamonds.

THE BURGLAR. Well, youve got them back, lady: havnt you? Can you give me back the years of my life you are going to take from me?

MRS HUSHABYE. Oh, we cant bury a man alive for ten years for a few diamonds.

THE BURGLAR. Ten little shining diamonds! Ten long black years!

LADY UTTERWORD. Think of what it is for us to be dragged through the horrors of a criminal court, and have all our family affairs in the papers! If you were a native, and Hastings could order you a good beating and send you away, I shouldnt mind; but here in England there is no real protection for any respectable person.

THE BURGLAR. I'm too old to be giv a hiding, lady. Send for the police and have done with it. It's only just and right you should.

RANDALL [*who has relaxed his vigilance on seeing the burglar so pacifically disposed, and comes forward swinging the poker between his fingers like a well-folded umbrella*] It is neither just nor right that we should be put to a lot of inconvenience to gratify your moral enthusiasm, my friend. You had better get out, while you have the chance.

THE BURGLAR [*inexorably*] No. I must work my sin off my conscience. This has come as a sort of call to me. Let me spend the rest of my life repenting in a cell. I shall have my reward above.

MANGAN [*exasperated*] The very burglars cant behave naturally in this house.

HECTOR. My good sir: you must work out your salvation at somebody else's expense. Nobody here is going to charge you.

THE BURGLAR. Oh, you wont charge me, wont you?

HECTOR. No. I'm sorry to be inhospitable; but will you kindly leave
the house?

THE BURGLAR. Right. I'll go to the police station and give myself up.
[*He turns resolutely to the door; but Hector stops him*].

HECTOR.   Oh no. You mustnt do that.

RANDALL.   No, no. Clear out, man, cant you; and dont be
                               a fool.

MRS HUSHABYE.   Dont be so silly. Cant you repent at home?

LADY UTTERWORD. You will have to do as you are told.

THE BURGLAR. It's compounding a felony, you know.

MRS HUSHABYE. This is utterly ridiculous. Are we to be forced to
prosecute this man when we dont want to?

THE BURGLAR. Am I to be robbed of my salvation to save you the
trouble of spending a day at the sessions? Is that justice? Is it right?
Is it fair to me?

MAZZINI [*rising and leaning across the table persuasively as if it were
a pulpit desk or a shop counter*] Come, come! let me shew you how you
can turn your very crimes to account. Why not set up as a locksmith?
You must know more about locks than most honest men?

THE BURGLAR. Thats true, sir. But I couldnt set up as a locksmith
under twenty pounds.

RANDALL. Well, you can easily steal twenty pounds. You will find it in
the nearest bank.

THE BURGLAR [*horrified*] Oh what a thing for a gentleman to put into
the head of a poor criminal scrambling out of the bottomless pit as it
were! Oh, shame on you, sir! Oh, God forgive you! [*He throws
himself into the big chair and covers his face as if in prayer*].

LADY UTTERWORD. Really, Randall!

HECTOR. It seems to me that we shall have to take up a collection for
this inopportunely contrite sinner.

LADY UTTERWORD. But twenty pounds is ridiculous.

THE BURGLAR [*looking up quickly*] I shall have to buy a lot of tools, lady.

LADY UTTERWORD. Nonsense: you have your burgling kit.

THE BURGLAR. Whats a jemmy* and a centrebit and an acetylene welding plant and a bunch of skeleton keys?* I shall want a forge, and a smithy, and a shop, and fittings. I cant hardly do it for twenty.

HECTOR. My worthy friend, we havnt got twenty pounds.

THE BURGLAR [*now master of the situation*] You can raise it among you, cant you?

MRS HUSHABYE. Give him a sovereign, Hector; and get rid of him.

HECTOR [*giving him a pound*] There! Off with you.

THE BURGLAR [*rising and taking the money very ungratefully*] I wont promise nothing. You have more on you than a quid:* all the lot of you, I mean.

LADY UTTERWORD [*vigorously*] Oh, let us prosecute him and have done with it. I have a conscience too, I hope; and I do not feel at all sure that we have any right to let him go, especially if he is going to be greedy and impertinent.

THE BURGLAR [*quickly*] All right, lady, all right. Ive no wish to be anything but agreeable. Good evening, ladies and gentlemen; and thank you kindly.

He is hurrying out when he is confronted in the doorway by Captain Shotover.

CAPTAIN SHOTOVER [*fixing the burglar with a piercing regard*] *Whats this?* Are there two of you?

THE BURGLAR [*falling on his knees before the Captain in abject terror*] Oh my good Lord, what have I done? Dont tell me it's *your* house Ive broken into, Captain Shotover.

The Captain seizes him by the collar; drags him to his feet; and leads him to the middle of the group, Hector falling back beside his wife to make way for them.

CAPTAIN SHOTOVER [*turning him towards Ellie*] Is that your daughter? [*He releases him*].

THE BURGLAR. Well, how do I know, Captain? You know the sort of life you and me has led. Any young lady of that age might be my daughter anywhere in the wide world, as you might say.

CAPTAIN SHOTOVER [*to Mazzini*] You are not Billy Dunn. This is Billy Dunn. Why have you imposed on me?

THE BURGLAR [*indignantly to Mazzini*] Have you been giving yourself out to be me? You, that nigh* blew my head off! Shooting *yourself*, in a manner of speaking!

MAZZINI. My dear Captain Shotover, ever since I came into this house I have done hardly anything else but assure you that I am not Mr William Dunn, but Mazzini Dunn, a very different person.

THE BURGLAR. He dont belong to my branch, Captain.* Theres two sets in the family: the thinking Dunns and the drinking Dunns, each going their own ways. I'm a drinking Dunn: he's a thinking Dunn. But that didnt give him any right to shoot me.

CAPTAIN SHOTOVER. So youve turned burglar, have you?

THE BURGLAR. No, Captain: I wouldnt disgrace our old sea calling by such a thing. I am no burglar.

LADY UTTERWORD. What were you doing with my diamonds?

GUINNESS. What did you break into the house for if youre no burglar?

RANDALL. Mistook the house for your own and came in by the wrong window, eh?

THE BURGLAR. Well, it's no use my telling you a lie: I can take in most captains, but not Captain Shotover, because he sold himself to the devil in Zanzibar, and can divine water, spot gold, explode a cartridge in your pocket with a glance of his eye, and see the truth hidden in the heart of man. But I'm no burglar.

CAPTAIN SHOTOVER. Are you an honest man?

THE BURGLAR. I dont set up to be better than my fellow-creatures, and never did, as you well know, Captain. But what I do is innocent and pious. I enquire about for houses where the right sort of people live. I work it on them same as I worked it here. I break into the house; put a few spoons or diamonds in my pocket; make a noise; get caught; and take up a collection. And you wouldnt believe how hard it is to get caught when youre actually trying to. I have knocked over all the chairs in a room without a soul paying any attention to me. In the end I have had to walk out and leave the job.

RANDALL. When that happens, do you put back the spoons and diamonds?

THE BURGLAR. Well, I dont fly in the face of Providence, if thats what you want to know.

CAPTAIN SHOTOVER. Guinness: you remember this man?

GUINNESS. I should think I do, seeing I was married to him, the blackguard!

HESIONE ⎱ *exclaiming* ⎰ Married to him!
LADY UTTERWORD ⎰ *together* ⎱ Guinness!!

THE BURGLAR. It wasnt legal. Ive been married to no end of women. No use coming that over me.

CAPTAIN SHOTOVER. Take him to the forecastle* [*he flings him to the door with a strength beyond his years*].

GUINNESS. I suppose you mean the kitchen. They wont have him there. Do you expect servants to keep company with thieves and all sorts?

CAPTAIN SHOTOVER. Land-thieves and water-thieves are the same flesh and blood. I'll have no boatswain on my quarter-deck. Off with you both.

THE BURGLAR. Yes, Captain. [*He goes out humbly*].

MAZZINI. Will it be safe to have him in the house like that?

GUINNESS. Why didnt you shoot him, sir? If I'd known who he was, I'd have shot him myself. [*She goes out*].

MRS HUSHABYE. Do sit down, everybody. [*She sits down on the sofa*].

They all move except Ellie. Mazzini resumes his seat. Randall sits down in the window seat near the starboard door, again making a pendulum of his poker, and studying it as Galileo* might have done. Hector sits on his left, in the middle. Mangan, forgotten, sits in the port corner. Lady Utterword takes the big chair. Captain Shotover goes into the pantry in deep abstraction. They all look after him; and Lady Utterword coughs consciously.

MRS HUSHABYE. So Billy Dunn was poor nurse's little romance. I knew there had been somebody.

RANDALL. They will fight their battles over again and enjoy themselves immensely.

LADY UTTERWORD [*irritably*] You are not married; and you know nothing about it, Randall. Hold your tongue.

RANDALL. Tyrant!

MRS HUSHABYE. Well, we have had a very exciting evening. Everything will be an anticlimax after it. We'd better all go to bed.

RANDALL. Another burglar may turn up.

MAZZINI. Oh, impossible! I hope not.

RANDALL. Why not? There is more than one burglar in England.

MRS HUSHABYE. What do you say, Alf?

MANGAN [*huffily*] Oh, I dont matter. I'm forgotten. The burglar has put my nose out of joint. Shove me into a corner and have done with me.

MRS HUSHABYE [*jumping up mischievously, and going to him*] Would you like a walk on the heath, Alfred? With me?

ELLIE. Go, Mr Mangan. It will do you good. Hesione will soothe you.

MRS HUSHABYE [*slipping her arm under his and pulling him upright*] Come, Alfred. There is a moon: it's like the night in Tristan and Isolde.* [*She caresses his arm and draws him to the port garden door*].

MANGAN [*writhing but yielding*] How you can have the face—the heart—[*he breaks down and is heard sobbing as she takes him out*].

LADY UTTERWORD. What an extraordinary way to behave! What is the matter with the man?

ELLIE [*in a strangely calm voice, staring into an imaginary distance*] His heart is breaking: that is all. [*The Captain appears at the pantry door, listening*]. It is a curious sensation: the sort of pain that goes mercifully beyond our powers of feeling. When your heart is broken, your boats are burned: nothing matters any more. It is the end of happiness and the beginning of peace.

LADY UTTERWORD [*suddenly rising in a rage, to the astonishment of the rest*] How dare you?

HECTOR. Good heavens! Whats the matter?*

RANDALL [*in a warning whisper*] Tch—tch—tch! Steady.

ELLIE [*surprised and haughty*] I was not addressing you particularly, Lady Utterword. And I am not accustomed to be asked how dare I.

LADY UTTERWORD. Of course not. Anyone can see how badly you have been brought up.

MAZZINI. Oh, I hope not, Lady Utterword. Really!

LADY UTTERWORD. I know very well what you meant. The impudence!

ELLIE. What on earth do you mean?

CAPTAIN SHOTOVER [*advancing to the table*] She means that her heart will not break. She has been longing all her life for someone to break it. At last she has become afraid she has none to break.

LADY UTTERWORD [*flinging herself on her knees and throwing her arms round him*] Papa: dont say you think Ive no heart.

CAPTAIN SHOTOVER [*raising her with grim tenderness*] If you had no heart how could you want to have it broken, child?

HECTOR [*rising with a bound*] Lady Utterword: you are not to be trusted. You have made a scene [*he runs out into the garden through the starboard door*].

LADY UTTERWORD. Oh! Hector, Hector! [*she runs out after him*].

RANDALL. Only nerves, I assure you. [*He rises and follows her, waving the poker in his agitation*] Ariadne! Ariadne! For God's sake be careful. You will—[*he is gone*].

MAZZINI [*rising*] How distressing! Can I do anything, I wonder?

CAPTAIN SHOTOVER [*promptly taking his chair and setting to work at the drawing-board*] No. Go to bed. Goodnight.

MAZZINI [*bewildered*] Oh! Perhaps you are right.

ELLIE. Goodnight, dearest. [*She kisses him*].

MAZZINI. Goodnight, love. [*He makes for the door, but turns aside to the bookshelves*]. I'll just take a book [*he takes one*]. Goodnight. [*He goes out, leaving Ellie alone with the Captain*].

The Captain is intent on his drawing. Ellie, standing sentry over his chair, contemplates him for a moment.

ELLIE. Does nothing ever disturb you, Captain Shotover?

CAPTAIN SHOTOVER. Ive stood on the bridge for eighteen hours in a typhoon. Life here is stormier; but I can stand it.

ELLIE. Do you think I ought to marry Mr Mangan?

CAPTAIN SHOTOVER [*never looking up*] One rock is as good as another to be wrecked on.

ELLIE. I am not in love with him.

CAPTAIN SHOTOVER. Who said you were?

ELLIE. You are not surprised?

CAPTAIN SHOTOVER. Surprised! At *my* age!

ELLIE. It seems to me quite fair. He wants me for one thing: I want him for another.

CAPTAIN SHOTOVER. Money?

ELLIE. Yes.

CAPTAIN SHOTOVER. Well, one turns the cheek: the other kisses it. One provides the cash: the other spends it.

ELLIE. Who will have the best of the bargain, I wonder?

CAPTAIN SHOTOVER. You. These fellows live in an office all day. You will have to put up with him from dinner to breakfast; but you will both be asleep most of that time. All day you will be quit of him; and you will be shopping with his money. If that is too much for you, marry a seafaring man: you will be bothered with him only three weeks in the year, perhaps.

ELLIE. That would be best of all, I suppose.

CAPTAIN SHOTOVER. It's a dangerous thing to be married right up to the hilt,* like my daughter's husband. The man is at home all day, like a damned soul in hell.

ELLIE. I never thought of that before.

CAPTAIN SHOTOVER. If youre marrying for business, you cant be too businesslike.

ELLIE. Why do women always want other women's husbands?

CAPTAIN SHOTOVER. Why do horse-thieves prefer a horse that is broken-in to one that is wild?

ELLIE [*with a short laugh*] I suppose so. What a vile world it is!

CAPTAIN SHOTOVER. It doesnt concern me. I'm nearly out of it.

ELLIE. And I'm only just beginning.

CAPTAIN SHOTOVER. Yes; so look ahead.

ELLIE. Well, I think I am being very prudent.

CAPTAIN SHOTOVER. I didnt say prudent. I said look ahead.

ELLIE. Whats the difference?

CAPTAIN SHOTOVER. It's prudent to gain the whole world and lose your own soul. But dont forget that your soul sticks to you if you stick to it; but the world has a way of slipping through your fingers.

ELLIE [*wearily, leaving him and beginning to wander restlessly about the room*] I'm sorry, Captain Shotover; but it's no use talking like that to me. Old-fashioned people are no use to me. Old-fashioned people think you can have a soul without money. They think the less money you have, the more soul you have. Young people nowadays know better. A soul is a very expensive thing to keep: much more so than a motor car.

CAPTAIN SHOTOVER. Is it? How much does your soul eat?

ELLIE. Oh, a lot. It eats music and pictures and books and mountains and lakes and beautiful things to wear and nice people to be with. In this country you cant have them without lots of money: that is why our souls are so horribly starved.

CAPTAIN SHOTOVER. Mangan's soul lives on pigs' food.

ELLIE. Yes: money is thrown away on him. I suppose his soul was starved when he was young. But it will not be thrown away on me. It is just because I want to save my soul that I am marrying for money. All the women who are not fools do.

CAPTAIN SHOTOVER. There are other ways of getting money. Why dont you steal it?

ELLIE. Because I dont want to go to prison.

CAPTAIN SHOTOVER. Is that the only reason? Are you quite sure honesty has nothing to do with it?

ELLIE. Oh, you are very very old-fashioned, Captain. Does any modern girl believe that the legal and illegal ways of getting money are the honest and dishonest ways? Mangan robbed my father and my father's friends. I should rob all the money back from Mangan if the police would let me. As they wont, I must get it back by marrying him.

CAPTAIN SHOTOVER. I cant argue: I'm too old: my mind is made up and finished. All I can tell you is that, old-fashioned or new-fashioned, if you sell yourself, you deal your soul a blow that all the books and pictures and concerts and scenery in the world wont heal [*he gets up suddenly and makes for the pantry*].

ELLIE [*running after him and seizing him by the sleeve*] Then why did you sell yourself to the devil in Zanzibar?

CAPTAIN SHOTOVER [*stopping, startled*] What?

ELLIE. You shall not run away before you answer. I have found out that trick of yours. If you sold yourself, why shouldnt I?

CAPTAIN SHOTOVER. I had to deal with men so degraded that they wouldnt obey me unless I swore at them and kicked them and beat them with my fists. Foolish people took young thieves off the streets; flung them into a training ship where they were taught to fear the cane instead of fearing God; and thought theyd made men and sailors of them by private subscription. I tricked these thieves into believing I'd sold myself to the devil. It saved my soul from the kicking and swearing that was damning me by inches.

ELLIE [*releasing him*] I shall pretend to sell myself to Boss Mangan to save my soul from the poverty that is damning *me* by inches.

CAPTAIN SHOTOVER. Riches will damn you ten times deeper. Riches wont save even your body.

ELLIE. Old-fashioned again. We know now that the soul is the body, and the body the soul. They tell us they are different because they want to persuade us that we can keep our souls if we let them make slaves of our bodies. I am afraid you are no use to me, Captain.

CAPTAIN SHOTOVER. What did you expect? A Savior, eh? Are you old-fashioned enough to believe in that?

ELLIE. No. But I thought you were very wise, and might help me. Now I have found you out. You pretend to be busy, and think of fine things to say, and run in and out to surprise people by saying them, and get away before they can answer you.

CAPTAIN SHOTOVER. It confuses me to be answered. It discourages me. I cannot bear men and women. I *have* to run away. I must run away now [*he tries to*].

ELLIE [*again seizing his arm*] You shall not run away from me. I can hypnotize you. You are the only person in the house I can say what I like to. I know you are fond of me. Sit down. [*She draws him to the sofa*].

CAPTAIN SHOTOVER [*yielding*] Take care: I am in my dotage.* Old men are dangerous: it doesnt matter to them what is going to happen to the world.

They sit side by side on the sofa. She leans affectionately against him with her head on his shoulder and her eyes half closed.

ELLIE [*dreamily*] I should have thought nothing else mattered to old men. They cant be very interested in what is going to happen to themselves.

CAPTAIN SHOTOVER. A man's interest in the world is only the overflow from his interest in himself. When you are a child your vessel is not yet full; so you care for nothing but your own affairs. When you grow up, your vessel overflows; and you are a politician, a philosopher, or an explorer and adventurer. In old age the vessel dries up: there is no overflow: you are a child again. I can give you the memories of my ancient wisdom: mere scraps and leavings; but I no longer really care for anything but my own little wants and hobbies. I sit here working out my old ideas as a means of destroying my fellow-creatures. I see my daughters and their men living foolish lives of romance and sentiment and snobbery. I see you, the younger generation, turning from their romance and sentiment and snobbery to money and comfort and hard common sense. I was ten times happier on the bridge in the typhoon, or frozen into Arctic ice for months in darkness, than you or they have ever been. You are looking for a rich husband. At your age I looked for hardship, danger, horror, and death, that I might feel the life in me more intensely.* I did not let the fear of death govern my life; and my reward was, I had my life. You are going to let the fear of poverty govern your life; and your reward will be that you will eat, but you will not live.

ELLIE [*sitting up impatiently*] But what can I do? I am not a sea captain: I cant stand on bridges in typhoons, or go slaughtering seals and

whales in Greenland's icy mountains. They wont let women be
captains. Do you want me to be a stewardess?

CAPTAIN SHOTOVER. There are worse lives. The stewardesses could
come ashore if they liked; but they sail and sail and sail.

ELLIE. What could they do ashore but marry for money? I dont want
to be a stewardess: I am too bad a sailor. Think of something else
for me.

CAPTAIN SHOTOVER. I cant think so long and continuously. I am too
old. I must go in and out. [*He tries to rise*].

ELLIE [*pulling him back*] You shall not. You are happy here, arnt you?

CAPTAIN SHOTOVER. I tell you it's dangerous to keep me. I cant keep
awake and alert.

ELLIE. What do you run away for? To sleep?

CAPTAIN SHOTOVER. No. To get a glass of rum.

ELLIE [*frightfully disillusioned*] Is *that* it? How disgusting! Do you like
being drunk?

CAPTAIN SHOTOVER. No: I dread being drunk more than anything in
the world. To be drunk means to have dreams; to go soft; to be easily
pleased and deceived; to fall into the clutches of women. Drink does
that for you when you are young. But when you are old: very very old,
like me, the dreams come by themselves. You dont know how terrible
that is: you are young: you sleep at night only, and sleep soundly. But
later on you will sleep in the afternoon. Later still you will sleep even
in the morning; and you will awake tired, tired of life. You will never
be free from dozing and dreams: the dreams will steal upon your
work every ten minutes unless you can awaken yourself with rum.
I drink now to keep sober; but the dreams are conquering: rum is not
what it was: I have had ten glasses* since you came; and it might be
so much water. Go get me another: Guinness knows where it is. You
had better see for yourself the horror of an old man drinking.

ELLIE. You shall not drink. Dream. I like you to dream. You must
never be in the real world when we talk together.

CAPTAIN SHOTOVER. I am too weary to resist or too weak. I am in my
second childhood. I do not see you as you really are. I cant remember
what I really am. I feel nothing but the accursed happiness I have

dreaded all my life long: the happiness that comes as life goes, the happiness of yielding and dreaming instead of resisting and doing, the sweetness of the fruit that is going rotten.

ELLIE. You dread it almost as much as I used to dread losing my dreams and having to fight and do things. But that is all over for me: *my* dreams are dashed to pieces. I should like to marry a very old, very rich man. I should like to marry you. I had much rather marry you than marry Mangan. Are you very rich?

CAPTAIN SHOTOVER. No. Living from hand to mouth. And I have a wife somewhere in Jamaica: a black one. My first wife. Unless she's dead.

ELLIE. What a pity! I feel so happy with you. [*She takes his hand, almost unconsciously, and pats it*]. I thought I should never feel happy again.

CAPTAIN SHOTOVER. Why?

ELLIE. Dont you know?

CAPTAIN SHOTOVER. No.

ELLIE. Heartbreak. I fell in love with Hector, and didnt know he was married.

CAPTAIN SHOTOVER. Heartbreak?* Are you one of those who are so sufficient to themselves that they are only happy when they are stripped of everything, even of hope?

ELLIE [*gripping the hand*] It seems so; for I feel now as if there was nothing I could not do, because I want nothing.

CAPTAIN SHOTOVER. Thats the only real strength. Thats genius. Thats better than rum.

ELLIE [*throwing away his hand*] Rum! Why did you spoil it?

Hector and Randall come in from the garden through the starboard door.

HECTOR. I beg your pardon. We did not know there was anyone here.

ELLIE [*rising*] That means that you want to tell Mr Randall the story about the tiger. Come, Captain: I want to talk to my father; and you had better come with me.

CAPTAIN SHOTOVER [*rising*] Nonsense! the man is in bed.

ELLIE. Aha! Ive caught you. My real father has gone to bed; but the father you gave me is in the kitchen. You knew quite well all along. Come. [*She draws him out into the garden with her through the port door*].

HECTOR. Thats an extraordinary girl. She has the Ancient Mariner* on a string like a Pekinese dog.*

RANDALL. Now that they have gone, shall we have a friendly chat?

HECTOR. You are in what is supposed to be my house. I am at your disposal.

Hector sits down in the draughtsman's chair, turning it to face Randall, who remains standing, leaning at his ease against the carpenter's bench.

RANDALL. I take it that we may be quite frank. I mean about Lady Utterword.

HECTOR. You may. I have nothing to be frank about. I never met her until this afternoon

RANDALL [*straightening up*] What! But you are her sister's husband.

HECTOR. Well, if you come to that, you are her husband's brother.

RANDALL. But you seem to be on intimate terms with her.

HECTOR. So do you.

RANDALL. Yes; but I *am* on intimate terms with her. I have known her for years.

HECTOR. It took her years to get to the same point with you that she got to with me in five minutes, it seems.

RANDALL [*vexed*] Really, Ariadne is the limit [*he moves away huffishly towards the windows*].

HECTOR [*coolly*] She is, as I remarked to Hesione, a very enterprising woman.

RANDALL [*returning, much troubled*] You see, Hushabye, you are what women consider a good-looking man.

HECTOR. I cultivated that appearance in the days of my vanity; and Hesione insists on my keeping it up. She makes me wear these ridiculous things [*indicating his Arab costume*] because she thinks me absurd in evening dress.

RANDALL. Still, you *do* keep it up, old chap. Now, I assure you I have not an atom of jealousy in my disposition—

HECTOR. The question would seem to be rather whether your brother has any touch of that sort.

RANDALL. What! Hastings! Oh, dont trouble about Hastings. He has the gift of being able to work sixteen hours a day at the dullest detail, and actually likes it. That gets him to the top wherever he goes. As long as Ariadne takes care that he is fed regularly, he is only too thankful to anyone who will keep her in good humour for him.

HECTOR. And as she has all the Shotover fascination,* there is plenty of competition for the job, eh?

RANDALL [*angrily*] She encourages them. Her conduct is perfectly scandalous. I assure you, my dear fellow, I havnt an atom of jealousy in my composition; but she makes herself the talk of every place she goes to by her thoughtlessness. It's nothing more: she doesnt really care for the men she keeps hanging about her; but how is the world to know that? It's not fair to Hastings. It's not fair to me.

HECTOR. Her theory is that her conduct is so correct—

RANDALL. Correct! She does nothing but make scenes from morning til night. You be careful, old chap. She will get you into trouble: that is, she would if she really cared for you.

HECTOR. Doesnt she?

RANDALL. Not a scrap. She may want your scalp to add to her collection; but her true affection has been engaged years ago. You had really better be careful.

HECTOR. Do you suffer much from this jealousy?

RANDALL. Jealousy! I jealous! My dear fellow, havnt I told you that there is not an atom of—

HECTOR. Yes. And Lady Utterword told me she never made scenes. Well, dont waste your jealousy on my moustache. Never waste jealousy on a real man: it is the imaginary hero that supplants us all in the long run. Besides, jealousy does not belong to your easy man-of-the-world pose, which you carry so well in other respects.

RANDALL. Really, Hushabye, I think a man may be allowed to be a gentleman without being accused of posing.

HECTOR. It is a pose like any other. In this house we know all the poses: our game is to find out the man under the pose. The man under your pose is apparently Ellie's favorite, Othello.

RANDALL. Some of your games in this house are damned annoying, let me tell you.

HECTOR. Yes: I have been their victim for many years. I used to writhe under them at first; but I became accustomed to them. At last I learned to play them.

RANDALL. If it's all the same to you, I had rather you didnt play them on me. You evidently dont quite understand my character, or my notions of good form.

HECTOR. Is it your notion of good form to give away Lady Utterword?

RANDALL [*a childishly plaintive note breaking into his huff*] I have not said a word against Lady Utterword. This is just the conspiracy over again.

HECTOR. What conspiracy?

RANDALL. You know very well, sir. A conspiracy to make me out to be pettish and jealous and childish and everything I am not. Everyone knows I am just the opposite.

HECTOR [*rising*] Something in the air of the house has upset you. It often does have that effect. [*He goes to the garden door and calls Lady Utterword with commanding emphasis*] Ariadne!

LADY UTTERWORD [*at some distance*] Yes.

RANDALL. What are you calling her for? I want to speak—

LADY UTTERWORD [*arriving breathless*] Yes. You really are a terribly commanding person. Whats the matter?

HECTOR. I do not know how to manage your friend Randall. No doubt you do.

LADY UTTERWORD. Randall: have you been making yourself ridiculous, as usual? I can see it in your face. Really, you are the most pettish creature.

RANDALL. You know quite well, Ariadne, that I have not an ounce of pettishness in my disposition. I have made myself perfectly pleasant here. I have remained absolutely cool and imperturbable in the face of a burglar. Imperturbability is almost too strong a point of mine.

But [*putting his foot down with a stamp, and walking angrily up and down the room*] I insist on being treated with a certain consideration. I will not allow Hushabye to take liberties with me. I will not stand your encouraging people as you do.

HECTOR. The man has a rooted delusion that he is your husband.

LADY UTTERWORD. I know. He is jealous. As if he had any right to be! He compromises me everywhere. He makes scenes all over the place. Randall: I will not allow it. I simply will not allow it. You had no right to discuss me with Hector. I will not be discussed by men.

HECTOR. Be reasonable, Ariadne.* Your fatal gift of beauty forces men to discuss you.

LADY UTTERWORD. Oh indeed! what about *your* fatal gift of beauty?

HECTOR. How can I help it?

LADY UTTERWORD. You could cut off your moustache: I cant cut off my nose. I get my whole life messed up with people falling in love with me. And then Randall says I run after men.

RANDALL. I—

LADY UTTERWORD. Yes you do:* you said it just now. Why cant you think of something else than women? Napoleon was quite right when he said that women are the occupation of the idle man.* Well, if ever there was an idle man on earth, his name is Randall Utterword.

RANDALL. Ariad—

LADY UTTERWORD [*overwhelming him with a torrent of words*] Oh yes you are: it's no use denying it. What have you ever done? What good are you? You are as much trouble in the house as a child of three. You couldnt live without your valet.

RANDALL. This is—

LADY UTTERWORD. Laziness! You are laziness incarnate. You are selfishness itself. You are the most uninteresting man on earth. You cant even gossip about anything but yourself and your grievances and your ailments and the people who have offended you. [*Turning to Hector*] Do you know what they call him, Hector?

HECTOR } [*speaking { Please dont tell me.
RANDALL } together*] { I'll not stand it—

LADY UTTERWORD. Randall the Rotter: that is his name in good society.

RANDALL [*shouting*] I'll not bear it, I tell you. Will you listen to me, you infernal—[*he chokes*].

LADY UTTERWORD. Well: go on. What were you going to call me? An infernal what? Which unpleasant animal is it to be this time?

RANDALL [*foaming*] There is no animal* in the world so hateful as a woman can be. You are a maddening devil. Hushabye: you will not believe me* when I tell you that I have loved this demon all my life; but God knows I have paid for it [*he sits down in the draughtsman's chair, weeping*].

LADY UTTERWORD [*standing over him with triumphant contempt*] Cry-baby!

HECTOR [*gravely, coming to him*] My friend: the Shotover sisters have two strange powers over men. They can make them love; and they can make them cry. Thank your stars that you are not married to one of them.

LADY UTTERWORD [*haughtily*] And pray, Hector—

HECTOR [*suddenly catching her round the shoulders; swinging her right round him and away from Randall; and gripping her throat with the other hand*] Ariadne: if you attempt to start on me, I'll choke you: do you hear? The cat-and-mouse game with the other sex is a good game; but I can play your head off at it. [*He throws her, not at all gently, into the big chair, and proceeds, less fiercely but firmly*] It is true that Napoleon said that woman is the occupation of the idle man. But he added that she is the relaxation of the warrior. Well, *I* am the warrior. So take care.

LADY UTTERWORD [*not in the least put out, and rather pleased by his violence*] My dear Hector: I have only done what you asked me to do.

HECTOR. How do you make that out, pray?

LADY UTTERWORD. You called me in to manage Randall, didnt you? You said you couldnt manage him yourself.

HECTOR. Well, what if I did? I did not ask you to drive the man mad.

LADY UTTERWORD. He isnt mad. Thats the way to manage him. If you were a mother, youd understand.

HECTOR. Mother! What are you up to now?

LADY UTTERWORD. It's quite simple. When the children got nerves and were naughty, I smacked them just enough to give them a good cry and a healthy nervous shock. They went to sleep and were quite good afterwards. Well, I cant smack Randall: he is too big; so when he gets nerves and is naughty, I just rag him til he cries. He will be all right now. Look: he is half asleep already [*which is quite true*].

RANDALL [*waking up indignantly*] I'm not. You are most cruel, Ariadne. [*Sentimentally*] But I suppose I must forgive you, as usual [*he checks himself in the act of yawning*].

LADY UTTERWORD [*to Hector*] Is the explanation satisfactory, dread warrior?

HECTOR. Some day I shall kill you, if you go too far. I thought you were a fool.

LADY UTTERWORD [*laughing*] Everybody does, at first. But I am not such a fool as I look. [*She rises complacently*]. Now, Randall: go to bed. You will be a good boy in the morning.

RANDALL [*only very faintly rebellious*] I'll go to bed when I like. It isnt ten yet.

LADY UTTERWORD. It is long past ten. See that he goes to bed at once, Hector. [*She goes into the garden*].

HECTOR. Is there any slavery on earth viler than this slavery of men to women?

RANDALL [*rising resolutely*] I'll not speak to her tomorrow. I'll not speak to her for another week. I'll give her *such* a lesson. I'll go straight to bed without bidding her goodnight. [*He makes for the door leading to the hall*].

HECTOR. You are under a spell, man. Old Shotover sold himself to the devil in Zanzibar. The devil gave him a black witch for a wife; and these two demon daughters are their mystical progeny. I am tied to Hesione's apron-string; but I'm her husband; and if I did go stark staring mad about her, at least we became man and wife. But why should *you* let yourself be dragged about and beaten by Ariadne as a toy donkey is dragged about and beaten by a child? What do you get by it? Are you her lover?

RANDALL. You must not misunderstand me. In a higher sense—in a Platonic sense—

HECTOR. Psha! Platonic sense! She makes you her servant; and when pay-day comes round, she bilks you: that is what you mean.

RANDALL [*feebly*] Well, if I dont mind, I dont see what business it is of yours. Besides, I tell you I am going to punish her. You shall see: *I* know how to deal with women. I'm really very sleepy. Say goodnight to Mrs Hushabye for me, will you, like a good chap. Goodnight. [*He hurries out*].

HECTOR. Poor wretch! Oh women! women! women! [*He lifts his fists in invocation to heaven*] Fall. Fall and crush. [*He goes out into the garden*].

ACT III

In the garden, Hector, as he comes out through the glass door of the poop, finds Lady Utterword lying voluptuously* in the hammock on the east side of the flagstaff, in the circle of light cast by the electric arc, which is like a moon in its opal globe. Beneath the head of the hammock, a camp-stool.* On the other side of the flagstaff, on the long garden seat, Captain Shotover is asleep, with Ellie beside him, leaning affectionately against him on his right hand. On his left is a deck chair. Behind them in the gloom, Hesione is strolling about with Mangan. It is a fine still night, moonless.

LADY UTTERWORD. What a lovely night! It seems made for us.

HECTOR. The night takes no interest in us. What are we to the night? [*He sits down moodily in the deck chair*].

ELLIE [*dreamily, nestling against the Captain*] Its beauty soaks into my nerves. In the night there is peace for the old and hope for the young.

HECTOR. Is that remark your own?

ELLIE. No. Only the last thing the Captain said before he went to sleep.

CAPTAIN SHOTOVER. I'm not asleep.

HECTOR. Randall is. Also Mr Mazzini Dunn. Mangan too, probably.

MANGAN. No.

HECTOR. Oh, you are there. I thought Hesione would have sent you to bed by this time.

MRS HUSHABYE [*coming to the back of the garden seat, into the light, with Mangan*] I think I shall. He keeps telling me he has a presentiment that he is going to die. I never met a man so greedy for sympathy.

MANGAN [*plaintively*] But I have a presentiment. I really have. And you wouldnt listen.

MRS HUSHABYE. I was listening for something else. There was a sort of splendid drumming in the sky. Did none of you hear it? It came from a distance and then died away.

MANGAN. I tell you it was a train.

MRS HUSHABYE. And *I* tell you, Alf, there is no train at this hour. The last is nine fortyfive.

MANGAN. But a goods train.

MRS HUSHABYE. Not on our little line. They tack a truck on to the passenger train. What can it have been, Hector?

HECTOR. Heaven's threatening growl of disgust at us useless futile creatures. [*Fiercely*] I tell you, one of two things must happen. Either out of that darkness some new creation will come to supplant us as we have supplanted the animals, or the heavens will fall in thunder and destroy us.

LADY UTTERWORD [*in a cool instructive manner, wallowing comfortably in her hammock*]* We have not supplanted the animals, Hector. Why do you ask heaven to destroy this house, which could be made quite comfortable if Hesione had any notion of how to live? Dont you know what is wrong with it?

HECTOR. We are wrong with it. There is no sense in us.* We are useless, dangerous, and ought to be abolished.

LADY UTTERWORD. Nonsense! Hastings told me the very first day he came here, nearly twentyfour* years ago, what is wrong with the house.

CAPTAIN SHOTOVER. What! The numskull said there was something wrong with my house!

LADY UTTERWORD. I said Hastings said it; and he is not in the least a numskull.

CAPTAIN SHOTOVER. Whats wrong with my house?*

LADY UTTERWORD. Just what is wrong with a ship, papa. Wasnt it clever of Hastings to see that?

CAPTAIN SHOTOVER. The man's a fool. Theres nothing wrong with a ship.

LADY UTTERWORD. Yes there is.

MRS HUSHABYE. But what is it? Dont be aggravating, Addy.

LADY UTTERWORD. Guess.

HECTOR. Demons. Daughters of the witch of Zanzibar. Demons.

LADY UTTERWORD. Not a bit. I assure you, all this house needs to make it a sensible, healthy, pleasant house, with good appetites and sound sleep in it, is horses.

MRS HUSHABYE. Horses! What rubbish!

LADY UTTERWORD. Yes: horses. Why have we never been able to let* this house? Because there are no proper stables. Go anywhere in England where there are natural, wholesome, contented, and really nice English people; and what do you always find? That the stables are the real centre of the household; and that if any visitor wants to play the piano the whole room has to be upset before it can be opened, there are so many things piled on it. I never lived until I learned to ride; and I shall never ride really well because I didnt begin as a child. There are only two classes in good society in England: the equestrian classes and the neurotic classes. It isnt mere convention: everybody can see that the people who hunt are the right people and the people who dont are the wrong ones.*

CAPTAIN SHOTOVER. There is some truth in this. My ship made a man of me; and a ship is the horse of the sea.

LADY UTTERWORD. Exactly how Hastings explained your being a gentleman.

CAPTAIN SHOTOVER. Not bad for a numskull. Bring the man here with you next time: I must talk to him.

LADY UTTERWORD. Why is Randall such an obvious rotter? He is well bred; he has been at a public school and a university; he has been in the Foreign Office; he knows the best people and has lived all his life among them. Why is he so unsatisfactory, so contemptible? Why cant he get a valet to stay with him longer than a few months? Just because he is too lazy and pleasure-loving to hunt and shoot. He strums the piano, and sketches, and runs after married women, and reads literary books and poems. He actually plays the flute; but I never let him bring it into my house. If he would only—[*she is interrupted by the melancholy strains of a flute coming from an open window above. She raises herself indignantly in the hammock*]. Randall: you have not gone to bed. Have you been listening? [*The flute replies pertly:*]

How vulgar! Go to bed instantly, Randall: how dare you? [*The window is slammed down. She subsides*]. How can anyone care for such a creature!*

MRS HUSHABYE. Addy: do you think Ellie ought to marry poor Alfred merely for his money?

MANGAN [*much alarmed*] Whats that? Mrs Hushabye: are my affairs to be discussed like this before everybody?

LADY UTTERWORD. I dont think Randall is listening now.

MANGAN. Everybody is listening. It isnt right.

MRS HUSHABYE. But in the dark, what does it matter? Ellie doesnt mind. Do you, Ellie?

ELLIE. Not in the least. What is your opinion, Lady Utterword? You have so much good sense.

MANGAN. But it isnt right. It—[*Mrs Hushabye puts her hand on his mouth*]. Oh, very well.

LADY UTTERWORD. How much money have you, Mr Mangan?

MANGAN. Really—No: I cant stand this.

LADY UTTERWORD. Nonsense, Mr Mangan! It all turns on your income, doesnt it?

MANGAN. Well, if you come to that, how much money has she?

ELLIE. None.

LADY UTTERWORD. You are answered, Mr Mangan. And now, as you have made Miss Dunn throw her cards on the table, you cannot refuse to shew your own.

MRS HUSHABYE. Come, Alf! out with it! How much?

MANGAN [*baited out of all prudence*] Well, if you want to know, I have no money and never had any.

MRS HUSHABYE. Alfred: you mustnt tell naughty stories.

MANGAN. I'm not telling you stories. I'm telling you the raw truth.

LADY UTTERWORD. Then what do you live on, Mr Mangan?

MANGAN. Travelling expenses. And a trifle of commission.

CAPTAIN SHOTOVER. What more have any of us but travelling expenses for our life's journey?*

MRS HUSHABYE. But you have factories and capital and things?

MANGAN. People think I have. People think I'm an industrial Napoleon. Thats why Miss Ellie wants to marry me. But I tell you I have nothing.

ELLIE. Do you mean that the factories are like Marcus's tigers? That they dont exist?

MANGAN. They exist all right enough. But theyre not mine. They belong to syndicates and shareholders and all sorts of lazy good-for-nothing capitalists.* I get money from such people to start the factories. I find people like Miss Dunn's father to work them, and keep a tight hand so as to make them pay. Of course I make them keep me going pretty well; but it's a dog's life;* and I dont own anything.*

MRS HUSHABYE. Alfred, Alfred: you are making a poor mouth of it to get out of marrying Ellie.

MANGAN. I'm telling the truth about my money for the first time in my life; and it's the first time my word has ever been doubted.

LADY UTTERWORD. How sad! Why dont you go in for politics, Mr Mangan?

MANGAN. Go in for politics! Where have you been living? I *am* in politics.

LADY UTTERWORD. I'm sure I beg your pardon. I never heard of you.

MANGAN. Let me tell you, Lady Utterword, that the Prime Minister of this country asked me to join the Government without even going through the nonsense of an election, as the dictator of a great public department.

LADY UTTERWORD. As a Conservative or a Liberal?

MANGAN. No such nonsense. As a practical business man. [*They all burst out laughing*]. What are you all laughing at?

MRS HUSHABYE. Oh, Alfred, Alfred!

ELLIE. You! who have to get my father to do everything for you!

MRS HUSHABYE. You! who are afraid of your own workmen!

HECTOR. You! with whom three women have been playing cat and mouse* all the evening!

LADY UTTERWORD. You must have given an immense sum to the party funds, Mr Mangan.

MANGAN. Not a penny out of my own pocket. The syndicate found the money: they knew how useful I should be to them in the Government.

LADY UTTERWORD. This is most interesting and unexpected, Mr Mangan. And what have your administrative achievements been, so far?

MANGAN. Achievements? Well, I dont know what you call achievements; but Ive jolly well put a stop to the games of the other fellows in the other departments. Every man of them thought he was going to save the country all by himself, and do me out of the credit and out of my chance of a title. I took good care that if they wouldnt let me do it they shouldnt do it themselves either. I may not know anything about my own machinery; but I know how to stick a ramrod into the other fellow's. And now they all look the biggest fools going.

HECTOR. And in heaven's name, what do *you* look like?

MANGAN. I look like the fellow that was too clever for all the others, dont I? If that isnt a triumph of practical business, what is?

HECTOR. Is this England, or is it a madhouse?

LADY UTTERWORD. Do you expect to save the country, Mr Mangan?*

MANGAN. Well, who else will? Will your Mr Randall save it?

LADY UTTERWORD. Randall the rotter! Certainly not.

MANGAN. Will your brother-in-law save it with his moustache and his fine talk?

HECTOR. Yes, if they will let me.

MANGAN [*sneering*] Ah! *Will* they let you?

HECTOR. No. They prefer you.

MANGAN. Very well then, as youre in a world where I'm appreciated and youre not, youd best be civil to me, hadnt you? Who else is there but me?

LADY UTTERWORD. There is Hastings. Get rid of your ridiculous sham democracy; and give Hastings the necessary powers, and a good supply of bamboo to bring the British native to his senses: he will save the country with the greatest ease.

CAPTAIN SHOTOVER. It had better be lost. Any fool can govern with a stick in his hand. *I* could govern that way. It is not God's way. The man is a numskull.

LADY UTTERWORD. The man is worth all of you rolled into one. What do *you* say, Miss Dunn?

ELLIE. I think my father would do very well if people did not put upon him and cheat him and despise him because he is so good.

MANGAN [*contemptuously*] I think I see Mazzini Dunn getting into parliament or pushing his way into the Government. Weve not come to that yet, thank God! What do *you* say, Mrs Hushabye?

MRS HUSHABYE. Oh, *I* say it matters very little which of you governs the country so long as we govern you.

HECTOR. We? Who is we, pray?

MRS HUSHABYE. The devil's granddaughters, dear. The lovely women.

HECTOR [*raising his hands as before*] Fall, I say; and deliver us from the lures of Satan!*

ELLIE. There seems to be nothing real in the world except my father and Shakespear. Marcus's tigers are false; Mr Mangan's millions are false; there is nothing really strong and true about Hesione but her beautiful black hair; and Lady Utterword's is too pretty to be real. The one thing that was left to me was the Captain's seventh degree of concentration; and that turns out to be—

CAPTAIN SHOTOVER. Rum.

LADY UTTERWORD [*placidly*] A good deal of my hair is quite genuine. The Duchess of Dithering* offered me fifty guineas for this [*touching her forehead*] under the impression that it was a transformation; but it is all natural except the color.

MANGAN [*wildly*] Look here: I'm going to take off all my clothes [*he begins tearing off his coat*].

LADY UTTERWORD.		Mr Mangan!
CAPTAIN SHOTOVER.	[*in consternation*]	Whats that?
HECTOR.		Ha! ha! Do. Do.
ELLIE.		Please dont.

MRS HUSHABYE [*catching his arm and stopping him*] Alfred: for shame! Are you mad?

MANGAN. Shame! What shame is there in this house? Let's all strip stark naked. We may as well do the thing thoroughly when we're about it. Weve stripped ourselves morally naked: well, let us strip ourselves physically naked as well, and see how we like it. I tell you I cant bear this. I was brought up to be respectable. I dont mind the women dyeing their hair and the men drinking: it's human nature. But it's not human nature to tell everybody about it. Every time one of you opens your mouth I go like this [*he cowers as if to avoid a missile*] afraid of what will come next. How are we to have any self-respect if we dont keep it up that we're better than we really are?

LADY UTTERWORD. I quite sympathize with you, Mr Mangan. I have been through it all; and I know by experience that men and women are delicate plants and must be cultivated under glass. Our family habit of throwing stones in all directions and letting the air in is not only unbearably rude, but positively dangerous. Still, there is no use catching physical colds as well as moral ones; so please keep your clothes on.

MANGAN. I'll do as I like: not what you tell me. Am I a child or a grown man? I wont stand this mothering tyranny. I'll go back to the city, where I'm respected and made much of.*

MRS HUSHABYE. Goodbye, Alf. Think of us sometimes in the city. Think of Ellie's youth!

ELLIE. Think of Hesione's eyes and hair!

CAPTAIN SHOTOVER. Think of this garden in which you are not a dog barking to keep the truth out!

HECTOR. Think of Lady Utterword's beauty! her good sense! her style!

LADY UTTERWORD. Flatterer. Think, Mr Mangan, whether you can really do any better for yourself elsewhere: that is the essential point, isnt it?

MANGAN [*surrendering*] All right: all right. I'm done. Have it your own way. Only let me alone. I dont know whether I'm on my head or my heels when you all start on me like this. I'll stay. I'll marry her. I'll do anything for a quiet life. Are you satisfied now?

ELLIE. No. I never really intended to make you marry me, Mr Mangan. Never in the depths of my soul. I only wanted to feel my strength: to know that you could not escape if I chose to take you.

MANGAN [*indignantly*] What! Do you mean to say you are going to throw me over after my acting so handsome?*

LADY UTTERWORD. I should not be too hasty, Miss Dunn. You can throw Mr Mangan over at any time up to the last moment. Very few men in his position go bankrupt. You can live very comfortably on his reputation for immense wealth.*

ELLIE. I cannot commit bigamy, Lady Utterword.

MRS HUSHABYE.		Bigamy! Whatever on earth are you talking about, Ellie?
LADY UTTERWORD.	[*exclaiming all together*]	Bigamy! What do you mean, Miss Dunn?
MANGAN.		Bigamy! Do you mean to say youre married already?
HECTOR.		Bigamy! This is some enigma.

ELLIE. Only half an hour ago I became Captain Shotover's white wife.

MRS HUSHABYE. Ellie! What nonsense! Where?

ELLIE. In heaven, where all true marriages are made.

LADY UTTERWORD. Really, Miss Dunn! Really, papa!

MANGAN. He told me *I* was too old! And him a mummy!

HECTOR [*quoting Shelley*]

'Their altar the grassy earth outspread,
And their priest the muttering wind.'*

ELLIE. Yes: I, Ellie Dunn, give my broken heart and my strong sound soul to its natural captain, my spiritual husband and second father.

She draws the Captain's arm through hers, and pats his hand. The Captain remains fast asleep.

MRS HUSHABYE. Oh, thats very clever of you, pettikins. *Very* clever. Alfred: you could never have lived up to Ellie. You must be content with a little share of me.

MANGAN [*sniffing and wiping his eyes*] It isnt kind—[*his emotion chokes him*].

LADY UTTERWORD. You are well out of it, Mr Mangan. Miss Dunn is the most conceited young woman I have met since I came back to England.

MRS HUSHABYE. Oh, Ellie isnt conceited. Are you, pettikins?

ELLIE. I know my strength now, Hesione.

MANGAN. Brazen, I call you. Brazen.

MRS HUSHABYE. Tut tut, Alfred: dont be rude. Dont you feel how lovely this marriage night is, made in heaven? Arnt you happy, you and Hector? Open your eyes: Addy and Ellie look beautiful enough to please the most fastidious man: we live and love and have not a care in the world. We women have managed all that for you. Why in the name of common sense do you go on as if you were two miserable wretches?

CAPTAIN SHOTOVER. I tell you happiness is no good. You can be happy when you are only half alive. I am happier now I am half dead than ever I was in my prime. But there is no blessing on my happiness.*

ELLIE [*her face lighting up*] Life with a blessing! that is what I want. Now I know the real reason why I couldnt marry Mr Mangan: there would be no blessing on our marriage. There is a blessing on my broken heart. There is a blessing on your beauty, Hesione. There is a blessing on your father's spirit. Even on the lies of Marcus there is a blessing; but on Mr Mangan's money there is none.

MANGAN. I dont understand a word of that.

ELLIE. Neither do I. But I know it means something.

MANGAN. Dont say there was any difficulty about the blessing. I was ready to get a bishop to marry us.

MRS HUSHABYE. Isnt he a fool, pettikins?

HECTOR [*fiercely*] Do not scorn the man. We are all fools.*

Mazzini, in pyjamas and a richly colored silk dressing-gown, comes from the house, on Lady Utterword's side.

MRS HUSHABYE. Oh! here comes the only man who ever resisted me.* Whats the matter, Mr Dunn? Is the house on fire?

MAZZINI. Oh no: nothing's the matter; but really it's impossible to go to sleep with such an interesting conversation going on under one's window, and on such a beautiful night too. I just had to come down and join you all. What has it all been about?

MRS HUSHABYE. Oh, wonderful things, soldier of freedom.

HECTOR. For example, Mangan, as a practical business man, has tried to undress himself and has failed ignominiously; whilst you, as an idealist, have succeeded brilliantly.

MAZZINI. I hope you dont mind my being like this, Mrs Hushabye. [*He sits down on the campstool*].

MRS HUSHABYE. On the contrary, I could wish you always like that.

LADY UTTERWORD. Your daughter's match is off, Mr Dunn. It seems that Mr Mangan, whom we all supposed to be a man of property, owns absolutely nothing.

MAZZINI. Well of course I knew that, Lady Utterword. But if people believe in him and are always giving him money, whereas they dont believe in me and never give me any, how can I ask poor Ellie to depend on what I can do for her?

MANGAN. Dont you run away with this idea that I have nothing. I—

HECTOR. Oh, dont explain. We understand. You have a couple of thousand pounds in exchequer bills,* 50,000 shares worth ten-pence a dozen, and half a dozen tabloids of cyanide of potassium* to poison yourself with when you are found out. Thats the reality of your millions.

MAZZINI. Oh no, no, no. He is quite honest: the businesses are genuine and perfectly legal.

HECTOR [*disgusted*] Yah! Not even a great swindler!*

MANGAN. So you think. But Ive been too many for some honest men, for all that.

LADY UTTERWORD. There is no pleasing you, Mr Mangan. You are determined to be neither rich nor poor, honest nor dishonest.*

MANGAN. There you go again.* Ever since I came into this silly house I have been made to look like a fool, though I'm as good a man in this house as in the city.

ELLIE [*musically*] Yes: this silly house, this strangely happy house, this agonizing house, this house without foundations. I shall call it Heartbreak House.

MRS HUSHABYE. Stop, Ellie; or I shall howl like an animal.

MANGAN [*breaks into a low snivelling*]!!!

MRS HUSHABYE. There! you have set Alfred off.

ELLIE. I like him best when he is howling.*

CAPTAIN SHOTOVER. Silence! [*Mangan subsides into silence*]. I say, let the heart break in silence.*

HECTOR. Do you accept that name for your house?

CAPTAIN SHOTOVER. It is not my house: it is only my kennel.*

HECTOR. We have been too long here. We do not live in this house: we haunt it.

LADY UTTERWORD [*heart torn*] It is dreadful to think how you have been here all these years while I have gone round the world. I escaped young; but it has drawn me back. It wants to break my heart too. But it shant. I have left you and it behind. It was silly of me to come back. I felt sentimental about papa and Hesione and the old place. I felt them calling to me.

MAZZINI. But what a very natural and kindly and charming human feeling, Lady Utterword!

LADY UTTERWORD. So I thought, Mr Dunn. But I know now that it was only the last of my influenza. I found that I was not remembered and not wanted.

CAPTAIN SHOTOVER. You left because you did not want us. Was there no heartbreak in that for your father? You tore yourself up by the roots; and the ground healed up and brought forth fresh plants and forgot you. What right had you to come back* and probe old wounds?

MRS HUSHABYE. You were a complete stranger to me at first, Addy; but now I feel as if you had never been away.

LADY UTTERWORD. Thank you, Hesione; but the influenza is quite cured. The place may be Heartbreak House to you, Miss Dunn, and to this gentleman from the city who seems to have so little self-control; but to me it is only a very ill-regulated and rather untidy villa without any stables.

HECTOR. Inhabited by——?

ELLIE. A crazy old sea captain and a young singer who adores him.

MRS HUSHABYE. A sluttish female, trying to stave off a double chin and an elderly spread, vainly wooing a born soldier of freedom.

MAZZINI. Oh, really, Mrs Hushabye——

MANGAN. A member of His Majesty's Government that everybody sets down as a nincompoop: dont forget him, Lady Utterword.

LADY UTTERWORD. And a very fascinating gentleman whose chief occupation is to be married to my sister.

HECTOR. All heartbroken imbeciles.

MAZZINI. Oh no. Surely, if I may say so, rather a favorable specimen of what is best in our English culture. You are very charming people, most advanced, unprejudiced, frank, humane, unconventional, democratic, freethinking, and everything that is delightful to thoughtful people.

MRS HUSHABYE. You do us proud, Mazzini.

MAZZINI. I am not flattering, really. Where else could I feel perfectly at ease in my pyjamas? I sometimes dream that I am in very distinguished society, and suddenly I have nothing on but my pyjamas! Sometimes I havnt even pyjamas. And I always feel overwhelmed with confusion. But here, I dont mind in the least: it seems quite natural.

LADY UTTERWORD. An infallible sign that you are not now in really distinguished society, Mr Dunn. If you were in my house, you *would* feel embarrassed.

MAZZINI. I shall take particular care to keep out of your house, Lady Utterword.

LADY UTTERWORD. You will be quite wrong, Mr Dunn. I should make you very comfortable; and you would not have the trouble and anxiety of wondering whether you should wear your purple and gold or your green and crimson dressing-gown at dinner. You complicate life instead of simplifying it by doing these ridiculous things.*

ELLIE. *Your* house is not Heartbreak House: is it, Lady Utterword?

HECTOR. Yet she breaks hearts, easy as her house is. That poor devil upstairs with his flute howls when she twists his heart, just as Mangan howls when my wife twists his.

LADY UTTERWORD. That is because Randall has nothing to do but have his heart broken. It is a change from having his head shampooed. Catch anyone breaking Hastings' heart!

CAPTAIN SHOTOVER. The numskull wins, after all.

LADY UTTERWORD. I shall go back to my numskull with the greatest satisfaction when I am tired of you all, clever as you are.

MANGAN [*huffily*]* I never set up to be clever.

LADY UTTERWORD. I forgot you, Mr Mangan.

MANGAN. Well, I dont see that quite, either.

LADY UTTERWORD. You may not be clever, Mr Mangan; but you are successful.*

MANGAN. But I dont want to be regarded merely as a successful man. I have an imagination like anyone else. I have a presentiment—

MRS HUSHABYE. Oh, you are impossible, Alfred. Here I am devoting myself to you; and you think of nothing but your ridiculous presentiment. You bore me. Come and talk poetry to me under the stars. [*She drags him away into the darkness*].

MANGAN [*tearfully, as he disappears*] Yes: it's all very well to make fun of me; but if you only knew—

HECTOR [*impatiently*] How is all this going to end?

MAZZINI. It wont end, Mr Hushabye. Life doesnt end: it goes on.

ELLIE. Oh, it cant go on for ever. I'm always expecting something. I dont know what it is; but life must come to a point sometime.

LADY UTTERWORD. The point for a young woman of your age is a baby.

HECTOR. Yes, but, damn it, I have the same feeling; and *I* cant have a baby.

LADY UTTERWORD. By deputy, Hector.

HECTOR. But I *have* children. All that is over and done with for me: and yet I too feel that this cánt last. We sit here talking, and leave everything to Mangan and to chance and to the devil. Think of the powers of destruction that Mangan and his mutual admiration gang wield! It's madness: it's like giving a torpedo to a badly brought up child to play at earthquakes with.

MAZZINI. I know. I used often to think about that when I was young.

HECTOR. Think! Whats the good of thinking about it? Why didnt you do something?

MAZZINI. But I did. I joined societies and made speeches and wrote pamphlets. That was all I could do. But, you know, though the people in the societies thought they knew more than Mangan, most of them wouldnt have joined if they had known as much. You see they had never had any money to handle or any men to manage. Every year I expected a revolution, or some frightful smash-up: it seemed impossible that we could blunder and muddle on any longer. But nothing happened, except, of course, the usual poverty and crime and drink that we are used to. Nothing ever does happen. It's amazing how well we get along, all things considered.

LADY UTTERWORD. Perhaps somebody cleverer than you and Mr Mangan was at work all the time.

MAZZINI. Perhaps so. Though I was brought up not to believe in anything, I often feel that there is a great deal to be said for the theory of an overruling Providence, after all.

LADY UTTERWORD. Providence! I meant Hastings.

MAZZINI. Oh, I *beg* your pardon, Lady Utterword.

CAPTAIN SHOTOVER. Every drunken skipper trusts to Providence. But one of the ways of Providence with drunken skippers is to run them on the rocks.

MAZZINI. Very true, no doubt, at sea. But in politics, I assure you, they only run into jellyfish.* Nothing happens.

CAPTAIN SHOTOVER. At sea nothing happens to the sea. Nothing happens to the sky. The sun comes up from the east and goes down to the west. The moon grows from a sickle to an arc lamp, and comes later and later until she is lost in the light as other things are lost in the darkness. After the typhoon, the flying-fish glitter in the sunshine like birds. It's amazing how *they* get along, all things considered. Nothing happens, except something not worth mentioning.

ELLIE. What is that, O Captain, my captain?*

CAPTAIN SHOTOVER [*savagely*] Nothing but the smash of the drunken skipper's ship on the rocks, the splintering of her rotten timbers, the tearing of her rusty plates, the drowning of the crew like rats in a trap.

ELLIE. Moral: dont take rum.

CAPTAIN SHOTOVER [*vehemently*] That is a lie, child. Let a man drink ten barrels of rum a day, he is not a drunken skipper until he is a drifting skipper. Whilst he can lay his course and stand on his bridge and steer it, he is no drunkard. It is the man who lies drinking in his bunk and trusts to Providence that I call the drunken skipper, though he drank nothing but the waters of the River Jordan.*

ELLIE. Splendid! And you havnt had a drop for an hour. You see you dont need it: your own spirit is not dead.

CAPTAIN SHOTOVER. Echoes: nothing but echoes. The last shot was fired years ago.

HECTOR. And this ship that we are all in? This soul's prison we call England?

CAPTAIN SHOTOVER. The captain is in his bunk, drinking bottled ditch-water; and the crew is gambling in the forecastle. She will strike and sink and split.* Do you think the laws of God will be suspended in favor of England because you were born in it?

HECTOR. Well, I dont mean to be drowned like a rat in a trap. I still have the will to live. What am I to do?

CAPTAIN SHOTOVER. Do? Nothing simpler. Learn your business as an Englishman.

HECTOR. And what may my business as an Englishman be, pray?

CAPTAIN SHOTOVER. Navigation. Learn it and live; or leave it and be damned.

ELLIE. Quiet, quiet: youll tire yourself.

MAZZINI. I thought all that once, Captain; but I assure you nothing will happen.

A dull distant explosion is heard.

HECTOR [*starting up*] What was that?

CAPTAIN SHOTOVER. Something happening [*he blows his whistle*]. Breakers ahead!*

The light goes out.

HECTOR [*furiously*] Who put that light out? Who dared put that light out?

NURSE GUINNESS [*running in from the house to the middle of the esplanade*] I did, sir. The police have telephoned to say we'll be summoned if we dont put that light out: it can be seen for miles.

HECTOR. It shall be seen for a hundred miles [*he dashes into the house*].

NURSE GUINNESS. The rectory is nothing but a heap of bricks, they say. Unless we can give the rector a bed he has nowhere to lay his head this night.

CAPTAIN SHOTOVER. The Church is on the rocks, breaking up.* I told him it would unless it headed for God's open sea.

NURSE GUINNESS. And you are all to go down to the cellars.

CAPTAIN SHOTOVER. Go there yourself, you and all the crew. Batten down the hatches.

NURSE GUINNESS. And hide beside the coward I married! I'll go on the roof first. [*The lamp lights up again*]. There! Mr Hushabye's turned it on again.

THE BURGLAR [*hurrying in and appealing to Nurse Guinness*] Here: wheres the way to that gravel pit? The boot-boy says theres a cave in the gravel pit. Them cellars is no use. Wheres the gravel pit, Captain?

NURSE GUINNESS. Go straight on past the flagstaff until you fall into it and break your dirty neck. [*She pushes him contemptuously towards the flagstaff, and herself goes to the foot of the hammock and waits there, as it were by Ariadne's cradle*].

Another and louder explosion is heard. The burglar stops and stands trembling.

ELLIE [*rising*] That was nearer.

CAPTAIN SHOTOVER. The next one will get us. [*He rises*]. Stand by, all hands, for judgment.

THE BURGLAR. Oh my Lordy God! [*He rushes away frantically past the flagstaff into the gloom*].

MRS HUSHABYE [*emerging panting from the darkness*] Who was that running away? [*She comes to Ellie*]. Did you hear the explosions? And the sound in the sky: it's splendid: it's like an orchestra: it's like Beethoven.

ELLIE. By thunder, Hesione: it *is* Beethoven.

She and Hesione throw themselves into one another's arms in wild excitement. The light increases.

MAZZINI [*anxiously*] The light is getting brighter.

NURSE GUINNESS [*looking up at the house*] It's Mr Hushabye turning on all the lights in the house and tearing down the curtains.

RANDALL [*rushing in in his pyjamas, distractedly waving a flute*] Ariadne: my soul, my precious, go down to the cellars: I beg and implore you, go down to the cellars!

LADY UTTERWORD [*quite composed in her hammock*] The governor's wife in the cellars with the servants! Really, Randall!

RANDALL. But what shall I do if you are killed?

LADY UTTERWORD. You will probably be killed, too, Randall. Now play your flute to shew that you are not afraid; and be good. Play us Keep the home fires burning.*

NURSE GUINNESS [*grimly*] *Theyll* keep the home fires burning for us: them up there.

RANDALL [*having tried to play*] My lips are trembling. I cant get a sound.*

MAZZINI. I hope poor Mangan is safe.

MRS HUSHABYE. He is hiding in the cave in the gravel pit.

CAPTAIN SHOTOVER. My dynamite drew him there. It is the hand of God.

HECTOR [*returning from the house and striding across to his former place*] There is not half light enough. We should be blazing to the skies.

ELLIE [*tense with excitement*] Set fire to the house, Marcus.

MRS HUSHABYE. My house! No.

HECTOR. I thought of that; but it would not be ready in time.

CAPTAIN SHOTOVER. The judgment has come. Courage will not save you; but it will shew that your souls are still alive.

MRS HUSHABYE. Sh-sh! Listen: do you hear it now? It's magnificent.

They all turn away from the house and look up, listening.

HECTOR [*gravely*] Miss Dunn: you can do no good here. We of this house are only moths flying into the candle. You had better go down to the cellar.

ELLIE [*scornfully*] I *dont* think.

MAZZINI. Ellie, dear, there is no disgrace in going to the cellar. An officer would order his soldiers to take cover. Mr Hushabye is behaving like an amateur. Mangan and the burglar are acting very sensibly; and it is they who will survive.*

ELLIE. Let them. I shall behave like an amateur. But why should you run any risk?

MAZZINI. Think of the risk those poor fellows up there are running!

NURSE GUINNESS. Think of *them*, indeed, the murdering blackguards! What next?

A terrific explosion shakes the earth. They reel back into their seats, or clutch the nearest support. They hear the falling of the shattered glass from the windows.

MAZZINI. Is anyone hurt?

HECTOR. Where did it fall?

NURSE GUINNESS [*in hideous triumph*] Right in the gravel pit: I seen it. Serve un* right! I seen it [*she runs away towards the gravel pit, laughing harshly*].

HECTOR. One husband gone.

CAPTAIN SHOTOVER. Thirty pounds of good dynamite wasted.*

MAZZINI. Oh, poor Mangan!

HECTOR. Are you immortal that you need pity him? Our turn next.

They wait in silence and intense expectation. Hesione and Ellie hold each other's hand tight.

A distant explosion is heard.

MRS HUSHABYE [*relaxing her grip*] Oh! they have passed us.

LADY UTTERWORD. The danger is over, Randall. Go to bed.

CAPTAIN SHOTOVER. Turn in, all hands. The ship is safe. [*He sits down and goes asleep*].

ELLIE [*disappointedly*] Safe!

HECTOR [*disgustedly*] Yes, safe. And how damnably dull the world has become again suddenly! [*He sits down*].

MAZZINI [*sitting down*] I was quite wrong, after all. It is we who have survived; and Mangan and the burglar——

HECTOR. ——the two burglars——

LADY UTTERWORD. ——the two practical men of business——

MAZZINI. ——both gone. And the poor clergyman will have to get a new house.

MRS HUSHABYE. But what a glorious experience! I hope theyll come again tomorrow night.

ELLIE [*radiant at the prospect*] Oh, I *hope* so.

*Randall at last succeeds in keeping the home fires burning on his flute.**

SAINT JOAN

A Chronicle Play* In Six Scenes
and an Epilogue*

PREFACE TO SAINT JOAN

Joan the Original and Presumptuous

JOAN OF ARC, a village girl from the Vosges,* was born about 1412; burnt for heresy, witchcraft, and sorcery in 1431; rehabilitated* after a fashion in 1456; designated Venerable in 1904; declared Blessed in 1908; and finally canonized* in 1920. She is the most notable Warrior Saint in the Christian calendar,* and the queerest fish among the eccentric worthies of the Middle Ages.* Though a professed and most pious Catholic, and the projector of a Crusade against the Husites,* she was in fact one of the first Protestant martyrs. She was also one of the first apostles of Nationalism, and the first French practitioner of Napoleonic realism in warfare as distinguished from the sporting ransom-gambling chivalry of her time. She was the pioneer of rational dressing for women, and, like Queen Christina of Sweden two centuries later, to say nothing of Catalina de Erauso* and innumerable obscure heroines who have disguised themselves as men to serve as soldiers and sailors, she refused to accept the specific woman's lot, and dressed and fought and lived as men did.

As she contrived to assert herself in all these ways with such force that she was famous throughout western Europe before she was out of her teens (indeed she never got out of them), it is hardly surprising that she was judicially burnt, ostensibly for a number of capital crimes which we no longer punish as such, but essentially for what we call unwomanly and insufferable presumption. At eighteen Joan's pretensions were beyond those of the proudest Pope or the haughtiest emperor. She claimed to be the ambassador and plenipotentiary of God, and to be, in effect, a member of the Church Triumphant* whilst still in the flesh on earth. She patronized her own king, and summoned the English king* to repentance and obedience to her commands. She lectured, talked down, and overruled statesmen and prelates. She pooh-poohed the plans of generals, leading their troops to victory on plans of her own. She had an unbounded and quite unconcealed contempt for official opinion, judgment, and authority, and for War Office tactics and strategy. Had she been a sage and monarch in whom the most venerable hierarchy and the most illustrious dynasty converged, her pretensions and proceedings would have been as trying to the official mind as the pretensions of Caesar were to Cassius.* As her actual condition was pure upstart, there were only two opinions about her. One was that she was miraculous: the other that she was unbearable.

Joan and Socrates*

If Joan had been malicious, selfish, cowardly or stupid, she would have been one of the most odious persons known to history instead of one of the most attractive. If she had been old enough to know the effect she was producing on the men whom she humiliated by being right when they were wrong, and had learned to flatter and manage them, she might have lived as long as Queen Elizabeth.* But she was too young and rustical and inexperienced to have any such arts. When she was thwarted by men whom she thought fools, she made no secret of her opinion of them or her impatience with their folly; and she was naïve enough to expect them to be obliged to her for setting them right and keeping them out of mischief. Now it is always hard for superior wits to understand the fury roused by their exposures of the stupidities of comparative dullards. Even Socrates, for all his age and experience, did not defend himself at his trial like a man who understood the long accumulated fury that had burst on him, and was clamoring for his death. His accuser, if born 2300 years later, might have been picked out of any first class carriage on a suburban railway during the evening or morning rush from or to the City; for he had really nothing to say except that he and his like could not endure being shewn up as idiots every time Socrates opened his mouth. Socrates, unconscious of this, was paralyzed by his sense that somehow he was missing the point of the attack. He petered out after he had established the fact that he was an old soldier and a man of honorable life, and that his accuser was a silly snob. He had no suspicion of the extent to which his mental superiority had roused fear and hatred against him in the hearts of men towards whom he was conscious of nothing but good will and good service.

Contrast with Napoleon

If Socrates was as innocent as this at the age of seventy, it may be imagined how innocent Joan was at the age of seventeen. Now Socrates was a man of argument, operating slowly and peacefully on men's minds, whereas Joan was a woman of action, operating with impetuous violence on their bodies. That, no doubt, is why the contemporaries of Socrates endured him so long, and why Joan was destroyed before she was fully grown. But both of them combined terrifying ability with

a frankness, personal modesty, and benevolence which made the furious
dislike to which they fell victims absolutely unreasonable, and therefore
inapprehensible by themselves. Napoleon, also possessed of terrifying
ability, but neither frank nor disinterested, had no illusions as to the
nature of his popularity. When he was asked how the world would take
his death, he said it would give a gasp of relief. But it is not so easy for
mental giants who neither hate nor intend to injure their fellows to realize that nevertheless their fellows hate mental giants and would like to
destroy them, not only enviously because the juxtaposition of a superior wounds their vanity, but quite humbly and honestly because it
frightens them. Fear will drive men to any extreme; and the fear
inspired by a superior being is a mystery which cannot be reasoned
away. Being immeasurable it is unbearable when there is no presumption or guarantee of its benevolence and moral responsibility: in other
words, when it has no official status. The legal and conventional superiority of Herod and Pilate, and of Annas and Caiaphas,* inspires fear;
but the fear, being a reasonable fear of measurable and avoidable consequences which seem salutary and protective, is bearable; whilst the
strange superiority of Christ and the fear it inspires elicit a shriek of
Crucify Him from all who cannot divine its benevolence. Socrates has
to drink the hemlock, Christ to hang on the cross, and Joan to burn at
the stake, whilst Napoleon, though he ends in St Helena,* at least dies
in his bed there; and many terrifying but quite comprehensible official
scoundrels die natural deaths in all the glory of the kingdoms of this
world, proving that it is far more dangerous to be a saint than to be
a conqueror. Those who have been both, like Mahomet* and Joan, have
found that it is the conqueror who must save the saint, and that defeat
and capture mean martyrdom. Joan was burnt without a hand lifted
on her own side to save her. The comrades she had led to victory and
the enemies she had disgraced and defeated, the French king she had
crowned and the English king whose crown she had kicked into the
Loire,* were equally glad to be rid of her.

Was Joan Innocent or Guilty?

As this result could have been produced by a crapulous* inferiority as
well as by a sublime superiority, the question which of the two was
operative in Joan's case has to be faced. It was decided against her by
her contemporaries after a very careful and conscientious trial; and the
reversal of the verdict twentyfive years later, in form a rehabilitation of
Joan, was really only a confirmation of the validity of the coronation of

Charles VII. It is the more impressive reversal by a unanimous Posterity, culminating in her canonization, that has quashed the original proceedings, and put her judges on their trial, which, so far, has been much more unfair than their trial of her. Nevertheless the rehabilitation of 1456, corrupt job as it was, really did produce evidence enough to satisfy all reasonable critics that Joan was not a common termagant,* not a harlot, not a witch, not a blasphemer, no more an idolater than the Pope himself, and not ill conducted in any sense apart from her soldiering, her wearing of men's clothes, and her audacity, but on the contrary good-humored, an intact virgin, very pious, very temperate (we should call her meal of bread soaked in the common wine which is the drinking water of France ascetic), very kindly, and, though a brave and hardy soldier, unable to endure loose language or licentious conduct. She went to the stake without a stain on her character except the overweening presumption, the superbity* as they called it, that led her thither. It would therefore be waste of time now to prove that the Joan of the first part of the Elizabethan chronicle play of Henry VI (supposed to have been tinkered by Shakespear) grossly libels her in its concluding scenes in deference to Jingo patriotism.* The mud that was thrown at her has dropped off by this time so completely that there is no need for any modern writer to wash up after it. What is far more difficult to get rid of is the mud that is being thrown at her judges, and the whitewash which disfigures her beyond recognition. When Jingo scurrility had done its worst to her, sectarian scurrility (in this case Protestant scurrility) used her stake to beat the Roman Catholic Church and the Inquisition.* The easiest way to make these institutions the villains of a melodrama was to make The Maid its heroine. That melodrama may be dismissed as rubbish. Joan got a far fairer trial from the Church and the Inquisition than any prisoner of her type and in her situation gets nowadays in any official secular court; and the decision was strictly according to law. And she was not a melodramatic heroine: that is, a physically beautiful lovelorn parasite on an equally beautiful hero, but a genius and a saint, about as completely the opposite of a melodramatic heroine as it is possible for a human being to be.

Let us be clear about the meaning of the terms. A genius is a person who, seeing farther and probing deeper than other people, has a different set of ethical valuations from theirs, and has energy enough to give effect to this extra vision and its valuations in whatever manner best suits his or her specific talents. A saint is one who having practised heroic virtues, and enjoyed revelations or powers of the order which The Church classes technically as supernatural, is eligible for canonization. If a historian is an Anti-Feminist, and does not believe women to be capable of genius in the traditional masculine departments, he will never make anything of Joan, whose genius was turned to practical account mainly in soldiering and politics. If he is Rationalist enough to deny that saints exist, and to hold that new ideas cannot come otherwise than by conscious ratiocination, he will never catch Joan's likeness. Her ideal biographer must be free from nineteenth century prejudices and biases; must understand the Middle Ages, the Roman Catholic Church, and the Holy Roman Empire* much more intimately than our Whig historians* have ever understood them; and must be capable of throwing off sex partialities and their romance, and regarding woman as the female of the human species, and not as a different kind of animal with specific charms and specific imbecilities.

Joan's Good Looks

To put the last point roughly, any book about Joan which begins by describing her as a beauty may be at once classed as a romance. Not one of Joan's comrades, in village, court, or camp, even when they were straining themselves to please the king by praising her, ever claimed that she was pretty. All the men who alluded to the matter declared most emphatically that she was unattractive sexually to a degree that seemed to them miraculous, considering that she was in the bloom of youth, and neither ugly, awkward, deformed, nor unpleasant in her person. The evident truth is that like most women of her hardy managing type she seemed neutral in the conflict of sex because men were too much afraid of her to fall in love with her. She herself was not sexless: in spite of the virginity she had vowed up to a point, and preserved to her death, she never excluded the possibility of marriage for herself. But marriage, with its preliminary of the attraction, pursuit, and capture of a husband, was not her business: she had something else to do. Byron's formula, 'Man's love is of man's life a thing apart: 'tis woman's whole existence,'* did not apply to her any more than to George Washington* or any other masculine worker on the heroic scale. Had she lived in our time, picture postcards might have been sold of her as a general: they would not have been sold of her as a sultana. Nevertheless there is one reason for crediting her with a very remarkable face. A sculptor of her time in Orleans made a statue of a helmeted young woman with a face that is unique in art in point of being evidently not an ideal face but a portrait, and yet so uncommon as to be unlike any real woman one has ever seen. It is surmised that Joan served unconsciously as the sculptor's model. There is no

proof of this; but those extraordinarily spaced eyes raise so powerfully
the question 'If this woman be not Joan, who is she?' that I dispense with
further evidence, and challenge those who disagree with me to prove
a negative. It is a wonderful face, but quite neutral from the point of
view of the operatic beauty fancier.

Such a fancier may perhaps be finally chilled by the prosaic fact that
Joan was the defendant in a suit for breach of promise of marriage, and
that she conducted her own case and won it.

Joan's Social Position

By class Joan was the daughter of a working farmer who was one of the
headmen of his village, and transacted its feudal business for it with
the neighboring squires and their lawyers. When the castle in which
the villagers were entitled to take refuge from raids became derelict, he
organized a combination of half a dozen farmers to obtain possession
of it so as to occupy it when there was any danger of invasion. As a child,
Joan could please herself at times with being the young lady of this
castle. Her mother and brothers were able to follow and share her fortune at court without making themselves notably ridiculous. These
facts leave us no excuse for the popular romance that turns every heroine into either a princess or a beggarmaid. In the somewhat similar case
of Shakespear a whole inverted pyramid of wasted research has been
based on the assumption that he was an illiterate laborer, in the face of
the plainest evidence that his father was a man of business, and at one
time a very prosperous one, married to a woman of some social pretensions. There is the same tendency to drive Joan into the position of
a hired shepherd girl, though a hired shepherd girl in Domrémy would
have deferred to her as the young lady of the farm.

The difference between Joan's case and Shakespear's is that
Shakespear was not illiterate. He had been to school, and knew as much
Latin and Greek as most university passmen* retain: that is, for practical purposes, none at all. Joan was absolutely illiterate. 'I do not know
A from B' she said. But many princesses at that time and for long after
might have said the same. Marie Antoinette,* for instance, at Joan's age
could not spell her own name correctly. But this does not mean that
Joan was an ignorant person, or that she suffered from the diffidence
and sense of social disadvantage now felt by people who cannot read or
write. If she could not write letters, she could and did dictate them and
attach full and indeed excessive importance to them. When she was called
a shepherd lass to her face she very warmly resented it, and challenged

any woman to compete with her in the household arts of the mistresses of well furnished houses. She understood the political and military situation in France much better than most of our newspaper fed university women-graduates understand the corresponding situation of their own country today. Her first convert was the neighboring commandant at Vaucouleurs;* and she converted him by telling him about the defeat of the Dauphin's troops at the Battle of Herrings* so long before he had official news of it that he concluded she must have had a divine revelation. This knowledge of and interest in public affairs was nothing extraordinary among farmers in a war-swept countryside. Politicians came to the door too often sword in hand to be disregarded: Joan's people could not afford to be ignorant of what was going on in the feudal world. They were not rich; and Joan worked on the farm as her father did, driving the sheep to pasture and so forth; but there is no evidence or suggestion of sordid poverty, and no reason to believe that Joan had to work as a hired servant works, or indeed to work at all when she preferred to go to confession, or dawdle about waiting for visions and listening to the church bells to hear voices in them. In short, much more of a young lady, and even of an intellectual, than most of the daughters of our petty bourgeoisie.

Joan's Voices and Visions

Joan's voices and visions have played many tricks with her reputation. They have been held to prove that she was mad, that she was a liar and impostor, that she was a sorceress (she was burned for this), and finally that she was a saint. They do not prove any of these things; but the variety of the conclusions reached shew how little our matter-of-fact historians know about other people's minds, or even about their own. There are people in the world whose imagination is so vivid that when they have an idea it comes to them as an audible voice, sometimes uttered by a visible figure. Criminal lunatic asylums are occupied largely by murderers who have obeyed voices. Thus a woman may hear voices telling her that she must cut her husband's throat and strangle her child as they lie asleep; and she may feel obliged to do what she is told. By a medico-legal superstition it is held in our courts that criminals whose temptations present themselves under these illusions are not responsible for their actions, and must be treated as insane. But the seers of visions and the hearers of revelations are not always criminals. The inspirations and intuitions and unconsciously reasoned conclusions of genius sometimes assume similar illusions. Socrates, Luther,

Swedenborg,* Blake saw visions and heard voices just as Saint Francis and Saint Joan did. If Newton's imagination had been of the same vividly dramatic kind he might have seen the ghost of Pythagoras* walk into the orchard and explain why the apples were falling. Such an illusion would have invalidated neither the theory of gravitation nor Newton's general sanity. What is more, the visionary method of making the discovery would not be a whit more miraculous than the normal method. The test of sanity is not the normality of the method but the reasonableness of the discovery. If Newton had been informed by Pythagoras that the moon was made of green cheese, then Newton would have been locked up. Gravitation, being a reasoned hypothesis which fitted remarkably well into the Copernican version of the observed physical facts of the universe,* established Newton's reputation for extraordinary intelligence, and would have done so no matter how fantastically he had arrived at it. Yet his theory of gravitation is not so impressive a mental feat as his astounding chronology, which establishes him as the king of mental conjurors, but a Bedlamite* king whose authority no one now accepts. On the subject of the eleventh horn of the beast seen by the prophet Daniel* he was more fantastic than Joan, because his imagination was not dramatic but mathematical and therefore extraordinarily susceptible to numbers: indeed if all his works were lost except his chronology we should say that he was as mad as a hatter. As it is, who dares diagnose Newton as a madman?

In the same way Joan must be judged a sane woman in spite of her voices because they never gave her any advice that might not have come to her from her mother wit exactly as gravitation came to Newton. We can all see now, especially since the late war threw so many of our women into military life,* that Joan's campaigning could not have been carried on in petticoats. This was not only because she did a man's work, but because it was morally necessary that sex should be left out of the question as between her and her comrades-in-arms. She gave this reason herself when she was pressed on the subject; and the fact that this entirely reasonable necessity came to her imagination first as an order from God delivered through the mouth of Saint Catherine* does not prove that she was mad. The soundness of the order proves that she was unusually sane; but its form proves that her dramatic imagination played tricks with her senses. Her policy was also quite sound: nobody disputes that the relief of Orleans, followed up by the coronation at Rheims* of the Dauphin as a counterblow to the suspicions then current of his legitimacy and consequently of his title, were military and political master-strokes that saved France. They might have been planned by Napoleon or any other illusionproof genius. They came to Joan as an instruction from her Counsel, as she called her visionary saints; but she was none the less an able leader of men for imagining her ideas in this way.

The Evolutionary Appetite

What then is the modern view of Joan's voices and visions and messages from God? The nineteenth century said that they were delusions, but that as she was a pretty girl, and had been abominably ill-treated and finally done to death by a superstitious rabble of medieval priests hounded on by a corrupt political bishop, it must be assumed that she was the innocent dupe of these delusions. The twentieth century finds this explanation too vapidly commonplace, and demands something more mystic. I think the twentieth century is right, because an explanation which amounts to Joan being mentally defective instead of, as she obviously was, mentally excessive, will not wash. I cannot believe, nor, if I could, could I expect all my readers to believe, as Joan did, that three ocularly visible well dressed persons, named respectively Saint Catherine, Saint Margaret, and Saint Michael,* came down from heaven and gave her certain instructions with which they were charged by God for her. Not that such a belief would be more improbable or fantastic than some modern beliefs which we all swallow; but there are fashions and family habits in belief, and it happens that, my fashion being Victorian and my family habit Protestant, I find myself unable to attach any such objective validity to the form of Joan's visions.

But that there are forces at work which use individuals for purposes far transcending the purpose of keeping these individuals alive and prosperous and respectable and safe and happy in the middle station in life, which is all any good bourgeois can reasonably require, is established by the fact that men will, in the pursuit of knowledge and of social readjustments for which they will not be a penny the better, and are indeed often many pence the worse, face poverty, infamy, exile, imprisonment, dreadful hardship, and death. Even the selfish pursuit of personal power does not nerve men to the efforts and sacrifices which are eagerly made in pursuit of extensions of our power over nature, though these extensions may not touch the personal life of the seeker at any point. There is no more mystery about this appetite for knowledge and power than about the appetite for food: both are known as facts and as facts only, the difference between them being that the appetite for food is necessary to the life of the hungry man and is therefore a personal appetite, whereas the other is an appetite for evolution, and therefore a superpersonal need.

The diverse manners in which our imaginations dramatize the approach of the superpersonal forces is a problem for the psychologist, not for the historian. Only, the historian must understand that visionaries are neither impostors nor lunatics. It is one thing to say that the figure Joan recognized as St Catherine was not really St Catherine, but the dramatization by Joan's imagination of that pressure upon her of the driving force that is behind evolution which I have just called the evolutionary appetite. It is quite another to class her visions with the vision of two moons seen by a drunken person, or with Brocken spectres,* echoes and the like. Saint Catherine's instructions were far too cogent for that; and the simplest French peasant who believes in apparitions of celestial personages to favored mortals is nearer to the scientific truth about Joan than the Rationalist and Materialist historians and essayists who feel obliged to set down a girl who saw saints and heard them talking to her as either crazy or mendacious. If Joan was mad, all Christendom was mad too; for people who believe devoutly in the existence of celestial personages are every whit as mad in that sense as the people who think they see them. Luther, when he threw his inkhorn at the devil, was no more mad than any other Augustinian monk:* he had a more vivid imagination, and had perhaps eaten and slept less: that was all.

The Mere Iconography does not Matter

All the popular religions in the world are made apprehensible by an array of legendary personages, with an Almighty Father, and sometimes a mother and divine child, as the central figures. These are presented to the mind's eye in childhood; and the result is a hallucination which persists strongly throughout life when it has been well impressed. Thus all the thinking of the hallucinated adult about the fountain of inspiration which is continually flowing in the universe, or about the promptings of virtue and the revulsions of shame: in short, about aspiration and conscience, both of which forces are matters of fact more obvious than electro-magnetism, is thinking in terms of the celestial vision. And when in the case of exceptionally imaginative persons, especially those practising certain appropriate austerities, the hallucination extends from the mind's eye to the body's, the visionary sees Krishna or the Buddha or the Blessed Virgin* or St Catherine as the case may be.

The Modern Education which Joan Escaped

It is important to everyone nowadays to understand this, because modern science is making short work of the hallucinations without regard to the vital importance of the things they symbolize. If Joan were reborn today she would be sent, first to a convent school in which she would be mildly taught to connect inspiration and conscience with St Catherine and St Michael exactly as she was in the fifteenth century, and then finished up with a very energetic training in the gospel of Saints Louis Pasteur and Paul Bert,* who would tell her (possibly in visions but more probably in pamphlets) not to be a superstitious little fool, and to empty out St Catherine and the rest of the Catholic hagiology as an obsolete iconography of exploded myths. It would be rubbed into her that Galileo was a martyr, and his persecutors incorrigible ignoramuses, and that St Teresa's hormones had gone astray and left her incurably hyperpituitary or hyperadrenal or hysteroid or epileptoid or anything but asteroid.* She would have been convinced by precept and experiment that baptism and receiving the body of her Lord were contemptible superstitions, and that vaccination and vivisection* were enlightened practices. Behind her new Saints Louis and Paul there would be not only Science purifying Religion and being purified by it, but hypochondria, melancholia, cowardice, stupidity, cruelty, muckraking curiosity, knowledge without wisdom, and everything that the eternal soul in Nature loathes, instead of the virtues of which St Catherine was the figure head. As to the new rites, which would be the saner Joan? the one who carried little children to be baptized of water and the spirit, or the one who sent the police to force their parents to have the most villainous racial poison we know thrust into their veins? the one who told them the story of the angel and Mary,* or the one who questioned them as to their experiences of the Edipus complex?* the one to whom the consecrated wafer was the very body of the virtue that was her salvation, or the one who looked forward to a precise and convenient regulation of her health and her desires by a nicely calculated diet of thyroid extract, adrenalin, thymin, pituitrin, and insulin, with pick-me-ups of hormone stimulants, the blood being first carefully fortified with antibodies against all possible infections by inoculations of infected bacteria and serum from infected animals, and against old age by surgical extirpation of the reproductive ducts or weekly doses of monkey gland?

It is true that behind all these quackeries there is a certain body of genuine scientific physiology. But was there any the less a certain body of genuine psychology behind St Catherine and the Holy Ghost? And which is the healthier mind? the saintly mind or the monkey gland mind? Does not the present cry of Back to the Middle Ages, which has been incubating ever since the pre-Raphaelite movement began, mean that it is no longer our Academy pictures that are intolerable, but our credulities that have not the excuse of being superstitions, our cruelties that have not the excuse of barbarism, our persecutions that have not the excuse of religious faith, our shameless substitution of successful swindlers and scoundrels and quacks for saints as objects of worship, and our deafness and blindness to the calls and visions of the inexorable power that made us, and will destroy us if we disregard it? To Joan and her contemporaries we should appear as a drove of Gadarene swine,* possessed by all the unclean spirits cast out by the faith and civilization of the Middle Ages, running violently down a steep place into a hell of high explosives. For us to set up our condition as a standard of sanity, and declare Joan mad because she never condescended to it, is to prove that we are not only lost but irredeemable. Let us then once for all drop all nonsense about Joan being cracked, and accept her as at least as sane as Florence Nightingale,* who also combined a very simple iconography of religious belief with a mind so exceptionally powerful that it kept her in continual trouble with the medical and military panjandrums of her time.

Failures of the Voices

That the voices and visions were illusory, and their wisdom all Joan's own, is shewn by the occasions on which they failed her, notably during her trial, when they assured her that she would be rescued. Here her hopes flattered her; but they were not unreasonable: her military colleague La Hire* was in command of a considerable force not so very far off; and if the Armagnacs,* as her party was called, had really wanted to rescue her, and had put anything like her own vigor into the enterprise, they could have attempted it with very fair chances of success. She did not understand that they were glad to be rid of her, nor that the rescue of a prisoner from the hands of the Church was a much more serious business for a medieval captain, or even a medieval king, than its mere physical difficulty as a military exploit suggested. According to her lights her expectation of a rescue was reasonable; therefore she heard Madame Saint Catherine assuring her it would happen, that being her way of finding out and making up her own mind. When it became evident that she had miscalculated: when she was led to the stake, and La Hire was not thundering at the gates of Rouen* nor charging Warwick's* men at arms, she threw over Saint Catherine at once, and recanted. Nothing could be more sane or practical. It was not until she discovered that she had gained nothing by her recantation but close imprisonment for life that she withdrew it, and deliberately and explicitly chose burning instead: a decision which shewed not only the extraordinary decision of her character, but also a Rationalism carried to its ultimate human test of suicide. Yet even in this the illusion persisted; and she announced her relapse as dictated to her by her voices.

Joan a Galtonic Visualizer

The most sceptical scientific reader may therefore accept as a flat fact, carrying no implication of unsoundness of mind, that Joan was what Francis Galton* and other modern investigators of human faculty call a visualizer. She saw imaginary saints just as some other people see imaginary diagrams and landscapes with numbers dotted about them, and are thereby able to perform feats of memory and arithmetic impossible to non-visualizers. Visualizers will understand this at once. Non-visualizers who have never read Galton will be puzzled and incredulous. But a very little inquiry among their acquaintances will reveal to them that the mind's eye is more or less a magic lantern, and that the street is full of normally sane people who have hallucinations of all sorts which they believe to be part of the normal permanent equipment of all human beings.

Joan's Manliness and Militarism

Joan's other abnormality, too common among uncommon things to be properly called a peculiarity, was her craze for soldiering and the masculine life. Her father tried to frighten her out of it by threatening to drown her if she ran away with the soldiers, and ordering her brothers to drown her if he were not on the spot. This extravagance was clearly not serious: it must have been addressed to a child young enough to imagine that he was in earnest. Joan must therefore as a child have wanted to run away and be a soldier. The awful prospect of being thrown into the Meuse and drowned by a terrible father and her big brothers kept her quiet until the father had lost his terrors and the brothers yielded to her natural leadership; and by that time she had sense enough to know that the masculine and military life was not a mere matter of running away from home. But the taste for it never left her, and was fundamental in determining her career.

If anyone doubts this, let him ask himself why a maid charged with a special mission from heaven to the Dauphin (this was how Joan saw her very able plan for retrieving the desperate situation of the uncrowned king) should not have simply gone to the court as a maid, in woman's dress, and urged her counsel upon him in a woman's way, as other women with similar missions had come to his mad father and his wise grandfather.* Why did she insist on having a soldier's dress and arms and sword and horse and equipment, and on treating her escort of soldiers as comrades, sleeping side by side with them on the floor at night as if there were no difference of sex between them? It may be answered that this was the safest way of travelling through a country infested with hostile troops and bands of marauding deserters from both sides. Such an answer has no weight because it applies to all the women who travelled in France at that time, and who never dreamt of travelling otherwise than as women. But even if we accept it, how does it account for the fact that when the danger was over, and she could present herself at court in feminine attire with perfect safety and obviously with greater propriety, she presented herself in her man's dress, and instead of urging Charles, like Queen Victoria urging the War Office to send Roberts to the Transvaal,* to send D'Alençon, De Rais, La Hire and the rest to the relief of Dunois* at Orleans, insisted that she must go herself and lead the assault in person? Why did she give exhibitions of her dexterity in handling a lance, and of her seat as a rider? Why did she accept presents of armor and chargers and masculine surcoats,* and in every action repudiate the conventional character of a woman? The simple answer to all these questions is that she was the sort of woman that wants to lead a man's life. They are to be found wherever there are armies on foot or navies on the seas, serving in male disguise, eluding detection for astonishingly long periods, and sometimes, no doubt, escaping it entirely. When they are in a position to defy public opinion they throw off all concealment. You have your Rosa Bonheur* painting in male blouse and trousers, and George Sand living a man's life and almost compelling her Chopins and De Mussets* to live women's lives to amuse her. Had Joan not been one of those 'unwomanly women,'* she might have been canonized much sooner.

But it is not necessary to wear trousers and smoke big cigars to live a man's life any more than it is necessary to wear petticoats to live a woman's. There are plenty of gowned and bodiced women in ordinary civil life who manage their own affairs and other people's, including those of their menfolk, and are entirely masculine in their tastes and pursuits. There always were such women, even in the Victorian days when women had fewer legal rights than men, and our modern women magistrates, mayors, and members of Parliament were unknown. In reactionary Russia in our own century a woman soldier organized an effective regiment of amazons, which disappeared only because it was Aldershottian* enough to be against the Revolution. The exemption of women from military service is founded, not on any natural inaptitude that men do not share, but on the fact that communities cannot reproduce themselves without plenty of women. Men are more largely dispensable, and are sacrificed accordingly.

Was Joan Suicidal?

These two abnormalities were the only ones that were irresistibly prepotent* in Joan; and they brought her to the stake. Neither of them was peculiar to her. There was nothing peculiar about her except the vigor and scope of her mind and character, and the intensity of her vital energy. She was accused of a suicidal tendency; and it is a fact that when she attempted to escape from Beaurevoir Castle by jumping from a tower said to be sixty feet high,* she took a risk beyond reason, though she recovered from the crash after a few days fasting. Her death was deliberately chosen as an alternative to life without liberty. In battle she challenged death as Wellington did at Waterloo, and as Nelson* habitually did when he walked his quarter-deck during his battles with all his decorations in full blaze. As neither Nelson nor Wellington nor any of those who have performed desperate feats, and preferred death to captivity, has been accused of suicidal mania, Joan need not be suspected of it. In the Beaurevoir affair there was more at stake than her freedom. She was distracted by the news that Compiègne* was about to fall; and she was convinced that she could save it if only she could get free. Still, the leap was so perilous that her conscience was not quite easy about it; and she expressed this, as usual, by saying that Saint Catherine had forbidden her to do it, but forgave her afterwards for her disobedience.

Joan Summed Up

We may accept and admire Joan, then, as a sane and shrewd country girl of extraordinary strength of mind and hardihood of body. Everything she did was thoroughly calculated; and though the process was so rapid that she was hardly conscious of it, and ascribed it all to her voices, she was a woman of policy and not of blind impulse. In war she was as much a realist as Napoleon: she had his eye for artillery and his knowledge of what it could do. She did not expect besieged cities to fall Jerichowise* at the sound of her trumpet, but, like Wellington, adapted her methods of attack to the peculiarities of the defence; and she anticipated the Napoleonic calculation that if you only hold on long enough the other fellow will give in: for example, her final triumph at Orleans was achieved after her commander Dunois had sounded the retreat at the end of a day's fighting without a decision. She was never for a moment what so many romancers and playwrights have pretended: a romantic young lady. She was a thorough daughter of the soil in her peasantlike matter-of-factness and doggedness, and her acceptance of great lords and kings and prelates as such without idolatry or snobbery, seeing at a glance how much they were individually good for. She had the respectable countrywoman's sense of the value of public decency, and would not tolerate foul language and neglect of religious observances, nor allow disreputable women to hang about her soldiers. She had one pious ejaculation 'En nom Dé!'* and one meaningless oath 'Par mon martin';* and this much swearing she allowed to the incorrigibly blasphemous La Hire equally with herself. The value of this prudery was so great in restoring the self-respect of the badly demoralized army that, like most of her policy, it justified itself as soundly calculated. She talked to and dealt with people of all classes, from laborers to kings, without embarrassment or affectation, and got them to do what she wanted when they were not afraid or corrupt. She could coax and she could hustle, her tongue having a soft side and a sharp edge. She was very capable: a born boss.

Joan's Immaturity and Ignorance

All this, however, must be taken with one heavy qualification. She was only a girl in her teens. If we could think of her as a managing woman of fifty we should seize her type at once; for we have plenty of managing women among us of that age who illustrate perfectly the sort of person she would have become had she lived. But she, being only a lass when all is said, lacked their knowledge of men's vanities and of the weight and proportion of social forces. She knew nothing of iron hands in velvet gloves: she just used her fists. She thought political changes much easier than they are, and, like Mahomet in his innocence of any world but the tribal world, wrote letters to kings calling on them to make millennial rearrangements. Consequently it was only in the enterprises that were really simple and compassable by swift physical force, like the coronation and the Orleans campaign, that she was successful.

Her want of academic education disabled her when she had to deal with such elaborately artificial structures as the great ecclesiastical and social institutions of the Middle Ages. She had a horror of heretics without suspecting that she was herself a heresiarch, one of the precursors of a schism that rent Europe in two, and cost centuries of bloodshed that is not yet staunched. She objected to foreigners on the sensible ground that they were not in their proper place in France; but she had no notion of how this brought her into conflict with Catholicism and Feudalism,* both essentially international. She worked by commonsense; and where scholarship was the only clue to institutions she was in the dark, and broke her shins against them, all the more rudely because of her enormous self-confidence, which made her the least cautious of human beings in civil affairs.

This combination of inept youth and academic ignorance with great natural capacity, push, courage, devotion, originality and oddity, fully accounts for all the facts in Joan's career, and makes her a credible historical and human phenomenon; but it clashes most discordantly both with the idolatrous romance that has grown up round her, and the belittling scepticism that reacts against that romance.

The Maid in Literature

English readers would probably like to know how these idolizations and reactions have affected the books they are most familiar with about Joan. There is the first part of the Shakespearean, or pseudo-Shakespearean trilogy of Henry VI, in which Joan is one of the leading characters. This portrait of Joan is not more authentic than the descriptions in the London papers of George Washington in 1780, of Napoleon in 1803, of the German Crown Prince in 1915, or of Lenin in 1917.* It ends in mere scurrility. The impression left by it is that the playwright, having begun by an attempt to make Joan a beautiful and romantic figure, was told by his scandalized company that English patriotism would never stand a sympathetic representation of a French conqueror of English troops, and that unless he at once introduced all the old charges against Joan of being a sorceress and a harlot, and assumed her to be guilty of all of them, his play could not be produced. As likely as not, this is what actually happened: indeed there is only one other apparent way of accounting for the sympathetic representation of Joan as a heroine culminating in her eloquent appeal to the Duke of Burgundy,* followed by the blackguardly scurrility of the concluding scenes. That other way is to assume that the original play was wholly scurrilous, and that

Shakespear touched up the earlier scenes. As the work belongs to a period at which he was only beginning his practice as a tinker of old works, before his own style was fully formed and hardened, it is impossible to verify this guess. His finger is not unmistakeably evident in the play, which is poor and base in its moral tone; but he may have tried to redeem it from downright infamy by shedding a momentary glamor on the figure of The Maid.

When we jump over two centuries to Schiller, we find Die Jungfrau von Orleans* drowned in a witch's caldron of raging romance. Schiller's Joan has not a single point of contact with the real Joan, nor indeed with any mortal woman that ever walked this earth. There is really nothing to be said of his play but that it is not about Joan at all, and can hardly be said to pretend to be; for he makes her die on the battlefield, finding her burning unbearable. Before Schiller came Voltaire, who burlesqued Homer in a mock epic called La Pucelle.* It is the fashion to dismiss this with virtuous indignation as an obscene libel; and I certainly cannot defend it against the charge of extravagant indecorum. But its purpose was not to depict Joan, but to kill with ridicule everything that Voltaire righteously hated in the institutions and fashions of his own day. He made Joan ridiculous, but not contemptible nor (comparatively) unchaste; and as he also made Homer and St Peter and St Denis* and the brave Dunois ridiculous, and the other heroines of the poem very unchaste indeed, he may be said to have let Joan off very easily. But indeed the personal adventures of the characters are so outrageous, and so Homerically free from any pretence at or even possibility of historical veracity, that those who affect to take them seriously only make themselves Pecksniffian.* Samuel Butler believed The Iliad to be a burlesque of Greek Jingoism and Greek religion, written by a hostage or a slave;* and La Pucelle makes Butler's theory almost convincing. Voltaire represents Agnes Sorel,* the Dauphin's mistress, whom Joan never met, as a woman with a consuming passion for the chastest concubinal fidelity, whose fate it was to be continually falling into the hands of licentious foes and suffering the worst extremities of rapine. The combats in which Joan rides a flying donkey, or in which, taken unaware with no clothes on, she defends Agnes with her sword, and inflicts appropriate mutilations on her assailants, can be laughed at as they are intended to be without scruple; for no sane person could mistake them for sober history; and it may be that their ribald irreverence is more wholesome than the beglamored sentimentality of Schiller. Certainly Voltaire should not have asserted that Joan's father was a priest; but when he was out to *écraser l'infâme** (the French Church) he stuck at nothing.

So far, the literary representations of The Maid were legendary. But the publication by Quicherat* in 1841 of the reports of her trial and rehabilitation placed the subject on a new footing. These entirely realistic documents created a living interest in Joan which Voltaire's mock Homerics and Schiller's romantic nonsense missed. Typical products of that interest in America and England are the histories of Joan by Mark Twain and Andrew Lang.* Mark Twain was converted to downright worship of Joan directly by Quicherat. Later on, another man of genius, Anatole France,* reacted against the Quicheratic wave of enthusiasm, and wrote a Life of Joan in which he attributed Joan's ideas to clerical prompting and her military success to an adroit use of her by Dunois as a *mascotte*: in short, he denied that she had any serious military or political ability. At this Andrew saw red, and went for Anatole's scalp in a rival Life of her which should be read as a corrective to the other. Lang had no difficulty in shewing that Joan's ability was not an unnatural fiction to be explained away as an illusion manufactured by priests and soldiers, but a straightforward fact.

It has been lightly pleaded in explanation that Anatole France is a Parisian of the art world, into whose scheme of things the able, hardheaded, hardhanded female, though she dominates provincial France and business Paris, does not enter; whereas Lang was a Scot, and every Scot knows that the grey mare is as likely as not to be the better horse. But this explanation does not convince me. I cannot believe that Anatole France does not know what everybody knows. I wish everybody knew all that he knows. One feels antipathies at work in his book. He is not anti-Joan; but he is anti-clerical, anti-mystic, and fundamentally unable to believe that there ever was any such person as the real Joan.

Mark Twain's Joan, skirted to the ground, and with as many petticoats as Noah's wife in a toy ark, is an attempt to combine Bayard with Esther Summerson from Bleak House* into an unimpeachable American school teacher in armor. Like Esther Summerson she makes her creator ridiculous, and yet, being the work of a man of genius, remains a credible human goodygoody in spite of her creator's infatuation. It is the description rather than the valuation that is wrong. Andrew Lang and Mark Twain are equally determined to make Joan a beautiful and most ladylike Victorian; but both of them recognize and insist on her capacity for leadership, though the Scots scholar is less romantic about it than the Mississippi pilot.* But then Lang was, by lifelong professional habit, a critic of biographies rather than a biographer, whereas Mark Twain writes his biography frankly in the form of a romance.

Protestant Misunderstandings of the Middle Ages

They had, however, one disability in common. To understand Joan's history it is not enough to understand her character: you must understand her environment as well. Joan in a nineteenth–twentieth century environment is as incongruous a figure as she would appear were she to walk down Piccadilly today in her fifteenth century armor. To see her in her proper perspective you must understand Christendom and the Catholic Church, the Holy Roman Empire and the Feudal System, as they existed and were understood in the Middle Ages. If you confuse the Middle Ages with the Dark Ages, and are in the habit of ridiculing your aunt for wearing 'medieval clothes,' meaning those in vogue in the eighteen-nineties,* and are quite convinced that the world has progressed enormously, both morally and mechanically, since Joan's time, then you will never understand why Joan was burnt, much less feel that you might have voted for burning her yourself if you had been a member of the court that tried her; and until you feel that you know nothing essential about her.

That the Mississippi pilot should have broken down on this misunderstanding is natural enough. Mark Twain, the Innocent Abroad, who saw the lovely churches of the Middle Ages without a throb of emotion, author of A Yankee at the Court of King Arthur, in which the heroes and heroines of medieval chivalry are guys seen through the eyes of a street arab,* was clearly out of court from the beginning. Andrew Lang was better read; but, like Walter Scott,* he enjoyed medieval history as a string of Border romances rather than as the record of a high European civilization based on a catholic faith. Both of them were baptized as Protestants, and impressed by all their schooling and most of their reading with the belief that Catholic bishops who burnt heretics were persecutors capable of any villainy; that all heretics were Albigensians* or Husites or Jews or Protestants of the highest character; and that the Inquisition was a Chamber of Horrors invented expressly and exclusively for such burnings. Accordingly we find them representing Peter Cauchon,* Bishop of Beauvais, the judge who sent Joan to the stake, as an unconscionable scoundrel, and all the questions put to her as 'traps' to ensnare and destroy her. And they assume unhesitatingly that the two or three score of canons and doctors of law and divinity who sat with Cauchon as assessors, were exact reproductions of him on slightly less elevated chairs and with a different headdress.

Comparative Fairness of Joan's Trial

The truth is that Cauchon was threatened and insulted by the English for being too considerate to Joan. A recent French writer denies that Joan was burnt, and holds that Cauchon spirited her away and burnt somebody or something else in her place, and that the pretender who subsequently personated her at Orleans and elsewhere was not a pretender but the real authentic Joan. He is able to cite Cauchon's pro-Joan partiality in support of his view. As to the assessors, the objection to them is not that they were a row of uniform rascals, but that they were political partisans of Joan's enemies. This is a valid objection to all such trials; but in the absence of neutral tribunals they are unavoidable. A trial by Joan's French partisans would have been as unfair as the trial by her French opponents; and an equally mixed tribunal would have produced a deadlock. Such recent trials as those of Edith Cavell* by a German tribunal and Roger Casement* by an English one were open to the same objection; but they went forward to the death nevertheless, because neutral tribunals were not available. Edith, like Joan, was an arch heretic: in the middle of the war she declared before the world that 'Patriotism is not enough.'* She nursed enemies back to health, and assisted their prisoners to escape, making it abundantly clear that she would help any fugitive or distressed person without asking whose side he was on, and acknowledging no distinction before Christ between Tommy and Jerry and Pitou the *poilu*.* Well might Edith have wished that she could bring the Middle Ages back, and have fifty civilians, learned in the law or vowed to the service of God, to support two skilled judges in trying her case according to the Catholic law of Christendom, and to argue it out with her at sitting after sitting for many weeks. The modern military Inquisition was not so squeamish. It shot her out of hand; and her countrymen, seeing in this a good opportunity for lecturing the enemy on his intolerance, put up a statue to her, but took particular care not to inscribe on the pedestal 'Patriotism is not enough,' for which omission, and the lie it implies, they will need Edith's intercession when they are themselves brought to judgment, if any heavenly power thinks such moral cowards capable of pleading to an intelligible indictment.

The point need be no further labored. Joan was persecuted essentially as she would be persecuted today. The change from burning to hanging or shooting may strike us as a change for the better. The change from careful trial under ordinary law to recklessly summary military terrorism may strike us a change for the worse. But as far as toleration is concerned the trial and execution in Rouen in 1431 might have been an event of today; and we may charge our consciences accordingly. If Joan had to be dealt with by us in London she would be treated with no more toleration than Miss Sylvia Pankhurst,* or the Peculiar People,* or the parents who keep their children from the elementary school, or any of the others who cross the line we have to draw, rightly or wrongly, between the tolerable and the intolerable.

Joan not tried as a Political Offender

Besides, Joan's trial was not, like Casement's, a national political trial. Ecclesiastical courts and the courts of the Inquisition (Joan was tried by a combination of the two) were Courts Christian: that is, international courts; and she was tried, not as a traitress, but as a heretic, blasphemer, sorceress and idolater. Her alleged offences were not political offences against England, nor against the Burgundian faction in France, but against God and against the common morality of Christendom. And although the idea we call Nationalism was so foreign to the medieval conception of Christian society that it might almost have been directly charged against Joan as an additional heresy, yet it was not so charged; and it is unreasonable to suppose that the political bias of a body of Frenchmen like the assessors would on this point have run strongly in favor of the English foreigners (even if they had been making themselves particularly agreeable in France instead of just the contrary) against a Frenchwoman who had vanquished them.

The tragic part of the trial was that Joan, like most prisoners tried for anything but the simplest breaches of the ten commandments, did not understand what they were accusing her of. She was much more like Mark Twain than like Peter Cauchon. Her attachment to the Church was very different from the Bishop's, and does not, in fact, bear close examination from his point of view. She delighted in the solaces the Church offers to sensitive souls: to her, confession and communion were luxuries beside which the vulgar pleasures of the senses were trash. Her prayers were wonderful conversations with her three saints. Her piety seemed superhuman to the formally dutiful people whose religion was only a task to them. But when the Church was not offering her her favorite luxuries, but calling on her to accept its interpretation of God's will, and to sacrifice her own, she flatly refused, and made it clear that her notion of a Catholic Church was one in which the Pope was Pope Joan. How could the Church tolerate that, when it had just destroyed Hus, and had watched the career of Wycliffe* with a growing anger that would have brought him, too, to the stake, had he not died a natural death before the wrath fell on him in his grave? Neither Hus nor Wycliffe was as bluntly defiant as Joan: both were reformers of the Church like Luther; whilst Joan, like Mrs Eddy,* was quite prepared to supersede St Peter as the rock on which the Church was built, and, like Mahomet, was always ready with a private revelation from God to settle every question and fit every occasion.

The enormity of Joan's pretension was proved by her own unconsciousness of it, which we call her innocence, and her friends called her simplicity. Her solutions of the problems presented to her seemed, and indeed mostly were, the plainest commonsense, and their revelation to her by her Voices was to her a simple matter of fact. How could plain commonsense and simple fact seem to her to be that hideous thing, heresy? When rival prophetesses came into the field, she was down on them at once for liars and humbugs; but she never thought of them as heretics. She was in a state of invincible ignorance as to the Church's view; and the Church could not tolerate her pretensions without either waiving its authority or giving her a place beside the Trinity* during her lifetime and in her teens, which was unthinkable. Thus an irresistible force met an immovable obstacle, and developed the heat that consumed poor Joan.

Mark and Andrew would have shared her innocence and her fate had they been dealt with by the Inquisition: that is why their accounts of the trial are as absurd as hers might have been could she have written one. All that can be said for their assumption that Cauchon was a vulgar villain, and that the questions put to Joan were traps, is that it has the support of the inquiry which rehabilitated her twentyfive years later. But this rehabilitation was as corrupt as the contrary proceeding applied to Cromwell by our Restoration* reactionaries. Cauchon had been dug up, and his body thrown into the common sewer. Nothing was easier than to accuse him of cozenage,* and declare the whole trial void on that account. That was what everybody wanted, from Charles the Victorious,* whose credit was bound up with The Maid's, to the patriotic Nationalist populace, who idolized Joan's memory. The English were gone; and a verdict in their favor would have been an outrage on the throne and on the patriotism which Joan had set on foot.

We have none of these overwhelming motives of political convenience and popularity to bias us. For us the first trial stands valid; and the rehabilitation would be negligible but for the mass of sincere testimony it produced as to Joan's engaging personal character. The question then arises: how did The Church get over the verdict at the first trial when it canonized Joan five hundred years later?

The Church Uncompromised by its Amends

Easily enough. In the Catholic Church, far more than in law, there is no wrong without a remedy. It does not defer to Joanesque private judgment as such, the supremacy of private judgment for the individual being the quintessence of Protestantism; nevertheless it finds a place for private judgment *in excelsis** by admitting that the highest wisdom may come as a divine revelation to an individual. On sufficient evidence it will declare that individual a saint. Thus, as revelation may come by way of an enlightenment of the private judgment no less than by the words of a celestial personage appearing in a vision, a saint may be defined as a person of heroic virtue whose private judgment is privileged. Many innovating saints, notably Francis and Clare,* have been in conflict with the Church during their lives, and have thus raised the question whether they were heretics or saints. Francis might have gone to the stake had he lived longer. It is therefore by no means impossible for a person to be excommunicated as a heretic, and on further consideration canonized as a saint. Excommunication* by a provincial ecclesiastical court is not one of the acts for which the Church claims infallibility. Perhaps I had better inform my Protestant readers that the famous Dogma of Papal Infallibility* is by far the most modest pretension of the kind in existence. Compared with our infallible democracies, our infallible medical councils, our infallible astronomers, our infallible judges, and our infallible parliaments, the Pope is on his knees in the dust confessing his ignorance before the throne of God, asking only that as to certain historical matters on which he has clearly more sources of information open to him than anyone else his decision shall be taken as final. The Church may, and perhaps some day will, canonize Galileo without compromising such infallibility as it claims for the Pope, if not without compromising the infallibility claimed for the Book of Joshua* by simple souls whose rational faith in more important things has become bound up with a quite irrational faith in the chronicle of Joshua's campaigns as a treatise on physics. Therefore the Church will probably not canonize Galileo yet awhile, though it might do worse. But it has been able to canonize Joan without any compromise at all. She never doubted that the sun went round the earth: she had seen it do so too often.

Still, there was a great wrong done to Joan and to the conscience of the world by her burning. *Tout comprendre, c'est tout pardonner,** which is the Devil's sentimentality, cannot excuse it. When we have admitted that the tribunal was not only honest and legal, but exceptionally merciful in respect of sparing Joan the torture which was customary when she was obdurate as to taking the oath, and that Cauchon was far more self-disciplined and conscientious both as priest and lawyer than any English judge ever dreams of being in a political case in which his party and class prejudices are involved, the human fact remains that the burning of Joan of Arc was a horror, and that a historian who would defend it would defend anything. The final criticism of its physical side is implied in the refusal of the Marquesas islanders* to be persuaded that the English did not eat Joan. Why, they ask, should anyone take the trouble to roast a human being except with that object? They cannot conceive its being a pleasure. As we have no answer for them that is not shameful to us, let us blush for our more complicated and pretentious savagery before we proceed to unravel the business further, and see what other lessons it contains for us.

Cruelty, Modern and Medieval

First, let us get rid of the notion that the mere physical cruelty of the burning has any special significance. Joan was burnt just as dozens of less interesting heretics were burnt in her time. Christ, in being cruci-fied, only shared the fate of thousands of forgotten malefactors. They have no pre-eminence in mere physical pain: much more horrible exe-cutions than theirs are on record, to say nothing of the agonies of so-called natural death at its worst.

Joan was burnt more than five hundred years ago. More than three hundred years later: that is, only about a hundred years before I was born, a woman was burnt on Stephen's Green* in my native city of Dublin for coining,* which was held to be treason. In my preface to the recent volume on English Prisons under Local Government, by Sidney and Beatrice Webb,* I have mentioned that when I was already a grown man I saw Richard Wagner conduct two concerts, and that when Richard Wagner was a young man he saw and avoided a crowd of people hastening to see a soldier broken on the wheel by the more cruel of the two ways of carrying out that hideous method of execution. Also that the penalty of hanging, drawing, and quartering,* unmentionable in its details, was abolished so recently that there are men living who have been sentenced to it. We are still flogging criminals, and clamoring for more flogging. Not even the most sensationally frightful of these atro-cities inflicted on its victim the misery, degradation, and conscious waste and loss of life suffered in our modern prisons, especially the model ones, without, as far as I can see, rousing any more compunction than the burning of heretics did in the Middle Ages. We have not even the excuse of getting some fun out of our prisons as the Middle Ages did out of their stakes and wheels and gibbets.* Joan herself judged this matter when she had to choose between imprisonment and the stake, and chose the stake. And thereby she deprived The Church of the plea that it was guiltless of her death, which was the work of the secular arm. The Church should have confined itself to excommunicating her. There it was within its rights: she had refused to accept its authority or comply with its conditions; and it could say with truth 'You are not one of us: go forth and find the religion that suits you, or found one for yourself.' It had no right to say 'You may return to us now that you have recanted; but you shall stay in a dungeon all the rest of your life.' Unfortunately, The Church did not believe that there was any genuine soul saving religion outside itself; and it was deeply corrupted, as all the Churches were and still are, by primitive Calibanism (in Browning's sense),* or the propitiation of a dreaded deity by suffering and sacrifice. Its method was not cruelty for cruelty's sake, but cruelty for the salvation of Joan's soul. Joan, however, believed that the saving of her soul was her own business, and not that of *les gens d'église*.* By using that term as she did, mistrustfully and contemptuously, she announced herself as, in germ, an anti-Clerical as thoroughgoing as Voltaire or Anatole France. Had she said in so many words 'To the dustbin with the Church Militant and its blackcoated officials: I recognize only the Church Triumphant in heaven,' she would hardly have put her view more plainly.

Catholic Anti-Clericalism

I must not leave it to be inferred here that one cannot be an anti-Clerical and a good Catholic too. All the reforming Popes have been vehement anti-Clericals, veritable scourges of the clergy. All the great Orders arose from dissatisfaction with the priests: that of the Franciscans with priestly snobbery, that of the Dominicans with priestly laziness and Laodiceanism,* that of the Jesuits with priestly apathy and ignorance and indiscipline. The most bigoted Ulster Orangeman or Leicester Low Church bourgeois (as described by Mr Henry Nevinson)* is a mere Gallio compared to Machiavelli,* who, though no Protestant, was a fierce anti-Clerical. Any Catholic may, and many Catholics do, denounce any priest or body of priests, as lazy, drunken, idle, dissolute, and unworthy of their great Church and their function as the pastors of their flocks of human souls. But to say that the souls of the people are no business of the Churchmen is to go a step further, a step across the Rubicon.* Joan virtually took that step.

Catholicism not yet Catholic Enough

And so, if we admit, as we must, that the burning of Joan was a mistake, we must broaden Catholicism sufficiently to include her in its charter. Our Churches must admit that no official organization of mortal men whose vocation does not carry with it extraordinary mental powers (and this is all that any Church Militant can in the face of fact and history pretend to be), can keep pace with the private judgment of persons of genius except when, by a very rare accident, the genius happens to be Pope, and not even then unless he is an exceedingly overbearing Pope. The Churches must learn humility as well as teach it. The Apostolic Succession* cannot be secured or confined by the laying on of hands: the tongues of fire have descended on heathens and outcasts too often for that, leaving anointed Churchmen to scandalize History as worldly rascals. When the Church Militant behaves as if it were already the Church Triumphant, it makes these appalling blunders about Joan and Bruno* and Galileo and the rest which make it so difficult for a Freethinker to join it; and a Church which has no place for Freethinkers: nay, which does not inculcate and encourage freethinking with a complete belief that thought, when really free, must by its own law take the path that leads to The Church's bosom, not only has no future in modern culture, but obviously has no faith in the valid science of its own tenets, and is guilty of the heresy that theology and science are two different and opposite impulses, rivals for human allegiance.

I have before me the letter of a Catholic priest.* 'In your play,' he writes, 'I see the dramatic presentation of the conflict of the Regal, sacerdotal, and Prophetical powers, in which Joan was crushed. To me it is not the victory of any one of them over the others that will bring peace and the Reign of the Saints in the Kingdom of God, but their fruitful interaction in a costly but noble state of tension.' The Pope himself could not put it better; nor can I. We must accept the tension, and maintain it nobly without letting ourselves be tempted to relieve it by burning the thread. This is Joan's lesson to The Church; and its formulation by the hand of a priest emboldens me to claim that her canonization was a magnificently Catholic gesture as the canonization of a Protestant saint by the Church of Rome. But its special value and virtue cannot be apparent until it is known and understood as such. If any simple priest for whom this is too hard a saying tells me that it was not so intended, I shall remind him that the Church is in the hands of God, and not, as simple priests imagine, God in the hands of the Church; so if he answers too confidently for God's intentions he may be asked 'Hast thou entered into the springs of the sea? or hast thou walked in the recesses of the deep?' And Joan's own answer is also the answer of old: 'Though He slay me, yet will I trust in Him; *but I will maintain my own ways before Him.*'*

The Law of Change is the Law of God

When Joan maintained her own ways she claimed, like Job, that there was not only God and the Church to be considered, but the Word made Flesh: that is, the unaveraged individual, representing life possibly at its highest actual human evolution and possibly at its lowest, but never at its merely mathematical average. Now there is no deification of the democratic average in the theory of the Church: it is an avowed hierarchy in which the members are sifted until at the end of the process an individual stands supreme as the Vicar of Christ. But when the process is examined it appears that its successive steps of selection and election are of the superior by the inferior (the cardinal vice of democracy), with the result that great popes are as rare and accidental as great kings, and that it has sometimes been safer for an aspirant to the Chair and the Keys* to pass as a moribund dotard than as an energetic saint. At best very few popes have been canonized, or could be without letting down the standard of sanctity set by the self-elected saints.

No other result could have been reasonably expected; for it is not possible that an official organization of the spiritual needs of millions of men and women, mostly poor and ignorant, should compete successfully in the selection of its principals with the direct choice of the Holy Ghost as it flashes with unerring aim upon the individual. Nor can any College of Cardinals pray effectively that its choice may be inspired. The conscious prayer of the inferior may be that his choice may light on a greater than himself; but the sub-conscious intention of his self-preserving individuality must be to find a trustworthy servant for his own purposes. The saints and prophets, though they may be accidentally in this or that official position or rank, are always really self-selected, like Joan. And since neither Church nor State, by the secular necessities of its constitution, can guarantee even the recognition of such self-chosen missions, there is nothing for us but to make it a point of honor to privilege heresy to the last bearable degree on the simple ground that all evolution in thought and conduct must at first appear as heresy and misconduct. In short, though all society is founded on intolerance, all improvement is founded on tolerance, or the recognition of the fact that the law of evolution is Ibsen's law of change.* And as the law of God in any sense of the word which can now command a faith proof against science is a law of evolution, it follows that the law of God is a law of change, and that when the Churches set themselves against change as such, they are setting themselves against the law of God.

Credulity, Modern and Medieval

When Abernethy,* the famous doctor, was asked why he indulged himself with all the habits he warned his patients against as unhealthy, he replied that his business was that of a direction post, which points out the way to a place, but does not go thither itself. He might have added that neither does it compel the traveller to go thither, nor prevent him from seeking some other way. Unfortunately our clerical direction posts always do coerce the traveller when they have the political power to do so. When the Church was a temporal as well as a spiritual power, and for long after to the full extent to which it could control or influence the temporal power, it enforced conformity by persecutions that were all the more ruthless because their intention was so excellent. Today, when the doctor has succeeded to the priest, and can do practically what he likes with parliament and the press through the blind faith in him which has succeeded to the far more critical faith in the parson, legal compulsion to take the doctor's prescription, however poisonous, is carried to an extent that would have horrified the Inquisition and staggered Archbishop Laud.* Our credulity is grosser than that of the Middle Ages, because the priest had no such direct pecuniary interest in our sins as the doctor has in our diseases: he did not starve when all was well with his flock, nor prosper when they were perishing, as our private commercial doctors must. Also the medieval cleric believed that something extremely unpleasant would happen to him after death if he was unscrupulous, a belief now practically extinct among persons receiving a dogmatically materialist education. Our professional corporations are Trade Unions without souls to be damned; and they will soon drive us to remind them that they have bodies to be kicked. The Vatican was never soulless: at worst it was a political conspiracy to make the Church supreme temporally as well as spiritually. Therefore the question raised by Joan's burning is a burning question still, though the penalties involved are not so sensational. That is why I am probing it. If it were only an historical curiosity I would not waste my readers' time and my own on it for five minutes.

Toleration, Modern and Medieval

The more closely we grapple with it the more difficult it becomes. At first sight we are disposed to repeat that Joan should have been excommunicated and then left to go her own way, though she would have protested vehemently against so cruel a deprivation of her spiritual food; for confession, absolution, and the body of her Lord were first necessaries of life to her. Such a spirit as Joan's might have got over that difficulty as the Church of England got over the Bulls of Pope Leo, by making a Church of her own,* and affirming it to be the temple of the true and original faith from which her persecutors had strayed. But as such a proceeding was, in the eyes of both Church and State at that time, a spreading of damnation and anarchy, its toleration involved a greater strain on faith in freedom than political and ecclesiastical human nature could bear. It is easy to say that the Church should have waited for the alleged evil results instead of assuming that they would occur, and what they would be. That sounds simple enough; but if a modern Public Health Authority were to leave people entirely to their own devices in the matter of sanitation, saying, 'We have nothing to do with drainage or your views about drainage; but if you catch smallpox or typhus we will prosecute you and have you punished very severely like the authorities in Butler's Erewhon,'* it would either be removed to the County Asylum or reminded that A's neglect of sanitation may kill the child of B two miles off, or start an epidemic in which the most conscientious sanitarians may perish.

We must face the fact that society is founded on intolerance. There are glaring cases of the abuse of intolerance; but they are quite as characteristic of our own age as of the Middle Ages. The typical modern example and contrast is compulsory inoculation replacing what was virtually compulsory baptism. But compulsion to inoculate is objected to as a crudely unscientific and mischievous anti-sanitary quackery, not in the least because we think it wrong to compel people to protect their children from disease. Its opponents would make it a crime, and will probably succeed in doing so; and that will be just as intolerant as making it compulsory. Neither the Pasteurians nor their opponents the Sanitarians* would leave parents free to bring up their children naked, though that course also has some plausible advocates. We may prate of toleration as we will; but society must always draw a line somewhere between allowable conduct and insanity or crime, in spite of the risk of mistaking sages for lunatics and saviors for blasphemers. We must persecute, even to the death; and all we can do to mitigate the danger of persecution is, first, to be very careful what we persecute, and second, to bear in mind that unless there is a large liberty to shock conventional people, and a well informed sense of the value of originality, individuality, and eccentricity, the result will be apparent stagnation covering a repression of evolutionary forces which will eventually explode with extravagant and probably destructive violence.

Variability of Toleration

The degree of tolerance attainable at any moment depends on the strain under which society is maintaining its cohesion. In war, for instance, we suppress the gospels and put Quakers in prison, muzzle the newspapers, and make it a serious offence to shew a light at night. Under the strain of invasion the French Government in 1792 struck off 4000 heads, mostly on grounds that would not in time of settled peace have provoked any Government to chloroform a dog; and in 1920 the British Government slaughtered and burnt in Ireland to persecute the advocates of a constitutional change which it had presently to effect itself.* Later on the Fascisti in Italy did everything that the Black and Tans* did in Ireland, with some grotesquely ferocious variations, under the strain of an unskilled attempt at industrial revolution by Socialists who understood Socialism even less than Capitalists understand Capitalism. In the United States an incredibly savage persecution of Russians took place during the scare spread by the Russian Bolshevik revolution after 1917.* These instances could easily be multiplied; but they are enough to shew that between a maximum of indulgent toleration and a ruthlessly intolerant Terrorism there is a scale through which toleration is continually rising or falling, and that there was not the smallest ground for the self-complacent conviction of the nineteenth century that it was more tolerant than the fifteenth, or that such an event as the execution of Joan could not possibly occur in what we call our own more enlightened times. Thousands of women, each of them a thousand times less dangerous and terrifying to our Governments than Joan was to the Government of her day, have within the last ten years been slaughtered, starved to death, burnt out of house and home, and what not that Persecution and Terror could do to them, in the course of Crusades far more tyrannically pretentious than the medieval Crusades which proposed nothing more hyperbolical than the rescue of the Holy Sepulchre from the Saracens.* The Inquisition, with its English equivalent the Star Chamber,* are gone in the sense that their names are now disused; but can any of the modern substitutes for the

Inquisition, the Special Tribunals and Commissions, the punitive expeditions, the suspensions of the Habeas Corpus Act,* the proclamations
of martial law and of minor states of siege, and the rest of them, claim
that their victims have as fair a trial, as well considered a body of law to
govern their cases, or as conscientious a judge to insist on strict legality
of procedure as Joan had from the Inquisition and from the spirit of the
Middle Ages even when her country was under the heaviest strain of
civil and foreign war? From us she would have had no trial and no law
except a Defence of The Realm Act* suspending all law; and for judge
she would have had, at best, a bothered major, and at worst a promoted
advocate in ermine and scarlet to whom the scruples of a trained ecclesiastic like Cauchon would seem ridiculous and ungentlemanly.

The Conflict between Genius and Discipline

Having thus brought the matter home to ourselves, we may now consider the special feature of Joan's mental constitution which made her
so unmanageable. What is to be done on the one hand with rulers who
will not give any reason for their orders, and on the other with people
who cannot understand the reasons when they are given? The government of the world, political, industrial, and domestic, has to be carried
on mostly by the giving and obeying of orders under just these conditions. 'Dont argue: do as you are told' has to be said not only to children
and soldiers, but practically to everybody. Fortunately most people do
not want to argue: they are only too glad to be saved the trouble of
thinking for themselves. And the ablest and most independent thinkers
are content to understand their own special department. In other
departments they will unhesitatingly ask for and accept the instructions
of a policeman or the advice of a tailor without demanding or desiring
explanations.

Nevertheless, there must be some ground for attaching authority to
an order. A child will obey its parents, a soldier his officer, a philosopher a railway porter, and a workman a foreman, all without question,
because it is generally accepted that those who give the orders understand what they are about, and are duly authorized and even obliged to
give them, and because, in the practical emergencies of daily life, there
is no time for lessons and explanations, or for arguments as to their
validity. Such obediences are as necessary to the continuous operation
of our social system as the revolutions of the earth are to the succession
of night and day. But they are not so spontaneous as they seem: they
have to be very carefully arranged and maintained. A bishop will defer

to and obey a king; but let a curate venture to give him an order, however necessary and sensible, and the bishop will forget his cloth and damn the curate's impudence. The more obedient a man is to accredited authority the more jealous he is of allowing any unauthorized person to order him about.

With all this in mind, consider the career of Joan. She was a village girl, in authority over sheep and pigs, dogs and chickens, and to some extent over her father's hired laborers when he hired any, but over no one else on earth. Outside the farm she had no authority, no prestige, no claim to the smallest deference. Yet she ordered everybody about, from her uncle to the king, the archbishop, and the military General Staff. Her uncle obeyed her like a sheep, and took her to the castle of the local commander, who, on being ordered about, tried to assert himself, but soon collapsed and obeyed. And so on up to the king, as we have seen. This would have been unbearably irritating even if her orders had been offered as rational solutions of the desperate difficulties in which her social superiors found themselves just then. But they were not so offered. Nor were they offered as the expression of Joan's arbitrary will. It was never 'I say so,' but always 'God says so.'

Joan as Theocrat

Leaders who take that line have no trouble with some people, and no end of trouble with others. They need never fear a lukewarm reception. Either they are messengers of God, or they are blasphemous impostors. In the Middle Ages the general belief in witchcraft greatly intensified this contrast, because when an apparent miracle happened (as in the case of the wind changing at Orleans) it proved the divine mission to the credulous, and proved a contract with the devil to the sceptical. All through, Joan had to depend on those who accepted her as an incarnate angel against those who added to an intense resentment of her presumption a bigoted abhorrence of her as a witch. To this abhorrence we must add the extreme irritation of those who did not believe in the voices, and regarded her as a liar and impostor. It is hard to conceive anything more infuriating to a statesman or a military commander, or to a court favorite, than to be overruled at every turn, or to be robbed of the ear of the reigning sovereign, by an impudent young upstart practising on the credulity of the populace and the vanity and silliness of an immature prince by exploiting a few of those lucky coincidences which pass as miracles with uncritical people. Not only were the envy, snobbery, and competitive ambition of the baser natures exacerbated by Joan's success, but among the friendly ones that were clever enough to be critical a quite reasonable scepticism and mistrust of her ability, founded on a fair observation of her obvious ignorance and temerity, were at work against her. And as she met all remonstrances and all criticisms, not with arguments or persuasion, but with a flat appeal to the authority of God and a claim to be in God's special confidence, she must have seemed, to all who were not infatuated by her, so insufferable that nothing but an unbroken chain of overwhelming successes in the military and political field could have saved her from the wrath that finally destroyed her.

Unbroken Success essential in Theocracy

To forge such a chain she needed to be the King, the Archbishop of Rheims, the Bastard of Orleans, and herself into the bargain; and that was impossible. From the moment when she failed to stimulate Charles to follow up his coronation with a swoop on Paris she was lost. The fact that she insisted on this whilst the king and the rest timidly and foolishly thought they could square the Duke of Burgundy, and effect a combination with him against the English, made her a terrifying nuisance to them; and from that time onward she could do nothing but prowl about the battlefields waiting for some lucky chance to sweep the captains into a big move. But it was to the enemy that the chance came: she was taken prisoner by the Burgundians fighting before Compiègne, and at once discovered that she had not a friend in the political world. Had she escaped she would probably have fought on until the English were gone, and then had to shake the dust of the court off her feet, and retire to Domrémy as Garibaldi had to retire to Caprera.*

Modern Distortions of Joan's History

This, I think, is all that we can now pretend to say about the prose of Joan's career. The romance of her rise, the tragedy of her execution, and the comedy of the attempts of posterity to make amends for that execution, belong to my play and not to my preface, which must be confined to a sober essay on the facts. That such an essay is badly needed can be ascertained by examining any of our standard works of reference. They give accurately enough the facts about the visit to Vaucouleurs, the annunciation to Charles at Chinon, the raising of the siege of Orleans and the subsequent battles, the coronation at Rheims, the capture at Compiègne, and the trial and execution at Rouen, with their dates and the names of the people concerned; but they all break down on the melodramatic legend of the wicked bishop and the entrapped maiden and the rest of it. It would be far less misleading if they were wrong as to the facts, and right in their view of the facts. As it is, they illustrate the too little considered truth that the fashion in which we think changes like the fashion of our clothes, and that it is difficult, if not impossible, for most people to think otherwise than in the fashion of their own period.

History always Out of Date

This, by the way, is why children are never taught contemporary history. Their history books deal with periods of which the thinking has passed out of fashion, and the circumstances no longer apply to active life. For example, they are taught history about Washington, and told lies about Lenin. In Washington's time they were told lies (the same lies) about Washington, and taught history about Cromwell. In the fifteenth and sixteenth centuries they were told lies about Joan, and by this time might very well be told the truth about her. Unfortunately the lies did not cease when the political circumstances became obsolete. The Reformation, which Joan had unconsciously anticipated, kept the questions which arose in her case burning up to our own day (you can see plenty of the burnt houses still in Ireland), with the result that Joan has remained the subject of anti-Clerical lies, of specifically Protestant lies, and of Roman Catholic evasions of her unconscious Protestantism. The truth sticks in our throats with all the sauces it is served with: it will never go down until we take it without any sauce at all.

The Real Joan not Marvellous Enough for Us

But even in its simplicity, the faith demanded by Joan is one which the anti-metaphysical temper of nineteenth century civilization, which remains powerful in England and America, and is tyrannical in France, contemptuously refuses her. We do not, like her contemporaries, rush to the opposite extreme in a recoil from her as from a witch self-sold to the devil, because we do not believe in the devil nor in the possibility of commercial contracts with him. Our credulity, though enormous, is not boundless; and our stock of it is quite used up by our mediums, clairvoyants, hand readers, slate writers, Christian Scientists, psycho-analysts, electronic vibration diviners, therapeutists of all schools registered and unregistered, astrologers, astronomers who tell us that the sun is nearly a hundred million miles away and that Betelgeuse* is ten times as big as the whole universe, physicists who balance Betelgeuse by describing the incredible smallness of the atom, and a host of other marvel mongers whose credulity would have dissolved the Middle Ages in a roar of sceptical merriment. In the Middle Ages people believed that the earth was flat, for which they had at least the evidence of their senses: we believe it to be round, not because as many as one per cent of us could give the physical reasons for so quaint a belief, but because modern science has convinced us that nothing that is obvious is true, and that everything that is magical, improbable, extraordinary, gigantic, microscopic, heartless, or outrageous is scientific.

I must not, by the way, be taken as implying that the earth is flat, or that all or any of our amazing credulities are delusions or impostures. I am only defending my own age against the charge of being less imaginative than the Middle Ages. I affirm that the nineteenth century, and still more the twentieth, can knock the fifteenth into a cocked hat* in point of susceptibility to marvels and miracles and saints and prophets and magicians and monsters and fairy tales of all kinds. The proportion of marvel to immediately credible statement in the latest edition of the Encyclopædia Britannica* is enormously greater than in the Bible. The medieval doctors of divinity who did not pretend to settle how many angels could dance on the point of a needle cut a very poor figure as far as romantic credulity is concerned beside the modern physicists who have settled to the billionth of a millimetre every movement and position in the dance of the electrons. Not for worlds would I question the precise accuracy of these calculations or the existence of electrons (whatever they may be). The fate of Joan is a warning to me against such heresy. But why the men who believe in electrons should regard themselves as less credulous than the men who believed in angels is not apparent to me. If they refuse to believe, with the Rouen assessors of 1431, that Joan was a witch, it is not because that explanation is too marvellous, but because it is not marvellous enough.

The Stage Limits of Historical Representation

For the story of Joan I refer the reader to the play which follows. It contains all that need be known about her; but as it is for stage use I have had to condense into three and a half hours a series of events which in their historical happening were spread over four times as many months; for the theatre imposes unities of time and place from which Nature in her boundless wastefulness is free. Therefore the reader must not suppose

that Joan really put Robert de Baudricourt in her pocket in fifteen minutes, nor that her excommunication, recantation, relapse, and death at
the stake were a matter of half an hour or so. Neither do I claim more for
my dramatizations of Joan's contemporaries than that some of them are
probably slightly more like the originals than those imaginary portraits of
all the Popes from Saint Peter onward through the Dark Ages which are
still gravely exhibited in the Uffizi in Florence* (or were when I was there
last). My Dunois would do equally well for the Duc d'Alençon. Both left
descriptions of Joan so similar that, as a man always describes himself
unconsciously whenever he describes anyone else, I have inferred that
these goodnatured young men were very like one another in mind; so
I have lumped the twain into a single figure, thereby saving the theatre
manager a salary and a suit of armor. Dunois' face, still on record at
Châteaudun,* is a suggestive help. But I really know no more about these
men and their circle than Shakespear knew about Falconbridge and the
Duke of Austria, or about Macbeth and Macduff.* In view of the things
they did in history, and have to do again in the play, I can only invent
appropriate characters for them in Shakespear's manner.

A Void in the Elizabethan Drama

I have, however, one advantage over the Elizabethans. I write in full
view of the Middle Ages, which may be said to have been rediscovered
in the middle of the nineteenth century after an eclipse of about four
hundred and fifty years. The Renascence of antique literature and art in
the sixteenth century, and the lusty growth of Capitalism, between
them buried the Middle Ages; and their resurrection is a second
Renascence. Now there is not a breath of medieval atmosphere in
Shakespear's histories. His John of Gaunt is like a study of the old age
of Drake.* Although he was a Catholic by family tradition, his figures
are all intensely Protestant, individualist, sceptical, self-centred in
everything but their love affairs, and completely personal and selfish
even in them. His kings are not statesmen: his cardinals have no religion: a novice can read his plays from one end to the other without
learning that the world is finally governed by forces expressing themselves in religions and laws which make epochs rather than by vulgarly
ambitious individuals who make rows. The divinity which shapes our
ends, rough hew them how we will,* is mentioned fatalistically only to be
forgotten immediately like a passing vague apprehension. To Shakespear
as to Mark Twain, Cauchon would have been a tyrant and a bully
instead of a Catholic, and the inquisitor Lemaître* would have been

a Sadist instead of a lawyer. Warwick would have had no more feudal quality than his successor the King Maker* has in the play of Henry VI. We should have seen them all completely satisfied that if they would only to their own selves be true they could not then be false to any man* (a precept which represents the reaction against medievalism at its intensest) as if they were beings in the air, without public responsibilities of any kind. All Shakespear's characters are so: that is why they seem natural to our middle classes, who are comfortable and irresponsible at other people's expense, and are neither ashamed of that condition nor even conscious of it. Nature abhors this vacuum in Shakespear; and I have taken care to let the medieval atmosphere blow through my play freely. Those who see it performed will not mistake the startling event it records for a mere personal accident. They will have before them not only the visible and human puppets, but the Church, the Inquisition, the Feudal System, with divine inspiration always beating against their too inelastic limits: all more terrible in their dramatic force than any of the little mortal figures clanking about in plate armor or moving silently in the frocks and hoods of the order of St Dominic.

Tragedy, not Melodrama

There are no villains in the piece. Crime, like disease, is not interesting: it is something to be done away with by general consent, and that is all about it. It is what men do at their best, with good intentions, and what normal men and women find that they must and will do in spite of their intentions, that really concern us. The rascally bishop and the cruel inquisitor of Mark Twain and Andrew Lang are as dull as pickpockets; and they reduce Joan to the level of the even less interesting person whose pocket is picked. I have represented both of them as capable and eloquent exponents of The Church Militant and The Church Litigant, because only by doing so can I maintain my drama on the level of high tragedy and save it from becoming a mere police court sensation. A villain in a play can never be anything more than a *diabolus ex machina*, possibly a more exciting expedient than a *deus ex machina*,* but both equally mechanical, and therefore interesting only as mechanism. It is, I repeat, what normally innocent people do that concerns us; and if Joan had not been burnt by normally innocent people in the energy of their righteousness her death at their hands would have no more significance than the Tokyo earthquake,* which burnt a great many maidens. The tragedy of such murders is that they are not committed by murderers. They are judicial murders, pious murders; and this contradiction at once brings an element of comedy into the tragedy: the angels may weep at the murder, but the gods laugh at the murderers.

The Inevitable Flatteries of Tragedy

Here then we have a reason why my drama of Saint Joan's career, though it may give the essential truth of it, gives an inexact picture of some accidental facts. It goes almost without saying that the old Jeanne d'Arc melodramas, reducing everything to a conflict of villain and hero, or in Joan's case villain and heroine, not only miss the point entirely, but falsify the characters, making Cauchon a scoundrel, Joan a prima donna, and Dunois a lover. But the writer of high tragedy and comedy, aiming at the innermost attainable truth, must needs flatter Cauchon nearly as much as the melodramatist vilifies him. Although there is, as far as I have been able to discover, nothing against Cauchon that convicts him of bad faith or exceptional severity in his judicial relations with Joan, or of as much anti-prisoner, pro-police, class and sectarian bias as we now take for granted in our own courts, yet there is hardly more warrant for classing him as a great Catholic churchman, completely proof against the passions roused by the temporal situation. Neither does the inquisitor Lemaître, in such scanty accounts of him as are now recoverable, appear quite so able a master of his duties and of the case before him as I have given him credit for being. But it is the business of the stage to make its figures more intelligible to themselves than they would be in real life; for by no other means can they be made intelligible to the audience. And in this case Cauchon and Lemaître have to make intelligible not only themselves but the Church and the Inquisition, just as Warwick has to make the feudal system intelligible, the three between them having thus to make a twentieth-century audience conscious of an epoch fundamentally different from its own. Obviously the real Cauchon, Lemaître, and Warwick could not have done this: they were part of the Middle Ages themselves, and therefore as unconscious of its peculiarities as of the atomic formula of the air they breathed. But the play would be unintelligible if I had not endowed them with enough of this consciousness to enable them to explain their attitude to the twentieth century. All I claim is that by this inevitable sacrifice of verisimilitude I have secured in the only possible way sufficient veracity to justify me in claiming that as far as I can gather from the available documentation, and from such powers of divination as I possess, the things I represent these three exponents of the drama as saying are the things they actually would have said if they had known what they were really doing. And beyond this neither drama nor history can go in my hands.

Some Well-meant Proposals for the Improvement of the Play

I have to thank several critics on both sides of the Atlantic, including some whose admiration for my play is most generously enthusiastic, for their heartfelt instructions as to how it can be improved. They point out that by the excision of the epilogue and all the references to such undramatic and tedious matters as the Church, the feudal system, the Inquisition, the theory of heresy and so forth, all of which, they point out, would be ruthlessly blue pencilled by any experienced manager, the play could be considerably shortened. I think they are mistaken. The experienced knights of the blue pencil, having saved an hour and a half by disembowelling the play, would at once proceed to waste two hours in building elaborate scenery, having real water in the river Loire and a real bridge across it, and staging an obviously sham fight for possession of it, with the victorious French led by Joan on a real horse. The coronation would eclipse all previous theatrical displays, shewing, first, the procession through the streets of Rheims, and then the service in the cathedral, with special music written for both. Joan would be burnt on the stage, as Mr Matheson Lang always is in The Wandering Jew,* on the principle that it does not matter in the least why a woman is burnt provided she is burnt, and people can pay to see it done. The intervals between the acts whilst these splendors were being built up and then demolished by the stage carpenters would seem eternal, to the great profit of the refreshment bars. And the weary and demoralized audience would lose their last trains and curse me for writing such inordinately long and intolerably dreary and meaningless plays. But the applause of the press would be unanimous. Nobody who knows the stage history of Shakespear will doubt that this is what would happen if I knew my business so little as to listen to these well intentioned but disastrous counsellors: indeed it probably will happen when I am no longer in control of the performing rights. So perhaps it will be as well for the public to see the play while I am still alive.

The Epilogue

As to the epilogue, I could hardly be expected to stultify myself by implying that Joan's history in the world ended unhappily with her execution, instead of beginning there. It was necessary by hook or crook to shew the canonized Joan as well as the incinerated one; for many a woman has got herself burnt by carelessly whisking a muslin skirt into the drawing room fireplace, but getting canonized is a different matter, and a more important one. So I am afraid the epilogue must stand.

To the Critics, lest they should feel Ignored

To a professional critic (I have been one myself) theatre-going is the curse of Adam.* The play is the evil he is paid to endure in the sweat of his brow; and the sooner it is over, the better. This would seem to place him in irreconcilable opposition to the paying playgoer, from whose point of view the longer the play, the more entertainment he gets for his money. It does in fact so place him, especially in the provinces, where the playgoer goes to the theatre for the sake of the play solely, and insists so effectively on a certain number of hours' entertainment that touring managers are sometimes seriously embarrassed by the brevity of the London plays they have to deal in.

For in London the critics are reinforced by a considerable body of persons who go to the theatre as many others go to church, to display their best clothes and compare them with other people's; to be in the fashion, and have something to talk about at dinner parties; to adore a pet performer; to pass the evening anywhere rather than at home: in short, for any or every reason except interest in dramatic art as such. In fashionable centres the number of irreligious people who go to church, of unmusical people who go to concerts and operas, and of undramatic people who go to the theatre, is so prodigious that sermons have been cut down to ten minutes and plays to two hours; and, even at that, congregations sit longing for the benediction and audiences for the final curtain, so that they may get away to the lunch or supper they really crave for, after arriving as late as (or later than) the hour of beginning can possibly be made for them.

Thus from the stalls and in the Press an atmosphere of hypocrisy spreads. Nobody says straight out that genuine drama is a tedious nuisance, and that to ask people to endure more than two hours of it (with two long intervals of relief) is an intolerable imposition. Nobody says 'I hate classical tragedy and comedy as I hate sermons and symphonies; but I like police news and divorce news and any kind of dancing or decoration that has an aphrodisiac effect on me or on my wife or husband. And whatever superior people may pretend, I cannot associate pleasure with any sort of intellectual activity; and I dont believe anyone else can either.' Such things are not said; yet nine-tenths of what is offered as criticism of the drama in the metropolitan Press of Europe and America is nothing but a muddled paraphrase of it. If it does not mean that, it means nothing.

I do not complain of this, though it complains very unreasonably of me. But I can take no more notice of it than Einstein of the people who are incapable of mathematics. I write in the classical manner for those who pay for admission to a theatre because they like classical comedy or tragedy for its own sake, and like it so much when it is good of its kind and well done that they tear themselves away from it with reluctance to catch the very latest train or omnibus that will take them home. Far from arriving late from an eight or half-past eight o'clock dinner so as to escape at least the first half-hour of the performance, they stand in queues outside the theatre doors for hours beforehand in bitingly cold weather to secure a seat. In countries where a play lasts a week, they bring baskets of provisions and sit it out. These are the patrons on whom I depend for my bread. I do not give them performances twelve hours long,* because circumstances do not at present make such entertainments feasible; though a performance beginning after breakfast and ending at sunset is as possible physically and artistically in Surrey or Middlesex as in Ober-Ammergau;* and an all-night sitting in a theatre would be at least as enjoyable as an all-night sitting in the House of Commons, and much more useful. But in St Joan I have done my best by going to the well-established classical limit of three and a half hours practically continuous playing, barring the one interval imposed by considerations which have nothing to do with art. I know that this is hard on the pseudo-critics and on the fashionable people whose play-going is a hypocrisy. I cannot help feeling some compassion for them when they assure me that my play, though a great play, must fail hopelessly, because it does not begin at a quarter to nine and end at eleven. The facts are overwhelmingly against them. They forget that all men are not as they are. Still, I am sorry for them; and though I cannot for their sakes undo my work and help the people who hate the theatre to drive out the people who love it, yet I may point out to them that they have several remedies in their own hands. They can escape the first part of the play by their usual practice of arriving late. They can escape the epilogue by not waiting for it. And if the irreducible minimum thus attained is still too painful, they can stay away altogether. But I deprecate this extreme course, because it is good neither for my pocket nor for their own souls. Already a few of them, noticing that what matters is not the absolute length of time occupied by a play, but the speed with which that time passes, are discovering that the theatre, though purgatorial in its Aristotelian moments,* is not necessarily always the dull place they have so often found it. What do its discomforts matter when the play makes us forget them?

AYOT ST LAWRENCE,
    May 1924.

SAINT JOAN

SCENE I

A fine spring morning on the river Meuse, between Lorraine and Champagne, in the year 1429 A.D., in the castle of Vaucouleurs.

Captain Robert de Baudricourt, a military squire, handsome and physically energetic, but with no will of his own, is disguising that defect in his usual fashion by storming terribly* at his steward, a trodden worm, scanty of flesh, scanty of hair, who might be any age from 18 to 55, being the sort of man whom age cannot wither because he has never bloomed.

The two are in a sunny stone chamber on the first floor of the castle. At a plain strong oak table, seated in chair to match, the captain presents his left profile. The steward stands facing him at the other side of the table, if so deprecatory a stance as his can be called standing. The mullioned thirteenth-century window* is open behind him. Near it in the corner is a turret with a narrow arched doorway leading to a winding stair which descends to the courtyard. There is a stout fourlegged stool under the table, and a wooden chest under the window.

ROBERT. No eggs! No eggs!! Thousand thunders, man, what do you mean by no eggs?

STEWARD. Sir: it is not my fault. It is the act of God.

ROBERT. Blasphemy. You tell me there are no eggs; and you blame your Maker* for it.

STEWARD. Sir: what can I do? I cannot lay eggs.

ROBERT [*sarcastic*] Ha! You jest about it.

STEWARD. No, sir, God knows. We all have to go without eggs just as you have, sir. The hens will not lay.

ROBERT. Indeed! [*Rising*] Now listen to me, you.

STEWARD [*humbly*] Yes, sir.

ROBERT. What am I?

STEWARD. What are you, sir?

ROBERT [*coming at him*] Yes: what am I? Am I Robert, squire of Baudricourt and captain of this castle of Vaucouleurs; or am I a cowboy?

STEWARD. Oh, sir, you know you are a greater man here than the king himself.

ROBERT. Precisely. And now, do you know what you are?

STEWARD. I am nobody, sir, except that I have the honor to be your steward.

ROBERT [*driving him to the wall, adjective by adjective*] You have not only the honor of being my steward, but the privilege of being the worst, most incompetent, drivelling snivelling jibbering jabbering idiot of a steward in France. [*He strides back to the table*].

STEWARD [*cowering on the chest*] Yes, sir: to a great man like you I must seem like that.

ROBERT [*turning*] My fault, I suppose. Eh?

STEWARD [*coming to him deprecatingly*] Oh, sir: you always give my most innocent words such a turn!

ROBERT. I will give your neck a turn if you dare tell me, when I ask you how many eggs there are, that you cannot lay any.

STEWARD [*protesting*] Oh sir, oh sir—

ROBERT. No: not oh sir, oh sir, but no sir, no sir. My three Barbary hens* and the black are the best layers in Champagne. And you come and tell me that there are no eggs! Who stole them? Tell me that, before I kick you out through the castle gate for a liar and a seller of my goods to thieves. The milk was short yesterday, too: do not forget that.

STEWARD [*desperate*] I know, sir. I know only too well. There is no milk: there are no eggs: tomorrow there will be nothing.

ROBERT. Nothing! You will steal the lot: eh?

STEWARD. No, sir: nobody will steal anything. But there is a spell on us: we are bewitched.

ROBERT. That story is not good enough for me. Robert de Baudricourt burns witches and hangs thieves. Go. Bring me four dozen eggs and two gallons of milk here in this room before noon, or Heaven have mercy on your bones! I will teach you to make a fool of me. [*He resumes his seat with an air of finality*].

STEWARD. Sir: I tell you there are no eggs. There will be none—not if you were to kill me for it—as long as The Maid is at the door.

ROBERT. The Maid! What maid? What are you talking about?

STEWARD. The girl from Lorraine, sir. From Domrémy.

ROBERT [*rising in fearful wrath*] Thirty thousand thunders! Fifty thousand devils! Do you mean to say that that girl, who had the impudence to ask to see me two days ago, and whom I told you to send back to her father with my orders that he was to give her a good hiding,* is here still?

STEWARD. I have told her to go, sir. She wont.

ROBERT. I did not tell you to tell her to go: I told you to throw her out. You have fifty men-at-arms and a dozen lumps of able-bodied servants to carry out my orders. Are they afraid of her?

STEWARD. She is so positive, sir.

ROBERT [*seizing him by the scruff of the neck*] Positive! Now see here. I am going to throw you downstairs.

STEWARD. No, sir. Please.

ROBERT. Well, stop me by being positive. It's quite easy: any slut of a girl can do it.*

STEWARD [*hanging limp in his hands*] Sir, sir: you cannot get rid of *her* by throwing *me* out. [*Robert has to let him drop. He squats on his knees on the floor, contemplating his master resignedly*]. You see, sir, you are much more positive than I am. But so is she.

ROBERT. I am stronger than you are, you fool.

STEWARD. No, sir: it isnt that: it's your strong character, sir. She is weaker than we are: she is only a slip of a girl; but we cannot make her go.

ROBERT. You parcel of curs:* you are afraid of her.

STEWARD [*rising cautiously*] No, sir: we are afraid of you; but she puts courage into us. She really doesnt seem to be afraid of anything. Perhaps you could frighten her, sir.

ROBERT [*grimly*] Perhaps. Where is she now?

STEWARD. Down in the courtyard, sir, talking to the soldiers as usual. She is always talking to the soldiers except when she is praying.

ROBERT. Praying! Ha! You believe she prays, you idiot. I know the sort of girl that is always talking to soldiers. She shall talk to me a bit. [*He goes to the window and shouts fiercely through it*] Hallo, you there!

A GIRL'S VOICE [*bright, strong and rough*] Is it me, sir?

ROBERT. Yes, you.

THE VOICE. Be you captain?

ROBERT. Yes, damn your impudence, I be captain. Come up here. [*To the soldiers in the yard*] Shew her the way, you. And shove her along quick. [*He leaves the window, and returns to his place at the table, where he sits magisterially*].

STEWARD [*whispering*] She wants to go and be a soldier herself. She wants you to give her soldier's clothes. Armor, sir! And a sword! Actually! [*He steals behind Robert*].

Joan appears in the turret doorway. She is an ablebodied country girl of 17 *or* 18, *respectably dressed in red, with an uncommon face: eyes very wide apart and bulging as they often do in very imaginative people, a long well-shaped nose with wide nostrils, a short upper lip, resolute but full-lipped mouth, and handsome fighting chin. She comes eagerly to the table, delighted at having penetrated to Baudricourt's presence at last, and full of hope as to the result. His scowl does not check or frighten her in the least. Her voice is normally a hearty coaxing voice, very confident, very appealing, very hard to resist.*

JOAN [*bobbing a curtsey**] Good morning, captain squire. Captain: you are to give me a horse and armor and some soldiers, and send me to the Dauphin. Those are your orders from my Lord.*

ROBERT [*outraged*] Orders from *your* lord! And who the devil may your lord be? Go back to him, and tell him that I am neither duke nor peer at his orders: I am squire of Baudricourt; and I take no orders except from the king.

JOAN [*reassuringly*] Yes, squire: that is all right. My Lord is the King of Heaven.

ROBERT. Why, the girl's mad. [*To the steward*] Why didnt you tell me so, you blockhead?

STEWARD. Sir: do not anger her: give her what she wants.

JOAN [*impatient, but friendly*] They all say I am mad until I talk to them, squire. But you see that it is the will of God that you are to do what He has put into my mind.

ROBERT. It is the will of God that I shall send you back to your father with orders to put you under lock and key and thrash the madness out of you. What have you to say to that?

JOAN. You think you will, squire; but you will find it all coming quite different. You said you would not see me; but here I am.

STEWARD [*appealing*] Yes, sir. You see, sir.

ROBERT. Hold your tongue, you.

STEWARD [*abjectly*] Yes, sir.

ROBERT [*to Joan, with a sour loss of confidence*] So you are presuming on my seeing you, are you?

JOAN [*sweetly*] Yes, squire.

ROBERT [*feeling that he has lost ground, brings down his two fists squarely on the table, and inflates his chest imposingly to cure the unwelcome and only too familiar* sensation*] Now listen to me. I am going to assert myself.

JOAN [*busily*] Please do, squire. The horse will cost sixteen francs. It is a good deal of money; but I can save it on the armor.* I can find a soldier's armor that will fit me well enough: I am very hardy; and I do not need beautiful armor made to my measure like you wear. I shall not want many soldiers: the Dauphin will give me all I need to raise the siege of Orleans.

ROBERT [*flabbergasted*] To raise the siege of Orleans!

JOAN [*simply*] Yes, squire: that is what God is sending me to do. Three men will be enough for you to send with me if they are good men and gentle to me. They have promised to come with me. Polly and Jack and—

ROBERT. Polly!! You impudent baggage, do you dare call squire Bertrand de Poulengey* Polly to my face?

JOAN. His friends call him so, squire: I did not know he had any other name. Jack—

ROBERT. That is Monsieur John of Metz,* I suppose?

JOAN. Yes, squire. Jack will come willingly: he is a very kind gentleman, and gives me money to give to the poor. I think John Godsave will come, and Dick the Archer, and their servants John of Honecourt and Julian.* There will be no trouble for you, squire: I have arranged it all: you have only to give the order.

ROBERT [*contemplating her in a stupor of amazement*] Well, I *am* damned!

JOAN [*with unruffled sweetness*] No, squire: God is very merciful; and the blessed saints Catherine and Margaret, who speak to me every day [*he gapes*], will intercede for you. You will go to paradise; and your name will be remembered for ever as my first helper.

ROBERT [*to the steward, still much bothered, but changing his tone as he pursues a new clue*] Is this true about Monsieur de Poulengey?

STEWARD [*eagerly*] Yes, sir, and about Monsieur de Metz too. They both want to go with her.

ROBERT [*thoughtful*] Mf! [*He goes to the window, and shouts into the courtyard*] Hallo! You there: send Monsieur de Poulengey to me, will you? [*He turns to Joan*] Get out; and wait in the yard.

JOAN [*smiling brightly at him*] Right, squire. [*She goes out*].

ROBERT [*to the steward*] Go with her, you, you dithering imbecile. Stay within call; and keep your eye on her. I shall have her up here again.

STEWARD. Do so in God's name, sir. Think of those hens, the best layers in Champagne; and—

ROBERT. Think of my boot; and take your backside out of reach of it.

The steward retreats hastily and finds himself confronted in the doorway by Bertrand de Poulengey, a lymphatic* French gentleman-at-arms, aged 36 or thereabout, employed in the department of the provost-marshal, dreamily absent-minded, seldom speaking unless spoken to, and then slow and obstinate* in reply: altogether in contrast to the self-assertive, loud-mouthed,* superficially energetic, fundamentally will-less Robert. The steward makes way for him,* and vanishes.

Poulengey salutes, and stands awaiting orders.

ROBERT [*genially*] It isnt service, Polly. A friendly talk. Sit down. [*He hooks the stool from under the table with his instep*].

Poulengey, relaxing, comes into the room; places the stool between the table and the window; and sits down ruminatively.* Robert, half sitting on the end of the table, begins the friendly talk.

ROBERT. Now listen to me, Polly. I must talk to you like a father.

Poulengey looks up at him gravely for a moment, but says nothing.

ROBERT. It's about this girl you are interested in. Now, I have seen her. I have talked to her. First, she's mad. That doesnt matter. Second, she's not a farm wench. She's a bourgeoise.* That matters a good deal. I know her class exactly. Her father came here last year to represent his village in a lawsuit: he is one of their notables. A farmer. Not a gentleman farmer: he makes money by it, and lives by it. Still, not a laborer. Not a mechanic. He might have a cousin a lawyer, or in the Church. People of this sort may be of no account socially; but they can give a lot of bother to the authorities. That is to say, to *me*. Now no doubt it seems to you a very simple thing to take this girl away, humbugging her into the belief that you are taking her to the Dauphin. But if you get her into trouble, you may get *me* into no end of a mess, as I am her father's lord, and responsible for her protection. So friends or no friends, Polly, hands off her.

POULENGEY [*with deliberate impressiveness*] I should as soon think of the Blessed Virgin herself in that way, as of this girl.

ROBERT [*coming off the table*] But she says you and Jack and Dick have offered to go with her. What for? You are not going to tell me that you take her crazy notion of going to the Dauphin seriously, are you?

POULENGEY [*slowly*] There is something about her. They are pretty foulmouthed and foulminded down there in the guardroom, some of them. But there hasnt been a word that has anything to do with her being a woman. They have stopped swearing before her. There is something. Something. It may be worth trying.

ROBERT. Oh, come, Polly! pull yourself together. Commonsense was never your strong point; but this is a little too much. [*He retreats disgustedly*].

POULENGEY [*unmoved*] What is the good of commonsense? If we had any commonsense we should join the Duke of Burgundy and the English king. They hold half the country, right down to the Loire. They have Paris. They have this castle: you know very well that we had to surrender it to the Duke of Bedford,* and that you are only holding it on parole. The Dauphin is in Chinon, like a rat in a corner, except that he wont fight. We dont even know that he *is* the Dauphin: his mother* says he isnt; and she ought to know. Think of that! the queen denying the legitimacy of her own son!

ROBERT. Well, she married her daughter to the English king.* Can you blame the woman?

POULENGEY. I blame nobody. But thanks to her,* the Dauphin is down and out; and we may as well face it. The English will take Orleans: the Bastard will not be able to stop them.

ROBERT. He beat the English the year before last at Montargis.* I was with him.

POULENGEY. No matter: his men are cowed now; and he cant work miracles. And I tell you that nothing can save our side now but a miracle.

ROBERT. Miracles are all right, Polly. The only difficulty about them is that they dont happen nowadays.

POULENGEY. I used to think so. I am not so sure now. [*Rising, and moving ruminatively towards the window*] At all events this is not a time to leave any stone unturned. There is something about the girl.

ROBERT. Oh! You think the girl can work miracles, do you?*

POULENGEY. I think the girl herself is a bit of a miracle. Anyhow, she is the last card left in our hand. Better play her than throw up the game. [*He wanders to the turret*].

ROBERT [*wavering*] You really think that?

POULENGEY [*turning*] Is there anything else left for us to think?

ROBERT [*going to him*] Look here, Polly. If you were in my place would you let a girl like that do you out of sixteen francs for a horse?

POULENGEY. I will pay for the horse.

ROBERT. You will!

POULENGEY. Yes: I will back my opinion.

ROBERT. You will really gamble on a forlorn hope to the tune of sixteen francs?

POULENGEY. It is not a gamble.

ROBERT. What else is it?

POULENGEY. It is a certainty. Her words and her ardent faith in God have put fire into me.*

ROBERT [*giving him up*] Whew! You are as mad as she is.

POULENGEY [*obstinately*] We want a few mad people now. See where the sane ones have landed us!

ROBERT [*his irresoluteness now openly swamping his affected decisiveness**]* I shall feel like a precious fool. Still, if you feel sure—?

POULENGEY. I feel sure enough to take her to Chinon—unless you stop me.

ROBERT. This is not fair. You are putting the responsibility on me.

POULENGEY. It is on you whichever way you decide.

ROBERT. Yes: thats just it. Which way am I to decide? You dont see how awkward this is for me. [*Snatching at a dilatory* step with an unconscious hope that Joan will make up his mind for him*] Do you think I ought to have another talk to her?

POULENGEY [*rising*] Yes. [*He goes to the window and calls*] Joan!

JOAN'S VOICE. Will he let us go, Polly?

POULENGEY. Come up. Come in. [*Turning to Robert*] Shall I leave you with her?

ROBERT. No: stay here; and back me up.

Poulengey sits down on the chest. Robert goes back to his magisterial chair, but remains standing to inflate himself more imposingly. Joan comes in, full of good news.

JOAN. Jack will go halves for the horse.

ROBERT. Well!! [*He sits, deflated*].

POULENGEY [*gravely*] Sit down, Joan.

JOAN [*checked a little, and looking to Robert*] May I?

ROBERT. Do what you are told.

Joan curtsies and sits down on the stool between them. Robert outfaces his perplexity with his most peremptory air.

ROBERT. What is your name?

JOAN [*chattily*] They always call me Jenny* in Lorraine. Here in France I am Joan. The soldiers call me The Maid.

ROBERT. What is your surname?

JOAN. Surname? What is that? My father sometimes calls himself d'Arc; but I know nothing about it. You met my father. He—

ROBERT. Yes, yes: I remember. You come from Domrémy in Lorraine, I think.

JOAN. Yes; but what does it matter? we all speak French.*

ROBERT. Dont ask questions: answer them. How old are you?

JOAN. Seventeen: so they tell me. It might be nineteen. I dont remember.

ROBERT. What did you mean when you said that St Catherine and St Margaret talked to you every day?

JOAN. They do.

ROBERT. What are they like?

JOAN [*suddenly obstinate*] I will tell you nothing about that: they have not given me leave.

ROBERT. But you actually see them; and they talk to you just as I am talking to you?

JOAN. No: it is quite different. I cannot tell you: you must not talk to me about my voices.

ROBERT. How do you mean? voices?

JOAN. I hear voices telling me what to do. They come from God.

ROBERT. They come from your imagination.

JOAN. Of course. That is how the messages of God come to us.

POULENGEY. Checkmate.*

ROBERT. No fear!* [*To Joan*] So God says you are to raise the siege of Orleans?

JOAN. And to crown the Dauphin in Rheims Cathedral.

ROBERT [*gasping*] Crown the D——! Gosh!

JOAN. And to make the English leave France.

ROBERT [*sarcastic*] Anything else?

JOAN [*charming*] Not just at present, thank you, squire.

ROBERT. I suppose you think raising a siege is as easy as chasing a cow out of a meadow. You think soldiering is anybody's job?

JOAN. I do not think it can be very difficult if God is on your side, and you are willing to put your life in His hand. But many soldiers are very simple.

ROBERT [*grimly*] Simple! Did you ever see English soldiers fighting?

JOAN. They are only men. God made them just like us; but He gave them their own country and their own language; and it is not His will that they should come into our country and try to speak our language.

ROBERT. Who has been putting such nonsense into your head? Dont you know that soldiers are subject to their feudal lord, and that it is nothing to them or to you whether he is the duke of Burgundy or the king of England or the king of France? What has their language to do with it?

JOAN. I do not understand that a bit. We are all subject to the King of Heaven; and He gave us our countries and our languages, and meant us to keep to them. If it were not so it would be murder to kill an Englishman in battle; and you, squire, would be in great danger of hell fire. You must not think about your duty to your feudal lord, but about your duty to God.

POULENGEY. It's no use, Robert: she can choke you like that every time.

ROBERT. Can she, by Saint Dennis! We shall see. [*To Joan*] We are not talking about God: we are talking about practical affairs. I ask you again, girl, have you ever seen English soldiers fighting? Have you ever seen them plundering, burning, turning the countryside into a desert? Have you heard no tales of their Black Prince who was blacker than the devil himself, or of the English king's father?*

JOAN. You must not be afraid, Robert—

ROBERT. Damn you, I am not afraid.* And who gave you leave to call me Robert?

JOAN. You were called so in church in the name of our Lord. All the other names are your father's or your brother's or anybody's.

ROBERT. Tcha!

JOAN. Listen to me, squire. At Domrémy we had to fly to the next village to escape from the English soldiers. Three of them were left behind, wounded. I came to know these three poor goddams quite well. They had not half my strength.

ROBERT. Do you know why they are called goddams?*

JOAN. No. Everyone calls them goddams.

ROBERT. It is because they are always calling on their God to condemn their souls to perdition.* That is what goddam means in their language. How do you like it?

JOAN. God will be merciful to them; and they will act like His good children when they go back to the country He made for them, and made them for. I have heard the tales of the Black Prince. The moment he touched the soil of our country the devil entered into him and made him a black fiend. But at home, in the place made for him by God, he was good. It is always so. If I went into England against the will of God to conquer England, and tried to live there and speak its language, the devil would enter into me; and when I was old I should shudder to remember the wickednesses I did.

ROBERT. Perhaps. But the more devil you were the better you might fight. That is why the goddams will take Orleans. And you cannot stop them, nor ten thousand like you.

JOAN. One thousand like me can stop them. Ten like me can stop them with God on our side. [*She rises impetuously, and goes at him, unable to sit quiet any longer*]. You do not understand, squire. Our soldiers are always beaten because they are fighting only to save their skins; and the shortest way to save your skin is to run away. Our knights are thinking only of the money they will make in ransoms: it is not kill or be killed with them, but pay or be paid. But I will teach them all to fight that the will of God may be done in France; and then they will drive the poor goddams before them like sheep. You and Polly will live to see the day when there will not be an English soldier on the soil of France; and there will be but one king there: not the feudal English king, but God's French one.

ROBERT [*to Poulengey*] This may be all rot, Polly;* but the troops might swallow it, though nothing that we can say seems able to put any fight into them. Even the Dauphin might swallow it. And if she can put fight into him,* she can put it into anybody.

POULENGEY. I can see no harm in trying. Can you? And there is something* about the girl—

ROBERT [*turning to Joan*] Now listen you to me; and [*desperately*] dont cut in before I have time to think.

JOAN [*plumping down on the stool again, like an obedient schoolgirl*] Yes, squire.

ROBERT. Your orders are, that you are to go to Chinon under the escort of this gentleman and three of his friends.

JOAN [*radiant, clasping her hands*] Oh, squire! Your head is all circled with light, like a saint's.

POULENGEY. How is she to get into the royal presence?

ROBERT [*who has looked up for his halo rather apprehensively*] I dont know: how did she get into *my* presence? If the Dauphin can keep her out he is a better man than I take him for. [*Rising*] I will send her to Chinon; and she can say I sent her. Then let come what may: I can do no more.

JOAN. And the dress? I may have a soldier's dress, maynt I, squire?

ROBERT. Have what you please. I wash my hands of it.

JOAN [*wildly excited by her success*] Come, Polly. [*She dashes out*].

ROBERT [*shaking Poulengey's hand*] Goodbye, old man, I am taking a big chance. Few other men would have done it. But as you say, there is something about her.

POULENGEY. Yes: there is something about her. Goodbye. [*He goes out*].

Robert, still very doubtful whether he has not been made a fool of by a crazy female, and a social inferior to boot,* scratches his head and slowly comes back from the door.

The steward runs in with a basket.

STEWARD. Sir, sir—

ROBERT. What now?

STEWARD. The hens are laying like mad, sir. Five dozen eggs!

ROBERT [*stiffens convulsively; crosses himself; and forms with his pale lips the words*] Christ in heaven! [*Aloud but breathless*] She *did* come from God.

SCENE II

Chinon, in Touraine.* An end of the throne room in the castle, curtained off to make an antechamber.* The Archbishop of Rheims,* close on 50, a full-fed political prelate with nothing of the ecclesiastic about him except his imposing bearing, and the Lord Chamberlain, Monseigneur de la Trémouille,* a monstrous arrogant wineskin of a man, are waiting for the Dauphin. There is a door in the wall to the right of the two men. It is late in the afternoon on the 8th of March, 1429. The Archbishop stands with dignity* whilst the Chamberlain, on his left, fumes about in the worst of tempers.

LA TRÉMOUILLE. What the devil does the Dauphin mean by keeping us waiting like this? I dont know how you have the patience to stand there like a stone idol.

THE ARCHBISHOP. You see, I am an archbishop; and an archbishop is a sort of idol. At any rate he has to learn to keep still and suffer fools patiently. Besides, my dear Lord Chamberlain, it is the Dauphin's royal privilege to keep you waiting, is it not?

LA TRÉMOUILLE. Dauphin be damned! saving your reverence. Do you know how much money he owes me?

THE ARCHBISHOP. Much more than he owes me, I have no doubt, because you are a much richer man. But I take it he owes you all you could afford to lend him. That is what he owes me.

LA TRÉMOUILLE. Twenty-seven thousand: that was his last haul. A cool twenty-seven thousand!

THE ARCHBISHOP. What becomes of it all? He never has a suit of clothes that I would throw to a curate.*

LA TRÉMOUILLE. He dines on a chicken or a scrap of mutton.* He borrows my last penny; and there is nothing to shew for it. [*A page appears in the doorway*]. At last!

THE PAGE. No, my lord: it is not His Majesty. Monsieur de Rais is approaching.

LA TRÉMOUILLE. Young Bluebeard! Why announce *him*?

THE PAGE. Captain La Hire is with him. Something has happened, I think.

Gilles de Rais, a young man of 25, very smart and self-possessed, and sporting the extravagance of a little curled beard dyed blue at a clean-shaven court, comes in. He is determined to make himself agreeable, but lacks nat-ural joyousness, and is not really pleasant. In fact when he defies the Church some eleven years later he is accused of trying to extract pleasure from hor-rible cruelties, and hanged. So far, however, there is no shadow of the gal-lows on him. He advances gaily to the Archbishop. The page withdraws.

BLUEBEARD. Your faithful lamb, Archbishop. Good day, my lord. Do you know what has happened to La Hire?

LA TRÉMOUILLE. He has sworn himself into a fit, perhaps.

BLUEBEARD. No: just the opposite. Foul Mouthed Frank, the only man in Touraine who could beat him at swearing, was told by a soldier that he shouldnt use such language when he was at the point of death.

THE ARCHBISHOP. Nor at any other point. But *was* Foul Mouthed Frank on the point of death?

BLUEBEARD. Yes: he has just fallen into a well and been drowned. La Hire is frightened out of his wits.

Captain La Hire comes in: a war dog with no court manners and pro-nounced camp ones.

BLUEBEARD. I have just been telling the Chamberlain and the Archbishop. The Archbishop says you are a lost man.

LA HIRE [*striding past Bluebeard, and planting himself between the Archbishop and La Trémouille*] This is nothing to joke about. It is worse than we thought. It was not a soldier, but an angel dressed as a soldier.

THE ARCHBISHOP
THE CHAMBERLAIN } [*exclaiming all together*] An angel!
BLUEBEARD

LA HIRE. Yes, an angel. She has made her way from Champagne with half a dozen men through the thick of everything: Burgundians, Goddams, deserters, robbers, and Lord knows who; and they never met a soul except the country folk. I know one of them: de Poulengey. He says she's an angel. If ever I utter an oath again may my soul* be blasted to eternal damnation!

THE ARCHBISHOP. A very pious beginning, Captain.

Bluebeard and La Trémouille laugh at him. The page returns.

THE PAGE. His Majesty.

They stand perfunctorily at court attention. The Dauphin, aged 26, really King Charles the Seventh since the death of his father, but as yet uncrowned, comes in through the curtains with a paper in his hands. He is a poor creature physically; and the current fashion of shaving closely, and hiding every scrap of hair under the headcovering or headdress, both by women and men, makes the worst of his appearance. He has little narrow eyes, near together, a long pendulous nose that droops over his thick short upper lip, and the expression of a young dog accustomed to be kicked, yet incorrigible and irrepressible. But he is neither vulgar nor stupid;* and he has a cheeky humor which enables him to hold his own in conversation. Just at present he is excited, like a child with a new toy. He comes to the Archbishop's left hand. Bluebeard and La Hire retire towards the curtains.

CHARLES. Oh, Archbishop, do you know what Robert de Baudricourt is sending me from Vaucouleurs?

THE ARCHBISHOP [*contemptuously*] I am not interested in the newest toys.

CHARLES [*indignantly*] It isnt a toy. [*Sulkily*] However, I can get on very well without your interest.

THE ARCHBISHOP. Your Highness is taking offence very unnecessarily.

CHARLES. Thank you. You are always ready with a lecture, arnt you?

LA TRÉMOUILLE [*roughly*] Enough grumbling. What have you got there?

CHARLES. What is that to you?

LA TRÉMOUILLE. It is my business to know what is passing between you and the garrison* at Vaucouleurs. [*He snatches the paper from the Dauphin's hand, and begins reading it with some difficulty, following the words with his finger and spelling them out syllable by syllable.*]

CHARLES [*mortified*] You all think you can treat me as you please because I owe you money, and because I am no good at fighting. But I have the blood royal in my veins.

THE ARCHBISHOP. Even that has been questioned, your Highness. One hardly recognizes in you the grandson of Charles the Wise.*

CHARLES. I want to hear no more of my grandfather. He was so wise that he used up the whole family stock of wisdom for five generations, and left me the poor fool I am, bullied and insulted by all of you.

THE ARCHBISHOP. Control yourself, sir. These outbursts of petulance are not seemly.

CHARLES. Another lecture! Thank you. What a pity it is that though you are an archbishop saints and angels dont come to see *you*!

THE ARCHBISHOP. What do you mean?

CHARLES. Aha! Ask that bully there [*pointing to La Trémouille*].

LA TRÉMOUILLE [*furious*] Hold your tongue. Do you hear?

CHARLES. Oh, I hear. You neednt shout. The whole castle can hear. Why dont you go and shout at the English, and beat them for me?

LA TRÉMOUILLE [*raising his fist*] You young—

CHARLES [*running behind the Archbishop*] Dont you raise your hand to me. It's high treason.

LA HIRE. Steady, Duke! Steady!

THE ARCHBISHOP [*resolutely*] Come, come! this will not do. My Lord Chamberlain: please! please! we must keep some sort of order. [*To the Dauphin*] And you, sir: if you cannot rule your kingdom, at least try to rule yourself.

CHARLES. Another lecture! Thank you.

LA TRÉMOUILLE [*handing the paper to the Archbishop*] Here: read the accursed thing for me. He has sent the blood boiling into my head: I cant distinguish the letters.

CHARLES [*coming back and peering round La Trémouille's left shoulder*] I will read it for you if you like. I *can* read, you know.

LA TRÉMOUILLE [*with intense contempt, not at all stung by the taunt*] Yes: reading is about all you are fit for. Can you make it out, Archbishop?

THE ARCHBISHOP. I should have expected more commonsense from De Baudricourt. He is sending some cracked country lass here—

CHARLES [*interrupting*] No: he is sending a saint: an angel. And she is coming to me: to *me*, the king, and not to you, Archbishop, holy as you are. She knows the blood royal if you dont. [*He struts up to the curtains between Bluebeard and La Hire*].

THE ARCHBISHOP. You cannot be allowed to see this crazy wench.

CHARLES [*turning*] But I am the king; and I will.

LA TRÉMOUILLE [*brutally*] Then she cannot be allowed to see *you*. Now!

CHARLES. I tell you I will. I am going to put my foot down—

BLUEBEARD [*laughing at him*] Naughty! What would your wise grandfather say?

CHARLES. That just shews your ignorance, Bluebeard. My grandfather had a saint who used to float in the air when she was praying, and told him everything he wanted to know. My poor father had two saints, Marie de Maillé and the Gasque of Avignon.* It is in our family; and I dont care what you say: I will have my saint too.

THE ARCHBISHOP. This creature is not a saint. She is not even a respectable woman. She does not wear women's clothes. She is dressed like a soldier, and rides round the country with soldiers. Do you suppose such a person can be admitted to your Highness's court?

LA HIRE. Stop. [*Going to the Archbishop*] Did you say a girl in armor, like a soldier?

THE ARCHBISHOP. So De Baudricourt describes her.

LA HIRE. But by all the devils in hell—Oh, God forgive me, what am I saying?—by Our Lady and all the saints, this must be the angel that struck Foul Mouthed Frank dead for swearing.

CHARLES [*triumphant*] You see! A miracle!

LA HIRE. She may strike the lot of us dead if we cross her. For Heaven's sake, Archbishop, be careful what you are doing.

THE ARCHBISHOP [*severely*] Rubbish! Nobody has been struck dead. A drunken blackguard who has been rebuked a hundred times for swearing has fallen into a well, and been drowned. A mere coincidence.

LA HIRE. I do not know what a coincidence is. I do know that the man is dead, and that she told him he was going to die.

THE ARCHBISHOP. We are all going to die, Captain.

LA HIRE [*crossing himself*] I hope not.* [*He backs out of the conversation*].

BLUEBEARD. We can easily find out whether she is an angel or not.* Let us arrange when she comes that I shall be the Dauphin, and see whether she will find me out.

CHARLES. Yes: I agree to that. If she cannot find the blood royal I will have nothing to do with her.

THE ARCHBISHOP. It is for the Church to make saints: let De Baudricourt mind his own business, and not dare usurp the function of his priest. I say the girl shall not be admitted.

BLUEBEARD. But, Archbishop—

THE ARCHBISHOP [*sternly*] I speak in the Church's name. [*To the Dauphin*] Do you dare say she shall?

CHARLES [*intimidated but sulky*] Oh, if you make it an excommunication matter, I have nothing more to say, of course. But you havnt read the end of the letter. De Baudricourt says she will raise the siege of Orleans, and beat the English for us.

LA TRÉMOUILLE. Rot!

CHARLES. Well, will *you* save Orleans for us, with all your bullying?

LA TRÉMOUILLE [*savagely*] Do not throw that in my face again: do you hear? I have done more fighting than you ever did or ever will. But I cannot be everywhere.

THE DAUPHIN. Well, thats something.

BLUEBEARD [*coming between the Archbishop and Charles*] You have Jack Dunois at the head of your troops in Orleans: the brave Dunois, the handsome Dunois, the wonderful invincible Dunois, the darling of all the ladies, the beautiful bastard. Is it likely that the country lass can do what he cannot do?

CHARLES. Why doesnt he raise the siege, then?

LA HIRE. The wind is against him.

BLUEBEARD. How can the wind hurt him at Orleans? It is not on the Channel.*

LA HIRE. It is on the river Loire; and the English hold the bridgehead.* He must ship his men across the river and upstream, if he is to take them in the rear. Well, he cannot, because there is a devil of a wind blowing the other way. He is tired of paying the priests to pray for a west wind. What he needs is a miracle. You tell me that what the girl did to Foul Mouthed Frank was no miracle. No matter: it finished Frank. If she changes the wind for Dunois, that may not be a miracle either; but it may finish the English. What harm is there in trying?

THE ARCHBISHOP [*who has read the end of the letter and become more thoughtful*] It is true that De Baudricourt seems extraordinarily impressed.

LA HIRE. De Baudricourt is a blazing ass; but he is a soldier; and if he thinks she can beat the English, all the rest of the army will think so too.

LA TRÉMOUILLE [*to the Archbishop, who is hesitating*] Oh, let them have their way. Dunois' men will give up the town in spite of him if somebody does not put some fresh spunk* into them.

THE ARCHBISHOP. The Church must examine the girl before anything decisive is done about her. However, since his Highness desires it, let her attend the Court.

LA HIRE. I will find her and tell her. [*He goes out*].

CHARLES. Come with me, Bluebeard; and let us arrange so that she will not know who I am. You will pretend to be me. [*He goes out through the curtains*].

BLUEBEARD. Pretend to be that thing! Holy Michael! [*He follows the Dauphin*].

LA TRÉMOUILLE. I wonder will she pick him out!

THE ARCHBISHOP. Of course she will.

LA TRÉMOUILLE. Why? How is she to know?

THE ARCHBISHOP. She will know what everybody in Chinon knows: that the Dauphin is the meanest-looking and worst-dressed figure in the Court, and that the man with the blue beard is Gilles de Rais.

LA TRÉMOUILLE. I never thought of that.

THE ARCHBISHOP. You are not so accustomed to miracles as I am. It is part of my profession.

LA TRÉMOUILLE [*puzzled and a little scandalized*] But that would not be a miracle at all.*

THE ARCHBISHOP [*calmly*] Why not?

LA TRÉMOUILLE. Well, come! what *is* a miracle?

THE ARCHBISHOP. A miracle, my friend, is an event which creates faith. That is the purpose and nature of miracles. They may seem very wonderful to the people who witness them, and very simple to those who perform them. That does not matter: if they confirm or create faith they are true miracles.

LA TRÉMOUILLE. Even when they are frauds, do you mean?

THE ARCHBISHOP. Frauds deceive. An event which creates faith does not deceive: therefore it is not a fraud, but a miracle.

LA TRÉMOUILLE [*scratching his neck in his perplexity*] Well, I suppose as you are an archbishop you must be right. It seems a bit fishy to me. But I am no churchman, and dont understand these matters.

THE ARCHBISHOP. You are not a churchman; but you are a diplomatist and a soldier. Could you make our citizens pay war taxes, or our soldiers sacrifice their lives, if they knew what is really happening instead of what seems to them to be happening?

LA TRÉMOUILLE. No, by Saint Dennis: the fat would be in the fire* before sundown.

THE ARCHBISHOP. Would it not be quite easy to tell them the truth?

LA TRÉMOUILLE. Man alive, they wouldnt believe it.

THE ARCHBISHOP. Just so. Well, the Church has to rule men for the good of their souls as you have to rule them for the good of their bodies. To do that, the Church must do as you do: nourish their faith by poetry.

LA TRÉMOUILLE. Poetry! I should call it humbug.

THE ARCHBISHOP. You would be wrong, my friend. Parables are not lies because they describe events that have never happened. Miracles are not frauds because they are often—I do not say always—very simple and innocent contrivances by which the priest fortifies the faith of his flock. When this girl picks out the Dauphin among his courtiers, it will not be a miracle for me, because I shall know how it has been done, and my faith will not be increased. But as for the others, if they feel the thrill of the supernatural, and forget their sinful clay* in a sudden sense of the glory of God, it will be a miracle and a blessed one. And you will find that the girl herself will be more affected than anyone else. She will forget how she really picked him out. So, perhaps, will you.

LA TRÉMOUILLE. Well, I wish I were clever enough to know how much of you is God's archbishop and how much the most artful fox in Touraine. Come on, or we shall be late for the fun; and I want to see it, miracle or no miracle.

THE ARCHBISHOP [*detaining him a moment*] Do not think that I am a lover of crooked ways. There is a new spirit rising in men: we are at the dawning of a wider epoch. If I were a simple monk, and had not to rule men, I should seek peace for my spirit with Aristotle and Pythagoras rather than with the saints and their miracles.

LA TRÉMOUILLE. And who the deuce was Pythagoras?

THE ARCHBISHOP. A sage who held that the earth is round, and that it moves round the sun.

LA TRÉMOUILLE. What an utter fool! Couldnt he use his eyes?

They go out together through the curtains, which are presently withdrawn, revealing the full depth of the throne room with the Court assembled. On the right are two Chairs of State on a dais.* Bluebeard is standing theatrically on the dais, playing the king, and, like the courtiers, enjoying the joke rather obviously. There is a curtained arch in the wall behind the dais; but the main door, guarded by men-at-arms, is at the other side of the room; and a clear path across is kept and lined by the courtiers. Charles is in this path in the middle of the room. La Hire is on his right. The Archbishop, on his left, has taken his place by the dais: La Trémouille at the other side of it. The Duchess de la Trémouille,* pretending to be the Queen, sits in the Consort's chair, with a group of ladies in waiting close by, behind the Archbishop.

The chatter of the courtiers makes such a noise that nobody notices the appearance of the page at the door.*

THE PAGE. The Duke of—[*Nobody listens*]. The Duke of—[*The chatter continues. Indignant at his failure to command a hearing, he snatches the halberd* of the nearest man-at-arms, and thumps the floor with it. The chatter ceases; and everybody looks at him in silence*]. Attention! [*He restores the halberd to the man-at-arms*]. The Duke of Vendôme* presents Joan the Maid to his Majesty.

CHARLES [*putting his finger on his lip*] Ssh! [*He hides behind the nearest courtier, peering out to see what happens*].

BLUEBEARD [*majestically*] Let her approach the throne.

Joan, dressed as a soldier, with her hair bobbed and hanging thickly round her face, is led in by a bashful and speechless nobleman, from whom she detaches herself to stop and look round eagerly for the Dauphin.*

THE DUCHESS [*to the nearest lady in waiting*] My dear! Her hair!

All the ladies explode in uncontrollable laughter.

BLUEBEARD [*trying not to laugh, and waving his hand in deprecation of their merriment*] Ssh—ssh! Ladies! Ladies!!

JOAN [*not at all embarrassed*] I wear it like this because I am a soldier. Where be Dauphin?

A titter runs through the Court as she walks to the dais.

BLUEBEARD [*condescendingly*] You are in the presence of the Dauphin.

Joan looks at him sceptically for a moment, scanning him hard up and down to make sure. Dead silence, all watching her. Fun dawns in her face.

JOAN. Coom,* Bluebeard! Thou canst not fool me. Where be Dauphin?

A roar of laughter breaks out as Gilles, with a gesture of surrender, joins in the laugh, and jumps down from the dais beside La Trémouille. Joan, also on the broad grin, turns back, searching along the row of courtiers, and presently makes a dive, and drags out Charles by the arm.

JOAN [*releasing him and bobbing him a little curtsey*] Gentle little Dauphin,* I am sent to you to drive the English away from Orleans and from France, and to crown you king in the cathedral at Rheims, where all true kings of France are crowned.

CHARLES [*triumphant, to the Court*] You see, all of you: she knew the blood royal. Who dare say now that I am not my father's son? [*To Joan*] But if you want me to be crowned at Rheims you must talk to the Archbishop, not to me. There he is [*he is standing behind her*]!

JOAN [*turning quickly, overwhelmed with emotion*] Oh, my lord! [*She falls on both knees before him, with bowed head, not daring to look up*]. My lord: I am only a poor country girl; and you are filled with the blessedness and glory of God Himself; but you will touch me with your hands, and give me your blessing, wont you?

BLUEBEARD [*whispering to La Trémouille*] The old fox blushes.*

LA TRÉMOUILLE. Another miracle!

THE ARCHBISHOP [*touched, putting his hand on her head*] Child: you are in love with religion.

JOAN [*startled: looking up at him*] Am I? I never thought of that. Is there any harm in it?

THE ARCHBISHOP. There is no harm in it, my child. But there is danger.

JOAN [*rising, with a sunflush of reckless happiness irradiating her face*]
There is always danger, except in heaven. Oh, my lord, you have
given me such strength, such courage. It must be a most wonderful
thing to be Archbishop.

The Court smiles broadly: even titters a little.

THE ARCHBISHOP [*drawing himself up sensitively*] Gentlemen: your
levity is rebuked by this maid's faith. I am, God help me, all unworthy; but your mirth is a deadly sin.

Their faces fall. Dead silence.

BLUEBEARD. My lord: we were laughing at her, not at you.

THE ARCHBISHOP. What? Not at my unworthiness but at her faith!
Gilles de Rais: this maid prophesied that the blasphemer should be
drowned in his sin—

JOAN [*distressed*] No!

THE ARCHBISHOP [*silencing her by a gesture*] I prophesy now that you
will be hanged in yours if you do not learn when to laugh and when
to pray.

BLUEBEARD. My lord: I stand rebuked. I am sorry: I can say no more.
But if you prophesy that I shall be hanged, I shall never be able to
resist temptation, because I shall always be telling myself that I may
as well be hanged for a sheep as a lamb.*

The courtiers take heart at this. There is more tittering.

JOAN [*scandalized*] You are an idle fellow, Bluebeard; and you have
great impudence to answer the Archbishop.

LA HIRE [*with a huge chuckle*] Well said, lass! Well said!

JOAN [*impatiently to the Archbishop*] Oh, my lord, will you send all
these silly folks away so that I may speak to the Dauphin alone?

LA HIRE [*goodhumoredly*] I can take a hint. [*He salutes; turns on his
heel; and goes out*].

THE ARCHBISHOP. Come, gentlemen. The Maid comes with God's
blessing, and must be obeyed.

*The courtiers withdraw, some through the arch, others at the opposite side.
The Archbishop marches across to the door, followed by the Duchess and*

La Trémouille. As the Archbishop passes Joan, she falls on her knees, and kisses the hem of his robe fervently. He shakes his head in instinctive remonstrance; gathers the robe from her; and goes out. She is left kneeling directly in the Duchess's way.

THE DUCHESS [*coldly*] Will you allow me to pass, please?

JOAN [*hastily rising, and standing back*] Beg pardon, maam, I am sure.

The Duchess passes on. Joan stares after her; then whispers to the Dauphin.

JOAN. Be that Queen?

CHARLES. No. She thinks she is.

JOAN [*again staring after the Duchess*] Oo-oo-oooh! [*Her awestruck amazement at the figure cut by the magnificently dressed lady is not wholly* complimentary*].

LA TRÉMOUILLE [*very surly*] I'll trouble your Highness not to gibe at my wife.* [*He goes out. The others have already gone*].

JOAN [*to the Dauphin*] Who be old Gruff-and-Grum?*

CHARLES. He is the Duke de la Trémouille.

JOAN. What be his job?

CHARLES. He pretends to command the army. And whenever I find a friend I can care for, he kills him.

JOAN. Why dost let him?

CHARLES [*petulantly moving to the throne side of the room to escape from her magnetic field*] How can I prevent him? He bullies me. They all bully me.

JOAN. Art afraid?*

CHARLES. Yes: I am afraid. It's no use preaching to me about it. It's all very well for these big men with their armor that is too heavy for me, and their swords that I can hardly lift, and their muscle and their shouting and their bad tempers. They like fighting: most of them are making fools of themselves all the time they are not fighting;* but I am quiet and sensible;* and I dont want to kill people: I only want to be left alone to enjoy myself in my own way. I never asked to be a king: it was pushed on me. So if you are going to say 'Son of

St Louis: gird on the sword of your ancestors, and lead us to victory'* you may spare your breath to cool your porridge;* for I cannot do it. I am not built that way; and there is an end of it.

JOAN [*trenchant and masterful*] Blethers!* We are all like that to begin with. I shall put courage into thee.

CHARLES. But I dont want to have courage put into me. I want to sleep in a comfortable bed, and not live in continual terror of being killed or wounded. Put courage into the others, and let them have their bellyful of fighting; but let me alone.

JOAN. It's no use, Charlie: thou must face what God puts on thee. If thou fail to make thyself king, thoult be a beggar: what else art fit for? Come! Let me see thee sitting on the throne. I have looked forward to that.

CHARLES. What is the good of sitting on the throne when the other fellows give all the orders? However! [*he sits enthroned, a piteous figure*] here is the king for you! Look your fill at the poor devil.

JOAN. Thourt not king yet, lad: thourt but Dauphin. Be not led away by them around thee. Dressing up dont fill empty noddle.* I know the people: the real people that make thy bread for thee; and I tell thee they count no man king of France until the holy oil has been poured on his hair,* and himself consecrated and crowned in Rheims Cathedral. And thou needs new clothes, Charlie. Why does not Queen* look after thee properly?

CHARLES. We're too poor. She wants all the money we can spare to put on her own back. Besides, I like to see her beautifully dressed; and I dont care what I wear myself: I should look ugly anyhow.

JOAN. There is some good in thee, Charlie; but it is not yet a king's good.

CHARLES. We shall see. I am not such a fool as I look. I have my eyes open; and I can tell you that one good treaty is worth ten good fights. These fighting fellows lose all on the treaties that they gain on the fights. If we can only have a treaty, the English are sure to have the worst of it, because they are better at fighting than at thinking.

JOAN. If the English win, it is they that will make the treaty; and then God help poor France! Thou must fight, Charlie, whether thou will or no. I will go first to hearten thee. We must take our courage in both hands: aye, and pray for it with both hands too.

CHARLES [*descending* from his throne and again crossing the room to escape from her dominating urgency*] Oh do stop talking about God and praying. I cant bear people who are always praying. Isnt it bad enough to have to do it at the proper times?

JOAN [*pitying him*] Thou poor child, thou hast never prayed in thy life. I must teach thee from the beginning.

CHARLES. I am not a child: I am a grown man and a father; and I will not be taught any more.

JOAN. Aye, you have a little son. He that will be Louis the Eleventh* when you die. Would you not fight for him?

CHARLES. No: a horrid boy. He hates me. He hates everybody, selfish little beast!* I dont want to be bothered with children. I dont want to be a father; and I dont want to be a son: especially a son of St Louis. I dont want to be any of these fine things you all have your heads full of: I want to be just what I am. Why cant you mind your own business, and let me mind mine?

JOAN [*again contemptuous*] Minding your own business is like minding your own body: it's the shortest way to make yourself sick. What is my business? Helping mother at home. What is thine? Petting lap-dogs and sucking sugar-sticks. I call that muck. I tell thee it is God's business we are here to do: not our own. I have a message to thee from God; and thou must listen to it, though thy heart break with the terror of it.

CHARLES. I dont want a message; but can you tell me any secrets? Can you do any cures? Can you turn lead into gold, or anything of that sort?

JOAN. I can turn thee into a king, in Rheims Cathedral; and that is a miracle that will take some doing, it seems.*

CHARLES. If we go to Rheims, and have a coronation, Anne* will want new dresses. We cant afford them. I am all right as I am.

JOAN. As you are! And what is that? Less than my father's poorest shepherd. Thourt not lawful owner of thy own land of France till thou be consecrated.

CHARLES. But I shall not be lawful owner of my own land anyhow. Will the consecration pay off my mortgages? I have pledged my last acre to the Archbishop and that fat bully. I owe money even to Bluebeard.

JOAN [*earnestly*] Charlie: I come from the land, and have gotten my strength working on the land; and I tell thee that the land is thine to rule righteously and keep God's peace in, and not to pledge at the pawnshop as a drunken woman pledges her children's clothes. And I come from God to tell thee to kneel in the cathedral and solemnly give thy kingdom to Him for ever and ever, and become the greatest king in the world as His steward and His bailiff, His soldier and His servant. The very clay of France will become holy: her soldiers will be the soldiers of God: the rebel dukes will be rebels against God: the English will fall on their knees and beg thee let them return to their lawful homes in peace. Wilt be a poor little Judas, and betray me and Him* that sent me?

CHARLES [*tempted at last*] Oh, if I only dare!

JOAN. I shall dare, dare, and dare again, in God's name! Art for or against me?

CHARLES [*excited*] I'll risk it, I warn you I shant be able to keep it up; but I'll risk it. You shall see. [*Running to the main door and shouting*] Hallo! Come back, everybody. [*To Joan, as he runs back to the arch opposite*] Mind you stand by and dont let me be bullied. [*Through the arch*] Come along, will you: the whole Court. [*He sits down in the royal chair as they all hurry in to their former places, chattering and wondering*]. Now I'm in for it; but no matter: here goes! [*To the page*] Call for silence, you little beast, will you?

THE PAGE [*snatching a halberd as before and thumping with it repeatedly*] Silence for His Majesty the King. The King speaks. [*Peremptorily*] Will you be silent there? [*Silence*].

CHARLES [*rising*] I have given the command of the army to The Maid. The Maid is to do as she likes with it. [*He descends from the dais*].

*General amazement. La Hire, delighted, slaps his steel thigh-piece with his gauntlet.**

LA TRÉMOUILLE [*turning threateningly towards Charles*] What is this? *I* command the army.

Joan quickly puts her hand on Charles's shoulder as he instinctively recoils. Charles, with a grotesque effort culminating in an extravagant gesture, snaps his fingers in the Chamberlain's face.

JOAN. Thourt answered, old Gruff-and-Grum. [*Suddenly flashing out her sword as she divines that her moment has come*] Who is for God and His Maid? Who is for Orleans with me?

LA HIRE [*carried away, drawing also*] For God and His Maid! To Orleans!

ALL THE KNIGHTS [*following his lead with enthusiasm*] To Orleans!

*Joan, radiant, falls on her knees in thanksgiving to God. They all kneel, except the Archbishop, who gives his benediction with a sign, and La Trémouille, who collapses, cursing.**

SCENE III

*Orleans, May 29th, 1429. Dunois, aged 26, is pacing up and down a patch
of ground on the south bank of the silver Loire, commanding a long view of
the river in both directions. He has had his lance stuck up with a pennon,*
which streams in a strong east wind. His shield with its bend sinister* lies
beside it. He has his commander's baton in his hand. He is well built, carrying his armor easily. His broad brow and pointed chin give him an equilat-
erally triangular face, already marked by active service and responsibility,
with the expression of a goodnatured and capable man who has no affect-
ations and no foolish illusions. His page is sitting on the ground, elbows on
knees, cheeks on fists, idly watching the water. It is evening; and both man
and boy are affected by the loveliness of the Loire.*

DUNOIS [*halting for a moment to glance up at the streaming pennon and
    shake his head wearily before he resumes his pacing*] West wind, west
    wind, west wind. Strumpet:* steadfast when you should be wanton,*
    wanton when you should be steadfast. West wind on the silver Loire:
    what rhymes to Loire? [*He looks again at the pennon, and shakes his fist
    at it*] Change, curse you, change, English harlot of a wind, change.
    West, west, I tell you. [*With a growl he resumes his march in silence, but
    soon begins again*] West wind, wanton wind, wilful wind, womanish
    wind, false wind from over the water, will you never blow again?

THE PAGE [*bounding to his feet*] See! There! There she goes!

DUNOIS [*startled from his reverie: eagerly*] Where? Who? The Maid?

THE PAGE. No: the kingfisher.* Like blue lightning. She went into
    that bush.

DUNOIS [*furiously disappointed*] Is that all? You infernal young idiot:
    I have a mind to pitch you into the river.

THE PAGE [*not afraid, knowing his man*] It looked frightfully jolly, that
    flash of blue. Look! There goes the other!

DUNOIS [*running eagerly to the river brim*] Where? Where?

THE PAGE [*pointing*] Passing the reeds.

DUNOIS [*delighted*] I see.

They follow the flight till the bird takes cover.

THE PAGE. You blew me up because you were not in time to see them
    yesterday.

DUNOIS. You knew I was expecting The Maid when you set up your yelping. I will give you something to yelp for next time.

THE PAGE. Arnt they lovely? I wish I could catch them.

DUNOIS. Let me catch you trying to trap them, and I will put you in the iron cage for a month to teach you what a cage feels like. You are an abominable boy.

THE PAGE [*laughs, and squats down as before*]!

DUNOIS [*pacing*] Blue bird, blue bird, since I am friend to thee, change thou the wind for me. No: it does not rhyme. He who has sinned for thee: thats better. No sense in it, though. [*He finds himself close to the page*] You abominable boy! [*He turns away from him*] Mary in the blue snood,* kingfisher color: will you grudge me a west wind?

A SENTRY'S VOICE WESTWARD. Halt! Who goes there?

JOAN'S VOICE. The Maid.

DUNOIS. Let her pass. Hither,* Maid! To me!

Joan, in splendid armor, rushes in in a blazing rage.* The wind drops; and the pennon flaps idly down the lance; but Dunois is too much occupied with Joan to notice it.

JOAN [*bluntly*] Be you Bastard of Orleans?

DUNOIS [*cool and stern, pointing to his shield**]* You see the bend sinister. Are you Joan the Maid?

JOAN. Sure.

DUNOIS. Where are your troops?

JOAN. Miles behind. They have cheated me. They have brought me to the wrong side of the river.

DUNOIS. I told them to.

JOAN. Why did you? The English are on the other side!

DUNOIS. The English are on both sides.

JOAN. But Orleans is on the other side. We must fight the English there. How can we cross the river?

DUNOIS [*grimly*] There is a bridge.

JOAN. In God's name, then, let us cross the bridge, and fall on them.

DUNOIS. It seems simple; but it cannot be done.

JOAN. Who says so?

DUNOIS. I say so;* and older and wiser heads than mine are of the same opinion.

JOAN [*roundly*] Then your older and wiser heads are fat-heads: they have made a fool of you; and now they want to make a fool of me too, bringing me to the wrong side of the river. Do you not know that I bring you better help than ever came to any general or any town?

DUNOIS [*smiling patiently*] Your own?

JOAN. No: the help and counsel of the King of Heaven. Which is the way to the bridge?

DUNOIS. You are impatient, Maid.

JOAN. Is this a time for patience? Our enemy is at our gates; and here we stand doing nothing. Oh, why are you not fighting? Listen to me: I will deliver you from fear. I—

DUNOIS [*laughing heartily, and waving her off*] No, no, my girl: if you delivered me from fear I should be a good knight for a story book, but a very bad commander of the army. Come! let me begin to make a soldier of you. [*He takes her to the water's edge*]. Do you see those two forts at this end of the bridge? the big ones?

JOAN. Yes. Are they ours or the goddams'?

DUNOIS. Be quiet, and listen to me. If I were in either of those forts with only ten men I could hold it against an army. The English have more than ten times ten goddams in those forts to hold them against us.

JOAN. They cannot hold them against God. God did not give them the land under those forts: they stole it from Him. He gave it to us. I will take those forts.

DUNOIS. Single-handed?

JOAN. Our men will take them. I will lead them.

DUNOIS. Not a man will follow you.

JOAN. I will not look back to see whether anyone is following me.

DUNOIS [*recognizing her mettle, and clapping her heartily on the shoulder*] Good. You have the makings of a soldier in you. You are in love with war.

JOAN [*startled*] Oh! And the Archbishop said I was in love with religion.

DUNOIS. I, God forgive me, am a little in love with war myself, the ugly devil! I am like a man with two wives. Do you want to be like a woman with two husbands?

JOAN [*matter-of-fact*] I will never take a husband.* A man in Toul took an action against me for breach of promise;* but I never promised him. I am a soldier: I do not want to be thought of as a woman. I will not dress as a woman. I do not care for the things women care for. They dream of lovers, and of money. I dream of leading a charge, and of placing the big guns. You soldiers do not know how to use the big guns: you think you can win battles with a great noise and smoke.

DUNOIS [*with a shrug*] True. Half the time the artillery is more trouble than it is worth.

JOAN. Aye, lad; but you cannot fight stone walls with horses: you must have guns, and much bigger guns too.

DUNOIS [*grinning at her familiarity, and echoing it*] Aye, lass; but a good heart and a stout ladder will get over the stoniest wall.

JOAN. I will be first up the ladder when we reach the fort, Bastard. I dare you to follow me.

DUNOIS. You must not dare a staff officer, Joan: only company officers are allowed to indulge in displays of personal courage. Besides, you must know that I welcome you as a saint, not as a soldier. I have daredevils enough at my call, if they could help me.

JOAN. I am not a daredevil: I am a servant of God. My sword is sacred: I found it behind the altar in the church of St Catherine,* where God hid it for me; and I may not strike a blow with it. My heart is full of courage, not of anger. I will lead; and your men will follow: that is all I can do. But I must do it: you shall not stop me.

DUNOIS. All in good time. Our men cannot take those forts by a sally* across the bridge. They must come by water, and take the English in the rear on this side.*

JOAN [*her military sense asserting itself*] Then make rafts and put big guns on them; and let your men cross to us.

DUNOIS. The rafts are ready; and the men are embarked. But they must wait for God.

JOAN. What do you mean? God is waiting for them.

DUNOIS. Let Him send us a wind then. My boats are downstream: they cannot come up against both wind and current. We must wait until God changes the wind. Come: let me take you to the church.

JOAN. No. I love church; but the English will not yield to prayers: they understand nothing but hard knocks and slashes. I will not go to church until we have beaten them.

DUNOIS. You must: I have business for you there.

JOAN. What business?

DUNOIS. To pray for a west wind. I have prayed; and I have given two silver candlesticks; but my prayers are not answered. Yours may be: you are young and innocent.

JOAN. Oh yes: you are right. I will pray:* I will tell St Catherine: she will make God give me a west wind. Quick: shew me the way to the church.

THE PAGE [*sneezes violently*] At-cha!!!

JOAN. God bless you, child! Coom, Bastard.

They go out. The page rises to follow. He picks up the shield, and is taking the spear as well when he notices the pennon, which is now streaming eastward.

THE PAGE [*dropping the shield and calling excitedly after them*] Seigneur!* Seigneur! Mademoiselle!

DUNOIS [*running back*] What is it? The kingfisher? [*He looks eagerly for it up the river*].

JOAN [*joining them*] Oh, a kingfisher! Where?

THE PAGE. No: the wind, the wind, the wind [*pointing to the pennon*]: that is what made me sneeze.

DUNOIS [*looking at the pennon*] The wind has changed. [*He crosses himself*] God has spoken. [*Kneeling and handing his baton to Joan*] You command the king's army. I am your soldier.

THE PAGE [*looking down the river*] The boats have put off. They are ripping upstream like anything.

DUNOIS [*rising*] Now for the forts. You dared me to follow. Dare you lead?

JOAN [*bursting into tears and flinging her arms round Dunois, kissing him on both cheeks*] Dunois, dear comrade in arms, help me. My eyes are blinded with tears. Set my foot on the ladder, and say 'Up, Joan.'

DUNOIS [*dragging her out*] Never mind the tears: make for the flash of the guns.

JOAN [*in a blaze of courage*] Ah!

DUNOIS [*dragging her along with him*] For God and Saint Dennis!

THE PAGE [*shrilly*] The Maid! The Maid! God and The Maid! Hurray-ay-ay! [*He snatches up the shield and lance, and capers out after them, mad with excitement*].

SCENE IV

*A tent in the English camp. A bullnecked English chaplain of 50 is sitting on
a stool at a table, hard at work writing. At the other side of the table an
imposing nobleman, aged 46, is seated in a handsome chair turning over the
leaves of an illuminated Book of Hours.* The nobleman is enjoying himself:
the chaplain is struggling with suppressed wrath. There is an unoccupied
leather stool on the nobleman's left. The table is on his right.*

THE NOBLEMAN. Now this is what I call workmanship. There is nothing on earth more exquisite than a bonny* book, with well-placed
columns of rich black writing in beautiful borders, and illuminated
pictures cunningly inset. But nowadays, instead of looking at books,
people read them. A book might as well be one of those orders for
bacon and bran that you are scribbling.

THE CHAPLAIN. I must say, my lord, you take our situation very coolly.
Very coolly indeed.

THE NOBLEMAN [*supercilious*] What is the matter?

THE CHAPLAIN. The matter, my lord, is that we English have been
defeated.

THE NOBLEMAN. That happens, you know. It is only in history books
and ballads that the enemy is always defeated.

THE CHAPLAIN. But we are being defeated over and over again. First,
Orleans—

THE NOBLEMAN [*poohpoohing**] Oh, Orleans!

THE CHAPLAIN. I know what you are going to say, my lord: that was
a clear case of witchcraft and sorcery. But we are still being defeated.*
Jargeau, Meung, Beaugency, just like Orleans. And now we have
been butchered at Patay,* and Sir John Talbot taken prisoner.* [*He
throws down his pen, almost in tears*] I feel it, my lord: I feel it very
deeply. I cannot bear to see my countrymen defeated by a parcel of
foreigners.

THE NOBLEMAN. Oh! you are an Englishman, are you?

THE CHAPLAIN. Certainly not, my lord: I am a gentleman. Still, like
your lordship, I was born in England; and it makes a difference.

THE NOBLEMAN. You are attached to the soil, eh?

THE CHAPLAIN. It pleases your lordship to be satirical at my expense: your greatness privileges you to be so with impunity. But your lordship knows very well that I am not attached to the soil in a vulgar manner, like a serf.* Still, I have a feeling about it; [*with growing agitation*] and I am not ashamed of it; and [*rising wildly*] by God, if this goes on any longer I will fling my cassock* to the devil, and take arms myself, and strangle the accursed witch with my own hands.

THE NOBLEMAN [*laughing at him goodnaturedly*] So you shall, chaplain: so you shall, if we can do nothing better. But not yet, not quite yet.

The Chaplain resumes his seat very sulkily.

THE NOBLEMAN [*airily*] I should not care very much about the witch—you see, I have made my pilgrimage to the Holy Land;* and the Heavenly Powers, for their own credit, can hardly allow *me* to be worsted by a village sorceress—but the Bastard of Orleans is a harder nut to crack; and as he has been to the Holy Land too, honors are easy between us as far as that goes.

THE CHAPLAIN. He is only a Frenchman, my lord.

THE NOBLEMAN. A Frenchman! Where did you pick up that expression? Are these Burgundians and Bretons and Picards and Gascons beginning to call themselves Frenchmen, just as our fellows are beginning to call themselves Englishmen? They actually talk of France and England as their countries. *Theirs*, if you please! What is to become of me and you if that way of thinking comes into fashion?

THE CHAPLAIN. Why, my lord? Can it hurt us?

THE NOBLEMAN. Men cannot serve two masters. If this cant of serving their country once takes hold of them, goodbye to the authority of their feudal lords, and goodbye to the authority of the Church. That is, goodbye to you and me.

THE CHAPLAIN. I hope I am a faithful servant of the Church; and there are only six cousins between me and the barony of Stogumber, which was created by the Conqueror.* But is that any reason why I should stand by and see Englishmen beaten by a French bastard and a witch from Lousy Champagne?

THE NOBLEMAN. Easy, man, easy: we shall burn the witch and beat the bastard all in good time. Indeed I am waiting at present for the Bishop of Beauvais, to arrange the burning with him. He has been turned out of his diocese* by her faction.

THE CHAPLAIN. You have first to catch her, my lord.

THE NOBLEMAN. Or buy her. I will offer a king's ransom.*

THE CHAPLAIN. A king's ransom! For that slut!*

THE NOBLEMAN. One has to leave a margin. Some of Charles's people will sell her to the Burgundians; the Burgundians will sell her to us; and there will probably be three or four middlemen who will expect their little commissions.

THE CHAPLAIN. Monstrous. It is all those scoundrels of Jews: they get in every time money changes hands. I would not leave a Jew alive in Christendom if I had my way.

THE NOBLEMAN. Why not? The Jews generally give value. They make you pay; but they deliver the goods. In my experience the men who want something for nothing are invariably Christians.

A page appears.

THE PAGE. The Right Reverend the Bishop of Beauvais: Monseigneur Cauchon.

Cauchon, aged about 60, comes in. The page withdraws. The two Englishmen rise.

THE NOBLEMAN [*with effusive courtesy*] My dear Bishop, how good of you to come! Allow me to introduce myself: Richard de Beauchamp, Earl of Warwick,* at your service.

CAUCHON. Your lordship's fame is well known to me.

WARWICK. This reverend cleric is Master John de Stogumber.*

THE CHAPLAIN [*glibly*] John Bowyer Spenser Neville de Stogumber, at your service, my lord: Bachelor of Theology, and Keeper of the Private Seal to His Eminence the Cardinal of Winchester.*

WARWICK [*to Cauchon*] You call him the Cardinal of England, I believe. Our king's uncle.

CAUCHON. Messire John de Stogumber: I am always the very good friend of His Eminence. [*He extends his hand to the chaplain, who kisses his ring*].

WARWICK. Do me the honor to be seated. [*He gives Cauchon his chair, placing it at the head of the table*].

Cauchon accepts the place of honor with a grave inclination. Warwick fetches the leather stool carelessly, and sits in his former place. The chaplain goes back to his chair.

Though Warwick has taken second place in calculated deference to the Bishop, he assumes the lead in opening the proceedings as a matter of course. He is still cordial and expansive; but there is a new note in his voice which means that he is coming to business.

WARWICK. Well, my Lord Bishop, you find us in one of our unlucky moments. Charles is to be crowned at Rheims, practically by the young woman from Lorraine; and—I must not deceive you, nor flatter your hopes—we cannot prevent it. I suppose it will make a great difference to Charles's position.

CAUCHON. Undoubtedly. It is a masterstroke of The Maid's.

THE CHAPLAIN [*again agitated*] We were not fairly beaten, my lord. No Englishman is ever fairly beaten.

Cauchon raises his eyebrow slightly, then quickly composes his face.

WARWICK. Our friend here takes the view that the young woman is a sorceress. It would, I presume, be the duty of your reverend lordship to denounce her to the Inquisition, and have her burnt for that offence.

CAUCHON. If she were captured in my diocese: yes.

WARWICK [*feeling that they are getting on capitally*] Just so. Now I suppose there can be no reasonable doubt that she is a sorceress.

THE CHAPLAIN. Not the least. An arrant witch.

WARWICK [*gently reproving the interruption*] We are asking for the Bishop's opinion, Messire John.

CAUCHON. We shall have to consider not merely our own opinions here, but the opinions—the prejudices, if you like—of a French court.

WARWICK [*correcting*] A Catholic court,* my lord.

CAUCHON. Catholic courts are composed of mortal men, like other courts, however sacred their function and inspiration may be. And if the men are Frenchmen, as the modern fashion calls them, I am afraid the bare fact that an English army has been defeated by a French one will not convince them that there is any sorcery in the matter.

THE CHAPLAIN. What! Not when the famous Sir John Talbot himself has been defeated and actually taken prisoner by a drab from the ditches of Lorraine!

CAUCHON. Sir John Talbot, we all know, is a fierce and formidable soldier, Messire; but I have yet to learn that he is an able general. And though it pleases you to say that he has been defeated by this girl, some of us may be disposed to give a little of the credit to Dunois.

THE CHAPLAIN [*contemptuously*] The Bastard of Orleans!

CAUCHON. Let me remind—

WARWICK [*interposing*] I know what you are going to say, my lord. Dunois defeated *me* at Montargis.

CAUCHON [*bowing*] I take that as evidence that the Seigneur Dunois is a very able commander indeed.

WARWICK. Your lordship is the flower of courtesy.* I admit, on our side, that Talbot is a mere fighting animal,* and that it probably served him right to be taken at Patay.

THE CHAPLAIN [*chafing*] My lord: at Orleans this woman had her throat pierced by an English arrow, and was seen to cry like a child from the pain of it. It was a death wound; yet she fought all day; and when our men had repulsed all her attacks like true Englishmen, she walked alone to the wall of our fort with a white banner in her hand; and our men were paralyzed, and could neither shoot nor strike whilst the French fell on them and drove them on to the bridge, which immediately burst into flames and crumbled under them, letting them down into the river, where they were drowned in heaps. Was this your bastard's generalship? or were those flames the flames of hell, conjured up by witchcraft?

WARWICK. You will forgive Messire John's vehemence, my lord; but he has put our case. Dunois is a great captain, we admit; but why could he do nothing until the witch came?

CAUCHON. I do not say that there were no supernatural powers on her side. But the names on that white banner were not the names of Satan and Beelzebub,* but the blessed names of our Lord and His holy mother. And your commander who was drowned—Clahz-da I think you call him—

WARWICK. Glasdale. Sir William Glasdale.*

CAUCHON. Glass-dell, thank you. He was no saint; and many of our people think that he was drowned for his blasphemies against The Maid.

WARWICK [*beginning to look very dubious*] Well, what are we to infer from all this, my lord? Has The Maid converted you?

CAUCHON. If she had, my lord, I should have known better than to have trusted myself here within your grasp.

WARWICK [*blandly deprecating*] Oh! oh! My lord!

CAUCHON. If the devil is making use of this girl—and I believe he is—

WARWICK [*reassured*] Ah! You hear, Messire John? I knew your lordship would not fail us. Pardon my interruption. Proceed.

CAUCHON. If it be so, the devil has longer views than you give him credit for.

WARWICK. Indeed? In what way? Listen to this, Messire John.

CAUCHON. If the devil wanted to damn a country girl, do you think so easy a task would cost him the winning of half a dozen battles? No, my lord: any trumpery imp could do that much if the girl could be damned at all. The Prince of Darkness does not condescend to such cheap drudgery. When he strikes, he strikes at the Catholic Church,* whose realm is the whole spiritual world. When he damns, he damns the souls of the entire human race. Against that dreadful design The Church stands ever on guard. And it is as one of the instruments of that design that I see this girl. She is inspired, but diabolically inspired.

THE CHAPLAIN. I told you she was a witch.

CAUCHON [*fiercely**] She is not a witch. She is a heretic.*

THE CHAPLAIN. What difference does that make?

CAUCHON. You, a priest, ask me that! You English are strangely blunt in the mind. All these things that you call witchcraft are capable of a natural explanation. The woman's miracles would not impose on a rabbit: she does not claim them as miracles herself. What do her victories prove but that she has a better head on her shoulders than your swearing Glass-dells and mad bull Talbots, and that the courage of faith, even though it be a false faith, will always outstay the courage of wrath?

THE CHAPLAIN [*hardly able to believe his ears*] Does your lordship
   compare Sir John Talbot, three times Governor of Ireland, to a mad
   bull?!!!

WARWICK. It would not be seemly for you to do so, Messire John, as
   you are still six removes from a barony. But as I am an earl, and
   Talbot is only a knight, I may make bold to accept the comparison.
   [*To the Bishop*] My lord: I wipe the slate as far as the witchcraft goes.
   None the less, we must burn the woman.

CAUCHON. I cannot burn her. The Church cannot take life. And my
   first duty is to seek this girl's salvation.*

WARWICK. No doubt. But you do burn people occasionally.

CAUCHON. No. When The Church cuts off an obstinate heretic as
   a dead branch from the tree of life, the heretic is handed over to the
   secular arm.* The Church has no part in what the secular arm may
   see fit to do.

WARWICK. Precisely. And I shall be the secular arm in this case. Well,
   my lord, hand over your dead branch; and I will see that the fire is
   ready for it. If you will answer for The Church's part, I will answer
   for the secular part.

CAUCHON [*with smouldering anger*] I can answer for nothing. You
   great lords are too prone to treat The Church as a mere political
   convenience.

WARWICK [*smiling and propitiatory*] Not in England, I assure you.

CAUCHON. In England more than anywhere else. No, my lord: the soul
   of this village girl is of equal value with yours or your king's before
   the throne of God; and my first duty is to save it. I will not suffer
   your lordship to smile at me as if I were repeating a meaningless
   form of words, and it were well understood between us that I should
   betray the girl to you. I am no mere political bishop: my faith is to me
   what your honor is to you; and if there be a loophole through which
   this baptized child of God can creep to her salvation, I shall guide
   her to it.

THE CHAPLAIN [*rising in a fury*] You are a traitor.

CAUCHON [*springing up*] You lie, priest. [*Trembling with rage*] If you
   dare do what this woman has done—set your country above the holy
   Catholic Church—you shall go to the fire with her.

THE CHAPLAIN. My lord: I—I went too far. I—[*he sits down with a submissive gesture*].*

WARWICK [*who has risen apprehensively*] My lord: I apologize to you for the word used by Messire John de Stogumber. It does not mean in England what it does in France. In your language traitor means betrayer: one who is perfidious, treacherous, unfaithful, disloyal. In our country it means simply one who is not wholly devoted to our English interests.*

CAUCHON. I am sorry: I did not understand.* [*He subsides into his chair with dignity*].

WARWICK [*resuming his seat, much relieved*] I must apologize on my own account if I have seemed to take the burning of this poor girl too lightly. When one has seen whole countrysides burnt over and over again as mere items in military routine, one has to grow a very thick skin.* Otherwise one might go mad: at all events, I should. May I venture to assume that your lordship also, having to see so many heretics burned from time to time, is compelled to take—shall I say a professional view of what would otherwise be a very horrible incident?

CAUCHON. Yes: it is a painful duty: even, as you say, a horrible one. But in comparison with the horror of heresy it is less than nothing. I am not thinking of this girl's body, which will suffer for a few moments only, and which must in any event die in some more or less painful manner, but of her soul, which may suffer to all eternity.

WARWICK. Just so; and God grant that her soul may be saved! But the practical problem would seem to be how to save her soul without saving her body. For we must face it, my lord: if this cult of The Maid goes on, our cause is lost.

THE CHAPLAIN [*his voice broken like that of a man who has been crying*] May I speak, my lord?

WARWICK. Really, Messire John, I had rather you did not, unless you can keep your temper.

THE CHAPLAIN. It is only this. I speak under correction; but The Maid is full of deceit: she pretends to be devout. Her prayers and confessions are endless. How can she be accused of heresy when she neglects no observance of a faithful daughter of The Church?

CAUCHON [*flaming up*] A faithful daughter of The Church! The Pope himself at his proudest dare not presume as this woman presumes.

She acts as if she herself were The Church. She brings the message of God to Charles; and The Church must stand aside. She will crown him in the cathedral of Rheims: *she*, not The Church! She sends letters to the king of England* giving him God's command through *her* to return to his island on pain of God's vengeance, which *she* will execute. Let me tell you that the writing of such letters was the practice of the accursed Mahomet, the anti-Christ. Has she ever in all her utterances said one word of The Church? Never. It is always God and herself.

WARWICK. What can you expect? A beggar on horseback!* Her head is turned.

CAUCHON. Who has turned it? The devil. And for a mighty purpose. He is spreading this heresy everywhere. The man Hus, burnt only thirteen years ago at Constance, infected all Bohemia with it. A man named WcLeef,* himself an anointed priest, spread the pestilence in England; and to your shame you let him die in his bed. We have such people here in France too: I know the breed. It is cancerous: if it be not cut out, stamped out, burnt out, it will not stop until it has brought the whole body of human society into sin and corruption, into waste and ruin. By it an Arab camel driver* drove Christ and His Church out of Jerusalem,* and ravaged his way west like a wild beast until at last there stood only the Pyrenees and God's mercy between France and damnation.* Yet what did the camel driver do at the beginning more than this shepherd girl is doing? He had his voices from the angel Gabriel: *she* has her voices from St Catherine and St Margaret and the Blessed Michael. He declared himself the messenger of God, and wrote in God's name to the kings of the earth. Her letters to them are going forth daily. It is not the Mother of God now to whom we must look for intercession, but to Joan the Maid. What will the world be like when The Church's accumulated wisdom and knowledge and experience, its councils of learned, venerable pious men, are thrust into the kennel by every ignorant laborer or dairymaid whom the devil can puff up with the monstrous self-conceit of being directly inspired from heaven? It will be a world of blood, of fury, of devastation, of each man striving for his own hand: in the end a world wrecked back into barbarism. For now you have only Mahomet and his dupes, and the Maid and her dupes; but what will it be when every girl thinks herself a Joan and every man a Mahomet? I shudder to the very marrow of my bones when I think of it. I have fought it all my life; and I will fight it to the end. Let all this woman's sins be forgiven her except only this sin; for it is the sin against the Holy Ghost; and if she does not recant in the dust before the world, and submit herself to the last inch of her soul to her Church, to the fire she shall go if she once falls into my hand.

WARWICK [*unimpressed*] You feel strongly about it, naturally.

CAUCHON. Do not you?

WARWICK. I am a soldier, not a churchman. As a pilgrim I saw something of the Mahometans. They were not so ill-bred as I had been led to believe. In some respects their conduct compared favorably with ours.

CAUCHON [*displeased*] I have noticed this before. Men go to the East to convert the infidels. And the infidels pervert them. The Crusader comes back more than half a Saracen.* Not to mention that all Englishmen are born heretics.

THE CHAPLAIN. Englishmen heretics!!!* [*Appealing to Warwick*] My lord: must we endure this? His lordship is beside himself. How can what an Englishman believes be heresy? It is a contradiction in terms.

CAUCHON. I absolve you, Messire de Stogumber, on the ground of invincible ignorance. The thick air of your country does not breed theologians.

WARWICK. You would not say so if you heard us quarrelling about religion, my lord! I am sorry you think I must be either a heretic or a blockhead because, as a travelled man, I know that the followers of Mahomet profess great respect for our Lord, and are more ready to forgive St Peter for being a fisherman than your lordship is to forgive Mahomet for being a camel driver. But at least we can proceed in this matter without bigotry.

CAUCHON. When men call the zeal of the Christian Church bigotry I know what to think.

WARWICK. They are only east and west views of the same thing.

CAUCHON [*bitterly ironical*] Only east and west! Only!!

WARWICK. Oh, my Lord Bishop, I am not gainsaying you. You will carry The Church with you; but you have to carry the nobles also. To my mind there is a stronger case against The Maid than the one you have so forcibly put. Frankly, I am not afraid of this girl becoming another Mahomet, and superseding The Church by a great heresy.

I think you exaggerate that risk. But have you noticed that in these letters of hers, she proposes to all the kings of Europe, as she has already pressed on Charles, a transaction which would wreck the whole social structure of Christendom?

CAUCHON. Wreck The Church. I tell you so.

WARWICK [*whose patience is wearing out*] My lord: pray get The Church out of your head for a moment; and remember that there are temporal institutions in the world as well as spiritual ones. I and my peers represent the feudal aristocracy as you represent The Church. We are the temporal power. Well, do you not see how this girl's idea strikes at us?

CAUCHON. How does her idea strike at you, except as it strikes at all of us, through The Church?

WARWICK. Her idea is that the kings should give their realms to God, and then reign as God's bailiffs.

CAUCHON [*not interested*] Quite sound theologically, my lord. But the king will hardly care, provided he reign. It is an abstract idea: a mere form of words.

WARWICK. By no means. It is a cunning device to supersede the aristocracy, and make the king sole and absolute autocrat. Instead of the king being merely the first among his peers, he becomes their master. That we cannot suffer: we call no man master. Nominally we hold our lands and dignities from the king, because there must be a keystone to the arch of human society; but we hold our lands in our own hands, and defend them with our own swords and those of our own tenants. Now by The Maid's doctrine the king will take our lands—*our* lands!—and make them a present to God; and God will then vest them wholly in the king.

CAUCHON. Need you fear that? You are the makers of kings after all. York or Lancaster in England, Lancaster or Valois in France: they reign according to your pleasure.

WARWICK. Yes; but only as long as the people follow their feudal lords, and know the king only as a travelling show, owning nothing but the highway that belongs to everybody. If the people's thoughts and hearts were turned to the king, and their lords became only the king's servants in their eyes, the king could break us across his knee one by one; and then what should we be but liveried courtiers* in his halls?

CAUCHON. Still you need not fear, my lord. Some men are born kings; and some are born statesmen. The two are seldom the same. Where would the king find counsellors to plan and carry out such a policy for him?

WARWICK [*with a not too friendly smile*] Perhaps in the Church, my lord.

Cauchon, with an equally sour smile, shrugs his shoulders, and does not contradict him.

WARWICK. Strike down the barons; and the cardinals will have it all their own way.

CAUCHON [*conciliatory, dropping his polemical tone**] My lord: we shall not defeat The Maid if we strive against one another. I know well that there is a Will to Power in the world. I know that while it lasts there will be a struggle between the Emperor and the Pope, between the dukes and the political cardinals, between the barons and the kings. The devil divides us and governs. I see you are no friend to The Church: you are an earl first and last, as I am a churchman first and last. But can we not sink our differences in the face of a common enemy? I see now that what is in your mind is not that this girl has never once mentioned The Church, and thinks only of God and herself, but that she has never once mentioned the peerage, and thinks only of the king and herself.

WARWICK. Quite so. These two ideas of hers are the same idea at bottom. It goes deep, my lord. It is the protest of the individual soul against the interference of priest or peer between the private man and his God. I should call it Protestantism if I had to find a name for it.

CAUCHON [*looking hard at him*] You understand it wonderfully well, my lord. Scratch an Englishman, and find a Protestant.

WARWICK [*playing the pink of courtesy**] I think you are not entirely void of sympathy with The Maid's secular heresy, my lord. I leave you to find a name for it.

CAUCHON. You mistake me, my lord. I have no sympathy with her political presumptions. But as a priest I have gained a knowledge of the minds of the common people; and there you will find yet another most dangerous idea. I can express it only by such phrases as France for the French, England for the English, Italy for the Italians, Spain for the Spanish, and so forth. It is sometimes so narrow and bitter in country folk that it surprises me that this country girl can rise above the idea of her village for its villagers. But she can. She does. When she threatens to drive the English from the soil of France she is undoubtedly thinking of the whole extent of country in which French is spoken. To her the French-speaking people are what the Holy Scriptures describe as a nation. Call this side of her heresy Nationalism if you will: I can find you no better name for it. I can only tell you that it is essentially anti-Catholic and anti-Christian; for the Catholic Church knows only one realm, and that is the realm of Christ's kingdom. Divide that kingdom into nations, and you dethrone Christ. Dethrone Christ, and who will stand between our throats and the sword? The world will perish in a welter of war.

WARWICK. Well, if you will burn the Protestant, I will burn the Nationalist, though perhaps I shall not carry Messire John with me there. England for the English will appeal to him.

THE CHAPLAIN. Certainly England for the English goes without saying: it is the simple law of nature. But this woman denies to England her legitimate conquests, given her by God because of her peculiar fitness to rule over less civilized races for their own good. I do not understand what your lordships mean by Protestant and Nationalist: you are too learned and subtle for a poor clerk like myself. But I know as a matter of plain commonsense that the woman is a rebel;* and that is enough for me. She rebels against Nature by wearing man's clothes, and fighting. She rebels against The Church by usurping the divine authority of the Pope. She rebels against God by her damnable league with Satan and his evil spirits against our army. And all these rebellions are only excuses for her great rebellion against England. That is not to be endured. Let her perish. Let her burn. Let her not infect the whole flock. It is expedient that one woman die for the people.

WARWICK [*rising*] My lord: we seem to be agreed.

CAUCHON [*rising also, but in protest*] I will not imperil my soul. I will uphold the justice of the Church. I will strive to the utmost for this woman's salvation.

WARWICK. I am sorry for the poor girl. I hate these severities. I will spare her if I can.

THE CHAPLAIN [*implacably*] I would burn her with my own hands.

CAUCHON [*blessing him*] Sancta simplicitas!*

SCENE V

The ambulatory* in the cathedral of Rheims, near the door of the vestry. A pillar bears one of the stations of the cross.* The organ is playing the people out of the nave* after the coronation. Joan is kneeling in prayer before the station. She is beautifully dressed, but still in male attire. The organ ceases as Dunois, also splendidly arrayed, comes into the ambulatory from the vestry.*

DUNOIS. Come, Joan!* you have had enough praying. After that fit of crying you will catch a chill if you stay here any longer. It is all over: the cathedral is empty; and the streets are full. They are calling for The Maid. We have told them you are staying here alone to pray; but they want to see you again.

JOAN. No: let the king have all the glory.

DUNOIS. He only spoils the show, poor devil. No, Joan: you have crowned him; and you must go through with it.

JOAN [*shakes her head reluctantly*].

DUNOIS [*raising her*] Come come! it will be over in a couple of hours. It's better than the bridge at Orleans: eh?

JOAN. Oh, dear Dunois, how I wish it were the bridge at Orleans again! We *lived* at that bridge.

DUNOIS. Yes, faith, and died too: some of us.

JOAN. Isnt it strange, Jack? I am such a coward: I am frightened beyond words before a battle; but it is so dull afterwards when there is no danger: oh, so dull! dull! dull!

DUNOIS. You must learn to be abstemious in war, just as you are in your food and drink, my little saint.*

JOAN. Dear Jack: I think you like me as a soldier likes his comrade.

DUNOIS. You need it, poor innocent child of God. You have not many friends at court.

JOAN. Why do all these courtiers and knights and churchmen hate me? What have I done to them? I have asked nothing for myself except that my village shall not be taxed; for we cannot afford war taxes. I have brought them luck and victory: I have set them right when they were doing all sorts of stupid things: I have crowned

Charles and made him a real king; and all the honors he is handing out have gone to them. Then why do they not love me?

DUNOIS [*rallying her*] Sim-ple-ton! Do you expect stupid people to love you for shewing them up? Do blundering old military dug-outs* love the successful young captains who supersede them? Do ambitious politicians love the climbers who take the front seats from them? Do archbishops enjoy being played off their own altars, even by saints? Why, I should be jealous of you myself if I were ambitious enough.

JOAN. You are the pick of the basket here, Jack: the only friend I have among all these nobles. I'll wager your mother was from the country. I will go back to the farm when I have taken Paris.

DUNOIS. I am not so sure that they will let you take Paris.

JOAN [*startled*] What!

DUNOIS. I should have taken it myself before this if they had all been sound about it. Some of them would rather Paris took you, I think. So take care.

JOAN. Jack: the world is too wicked for me. If the goddams and the Burgundians do not make an end of me, the French will. Only for my voices I should lose all heart. That is why I had to steal away to pray here alone after the coronation. I'll tell you something, Jack. It is in the bells I hear my voices.* Not to-day, when they all rang: that was nothing but jangling. But here in this corner, where the bells come down from heaven, and the echoes linger, or in the fields, where they come from a distance through the quiet of the countryside, my voices are in them. [*The cathedral clock chimes the quarter*] Hark! [*She becomes rapt*] Do you hear? 'Dear-child-of-God': just what you said. At the half-hour they will say 'Be-brave-go-on.' At the three-quarters they will say 'I-am-thy-Help.' But it is at the hour, when the great bell goes after 'God-will-save-France': it is then that St Margaret and St Catherine and sometimes even the blessed Michael will say things that I cannot tell beforehand. Then, oh then—

DUNOIS [*interrupting her kindly but not sympathetically*] Then, Joan, we shall hear whatever we fancy in the booming of the bell. You make me uneasy when you talk about your voices: I should think you were a bit cracked if I hadnt noticed that you give me very sensible reasons for what you do, though I hear you telling others you are only obeying Madame Saint Catherine.

JOAN [*crossly*] Well, I have to find reasons for you, because you do not believe in my voices. But the voices come first; and I find the reasons after: whatever you may choose to believe.

DUNOIS. Are you angry, Joan?

JOAN. Yes. [*Smiling*] No: not with you. I wish you were one of the village babies.

DUNOIS. Why?

JOAN. I could nurse you for awhile.

DUNOIS. You are a bit of a woman after all.

JOAN. No: not a bit: I am a soldier and nothing else. Soldiers always nurse children when they get a chance.

DUNOIS. That is true. [*He laughs*].

King Charles, with Bluebeard on his left and La Hire on his right, comes from the vestry, where he has been disrobing. Joan shrinks away behind the pillar. Dunois is left between Charles and La Hire.

DUNOIS. Well, your Majesty is an anointed king at last. How do you like it?

CHARLES. I would not go through it again to be emperor of the sun and moon. The weight of those robes! I thought I should have dropped when they loaded that crown on to me. And the famous holy oil they talked so much about was rancid: phew! The Archbishop must be nearly dead: his robes must have weighed a ton: they are stripping him still in the vestry.

DUNOIS [*drily*] Your majesty should wear armor oftener. That would accustom you to heavy dressing.

CHARLES. Yes: the old jibe! Well, I am not going to wear armor: fighting is not my job. Where is The Maid?

JOAN [*coming forward between Charles and Bluebeard, and falling on her knee*] Sire: I have made you king: my work is done. I am going back to my father's farm.

CHARLES [*surprised, but relieved*] Oh, are you? Well, that will be very nice.

Joan rises, deeply discouraged.

CHARLES [*continuing heedlessly*] A healthy life, you know.

DUNOIS. But a dull one.

BLUEBEARD. You will find the petticoats tripping you up after leaving them off for so long.

LA HIRE. You will miss the fighting. It's a bad habit, but a grand one, and the hardest of all to break yourself of.

CHARLES [*anxiously*] Still, we dont want you to stay if you would really rather go home.

JOAN [*bitterly*] I know well that none of you will be sorry to see me go. [*She turns her shoulder to Charles and walks past him to the more congenial neighborhood of Dunois and La Hire*].

LA HIRE. Well, I shall be able to swear when I want to. But I shall miss you at times.

JOAN. La Hire: in spite of all your sins and swears we shall meet in heaven; for I love you as I love Pitou, my old sheep dog.* Pitou could kill a wolf. You will kill the English wolves until they go back to their country and become good dogs of God, will you not?

LA HIRE. You and I together: yes.

JOAN. No: I shall last only a year from the beginning.*

ALL THE OTHERS. What!

JOAN. I know it somehow.

DUNOIS. Nonsense!

JOAN. Jack: do you think you will be able to drive them out?

DUNOIS [*with quiet conviction*] Yes: I shall drive them out. They beat us because we thought battles were tournaments and ransom markets. We played the fool while the goddams took war seriously. But I have learnt my lesson, and taken their measure. They have no roots here. I have beaten them before; and I shall beat them again.

JOAN. You will not be cruel to them, Jack?

DUNOIS. The goddams will not yield to tender handling. We did not begin it.

JOAN [*suddenly*] Jack: before I go home, let us take Paris.

CHARLES [*terrified*] Oh no no. We shall lose everything we have gained. Oh dont let us have any more fighting. We can make a very good treaty with the Duke of Burgundy.

JOAN. Treaty! [*She stamps with impatience*].

CHARLES. Well, why not, now that I am crowned and anointed? Oh, that oil!

The Archbishop comes from the vestry, and joins the group between Charles and Bluebeard.

CHARLES. Archbishop: The Maid wants to start fighting again.

THE ARCHBISHOP. Have we ceased fighting, then? Are we at peace?

CHARLES. No: I suppose not; but let us be content with what we have done. Let us make a treaty. Our luck is too good to last; and now is our chance to stop before it turns.

JOAN. Luck! God has fought for us; and you call it luck! And you would stop while there are still Englishmen on this holy earth of dear France!

THE ARCHBISHOP [*sternly*] Maid: the king addressed himself to me, not to you. You forget yourself. You very often forget yourself.

JOAN [*unabashed, and rather roughly*] Then speak, you; and tell him that it is not God's will that he should take his hand from the plough.

THE ARCHBISHOP. If I am not so glib with the name of God as you are, it is because I interpret His will with the authority of the Church and of my sacred office. When you first came you respected it, and would not have dared to speak as you are now speaking. You came clothed with the virtue of humility; and because God blessed your enterprises accordingly, you have stained yourself with the sin of pride. The old Greek tragedy is rising among us. It is the chastisement of hubris.*

CHARLES. Yes: she thinks she knows better than everyone else.

JOAN [*distressed, but naïvely incapable of seeing the effect she is producing*] But I *do* know better than any of you seem to. And I am not proud: I never speak unless I know I am right.

BLUEBEARD ⎱ [*exclaiming* ⎰ Ha ha!
CHARLES ⎰ *together*] ⎱ Just so.

THE ARCHBISHOP. How do you know you are right?

JOAN. I always know. My voices—

CHARLES. Oh, your voices, your voices. Why dont the voices come to me? I am king, not you.

JOAN. They do come to you; but you do not hear them. You have not sat in the field in the evening listening for them. When the angelus* rings you cross yourself and have done with it; but if you prayed from your heart, and listened to the thrilling of the bells in the air after they stop ringing, you would hear the voices as well as I do. [*Turning brusquely from him*] But what voices do you need to tell you what the blacksmith can tell you: that you must strike while the iron is hot?* I tell you we must make a dash at Compiègne and relieve it as we relieved Orleans. Then Paris will open its gates; or if not, we will break through them. What is your crown worth without your capital?

LA HIRE. That is what I say too. We shall go through them like a red hot shot through a pound of butter. What do you say, Bastard?

DUNOIS. If our cannon balls were all as hot as your head, and we had enough of them, we should conquer the earth, no doubt. Pluck and impetuosity are good servants in war, but bad masters: they have delivered us into the hands of the English every time we have trusted to them. We never know when we are beaten: that is our great fault.

JOAN. You never know when you are victorious: that is a worse fault. I shall have to make you carry looking-glasses in battle to convince you that the English have not cut off all your noses. You would have been besieged in Orleans still, you and your councils of war, if I had not made you attack. You should always attack; and if you only hold on long enough the enemy will stop first. You dont know how to begin a battle; and you dont know how to use your cannons. And I do.

She squats down on the flags with crossed ankles, pouting.*

DUNOIS. I know what you think of us, General Joan.

JOAN. Never mind that, Jack. Tell them what you think of me.

DUNOIS. I think that God was on your side; for I have not forgotten how the wind changed, and how our hearts changed when you came; and by my faith I shall never deny that it was in your sign that we conquered.* But I tell you as a soldier that God is no man's daily drudge, and no maid's either. If you are worthy of it He will some-times snatch you out of the jaws of death and set you on your feet again; but that is all: once on your feet you must fight with all your might and all your craft. For He has to be fair to your enemy too:

dont forget that. Well, He set us on our feet through you at Orleans; and the glory of it has carried us through a few good battles here to the coronation. But if we presume on it further, and trust to God to do the work we should do ourselves, we shall be defeated; and serve us right!

JOAN. But—

DUNOIS. Sh! I have not finished. Do not think, any of you, that these victories of ours were won without generalship. King Charles: you have said no word in your proclamations of my part in this campaign; and I make no complaint of that; for the people will run after The Maid and her miracles and not after the Bastard's hard work finding troops for her and feeding them. But I know exactly how much God did for us through The Maid, and how much He left me to do by my own wits; and I tell you that your little hour of miracles is over, and that from this time on he who plays the war game best will win—if the luck is on his side.

JOAN. Ah!* if, if, if, if! If ifs and ans were pots and pans there'd be no need of tinkers.* [*Rising impetuously*] I tell *you*, Bastard, your art of war is no use, because your knights are no good for real fighting. War is only a game to them, like tennis and all their other games: they make rules as to what is fair and what is not fair, and heap armor on themselves and on their poor horses to keep out the arrows; and when they fall they cant get up, and have to wait for their squires to come and lift them to arrange about the ransom with the man that has poked them off their horse. Cant you see that all the like of that is gone by and done with? What use is armor against gunpowder? And if it was, do you think men that are fighting for France and for God will stop to bargain about ransoms, as half your knights live by doing? No: they will fight to win; and they will give up their lives out of their own hand into the hand of God when they go into battle, as I do. Common folks understand this. They cannot afford armor and cannot pay ransoms; but they followed me half naked into the moat and up the ladder and over the wall. With them it is my life or thine, and God defend the right! You may shake your head, Jack; and Bluebeard may twirl his billygoat's beard and cock his nose at me; but remember the day your knights and captains refused to follow me to attack the English at Orleans! You locked the gates to keep me in; and it was the townsfolk and the common people that followed me, and forced the gate, and shewed you the way to fight in earnest.

BLUEBEARD [*offended*] Not content with being Pope Joan, you must be Caesar and Alexander* as well.

THE ARCHBISHOP. Pride will have a fall, Joan.

JOAN. Oh, never mind whether it is pride or not: is it true? is it commonsense?

LA HIRE. It is true. Half of us are afraid of having our handsome noses broken; and the other half are out for paying off their mortgages. Let her have her way, Dunois: she does not know everything; but she has got hold of the right end of the stick. Fighting is not what it was; and those who know least about it often make the best job of it.

DUNOIS. I know all that. I do not fight in the old way: I have learnt the lesson of Agincourt, of Poitiers and Crecy.* I know how many lives any move of mine will cost; and if the move is worth the cost I make it and pay the cost. But Joan never counts the cost at all: she goes ahead and trusts to God: she thinks she has God in her pocket. Up to now she has had the numbers on her side; and she has won. But I know Joan; and I see that some day she will go ahead when she has only ten men to do the work of a hundred. And then she will find that God is on the side of the big battalions. She will be taken by the enemy. And the lucky man that makes the capture will receive sixteen thousand pounds from the Earl of Ouareek.*

JOAN [*flattered*] Sixteen thousand pounds! Eh, laddie,* have they offered that for me? There cannot be so much money in the world.

DUNOIS. There is, in England. And now tell me, all of you, which of you will lift a finger to save Joan once the English have got her? I speak first, for the army. The day after she has been dragged from her horse by a goddam or a Burgundian, and he is not struck dead: the day after she is locked in a dungeon, and the bars and bolts do not fly open at the touch of St Peter's angel: the day when the enemy finds out that she is as vulnerable as I am and not a bit more invincible, she will not be worth the life of a single soldier to us; and I will not risk that life, much as I cherish her as a companion-in-arms.

JOAN. I dont blame you, Jack: you are right. I am not worth one soldier's life if God lets me be beaten; but France may think me worth my ransom after what God has done for her through me.

CHARLES. I tell you I have no money; and this coronation, which is all your fault, has cost me the last farthing I can borrow.

JOAN. The Church is richer than you. I put my trust in the Church.

THE ARCHBISHOP. Woman: they will drag you through the streets, and burn you as a witch.

JOAN [*running to him*] Oh, my lord, do not say that. It is impossible. I a witch!

THE ARCHBISHOP. Peter Cauchon knows his business. The University of Paris* has burnt a woman for saying that what you have done was well done, and according to God.

JOAN [*bewildered*] But why? What sense is there in it? What I have done *is* according to God. They could not burn a woman for speaking the truth.

THE ARCHBISHOP. They did

JOAN. But you know that she was speaking the truth. You would not let them burn me.

THE ARCHBISHOP. How could I prevent them?

JOAN. You would speak in the name of the Church. You are a great prince of the Church. I would go anywhere with your blessing to protect me.

THE ARCHBISHOP. I have no blessing for you while you are proud and disobedient.

JOAN. Oh, why will you go on saying things like that? I am not proud and disobedient. I am a poor girl, and so ignorant that I do not know A from B. How could I be proud? And how can you say that I am disobedient when I always obey my voices, because they come from God.

THE ARCHBISHOP. The voice of God on earth is the voice of the Church Militant; and all the voices that come to you are the echoes of your own wilfulness.

JOAN. It is not true.

THE ARCHBISHOP [*flushing angrily*] You tell the Archbishop in his cathedral that he lies; and yet you say you are not proud and disobedient.

JOAN. I never said you lied. It was you that as good as said my voices lied. When have they ever lied? If you will not believe in them: even if they are only the echoes of my own commonsense, are they not always right? and are not your earthly counsels always wrong?

THE ARCHBISHOP [*indignantly*] It is waste of time admonishing you.

CHARLES. It always comes back to the same thing. She is right; and everyone else is wrong.

THE ARCHBISHOP. Take this as your last warning. If you perish through setting your private judgment above the instructions of your spiritual directors, the Church disowns you, and leaves you to whatever fate your presumption may bring upon you. The Bastard has told you that if you persist in setting up your military conceit above the counsels of your commanders—

DUNOIS [*interposing*] To put it quite exactly, if you attempt to relieve the garrison in Compiègne without the same superiority in numbers you had at Orleans—

THE ARCHBISHOP. The army will disown you, and will not rescue you. And His Majesty the King has told you that the throne has not the means of ransoming you.

CHARLES. Not a penny.

THE ARCHBISHOP. You stand alone: absolutely alone, trusting to your own conceit, your own ignorance, your own headstrong presumption, your own impiety in hiding all these sins under the cloak of a trust in God. When you pass through these doors into the sunlight, the crowd will cheer you. They will bring you their little children and their invalids to heal: they will kiss your hands and feet, and do what they can, poor simple souls, to turn your head, and madden you with the self-confidence that is leading you to your destruction. But you will be none the less alone: they cannot save you. We and we only can stand between you and the stake at which our enemies have burnt that wretched woman in Paris.

JOAN [*her eyes skyward*] I have better friends and better counsel than yours.

THE ARCHBISHOP. I see that I am speaking in vain to a hardened heart. You reject our protection, and are determined to turn us all against you. In future, then, fend for yourself; and if you fail, God have mercy on your soul.

DUNOIS. That is the truth, Joan. Heed it.

JOAN. Where would you all have been now if I had heeded that sort of truth? There is no help, no counsel, in any of you. Yes: I *am* alone on earth: I have always been alone. My father told my brothers to drown me if I would not stay to mind his sheep while France was bleeding to death: France might perish if only our lambs were safe. I thought France would have friends at the court of the king of France; and I find only wolves fighting for pieces of her poor torn body. I thought God would have friends everywhere, because He is the friend of everyone; and in my innocence I believed that you who now cast me out would be like strong towers to keep harm from me. But I am wiser now; and nobody is any the worse for being wiser. Do not think you can frighten me by telling me that I am alone. France is alone; and God is alone; and what is my loneliness before the loneliness of my country and my God? I see now that the loneliness of God is His strength: what would He be if He listened to your jealous little counsels? Well, my loneliness shall be my strength too; it is better to be alone with God: His friendship will not fail me, nor His counsel, nor His love. In His strength I will dare, and dare, and dare, until I die. I will go out now to the common people, and let the love in their eyes comfort me for the hate in yours.* You will all be glad to see me burnt; but if I go through the fire I shall go through it to their hearts for ever and ever. And so, God be with me!

She goes from them. They stare after her in glum silence for a moment. Then Gilles de Rais twirls his beard.

BLUEBEARD. You know, the woman is quite impossible. I dont dislike her, really; but what are you to do with such a character?

DUNOIS. As God is my judge, if she fell into the Loire I would jump in in full armor to fish her out. But if she plays the fool at Compiègne, and gets caught, I must leave her to her doom.

LA HIRE. Then you had better chain me up; for I could follow her to hell when the spirit rises in her like that.

THE ARCHBISHOP. She disturbs my judgment too: there is a dangerous power in her outbursts. But the pit is open at her feet; and for good or evil we cannot turn her from it.

CHARLES. If only she would keep quiet, or go home!

They follow her dispiritedly.

SCENE VI

Rouen, 30th May 1431.* A great stone hall in the castle, arranged for a trial-at-law, but not a trial-by-jury, the court being the Bishop's court with the Inquisition participating: hence there are two raised chairs side by side for the Bishop and the Inquisitor as judges. Rows of chairs radiating from them at an obtuse angle* are for the canons,* the doctors of law and theology, and the Dominican monks, who act as assessors. In the angle is a table for the scribes, with stools. There is also a heavy rough wooden stool for the prisoner. All these are at the inner end of the hall. The further end is open to the courtyard through a row of arches. The court is shielded from the weather by screens and curtains.*

Looking down the great hall from the middle of the inner end, the judicial chairs and scribes' table are to the right. The prisoner's stool is to the left. There are arched doors right and left. It is a fine sunshiny May morning.

Warwick comes in through the arched doorway on the judges' side, followed by his page.

THE PAGE [*pertly*] I suppose your lordship is aware that we have no business here. This is an ecclesiastical court; and we are only the secular arm.

WARWICK. I am aware of that fact. Will it please your impudence to find the Bishop of Beauvais for me, and give him a hint that he can have a word with me here before the trial, if he wishes?

THE PAGE [*going*] Yes, my lord.

WARWICK. And mind you behave yourself. Do not address him as Pious Peter.

THE PAGE. No, my lord. I shall be kind to him, because, when The Maid is brought in, Pious Peter will have to pick a peck of pickled pepper.*

Cauchon enters through the same door with a Dominican monk and a canon, the latter carrying a brief.

THE PAGE. The Right Reverend his lordship the Bishop of Beauvais. And two other reverend gentlemen.

WARWICK. Get out; and see that we are not interrupted.

THE PAGE. Right, my lord [*he vanishes airily*].

CAUCHON. I wish your lordship good-morrow.

WARWICK. Good-morrow to your lordship. Have I had the pleasure of meeting your friends before? I think not.

CAUCHON [*introducing the monk, who is on his right*] This, my lord, is Brother John Lemaître, of the order of St Dominic. He is acting as deputy for the Chief Inquisitor into the evil of heresy in France. Brother John: the Earl of Warwick.

WARWICK. Your Reverence is most welcome. We have no Inquisitor in England, unfortunately; though we miss him greatly, especially on occasions like the present.

The Inquisitor smiles patiently, and bows. He is a mild elderly gentleman, but has evident reserves of authority and firmness.

CAUCHON [*introducing the Canon, who is on his left*] This gentleman is Canon John D'Estivet, of the Chapter of Bayeux.* He is acting as Promoter.

WARWICK. Promoter?

CAUCHON. Prosecutor, you would call him in civil law.

WARWICK. Ah! prosecutor. Quite, quite. I am very glad to make your acquaintance, Canon D'Estivet.

D'Estivet bows. [He is on the young side of middle age, well mannered, but vulpine beneath his veneer].*

WARWICK. May I ask what stage the proceedings have reached? It is now more than nine months since The Maid was captured* at Compiègne by the Burgundians. It is fully four months since I bought her from the Burgundians for a very handsome sum, solely that she might be brought to justice. It is very nearly three months* since I delivered her up to you, my Lord Bishop, as a person suspected of heresy. May I suggest that you are taking a rather unconscionable time to make up your minds about a very plain case? Is this trial never going to end?

THE INQUISITOR [*smiling*] It has not yet begun, my lord.

WARWICK. Not yet begun! Why, you have been at it eleven weeks!*

CAUCHON. We have not been idle, my lord. We have held fifteen examinations of The Maid: six public and nine private.

THE INQUISITOR [*always patiently smiling*] You see, my lord, I have been present at only two of these examinations. They were proceedings of the Bishop's court solely, and not of the Holy Office. I have only just decided to associate myself—that is, to associate the Holy Inquisition—with the Bishop's court. I did not at first think that this was a case of heresy at all. I regarded it as a political case, and The Maid as a prisoner of war. But having now been present at two of the examinations, I must admit that this seems to be one of the gravest cases of heresy within my experience. Therefore everything is now in order, and we proceed to trial this morning. [*He moves towards the judicial chairs*].

CAUCHON. This moment, if your lordship's convenience allows.

WARWICK [*graciously*] Well, that is good news, gentlemen. I will not attempt to conceal from you that our patience was becoming strained.

CAUCHON. So I gathered from the threats of your soldiers to drown those of our people who favor The Maid.

WARWICK. Dear me! At all events their intentions were friendly to *you*, my lord.

CAUCHON [*sternly*] I hope not.* I am determined that the woman shall have a fair hearing. The justice of the Church is not a mockery, my lord.

THE INQUISITOR [*returning*] Never has there been a fairer examination within my experience, my lord. The Maid needs no lawyers to take her part: she will be tried by her most faithful friends, all ardently desirous to save her soul from perdition.

D'ESTIVET. Sir: I am the Promoter; and it has been my painful duty to present the case against the girl; but believe me, I would throw up my case today and hasten to her defence if I did not know that men far my superiors in learning and piety, in eloquence and persuasiveness, have been sent to reason with her, to explain to her the danger she is running, and the ease with which she may avoid it. [*Suddenly bursting into forensic eloquence, to the disgust of Cauchon and the Inquisitor, who have listened to him so far with patronizing approval*] Men have dared* to say that we are acting from hate; but God is our witness that they lie. Have we tortured her? No. Have we ceased to exhort her; to implore her to have pity on herself; to come to the bosom of her Church as an erring but beloved child? Have we—

CAUCHON [*interrupting drily*] Take care, Canon. All that you say is true; but if you make his lordship believe it I will not answer for your life, and hardly for my own.

WARWICK [*deprecating, but by no means denying*] Oh, my lord, you are very hard on us poor English. But we certainly do not share your pious desire to save The Maid: in fact I tell you now plainly that her death is a political necessity which I regret but cannot help. If the Church lets her go—

CAUCHON [*with fierce and menacing pride*] If the Church lets her go, woe to the man, were he the Emperor himself, who dares lay a finger on her! The Church is not subject to political necessity, my lord.

THE INQUISITOR [*interposing smoothly*] You need have no anxiety about the result, my lord. You have an invincible ally in the matter: one who is far more determined than you that she shall burn.

WARWICK. And who is this very convenient partisan, may I ask?

THE INQUISITOR. The Maid herself. Unless you put a gag in her mouth you cannot prevent her from convicting herself ten times over every time she opens it.

D'ESTIVET. That is perfectly true, my lord. My hair bristles on my head when I hear so young a creature utter such blasphemies.

WARWICK. Well, by all means do your best for her if you are quite sure it will be of no avail. [*Looking hard at Cauchon*] I should be sorry to have to act without the blessing of the Church.

CAUCHON [*with a mixture of cynical admiration and contempt*] And yet they say Englishmen are hypocrites! You play for your side, my lord, even at the peril of your soul. I cannot but admire such devotion; but I dare not go so far myself. I fear damnation.*

WARWICK. If we feared anything we could never govern England, my lord. Shall I send your people in to you?

CAUCHON. Yes: it will be very good of your lordship to withdraw and allow the court to assemble.

Warwick turns on his heel, and goes out through the courtyard. Cauchon takes one of the judicial seats; and D'Estivet sits at the scribes' table, studying his brief.

CAUCHON [*casually, as he makes himself comfortable*] What scoundrels these English nobles are!

THE INQUISITOR [*taking the other judicial chair on Cauchon's left*] All secular power makes men scoundrels. They are not trained for the work; and they have not the Apostolic Succession. Our own nobles are just as bad.

The Bishop's assessors hurry into the hall, headed by Chaplain de Stogumber and Canon de Courcelles,* a young priest of 30. The scribes sit at the table, leaving a chair vacant opposite D'Estivet. Some of the assessors take their seats: others stand chatting, waiting for the proceedings to begin formally.* De Stogumber, aggrieved and obstinate, will not take his seat: neither will the Canon, who stands on his right.

CAUCHON. Good morning, Master de Stogumber. [*To the Inquisitor*] Chaplain to the Cardinal of England.

THE CHAPLAIN [*correcting him*] Of Winchester, my lord. I have to make a protest, my lord.

CAUCHON. You make a great many.

THE CHAPLAIN. I am not without support, my lord. Here is Master de Courcelles, Canon of Paris, who associates himself with me in my protest.

CAUCHON. Well, what is the matter?

THE CHAPLAIN [*sulkily*] Speak you, Master de Courcelles, since I do not seem to enjoy his lordship's confidence. [*He sits down in dudgeon* next to Cauchon, on his right*].

COURCELLES. My lord: we have been at great pains to draw up an indictment of The Maid on sixty-four counts. We are now told that they have been reduced, without consulting us.

THE INQUISITOR. Master de Courcelles: I am the culprit.* I am overwhelmed with admiration for the zeal displayed in your sixty-four counts; but in accusing a heretic, as in other things, enough is enough. Also you must remember that all the members of the court are not so subtle and profound as you, and that some of your very great learning might appear to them to be very great nonsense.* Therefore I have thought it well to have your sixty-four articles cut down to twelve—*

COURCELLES [*thunderstruck*] Twelve!!!

THE INQUISITOR. Twelve will, believe me, be quite enough for your purpose.

THE CHAPLAIN. But some of the most important points have been reduced almost to nothing. For instance, The Maid has actually declared that the blessed saints Margaret and Catherine, and the holy Archangel Michael, spoke to her in French.* That is a vital point.

THE INQUISITOR. You think, doubtless, that they should have spoken in Latin?

CAUCHON. No: he thinks they should have spoken in English.

THE CHAPLAIN. Naturally, my lord.

THE INQUISITOR. Well, as we are all here agreed, I think, that these voices of The Maid are the voices of evil spirits tempting her to her damnation, it would not be very courteous to you, Master de Stogumber, or to the King of England, to assume that English is the devil's native language. So let it pass. The matter is not wholly omitted from the twelve articles. Pray take your places, gentlemen; and let us proceed to business.

All who have not taken their seats, do so.

THE CHAPLAIN. Well, I protest. That is all.

COURCELLES. I think it hard that all our work should go for nothing. It is only another example of the diabolical influence which this woman exercises over the court. [*He takes his chair, which is on the Chaplain's right*].

CAUCHON. Do you suggest that I am under diabolical influence?

COURCELLES. I suggest nothing, my lord. But it seems to me that there is a conspiracy here to hush up the fact that The Maid stole the Bishop of Senlis's horse.*

CAUCHON [*keeping his temper with difficulty*] This is not a police court. Are we to waste our time on such rubbish?

COURCELLES [*rising, shocked*] My lord: do you call the Bishop's horse rubbish?

THE INQUISITOR [*blandly*] Master de Courcelles: The Maid alleges that she paid handsomely for the Bishop's horse, and that if he did not get the money the fault was not hers. As that may be true, the point is one on which The Maid may well be acquitted.

COURCELLES. Yes, if it were an ordinary horse. But the Bishop's horse! how can she be acquitted for that? [*He sits down again, bewildered and discouraged*].

THE INQUISITOR. I submit to you, with great respect, that if we persist in trying The Maid on trumpery issues on which we may have to declare her innocent, she may escape us on the great main issue of heresy, on which she seems so far to insist on her own guilt. I will ask you, therefore, to say nothing, when The Maid is brought before us, of these stealings of horses, and dancings round fairy trees with the village children, and prayings at haunted wells, and a dozen other things which you were diligently inquiring into until my arrival. There is not a village girl in France against whom you could not prove such things: they all dance round haunted trees, and pray at magic wells.* Some of them would steal the Pope's horse if they got the chance. Heresy, gentlemen, heresy is the charge we have to try. The detection and suppression of heresy is my peculiar business: I am here as an inquisitor, not as an ordinary magistrate. Stick to the heresy, gentlemen; and leave the other matters alone.

CAUCHON. I may say that we have sent to the girl's village to make inquiries about her? and there is practically nothing serious against her.

THE CHAPLAIN ⎰ [*rising and*   ⎰ Nothing serious, my lord—
COURCELLES   ⎱ *clamoring*   ⎱ What! The fairy tree not—
                 together]

CAUCHON [*out of patience*] Be silent, gentlemen; or speak one at a time.

Courcelles collapses into his chair, intimidated.

THE CHAPLAIN [*sulkily resuming his seat*] That is what The Maid said to us last Friday.

CAUCHON. I wish you had followed her counsel, sir. When I say nothing serious, I mean nothing that men of sufficiently large mind to conduct an inquiry like this would consider serious. I agree with my colleague the Inquisitor that it is on the count of heresy that we must proceed.

LADVENU* [*a young but ascetically fine-drawn Dominican who is sitting next Courcelles, on his right*] But is there any great harm in the girl's heresy? Is it not merely her simplicity? Many saints have said as much as Joan.

THE INQUISITOR [*dropping his blandness and speaking very gravely*] Brother Martin: if you had seen what I have seen of heresy, you would not think it a light thing even in its most apparently harmless and even lovable and pious origins. Heresy begins* with people who are to all appearance better than their neighbors. A gentle and pious

girl, or a young man who has obeyed the command of our Lord by
giving all his riches to the poor, and putting on the garb of poverty,
the life of austerity, and the rule of humility and charity, may be the
founder of a heresy that will wreck both Church and Empire if not
ruthlessly stamped out in time. The records of the holy Inquisition
are full of histories we dare not give to the world, because they are
beyond the belief of honest men and innocent women; yet they all
began* with saintly simpletons. I have seen this again and again.
Mark what I say: the woman who quarrels with her clothes, and puts
on the dress of a man, is like the man who throws off his fur gown and
dresses like John the Baptist: they are followed, as surely as the night
follows the day, by bands of wild women and men who refuse to wear
any clothes at all. When maids will neither marry nor take regular
vows, and men reject marriage and exalt their lusts into divine inspirations, then, as surely as the summer follows the spring, they begin
with polygamy, and end by incest. Heresy at first seems innocent and
even laudable; but it ends in such a monstrous horror of unnatural
wickedness that the most tender-hearted among you, if you saw it at
work as I have seen it, would clamor against the mercy of the Church
in dealing with it. For two hundred years the Holy Office has striven
with these diabolical madnesses; and it knows that they begin always
by vain and ignorant persons setting up their own judgment against
the Church, and taking it upon themselves to be the interpreters of
God's will. You must not fall into the common error of mistaking
these simpletons for liars and hypocrites. They believe honestly and
sincerely that their diabolical inspiration is divine. Therefore you
must be on your guard against your natural compassion.* You are all,
I hope, merciful men: how else could you have devoted your lives to
the service of our gentle Savior? You are going to see before you
a young girl, pious and chaste; for I must tell you, gentlemen, that
the things said of her by our English friends are supported by no
evidence,* whilst there is abundant testimony that her excesses have
been excesses of religion and charity and not of worldliness and wan-
tonness. This girl* is not one of those whose hard features are the
sign of hard hearts, and whose brazen looks and lewd demeanor condemn them before they are accused. The devilish pride that has led
her into her present peril has left no mark on her countenance.
Strange as it may seem to you, it has even left no mark on her character outside those special matters in which she is proud; so that you
will see a diabolical pride and a natural humility seated side by side
in the selfsame soul. Therefore be on your guard. God forbid that

I should tell you to harden your hearts; for her punishment if we condemn her will be so cruel that we should forfeit our own hope of divine mercy were there one grain of malice against her in our hearts. But if you hate cruelty—and if any man here does not hate it I command him on his soul's salvation to quit this holy court—I say, if you hate cruelty, remember that nothing is so cruel in its consequences as the toleration of heresy. Remember also that no court of law can be so cruel as the common people are to those whom they suspect of heresy. The heretic in the hands of the Holy Office is safe from violence, is assured of a fair trial, and cannot suffer death, even when guilty, if repentance follows sin. Innumerable lives* of heretics have been saved because the Holy Office has taken them out of the hands of the people, and because the people have yielded them up, knowing that the Holy Office would deal with them. Before the Holy Inquisition existed, and even now when its officers are not within reach, the unfortunate wretch suspected of heresy, perhaps quite ignorantly and unjustly, is stoned, torn in pieces, drowned, burned in his house with all his innocent children, without a trial, unshriven,* unburied save as a dog is buried: all of them deeds hateful to God and most cruel to man. Gentlemen: I am compassionate by nature as well as by my profession; and though the work I have to do may seem cruel to those who do not know how much more cruel it would be to leave it undone, I would go to the stake myself sooner than do it if I did not know its righteousness, its necessity, its essential mercy. I ask you to address yourself to this trial in that conviction. Anger is a bad counsellor: cast out anger. Pity is sometimes worse: cast out pity. But do not cast out mercy. Remember only that justice comes first. Have you anything to say, my lord, before we proceed to trial?

CAUCHON. You have spoken for me, and spoken better than I could. I do not see how any sane man could disagree with a word that has fallen from you. But this I will add. The crude heresies of which you have told us are horrible; but their horror is like that of the black death:* they rage for a while and then die out, because sound and sensible men will not under any incitement be reconciled to nakedness and incest and polygamy and the like. But we are confronted today throughout Europe with a heresy that is spreading among men not weak in mind nor diseased in brain: nay, the stronger the mind, the more obstinate the heretic. It is neither discredited by fantastic extremes nor corrupted by the common lusts of the flesh; but it, too, sets up the private judgment of the single erring mortal against the considered wisdom and experience of the Church. The mighty structure of Catholic Christendom will never be shaken by naked madmen or by the sins of Moab and Ammon.* But it may be betrayed from within, and brought to barbarous ruin and desolation, by this arch heresy which the English Commander calls Protestantism.

THE ASSESSORS [*whispering*] Protestantism! What was that? What does the Bishop mean? Is it a new heresy? The English Commander, he said. Did *you* ever hear of Protestantism? etc., etc.

CAUCHON [*continuing*] And that reminds me. What provision has the Earl of Warwick made for the defence of the secular arm should The Maid prove obdurate, and the people be moved to pity her?

THE CHAPLAIN. Have no fear on that score, my lord. The noble earl has eight hundred men-at-arms at the gates. She will not slip through our English fingers even if the whole city be on her side.

CAUCHON [*revolted*] Will you not add, God grant that she repent and purge her sin?

THE CHAPLAIN. That does not seem to me to be consistent; but of course I agree with your lordship.

CAUCHON [*giving him up with a shrug of contempt*] The court sits.

THE INQUISITOR. Let the accused be brought in.

LADVENU [*calling*] The accused. Let her be brought in.

Joan, chained by the ankles, is brought in through the arched door behind the prisoner's stool by a guard of English soldiers. With them is the Executioner and his assistants. They lead her to the prisoner's stool, and place themselves behind it after taking off her chain. She wears a page's black suit. Her long imprisonment and the strain of the examinations which have preceded the trial have left their mark on her; but her vitality still holds: she confronts the court unabashed, without a trace of the awe which their formal solemnity seems to require for the complete success of its impressiveness.

THE INQUISITOR [*kindly*] Sit down, Joan. [*She sits on the prisoner's stool*]. You look very pale today. Are you not well?

JOAN. Thank you kindly: I am well enough. But the Bishop sent me some carp;* and it made me ill.

CAUCHON. I am sorry. I told them to see that it was fresh.

JOAN. You meant to be good to me, I know; but it is a fish that does not agree with me. The English thought you were trying to poison me—

CAUCHON   } [*together*] {   What!
THE CHAPLAIN }   {   No, my lord.

JOAN [*continuing*] They are determined that I shall be burnt as a witch; and they sent their doctor to cure me; but he was forbidden to bleed me because the silly people* believe that a witch's witchery leaves her if she is bled;* so he only called me filthy names. Why do you leave me in the hands of the English? I should be in the hands of the Church. And why must I be chained by the feet* to a log of wood? Are you afraid I will fly away?

D'ESTIVET [*harshly*] Woman: it is not for you to question the court: it is for us to question you.

COURCELLES. When you were left unchained, did you not try to escape by jumping from a tower sixty feet high? If you cannot fly like a witch, how is it that you are still alive?

JOAN. I suppose because the tower was not so high then. It has grown higher every day since you began asking me questions about it.

D'ESTIVET. Why did you jump from the tower?

JOAN. How do you know that I jumped?

D'ESTIVET. You were found lying in the moat. Why did you leave the tower?

JOAN. Why would anybody leave a prison if they could get out?

D'ESTIVET. You tried to escape?

JOAN. Of course I did; and not for the first time either. If you leave the door of the cage open the bird will fly out.

D'ESTIVET [*rising*] That is a confession of heresy. I call the attention of the court to it.

JOAN. Heresy, he calls it! Am I a heretic because I try to escape from prison?

D'ESTIVET. Assuredly, if you are in the hands of the Church, and you wilfully take yourself out of its hands, you are deserting the Church; and that is heresy.

JOAN. It is great nonsense.* Nobody could be such a fool as to think that.

D'ESTIVET. You hear, my lord, how I am reviled in the execution of my duty by this woman. [*He sits down indignantly*].

CAUCHON. I have warned you before, Joan, that you are doing yourself no good by these pert answers.*

JOAN. But you will not talk sense to me. I am reasonable if you will be reasonable.

THE INQUISITOR [*interposing*] This is not yet in order. You forget, Master Promoter, that the proceedings have not been formally opened. The time for questions is after she has sworn on the Gospels to tell us the whole truth.

JOAN. You say this to me every time. I have said again and again that I will tell you all that concerns this trial. But I cannot tell you the whole truth: God does not allow the whole truth to be told. You do not understand it when I tell it. It is an old saying that he who tells too much truth is sure to be hanged. I am weary of this argument:* we have been over it nine times already. I have sworn as much as I will swear; and I will swear no more.

COURCELLES. My lord: she should be put to the torture.*

THE INQUISITOR. You hear, Joan? That is what happens to the obdurate. Think before you answer. Has she been shewn the instruments?

THE EXECUTIONER. They are ready, my lord. She has seen them.

JOAN. If you tear me limb from limb until you separate my soul from my body you will get nothing out of me beyond what I have told you. What more is there to tell that you could understand? Besides, I cannot bear to be hurt; and if you hurt me I will say anything you like to stop the pain. But I will take it all back afterwards; so what is the use of it?*

LADVENU. There is much in that. We should proceed mercifully.

COURCELLES. But the torture is customary.

THE INQUISITOR. It must not be applied wantonly. If the accused will confess voluntarily, then its use cannot be justified.

COURCELLES. But this is unusual and irregular. She refuses to take the oath.

LADVENU [*disgusted*] Do you want to torture the girl for the mere pleasure of it?

COURCELLES [*bewildered*] But it is not a pleasure.* It is the law. It is customary. It is always done.

THE INQUISITOR. That is not so, Master, except when the inquiries are carried on by people who do not know their legal business.

COURCELLES. But the woman is a heretic. I assure you it is always done.

CAUCHON [*decisively*] It will not be done today if it is not necessary. Let there be an end of this. I will not have it said that we proceeded on forced confessions. We have sent our best preachers and doctors to this woman to exhort and implore her to save her soul and body from the fire: we shall not now send the executioner to thrust her into it.

COURCELLES. Your lordship is merciful, of course. But it is a great responsibility to depart from the usual practice.

JOAN. Thou art a rare noodle, Master.* Do what was done last time is thy rule, eh?

COURCELLES [*rising*] Thou wanton: dost thou dare call me noodle?

THE INQUISITOR. Patience, Master, patience: I fear you will soon be only too terribly avenged.

COURCELLES [*mutters*] Noodle indeed! [*He sits down, much discontented*].

THE INQUISITOR. Meanwhile, let us not be moved by the rough side of a shepherd lass's tongue.

JOAN. Nay: I am no shepherd lass,* though I have helped with the sheep like anyone else. I will do a lady's work in the house—spin or weave—against any woman in Rouen.

THE INQUISITOR. This is not a time for vanity, Joan. You stand in great peril.

JOAN. I know it: have I not been punished for my vanity? If I had not worn my cloth of gold surcoat in battle like a fool, that Burgundian soldier* would never have pulled me backwards off my horse; and I should not have been here.

THE CHAPLAIN. If you are so clever at woman's work why do you not stay at home and do it?

JOAN.   There are plenty of other women to do it; but there is nobody to do my work.

CAUCHON.   Come! we are wasting time on trifles. Joan: I am going to put a most solemn question to you. Take care how you answer; for your life and salvation are at stake on it. Will you for all you have said and done, be it good or bad, accept the judgment of God's Church on earth? More especially as to the acts and words that are imputed to you in this trial by the Promoter here, will you submit your case to the inspired interpretation of the Church Militant?

JOAN.   I am a faithful child of the Church. I will obey the Church—

CAUCHON [*hopefully leaning forward*] You will?

JOAN.   —provided it does not command anything impossible.

Cauchon sinks back in his chair with a heavy sigh. The Inquisitor purses his lips and frowns. Ladvenu shakes his head pitifully.

D'ESTIVET.   She imputes to the Church the error and folly of commanding the impossible.

JOAN.   If you command me to declare that all that I have done and said, and all the visions and revelations I have had, were not from God, then that is impossible: I will not declare it for anything in the world. What God made me do I will never go back on; and what He has commanded or shall command I will not fail to do in spite of any man alive. That is what I mean by impossible. And in case the Church should bid me do anything contrary to the command I have from God, I will not consent to it, no matter what it may be.

THE ASSESSORS [*shocked and indignant*] Oh! The Church contrary to God! What do you say now? Flat heresy. This is beyond everything, etc., etc.

D'ESTIVET [*throwing down his brief*] My lord: do you need anything more than this?

CAUCHON.   Woman: you have said enough to burn ten heretics.* Will you not be warned? Will you not understand?

THE INQUISITOR.   If the Church Militant tells you that your revelations and visions are sent by the devil to tempt you to your damnation, will you not believe that the Church is wiser than you?

JOAN.   I believe that God is wiser than I; and it is His commands that I will do. All the things that you call my crimes have come to me by the command of God. I say that I have done them by the order of God: it is impossible for me to say anything else. If any Churchman says the contrary I shall not mind him: I shall mind God alone, whose command I always follow.

LADVENU [*pleading with her urgently*] You do not know what you are saying, child. Do you want to kill yourself? Listen. Do you not believe that you are subject to the Church of God on earth?

JOAN. Yes. When have I ever denied it?

LADVENU. Good. That means, does it not, that you are subject to our Lord the Pope, to the cardinals, the archbishops, and the bishops for whom his lordship stands here today?

JOAN. God must be served first.

D'ESTIVET. Then your voices command you not to submit yourself to the Church Militant?

JOAN. My voices do not tell me to disobey the Church; but God must be served first.

CAUCHON. And you, and not the Church, are to be the judge?

JOAN. What other judgment can I judge by but my own?

THE ASSESSORS [*scandalized*] Oh! [*They cannot find words*].

CAUCHON. Out of your own mouth you have condemned yourself. We have striven for your salvation to the verge of sinning ourselves: we have opened the door to you again and again; and you have shut it in our faces and in the face of God. Dare you pretend, after what you have said, that you are in a state of grace?

JOAN. If I am not, may God bring me to it: if I am, may God keep me in it!*

LADVENU. That is a very good reply, my lord.

COURCELLES. Were you in a state of grace when you stole the Bishop's horse?

CAUCHON [*rising in a fury*] Oh, devil take the Bishop's horse and you too! We are here to try a case of heresy; and no sooner do we come to the root of the matter than we are thrown back by idiots who understand nothing but horses. [*Trembling with rage, he forces himself to sit down*].

THE INQUISITOR. Gentlemen, gentlemen: in clinging to these small issues you are The Maid's best advocates. I am not surprised that his lordship has lost patience with you. What does the Promoter say? Does he press these trumpery matters?

D'ESTIVET. I am bound by my office to press everything; but when the woman confesses a heresy that must bring upon her the doom of excommunication, of what consequence is it that she has been guilty also of offences which expose her to minor penances? I share the impatience* of his lordship as to these minor charges. Only, with great respect, I must emphasize the gravity of two very horrible and blasphemous crimes which she does not deny. First, she has intercourse with evil spirits, and is therefore a sorceress. Second, she wears men's clothes, which is indecent, unnatural, and abominable; and in spite of our most earnest remonstrances and entreaties, she will not change them even to receive the sacrament.

JOAN. Is the blessed St Catherine an evil spirit? Is St Margaret? Is Michael the Archangel?

COURCELLES. How do you know that the spirit which appears to you is an archangel? Does he not appear to you as a naked man?

JOAN. Do you think God cannot afford clothes for him?*

The assessors cannot help smiling, especially as the joke is against Courcelles.

LADVENU. Well answered, Joan.

THE INQUISITOR. It is, in effect, well answered. But no evil spirit would be so simple as to appear to a young girl in a guise that would scandalize her when he meant her to take him for a messenger from the Most High? Joan: the Church instructs you that these apparitions are demons seeking your soul's perdition. Do you accept the instruction of the Church?

JOAN. I accept the messenger of God. How could any faithful believer in the Church refuse him?

CAUCHON. Wretched woman: again I ask you, do you know what you are saying?

THE INQUISITOR. You wrestle in vain with the devil for her soul, my lord: she will not be saved. Now as to this matter of the man's dress. For the last time, will you put off that impudent attire, and dress as becomes your sex?

JOAN. I will not.

D'ESTIVET [*pouncing*] The sin of disobedience, my lord.

JOAN [*distressed*] But my voices tell me I must dress as a soldier.

LADVENU. Joan, Joan: does not that prove to you that the voices are the voices of evil spirits? Can you suggest to us one good reason why an angel of God should give you such shameless advice?

JOAN. Why, yes: what can be plainer commonsense?* I was a soldier living among soldiers. I am a prisoner guarded by soldiers. If I were to dress as a woman they would think of me as a woman; and then what would become of me? If I dress as a soldier they think of me as a soldier, and I can live with them as I do at home with my brothers.* That is why St Catherine tells me I must not dress as a woman until she gives me leave.

COURCELLES. When will she give you leave?

JOAN. When you take me out of the hands of the English soldiers. I have told you that I should be in the hands of the Church, and not left night and day with four soldiers of the Earl of Warwick. Do you want me to live with them in petticoats?

LADVENU. My lord: what she says is, God knows, very wrong and shocking; but there is a grain of worldly sense in it such as might impose on a simple village maiden.

JOAN. If we were as simple in the village as you are in your courts and palaces, there would soon be no wheat to make bread for you.

CAUCHON. That is the thanks you get for trying to save her, Brother Martin.

LADVENU. Joan: we are all trying to save you.* His lordship is trying to save you. The Inquisitor could not be more just to you if you were his own daughter. But you are blinded by a terrible pride and self-sufficiency.

JOAN. Why do you say that? I have said nothing wrong. I cannot understand.

THE INQUISITOR. The blessed St Athanasius has laid it down in his creed that those who cannot understand are damned.* It is not enough to be simple. It is not enough even to be what simple people call good. The simplicity of a darkened mind is no better than the simplicity of a beast.

JOAN. There is great wisdom in the simplicity of a beast, let me tell you; and sometimes great foolishness in the wisdom of scholars.

LADVENU. We know that, Joan: we are not so foolish as you think us. Try to resist the temptation to make pert replies to us. Do you see that man who stands behind you [*he indicates the Executioner*]?

JOAN [*turning and looking at the man*] Your torturer? But the Bishop said I was not to be tortured.

LADVENU. You are not to be tortured because you have confessed everything that is necessary to your condemnation. That man is not only the torturer: he is also the Executioner. Executioner: let The Maid hear your answers to my questions. Are you prepared for the burning of a heretic this day?

THE EXECUTIONER. Yes, Master.

LADVENU. Is the stake ready?

THE EXECUTIONER. It is. In the market-place. The English have built it too high for me to get near her and make the death easier. It will be a cruel death.

JOAN [*horrified*] But you are not going to burn me now?

THE INQUISITOR. You realize it at last.

LADVENU. There are eight hundred English soldiers waiting to take you to the market-place the moment the sentence of excommunication has passed the lips of your judges. You are within a few short moments of that doom.

JOAN [*looking round desperately for rescue*] Oh God!

LADVENU. Do not despair, Joan. The Church is merciful. You can save yourself.

JOAN [*hopefully*] Yes: my voices promised me I should not be burnt. St Catherine bade me be bold.

CAUCHON. Woman: are you quite mad?* Do you not yet see that your voices have deceived you?

JOAN. Oh no: that is impossible.

CAUCHON. Impossible! They have led you straight to your excommunication, and to the stake which is there waiting for you.

LADVENU [*pressing the point hard*] Have they kept a single promise*
to you since you were taken at Compiègne? The devil has betrayed
you. The Church holds out its arms to you.

JOAN [*despairing*] Oh, it is true: it is true: my voices have deceived me.
I have been mocked by devils: my faith is broken. I have dared and
dared; but only a fool will walk into a fire: God, who gave me my
commonsense, cannot will me to do that.

LADVENU. Now God be praised that He has saved you at the eleventh
hour! [*He hurries to the vacant seat at the scribes' table, and snatches
a sheet of paper, on which he sets to work writing eagerly*].

CAUCHON. Amen!

JOAN. What must I do?

CAUCHON. You must sign a solemn recantation of your heresy.

JOAN. Sign? That means to write my name. I cannot write.

CAUCHON. You have signed many letters before.

JOAN. Yes; but someone held my hand and guided the pen. I can make
my mark.

THE CHAPLAIN [*who has been listening with growing alarm and indignation*] My lord: do you mean that you are going to allow this woman
to escape us?

THE INQUISITOR. The law must take its course, Master de Stogumber.
And you know the law.

THE CHAPLAIN [*rising, purple with fury*] I know that there is no faith
in a Frenchman. [*Tumult, which he shouts down*]. I know what my
lord the Cardinal of Winchester will say when he hears of this. I know
what the Earl of Warwick will do when he learns that you intend to
betray him. There are eight hundred men at the gate who will see
that this abominable witch is burnt in spite of your teeth.

THE ASSESSORS [*meanwhile*] What is this? What did he say? He
accuses us of treachery! This is past bearing. No faith in a Frenchman!
Did you hear that? This is an intolerable fellow. Who is he? Is this
what English Churchmen are like? He must be mad or drunk, etc., etc.

THE INQUISITOR [*rising*] Silence, pray! Gentlemen: pray silence!
Master Chaplain: bethink you a moment of your holy office: of what
you are, and where you are. I direct you to sit down.

THE CHAPLAIN [*folding his arms doggedly, his face working convulsively*] I will NOT sit down.

CAUCHON. Master Inquisitor: this man has called me a traitor to my face before now.

THE CHAPLAIN. So you are a traitor. You are all traitors. You have been doing nothing but begging this damnable witch on your knees to recant all through this trial.

THE INQUISITOR [*placidly resuming his seat*] If you will not sit, you must stand: that is all.

THE CHAPLAIN. I will NOT stand [*he flings himself back into his chair**].

LADVENU [*rising with the paper in his hand*] My lord: here is the form of recantation for The Maid to sign.

CAUCHON. Read it to her.

JOAN. Do not trouble. I will sign it.

THE INQUISITOR. Woman: you must know what you are putting your hand to. Read it to her, Brother Martin. And let all be silent.

LADVENU [*reading quietly*] 'I, Joan, commonly called The Maid, a miserable sinner, do confess that I have most grievously sinned in the following articles. I have pretended to have revelations from God and the angels and the blessed saints, and perversely rejected the Church's warnings that these were temptations by demons. I have blasphemed abominably by wearing an immodest dress, contrary to the Holy Scripture and the canons of the Church. Also I have clipped my hair in the style of a man, and, against all the duties which have made my sex specially acceptable in heaven, have taken up the sword, even to the shedding of human blood, inciting men to slay each other, invoking evil spirits to delude them, and stubbornly and most blasphemously imputing these sins to Almighty God. I confess to the sin of sedition, to the sin of idolatry, to the sin of disobedience, to the sin of pride, and to the sin of heresy. All of which sins I now renounce and abjure and depart from, humbly thanking you Doctors and Masters who have brought me back to the truth and into the grace of our Lord. And I will never return to my errors, but will remain in communion with our Holy Church and in obedience to our Holy Father the Pope of Rome. All this I swear by God Almighty and the Holy Gospels, in witness whereto I sign my name to this recantation.'

THE INQUISITOR. You understand this, Joan?

JOAN [*listless*] It is plain enough, sir.

THE INQUISITOR. And it is true?

JOAN. It may be true. If it were not true, the fire would not be ready for me in the market-place.

LADVENU [*taking up his pen and a book, and going to her quickly lest she should compromise herself again*] Come, child: let me guide your hand. Take the pen. [*She does so; and they begin to write, using the book as a desk*] J.E.H.A.N.E. So. Now make your mark by yourself.

JOAN [*makes her mark, and gives him back the pen, tormented by the rebellion of her soul against her mind and body*] There!*

LADVENU [*replacing the pen on the table, and handing the recantation to Cauchon with a reverence*] Praise be to God, my brothers, the lamb has returned to the flock; and the shepherd rejoices in her more than in ninety and nine just persons.* [*He returns to his seat*].

THE INQUISITOR [*taking the paper from Cauchon*] We declare thee by this act set free from the danger of excommunication in which thou stoodest. [*He throws the paper down to the table*].

JOAN. I thank you.

THE INQUISITOR. But because thou hast sinned most presumptuously against God and the Holy Church, and that thou mayst repent thy errors in solitary contemplation, and be shielded from all temptation to return to them, we, for the good of thy soul, and for a penance that may wipe out thy sins and bring thee finally unspotted to the throne of grace, do condemn thee to eat the bread of sorrow and drink the water of affliction to the end of thy earthly days in perpetual imprisonment.

JOAN [*rising in consternation and terrible anger*] Perpetual imprisonment! Am I not then to be set free?

LADVENU [*mildly shocked*] Set free, child, after such wickedness as yours! What are you dreaming of?

JOAN. Give me that writing. [*She rushes to the table; snatches up the paper; and tears it into fragments*] Light your fire: do you think I dread it as much as the life of a rat in a hole? My voices were right.*

LADVENU. Joan! Joan!

JOAN. Yes: they told me you were fools [*the word gives great offence*], and that I was not to listen to your fine words nor trust to your charity. You promised me my life; but you lied [*indignant exclamations*]. You think that life is nothing but not being stone dead. It is not the bread and water I fear: I can live on bread: when have I asked for more? It is no hardship to drink water if the water be clean. Bread has no sorrow for me, and water no affliction. But to shut me from the light of the sky and the sight of the fields and flowers; to chain my feet so that I can never again ride with the soldiers nor climb the hills; to make me breathe foul damp darkness, and keep from me everything that brings me back to the love of God when your wickedness and foolishness tempt me to hate Him: all this is worse than the furnace in the Bible that was heated seven times.* I could do without my warhorse; I could drag about in a skirt; I could let the banners and the trumpets and the knights and soldiers pass me and leave me behind as they leave the other women, if only I could still hear the wind in the trees, the larks in the sunshine, the young lambs crying through the healthy frost, and the blessed blessed church bells that send my angel voices floating to me on the wind. But without these things I cannot live; and by your wanting to take them away from me, or from any human creature, I know that your counsel is of the devil, and that mine is of God.

THE ASSESSORS [*in great commotion*] Blasphemy! blasphemy! She is possessed. She said our counsel was of the devil. And hers of God. Monstrous! The devil is in our midst, etc., etc.

D'ESTIVET [*shouting above the din*] She is a relapsed heretic, obstinate, incorrigible, and altogether unworthy of the mercy we have shewn her. I call for her excommunication.

THE CHAPLAIN [*to the Executioner*] Light your fire, man. To the stake with her.

The Executioner and his assistants hurry out through the courtyard.

LADVENU. You wicked girl: if your counsel were of God would He not deliver you?

JOAN. His ways are not your ways. He wills that I go through the fire to His bosom; for I am His child, and you are not fit that I should live among you. That is my last word to you.

The soldiers seize her.

CAUCHON [*rising*] Not yet.

They wait. There is a dead silence. Cauchon turns to the Inquisitor with an inquiring look. The Inquisitor nods affirmatively. They rise solemnly, and intone the sentence antiphonally.*

CAUCHON. We decree that thou art a relapsed heretic.

THE INQUISITOR. Cast out from the unity of the Church.

CAUCHON. Sundered from her body.

THE INQUISITOR. Infected with the leprosy* of heresy.

CAUCHON. A member of Satan.

THE INQUISITOR. We declare that thou must be excommunicate.

CAUCHON. And now we do cast thee out, segregate thee, and abandon thee to the secular power.

THE INQUISITOR. Admonishing the same secular power that it moderate its judgment of thee in respect of death and division of the limbs.* [*He resumes his seat*].

CAUCHON. And if any true sign of penitence appear in thee, to permit our Brother Martin to administer to thee the sacrament of penance.*

THE CHAPLAIN. Into the fire with the witch [*he rushes at her, and helps the soldiers to push her out*].

Joan is taken away through the courtyard. The assessors rise in disorder, and follow the soldiers, except Ladvenu, who has hidden his face in his hands.

CAUCHON [*rising again in the act of sitting down*] No, no: this is irregular. The representative of the secular arm should be here to receive her from us.

THE INQUISITOR [*also on his feet again*] That man is an incorrigible fool.

CAUCHON. Brother Martin: see that everything is done in order.

LADVENU. My place is at her side, my lord. You must exercise your own authority. [*He hurries out*].

CAUCHON. These English are impossible: they will thrust her straight into the fire. Look!

He points to the courtyard, in which the glow and flicker of fire can now be seen reddening the May daylight. Only the Bishop and the Inquisitor are left in the court.

CAUCHON [*turning to go*] We must stop that.

THE INQUISITOR [*calmly*] Yes; but not too fast, my lord.

CAUCHON [*halting*] But there is not a moment to lose.

THE INQUISITOR. We have proceeded in perfect order. If the English*
choose to put themselves in the wrong, it is not our business to put
them in the right. A flaw in the procedure may be useful later on: one
never knows. And the sooner it is over, the better for that poor girl.

CAUCHON [*relaxing*] That is true. But I suppose we must see this
dreadful thing through.

THE INQUISITOR. One gets used to it. Habit is everything. I am
accustomed to the fire: it is soon over. But it is a terrible thing to see
a young and innocent creature crushed between these mighty forces,
the Church and the Law.

CAUCHON. You call her innocent!

THE INQUISITOR. Oh, quite innocent. What does she know of the
Church and the Law? She did not understand a word we were saying.
It is the ignorant who suffer. Come, or we shall be late for the end.

CAUCHON [*going with him*] I shall not be sorry if we are: I am not so
accustomed as you.

They are going out when Warwick comes in, meeting them.

WARWICK. Oh, I am intruding. I thought it was all over. [*He makes
a feint of retiring*].

CAUCHON. Do not go, my lord. It is all over.

THE INQUISITOR. The execution is not in our hands, my lord; but it
is desirable that we should witness the end. So by your leave—[*He
bows, and goes out through the courtyard*].

CAUCHON. There is some doubt whether your people have observed
the forms of law, my lord.

WARWICK. I am told that there is some doubt whether your authority
runs in this city, my lord. It is not in your diocese. However, if you
will answer for that I will answer for the rest.

CAUCHON. It is to God that we both must answer. Good morning,
my lord.

WARWICK. My lord: good morning.

They look at one another for a moment with unconcealed hostility. Then Cauchon follows the Inquisitor out. Warwick looks round. Finding himself alone, he calls for attendance.

WARWICK. Hallo: some attendance here! [*Silence*]. Hallo, there! [*Silence*]. Hallo! Brian, you young blackguard, where are you? [*Silence*]. Guard! [*Silence*]. They have all gone to see the burning: even that child.

The silence is broken by someone frantically howling and sobbing.

WARWICK. What in the devil's name—?

The Chaplain staggers in from the courtyard like a demented creature, his face streaming with tears, making the piteous sounds that Warwick has heard. He stumbles to the prisoner's stool, and throws himself upon it with heartrending sobs.

WARWICK [*going to him and patting him on the shoulder*] What is it, Master John? What is the matter?

THE CHAPLAIN [*clutching at his hands*] My lord, my lord: for Christ's sake pray for my wretched guilty soul.

WARWICK [*soothing him*] Yes, yes: of course I will. Calmly, gently—

THE CHAPLAIN [*blubbering miserably*] I am not a bad man, my lord.

WARWICK. No, no: not at all.

THE CHAPLAIN. I meant no harm. I did not know what it would be like.

WARWICK [*hardening*] Oh! You saw it, then?

THE CHAPLAIN. I did not know what I was doing. I am a hot-headed fool; and I shall be damned to all eternity for it.

WARWICK. Nonsense! Very distressing, no doubt; but it was not your doing.

THE CHAPLAIN [*lamentably*] I let them do it. If I had known, I would have torn her from their hands. You dont know: you havnt seen: it is so easy to talk when you dont know. You madden yourself with words: you damn yourself because it feels grand to throw oil on the flaming hell of your own temper. But when it is brought home to you; when you see the thing you have done; when it is blinding your eyes, stifling your nostrils, tearing your heart, then—then—[*Falling on his knees*] O God, take away this sight from me! O Christ, deliver me from this fire that is consuming me! She cried to Thee in the midst of it: Jesus! Jesus! Jesus! She is in Thy bosom; and I am in hell for evermore.

WARWICK [*summarily hauling him to his feet*] Come come, man! you must pull yourself together. We shall have the whole town talking of this. [*He throws him not too gently into a chair at the table*] If you have not the nerve to see these things, why do you not do as I do, and stay away?

THE CHAPLAIN [*bewildered and submissive*] She asked for a cross. A soldier gave her two sticks tied together. Thank God he was an Englishman! I might have done it; but I did not: I am a coward, a mad dog, a fool. But he was an Englishman too.

WARWICK. The fool! they will burn him too if the priests get hold of him.

THE CHAPLAIN [*shaken with a convulsion*] Some of the people laughed at her. They would have laughed at Christ. They were French people, my lord: I know they were French.

WARWICK. Hush! someone is coming. Control yourself.

Ladvenu comes back through the courtyard to Warwick's right hand, carrying a bishop's cross which he has taken from a church. He is very grave and composed.

WARWICK. I am informed that it is all over, Brother Martin.

LADVENU [*enigmatically*] We do not know, my lord. It may have only just begun.

WARWICK. What does that mean, exactly?

LADVENU. I took this cross from the church for her that she might see it to the last: she had only two sticks that she put into her bosom. When the fire crept round us, and she saw that if I held the cross before her I should be burnt myself, she warned me to get down and save myself.* My lord: a girl who could think of another's danger in such a moment was not inspired by the devil. When I had to snatch the cross from her sight, she looked up to heaven. And I do not believe that the heavens were empty. I firmly believe that her Savior appeared to her then in His tenderest glory. She called to Him and died. This is not the end for her, but the beginning.

WARWICK. I am afraid it will have a bad effect on the people.

LADVENU. It had, my lord, on some of them. I heard laughter. Forgive me for saying that I hope and believe it was English laughter.

THE CHAPLAIN [*rising frantically*] No: it was not. There was only one Englishman there that disgraced his country; and that was the mad dog, de Stogumber. [*He rushes wildly out, shrieking*] Let them torture him. Let them burn him. I will go pray among her ashes. I am no better than Judas: I will hang myself.

WARWICK. Quick, Brother Martin: follow him: he will do himself some mischief. After him, quick.

Ladvenu hurries out, Warwick urging him. The Executioner comes in by the door behind the judges' chairs; and Warwick, returning, finds himself face to face with him.

WARWICK. Well, fellow: who are you?

THE EXECUTIONER [*with dignity*] I am not addressed as fellow, my lord. I am the Master Executioner of Rouen: it is a highly skilled mystery.* I am come to tell your lordship that your orders have been obeyed.

WARWICK. I crave your pardon, Master Executioner; and I will see that you lose nothing by having no relics to sell. I have your word, have I, that nothing remains, not a bone, not a nail, not a hair?

THE EXECUTIONER. Her heart would not burn, my lord; but everything that was left is at the bottom of the river. You have heard the last of her.

WARWICK [*with a wry smile, thinking of what Ladvenu said*] The last of her? Hm! I wonder!

EPILOGUE

A restless fitfully windy night in June 1456, full of summer lightning after many days of heat. King Charles the Seventh of France, formerly Joan's Dauphin, now Charles the Victorious, aged 51, is in bed in one of his royal chateaux. The bed, raised on a dais of two steps, is towards the side of the room so as to avoid blocking a tall lancet window* in the middle. Its canopy bears the royal arms in embroidery. Except for the canopy and the huge down pillows there is nothing to distinguish it from a broad settee* with bedclothes* and a valance.* Thus its occupant is in full view from the foot.

Charles is not asleep: he is reading in bed, or rather looking at the pictures in Fouquet's Boccaccio* with his knees doubled up to make a reading desk. Beside the bed on his left is a little table with a picture of the Virgin, lighted by candles of painted wax. The walls are hung from ceiling to floor with painted curtains which stir at times in the draughts. At first glance the prevailing yellow and red in these hanging pictures is somewhat flamelike when the folds breathe in the wind.

The door is on Charles's left, but in front of him close to the corner farthest from him. A large watchman's rattle,* handsomely designed and gaily painted, is in the bed under his hand.

Charles turns a leaf. A distant clock strikes the half-hour softly. Charles shuts the book with a clap; throws it aside; snatches up the rattle; and whirls it energetically, making a deafening clatter. Ladvenu enters, 25 years older, strange and stark in bearing, and still carrying the cross from Rouen. Charles evidently does not expect him; for he springs out of bed on the farther side from the door.

CHARLES. Who are you? Where is my gentleman of the bedchamber? What do you want?

LADVENU [*solemnly*] I bring you glad tidings of great joy. Rejoice, O king; for the taint is removed from your blood, and the stain from your crown. Justice, long delayed, is at last triumphant.

CHARLES. What are you talking about? Who are you?

LADVENU. I am brother Martin.

CHARLES. And who, saving your reverence, may Brother Martin be?

LADVENU. I held this cross when The Maid perished in the fire. Twenty-five years have passed since then: nearly ten thousand days. And on every one of those days I have prayed God to justify* His daughter on earth as she is justified in heaven.

CHARLES [*reassured, sitting down on the foot of the bed*] Oh, I remember now. I have heard of you. You have a bee in your bonnet* about The Maid. Have you been at the inquiry?

LADVENU. I have given my testimony.

CHARLES. Is it over?

LADVENU. It is over.

CHARLES. Satisfactorily?

LADVENU. The ways of God are very strange.

CHARLES. How so?

LADVENU. At the trial which sent a saint to the stake as a heretic and a sorceress, the truth was told; the law was upheld; mercy was shewn beyond all custom; no wrong was done but the final and dreadful wrong of the lying sentence and the pitiless fire. At this inquiry from which I have just come, there was shameless perjury, courtly corruption, calumny of the dead who did their duty according to their lights, cowardly evasion of the issue, testimony made of idle tales that could not impose on a plough-boy. Yet out of this insult to justice, this defamation of the Church, this orgy of lying and foolishness, the truth is set in the noonday sun on the hilltop; the white robe of innocence is cleansed from the smirch of the burning faggots; the holy life is sanctified; the true heart that lived through the flame is consecrated; a great lie is silenced for ever; and a great wrong is set right before all men.*

CHARLES. My friend: provided they can no longer say that I was crowned by a witch and a heretic, I shall not fuss about how the trick has been done. Joan would not have fussed about it if it came all right in the end: she was not that sort: I knew her. Is her rehabilitation complete?* I made it pretty clear that there was to be no nonsense about it.

LADVENU. It is solemnly declared that her judges were full of corruption, cozenage, fraud, and malice. Four falsehoods.

CHARLES. Never mind the falsehoods: her judges are dead.

LADVENU. The sentence on her is broken, annulled, annihilated, set aside as non-existent, without value or effect.

CHARLES. Good. Nobody can challenge my consecration now, can they?

LADVENU. Not Charlemagne nor King David* himself was more sacredly crowned.

CHARLES [*rising*] Excellent. Think of what that means to me!

LADVENU. I think of what it means to her!

CHARLES. You cannot. None of us ever knew what anything meant to her. She was like nobody else; and she must take care of herself wherever she is; for *I* cannot take care of her; and neither can you, whatever you may think: you are not big enough. But I will tell you this about her. If you could bring her back to life, they would burn her again within six months, for all their present adoration of her. And you would hold up the cross, too, just the same. So [*crossing himself*] let her rest; and let you and I mind our own business, and not meddle with hers.

LADVENU. God forbid that I should have no share in her, nor she in me! [*He turns and strides out as he came, saying*] Henceforth my path will not lie through palaces, nor my conversation be with kings.

CHARLES [*following him towards the door, and shouting after him*] Much good may it do you, holy man! [*He returns to the middle of the chamber, where he halts, and says quizzically to himself*] That was a funny chap. How did he get in? Where are my people? [*He goes impatiently to the bed, and swings the rattle. A rush of wind through the open door sets the walls swaying agitatedly. The candles go out. He calls in the darkness*] Hallo! Someone come and shut the windows: everything is being blown all over the place. [*A flash of summer lightning shews up the lancet window. A figure is seen in silhouette against it*] Who is there? Who is that? Help! Murder! [*Thunder. He jumps into bed, and hides under the clothes*].

JOAN'S VOICE. Easy, Charlie, easy. What art making all that noise for? No one can hear thee. Thourt asleep. [*She is dimly seen in a pallid greenish light by the bedside*].

CHARLES [*peeping out*] Joan! Are you a ghost, Joan?

JOAN. Hardly even that, lad. Can a poor burnt-up lass have a ghost? I am but a dream that thourt dreaming.* [*The light increases: they become plainly visible as he sits up*] Thou looks older, lad.

CHARLES. I *am* older. Am I really asleep?

JOAN. Fallen asleep over thy silly book.

CHARLES. That's funny.

JOAN. Not so funny as that I am dead, is it?

CHARLES. Are you really dead?

JOAN. As dead as anybody ever is, laddie. I am out of the body.

CHARLES. Just fancy! Did it hurt much?

JOAN. Did what hurt much?

CHARLES. Being burnt.

JOAN. Oh, *that*! I cannot remember very well. I think it did at first; but then it all got mixed up; and I was not in my right mind until I was free of the body. But do not thou go handling fire and thinking it will not hurt thee. How hast been ever since?

CHARLES. Oh, not so bad. Do you know, I actually lead my army out and win battles? Down into the moat up to my waist in mud and blood. Up the ladders with the stones and hot pitch raining down. Like you.

JOAN. No! Did I make a man of thee after all, Charlie?

CHARLES. I am Charles the Victorious now. I had to be brave because you were. Agnes put a little pluck into me too.

JOAN. Agnes! Who was Agnes?

CHARLES. Agnes Sorel. A woman I fell in love with. I dream of her often. I never dreamed of you before.

JOAN. Is she dead, like me?

CHARLES. Yes. But she was not like you. She was very beautiful.

JOAN [*laughing heartily*] Ha ha! I was no beauty: I was always a rough one: a regular soldier. I might almost as well have been a man. Pity I wasnt: I should not have bothered you all so much then. But my head was in the skies; and the glory of God was upon me; and, man or woman, I should have bothered you as long as your noses were in the mud. Now tell me what has happened since you wise men knew no better than to make a heap of cinders of me?*

CHARLES. Your mother and brothers have sued the courts to have your case tried over again. And the courts have declared that your judges were full of corruption and cozenage, fraud and malice.

JOAN. Not they. They were as honest a lot of poor fools as ever burned their betters.

CHARLES. The sentence on you is broken, annihilated, annulled: null, non-existent, without value or effect.

JOAN. I was burned,* all the same. Can they unburn me?

CHARLES. If they could, they would think twice before they did it. But they have decreed that a beautiful cross be placed where the stake stood, for your perpetual memory and for your salvation.*

JOAN. It is the memory and the salvation that sanctify the cross, not the cross that sanctifies the memory and the salvation. [*She turns away, forgetting him*] I shall outlast that cross. I shall be remembered when men will have forgotten where Rouen stood.

CHARLES. There you go with your self-conceit, the same as ever! I think you might say a word of thanks to me for having had justice done at last.

CAUCHON [*appearing at the window between them*] Liar!

CHARLES. Thank you.

JOAN. Why, if it isnt Peter Cauchon! How are you, Peter? What luck have you had since you burned me?

CAUCHON. None. I arraign the justice of Man. It is not the justice of God.

JOAN. Still dreaming of justice, Peter? See what justice came to with me! But what has happened to thee? Art dead or alive?

CAUCHON. Dead. Dishonored. They pursued me beyond the grave. They excommunicated my dead body: they dug it up and flung it into the common sewer.

JOAN. Your dead body did not feel the spade and the sewer as my live body felt the fire.

CAUCHON. But this thing that they have done against me hurts justice; destroys faith; saps the foundation of the Church. The solid earth sways like the treacherous sea beneath the feet of men and spirits alike when the innocent are slain in the name of law, and their wrongs are undone by slandering the pure of heart.

JOAN. Well, well, Peter, I hope men will be the better for remembering me; and they would not remember me so well if you had not burned me.

CAUCHON. They will be the worse for remembering *me*: they will see in me evil triumphing over good, falsehood over truth, cruelty over mercy, hell over heaven. Their courage will rise as they think of you, only to faint as they think of me. Yet God is my witness I was just: I was merciful: I was faithful to my light: I could do no other than I did.

CHARLES [*scrambling out of the sheets and enthroning himself on the side of the bed**] Yes: it is always you good men that do the big mischiefs. Look at me! I am not Charles the Good, nor Charles the Wise, nor Charles the Bold. Joan's worshippers may even call me Charles the Coward because I did not pull her out of the fire. But I have done less harm than any of you. You people with your heads in the sky spend all your time trying to turn the world upside down; but I take the world as it is, and say that top-side-up is right-side-up; and I keep my nose pretty close to the ground. And I ask you, what king of France has done better, or been a better fellow in his little way?

JOAN. Art really king of France, Charlie? Be the English gone?

DUNOIS [*coming through the tapestry on Joan's left, the candles relighting themselves at the same moment, and illuminating his armor and surcoat cheerfully*] I have kept my word: the English are gone.

JOAN. Praised be God! now is fair France a province in heaven. Tell me all about the fighting, Jack. Was it thou that led them? Wert thou God's captain to thy death?

DUNOIS. I am not dead.* My body is very comfortably asleep in my bed at Chateaudun; but my spirit is called here by yours.

JOAN. And you fought them *my* way, Jack: eh? Not the old way, chaffering* for ransoms; but The Maid's way: staking life against death, with the heart high and humble and void of malice, and nothing counting under God but France free and French. Was it my way, Jack?

DUNOIS. Faith, it was any way that would win. But the way that won was always your way. I give you best, lassie. I wrote a fine letter to set you right at the new trial. Perhaps I should never have let the priests burn you; but I was busy fighting; and it was the Church's business, not mine. There was no use in both of us being burned, was there?

CAUCHON. Ay! put the blame on the priests. But I, who am beyond praise and blame, tell you that the world is saved neither by its priests nor its soldiers, but by God and His Saints. The Church Militant sent this woman to the fire; but even as she burned, the flames whitened into the radiance of the Church Triumphant.

*The clock strikes the third quarter. A rough male voice is heard trolling an improvised tune.**

> Rum tum trumpledum,
> Bacon fat and rumpledum,
> Old Saint mumpledum,
> Pull his tail and stumpledum
>   O my Ma—ry Ann!

*A ruffianly English soldier comes through the curtains and marches between Dunois and Joan.**

DUNOIS. What villainous troubadour taught you that doggrel?*

THE SOLDIER. No troubadour. We made it up ourselves as we marched. We were not gentlefolks and troubadours. Music straight out of the heart of the people, as you might say. Rum tum trumpledum, Bacon fat and rumpledum, Old Saint mumpledum, Pull his tail and stumpledum: that dont mean anything, you know; but it keeps you marching. Your servant, ladies and gentlemen. Who asked for a saint?

JOAN. Be you a saint?

THE SOLDIER. Yes, lady, straight from hell.*

DUNOIS. A saint, and from hell!

THE SOLDIER. Yes, noble captain: I have a day off. Every year, you know. Thats my allowance for my one good action.

CAUCHON. Wretch! In all the years of your life did you do only one good action?

THE SOLDIER. I never thought about it: it came natural like. But they scored it up for me.

CHARLES. What was it?

THE SOLDIER. Why, the silliest thing you ever heard of. I—

JOAN [*interrupting him by strolling across to the bed, where she sits beside Charles*] He tied two sticks together, and gave them to a poor lass that was going to be burned.

THE SOLDIER. Right. Who told you that?

JOAN. Never mind. Would you know her if you saw her again?

THE SOLDIER. Not I. There are so many girls! and they all expect you to remember them as if there was only one in the world. This one must have been a prime sort; for I have a day off every year for her; and so, until twelve o'clock punctually, I am a saint, at your service, noble lords and lovely ladies.

CHARLES. And after twelve?

THE SOLDIER. After twelve, back to the only place fit for the likes of me.

JOAN [*rising*] Back there! You! that gave the lass the cross!

THE SOLDIER [*excusing his unsoldierly conduct*] Well, she asked for it; and they were going to burn her. She had as good a right to a cross as they had; and they had dozens of them. It was her funeral, not theirs. Where was the harm in it?

JOAN. Man: I am not reproaching* you. But I cannot bear to think of you in torment.

THE SOLDIER [*cheerfully*] No great torment, lady. You see I was used to worse.

CHARLES. What! worse than hell?

THE SOLDIER. Fifteen years' service in the French wars. Hell was a treat after that.

Joan throws up her arms, and takes refuge from despair of humanity before the picture of the Virgin.

THE SOLDIER [*continuing*]—Suits me somehow. The day off was dull at first, like a wet Sunday. I dont mind it so much now. They tell me I can have as many as I like as soon as I want them.

CHARLES. What is hell like?

THE SOLDIER. You wont find it so bad, sir.* Jolly. Like as if you were always drunk without the trouble and expense of drinking. Tip top company too: emperors and popes and kings and all sorts. They chip* me about giving that young judy* the cross; but I dont care: I stand up to them proper, and tell them that if she hadnt a better right to it than they, she'd be where they are. That dumbfounds them, that does. All they can do is gnash their teeth, hell fashion; and

I just laugh, and go off singing the old chanty: Rum tum trumple—
Hullo! Who's that knocking at the door?

They listen. A long gentle knocking is heard.

CHARLES. Come in.

The door opens; and an old priest, white-haired, bent, with a silly but benevolent smile, comes in and trots over to Joan.

THE NEWCOMER. Excuse me, gentle lords and ladies. Do not let me disturb you. Only a poor old harmless English rector. Formerly chaplain to the cardinal: to my lord of Winchester. John de Stogumber, at your service. [*He looks at them inquiringly*] Did you say anything? I am a little deaf, unfortunately. Also a little—well, not always in my right mind, perhaps; but still, it is a small village with a few simple people. I suffice: I suffice: they love me there; and I am able to do a little good. I am well connected, you see; and they indulge me.

JOAN. Poor old John! What brought thee to this state?

DE STOGUMBER. I tell my folks they must be very careful. I say to them, 'If you only saw what you think about you would think quite differently about it. It would give you a great shock. Oh, a great shock.' And they all say 'Yes, parson: we all know you are a kind man, and would not harm a fly.' That is a great comfort to me. For I am not cruel by nature, you know.

THE SOLDIER. Who said you were?

DE STOGUMBER. Well, you see, I did a very cruel thing once because I did not know what cruelty was like. I had not seen it, you know. That is the great thing: you must see it. And then you are redeemed and saved.

CAUCHON. Were not the sufferings of our Lord Christ enough for you?

DE STOGUMBER. No. Oh no: not at all. I had seen them in pictures, and read of them in books, and been greatly moved by them, as I thought. But it was no use: it was not our Lord that redeemed me, but a young woman whom I saw actually burned to death. It was dreadful: oh, most dreadful. But it saved me. I have been a different man ever since, though a little astray in my wits sometimes.

CAUCHON. Must then a Christ perish in torment in every age* to save those that have no imagination?

JOAN. Well, if I saved all those he would have been cruel to if he had not been cruel to me, I was not burnt for nothing, was I?

DE STOGUMBER. Oh no; it was not you. My sight is bad: I cannot distinguish your features: but you are not she: oh no: she was burned to a cinder: dead and gone, dead and gone.

THE EXECUTIONER [*stepping from behind the bed curtains on Charles's right, the bed being between them*] She is more alive than you, old man. Her heart would not burn; and it would not drown. I was a master at my craft: better than the master of Paris, better than the master of Toulouse;* but I could not kill The Maid. She is up and alive everywhere.

THE EARL OF WARWICK [*sallying from the bed curtains on the other side, and coming to Joan's left hand*] Madam: my congratulations on your rehabilitation. I feel that I owe you an apology.

JOAN. Oh, please dont mention it.

WARWICK [*pleasantly*] The burning was purely political. There was no personal feeling against you, I assure you.

JOAN. I bear no malice, my lord.

WARWICK. Just so. Very kind of you to meet me in that way: a touch of true breeding. But I must insist on apologizing very amply. The truth is, these political necessities sometimes turn out to be political mistakes; and this one was a veritable howler;* for your spirit conquered us, madam, in spite of our faggots. History will remember me for your sake, though the incidents of the connection were perhaps a little unfortunate.

JOAN. Ay, perhaps just a little, you funny man.

WARWICK. Still, when they make you a saint, you will owe your halo to me, just as this lucky monarch owes his crown to you.

JOAN [*turning from him*] I shall owe nothing to any man: I owe everything to the spirit of God that was within me. But fancy me a saint! What would St Catherine and St Margaret say if the farm girl was cocked up* beside them!

A clerical-looking gentleman in black frockcoat and trousers, and tall hat, in the fashion of the year 1920, suddenly appears before them in the corner on their right. They all stare at him. Then they burst into uncontrollable laughter.

THE GENTLEMAN. Why this mirth, gentlemen?

WARWICK. I congratulate you on having invented a most extraordinarily comic dress.

THE GENTLEMAN. I do not understand. You are all in fancy dress: I am properly dressed.

DUNOIS. All dress is fancy dress, is it not, except our natural skins?

THE GENTLEMAN. Pardon me: I am here on serious business, and cannot engage in frivolous discussions. [*He takes out a paper, and assumes a dry official manner*]. I am sent to announce to you that Joan of Arc, formerly known as The Maid, having been the subject of an inquiry instituted by the Bishop of Orleans—*

JOAN [*interrupting*] Ah! They remember me still in Orleans.

THE GENTLEMAN [*emphatically, to mark his indignation at the interruption*]—by the Bishop of Orleans into the claim of the said Joan of Arc to be canonized as a saint—

JOAN [*again interrupting*] But I never made any such claim.

THE GENTLEMAN [*as before*]—the Church has examined the claim exhaustively in the usual course, and, having admitted the said Joan successively to the ranks of Venerable and Blessed,—*

JOAN [*chuckling*] Me venerable!

THE GENTLEMAN. —has finally declared her to have been endowed with heroic virtues and favored with private revelations, and calls the said Venerable and Blessed Joan to the communion of the Church Triumphant as Saint Joan.

JOAN [*rapt*] Saint Joan!

THE GENTLEMAN. On every thirtieth day of May, being the anniversary of the death of the said most blessed daughter of God, there shall in every Catholic church to the end of time be celebrated a special office in commemoration of her; and it shall be lawful to dedicate a special chapel to her, and to place her image on its altar in every such church. And it shall be lawful and laudable for the faithful to kneel and address their prayers through her to the Mercy Seat.*

JOAN. Oh no. It is for the saint to kneel. [*She falls on her knees, still rapt*].

THE GENTLEMAN [*putting up his paper, and retiring beside the Executioner*] In Basilica Vaticana,* the sixteenth day of May, nineteen hundred and twenty.

DUNOIS [*raising Joan*] Half an hour to burn you, dear Saint; and four centuries to find out the truth about you!

DE STOGUMBER. Sir: I was chaplain to the Cardinal of Winchester once. They always would call him the Cardinal of England. It would be a great comfort to me and to my master to see a fair statue to The Maid in Winchester Cathedral. Will they put one there, do you think?

THE GENTLEMAN. As the building is temporarily in the hands of the Anglican heresy, I cannot answer for that.

A vision of the statue in Winchester Cathedral is seen through the window.*

DE STOGUMBER. Oh look! look! that is Winchester.

JOAN. Is that meant to be me? I was stiffer on my feet.

The vision fades.

THE GENTLEMAN. I have been requested by the temporal authorities of France to mention that the multiplication of public statues to The Maid threatens to become an obstruction to traffic. I do so as a matter of courtesy to the said authorities, but must point out on behalf of the Church that The Maid's horse is no greater obstruction to traffic than any other horse.

JOAN. Eh! I am glad they have not forgotten my horse.

A vision of the statue before Rheims Cathedral appears.*

JOAN. Is that funny little thing me too?

CHARLES. That is Rheims Cathedral where you had me crowned. It must be you.

JOAN. Who has broken my sword? My sword was never broken. It is the sword of France.

DUNOIS. Never mind. Swords can be mended. Your soul is unbroken; and you are the soul of France.

The vision fades. The Archbishop and the Inquisitor are now seen on the right and left of Cauchon.

JOAN. My sword shall conquer yet: the sword that never struck a blow. Though men destroyed my body, yet in my soul I have seen God.

CAUCHON [*kneeling to her*] The girls in the field praise thee; for thou hast raised their eyes; and they see that there is nothing between them and heaven.

DUNOIS [*kneeling to her*] The dying soldiers praise thee, because thou art a shield of glory between them and the judgment.

THE ARCHBISHOP [*kneeling to her*] The princes of the Church praise thee, because thou hast redeemed the faith their worldlinesses have dragged through the mire.

WARWICK [*kneeling to her*] The cunning counsellors praise thee, because thou hast cut the knots in which they have tied their own souls.

DE STOGUMBER [*kneeling to her*] The foolish old men on their deathbeds praise thee, because their sins against thee are turned into blessings.

THE INQUISITOR [*kneeling to her*] The judges in the blindness and bondage of the law praise thee, because thou hast vindicated the vision and the freedom of the living soul.

THE SOLDIER [*kneeling to her*] The wicked out of hell praise thee, because thou hast shewn them that the fire that is not quenched is a holy fire.

THE EXECUTIONER [*kneeling to her*] The tormentors and executioners praise thee, because thou hast shewn that their hands are guiltless of the death of the soul.*

CHARLES [*kneeling to her*] The unpretending praise thee, because thou hast taken upon thyself the heroic burdens that are too heavy for them.

JOAN. Woe unto me when all men praise me! I bid you remember that I am a saint, and that saints can work miracles. And now tell me: shall I rise from the dead, and come back to you a living woman?

A sudden darkness blots out the walls of the room as they all spring to their feet in consternation. Only the figures and the bed remain visible.

JOAN. What! Must I burn again? Are none of you ready to receive me?

CAUCHON. The heretic is always better dead.* And mortal eyes cannot distinguish the saint from the heretic. Spare them.* [*He goes out as he came*].

DUNOIS. Forgive us, Joan: we are not yet good enough for you. I shall go back to my bed. [*He also goes*].

WARWICK. We sincerely regret our little mistake; but political necessities, though occasionally erroneous, are still imperative; so if you will be good enough to excuse me—[*He steals discreetly away*].

THE ARCHBISHOP. Your return would not make me the man you once thought me. The utmost I can say is that though I dare not bless you, I hope I may one day enter into your blessedness. Meanwhile, however—[*He goes*].

THE INQUISITOR. I who am of the dead, testified that day that you were innocent. But I do not see how The Inquisition could possibly be dispensed with under existing circumstances. Therefore—[*He goes*].

DE STOGUMBER. Oh, do not come back: you must not come back. I must die in peace. Give us peace in our time, O Lord! [*He goes*].

THE GENTLEMAN. The possibility of your resurrection was not contemplated in the recent proceedings for your canonization. I must return to Rome for fresh instructions. [*He bows formally, and withdraws*].

THE EXECUTIONER. As a master in my profession I have to consider its interests. And, after all, my first duty is to my wife and children. I must have time to think over this. [*He goes*].

CHARLES. Poor old Joan! They have all run away from you except this blackguard who has to go back to hell at twelve o'clock. And what can I do but follow Jack Dunois' example, and go back to bed too? [*He does so*].

JOAN [*sadly*] Goodnight, Charlie.

CHARLES [*mumbling in his pillows*] Goo ni. [*He sleeps. The darkness envelops the bed*].

JOAN [*to the soldier*] And you, my one faithful? What comfort have you for Saint Joan?

THE SOLDIER. Well, what do they all amount to, these kings and captains and bishops and lawyers and such like? They just leave you in the ditch to bleed to death; and the next thing is, you meet them down there, for all the airs they give themselves. What I say is, you have as good a right to your notions as they have to theirs, and perhaps better. [*Settling himself for a lecture on the subject*] You see, it's like this. If—[*the first stroke of midnight is heard softly from a distant bell*]. Excuse me: a pressing appointment—[*He goes on tiptoe*].

The last remaining rays of light gather into a white radiance descending on Joan. The hour continues to strike.

JOAN. O God that madest this beautiful earth, when will it be ready to receive Thy saints? How long, O Lord, how long?

EXPLANATORY NOTES

PYGMALION

2 *Note for Technicians*: this note first appeared in the 1941 Constable edition, which includes scenes and dialogue from the film script.

e upside down: this symbol is not used in editions prior to 1941.

3 *They cannot spell . . . Frenchmen*: in previous editions, this reads: 'They spell it so abominably that no man can teach himself what it sounds like. It is impossible for an Englishman to open his mouth without making some other Englishman hate or despise him. German and Spanish are accessible to foreigners: English is not accessible even to Englishmen' (CON P 1939).

Alexander Melville Bell . . . telephone: visible speech was a phonetic system invented by Alexander Melville Bell (1819–1905) to teach the deaf. His son, Alexander Graham Bell (1847–1922), invented the telephone in 1876.

Alexander J. Ellis: an English mathematician and philologist who also worked in the field of musicology, Alexander John Ellis (1814–90) developed two phonetic alphabets and authored *Phonetics: A Familiar Exposition of the Principles of that Science* (1844), *A Plea for Phonotypy and Phonography: or, Speech-printing Speech-writing* (1845), *A Plea for Phonetic Spelling: or, the Necessity of Orthographic Reform* (1848), and *On Early English Pronunciation* (1869).

Tito Pagliardini: Tito Pagliardini (1817–95) was the author of *National Education and the English Language* (1868) and *The Advantages of Phonetic Spelling in Elementary Schools* (1882).

Henry Sweet: Henry Sweet (1845–1912) was an English grammarian, philologist, and phonetician who authored several studies, including *A Handbook of Phonetics* (1877), *The History of Language* (1900), and *The Sounds of English* (1908). As known for his bluntness in social situations as he was for his scholarship, he was awarded the readership in phonetics at the University of Oxford in 1901.

Ibsen: the Norwegian writer Henrik Ibsen (1828–1906) is one of the world's most renowned playwrights. He was celebrated by many intellectuals in his day as a destroyer of ideals. Shaw wrote the first major study of him, *The Quintessence of Ibsenism* (1891), and played a key role in promoting his work.

Samuel Butler: English writer Samuel Butler (1835–1902) was an early devotee of Darwinian evolutionary science and author of the canonical utopian novel *Erewhon* (1872), which was greatly admired by Shaw.

Imperial Institute . . . Kensington: the Imperial Institute was established in 1888; it was built to celebrate Queen Victoria's Golden Jubilee and opened in 1893. In the mid-twentieth century, it was renamed the Commonwealth Institute to align it with contemporary politics. The institute conducted research into the colonies and dominions to explore their commercial and industrial possibilities. It was declared no longer sustainable and shuttered in 2015.

3 *Joseph Chamberlain . . . Empire*: Joseph Chamberlain (1836–1914) was a British politician and fervent imperialist. In 1886, he broke from the Liberal Party over the issue of Home Rule for Ireland, which he was against, to form the Liberal Unionists. As secretary of state for the colonies, he promoted the British cause in the Second Boer War (1899–1902).

4 *four and sixpenny . . . Clarendon Press*: the publication to which Shaw refers is Sweet's *Manual of Current Shorthand, Orthographic and Phonetic*. Oxford University Press became known as the Clarendon Press following its move from the Sheldonian Theatre to the Clarendon Building in Broad Street in 1713.

postcards . . . describes: in Act III, Mrs Higgins says to Henry that 'though I like to get pretty postcards in your patent shorthand, I always have to read the copies in ordinary writing you so thoughtfully send me' (p. 50).

Pitman . . . shorthand: Sir Isaac Pitman (1813–97) was an English educator and inventor. He created a shorthand style of writing that was named after him. Shaw wrote the first drafts of many of his plays in Pitman shorthand, which his secretaries then typed for him to revise.

5 *the Sybil . . . attend to*: the sybils were oracles in ancient Greece.

The Times: founded in 1785, *The Times* is a major daily newspaper published in London.

Encyclopædia Britannica: first published in 1768, this is the world's oldest English-language encyclopedia.

Gregg shorthand: created by and named after the Irishman John Robert Gregg (1867–1948), Gregg shorthand, like Pitman, is a rapid writing system based on sounds. The first pamphlet promoting it was published in 1888. It is the most popular form of shorthand in the United States and has been adopted into other languages.

In America . . . prodigious: in previous editions, this reads: 'Therefore, Sweet railed at Pitman as vainly as Thersites railed at Ajax: his raillery, however it may have eased his soul, gave no popular vogue to Current Shorthand' (CON P 1939). In Shakespeare's *Troilus and Cressida* (1601–2), Thersites is portrayed as Ajax's comical slave who curses his master.

Robert Bridges . . . Miltonic sympathies: English poet Robert Bridges (1844–1930) became Poet Laureate of the United Kingdom in 1913 and held that office until his death; he published *Milton's Prosody* (1901), a study of the verse style of English poet John Milton (1608–74). When the BBC formed its Advisory Committee on Pronunciation in 1926, Bridges presided as chair and Shaw sat as a member. Upon Bridges's death in 1930, Shaw chaired the committee until 1937; it was dissolved in 1939. L. W. Conolly notes: 'During its thirteen years of operation the committee published seven pamphlets with 9000 pronunciation recommendations, pronunciations that in nearly all cases became Standard English usage' (*Bernard Shaw and the BBC* (Toronto: University of Toronto Press, 2009), 18).

6 *Ruy Blas*: set in Madrid in 1699, the play *Ruy Blas* (1838) is a melodrama by French writer Victor Hugo (1802–85). The queen depicted is Maria Anna of Neuburg (1667–1740), wife of King Charles II of Spain (1661–1700).

Théâtre Français: this is the national theatre of France and has its origins in the company of actors who worked under the direction of French playwright Molière (né Jean-Baptiste Poquelin, 1622–73). In 1791, it established its current headquarters in Paris. The theatre is now more usually known as the Comédie-Française.

7 *St Paul's church (. . . Covent Garden vegetable market)*: Sir Christopher Wren (1632–1723) was the architect of fifty-three London churches, including St Paul's Cathedral, which was completed in 1710. Inigo Jones (1573–1652) founded the English classical tradition of architecture. His design of Covent Garden is the first instance of formal town planning in London, evocative of an Italian piazza with St Paul's church, completed in 1633, at its western end. Coincidentally, Jones also led the restoration of St Paul's Cathedral and his work was a major influence on Wren.

London at 11.15 p.m. . . . first quarter: in the typescript, these stage directions read:

> ~~London~~ *Covent Garden* at 11.15 p.m. Torrents of *heavy summer* rain. ~~An Archway. Some people sheltering. A~~ *Pedestrians running for shelter into the market and under the Portico of St Paul's Church, where there are already several people, among them a* lady and her daughter in evening dress ~~among them. A gentle~~ *They are all peering gloomily at the rain, except one* man in the background, *who is with his face to the church door, and seems wholly preoccupied with his note book* making notes. Cab whistles ~~heard~~ blowing in all directions. *The church clock strikes the first quarter.*
>
> (P Type, 1)

(Italics represent additions that Shaw made to the typescript.) The opening location was switched back to London when Shaw added the line 'not Wren's Cathedral but Inigo Jones's church in Covent Garden vegetable garden' for the 1941 edition.

It's too bad: the Mother originally said 'It's outrageous' (P Type, 1).

young man of twenty: originally, Freddy was more vaguely described as a 'youth' (P Type, 1).

8 *Charing Cross . . . Ludgate Circus . . . Trafalgar Square*: from St Paul's church, Charing Cross is 0.3 miles to the south-west, Trafalgar Square is a further 0.1 miles, and Ludgate Circus is 0.9 miles to the east.

Hammersmith: from Covent Garden, the neighbourhood of Hammersmith is 4.8 miles to the west.

8 *Strandwards*: the Strand is a major thoroughfare running between the Aldwych and Trafalgar Square directly to the south of Covent Garden.

a flower girl: Shaw originally wrote 'LIZZIE DOOLITTLE.' He also crossed out 'violent' before 'collision' (P Type, 2–3).

Theres . . . mad: Shaw transcribes a cockney accent. In Standard English, the passage would read: 'There's manners for you! Two bunches of violets trod into the mud.'

romantic: Shaw changed this from 'attractive' for the 1941 edition.

9 *Ow . . . f'them?*: another transcription of cockney. In Standard English this reads: 'Oh, he's your son, is he? Well, if you'd done your duty by him as a mother should, he'd know better than to spoil a poor girl's flowers, then run away without paying. Will you pay me for them?' Eliza's cockney English originally appeared as Standard English in the typescript. Shaw rendered it phonetically in holograph revisions (P Type, 3).

tanner: a sixpence piece in British old currency. Most of the references to coins and money in the play are now dated, with British currency having been modernized with the introduction of decimalization in 1971.

10 *poor girl*: originally, before The Gentleman speaks, The Daughter remarked: 'The impertinence!' Shaw deleted this in the typescript (P Type, 5).

sovereign: the smallest amount Pickering originally had was a 'five pound note' (P Type, 5). It is more probable that a flower girl could make change for a sovereign, which was a gold coin worth a pound.

half-a-crown . . . tuppence: a half-crown was worth an eighth of a pound; tuppence refers to twopence.

hapence: also known as a ha'penny or a halfpence.

bloke: man or fellow.

Hysterically: originally, Eliza became hysterical before the preceding sentence (P Type, 5).

11 *tec*: slang for 'detective'.

breaking through them: in the 1939 edition, Eliza was described just before this line as '*distraught and mobbed*'.

It's aw . . . bə-oots: in Standard English, this reads: 'It's all right: he's a gentleman: look at his boots.'

much distressed: originally, Eliza was only 'distressed' (P Type, 6).

agen: against.

12 *THE BYSTANDERS GENERALLY . . . etc.*: Shaw added this in the typescript, though he did not include the stage directions that follow their remarks until the play was published (P Type, 6–7; CON P 1916).

Selsey: a coastal town in West Sussex.

Lisson Grove: a London neighbourhood just to the west of Regent's Park.

four-and-six: this refers to paying a weekly rent of four shillings and six-pence. A shilling was worth twelvepence, and there were twenty shillings in a pound.

Park Lane: this road, which is notable for its expensive housing, runs along the eastern boundary of Hyde Park.

Housing Question: this refers to the issue of housing quality and availabil-ity. Because of the rapid rate of urbanization, it was a pressing concern in the nineteenth century. As a borough councillor and vestryman in St Pancras (1897–1903), Shaw spent numerous hours on the issue. He also wrote a number of essays on the subject and it forms the crux of his first play, *Widowers' Houses* (1892).

Hoxton: a neighbourhood of east London, renowned for its slums at this time.

Bly me!: most often written 'blimey'; an expression of surprise.

13 *meddle with you?*: at this point in the 1939 edition, the bystander asks 'Wheres your warrant?', which is repeated by several others.

have no truck with him: have nothing to do with him.

Cheltenham, Harrow, Cambridge: Cheltenham is a town in Gloucestershire; Harrow, founded in 1572, is one of the most prestigious secondary schools in England; and the University of Cambridge, founded in 1209, is a world-renowned third-level institution.

toff: slang term for someone from the upper classes.

Earlscourt: Clara was originally from Bayswater, but Shaw changed this in early proofs (CON P 1913). Both neighbourhoods are a few miles to the west of Covent Garden. Earls Court was a less expensive part of the borough of Kensington and Chelsea.

Epsom: a market town in Surrey known for the Derby horse race.

14 *copper*: slang for police officer.

Hanwell: a town at the western extremity of London.

15 *worried and chivied*: worried and harassed.

The science of speech: this line was added in the typescript (P Type, 10), perhaps to explain to the audience what exactly phonetics is.

brogue: a strong accent or dialect.

Sometimes within two streets: this line was added in the typescript (P Type, 10), evidently to make Higgins even more impressive.

Kentish Town: a neighbourhood in north London that was rampant with poverty at the time.

with feeble defiance: the typescript reads 'with feeble, ~~deprecating,~~ defiance' (P Type, 11).

daring to raise: Shaw changed it to this from the plainer and less psycho-logically revelatory 'raising' (P Type, 11).

Garn!: slang for 'Go on!', generally uttered in disbelief or ridicule.

16 *an ambassador's garden party*: Higgins's boast was originally bolder in the typescript: 'a Buckingham Palace garden party: and I could pass her father off—if she has one—as a Lord Chief Justice' (P Type, 12).

Queen of Sheba: an extremely wealthy queen who lived in the tenth century BCE. She visited King Solomon to test his wisdom with a series of riddles.

Colonel Pickering: originally 'General Pickering' (P Type, 12).

Henry Higgins: the names of Shaw's characters have provided a great deal of academic speculation and in many cases open up provocative readings of the plays. From 1901 to 1943, Shaw's head gardener at his home in Ayot St Lawrence was Henry Higgs; Higgs's wife, who was Shaw's housekeeper over the same years, was named Clara, like the daughter of Mrs Eynsford Hill. This would suggest a rather unlikely match between these two characters—or it was, perhaps, Shaw having a bit of fun with an inside joke at his employees' expense.

the Carlton: a luxury hotel in Haymarket, central London, which operated from 1899 to 1940 and was demolished in 1958. It stood beside His Majesty's Theatre, where *Pygmalion* had its English-language premiere in 1914.

half-a-crown: originally 'a shilling' (P Type, 13).

17 *Pharisaic want of charity*: the Pharisees were a Jewish religious party known for ostentatious demonstrations of piety. The motivations behind their charitable acts have been questioned, many believing that the Pharisees gave for their own glory rather than for the welfare of others.

florins: a florin is an English coin worth two shillings, but the term can also refer to coins in a more general sense. The name is derived from the Italian city of Florence, where some English coins were made.

18 *Drury Lane*: the taxi ride from Covent Garden to Drury Lane is comically short, the distance between them being only 0.3 miles, thus emphasizing Eliza's extravagance. As we see in the next scene, it takes her all of two minutes to get home. Drury Lane was a slum notorious for prostitution and drinking establishments.

Impidence!: 'Impudence!'

20 *Wimpole Street*: Higgins lives in Wimpole Street, part of the affluent London neighbourhood of Marylebone.

bellows: Shaw originally described the pipes as being 'in a medieval case' and 'looking like those played by angels in 14th century paintings' (P Type, 14).

On the piano . . . mostly chocolates: this sentence did not originally appear in the typescript, to which Shaw only added 'On the piano is a box of chocolates' (P Type, 15). The sentence was emended to the longer description for the 1916 edition.

Piranesis and mezzotint portraits: Giovanni Battista Piranesi (1720–78), also known as Giambattista Piranesi, was an Italian neoclassical printmaker and architect. Mezzotint, a method of printmaking, is derived from the Italian *mezza tinta*, meaning half-tone, which refers to the art's ability to gradate black ink on a white background.

frock-coat: double-breasted coat, with long skirts both in front and behind.

Next day . . . moments: the opening stage directions for Act II originally read: 'Higgins's laboratory in Wimpole Street. Phonographs, records, a laryngoscope, working model of the vocal organ, etc. HIGGINS and PICKERING' (P Type, 16).

21 *It's for you to say*: originally, before Mrs Pearce leaves, Higgins added: '(as she goes out) And oh, by the way, Mrs Pearce. Stay here with us when she comes up. You understand.' She then responded before leaving: 'Yessir' (P Type, 17). This would have shown that Higgins was more aware of the potential impropriety of the situation and/or that he wished Mrs Pearce to be there to escort the girl out should the situation require it.

22 *broad Romic*: phonetic alphabet created by Henry Sweet and the direct precursor of the International Phonetic Alphabet.

saucy: insolent.

stupent: stupefied.

bringing you business?: Shaw deleted a brief exchange between Higgins and Eliza here:

HIGGINS. Patronizing me!
THE FLOWER GIRL. Oh well, I didnt say so, did I? Oh, dont rumple your hair like that. I'm not going to eat you.
(P Type, 19)

23 *Tottenham Court Road*: major commercial street in central London.

zif: this reads 'as if' in all editions of the play previous to 1941.

Youd had a drop in, hadnt you?: Shaw added this line in the typescript (P Type, 20).

peremptorily: decisively.

24 *Take it or leave it*: Eliza originally said, rather less assertively: 'That's fair, now, aint it?' (P Type, 21).

guineas: a guinea was worth twenty-one shillings, or one pound one shilling.

25 *Dont cry, you silly girl. Sit down*: Mrs Pearce was slightly more coaxing in the original: 'Come come come now, you silly girl. You dont understand. Now be quiet' (P Type, 21).

the ambassador's garden party: to follow the bet from Act I, Pickering originally referred here to 'the garden party at Buckingham Palace' (P Type, 22).

horribly dirty: Shaw has the actor emphasize 'horribly' (RN P 1920).

I washed . . . I did: originally, Eliza added that she washed her face 'with scented soap' (P Type, 22).

26 *inspired follies?*: Shaw directs the actor to emphasize 'follies' (RN P 1920).

Monkey Brand: a scouring soap.

Take all her clothes off and burn them: Shaw instructs Higgins throughout this scene to 'Walk over everybody' and say 'WALLOP her' (RN P 1936).

Whiteley: first opened in 1863 in Westbourne Grove, Whiteleys is considered London's first department store. In 1911, it was relocated to Queensway in Bayswater, not far from Higgins's house in Marylebone. In 2018 it was closed for redevelopment.

27 *I walk over everybody!*: Shaw tells the actor that the charge has 'no effect' on Higgins because he believes that 'he has not walked over anybody' (RN P 1920).

Married indeed!: Shaw excised the sentence 'Cant you see that shes still young—that she'll look quite fresh when you clean her up' that originally followed this line (CON P 1913).

balmies: crazy people. The terms 'balmy' and 'barmy' were used more interchangeably in the past, with 'balmy' now tending to mean mild weather and 'barmy' retaining the meaning of crazy.

You see now what comes of being saucy: originally, instead of this line, Mrs Pearce said: 'Dont be silly, child. Cant you see that the gentleman doesnt mean what he says?' (P Type, 25).

28 *I aint got no mother*: Eliza originally responded: 'Dead' (P Type, 26).

Oh you are a brute: Shaw originally had Eliza emphasize 'are'. He also had Eliza stand 'akimbo', but in the proofs, he wrote that she was to deliver these lines after 'turning on him'. The revisions make her less defensive and more on the counter-attack (CON P 1913).

[To Pickering] Oh, sir . . . like that: this stage direction and line did not appear in earlier editions. In their place was the stage direction '*She goes back to her chair and plants herself there defiantly*' (CON P 1916; CON P 1931).

29 *in a flower shop*: Shaw added this phrase in the 1941 edition.

Have some chocolates, Eliza: Shaw directs Eliza that her 'mouth waters' (RN P 1920).

30 *Tower of London . . flower girls*: first built in the eleventh century, the Tower of London was a renowned prison and site of execution. When Shaw wrote the play, it still served these purposes.

31 *no longer audible*: Shaw added the next scene in the 1941 edition. In the 1931 edition, the stage direction continues: 'Pickering comes from the hearth to the chair and sits astride it with his arms on the back.' It then picks up with his line 'Excuse the straight question, Higgins.' When this scene was added for performance, the Lord Chamberlain commented that it could be played as long as Eliza's robe was snatched from her offstage, adding: 'I think it would make a nice scene' (LC P).

scullery: a room attached to the kitchen where washing is done.

32 *Funny sort of copper*: having believed that she would be taken to the scullery, she now mistakes the bath for a cooking or laundry boiling vat, vessels
traditionally made of copper.

   slut: while the more contemporary use of slut tends to refer to a sexually
promiscuous woman, it has historically also referred to one who is dirty
and slovenly in appearance and habits.

35 *She has Eliza's hat ... Not at all, sir*: Shaw added this dialogue and the
references to Eliza's hat in the typescript (P Type, 32–3).

   She knows no better: originally, Mrs Pearce said: 'She was quite surprised
when I told her not to repeat it' (P Type, 33).

36 *benzine*: now most commonly written as 'benzene', this is a cleaning fluid
and a product used in petrol. Higgins likely uses it for his laboratory
equipment.

37 *dustman*: a refuse/garbage collector. Mrs Pearce originally called him 'a
man' (P Type, 35).

   blackguard: someone who acts in a dishonourable way; also a villain.

   He may not be a blackguard ... not I with him: Shaw added this exchange in
the typescript (P Type, 36), emphasizing that both men are aware of the
potential impropriety of the situation and the possibility that Eliza's father
will want to profit by it.

38 *Hounslow*: a borough on the western periphery of London. It is home to
Heathrow, London's major airport.

   menacingly: Shaw originally wrote 'aggressively', then changed it to
'sternly' (P Type, 36). It appears as 'menacingly' in the 1916 edition.

   some spark of family feeling left: Shaw has Higgins emphasize 'some' (RN
P 1920).

   Is this reasonable?: Shaw directs Doolittle to 'sing' the line (RN P 1920).

   fairity: fair.

   farthing: a coin worth one-quarter of a penny.

   a poser: a question.

   Well, what would a man come for?: Shaw instructs Higgins to 'hold him'
(RN P 1920). This means to fix him in his gaze, not to physically
embrace him.

39 *'most musical, most melancholy'*: a quote from John Milton's poem 'Il
Penseroso' (1631).

   I'm willing to tell you. I'm wanting to tell you. I'm waiting to tell you: for
these lines to have their desired effects, Shaw instructs the actor that he
should 'begin low' (RN P 1920).

   his native woodnotes wild: Higgins here quotes directly from Milton's pas-
toral poem 'L'Allegro' (1631), which is a companion to 'Il Penseroso'.
While 'L'Allegro' invokes the goddess Mirth, 'Il Penseroso' invokes the
goddess Melancholy.

402 | *Explanatory Notes*

39 *please*: Shaw emphasized this only in the first edition (CON P 1916).

the corner of Long Acre and Endell Street: this intersection is close to half-way between Covent Garden and Eliza's former home in Drury Street; it is a very short walk to each.

Public house: a drinking establishment, more commonly called by its abbreviated name, pub.

40 *You'd better go ... with dignity*: Shaw added this in the typescript (P Type, 40), evidently feeling that it would be better in terms of the propriety of the scene were Mrs Pearce not present for the discussion between Higgins and Doolittle.

41 *Do you mean to say*: Shaw originally had Higgins charge Doolittle here as 'you infernal scoundrel', then changed it to 'callous rascal', before deleting all name-calling (P Type, 41).

Have you no morals, man?: Shaw has Pickering emphasize 'morals' (RN P 1920).

42 *What is middle class morality?*: Shaw instructs the actor to 'expand' here (RN P 1920).

43 *it makes a man feel prudent like*: Shaw instructs Doolittle to be 'slow' when delivering this line (RN P 1920).

44 *conceited*: this originally read 'conscious' (P Type, 46).

towel horse: a rack on which one hangs a towel.

Me!: in the first edition, Shaw added emphasis here, but he did away with it in later editions.

to give her a lick of a strap: to hit her with a strap made out of leather, to flog her.

45 *Your blessing, for instance*: instead of this line, Higgins originally turned to Pickering and said: 'I should think our friend would come out strong as Polonius, if he let himself go.' Before picking up where he does in the script here, Doolittle responded: 'I know all about that, sir. Him in the play, you mean. "Costly thy habit as thy purse can buy." She dont need me to tell her' (P Type, 48). In Shakespeare's *Hamlet* (1599–1601), Polonius offers his son Laertes a good deal of fatherly advice on how to lead his life, including the line that Doolittle quoted, before Laertes leaves Denmark for Paris (*Hamlet*, I. iii. 60–87).

navvy: a labourer employed in the construction of canals, roads, and railways.

46 *Higgins: we have*: all editions prior to that of 1941 ended Act II here.

47 *nine years in school at our expense*: beginning in 1870, a series of educational acts made school mandatory for children. As a local politician, Shaw was well aware of such legislation and the Fabian Society published a pamphlet on the subject, *The Education Act, 1902: How to Make the Best of It* (1903), to help borough and county councillors better understand and administer the law.

Fortissimo: Italian musical term meaning 'very loud'.

cep: except.

49 *Chelsea Embankment*: a road and walkway on the southernmost border of Chelsea, in south-west London. It runs along the northern bank of the River Thames, between the Chelsea and Albert bridges, and directly across from Battersea Park, which Higgins looks out at when he turns away from the Eynsford Hills.

Morris and Burne Jones: William Morris (1834–96) and Sir Edward Coley Burne-Jones (1833–98) were leading artists and designers in the Victorian period; their work was in the romantic vein and employed medieval imagery.

Grosvenor Gallery: a private gallery that operated from 1877 to 1890 and is best remembered for introducing such avant-garde artists as Burne-Jones and Whistler. It served as the more progressive counterpoint to the conservative Royal Academy.

Whistler: American artist James McNeill Whistler (1834–1903), who helped to introduce modern French painting to England.

Cecil Lawson ... Rubens: Scottish painter Cecil Lawson (1849–82) was likewise celebrated by the Grosvenor Gallery; Peter Paul Rubens (1577–1640) was a Flemish Baroque painter.

portrait of Mrs Higgins ... Rossettian costumes: English artist Dante Gabriel Rossetti (1828–82) was a founder of the Pre-Raphaelite Brotherhood and a friend of Edward Burne-Jones and William Morris. The painting of Mrs Higgins would have depicted her in a dress in the fashion of the aesthetic movement, the forerunners of which were Rossetti and Morris. Aesthetic dress countered the stiffly tailored clothing of Victorian fashion in favour of the flowing, softer, and more comfortable clothing of medieval times.

Chippendale chair: a generally rococo style of furniture that was fashionable in the third quarter of the eighteenth century. It was named after Thomas Chippendale (1718–79), a leading English cabinetmaker. Like aesthetic dress, it favours more natural, curving forms.

in the taste of Inigo Jones: in the neoclassical style favoured by Inigo Jones.

50 *You offend ... meet you*: Mrs Pearce originally said: 'Three friends whom I particularly like dropped me after your behavior last time' (P Type, 52). Shaw's revision conveys that Higgins's loutish behaviour is more habitual.

large talk?: Mrs Higgins originally added a few lines here: 'If youd only hold your tongue, it wouldnt matter, but that is the one thing you cannot do. You are a perfect bull in a china shop' (P Type, 53).

Henry! ... I must: the opening of Act III was originally briefer:

MRS HIGGINS Henry.

HIGGINS (kissing her) Mother.

MRS HIGGINS And to what do I owe the unexpected honor?

HIGGINS I ought to come oftener. But you know I'm becoming an awful brute. Always on the job. I never see anyone I care about. I'm always with people I'm interested in.

MRS HIGGINS   Then how have I managed to interest you today?
(P Type Ins)

51 *she must talk about something*: Shaw has the actor emphasize 'something'
    (RN P 1920).

52 *Ive seen you before somewhere*: Shaw has Higgins emphasize 'you' (RN
    P 1920).

53 *as anybody else*: Mrs Higgins originally intervened before the parlourmaid
    appears, saying: 'Henry is being very nice to you,—in his way. Youll get
    used to him' (P Type, 58).

    Ahdedo?: How do you do?

    Royal Society's soirées: evening sessions, including lectures and debates,
    held by the Royal Society, which was founded in 1660 to promote scientific
    learning.

54 *Or of manners, Henry?*: before the parlourmaid appears, Shaw had origin-
    ally written a longer exchange, which continued:

    HIGGINS   Oh, theres nothing wrong with my manners. (Resuming his
       catechism) You dont mind, do you?
    MRS E.H.   Oh, not at all.
    HIGGINS   (to MISS E.H.) Do you?
    MISS E.H.   (rising to the occasion) Of course I do. Youre the rudest man
       I ever met.
    MRS HIGGINS   (laughs) !!!
    HIGGINS   (laughing also) Well, isnt it just as good fun as the other thing,
       anyhow?
    MRS HIGGINS   You have forgotten to apologize to Mr. Eynsford Hill.
    FREDDY   (blushing) Oh, not at all. When a chap has a sister he gets
       accustomed to home truths. (MISS E.H. looks daggers)
    HIGGINS   (breaking a momentary silence) I daresay youre right. We were
       a lot of brothers with just one little sister at the tail end of the family.
       We spoilt her like anything. But it must be a devil of a thing to have an
       older sister, especially if she has a bit of tongue.
    FREDDY   (with conviction) It is; and no mistake.
    MRS HIGGINS   (to MISS EYNSFORD HILL, who is furious) I was an elder
       sister, Miss Eynsford Hill. Imagine my feelings! I have been elder sis-
       tering and mothering all my life; and this is my reward.
    MISS E.H.   (disarmed) We are fellow-sufferers. I am older than Freddy,
       I am sorry to say.
    MRS HIGGINS   Are you, by George!
    MISS E.H.   I am delighted to find that I look younger.
    HIGGINS   You dont. I should say theres a good six years between.
    (P Type, 59–60)

    The original dialogue makes Clara considerably more aware and assertive
    and reveals more about Higgins's family story. It also suggests that his
    interest in and treatment of Eliza might be determined in part by his rela-
    tionship with his younger sister.

55 *The shallow depression . . . barometrical situation*: Eliza originally said: 'The weather is fine; but the depression is advancing from the South West of Ireland and mild showers may be expected later' (P Type 60b).

56 *Why should she die of influenza?*: Shaw has Eliza emphasize 'she' (RN P 1920).

pinched it: slang for 'stole it'.

Not her . . . Besides: Shaw added this in the typescript (P Type, 63).

57 *Not bloody likely*: the Reader's Report for the Lord Chamberlain, dated 23 February 1914, reads: 'On Page 46, the word "bloody" slips out of the as yet only partially educated Liza and on the next page a silly young woman uses it under the impression that it is part of the new "small talk". The word is not used in anger, of course, and the incident is merely funny. I think it would be a mistake to be particular about it, but since the word has been forbidden in other plays—in a different sort of connection, however—I mention it' (LC P). An 'X' is pencilled in the margins beside both Eliza's 'bloody' and Clara's 'bloody.'

Sensation: originally the stage direction read 'Freddy reels. Higgins falls back on the divan' (P Type).

60 *review the volunteers in Hyde Park*: soldiers (volunteers) were periodically inspected (reviewed) by the royal family and ranking officers in London's Hyde Park. Closely akin to military parades, such reviews provided impressive spectacles and the public attended them in large numbers.

talk like a bishop: originally, Mrs Higgins then added: 'Thank you for saying bishop without any adjective, Henry.' To this, Higgins explodes: 'Well, damn him', which Shaw changed to 'dash him'. Before Mrs Higgins addresses Colonel Pickering, she continued: 'Sh-sh-sh! Thats quite enough on that subject. I want to ask you something else' (P Type, 69).

61 *Hottentot clicks*: the Khoekhoe, also spelled Khoikhoi, are an African people who were formerly pejoratively known as the Hottentots, an Afrikaner nomenclature that imitates the clicks of the Khoekhoe language.

62 *Beethoven . . . Monckton*: German classical composers Ludwig van Beethoven (1770–1827) and Johannes Brahms (1833–97), Hungarian operetta composer Franz Lehár (1870–1948), and English musical-comedy composer Lionel Monckton (1861–1924). In the years around which Shaw wrote *Pygmalion*, Lehár and Monckton enjoyed considerable success on London stages.

dont you realize . . . walked in with her: originally, Mrs Higgins asked Pickering 'have you known Henry long enough to find him out?' After this, the conversation took a different tack:

HIGGINS What the—

MRS HIGGINS Be quiet, Henry. I am speaking to Colonel Pickering, not to you.

PICKERING I dont quite understand. Found out what?

HIGGINS   The old story—

MRS HIGGINS   Do hold your tongue, Henry, to oblige me.

HIGGINS   O, very well, very well, very well. Have it your own way. I have devoted my life to the regeneration of the Human race through the most difficult science in the world; and then I am told I am selfish. Go on. Go on.

PICKERING   I find him a very good fellow, Mrs Higgins. I get on very well with him.

MRS HIGGINS   No doubt. He _is_ a very good fellow.

HIGGINS   Thank you.

MRS HIGGINS   (Continuing) If he were not, he would be in prison or in the Cape Police, or some other refuge for gentlemen criminals. He has always been a headstrong, ungovernable, perfectly unscrupulous boy; and if it were not that by the mercy of heaven his impulses are mostly good ones I dont know what would have become of him.

PICKERING   We are all creatures of impulse, Mrs Higgins.

MRS HIGGINS   Dont talk nonsense, Colonel Pickering.

HIGGINS   (Uproariously) Ha ha! Ha ha! Your turn now, Pick.

MRS HIGGINS   Less noise, Henry, please. (To Pickering) Soldiering may be a matter of impulses: at least it doesnt seem to require much fore-thought in our army; but housekeeping and mothering and women's work in general teach them some conscience and consideration, dont they?

PICKERING   Yes; but what is all this leading to, my dear lady?

MRS HIGGINS   Patience, Colonel: I am not as amusing as Eliza; but what I say is for your good.

PICKERING   I am sure of that, Mrs Higgins.

HIGGINS   Ha ha! O Lord! If you could only see your face, Pick!

The conversation then picked up with Mrs Higgins noting that when Eliza walked into Wimpole Street, something came with her (P Type, 72–3).

63   *Shakespear exhibition at Earlscourt*: from May to October 1912, an exhib-ition on 'Shakespeare's England' was held at Earl's Court. It was organ-ized by Lady Randolph Churchill (1854–1921), known then as Mrs George Cornwallis-West by virtue of her second marriage, to raise funds for the Shakespeare Memorial National Theatre Fund, a project for which Shaw had long campaigned. Lady Churchill is best known today as the mother of British prime minister Sir Winston Churchill (1874–1965).

Oh, men! men!! men!!!: in all editions prior to that of 1941, Act III ends here.

64   *Pandour from Hungary*: a Hungarian guard or police officer.

65   *Clerkenwell*: a neighbourhood now in the London borough of Islington that has had a tradition of making clocks and watches since the eighteenth century.

66   *somnambulist*: sleepwalker.

débutante: in high society circles, a debutante is a young woman making her first public appearance. Until 1958, debutantes were presented at Court each year.

Mrs Langtry: English actor Lillie Langtry (1853–1929). Her second marriage was to Hugo de Bathe (1871–1940), a baronet, thereby making her Lady Bathe at the time of the play. Considered one of the most beautiful women of her time and at one time mistress of the future Edward VII (1841–1910), she caused some sensation in 1881 when she became the first society woman to appear on stage.

67 *Magyar races*: a member of a Hungarian-speaking people who are mostly concentrated in Hungary; however, they also have significant numbers in Romania, Croatia, Slovakia, and Ukraine.

68 *Morganatic*: relating to a marriage between a man of high rank and a woman of lower rank in which the woman and her children have no claim to the husband's title and possessions.

69 *all the finery . . . bet for him*: instead of this phrase, the 1939 edition reads: '*opera cloak, brilliant evening dress, and diamonds, with fan, flowers, and all accessories*'.

La Fanciulla del Golden West: a three-act opera whose title is *La fanciulla del West*, the English version being *The Girl of the Golden West*. Written by Giacomo Puccini (1858–1924), the Italian composer of such major operas as *La Bohème*, *Tosca*, and *Madame Butterfly*, it premiered at the Metropolitan Opera in New York in December 1910 and had its first English performance at London's Covent Garden Theatre in May 1911, the year before Shaw wrote *Pygmalion*.

70 *coroneted billet-doux*: a love letter bearing the seal of a member of the peerage. As Higgins's reaction in the next line suggests, Pickering is being ironic.

71 *Theres always something professional*: Shaw has Eliza emphasize 'always' (RN P 1920).

may you never have a day's luck with them!: Eliza originally said: 'be damned to you' (P Type, 78).

crisps: curls.

74 *shied*: carelessly threw.

75 *perfunctorily*: quick and carelessly.

This ring . . . Brighton: this is a curious and unexplained reference. Brighton is a coastal resort in East Sussex. Eliza wearing the ring for such an important day and evening suggests that it is of some value. Given that Shaw denies that there is any romance between Higgins and Eliza, this ring and their trip to Brighton injects some peculiar ambiguity into their relationship.

Dont you hit me . . . to the heart: Shaw added this exchange in the typescript (P Type, 84).

slamming the door savagely: in earlier editions, following this stage direction, Shaw continues differently: '*Eliza smiles for the first time; expresses her feelings by a wild pantomime in which an imitation of Higgins's exit is confused with her own triumph; and finally goes down on her knees on the hearthrug to look for the ring*' (CON P 1916; CON P 1931). Act IV then ends. The scene between Freddy and Eliza was added in the 1941 edition.

77 *Cavendish Square*: one block east of Wimpole Street.

Hanover Square: two blocks south of Cavendish Square.

78 *Wimbledon Common*: a 460-hectare parkland located 8 miles south-west of Hanover Square. Its size and wilderness would have afforded them considerably more privacy than the squares of the city.

79 *Ask her not to come down til I send for her*: this line originally read: 'Say she can do as she likes about coming down' (P Type, 86).

What am I to do?: in the typescript, Shaw included a brief exchange before Higgins says this line:

MRS HIGGINS   Were you in bed, asleep?
HIGGINS   Yes; but she could have called me.
MRS HIGGINS   Are you always very amiable when you are disturbed?
HIGGINS   But, Good Heavens! this was something serious. Theyd have to call me if the house was on fire. Well: this was worse than ten fires. What am I to do?
(P Type, 87)

81 *He is resplendently ... the bridegroom*: in all earlier editions, this line reads: '*He is brilliantly dressed in a new fashionable frock-coat, with white waistcoat and grey trousers.*' In the typescript, the line originally read: 'He is well—indeed brilliantly—dressed and looks rather like Abraham Lincoln' (P Type, 89).

Why would she buy me clothes?: Doolittle originally said: 'Catch her throwing her money away' (P Type, 89).

82 *Moral Reform Societies*: from the eighteenth century to well into the twentieth century, Britain and the United States had a number of such organizations. They were founded to combat prostitution, sexual promiscuity, alcohol, and Godlessness.

Ezra D. Wannafeller: a satirical hybrid of two American business titans: John Wanamaker (1838–1922) and John D. Rockefeller (1839–1937). Rockefeller became a generous philanthropist in the twentieth century.

three thousand a year: in the sequel at the end of Act V, Shaw says that Doolittle lives on four thousand a year (p. 102).

83 *Skilly ... Char Bydis*: Doolittle's malapropisms; he means Scylla and Charybdis. In the *Odyssey*, by Greek poet Homer (ninth or eighth century BCE), Odysseus must navigate his boat through a narrow channel, on one side of which is Scylla, a horrible sea creature, and on the other side Charybdis, a monster who personifies a deadly whirlpool. To be caught between Scylla and Charybdis means to be confronted by two unpleasant alternatives.

84 *Happier men than me*: Shaw instructs Doolittle to 'sing it' (RN P 1920).

this morning: in earlier editions, following this sentence and before the next, Mrs Higgins says: 'She passed the night partly walking about in a rage, partly trying to throw herself into the river and being afraid to, and partly in the Carlton Hotel' (CON P 1916; CON P 1931). The deletion was evidently necessary because of the addition of the scene at the end of Act IV when Freddy and Eliza leave to spend the night on Wimbledon Common.

85 *But why? What did we do to her?*: instead of Pickering's line, it originally read:

MRS HIGGINS   Which she learnt, I'm afraid, from you, dear.
HIGGINS   Certainly not. I am always particularly careful what I say in her presence—except of course when something upsets me.
(P Type, 96)

a girl of her class: originally, Mrs Higgins instead said 'a girl like that'. She then continued before her next sentence: 'She studied all your ways. You said just now that you cant find anything and cant remember anything now shes gone. That means that shes been finding everything and remembering everything, I suppose' (P Type, 96).

the whole thing: Mrs Higgins originally added: 'as if the girl was a doormat' (P Type, 96).

We said nothing . . . Wimpole Street: the dialogue originally read:

HIGGINS   You know, mother, all this is pure imagination. We said nothing except that we were tired and wanted to go to bed. It's all her fancy. It's the most infernal nonsense. Isn't it, Pick?
PICKERING   Well, women do go on like that. I didnt mean to be unkind to the girl.
HIGGINS   (Intolerantly, rising). Oh, tell her to come down, and not be a damned fool.
MRS HIGGINS   Henry: will you please sit down and stop using bad language.
HIGGINS   (With a snort of protest). !! (he sits down).
MRS HIGGINS   I have tried to make Eliza understand that this kind of stupidity is part of what people call manliness. I did my best to persuade her at the same time that you, Henry, are not quite incapable of feeling; but I dont think I should have convinced her if you hadnt fortunately parted from her with some words which betrayed on your—
HIGGINS   She lies. She hurt my feelings very much; and I damned her up hill and down dale.
MRS HIGGINS   Yes, I gathered that that was the particular form of endearment that just saved the situation. Well, I am afraid she will not go back to Wimpole Street...
(P Type, 97)

86 *Henry, I'll ask her to come down*: this line originally read: 'and remember that she is a lady and that you are a gentleman, I will call her down and let her see you' (P Type, 98).

86 *He is doing his best, Mrs Higgins*: Pickering originally said: 'I really dont see what more we can do' (P Type, 99).

87 *It's very kind of you to say so, Miss Doolittle*: Shaw added this line in the typescript (P Type, 100).

88 *I was brought up to be just like him*: Shaw has Eliza emphasize 'I' (RN P 1920).
But you see I did it: Shaw has Eliza emphasize 'did' (RN P 1920).

89 *your teeth, Henry*: Mrs Higgins originally continued: 'I shall have to get you a coral if you do' (P Type).

I cant go back to it: in earlier editions, before she continues with the next sentence, Eliza says: 'Last night, when I was wandering about, a girl spoke to me; and I tried to get back into the old way with her; but it was no use' (CON P 1916; CON P 1931). As above, Shaw would have cut this line in the 1941 edition because he added the scene between Freddy and Eliza at the end of Act IV.

90 *spraddling*: sprawling.

St George's, Hanover Square: St George's church lies just south of Hanover Square, where Freddy and Eliza are last seen in Act IV. Built in the eighteenth century, the church is located in the wealthy neighbourhood of Mayfair, which has made it a common site for high society weddings.

91 *Quite right . . . bachelor can*: instead of this exchange, Shaw originally had Eliza return here and announce: 'I'm quite ready' (P Type, 105).

tremenjous: tremendous; not a typographical error.

brougham: a closed, horse-drawn carriage.

dad: in earlier editions, Eliza calls Doolittle 'papa' (CON P 1916; CON P 1931).

92 *Amen . . . preacher*: Shaw added this line in the typescript (P Type, 107).

93 *I wont be passed over . . . no consideration for anyone*: Shaw originally followed Eliza's comment about refusing to be passed over with a different dialogue:

HIGGINS   Indeed? And who has passed you over, pray?

ELIZA   You did. You looked at your slippers and you never looked at me. You said I had served your turn, and you were sick of me, and had been, all along, after the first fortnight. You took everything I did for you as a matter of course. You said I had no feelings; and what was worse, you didnt care whether I had or not. When I won your bet for you, and was sitting there sore all over with having had my heart in my mouth all day, you hadnt a kind word for me: you thought of nothing but your slippers and your satisfaction that you were done with me and wouldnt have to touch me or trouble yourself about me any more.

HIGGINS   (grinning) A-a-a-a-ahowooh!

ELIZA   (annoyed, turning away from him) No: its no use: you cant turn it off by making fun of me. (Over her shoulder) I can do without you: dont think I cant.

(P Type, 108)

[*selling violets*]: Shaw's own insertion.

94 *Dont sneer at me . . . trade in affection*: instead of this exchange, after making the analogy to selling violets Higgins originally continued: 'But let me tell you something. A person who cares for you is a person that wont let you call your soul your own. Its the people that dont care a damn for you that keep you alive. What do you suppose all this flower girl's snivel about wanting people to care for you matters to me? I am a man; and independence of that sort of thing is a man's advantage. I know that you women are always trying to fasten on the weak spot in us—the womanly spot, as it's called—to make us sentimental and personal like yourselves, and tie us up feet and hands so that we darent say a word we really think, or go away for a day by ourselves, for fear of hurting your feelings and making you cry. But you shant fasten yourself on me that way. No use slaving for me and then saying you want to be cared for: who cares for a slave? You call me a brute . . .' (P Type, 110).

You never thought of the trouble it would make for me: Shaw directs Eliza to emphasize 'me' (RN P 1920).

97 [*thunderstruck*] *Freddy!!! . . . be a teacher*: Shaw changed the dialogue to these lines in the 1941 edition. In earlier editions, it reads:

HIGGINS [*sitting down beside her*] Rubbish! you shall marry an ambassador. You shall marry the Governor-General of India or the Lord-Lieutenant of Ireland, or somebody who wants a deputy-queen. I'm not going to have my masterpiece thrown away on Freddy.

LIZA. You think I like you to say that. But I havnt forgot what you said a minute ago; and I wont be coaxed round as if I was a baby or a puppy. If I cant have kindness, I'll have independence.

HIGGINS. Independence? Thats middle class blasphemy. We are all dependent on one another, every soul of us on earth.

LIZA [*rising determinedly*] I'll let you see whether I'm dependent on you. If you can preach, I can teach. I'll go and be a teacher.

(CON P 1916; CON 1931)

that hairyfaced Hungarian: 'Professor Nepean' in earlier editions (CON P 1916; CON 1931). Shaw changed this line for the 1941 edition with the addition of the scene at the ambassador's party at the end of Act III. The Hungarian's name was also changed.

Aha . . . Enry Iggins: Shaw instructs Eliza to 'dance around' (RN P 1936).

98 *I like you like this*: Shaw directs Higgins: 'Youre alive at last' (RN P 1920).

new suit of mine: in earlier editions, Higgins continues the sentence to specify from which store he wants the gloves and tie to be purchased: 'at Eale & Binmans'.

incorrigible: the end of the dialogue from this point changes in various editions. The 1916 and 1931 editions read:

LIZA [*disdainfully*] Buy them yourself. [*She sweeps out*].

MRS HIGGINS. I'm afraid youve spoiled that girl, Henry. But never mind, dear: I'll buy you the tie and gloves.

HIGGINS [*sunnily*] Oh, dont bother. She'll buy em all right enough. Goodbye.

(CON P 1916; CON P 1931)

The 1939 edition reads:

LIZA [*disdainfully*] Buy them yourself. [*She sweeps out*].

MRS HIGGINS. I'm afraid youve spoilt that girl, Henry. I should be uneasy about you and her if she were less fond of Colonel Pickering.

HIGGINS. Pickering! Nonsense: she's going to marry Freddy. Ha ha! Freddy! Freddy!! Ha ha ha ha ha!!!!! [He roars with laughter as the play ends].

(CON P 1939)

99 *Nell Gwynne*: a leading actor of her day and a mistress of Charles II, Nell Gwyn (1650–87) started out selling oranges at the Drury Lane Theatre.

in particular: Shaw originally included another sentence here: 'It is almost enough to drive an unfortunate author to write novels, since in that childish pursuit he can at least stop the progress of his narrative to warn his romantic readers not to jump to silly conclusions' (P Pre/Ep).

between them: Shaw originally included another sentence here: 'I do not pretend to understand this; but I know it' (P Pre/Ep).

100 *intelligence*: originally 'indulgence' (P Pre/Ep).

Landor: English Romantic poet Walter Savage Landor (1775–1864). In Landor's dramatic sketch 'Roger Ascham and Lady Jane Grey', Ascham says to his pupil: 'Love is a secondary passion in those who love most, a primary in those who love least.'

101 '*When you go to women . . . take your whip with you*': from *Thus Spake Zarathustra* (1883–5), by German philosopher Friedrich Nietzsche (1844–1900).

'*the first lion thinks the last a bore*': from *Bombastes Furioso* (1810), a burlesque by English author William Barnes Rhodes (1772–1826). The line has been slightly altered from the original. The relevant passage reads: 'So I have heard, on Afric's burning shore | A hungry lion give a grievous roar; | The grievous roar echo'd along the shore.' To this is replied: 'So I have heard on Afric's burning shore | Another lion give a grievous roar, | And the first lion thought the last a bore.'

102 *sinecure*: a position in which one is paid for doing no work.

Nietzschean transcendence of good and evil: a reference to Nietzsche's *Beyond Good and Evil* (1886). This work was a major influence on Shaw.

four thousand a year: his income in the play is three thousand a year (p. 82).

103 *shift*: make a living by one's own devices.

the city: usually capitalized as 'the City', this is the central borough of London known for financial institutions, including the Bank of England and the Stock Exchange.

vouchsafed: given in a condescending manner.

104 *H. G. Wells*: a noted socialist and advocate for international cooperation and free love, H. G. Wells (1866–1946) was a leading writer of the time, authoring the novels *The Time Machine* (1895), *The Island of Doctor Moreau* (1896), *The Invisible Man* (1897), and *War of the Worlds* (1898). He was also a friend of Shaw's from the Fabian Society.

Acts of the Apostles: often shortened to Acts, this book of the New Testament details how the Apostles spread Christianity to the Gentiles and broke from Jewish traditions.

105 *General Booth or Gypsy Smith*: William Booth (1829–1912) was founder and general of the Salvation Army, an international Christian charitable organization. Booth recruited Rodney 'Gypsy' Smith (1860–1947), whose nickname was derived from his Romani (Gypsy) background, as an evangelist for the Salvation Army. For a depiction of the Salvation Army's work, see Shaw's play *Major Barbara* (1905).

Galsworthy: English novelist and playwright John Galsworthy (1867–1933), whose novel sequence *The Forsyte Saga* (1906–21) investigates the moral implications of accumulated wealth and property. His play *Justice* (1910) notably led to reform of the judicial-penal system.

106 *blackening the Largelady scutcheon*: 'scutcheon' is an archaic form of 'escutcheon', the shield on which a heraldic coat of arms is depicted. To blacken one's scutcheon is a figure of speech, meaning to stain one's reputation.

Dover Street: located in the Mayfair neighbourhood.

Age had not . . . half an hour: in Shakespeare's *Antony and Cleopatra*, Enobarbus praises Cleopatra: 'Age cannot wither her, nor custom stale | Her infinite variety' (II. ii. 276–7).

Victoria and Albert Museum: named after Queen Victoria (1819–1901) and her consort Prince Albert (1819–61), the Victoria and Albert Museum was founded in 1852. Its current building in South Kensington was completed in 1909 and houses an incredible collection of the decorative arts. Eliza's shop is near South Kensington tube station.

Porson or Bentley: Classical scholars Richard Porson (1759–1808) and Richard Bentley (1662–1742).

107 *that Balbus built a wall and that Gaul was divided into three parts*: Lucius Cornelius Balbus (*c.*100–*c.*32 BCE) was Julius Caesar's chief of staff and chief engineer. Gaul was the region inhabited by the Gauls; it comprises modern-day France, Luxembourg, northern Italy, western Germany, most of Switzerland, and parts of Belgium. Gaul was divided into four provinces, not three: Narbonensis (southern France), Aquitania (south-west France), Celtica (central France and Switzerland), and Belgica (north-east France). However, Caesar divided the Gauls into three people: the Aquitani, the Galli (or Celtae), and the Belgae.

London School of Economics: located in Westminster, the London School of Economics and Political Science is an international leader in social

sciences research. It was founded in 1895 by members of the Fabian
Society, including Sidney and Beatrice Webb (1859–1947 and 1858–1943
respectively) and Bernard Shaw. In 1900, it became a college of the
University of London.

107 *Dickensian essay . . . combined the information*: Mr Potts describes such an
incident in *The Pickwick Papers* (1836–7) by Charles Dickens (1812–70).

Kew Gardens: established in 1759, the Royal Botanic Gardens are situated
in Kew, in the south-west London borough of Richmond upon Thames.

108 *Esquire*: in Britain, the title esquire has its roots in the peerage to denote
those who were landowners, but over the years it has come to be appended
to the surnames of any professional man in lieu of Dr or Mr.

swank: ostentatious or pretentious behaviour.

HEARTBREAK HOUSE

111 *A Fantasia*: in music, a free instrumental composition springing solely
from the imagination of the author, and consequently varying widely in
form and style.

113 *Tchekov*: Anton Chekhov (1860–1904), author of *The Cherry Orchard*
(1904), *Uncle Vanya* (1897), and *The Seagull* (1896). The fourth play to
which Shaw refers is *Three Sisters* (1901). Chekhov's plays are devoid of
complex plots and have haunting atmospheres, something Shaw evokes in
Heartbreak House, which borrows other elements from Chekhov's plays.

Tolstoy . . . Enlightenment: Russian author Leo Tolstoy (1828–1910), a major
novelist, is best-known for *War and Peace* (1865–9) and *Anna Karenina*
(1875–7). He also penned a few plays, including *The Power of Darkness*
(1886) and *The Fruits of Enlightenment* (1889–90).

the Stage Society: founded in 1899 as a private theatre club, the Stage Society
produced new and experimental plays and those that had been refused
licence for public performance. Shaw was an active founding member for
many years and the Stage Society performed a number of his plays.

114 *Capua*: a prosperous ancient Italian city famous for its bronzes and perfumes, Capua was known as a place of luxury, having baths and the
second-largest amphitheatre in the Roman Empire.

Schumann: German Romantic composer Robert Schumann (1810–56).

the garden of Klingsor: Klingsor is an evil sorcerer whose garden enchants
the eponymous hero in *Parsifal* (1882), an opera by the German composer
Richard Wagner (1813–83). Shaw excised dialogue in *Heartbreak House* in
which Parsifal is evoked; see note to p. 234.

115 *Sabbath*: the sacred day of rest; Saturday in the Jewish faith, Sunday in the
Christian faith.

Granville Barker: Harley Granville-Barker (1877–1946) was a leading
English dramatist, producer, and actor. From 1904 to 1907 he managed

Explanatory Notes

the Court Theatre, which was important for establishing Shaw's reputation as a major playwright.

Bennett: English writer Arnold Bennett (1867–1931), author of several novels, including *Anna of the Five Towns* (1902) and *The Old Wives' Tale* (1908), is a central figure in the histories of both English and European realism.

Blake ... Hardy: English visionary, poet, and artist William Blake (1757–1827); French philosopher Henri Bergson (1859–1941), who, like Shaw, contributed to the interlinked notions of Creative Evolution and the Life Force that prioritized individual agency over biological determinism; Samuel Butler, see notes to pp. 3, 118, 264, and 277; physiologist John Scott Haldane (1860–1936); and leading English poets and novelists George Meredith (1828–1909) and Thomas Hardy (1840–1928).

Home Secretary: in British politics, the Home Secretary is the minister responsible for interior affairs of state.

liner: a steamship.

Bond Street: street in the wealthy Mayfair neighbourhood, renowned for luxury goods and designer brands.

Erasmus ... Sir Thomas More: Dutch humanist and scholar Desiderius Erasmus (1469–1536) and English humanist and statesman Sir Thomas More (1478–1535).

Votes for Everybody: a reference to the movement for universal suffrage in which every adult citizen would vote, regardless of sex, race, and class. Shaw had long supported women's suffrage, and the year before *Heartbreak House* was published women won the vote through the Representation of the People Act of 1918; however, until 1928 only women aged 30 and older could vote.

116 *Charles the Second*: Charles II (1630–85) was king of Great Britain and Ireland from 1660 to 1685.

117 *having to hide ... from the shells of an enemy*: in both world wars, stations of the London Underground (the city's subway system) functioned as air-raid shelters.

Kensington Gardens: a vast Royal Park in west London, situated between Kensington Palace to the west and Hyde Park to the east.

she smote our firstborn ... plagues of which Egypt never dreamed: in the Book of Exodus, God inflicts several plagues on Egypt, including the deaths of all firstborn sons, to persuade the Pharaoh to free the Israelites from slavery.

the great Plague of London: the Great Plague of London of 1665–6 ravaged the city's population, with some estimates that it killed nearly a quarter of its inhabitants.

the blackest Calvinism: blackest here means gloomiest. Calvinism is a Christian faith founded by John Calvin (1509–64), a French Protestant reformer whose teachings informed English Puritanism.

117 *Prussia*: the Kingdom of Prussia comprised large parts of Germany, Belgium, Denmark, Poland, Lithuania, Russia, and the Czech Republic from 1701 to 1918. In the wake of the Austro-Prussian War of 1866 and the Franco-Prussian War of 1870–1, Prussia became the leading state in the imperial German Reich. After the First World War, it was incorporated into the Weimar Republic.

118 *my next volume of plays*: Shaw's next volume of plays was his five-play cycle *Back to Methuselah* (1922), which illustrates the philosophy of Creative Evolution and runs from the Garden of Eden to the year 31920 CE.

Charles Darwin: English naturalist Charles Darwin (1809–82). As he suggests here, in emphasizing individual agency, Shaw's Creative Evolution differs from the determinism of Darwin's natural selection.

'of mind from the universe': a major influence on Shaw's thought, Butler wrote three books critical of Darwin's theories—*Evolution, Old and New* (1879), *Unconscious Memory* (1880), and *Luck, or Cunning?* (1887)—that emphasize the agency of creatures.

stop eating meat . . . Shelleyan grounds: the English Romantic poet Percy Bysshe Shelley (1792–1822) promoted vegetarianism in the essay 'A Vindication of Natural Diet', which was published initially as a note to his first major poem *Queen Mab* (1813) and later as a separate pamphlet. The essay argues for a compassionate view of animals and emphasizes his disgust and horror at eating flesh. For reasons similar to those of Shelley, Shaw was a devoted vegetarian.

Uric Acid: a chemical that aids with digestion but in large quantities can lead to gout and diabetes.

Pyorrhea: an inflammation of the gums.

table-rapping . . . drift to the abyss: here Shaw mocks the various fads of mysticism that were prevalent in Victorian society.

119 *child of Adam*: any human being; the term is derived from the biblical account that all humans are descendants of Adam, the first man.

The Inquisition: a judicial procedure and later an institution founded by the Catholic Church to combat heresy. It functioned in various forms from the twelfth to the nineteenth century. For a depiction of the Inquisition, see Scene VI of Shaw's *Saint Joan*.

General Medical Council: founded in 1858, the General Medical Council oversees the training and certification of the medical profession in Britain. As this paragraph attests, Shaw was a sceptic of modern medicine. For more on the subject, see his play *The Doctor's Dilemma* (1906) and its preface.

Larochefoucauld's . . . never read about it: French author François de La Rochefoucauld (1613–80). The line to which Shaw refers is maxim 136 from La Rochefoucauld's *Réflexions; ou, Sentences et maximes morales* (1665).

Swift: Irish satirist Jonathan Swift (1667–1745).

Peer Gynt: Shaw describes an episode from Henrik Ibsen's play *Peer Gynt* (1867).

120 *hyperaesthesia*: excessive sensitiveness.

British Museum: established in 1753, the British Museum is the national museum of Great Britain. Its present building, completed in 1852, is located in the Bloomsbury district of London. Shaw spent many of his early adult years working in its Reading Room.

the passionate penny collecting . . . some sort of regulation: on a Flag Day, money is raised for a charity or a community group by the sale of small paper flags or other tokens; these are worn as evidence that the wearer has contributed. The local council generally issues permits for such collections of funds.

121 *Victoria Cross*: established in 1856, the Victoria Cross is the highest military distinction in the British armed forces. It is awarded for extreme bravery in the face of the enemy.

Compulsory Military Service: in 1916, Britain adopted conscription to enforce military service for civilians.

Officers' Training Corps: now called the University Officers' Training Corps, it was founded in 1906. During the First World War, it was responsible for training a large number of officers.

Lynch law: punishment without trial.

Jaurès: French Socialist statesman Jean Jaurès (1859–1914) was assassinated by a fanatic who feared that his pacifism was helping the cause of the German forces.

Clemenceau: French prime minister Georges Clemenceau (1841–1929) was an ardent supporter of the war effort. In 1919, an anarchist failed in his attempt to assassinate Clemenceau during the Paris Peace Conference, where Clemenceau advocated for the harsh conditions on Germany that formed the foundations of the Treaty of Versailles.

Keir Hardie . . . Lloyd George: British Labour Party leader J. Keir Hardie (1856–1915), a dedicated socialist and pacifist, and David Lloyd George (1863–1945), a staunch member of the Liberal Party and advocate for armament who served as secretary of state for war (1916) and later as prime minister (1916–22).

influenza: the influenza pandemic of 1918–19, known as the Spanish flu, was the most severe and devastating outbreak in the twentieth century, causing an estimated 25 million deaths.

122 *'C'est la guerre'*: (Fr.) 'That's war.'

the Flood: the biblical flood that covered the earth and for which Noah built his ark; see Genesis 6–9.

American War Loans: in 1917–18, the American government sold Liberty Bonds, or Liberty Loans, to finance the war effort.

123 *à la Russe*: (Fr.) 'in the Russian manner'.

Thucydides: Greek historian Thucydides (c.460–404 BCE) authored the *History of the Peloponnesian War.*

123 *Luther and Goethe*: German theologian and religious reformer Martin Luther (1483–1546), who helped to usher in the Protestant Reformation in the sixteenth century, and the great German writer Johann Wolfgang von Goethe (1749–1832).

124 *Kaiser's*: during the First World War, the German Kaiser (emperor) was Wilhelm II (1859–1941).

changing the King's illustrious and historically appropriate surname for that of a traditionless locality: the British royal family is descended from the Saxe-Coburg-Gotha and Hanover dynasties of Germany. In 1917, they changed their surname to Windsor, the town in which the royal residence Windsor Castle is located, to reflect the patriotic atmosphere of the war years and to reject the outer vestiges of their German heritage.

St George and the Dragon: St George (third century) was a Christian warrior-martyr who reputedly saved the king of Libya's daughter from a dragon and then slayed the beast in return for baptism of the king's subjects. St George is the patron saint of England.

Archimedes: Greek mathematician and inventor Archimedes (*c.*287–212/11 BCE), who developed war machines to ward off the invading Roman forces, was killed by a Roman soldier.

carmagnoles: derived from the nickname of a French Revolutionary soldier, a carmagnole is the hyperbolic style of reporting successes in the French Revolutionary forces.

'Blood and destruction . . . the hands of war': in Shakespeare's *Julius Caesar*, Mark Antony describes the civil strife that will come to Italy following Caesar's murder:

> Blood and destruction shall be so in use,
> And dreadful objects so familiar,
> That mothers shall but smile when they behold
> Their infants quartered with the hands of war,
> All pity choked with custom of fell deeds,
> And Caesar's spirit, ranging for revenge,
> With Ate by his side come hot from hell,
> Shall in these confines with a monarch's voice
> Cry 'Havoc!' and let slip the dogs of war,
> That this foul deed shall smell above the earth
> With carrion men, groaning for burial.
>
> (III. i. 291–301)

125 *forming fours*: a military drill.

Frederick Keeling: Frederick 'Ben' Keeling (1886–1916), a noted socialist and active member of the Fabian Society, refused an officer's commission to serve as a private soldier. He earned a reputation as a particularly fierce fighter and was killed in action.

Newton: English physicist and mathematician Sir Isaac Newton (1643–1727).

Michael Angelo: Italian Renaissance sculptor, painter, and architect Michelangelo (1475–1564).

Napoleon: Napoleon Bonaparte (1769–1821), French post-Revolutionary general and emperor, is the eponymous hero of Shaw's play *The Man of Destiny* (1896).

126 *St Francis*: Italian saint Francis of Assisi (1181/2–1226) embraced a life of poverty and charitable acts to imitate the life of Christ. He was also a devoted lover of nature, seeing it as a reflection of God, and is the patron saint of ecology.

Richard III: Shaw draws on the popular view that English king Richard III (1452–85) was wicked, as promoted in Shakespeare's *Richard III* (1592–4).

Don Quixote: eponymous hero of the comic novel by Miguel de Cervantes (1547–1616); Quixote suffers from romantic delusions of grandeur.

Platos: Plato was a renowned Greek philosopher (428/7–348/7 BCE).

Bill Sikes: the violent criminal in Charles Dickens's novel *Oliver Twist* (1837–9).

Straining . . . Camel: adapted from Matthew 23: 24, in which Jesus berates the scribes and Pharisees, the hypocritical religious leaders of his day: 'You blind guides! You strain out a gnat but swallow a camel.' In this verse, he criticizes their tendency to focus on small matters while ignoring more important ones.

'the Huns': nomadic Asian people who attacked the Roman Empire. Under their great leader Attila (fifth century CE) the warrior Huns spread considerable fear, invading the southern Balkans, Greece, Gaul, and Italy. Hun became a byword for barbarian and the British applied it to the Germans in the First World War.

Neuve Chapelle . . . Gallipoli landing: Neuve Chapelle, in northern France, was the site of a British offensive in March 1915. The Gallipoli Campaign, which operated from February 1915 to January 1916, was mounted by Anglo-French forces to relieve pressure on the Russian army by attacking Turkey and taking control of the Dardanelles channel, which lies to the east of the Gallipoli peninsula. The landing began on 25 April 1915 and by the end of the campaign British Commonwealth forces had suffered 213,980 casualties.

127 *Lusitania*: ship sunk by a German U-boat (submarine) on 7 May 1915. The event caused major public outcry on both sides of the Atlantic.

Sir Hugh Lane: because of the unclear terms of his will, the extensive impressionist painting collection of Irish art dealer and gallery director Sir Hugh Percy Lane (1875–1915) is divided between museums in London and Dublin.

Ypres: a municipality in the Belgian province of West Flanders, Ypres was the site of three major battles during the First World War.

127 *I was well acquainted personally with the three best-known victims*: in addition to Lane, Shaw is likely referring to American theatre producer Charles Frohman (1860–1915) and American writer Elbright Hubbard (1856–1915).

the holocaust of Festubert: the Allied forces suffered massive casualties in the Battle of Festubert, in the Artois region of northern France, 15–25 May 1915.

128 *bombardments of Scarborough and Ramsgate*: German battleships bombarded the seaside towns of Scarborough, on 16 December 1914, and Ramsgate, on 27 April 1917. In Scarborough, there were seventeen casualties.

the battle of Jutland: the only major encounter between British and German fleets during the First World War took place from 31 May to 1 June 1916 off the coast of Denmark's Jutland peninsula. It involved 250 ships and over 100,000 men. It resulted in almost 10,000 casualties and Britain maintaining control of the North Sea.

khaki: the dull brownish-yellow colour of the British army's field uniforms.

the armistice . . . the following general election: the armistice, or cessation of hostilities that marked the end of the First World War, occurred on 11 November 1918; this remains a day of observation on which veterans are honoured. A general election was called in Britain following the end of the war; it was held on 14 December 1918.

129 *Bedlam*: founded in 1247, the Bethlem Royal Hospital, colloquially known as Bedlam, was England's first mental asylum. The word now colloquially signifies a general uproar or chaotic scene.

the submarine scare: during the First World War, and particularly from February 1917 on, German submarines were responsible for destroying a large number of ships coming from and bound for Britain. In April 1917 alone, they sank 430 Allied and neutral ships.

the Government . . to behave itself: during the conflict, the mistreatment of prisoners of war by both sides was a constant source of protest and tended to result in reprisals. Most belligerents used prisoners of war as cheap sources of labour to fuel the war effort.

131 *war rationing . . . coupon*: towards the end of the war in Britain, citizens were given coupon booklets to purchase such rationed goods as bread. There was a shortage of certain foods because the U-boat blockade around the British Isles made it difficult to import.

starving the enemies who had thrown down their arms: a reference to the harsh terms that the Treaty of Versailles imposed on Germany.

132 *The Yahoo and the Angry Ape*: in the final book of Jonathan Swift's *Gulliver's Travels* (1726), the Yahoo is a humanoid creature that is vicious and uncivilized; it is an extreme satirical depiction of humankind. The Yahoo lives in the land of the Houyhnhnms, a highly intelligent and virtuous race of horses. In Shakespeare's *Measure for Measure* (1603–4), Isabella compares man to an angry ape:

    But man, proud man,
   Dress'd in a little brief authority,
   Most ignorant of what he's most assur'd—
   His glassy essence—like an angry ape
   Plays such fantastic tricks before high heaven
   As makes the angels weep; who, with our spleens,
   Would all themselves laugh mortal.
           (II. ii. 146–52)

Wellington: Irish-born British general and prime minister Arthur Wellesley (1769–1852), 1st Duke of Wellington.

'Could great men . . . nothing but thunder': as above, Isabella speaks these lines in Shakespeare's *Measure for Measure* (II. ii. 139–43).

Messines Ridge: in 1917, the Allies undertook a vast mining operation under the Messines Ridge in Belgium. The detonation resulted in the utter destruction of the ridge and 17,000 casualties..

Stratford: Shakespeare was born in the Warwickshire town of Stratford-upon-Avon.

Byron said, 'not difficult to die': from *Manfred* (1817), by English Romantic poet Lord Byron (1788–1824). The actual line, the last spoken by the titular character, is "tis not so difficult to die' (III. iv. 151).

the traitor Bolo: Bolo Pasha (1867–1918), né Paul Bolo, was executed by the French as a traitor for accepting German money to finance French pacifist activities.

133 *'a man must live'*: from 'Of Managing the Will', by the French essayist Michel de Montaigne (1533–92). The line runs: 'a man must live by the world; and make his best of it, such as it is.'

the Prince of Peace: Jesus Christ.

'the grace of our Lord': from the apostolic benediction in 2 Corinthians 13: 14, which reads: 'May the grace of the Lord Jesus Christ, and the love of God, and the communion of the Holy Ghost, be with you all.'

Armada: fleet of warships, particularly as applied to the Spanish fleet that, under Philip II, was sent to attack England in 1588. Here Shaw uses the term to refer to the British navy.

Plague on Both your Houses!: in Shakespeare's *Romeo and Juliet* (1596), when Mercutio is dying from a wound sustained in a fight between the warring houses of Montague and Capulet, he curses them equally in anger: 'A plague o' both your houses!' (III. i. 103–4 and 111).

Bolshevist: the Bolshevik Party (the Russian Communist Party) seized power in Russia following the October (or Bolshevik) Revolution of 1917. Their leader was Vladimir Lenin (1870–1924).

Doubting Castle . . . Vanity Fair: characters, places, and events in the religious allegorical tale *Pilgrim's Progress* (1678–84), by English writer John Bunyan (1628–88).

133 *ancient public schools*: in Britain, the name given to a class of grammar
schools that were originally founded or endowed for public use, and later,
chiefly from the nineteenth century, developed into fee-paying private
secondary schools. Examples are Eton and Harrow.

Sir Douglas Haig: Douglas Haig (1861–1928) was commander in chief of
the British forces in France during the First World War.

Waterloos: a reference to the Battle of Waterloo (18 June 1815), the decisive
battle of the Napoleonic wars won by British and Prussian forces that took
place near the Belgian town of Waterloo.

134 *Heartbreak House has not yet reached the stage*: Shaw wrote the preface in
June 1919; the first performance of *Heartbreak House* was at New York's
Garrick Theatre on 10 November 1920.

Alboni: Italian opera singer Marietta Alboni (*c.*1826–94).

135 *flappers*: slang term for young women considered to lack decorum and to
be given to vice.

George Barnwell ... the Demon Barber of Fleet Street: references to English
playwright George Lillo's (1693–1739) tragedy *The London Merchant: or,
the History of George Barnwell* (1731), the protagonist of which begins as
an innocent young man but is lured into a life of crime and vice by a prostitute. Maria Marten was killed by her lover in what is known as the Red
Barn Murder, named after the scene of the crime; many Victorian melodramas and later films were made on the subject. Sweeney Todd is known
as the Demon Barber of Fleet Street; several plays and films have
recounted his story. His character first appeared in the penny dreadful
serial *The String of Pearls* (1846–7).

136 *Charles Wyndham*: popular English actor and theatre manager Sir Charles
Wyndham (1837–1919); he was known for his charitable performances for
injured servicemen as well as for his stage successes.

Pink Dominos: a farce by English playwright James Albery (1838–89); after
Albery's death, his wife, the actress Mary Moore (1861–1931), married
Charles Wyndham.

Wellington said that an army moves on its belly: this quote is actually attributed to Wellington's adversary Napoleon.

Mozart: Austrian composer Wolfgang Amadeus Mozart (1756–91).

Unser: (Ger.) 'our'.

the tercentenary of the death of Shakespear: as Shakespeare died in 1616, the
tercentenary of his death was in 1916.

137 *The Dark Lady of The Sonnets*: as he recounts here, Shaw wrote his
Shakespeare-inspired one-act comedy *The Dark Lady of the Sonnets*
(1910) as a fundraiser for the construction of a national theatre.

a single handsome subscription from a German gentleman: Carl Meyer
(1851–1922), who was born in Germany but spent most of his adult
life in England where he was a banker and mining magnate, donated

£70,000 to the National Theatre project in 1909. He was made a baronet in 1910.

Richard Mansfield: American actor and theatre manager Richard Mansfield (1854/7–1907) launched Shaw's career in the United States with *Arms and the Man* in 1894. His production of *The Devil's Disciple* in 1897–8 was Shaw's first hit.

the sole official attention ... the chief officer of its household: Shaw refers here to the censorship of plays, which was established in 1737 and continued until 1968. The censorship was run under the authority of the Lord Chamberlain, who is charged with organizing the monarch's daily activities; theatre managers had to submit plays to obtain a licence before mounting a public production. Shaw had had three of his plays banned in Britain: *Mrs Warren's Profession* (1893), *Press Cuttings* (1909), and *The Shewing-up of Blanco Posnet* (1909).

138 *Murray ... Drinkwater*: English Classics scholar Gilbert Murray (1866–1957), whose translations of ancient Greek plays renewed their popularity on the modern stage. He was a close friend of Shaw's and served as the model for Adolphus Cusins in *Major Barbara*. Like the others in this list, he was a major force in the development of modern drama in Britain. English author John Masefield (1878–1967) was a playwright, novelist, and poet; St John Hankin (1869–1909) was an English playwright; Laurence Housman (1865–1959) was an English artist and writer; English poet, playwright, and critic John Drinkwater (1882–1937) founded what would become the Birmingham Repertory Theatre Company in 1907.

a restoration to the stage of Shakespear's plays as he wrote them: in his theatre reviews of the 1890s, Shaw repeatedly bemoaned the quality of contemporary productions of Shakespeare. See *Our Theatres in the Nineties*, his three-volume collection of criticism.

Potiphar's wife: in Genesis 39, Potiphar's wife repeatedly attempts to seduce her husband's slave Joseph, but the latter resists. Joseph is put in prison when Potiphar's wife, frustrated with his rejections, falsely accuses him of attempting to seduce her.

Song of Songs: a book of the Old Testament also called the Song of Solomon, Song of Songs is a collection of love poems.

Schubert ... Brahms: Romantic composers: the Austrian Franz Schubert (1797–1828), the Germans Felix Mendelssohn (1809–47) and Johannes Brahms (1833–97), and the Frenchman Charles Gounod (1818–93).

139 *Cathedral of Rheims*: in 1429, the cathedral of this eastern French city saw the coronation of Charles VII, which Shaw depicts in Scene V of *Saint Joan*. It was seriously damaged by shelling in September 1914.

Little Theatre in the Adelphi: opened in 1910, this West End theatre was bombed in 1917 and later again in 1941.

fane: temple.

139 *the glass at Chartres*: Chartres Cathedral is renowned for its stained glass windows.

Blondin Donkey: possibly a reference to renowned French tightrope walker and showman Blondin (1824–97), né Jean-François Gravelet. One of his stunts was to carry someone on his back (like a donkey) as he walked across a chasm.

Miss Kingston: English actor Gertrude Kingston (1862–1937), who was the first manager of the Little Theatre in the Adelphi. She acted in a number of Shaw's plays.

Mr Chesterton's Magic or Brieux's Les Avariés: the comedic play *Magic* (1913), by English author and critic G. K. Chesterton (1874–1936). The play *Les Avariés* (1901), by French playwright Eugène Brieux (1858–1932), frankly discusses the subject of venereal disease. Shaw knew Chesterton well and he and his wife Charlotte were responsible for translating and introducing Brieux to English audiences.

140 *Westminster Abbey*: like Rheims Cathedral, Westminster Abbey is the site of coronations.

super tax: a tax that is levied in addition to one's income tax.

death duties: taxes levied on the estate of a person who has recently died.

141 *American President*: Woodrow Wilson (1856–1924) was president of the United States from 1913 to 1921. He was a professor of history and later president at Princeton University.

Hegel . . . never learn anything from history: German philosopher Georg Wilhelm Friedrich Hegel (1770–1831). The quote is from his posthumously published *Lectures on the Philosophy of History* (1832).

Lincoln: American president Abraham Lincoln (1809–65).

'the considerate judgment . . . Almighty God': from the *Emancipation Proclamation* (1863), an edict issued by Lincoln that freed the slaves of the Confederate states during the American Civil War (1861–5).

Zabern: the French Alsatian town of Saverne (known as Zabern under German occupation) was the site of unrest in 1913. After locals were insulted by a German army officer, there was popular protest, which the military brutally quelled. This led to the term 'zabernism', which refers to the aggressive misuse of military force.

142 *Bastilles*: the Bastille, a prison in Paris, was stormed at the beginning of the French Revolution on 14 July 1789, and is commemorated as France's national holiday on that date each year. It had come to symbolize the despotic rule of the Bourbon monarchy.

Hapsburg: the Habsburg dynasty ruled over the Austro–Hungarian Empire from 1867 until the end of the First World War in 1918.

All Highest Hohenzollern: Kaiser Willhelm II was the head of the Hohenzollern dynasty. He sought asylum in the Netherlands in 1919 and lived out his days there until his death in 1941.

Imperial Romanoff: Nicholas Romanov (1868–1918) was the last of the Russian tsars. He and his family were executed by the Bolsheviks following the October Revolution of 1917.

lord of Hellas: Constantine I (1868–1923) was king of Greece from 1913 to 1917, when he was deposed by the Allies and his political opponents for his pro-German views. He was restored to the throne in 1920, the year after Shaw wrote his preface, but was deposed again in 1922. Hellas is a historical name for Greece.

Solons: a reference to the Athenian statesman and poet Solon (*c*.630–*c*.560 BCE).

Banquo: a general in Shakespeare's *Macbeth* (1606–7), Banquo is murdered on Macbeth's orders after the Weird Sisters prophesy that he will beget kings.

Euripides . . . Aristophanes: Greek tragic playwright Euripides (*c*.484–406 BCE); in Shaw's *Major Barbara*, Adolphus Cusins, a Greek scholar, is repeatedly referred to as Euripides. Aristophanes (*c*.450–*c*.388 BCE) was a Greek comedic playwright.

two pamphlets: Shaw's polemical pamphlets *Common Sense about the War* (1914) and *More Common Sense about the War* (1915).

Pharisaism: in the New Testament, the Pharisees are a religious party within Judaism who are known for their rigorous legalism, self-righteousness, and hypocrisy.

143 *Brynhild, 'Lass . . . geh'n'*: Brünnhilde (Brynhild) is a beautiful princess of warrior stature in Richard Wagner's opera cycle *Der Ring des Nibelungen* (*The Ring of the Nibelung*) (1869–76). Shaw knew her story well, having authored the book-length study *The Perfect Wagnerite: A Commentary on the Niblung's Ring* (1898). Shaw cut the word 'Lachund' from the opening of the original. The German line, with the word restored, translates as 'Laughing let us be lost, with laughter go down to death.'

trinitrotoluene: an explosive better known by its acronym, TNT.

145 *high-pooped*: the poop is the rear-most and highest deck of a ship and often includes the captain's cabin.

stern gallery: a balcony at the stern, or rear-most part of the ship.

port side: left side of a ship when facing forward to the bow, or the front of the ship.

starboard side: right side of a ship when facing forward to the bow.

Indian ink: a black pigment in stick form that is moistened before use in drawing. It is valued for its opacity and durability. Despite its name, it was particularly used in ancient China and Egypt.

fire bucket: a receptacle used to extinguish a fire; it generally holds water.

mahogany: native to the Caribbean and Latin and South America, mahogany is a tree whose reddish-brown wood is prized for furniture. Like many of the furnishings and food in the play, this emphasizes the circuits of colonialism followed by a number of the characters.

145 *teak*: native to southern and south-east Asia, teak is a tree whose durable wood has long been prized in shipbuilding.

caulked and holystoned: to caulk a ship is to use oakum (a sticky resin) to block the pores and prevent leaking. Sailors scour and scrub the ship with a holystone, which is a soft sandstone.

146 *cupola*: dome.

Temple Shakespear: a forty-volume edition of Shakespeare's plays, published in London by J. M. Dent, 1894–7.

The hilly country . . . let the tray fall: these long stage directions were added in the typescript (HH Type, 1–3). The original stage directions were simply: 'Ellie Dunn sits, gloved and hatted. Nurse Guinness enters and stares at Ellie curiously.' Preceding the stage directions, the play's original title—'The Studio at the Clouds'—was indicated (HH Type, 4).

I heard him roaring: Shaw directs Nurse Guinness to emphasize 'roaring' (RN HH 1921).

ducky: most instances when Nurse Guinness calls Ellie 'ducky' were changed from 'deary' in the typescript; in some cases, they were added where there was no address (HH Type, 4).

147 *reefer jacket*: a sailor's coat; it is thick and double-breasted.

I'm afraid: in the typescript, this line was followed by the deleted 'Please, can I have a fly sent for to take them—and myself—away' (HH Type, 5).

148 *Ellie Dunn*: given the prevalence of classical name references in the play, it is likely that Ellie is a link to the Greek mythological character Helen of Troy, whose famed beauty led, indirectly, to the Trojan War. The name is relevant in terms of plot (she is vied for by three of the men in the play) and theme (the First World War forms the play's backdrop).

certainly not: in the typescript, Shaw deleted an interjection here before Ellie continues with the next sentence. The Captain says: 'Why not? Such men have daughters—attractive daughters. If we were all the daughters of thoroughly bad men and the sons of thoroughly bad women, this world would be paradise. I dont know why, but it is so' (HH Type, 6).

the seventh degree of concentration: in the typescript, Shaw changed this from 'the seventh degree of contemplation' (HH Type, 7).

Hesione Hushabye: in Greek legend, Laomedon is told by an oracle that the only way to save Troy is to sacrifice his daughter Hesione to the sea monster. The gods had sent the monster to plague the city because Laomedon had refused to give them a promised reward for building Troy's walls. Heracles saves Hesione and slays the monster, then kills Laomedon when, again, Laomedon refuses to give the reward he had promised. Hushabye is a word used to lull a child to sleep. It is also a composite of the refrain of the children's song 'Ring-around-the Rosie', which ends 'husha, husha, we all fall down', and the lullaby 'Rock-a-bye baby'.

numskull of a husband: the remainder of Shotover's speech here was added in the typescript. The original sentence, which Shaw deleted, continued to describe the husband: 'the only man on earth sufficiently like a ship's figure head to endure her incessant gush of sentiment and scandal' (HH Type, 7).

figure-head: the ornamental carving at the bow of a ship.

forty-six: changed from thirty-two in the typescript (HH Type, 8).

eighty-eight: before the next sentence begins, the typescript reads: 'Do you expect me to keep up my interest in a ~~stupid gabbling woman~~ *thankless girl* for ~~fifty six years~~ *nearly half a century* merely because I was the innocent instrument by which she was let loose in this miserable world?' (HH Type, 8). (Italics represent additions that Shaw made to the typescript.)

149 *leathern*: made of leather.

dogs: before he disappears, the typescript directed Shotover to turn to the nurse and say: 'Take the damned things away, or I shall smash them' (HH Type, 8).

Zanzibar: island off the east coast of Africa, now a part of Tanzania.

I believe them: in the typescript, Nurse Guinness continues: 'But youll get used to him, like me. Youll get used to all of us' (HH Type, 9).

150 *Hastings*: likely named after Warren Hastings (1732–1818), the first British governor general of India, from 1772 to 1785, who was subjected to an impeachment trial but was ultimately acquitted. His time in power was important for establishing British rule in the subcontinent and raised questions regarding the standards of integrity and responsibility towards the colonized natives of the British Empire.

Government House: the official residence of the governor or official representative of the Crown in the former British colonies.

Chinese lacquer: opaque varnish.

151 *Lady Utterword...her tears*: Shaw adopted this stage direction in the typescript, changing it from 'Lady Utterword breaks down, burying her face in her hands' (HH Type, 11).

Ariadne: in Greek mythology, Ariadne gave Theseus a thread to help him escape the labyrinth after he killed the Minotaur. Some versions have her later marrying the god Dionysus and she is often depicted in ancient art as asleep on the shore of Naxos while Dionysus admires her.

Paddy Patkins: in keeping with the diminutives and child imagery, this is likely a nickname derived from the nursery rhyme 'Patty cake'.

seventh degree of concentration...the worse: Lady Utterword's line 'But I'm your daughter...' was added in the typescript. Shotover's speech from the stage direction originally ran: 'That is true, my child. I dont remember you by the years you were away, but by the years you werent away. (He kisses her and puts his hands on her shoulders, holding her at arms length). Come: you are not so bad after all. (He makes her sit down). You see, my pet, when one's relatives are at home...' (HH Type, 12).

151 *so do not ... impersonating her*: Shaw changed the line to this in the typescript, which originally read: 'but now that we meet I dont see anything particularly wrong about you' (HH Type, 12). In the typescript, in the sentence preceding this, 'my absent daughter Ariadne' becomes 'you'. This alteration and the change above make Shotover more absent-minded and less tender towards his daughter.

152 *No—*: following this and before the stage direction, the typescript included a short exchange between Shotover and Ariadne that Shaw deleted:

THE CAPTAIN.	(Continuing) What's become of the fellow Ariadne married—the numskull?

LADY UTTERWORD	(flying into a rage) Papa: once for all, I will not have Sir Hastings spoken of in that way. I should have thought his distinguished career and high position must have convinced you long ago how unjust and prejudiced you were about him.

THE CAPTAIN.	Oh, Sir Hastings, is he. Ha ha!

(HH Type, 13)

hogwash: kitchen scraps and rubbish fit only for swine.

Nurse: will you please: Shaw directs Ariadne to be 'explosive' here (RN HH 1921).

Oh, dont ask me: Shaw suggests that Ariadne emphasize 'me' and deliver the line with 'flounce' (RN HH 1921).

153 *he is worse*: the typescript includes a line following this that Shaw deleted: 'Besides, though it grieves me deeply to have to hint such a thing about papa, I must...' (HH Type, 15). Just as Shotover becomes tougher towards Ariadne through the revisions noted above, she, too, becomes a bit more hardened.

fishpools of Heshbon: the phrase is from Song of Solomon 7: 4: 'Thy neck is as a tower of ivory; thine eyes like the fishpools in Heshbon, by the gate of Bathrabbim: thy nose is as the tower of Lebanon which looketh towards Damascus.' Heshbon was a town in ancient Jordan.

154 *as poor as a church mouse*: extremely poor.

My pettikins ... persecuting you: Shaw directs Hesione to 'jump down her throat', in reference to how she should speak to Ellie here (RN HH 1921).

[to Lady Utterword]: in the typescript, before she says to Ariadne that Mazzini is a very remarkable man, she begins: 'I wonder how you will get on with her father, Addy? ~~He is a funny old bird   (quickly, to Ellie) there, dear, you know how I talk about everybody~~' (HH Type, 17).

the Brownings: husband and wife poets Robert Browning and Elizabeth Barrett Browning (1806–61).

Mazzini: Italian republican revolutionary Giuseppe Mazzini (1805–72). While in exile following the failed Young Italy uprising in 1833, he spent a number of years living in London, where he was embraced by many English Liberals.

155 *What about my sheets?*: Shaw directs Ariadne to be 'indignant' (RN HH 1921).

Take my advice . . . blankets: after this sentence, the typescript reads: 'You were asking after my daughter Ariadne. I have brought you down her portrait. She was fairer than she looks here: freckles used to come out black in a photograph in those days' (HH Type, 18–19). The emphasis on Ariadne's complexion and the anxiety to distinguish her skin as fair and not black might relate to her current life in the colonies and her father's marriage to a black woman.

mackintosh: a coat made of waterproof, rubber material.

as mad as a hatter: a colloquial expression meaning that someone is insane. It is believed that the phrase comes from the fact that mercury was widely used in the hat-making industry, which exposed labourers, known as hatters, to high levels of mercury poisoning. Mercury poisoning leads to many physical ailments, but also erethism, or mental deterioration, which can include depression, anxiety, delirium, memory loss, and personality change.

156 *Mangan*: perhaps ironically named after Irish poet James Clarence Mangan (1803–49), who had many acquaintances in the nationalist Young Ireland movement and published some of his poetry in their periodical *The Nation*.

157 *Bosun ahoy!*: a bosun is a boatswain, a ship's officer in charge of the crew and equipment; ahoy is a nautical greeting.

their eyes in fine frenzy rolling: from Shakespeare's *A Midsummer Night's Dream* (1595–6): 'The poet's eye, in a fine frenzy rolling, | Doth glance from heaven to Earth, from Earth to heaven' (V. i. 12–13).

Pulling the devil by the tail: Being in reduced circumstances; just getting by.

158 *he had to incur liabilities*: Shaw directs Ellie to emphasize 'had' (RN HH 1921).

160 *dear father*: Shaw directs Hesione to emphasize 'dear' (RN HH 1921).

Othello: in Shakespeare's play *Othello* (1603–4), the eponymous character is a military general and a Moor, a Muslim of North African descent. Othello is considerably older and worldlier than his white wife, Desdemona, whom he kills in a jealous rage when he is tricked into believing rumours of her infidelity.

161 *Ellie darling . . . happened?*: in the typescript, Shaw deleted Hesione's next line: 'Othello was drawing the long bow' (HH Type, 29). To draw the long bow is to make exaggerated or untrue claims.

green-room: a place backstage in which performers can relax.

162 *National Gallery*: founded in 1824 and located on the north side of London's Trafalgar Square since 1838, the National Gallery houses Britain's national collection of European paintings.

162 *Richmond Park*: a Royal Park and nature reserve of 2,500 acres, Richmond Park is situated in south-west London.

   you have been going it: Shaw directs Hesione to emphasize 'have' (RN HH 1921).

   Marcus Darnley: given the prominence of well-known family names in the play, it is possible that the name Darnley was chosen to recall Henry Stewart, Lord Darnley (1545–67), the prince consort of Mary, Queen of Scots (1542–87), and father of James I (1566–1625). Darnley was estranged from his wife due in part to his vanity and arrogance. Born in Yorkshire, he died in Scotland, though in Edinburgh, not Aberdeen.

   He was found in an antique chest: this is a plot element of a number of nineteenth–century farces in which children are found in the most unlikely of places, such as a handbag in *The Importance of Being Earnest* (1895), by Shaw's fellow Irishman Oscar Wilde (1854–1900).

163 *Viscount . . . de Rougemont*: the lords or viscounts of Rougemont ruled Besançon in the Franche-Comté region of eastern France. Rougemont is a village near Besançon.

   Larochejaquelin: Shaw directs Ellie to say 'Larochejaquelin' with an 'affectedly correct pronunciation' (RN HH 1921). It could possibly be a reference to Henri du Vergier, Count de la Rochejaquelein (1772–94), who led the counter-revolutionary forces in the Vendée region. He is often romanticized for his bravery.

   King Edward's . . . India: the second child and eldest son of Queen Victoria, Edward VII was king of the United Kingdom of Great Britain and Ireland and emperor of India from 1901 until his death in 1910. He was also an uncle of the Kaiser, Wilhelm II.

164 *It makes the hours go fast, doesnt it?*: Shaw directs Ellie that, throughout this passage, she should 'Hang on breathless' (RN HH 1921).

   mousquetaire moustaches: a moustache with curly ends, often accompanied by a pointed goatee.

   dandified: exemplifying elegant or fashionable style.

   Hector: in Greek mythology, Hector, who is often depicted as an ideal warrior, is the eldest son of Priam, King of Troy. It was not Hector but rather his brother Paris who seduced Helen (see note to p. 148) and refused to give her up, thereby leading to the Trojan War.

165 *Albert Medals for saving people's lives*: the Albert Medal for Lifesaving, named in memory of Prince Albert, was first instituted in 1866 and discontinued in 1971.

166 *believed it*: in the typescript, Shaw deleted Hector's response to Ellie: 'Unless a story is too good to be true, its [*sic*] not worth telling. Hang it, Miss Dunn, I'm not a newspaper' (HH Type, 39).

167 *delirium tremens*: a severe form of alcohol withdrawal that can include physical symptoms of shaking and mental symptoms such as hallucinations.

I congratulate you, Mr Dunn: Shaw directs Hesione: 'Shake hands with Mazy on I congratulate you & hold on to him for the warning about her father' (RN HH 1921).

teetotaler: one who, like Shaw, abstains from alcohol.

168 *movy*: movie.

Chinese tray: in the typescript, Shaw deleted a part of the exchange between Shotover and Mangan here:

MANGAN (laughing sorely) I guess that is so. But a man may be a fool and yet strike oil. The question is, how did he make it.
CAPTAIN SHOTOVER. He is a motion picture actor.
MANGAN (contemptuously) Oh, that! Plays the fool does he?
CAPTAIN SHOTOVER. Yes: plays the fool. He could not do that if he was a fool.
MANGAN. Mm!
CAPTAIN SHOTOVER. Unless he married a young wife.
(HH Type, 42–3)

169 *West Indian*: Caribbean.

I thought so: Shaw directs Mangan to react 'verblufft!' (RN HH 1921). *Verblüfft* is German for 'amazed'.

West Ender: person from the well-to-do West End of London.

171 *Claridge's*: a luxury hotel in London's Mayfair neighbourhood.

Pleased to meet you, Lady Utterword: in the typescript, Shaw deleted a brief exchange here between Hesione and Mangan:

MRS HUSHABYE. I never know whether I should introduce you as Mr Mangan or as Boss Mangan. Boss means a millionaire, doesnt it?
MANGAN. Not always, Mrs Hushabye. Every millionaire is a boss; but every boss is not a millionaire.
(HH Type, 48)

172 *Dont be vulgar, Randall*: Shaw directs Ariadne to 'emphasize the 'v' in 'vulgar' (RN HH 1921).

174 *keeps dynamite and things of that sort*: Shaw directs Hesione to be 'trivial' when speaking here (RN HH 1921).

Mahatma: someone with preternatural powers; also the title given to a respected person.

175 *No child ... Bohemianism*: Shaw directs Ariadne to say these lines 'strascinando' (RN HH 1921). From the Italian meaning 'dragging', this is a musical term directing a passage to be performed in a slow, heavily slurred manner. A bohemian is one who leads an unconventional life, whereas a puritan lives according to strict principles.

176 *I am deliberately playing the fool*: Shaw directs Hector to say this line with 'Real self-contempt' (RN HH 1921).

I see ... sheer worthlessness: the typescript does not include the dialogue between these phrases. In their place it reads:

HECTOR.   How true! Oh, how true! Well, do I look an ill conducted, careless man?

LADY UTTERWORD.   You look one of the nicest men I have ever met. And
I am greatly flattered that you dont think me plain—though of course
you know my age.

HECTOR.   You are quite charming. And you are intelligent. You can be
trusted.

LADY UTTERWORD. Oh, you appreciate that.

HECTOR.   Thoroughly.

(HH Type, 54–5)

176 *Your husband is quite charming, darling*: Shaw instructs Ariadne to deliver
this line with a 'Monna Lisa smile' (RN HH 1921). The *Mona Lisa*
(*c*.1503–19), painted by the Italian Renaissance artist Leonardo da Vinci
(1452–1519), is famous for the figure's mysterious smile.

177 *I have never been able to grudge*: Shaw directs Hesione to emphasize
'grudge' (RN HH 1921).

You fascinated me . . . [She is going . . . in his hand]: Shaw added this passage
in the typescript, deleting the shorter original:

HECTOR.   I dont know that I want it to come off. It was damned dangerous. If I hadnt chanced on the right woman, I hardly think about what
might have happened.

MRS HUSHABYE.   I'm afraid it doesnt happen twice in a lifetime.

(HH Type, 57)

178 *'Do you love me!'*: the exclamation mark, not a question mark as might be
expected, appears in all editions of the play.

Are we . . . their snouts: the typescript reads: 'Are we to ~~work hand in hand
with God for the raising of our kind to the planes of heaven to~~ be kept for
ever in the mud by these hogs to whom the universe is nothing but a machine
for greasing their bristles and filling their snouts?' (HH Type, 58–9).

lovelocks?: in the typescript, Hector continues: 'Is greed less terrible than
the twaddling futility of your converted pirate?' (HH Type, 59).

179 *Precisely . . . mine also*: Shaw added these lines in the typescript after deleting a different exchange:

HECTOR.   Precisely. And your own daughter Ariadne?

CAPTAIN SHOTOVER.   When my dynamite is perfect I shall ask you to
spare a father's feelings and kill her for me.

(HH Type, 59)

I tell you I have often thought of this killing of . . . human vermin: Shaw
directs Hector to say this line 'slow—bored' (RN HH 1921).

blackmailers: before the next sentence, the typescript reads here: 'Their
survival also is a miracle; and they too, do not always survive. ~~When they
escape, they dig their graves with their teeth. And they are the slaves of all
sorts of vampires: blackmailers who trade in the exposure of their vices,~~

~~or worse still—blackmailers who trade in their dread of death by disease, blackmailers who trade in their dread of hell, in their ignorance of the law, in their desire to live for ever and transmute into gold~~' (HH Type, 60).

180 *none the less*: in the typescript, Shotover speaks a few more sentences here before saying that he will discover a mighty ray: 'If I do not go according to my lights I shall be enslaved by men who go according to theirs. And my own lights leads me to seek power for self-defence, for the power to resist evil wills. Remember, we are no longer free as we were. They have made hell and cast us into the cauldron. I will fight for my own soul and yours' (HH Type, 61).

I must change: instead of delivering this line, the typescript has a conversation between Shotover, Hesione, and Hector on the impossibility of Ellie's relationship with Mangan (HH Type, 62–4). Hesione notes that Ellie will become disgusted as she is confronted by realities, thus leading her to be cruel to Mangan.

SHOTOVER.   She should not be cruel to a hog. Let her be cruel to men: it may teach them something.

HECTOR   [*restless*] These comparisons make me uneasy. They are unfair to the hog and unfair to the man. They are snobbish. What has Mangan done that he should be compared to a hog? What has the hog done that he should be compared to Mangan? I accuse you of dating, Captain.

MRS HUSHABYE.   Of what?

CAPTAIN SHOTOVER.   Of dating. Of being old-fashioned. You are right. I am frightfully old. My generation called men asses and hounds and hogs. We called women by the female equivalents. Hector has a sense of honor towards the animals.

(HH Type, 63–4)

182 *food in the house*: Shaw deleted a short exchange between Hesione and Hector after this line:

HECTOR.   If I were you I should hand over the commissariat to that keen old sportswoman your sister Ariadne. She will enjoy ordering dinner.

MRS HUSHABYE.   What a splendid idea! Just the thing! How clever of you, darling!

(HH Type, 67)

Give me . . . in the light: Shaw wrote this line in the typescript, deleting the original: 'Only in the darkness is there any light for me' (HH Type, 68).

183 *What did he say?*: in the typescript, this appears as 'What has he to do with our affairs?' Mangan then responds: 'I asked him that; but ~~he has a way of getting round such questions:~~ he is not a man you can snub, exactly. Besides, there was a good deal in what he said' (HH Type, 69–70).

He notices everything: in the typescript, this line reads: 'That is my business, not his' (HH Type, 70). Given the thrust of the original lines here and just above, in early drafts Ellie was considerably more standoffish with regards to Shotover at the outset of ACT II.

184 *Was I? I forget*: in lieu of this line, the typescript has a longer exchange between Ellie and Mangan:

> ELLIE.   I was saying that I know very well our engagement is not a roman-tic one. But I can never forget your great kindness to my father; and—
>
> MANGAN.   Oh, is that all? Listen to me, Miss Ellie. I dont want to sail under false colors with you. I want to put this thing straight. You have no reason to be grateful to me on your father's account. The fact is, you dont quite know the sort of man I am.
>
> ELLIE.   Oh, I know you dont like to be thanked and treated as a benefac-tor and so forth. I understand. Please say no more about it. Tell me...
>
> (HH Type, 70–1)

The conversation then continues with Ellie asking if he likes this part of the country.

I like the place. The air suits me: Shaw directs Mangan: 'Imply why he says this' (RN HH 1921).

Yes I did: Shaw directs Ellie to 'Play' to the line (RN HH 1921).

185 *no risks in ideas*: Shaw directs Mangan to emphasize 'ideas' (RN HH 1921).

186 *He has nothing to say*: the original stage direction was longer, adding a few sentences before Mangan whistles: 'He has nothing to say, and looks at her in great perplexity. She looks at him with an air of polite enquiry. He can-not meet her gaze. He looks about him as if he had lost something' (HH Type, 76).

188 *hypnotism*: although it dates back to ancient times, hypnotism's scientific history began in the eighteenth century with the work of German phys-ician Franz Mesmer (1734–1815), after whom the system of therapeutics known as mesmerism was named. The word 'hypnosis' is derived from Hypnos, the Graeco-Roman god of sleep. Central features of one in a hyp-notic state are heightened awareness and receptiveness.

190 *look. Just look. Look hard*: Shaw changed the lines to this in the typescript; he deleted: 'we can talk without any fear of being overheard or interrupted by Boss Mangan. Let us make the most of the opportunity' (HH Type, 84).

191 *halfpenny*: Shaw changed this from 'penny' (HH Type, 85).

captain of industry: in his essay *Past and Present* (1843), British historian Thomas Carlyle (1795–1881) writes on 'the captains of industry', the industrialists who control the factories. Carlyle argues that these captains mercilessly exploit labour and that they need to be more responsible and sympathetic leaders of society.

dog's chance: Shaw directs Mazzini to 'Play to' this phrase (RN HH 1921). Both to have and not to have a dog's chance is to have a small chance of success.

192 *he is really the most helpless of mortals*: Shaw changed this in the transcript from 'he really doesnt know anything' (HH Type, 87).

And pray why dont you do without him if youre all so much cleverer?: Shaw directs Hesione to be 'surprised at his brilliancy' (RN HH 1921).

193 *Now if ... say it wittily*: in place of these lines, Shaw originally included the
following exchange:

MRS HUSHABYE.   So <u>youre</u> coming out as a cynic now, Mr Mazzini. My
compliments.

MAZZINI.   I'm sure you dont think that Mrs Hushabye. There never was
a man less a cynic than I am. I sometimes think it would have been
better for my family if I had been one.

(HH Type, 88)

194 *Come here ... shew you*: Shaw added this after deleting 'The boss is in
a cataleptic trance' (HH Type, 92).

195 *my own sake*: Ellie originally continued: '~~I know you wouldnt let me.~~ Is that
enough?' (HH Type, 93).

telegraph: developed in the mid-nineteenth century, telegraphy is
a long-distance system of communicating messages, or telegraphs, by
radio wave. With the advent of digital systems of communication in the
second half of the twentieth century, telegraphy became obsolete.

196 *siren*: in Greek mythology, the Sirens were creatures, half-bird half-
woman, who lured sailors to destruction with their enticing song.

can feel a few hard words: originally 'has time for squabbling' (HH
Type, 96).

You are just foolish and stupid and selfish: in reaction to this line, Shaw
directs Hesione to begin an 'irritated walk' (RN HH 1921).

smasher: a heavy blow.

197 *damnable world*: before continuing with the next sentence, Hesione originally spoke for a few more lines: 'If you think that the hardness of a girl who
has had nothing that the world can give her is as hard as the hardness of
a woman who has had everything it can give her, you will find yourself
more mistaken than you ever thought so clever a young woman could be.
I can be all things to all men and to all women too' (HH Type, 96).

grindstone: a revolving stone used to sharpen or polish.

despicable and wicked: Hesione originally continued: 'That will soon make
an end of your youth and your niceness: thats all' (HH Type, 97).

Sick and Indigent Room-keepers' Association: there is a Sick and Indigent
Roomkeepers' Society in Shaw's native Dublin. Founded in 1790 to help
people experiencing difficulties become self-sufficient, it claims to be the
city's oldest charity.

my heart is broken: Shaw directs Ellie to emphasize 'is' (RN HH 1921).

198 *I have taken the Boss's measure*: Shaw directs Ellie to 'measure his head
with the fingers' (RN HH 1921).

Hector: Shaw directs Hesione to turn away from Ellie as she says Hector's
name (RN HH 1921).

199 *but I can swing a baby on mine*: Shaw directs Hesione to deliver the line in
a 'prosaic and cheery' way (RN HH 1921).

199 *You couldnt help it*: Shaw directs Ellie to 'kiss' Hesione here (RN HH 1921).

disgusting old skinflint: Shaw directs Mangan to 'sob' as he says this line (RN HH 1921). In the typescript, it was changed from 'old ugly skinflint' (HH Type, 101). A skinflint is a miser.

200 *I shant forget*: in this scene, Shaw directs Mangan to be 'very sincere' (RN HH 1921).

201 *Tennyson*: Alfred, Lord Tennyson (1809–92) was the most renowned poet of Victorian England and held the title of Poet Laureate of the United Kingdom from 1850 until his death.

you are a real person: Shaw directs Hesione to 'get him by the shoulders' (RN HH 1921).

202 *Providence*: benevolent divine intervention.

Arab costume: a white robe.

203 *latitude and longitude*: the coordinate system of locating places on earth. Being a sailor, Shotover would know it well.

heath: an extensive tract of land generally covered in low-lying vegetation, such as heather.

waterproof: a coat that is impervious to water.

Alfred: here and in Hector's next lines, Shaw had originally written the name as 'Albert', then corrected it to 'Alfred'. However, Hesione then refers to him as 'Alf' (HH Type, 108). It is unclear if Shaw simply made a mistake and lost track of his name, which is indicated as Alfred earlier in the typescript, or if he was playing with both names as possibilities at this time.

menagerie: a collection of wild animals kept for exhibition.

204 *tell the truth*: Shaw revised the stage directions to introduce the characters one by one. Originally he had written here: 'They all return, except the Captain, bringing in an old and villainous looking man. Nurse Guinness is with them' (HH Type, 109).

205 *cop*: slang for 'capture'.

Beginning with solitary: in the British penal system of the time, convicts spent the first few months of their sentence in solitary confinement. Penal reform legislation had cut this time down from as many as nine months in the latter decades of the nineteenth century.

207 *jemmy*: a crowbar used by burglars.

skeleton keys: master keys that fit many locks.

quid: a colloquialism for a pound in English money, not weight.

208 *nigh*: nearly.

He dont belong to my branch, Captain: Shaw added this line in the typescript after deleting the original: 'I know he is: he's my cousin' (HH Type, 116).

209 *forecastle*: a raised deck at the bow of a ship.

Galileo: Italian astronomer and mathematician Galileo Galilei (1564–1642). Though they were initially censured by the Inquisition, his discoveries led to later acceptance of the heliocentric model of the universe. In his day, authorities enforced acceptance of the geocentric model, which proposed that the universe revolved around the earth as opposed to the sun.

210 *Tristan and Isolde*: eponymous characters of a Celtic legend that became a well-known medieval love romance and later the subject of Richard Wagner's opera *Tristan und Isolde* (1865).

Good heavens! Whats the matter?: Shaw tells Hector 'don't rise—light surprise' (RN HH 1921).

212 *up to the hilt*: completely, thoroughly.

215 *dotage*: state of feebleness in old age.

feel the life in me more intensely: in the typescript, Ellie intervenes here: 'A lot of women must have stayed at home without any adventures to provide for your adventures.' Shotover then says: ~~'Young woman: I am too old to be touched by these feminist recriminations.~~ Without my adventures they would not have had the tea they drug themselves with, or the whalebone they stiffen their corsets with' (HH Type, 130). It then picks up with 'I did not let the fear of death...'

216 *ten glasses*: Shaw directs Shotover to emphasize 'ten' (RN HH 1921).

217 *Heartbreak?*: Shaw instructs Shotover to say this word with a 'chest voice—powerful' (RN HH 1921).

218 *Ancient Mariner*: a reference to 'The Rime of the Ancient Mariner' (1798), a poem by English Romantic poet Samuel Taylor Coleridge (1772–1834). The eponymous character recounts bringing bad luck to his ship by killing an albatross, which leads to the death of his crew.

Pekinese dog: a long-haired breed of toy dog.

219 *fascination*: Shaw changed this from 'good looks' (HH Type, 137).

221 *Be reasonable, Ariadne*: Shaw directs Hector to be 'grave' and, referring to Ariadne, tells him 'don't catch her tone'. He asks Ariadne to 'Hold him, don't turn away' (RN HH 1921).

Yes you do: Shaw directs Ariadne to speak this line with a 'low pitch' (RN HH 1921).

Napoleon . . . idle man: Napoleon claimed: 'L'amour est l'occupation de l'homme oisif, la distraction du guerrier, l'écueil du Souverain' (Love is the occupation of the idle man, the distraction of the warrior, the peril of the Sovereign).

222 *There is no animal*: Shaw directs Randall to emphasize 'no' (RN HH 1921).

you will not believe me: Shaw tells Randall that this is where his 'tears begin' (RN HH 1921).

225 *lying voluptuously*: in the transcript, Shaw changed this line from 'very comfortably established' (HH Type, 147).

campstool: a portable folding stool.

226 *wallowing . . . hammock*: Shaw added this phrase in the typescript (HH Type, 148).

There is no sense in us: Shaw deleted the line that followed this in the typescript: 'We are the true House of Lords' (HH Type, 148).

nearly twentyfour: in the typescript, Shaw changed this phrase from 'more than thirty' (HH Type, 149). He was evidently still working through the play's historical chronology.

What's wrong with my house?: in the typescript, before this line, Shaw deleted the opening of Shotover's response: 'Aye: did he?' (HH Type, 149).

227 *to let*: to rent.

It isnt mere convention . . . the wrong ones: Shaw changed these lines in the typescript from: 'It isnt mere convention: you just look at the people and you see that even if you had just come down from another planet and knew nothing about it you would see that the people who hunt are the right people and the people who dont are the wrong ones. If papa had been the captain of a canal barge he would have know [*sic*] that what Hesione and I needed to make women of us was horses' (HH Type, 150).

228 *such a creature*: In the typescript, Shaw deleted a brief exchange here between Ariadne, Hector, and Hesione. Ariadne's next line was: 'A coster-monger would have more respect' (HH Type, 151). It then continued:

HECTOR.   Costermongers do not hunt.

LADY UTTERWORD.   They keep donkeys.

MRS HUSHABYE.   Who would not be proud of so distinguished a grand-father. Addy: do you think . . .

(HH Type, 151–2)

A costermonger is a fruit seller.

for our life's journey: Shaw added this phrase after deleting 'through a vale of tears' (HH Type, 153).

229 *lazy good-for-nothing capitalists*: Shaw directs Mangan that out of the three terms in this phrase, it is 'good-for-nothing' that should be emphasized (RN HH 1921).

a dog's life: an unhappy existence.

I dont own anything: Shaw deleted a brief exchange in the typescript here:

CAPTAIN SHOTOVER.   You said this afternoon that you could leave your widow well off.

MANGAN.   My widow will expect millions. Well, she'll be jolly lucky if she gets a few hundred a year. How can I tell? She may do pretty well; and she may get nothing. (HH Type, 154)

playing cat and mouse: cruelly toying.

230 *Is this England . . . Mr Mangan?*: in place of these lines, the typescript has the following exchange:

HECTOR. And what becomes of the country?

MANGAN. Dont you trouble about the country. The country is all right as long as you do your bit and I do my bit and everybody else does the same. If I am all right, my bit of the country is all right. If youre all right, your bit of the country is all right. Mind your own business and youll be minding the country's own business too.

THE VOICE OF THE BURGLAR. [enthusiastically] Hurray! Hear hear! (He emerges from the darkness beside Mangan putting a pipe in his pocket). Thats what I call good sense. (To Mangan) You and me is all right, governor, aint we?

CAPTAIN SHOTOVER. [waking up] What are you doing here, you black-guard? This is not the forecastle.

THE BURGLAR. Well, the old woman wouldnt let me smoke and wouldnt stop jawing me: so I came out for a turn in the garden. Wants to put me away for bigamy, she does. She would, too, if she could do it without making herself ridiculous.

HECTOR. Did you threaten to give yourself up unless she gave you a couple of pounds?

THE BURGLAR. (startled) Never thought of it, sir. Fancy that! I'll go and have a word with her. Goodnight, ladies and gentlemen (he vanishes into the direction of the house past Lady Utterword with an air of urgent business).

HECTOR. Is this England, or is it a madhouse?

MANGAN. You may well ask. Just imagine that common swine talking to me as if he was my equal! What's the country coming to?

LADY UTTERWORD. I'm afraid you will not be able to save it, Mr Mangan.

(HH Type, 162–3)

231 *and deliver us from the lures of Satan!*: the typescript instead reads: 'Women: I hate you' (HH Type, 165).

Duchess of Dithering: no such title exists; it is evidently an ironic name to suggest that the nobility dithers, that is, acts indecisively.

232 *I'll do as I like . . . made much of*: Shaw deleted an earlier exchange of which this was part. Following Ariadne asking him to keep his clothes on, it runs:

ELLIE. ~~But if life is to be unreal, if it is to be all pictures and acting and romance, if we must disguise ourselves with clothes, then what is to happen to people like myself who cant stand bad amateur painting and badly printed books and cheap dowdy dresses and furniture? I want the best and that means money, money, money.~~ If you really have no money Mr Mangan, you might at least find a rich husband for me. You say you can find capitalists to invest money in you. Cant you find one to invest in me? ~~My father says that it is in people, and not in factories that capital should be invested.~~ I offer myself as an eligible investment.

~~MANGAN.~~ ~~I can get a syndicate to invest in you fast enough. But you are not content with capital: you want marriage and respectability. Capital has no sentimentalities of that sort.~~

HECTOR.   ~~Rot. Where would capital be without contracts and the police~~
~~to enforce them? Miss Dunn is entitled to her contract and to police~~
~~protection.~~

LADY UTTERWORD.   I'm afraid you will have to find Miss Dunn a husband or marry her yourself, Mr Mangan.

MANGAN.   Why must I marry her? Am I a child or a slave? Maynt I do as
I please? I wont stand this tyranny.

CAPTAIN SHOTOVER.   I opened the door: you have passed through: you
are free under the stars.

(HH Type, 156–7)

The dialogue then picks up with Ariadne saying: 'Goodbye, Alf.'

233   *my acting so handsome*: Shaw originally included a brief exchange after this
line before Ariadne counsels Ellie not to be too hasty:

ELLIE.   I thought you wanted me to.

MANGAN.   Well, perhaps I did; but its [*sic*] one thing for me to want to
get out of it, and another for you to throw me over. Do you suppose
a man has no natural pride? Besides, as Lady Utterword says, how do
I know that I shall do any better?

LADY UTTERWORD.   How does Miss Dunn know that she will do any
better?

MANGAN.   Just so.

(HH Type, 158)

immense wealth: before Ellie announces that she cannot commit bigamy,
which Shaw added to the typescript, there was the following exchange that
drew out the suspense but perhaps minimized the shock value of her
announcement:

ELLIE.   I know he will always have money enough to be a very good
match for me: that is not the obstacle. I assure you I have faced this
question and reasoned it thoroughly out. Hesione has said her utmost
against my marrying Mr Mangan. The Captain has said his utmost
against it. Neither of them has had anything to say but sheer sentimentality. They have convinced me that my reasoning was right.

LADY UTTERWORD.   Quite. Then why throw Mr Mangan over?

ELLIE.   Well, I suppose because when people thoroughly understand
what they are going to do, they never do it. If I knew I was really going
to do a thing, I should take care not to reason about it.

HECTOR.   In heaven's name, why?

ELLIE.   For fear I should find out it was wrong. I should not like to have
to do a thing, knowing it to be wrong.

HECTOR.   ~~On the same principle, when you know you are not going to do~~
~~a thing, you should not reason about it lest you should find out that you~~
~~ought to do it.~~

ELLIE: ~~Precisely.~~

MRS HUSHABYE.   Moral: be a good Englishwoman and dont reason
at all.

LADY UTTERWORD.   That is all very well here in England, Miss Dunn, where there is no real government, and where it does not matter what anybody does or says. But if you had to govern a Crown Colony, or even to manage a household of native servants, you would have to think. If you didnt there would soon be no Crown Colony and no household and even no you. You had better make sure of Mr Mangan while you have the chance.

(HH Type, 158–9)

'Their altar . . . muttering wind': from Percy Bysshe Shelley's *Rosalind and Helen: A Modern Eclogue* (1819). The line differs in its pronouns, being spoken in the first-person collective: 'Our altar the grassy earth outspread, | And our priest the muttering wind.'

234 *But there is no blessing on my happiness*: Shaw directs Shotover to emphasize 'blessing' and to deliver the line 'low & brooding' (RN HH 1921).

We are all fools: the typescript includes an exchange between this line and the stage directions indicating Mazzini's entrance:

ELLIE.   I might marry him if he were only a fool, Hesione. Perhaps he would step in where angels fear to tread. Parsifal was a fool. ~~But how can I marry a practical business man who doesnt own anything and cant make anything or do anything? He cant afford to marry me. I should only take his mind off his money, and then it would vanish.~~

MRS HUSHABYE.   I believe Addy or I could have put Parsifal in our pockets in ten minutes.

ELLIE.   Then there would have been no Parsifal. Parsifal is only the name of the man you could not put in your pocket.

(HH Type, 166–7)

Oh! . . . resisted me: Hesione's line in the typescript reads: 'Oh! here <u>is</u> Parsifal: the only man who ever resisted me (HH Type, 167).

235 *exchequer bills*: saving bonds issued by the British parliament that pay interest.

cyanide of potassium: also referred to as potassium cyanide, a soluble, highly toxic chemical compound used in gold mining, electroplating, and jewellery buffing.

[disgusted] Yah! Not even a great swindler!: there is no stage direction in the typescript, and Hector speaks more gently: 'Then the last ray of romance fades from his brow. He is not even a great swindler' (HH Type, 169).

nor dishonest: Shaw deleted a brief exchange in the typescript before Mangan says 'There you go again':

MAZZINI.   He has no head for ethics, Lady Utterword. But I will say for him that he subscribes to the Moral Instruction League.

They all laugh except Mazzini and Mangan.

MANGAN.   Well, you dont suppose I do it for nothing, do you? I do it because if men like me didnt keep a hand on these sort of people God

only knows what they might be teaching next. Theres too much socialism about that League as it is.

HESIONE. Tell us more about Alfred, Mr. Dunn: he is inexhaustible.
(HH Type, 169)

In the typescript, Shaw changed all indications of Hesione's lines from
'HESIONE' to 'MRS HUSHABYE'.

235 *There you go again*: Shaw added this line in the typescript after deleting the
following: 'You just drop the subject, Dunn: you and all the rest too. If you
cant talk about a man without making everything he does look ridiculous,
you had better not talk about him at all' (HH Type, 169).

236 *I like him best when he is howling*: before this line, Ellie originally said:
'I have touched the human spot in Alfred: the sore spot.' (HH Type, 170).

in silence: Shotover originally continued: '~~Mangan will be better without~~
~~one.~~ Do not encourage the man to behave like a frog yowling at night in
a pond' (HH Type, 170).

kennel: a dog's house; this continues the bestial and especially canine
imagery.

come back: Shaw directs Shotover to say this phrase sharply (RN HH
1921).

237 *You complicate . . . ridiculous things*: following this line, the typescript continues the discussion between Mazzini and Ariadne before Ellie speaks:

MAZZINI.   Oh, I am only too thankful to have what I wear settled for me,
if only I can afford to buy what is settled. But you see, the people who
insist on settling my dress insist on settling my religion and my politics
and my notions of right and wrong.

LADY UTTERWORD.   How kind of them! and how easy for you!

MAZZINI.   Thats perfectly true. Party politics and conventional religion
are so easy; and real politics are so fearfully difficult and require such
a lot of knowledge! You certainly have the best of it as far as an easy life
goes, Lady Utterword.

(HH Type, 174)

238 *[huffily]*: this stage direction does not appear in the typescript. Instead,
when Mangan says his next line, Shaw directs him to be 'offended' (HH
Type, 175).

You may . . . are successful: in the typescript, this line reads: 'You and I are
in a class by ourselves, Mr Mangan. We are successful' (HH Type, 175).

239 *run into jellyfish*: Shaw directs Mazzini to 'wait for possible laugh' after
'jellyfish' (RN HH 1921).

240 *O Captain, my captain*: in the typescript, Shaw changed to this from
simply 'Captain' (HH Type, 178). In 'Oh Captain! My Captain' (1865),
a poem by American poet Walt Whitman (1819–92), the narrator tells
of a ship that has braved a storm and arrived in port to be welcomed by
a cheering public while the captain lies dead on the deck. The poem is an
elegy for Abraham Lincoln and uses the metaphor of the ship of state to

refer to the United States having come through the Civil War. The ship-of-state analogy, which Shaw exploits throughout this scene, has a long pedigree, going back to Plato's *Republic* (488e–489c).

the River Jordan: body of water revered by Jews, Christians, and Muslims, where St John the Baptist baptized Jesus.

split: in the typescript, Shaw deleted a line here: 'What is she but one vessel in a fleet called a civilization. Well, civilizations have foundered before' (HH Type, 178–9).

241 *Breakers ahead!*: in the typescript, Shaw deleted Shotover's next line: 'Stand by, all hands, and waken Captain Mangan' (HH Type, 179). The expression 'Breakers ahead!' is used to warn of the danger of a breaker, a violent incoming wave that breaks over a reef or shallows.

The Church . . . breaking up: this line does not appear in the typescript (HH Type, 180).

242 *Keep the home fires burning*: a popular patriotic song from the First World War, composed in 1914 by Ivor Novello (1893–1951). The first lines of the chorus run: 'Keep the Home Fires Burning, | While your hearts are yearning, | Though your lads are far away | They dream of home.' The image of fires burning in a house is evidently ironic here given the zeppelin raid. The mention of soldiers dreaming is also in keeping with the play's dream imagery.

I cant get a sound: in the typescript, Shaw deleted Shotover's line that followed Randall's: 'Captain ahoy! Where is Captain Mangan?' (HH Type, 182).

243 *Ellie, dear, . . . will survive*: in the typescript, Shaw changed Mazzini's lines from an earlier version: 'I am much fonder of Ellie than you are, Mrs Hushabye: but this is her own business. Mangan and the Burglar are quite safe: it is they who will survive anyhow. It always happens that way' (HH Type, 183).

un: English regional dialect for 'him'.

Thirty pounds . . . wasted: this line was added in the typescript (HH Type, 183).

244 *Randall at last . . . on his flute*: Shaw added the concluding stage direction in the typescript (HH Type, 184).

SAINT JOAN

245 *Chronicle Play*: play that takes its inspiration from history and is composed of loosely connected, chronologically sequenced episodes.

Epilogue: the proofs of the 1924 Constable edition included an epigraph on the title page after the subtitle: '*Though he slay me, yet will I trust in him; but I will maintain mine own ways before him.*—Job xiii. 15' (SJ LC). Shaw deleted it from early proofs (SJ Proof 2). In a scenario he wrote in 1934, Shaw included a different epigraph: 'her cities and her towns defaced | By wasting ruin of the cruel foe' (SJ Scenario). The quote, which actually reads 'Look on thy country, look on fertile France, | And see the cities and the towns defaced | By wasting ruin of the cruel foe' (III. iii. 44–6), is from Shakespeare's *Henry VI, Part 1* (*c*.1589–92). Joan speaks this line as a part of her effort to convince the Duke of Burgundy to join Charles to join the battle against the English forces.

247 *the Vosges*: a department (French administrative division, somewhat similar to an English county) named after the Vosges mountain range; it is in the province of Lorraine, in eastern France. Joan was born in the village of Domrémy, since renamed in Joan's honour as Domrémy-la-Pucelle. 'Pucelle' means 'maid' in Old French.

rehabilitated: rehabilitation is a formal restoration of someone who had formerly been excommunicated (cast out of) the Catholic Church.

Venerable . . . Blessed . . . canonized: in the Catholic Church, there are three stages to becoming a saint. In the first stage, one is recognized as Venerable, a title given to people of spiritual merit. One can then pass to the second stage, in which one becomes Blessed, or Beatified. The final stage is canonization; at this point, one is acknowledged as a saint.

Christian calendar: the various Christian faiths have slightly different calendars in terms of what they celebrate or observe. In the Catholic calendar, each day of the year is allocated to a saint, with some exceptions including Christmas (25 December), Jesus's mother Mary's Nativity (8 September), the Archangel Gabriel's Annunciation to Mary (25 March), and the Assumption of Mary's body to heaven (15 August). Joan's feast day is 30 May.

Middle Ages: the approximately 1,000-year period from the fifth century to about the fifteenth century, extending from the collapse of the Roman Empire to the Renaissance.

Husites: Hussites were followers of Jan Hus (*c*.1370–1415), a Czech religious reformer. His work anticipated that of Martin Luther (1483–1546) and the Reformation, a religious revolution against the Catholic Church in the sixteenth century CE that led to the foundation of Protestantism. Like Joan, Hus was tried and burned at the stake for heresy.

Queen Christina of Sweden . . . Catalina de Erauso: Christina (1626–89), or Kristina, was queen of Sweden from 1644 to 1654, then shocked Europe by abdicating her throne and converting to Catholicism. Nicknamed 'the Minerva of the North', she was learned and sponsored the arts. Christina was also controversial for often adopting men's clothes. Catalina de Erauso (1592–1650) escaped the Spanish convent in which she had been educated since childhood, cut her hair, dressed and passed as a man, and led a swashbuckling life, including leading military adventures in the Americas.

Church Triumphant: one of the three divisions of the Christian Church, the Church Triumphant is composed of those who are in heaven. The other two divisions are the Church Militant, composed of those on earth who fight for Christ against sin and evil, and the Church Penitent, those who have died but have yet to accede to heaven from Purgatory.

her own king . . . English king: as the play shows, Joan helped install Charles VII (1403–61) as king of France, a position he held from his coronation on 17 July 1429 until his death. Some people considered him the king of France following the death of his father, Charles VI, on 21 October 1422; however, his reign was challenged because he could not be crowned in Rheims Cathedral, the site where French monarchs were officially invested, as the English controlled much of the north of France. Henry VI (1421–71) was king of England in Joan's time, although he was not even 1 year old when he assumed the throne; under the terms of the Treaty of Troyes (1420), he was proclaimed king of France following the death of Charles VI.

Caesar . . . Cassius: offended at being passed over for high office, Gaius Cassius Longinus (d. 42 BCE) participated in the conspiracy to assassinate Julius Caesar.

248 *Socrates*: Greek philosopher Socrates (c.470–399 BCE) was tried for impiety and corrupting youth. He defied the court by refusing to answer the charges and instead attacked his accusers for the ways in which they led their lives. In the end, he was sentenced to death by poisoning, most likely by drinking hemlock.

Queen Elizabeth: the Tudor Queen Elizabeth I (1533–1603) died short of her seventieth birthday. Queen Elizabeth II (b. 1926), who has lived even longer, was born less than two years after Shaw wrote the preface.

249 *Herod and Pilate . . . Annas and Caiaphas*: Herod (21 BCE–39 CE) was the ruler of Galilee who sentenced John the Baptist to death and attempted to have Jesus killed when he was an infant. Pontius Pilate (d. 36 CE) was the Roman prefect who presided over Jesus's trial. Annas and Caiaphus were the Jewish high priests who questioned Jesus on his teachings and ultimately sent him to Pilate.

St Helena: following his defeat at the hand of British and Prussian forces in 1815, Napoleon was exiled on St Helena, a small island off the west coast of Africa where he spent his final years.

Mahomet: older spelling of Muhammad (c.570–632), the founder of Islam; he is considered a prophet, but is not recognized as a saint.

English king . . . the Loire: the longest river in France, the Loire runs north from the Massif Central to Orléans, then west to Nantes where it empties into the Atlantic Ocean. Its valley is rich agricultural land and is famously studded with hundreds of castles. Joan did not actually kick the English king's crown into the Loire; Shaw means that her lifting of the Siege of Orléans was the beginning of the end of his rule in France.

crapulous: grossly excessive.

250 *termagant*: shrew, or bad-tempered woman.

superbity: archaic term for arrogance, or pride.

250 *Elizabethan chronicle play . . . Jingo patriotism*: some academics have argued that Shakespeare's *Henry VI, Part 1* was co-written by Christopher Marlowe (1564–93); in 2016, the New Oxford Shakespeare editors credited Marlowe as a collaborator of *Henry VI, Parts 1, 2,* and *3*. It is a thoroughly nationalist and pro-Protestant play, negatively depicting Joan, the French, and everything Catholic.

the Inquisition: a judicial procedure overseen by the Catholic Church to combat heresy. It was first used in the twelfth century and became permanently established bureaucratic organizations scattered across Europe by the fifteenth century. The singular Inquisition that Shaw refers to here was the one in France that tried Joan.

251 *the Holy Roman Empire*: although it changed in shape and size over the better part of a millennium (*c*.800–1806), the Holy Roman Empire was a conglomeration of territories covering much of central Europe, from eastern France and Belgium in the west to the Czech Republic and north-western Poland in the east, and from the Baltic Sea in the north to Sardinia and central Italy in the south. The Emperor was the temporal ruler and the Pope, as head of the Catholic Church, was the spiritual ruler.

Whig historians: those who interpret history as a continuum of progress.

'Man's love . . . whole existence': the quote is from Lord Byron's *Don Juan* (1819–24), canto i, verse 194.

George Washington: general and commander of the colonial armies that rebelled against England in the American Revolution, George Washington (1732–99) was also the first president of the United States (1789–97).

252 *university passmen*: as opposed to one who takes a degree with honours, a passman obtains a less-distinguished pass degree.

Marie Antoinette: best known to history for the remarks attributed to her on the suffering of the peasantry at the time of the French Revolution, Marie Antoinette (1755–93) was the queen consort of Louis XVI (1754–93). She was guillotined by revolutionary forces in part because of her intrigues with foreign powers to restore the monarchy.

253 *commandant at Vaucouleurs*: Robert de Baudricourt (*c*.1400–54) was named captain of Vaucouleurs, situated in the eastern French department of Meuse, in 1420; he sent Joan, accompanied with six soldiers, to Chinon.

Battle of Herrings: just north of Orléans, the Battle of the Herrings took place between French and English forces on 12 February 1429. The French attempted to cut the line of supply to the English army that had besieged Orléans. Decisively won by the English, the battle took its name from the presence of a large stock of herring that had been shipped in to feed the people during Lent, when practising Catholics abstain from eating meat.

254 *Swedenborg*: Swedish scientist, philosopher, and theologian Emanuel Swedenborg (1688–1772). He had visions of Christ beginning on 7 April 1744, after which he abandoned science to devote his life to interpreting the Bible.

Pythagoras: Greek philosopher and mathematician Pythagoras (*c*.570–490 BCE).

Copernican . . . universe: Polish astronomer Copernicus (1473–1543) proposed the heliocentric model of the universe, in which the planets revolve around the Sun; his theory was rejected by the Church; see note to p. 209.

Bedlamite: a lunatic, meaning a patient in Bedlam; see note to p. 129.

the eleventh horn of the beast . . . Daniel: reference to Daniel's dream, as recounted in Daniel 7.

the late war . . . military life: large numbers of women worked in factories during the First World War to make up for the loss of the male labour force that had been conscripted.

Saint Catherine: a popular Christian martyr, St Catherine of Alexandria (d. *c.* early fourth century) was among the heavenly voices that spoke to Joan.

the coronation at Rheims: built in the thirteenth century, Rheims Cathedral was the site of the coronations of twenty-five kings of France, from Louis VIII in 1223 to Charles X in 1825. Rheims is to the north-east of Paris, in the Marne department.

255 *Saint Margaret, and Saint Michael*: the other voices that Joan heard were St Margaret of Antioch (third or fourth century) and St Michael the Archangel. Like Joan, St Michael is a warrior, leading heaven's army against Satan and evil.

256 *Brocken spectres*: optical illusions in the form of huge haloed figures that are encountered on mountain peaks. Their name derives from Brocken, the highest peak in Germany's Harz Mountains, where the effect is particularly spectacular.

Luther . . . Augustinian monk: in one popular account, the Devil attempted to prevent Luther from translating the Bible into German. Luther responded by throwing his inkhorn (the small tub of ink he used for writing) at the Devil. A dark stain on the wall of his study at Wartburg Castle is said to be proof of the incident. Luther was a monk, or friar, of the Order of Saint Augustine, which was formally established in 1244 and was active in universities and ecclesiastical affairs.

Krishna . . . Buddha . . . Blessed Virgin: Krishna, an incarnation of the God Vishnu, is an important Hindu deity. Gautama Buddha (*c*.sixth–fourth century BCE) is the founder of Buddhism. Jesus's mother Mary is named the Blessed Virgin because Catholic dogma since 1854 asserts that she had an immaculate conception in which she was free from original sin.

257 *Saints Louis Pasteur and Paul Bert*: neither Louis Pasteur (1822–95) nor Paul Bert (1833–86) is a saint; they are, rather, French scientists, but Shaw refers to them as saints to emphasize their hallowed reputations and people's blind acceptance of their claims. Pasteur developed pasteurization, the process of heating beverages to avoid pathogenic microorganisms, and vaccines against anthrax and rabies. Bert is renowned for physiological research into the effects of air pressure.

257 *St Teresa's... asteroid*: St Teresa of Ávila (1515–82) reformed the Carmelite order of nuns to emphasize austerity and contemplation. The various health difficulties that Shaw lists as possibly inflicting her are likely references to her long-term fragile health, with the notable exception of the concluding joke.

vaccination and vivisection: as the following paragraph makes clear, Shaw was a confirmed sceptic of vaccination and he regularly denounced vivisection, the practice of experimenting upon living animals, usually involving painful dissection.

the story of the angel and Mary: a reference to the Annunciation, when the Archangel Gabriel visited Mary to announce that Jesus would be conceived through the power of the Holy Spirit.

Edipus complex: the Oedipus complex is a psychoanalytic model first posited by Sigmund Freud (1856–1939) in his book *Interpretation of Dreams* (1899). Named after the ancient Greek hero who unknowingly killed his father and married his mother, it describes the developmental phase of the child who desires a sexual relation with the parent of the opposite sex while competing with the parent of the same sex.

258 *Gadarene swine*: in the miracle of the Gadarene swine, Jesus exorcizes demons from a man and casts them into nearby swine who then rush to the sea to drown themselves. The tale is recounted in Mark 5: 1–20, Matthew 8: 28–34, and Luke 8: 26–39.

Florence Nightingale: Florence Nightingale (1820–1910) is famed for tirelessly nursing British and Allied soldiers in Turkey during the Crimean War (1853–6). She established the first school of nursing in London in 1860.

La Hire: born Étienne de Vignolles (1390–1443), La Hire was a French military commander and early supporter of Joan.

Armagnacs: a region in south-west France that the Treaty of Calais (1360) ceded to the English. The Armagnac party, which supported Charles VII, was in conflict with the Burgundians, who were allied with the English.

Rouen: major French city in Normandy, located along the River Seine to the north-west of Paris. It was the site of Joan's trial and execution.

Warwick's: Richard Beauchamp (1382–1439), 13th Earl of Warwick, was a soldier and diplomat who served under several kings. He died in Rouen, where he was English military governor in France.

259 *Francis Galton*: British scientist Francis Galton (1822–1911) coined the term 'eugenics' in developing his theory that intelligence was hereditary. The visions that Shaw describes in this passage are taken from Galton's essay 'The Visions of Sane Persons' (1881), which argues that visions are not necessarily a sign of insanity.

260 *father... grandfather*: Charles VII's father and grandfather were, respectively, Charles VI (1368–1422), known as Charles the Mad for his frequent convulsions and bouts of insanity, and Charles V (1338–80), known as Charles the Wise for his revered intellect.

send Roberts to the Transvaal: Frederick Roberts (1832–1914) was a field marshal who led British forces during the Second Boer War, capturing Bloemfontein, Johannesburg, and Pretoria in 1900. The Transvaal was the alternative name for the South African Republic, which lasted from 1852 to the end of the war in 1902.

D'Alençon, De Rais, La Hire . . . Dunois: John, Duke of Alençon (1409–76), was the commander of the French forces that liberated the Loire Valley; he was a prominent supporter of Joan. Gilles de Rais (1404–40), also known as Bluebeard, remained at Joan's side throughout her campaign to rid France of the English; he was executed for Satanism and infanticide. For La Hire, see note to p. 258. Jean d'Orléans (1403–68), the Count of Dunois, also known as the Bastard of Orléans because his father, the Duke of Orléans, had sired him with a mistress, was an important French military commander and diplomat; he was a trusted adviser to Charles VII.

surcoats: garments, emblazoned with heraldic arms, worn over armour.

Rosa Bonheur: French painter Rosa Bonheur (1822–99) donned male attire to visit the masculine territory of stockyards, horse fairs, and slaughterhouses, all of which she represented in her art. In 1852, she obtained police authorization to dress in male garb.

George Sand . . . Chopins and De Mussets: French novelist George Sand (1804–76), née Amantine-Lucile-Aurore Dupin, was an independent-minded woman; like Bonheur, she dressed in male attire to circulate more freely. Her lovers included the Polish composer Fryderyk Chopin (1810–49) and the French dramatist Alfred de Musset (1810–57).

'unwomanly women': a term that was common currency at the time to describe those who did not conform to social stereotypes of how women should dress, think, and behave. Shaw discusses the type in his study *The Quintessence of Ibsenism*.

261 *Aldershottian*: Aldershot is the location of England's largest permanent military base, established in 1854. The term 'Aldershottian' is a Shavian neologism that never became popular. He refers here to the military's conservative tendency to defend and preserve the status quo, as opposed to favouring change and progressive movements such as the Russian Revolution.

prepotent: very powerful.

Beaurevoir Castle . . . sixty feet high: the only remaining part of Beaurevoir Castle is the keep, in which Joan was imprisoned; it is now known as the Joan of Arc Tower. Beaurevoir is located in the Aisne department, in the north of France.

Wellington . . . Nelson: the Duke of Wellington is best known for his defeat of the Napoleonic French forces at the Battle of Waterloo (18 June 1815).

Horatio Nelson (1758–1805) led the British Navy to victory against the Napoleonic forces in several battles, most notably that of Trafalgar (21 October 1805), where he was killed; his tendency to wear full dress and walk the decks during battle made him easily recognized at a distance, which led to his being fatally shot by a sniper.

261 *Compiègne*: on 23 May 1430, Joan was captured by the Burgundians at Compiègne, located in the Oise department, to the north-east of Paris.

262 *Jerichowise*: the town of Jericho is located in the West Bank. In the biblical tale (Joshua 6), when the priests sounded their trumpets, the defensive walls of Jericho crumbled; Joshua and the Israelites then looted, murdered, and razed the town.

'*En nom Dé!*': more properly '*Au nom de Dieu*' (In the name of God).

'*Par mon martin*': 'By my staff.'

263 *Feudalism*: the social, political, and economic worlds of the Middle Ages were defined by feudalism, a system of local land holdings ruled over by lords in the absence of the larger, more central governing structure that would replace it with the rise of empires and, eventually, the modern state.

Washington . . . Napoleon . . . German Crown Prince . . . Lenin in 1917: all of these figures were demonized in the British press for threatening British interests. Washington led American forces against British colonial rule in 1780; Napoleon commanded the forces of the French Republic in 1803; the German Crown Prince was Wilhelm (1882–1951), the son of the Kaiser, Wilhelm II, and commander of German forces during the First World War; and Lenin, the founder of the Russian Communist Party, led the Bolshevik Revolution of 1917.

Duke of Burgundy: Philip III (1396–1467), also known as Philip the Good, was duke of Burgundy at the time that Joan led the French forces.

264 *Schiller . . . Die Jungfrau von Orleans*: German writer Friedrich Schiller (1759–1805) rewrote the story of Joan in his Romantic play *Die Jungfrau von Orleans* (1801; *The Maid of Orleans*) along the lines that Shaw describes.

Voltaire . . . La Pucelle: French writer Voltaire (1694–1778) published *La Pucelle*, a ribald mock-heroic poem, in 1752.

St Peter and St Denis: the Apostle St Peter (d. 64) was a Jewish fisherman; as the leader of Jesus's twelve disciples, he is considered the first pope of the Roman Catholic Church. Now the patron saint of France, St Denis (d. *c.*258) is alleged to have been the first bishop of Paris; it is supposed that he was sent from Rome to convert the Gauls, a Celtic people who lived in what is now modern-day France.

Pecksniffian: Seth Pecksniff is an insincere and hypocritical character in Charles Dickens's novel *Martin Chuzzlewit* (1843–4); someone who is Pecksniffian shares those traits.

Samuel Butler . . . a slave: in addition to being renowned for writing evolutionary tracts and utopian fiction, Samuel Butler produced a study of humour in Homer (1892) and prose translations of *The Iliad* (1898) and *The Odyssey* (1900). He also wrote a polemic arguing that a woman wrote *The Odyssey*.

Agnes Sorel: also known as 'La Dame de Beauté' (the Lady of Beauty), Agnès Sorel (*c.*1422–50) was the acknowledged mistress of Charles VII from 1444 to her death; she is considered to have induced him to take an active role in the conquest of Normandy. Shaw accurately depicts Voltaire's factually challenged satire in this passage.

écraser l'infâme: Shaw misspells Voltaire's famous quote, which is *écrasez l'infâme*, meaning 'crush the infamous', not '*to* crush the infamous', as Shaw's homonymous formulation would have it. Voltaire signed his letters with the phrase, an injunction directed at the Catholic Church because of the intolerance and superstition he believed it bred.

265 *Quicherat*: the five-volume *Procès de condemnation et de rehabilitation de Jeanne d'Arc, dite la Pucelle* (1841–9), edited and annotated by French historian Jules Quicherat (1814–82), published documents relating to the life of Joan. Consulting T. Douglas Murray's 1902 translation of Quicherat's work, Shaw drew extensively upon the official transcriptions of Joan's trial while composing the play.

Mark Twain and Andrew Lang: Mark Twain (1835–1910), the pseudonym of Samuel Clemens, was the popular author of *The Adventures of Tom Sawyer* (1876), *Adventures of Huckleberry Finn* (1885), and *A Connecticut Yankee in King Arthur's Court* (1889). He anonymously published *Personal Recollections of Joan of Arc* (1895–96), which was written as a memoir penned by Joan's page. Andrew Lang (1844–1912), best known for his books of fairy tales and translations of Homer, published *The Maid of France* in 1908. In their accounts of Joan's life, both men drew upon Quicherat.

Anatole France: French man of letters and Nobel Laureate Anatole France (1844–1924) wrote a two-volume biography, *La Vie de Jeanne d'Arc* (1904–8).

Bayard . . . Esther Summerson from Bleak House: Pierre Terrail (*c.*1473–1524), seigneur de Bayard, was known as 'the knight without fear and without reproach', that is, for his chivalry. Esther Summerson is the selfless heroine of Dickens's novel *Bleak House* (1852–3).

the Mississippi pilot: a reference to Mark Twain, who once worked as a steamboat pilot on the Mississippi River.

266 *'medieval clothes' . . . eighteen-nineties*: see note to p. 49.

street arab: a homeless person in general, it more commonly refers to a child who lives on the streets.

Walter Scott: the novelist Walter Scott, renowned for *Waverley* (1814), *Rob Roy* (1817), *The Heart of Midlothian* (1818), *The Bride of Mammermoor* (1819), and *Ivanhoe* (1819), also published *Minstrelsy of the Scottish Border*, a three-volume collection of border ballads (1802–3).

266 *Albigensians*: heretics who lived in the south of France in the late Middle Ages. They were crushed by a combination of papal crusades and the machinations of the Inquisition.

Peter Cauchon: Pierre Cauchon (1371–1442) became bishop of Beauvais, capital of the Oise department, in 1420. Following Joan's trial, he became bishop of Lisieux in 1432.

267 *Edith Cavell*: English nurse Edith Cavell (1865–1915), who had been working in Belgium since 1907, was executed by the German forces for helping Allied soldiers to escape from German-occupied territory.

Roger Casement: Irishman Roger Casement (1864–1916) was knighted for exposing rapacious and murderous exploitation of natives in Africa and South America. He was executed for his role in bringing guns aboard a German submarine to assist with the nationalist Easter Rising of 1916, which was to lead to Irish independence from British rule. Shaw was a staunch defender of Casement.

'Patriotism is not enough': the night before her execution, Cavell was quoted as saying, 'Patriotism is not enough. I must have no hatred or bitterness for anyone.' This statement is now engraved on her statue in St Martin's Place, London.

Tommy and Jerry and Pitou the poilu: slang terms for soldiers from Britain, Germany, and France respectively; *poilu* is French for 'hairy'.

268 *Sylvia Pankhurst*: radical suffragist and labour activist Sylvia Pankhurst (1882–1960), who was also a pacifist during the First World War.

the Peculiar People: Shaw could be referring to two groups here. The most likely is the Peculiar People, an Evangelical and puritanical movement founded in 1838. They believed in faith and prayer to heal, refusing the intervention of modern medicine, which led to cases of infant mortality and the incarceration of the parents. The Quakers, founded in the mid-seventeenth century, have also been variously known as the Society of Friends and the Peculiar People. They were conscientious objectors to both world wars.

Wycliffe: English theologian John Wycliffe (c.1330–84) promoted the first translation of the Bible into English, which, at the time, was considered heresy. He was a precursor of the Reformation in his criticism of the Church's materialism.

269 *Mrs Eddy*: American Mary Baker Eddy (1821–1910) was an energetic religious reformer. She founded the Christian Science movement, which promotes spiritual healing.

the Trinity: in Christian doctrine, the unity of the Father, the Son, and the Holy Spirit in one Godhead.

Cromwell . . . Restoration: having led the parliamentary forces to victory during the English Civil Wars, Oliver Cromwell (1599–1658) was the leader of England, Scotland, and Ireland when the republican government ruled over the Commonwealth. Following the Restoration of the monarchy in 1660, Cromwell's presumed corpse was exhumed and hung. His body was then ignominiously buried beneath the gallows, save for his head, which was stuck on a pole at the top of Westminster Hall.

cozenage: fraud.

Charles the Victorious: the byname for Charles VII.

270 *in excelsis*: (Lat.) 'in the highest'.

Clare: St Clare of Assisi (1194–1253) was a follower of St Francis of Assisi, sharing his anti-material beliefs.

Excommunication: when someone is excommunicated from the Catholic Church, they are excluded from it, meaning that they are barred from the sacraments and Christian burial.

Dogma of Papal Infallibility: in Roman Catholicism, this dogma asserts that the pope, as supreme leader and teacher, cannot err in matters of faith and morals when speaking *ex cathedra*, meaning in his official capacity as pope.

Book of Joshua: the sixth book of the Bible, the Book of Joshua recounts how the Israelites, under their leader Joshua, conquered and settled in the Promised Land of Canaan.

Tout comprendre, c'est tout pardonner: (Fr.) 'To understand all is to pardon all.'

271 *Marquesas islanders*: the Marquesas Islands are part of French Polynesia; following victory, the inhabitants sometimes cannibalized their enemies.

Stephen's Green: the oldest and largest of Dublin's squares, St Stephen's Green is a major central public park.

coining: counterfeiting.

English Prisons . . . Sidney and Beatrice Webb: Shaw's lifelong friends and Fabian Society colleagues Sidney (1859–1947) and Beatrice Webb (1858–1943) published *English Prisons under Local Government* in 1922. It was the sixth volume in their series of writings collectively titled *English Local Government from the Revolution to the Municipal Corporations*. As he notes, Shaw wrote the preface, which was characteristically lengthy.

drawing, and quartering: dragging and cutting the criminal's body into pieces.

272 *wheels and gibbets*: wheels were torture devices upon which the criminal's body was broken, while gibbets were poles used to expose executed bodies.

Calibanism (in Browning's sense): Shaw refers here to Robert Browning's (1812–89) poem 'Caliban upon Setebos' (1864), which describes Caliban, the native 'savage' in Shakespeare's *The Tempest* (1611). Caliban creates the godly figure Setebos, to whom he ascribes his own qualities of jealousy and impulsiveness.

les gens d'église: directly translated from French, this means 'the people of the Church', but it more specifically refers to the clergy.

Laodiceanism: politically or religiously indifferent. In Revelation 3: 14–16, the Laodiceans are condemned for their indifference.

272 *Henry Nevinson*: campaigning journalist and social activist Henry Nevinson (1856–1941).

Gallio ... Machiavelli: Junius Gallio (*c.* 5 BCE–65 CE) was the Roman official who dismissed the Jews' charges against the apostle Paul in Acts 18: 12–17. Italian statesman Niccolò Machiavelli (1469–1527) is renowned for the cynical political realism he promotes in his treatise *The Prince* (1513).

273 *a step across the Rubicon*: an idiomatic expression meaning to take a decisive and irrevocable step. The Rubicon was a small stream dividing Italy and Gaul. In crossing the Rubicon in 49 BCE, Julius Caesar's forces were in effect declaring war on Gaul. Caesar understood the importance of this act: upon breaching the frontier, he reportedly stated *iacta alea est* (the die is cast), which has the same meaning as 'crossing the Rubicon'.

Apostolic Succession: doctrine that bishops form a direct and uninterrupted continuity with Jesus's Apostles and thus bear divine sanction.

Bruno: the Italian philosopher and scientist Giordano Bruno (1548–1600), who promoted the Copernican heliocentric model of the universe (see note to p. 254), was burned at the stake for heresy.

the letter of a Catholic priest: while Shaw worked on *Saint Joan*, he corresponded with Father Joseph Leonard (1877–1964), a Catholic priest and teacher at St Mary's College, Hammersmith. The two men had met in 1919 while vacationing in Parknasilla, Co. Kerry. Shaw used Father Leonard's quote that follows after allowing him to amend it before publication. Letter of 25 May 1924, in *CL* iii. 876.

274 *'Though He slay me ... before Him'*: Job 13: 15. Shaw originally included this verse as the play's epigraph; see note to p. 245.

the Chair and the Keys: Shaw refers here to the office of the Pope. In Matthew 16: 19, Jesus promised to give St Peter, the first pope, the keys to heaven, which are depicted on the coat of arms of the Vatican.

275 *Ibsen's law of change*: in Ibsen's play *Little Eyolf* (1894), the protagonist Alfred Allmers coins the phrase 'law of change' to refer to the inevitable transformations that people and their relationships undergo over time.

Abernethy: English doctor John Abernethy (1764–1831) argued that many diseases were the result of digestive problems and accordingly prescribed purging and strict diets. He even created and promoted a digestive biscuit, appropriately called the Abernethy biscuit.

Archbishop Laud: William Laud (1573–1645), the Archbishop of Canterbury and adviser to Charles I (1600–49), severely persecuted Puritans. With the country's descent into civil war, his zeal eventually resulted in his execution.

276 *Church of England ... Church of her own*: in 1521, Pope Leo X (1475–1521) excommunicated Martin Luther in his papal bull *Decet Romanum Pontificem* after ordering Luther to recant his deviations from the Church in an earlier bull, *Exsurge Domini*, in 1520. The Church of England broke away from the papacy in 1534, following Rome's refusal to approve the

annulment of the marriage of Henry VIII (1491–1547) and Catherine of Aragon (1485–1536).

Butler's Erewhon: Samuel Butler's satirical utopia *Erewhon* (1872). The novel's title is an anagram of 'nowhere', which is the etymological equivalent of 'utopia', derived from the Greek *u* (no) and *topos* (place).

Pasteurians . . . Sanitarians: to curb the spread of disease, Pasteurians favoured inoculations whereas Sanitarians promoted developing sewage systems. Modern medicine and public health embrace the two viewpoints.

277 *constitutional change . . . to effect itself*: the insurrectionists in Ireland sought independence. The British government finally granted Irish independence under the terms of the Anglo-Irish Treaty (1922), after many Home Rule Bills had failed to do so.

Black and Tans: named after their makeshift uniforms composed of dark military shirts and khaki pants, the Black and Tans were the British recruits enrolled in the Royal Irish Constabulary from January 1920 to July 1921. They were mobilized to combat the Irish Republican Army during the Anglo-Irish War (1919–21) and quickly acquired a reputation for brutal reprisals.

United States . . . after 1917: in the United States, the years following the Russian Revolution led to the first 'Red Scare', so named because people were afraid of the Communists, whose identifying colour is red. While some of it was ethnically focused, the eruption of wide-scale labour activities and strikes in 1919 caused the authorities to crack down on Socialists and Communists more generally.

Holy Sepulchre . . . Saracens: Shaw refers here to the Crusades, the military expeditions first launched by European Christians in the late eleventh century to fight the spread of Islam and to regain control of the Holy Land. The church of the Holy Sepulchre is built on the traditional site of Jesus's crucifixion and burial in the Old City of Jerusalem. In the Middle Ages, Muslims were known as Saracens.

Star Chamber: in English law, the Court of Star Chamber falls under the monarch's prerogative and thus is not bound by the common law. As a result, it has achieved a reputation for oppression.

278 *Habeas Corpus Act*: passed in 1679, the Habeas Corpus Act ensures that a prisoner is not unlawfully detained and has a right to appear before the courts.

Defence of The Realm Act: passed just after the outbreak of war in August 1914, the Defence of the Realm Act, also known by its acronym DORA, suspended many normal rights and allowed the government greater powers, such as the ability to requisition property and to censor the press.

280 *Garibaldi . . . Caprera*: republican military leader Giuseppe Garibaldi (1807–82) contributed to the unification of Italy. In 1855, he bought the island of Caprera, which lies just off the Sardinian coast, where he lived out his final years in declining health.

282 *Betelgeuse*: a red supergiant that forms part of the constellation Orion, Betelgeuse is one of the largest known stars; it is 950 times bigger than the earth's Sun.

knock . . . into a cocked hat: to beat or defeat soundly. A cocked hat, which was a popular headwear at the end of the eighteenth century, has an upturned brim and tends to have three corners, making it triangular in shape.

Encyclopædia Britannica: see note to p. 5. The edition to which Shaw refers is the twelfth, which was published in 1922 and ran to thirty-two volumes.

283 *Uffizi in Florence*: the Uffizi Gallery in Florence houses what is generally considered to be one of the world's finest collections of Italian Renaissance paintings.

Châteaudun: Dunois owned and resided in the Château (Castle) of Châteaudun, which is in the Eure-et-Loir department.

Shakespear . . . Macduff: Shaw refers here to historical figures depicted in Shakespeare's *King John* (1594–6) and *Macbeth*.

John of Gaunt . . . Drake: John of Gaunt (1340–99) was an English prince whose name was derived from his birthplace, the Belgian city of Ghent. He appears as an elderly sick man in Shakespeare's *Richard II* (1595–6). Sir Francis Drake (c.1540/3–96) was renowned as a seaman who circumnavigated the earth. Drake and many of the men of his fleet died of fever in the West Indies.

The divinity . . . how we will: in the opening of the final scene of *Hamlet*, the eponymous character says: 'There's a divinity that shapes our ends, | Rough-hew them how we will' (V. ii. 11–12).

Lemaître: Jean Lemaître was the vice-inquisitor for northern France. Viewing Joan's trial as political, he refused to attend until he was forced to do so.

284 *King Maker*: Richard Neville (1428–71) was the 16th Earl of Warwick. He was known as 'kingmaker' for his role as arbiter between the houses of Lancaster and York during the Wars of the Roses (1455–85).

to their own selves be true . . . false to any man: another line from *Hamlet*, in this case uttered by Polonius when he dispenses fatherly advice to his son Laertes: 'This above all: to thine ownself be true, | And it must follow, as the night the day, | Thou canst not then be false to any man' (I. iii. 84–6).

diabiolus ex machina . . . deus ex machina: Latin for 'God out of the machine', *deus ex machina* is a theatrical term for a contrived solution to a difficult situation. It generally takes the form of the unexpected arrival of a person or an event. It has its roots in Greek drama wherein a god would suddenly appear from the sky (via a crane, hence 'out of the machine') to resolve the plot. Shaw substitutes God (*deus*) for the Devil (*diabolus*).

Tokyo earthquake: the Tokyo–Yokohama earthquake, which struck on 1 September 1923, had a magnitude of 7.9 and an estimated death toll of more than 140,000.

286 *Matheson Lang ... The Wandering Jew*: Canadian Matheson Lang (1879–1948) was a popular actor in movies and on the British stage. One of his most remembered roles was as the eponymous hero of *The Wandering Jew* (1920), by Temple Thurston (1879–1933); he also played the character in the silent film version (1923).

287 *curse of Adam*: in Genesis 3: 17, God condemns Adam to a life of toil for having eaten the forbidden fruit from the tree of knowledge.

288 *I do not give them performances twelve hours long*: Shaw's five-cycle play *Back to Methuselah*, written only a year earlier in 1922, comes close to doing so; it begins in the Garden of Eden and ends in the year 31920 CE.

Ober-Ammergau: since the seventeenth century, the villagers of Oberammergau, a town in the Bavarian alps, have performed a passion play, a religious drama that depicts the trial, suffering, death, and resurrection of Jesus Christ.

289 *Aristotelian moments*: Shaw refers here to the rhetorical, discursive, and philosophical aspects of his play, which are, as he admits in his preface, long and devoid of physical action. The adjective is derived from Greek philosopher and scientist Aristotle (384–322 BCE).

291 *military squire ... storming terribly*: this passage originally read: 'youngish gentleman with more energy than he can work off in the routine of his military command and housekeeping in his castle of Vaucouleurs, is expending its superfluity in storming' (SJ Proof 2).

mullioned ... window: a mullion is a dividing bar in a window.

your Maker: Shaw originally wrote 'God' but changed it in the typescript to 'your Maker' (SJ Folio).

292 *Barbary hens*: hens that come from the north coast of Africa, formerly a region referred to as Barbary. The etymological roots of the word are the same as 'barbarous', which was the predominant European perspective of the Islamic peoples who lived there.

293 *give her a good hiding*: in Shaw's research notes, this line appears as 'box her ears' (SJ Notes).

can do it: Shaw deleted a stage direction that followed this line: '*He drags the steward towards the door*' (SJ Proof 2).

parcel of curs: a bunch or a group of low-bred dogs.

294 *[bobbing a curtsey]*: a curtsey is generally a slow action, a mark of respect paid by women to people in authority by bending their knees and lowering their body. Bobbing, however, is a quick and fluid up-and-down action, indicating that Joan is energetic, impatient, and not given to formal signs of respect to those who normally merit them.

from my Lord: in her initial exchanges from her introduction to being sent back into the yard, Shaw directs Joan to speak at a slow pace because she 'must soothe the audience' (RN SJ n.d.).

295 *unwelcome and only too familiar*: Shaw changed this from '*unpleasant*' (SJ Proof 2).

   armor: Shaw's research notes indicate that Joan's 'official armor cost 100 livres' (SJ Notes).

   Bertrand de Poulengey: nicknamed Pollichon, Bertrand de Poulengey was one of Joan's escorts to Chinon.

   John of Metz: Jean de Metz was, like Poulengey, a nobleman who escorted Joan to Chinon.

296 *John Godsave . . . Dick the Archer . . . John of Honecourt . . . Julian*: all of these men accompanied Joan to Chinon, with the exception of John Godsave.

   lymphatic: pale and sluggish. In ancient medicine, there were four humours, that is, fluids of the body that were linked to people's health: blood, phlegm, yellow bile, and black bile. Their relative proportions in the body were thought to determine the person's characteristics. Phlegm belonged to the lymph, so someone who was considered lymphatic or phlegmatic was said to suffer from an excess of phlegm, which was supposed to lead to sluggishness.

   obstinate: Shaw changed this from '*amiably obstinate*' (SJ Proof 2).

   self-assertive, loud-mouthed: between these adjectives, Shaw earlier included 'ready tongued' (SJ Proof 2).

   makes way for him: Shaw originally wrote '*makes way for him servilely*' (SJ Proof 2).

   ruminatively: contemplatively, thoughtfully.

297 *bourgeoise*: as de Baudricourt explains, a bourgeois(e) is a person socially ranked between a peasant and a gentleman.

   Duke of Bedford: John Plantagenet (1389–1435), the Duke of Bedford, commanded the English forces in France during Joan's time.

   his mother: Isabeau of Bavaria (1371–1435) was regent of France for periods of time because of her husband Charles VI's insanity. She was the signatory of the Treaty of Troyes, which recognized Henry V (1387–1422) of England as heir to the French crown, in place of her own son, Charles VII, the Dauphin. Dauphin is the title for the eldest son of the King of France.

298 *she married her daughter to the English king*: Catherine de Valois (1401–37) was married to Henry V in 1420, once the Treaty of Troyes had been signed.

   Well, she married . . . But thanks to her: this exchange was inserted in the proofs. Formerly, Poulengey continued: 'And the old king was mad. Can you expect soldiers to fight for such a Dauphin when he has never been crowned king?' (SJ Proof 2).

   the Bastard . . . Montargis: Shaw's research notes indicate: 'Dunois, Bastard of Orleans 26, had defeated the English under Warwick at Montargis in 1427 (at 25)' (SJ Notes). Montargis, a city located in the Loiret department, was the site of an important attempted siege by English forces throughout the summer of 1427. The victory under Dunois's command, his first, marked a positive turn for the French forces.

You think the girl can work miracles, do you?: Shaw directs Robert to emphasize 'miracles' (RN SJ 1924).

Her words . . . fire into me: Shaw copied this passage almost word for word from his research, changing only the ending from 'God inflamed me' (SJ Notes).

299 *irresoluteness . . . decisiveness*: in the proofs, de Baudricourt's irresoluteness is 'fundamental' and his decisiveness is 'superficial' (SJ Proof 2).

dilatory: hesitant or delayed with an intent to defer decision or action.

Jenny: the people of Joan's village referred to her by the French diminutive Jeannette.

300 *we all speak French*: another historical anachronism. In Joan's day, France was a patchwork of regions that had their own dialects and languages distinct from French, which many people were not able to speak. Joan's Lorraine, for example, still has many living speakers of Lorrain (a dialect of Oïl, a Gallo-Romance language) and Lorraine Franconian (a Germanic dialect).

Checkmate: in chess, checkmate is the final move of the game, when the king cannot escape being taken.

No fear!: this appears as 'Gammon!' in the proofs (SJ Proof 2). Gammon is a decisive victory in the board game backgammon; it is an echo of Poulengey's 'Checkmate' that precedes it. Shaw's change indicates that de Baudricourt has not yet given in to Joan.

301 *Black Prince . . . English king's father*: Edward the Black Prince (1330–76) commanded the English to victory at the Battle of Poitiers (1356), where the French king, John II (1319–64), was captured for ransom. The Black Prince was the heir apparent to his father, Edward III (1312–77), but he died before acceding to the throne, leaving it to his son, Richard II (1367–1400). As the king of England in 1429 was Henry VI, his father was Henry V, who led the English forces to important victories at Harfleur and Agincourt in 1415 and the conquest of Normandy by 1419, the latter leading directly to the French concessions of the Treaty of Troyes.

Damn you, I am not afraid: Shaw directs Robert to say this with 'surprise' at Joan's charge (RN SJ n.d.).

302 *Do you know why they are called goddams?*: Shaw directs Robert, when saying this, to 'drop the tone' (RN SJ n.d.).

perdition: spiritual damnation.

This may be all rot, Polly: Shaw directs Robert to say this 'slowly & thoughtfully' (RN SJ n.d.).

put fight into him: Shaw directs Robert to emphasize 'him' (RN SJ n.d.).

And there is something: Shaw directs Poulengey to emphasize 'is' (RN SJ n.d.).

303 *to boot*: slang for 'also'.

304 *Touraine*: a historical French province, coextensive with the department of Indre-et-Loire and including small areas of Loir-et-Cher and Indre. Its capital was Tours, to the south-west of which lies Chinon.

antechamber: a small room leading to a larger one, normally used for waiting before access is granted to the latter.

Archbishop of Rheims: at the time, Regneault Chartres (1380–1444).

the Lord Chamberlain, Monseigneur de la Trémouille: Shaw's research notes indicate that in '1433 Yolande & the Constable (Richard) killed La T' (SJ Notes). Georges de La Trémoille (*c*.1382–1446), not Trémouille, was a powerful nobleman who had influence over Charles VII. A chamberlain is a male attendant for someone of royal or noble standing, while Lord Chamberlain is the title of the senior officer of the royal household.

dignity: Shaw originally had him stand with '*comparative dignity*' (SJ Proof 2).

curate: a parish clergyman, well below an archbishop in church hierarchy.

mutton: sheep flesh.

305 *may my soul*: Shaw directs La Hire to 'pick it out' (RN SJ n.d.).

306 *But he is neither vulgar nor stupid*: this originally read: '*His small rickety figure and spindle shanks make it impossible for him to achieve the dignity of hearing proper to his exalted person. He is not stupid . . .*' (SJ Proof 2).

garrison: fortress or stronghold.

Charles the Wise: Shaw's research notes state: 'Charles V the Wise 1337–1380 brother Philip the Bold of Burgundy d. 1404' (SJ Notes).

308 *Marie de Maillé . . . Gasque of Avignon*: Jeanne-Marie de Maillé (1331–1414) was renowned for her chastity and earnest devotion to attaining spiritual perfection. Marie Robine (d. 1399), the Gasque of Avignon, was a visionary, not a saint; one of her visions foretold of an armed maid who would rid France of the English.

I hope not: on three separate occasions during rehearsals, Shaw directed the actor: 'I HOPE not' (RN SJ n.d.).

We can easily find out whether she is an angel or not: originally, 'Give the saint a chance' (SJ Proof 2).

309 *the Channel*: the English Channel is the body of water that separates France and England.

bridgehead: a fortification that protects a bridge.

310 *spunk*: courage.

But that would not be a miracle at all: Shaw directs La Trémouille to say this line with 'Spunk' (RN SJ 1924).

311 *the fat would be in the fire*: a colloquial expression alluding to fat being dropped into a fire and causing a burst of flame, this means that something injudicious has been said or done, provoking an immense amount of trouble.

clay: body.

312 *a dais*: a stage. The sentence originally then went on to describe the chairs: '*with canopies, all of carved wood, painted and gilt*' (SJ Proof 2).

Duchess de la Trémouille: Catherine de l'Isle Bouchard (c.1399–1472) was La Trémouille's second wife.

page at the door: originally, Shaw then described the page: '*He is as haughty before the full Court as he was respectful in private*' (SJ Proof 2).

halberd: weapon consisting of a battle-axe mounted on a long staff.

the Duke of Vendôme: the Count of Vendôme (not the Duke) was Louis I (1376–1446), also known as Louis of Bourbon. He fought alongside Joan at Orléans.

is led in . . . the Dauphin: originally, this read: '*enters eagerly. She stops to take in the scene, and finds where the Dauphin is*' (SJ Proof 2).

313 *Coom*: 'come', in the North Country dialect that Joan speaks in Shaw's play.

Gentle little Dauphin: when Joan says this line, Shaw directs the rest of the cast: 'Fffff!' (RN SJ 1924).

The old fox blushes: Shaw directs Bluebeard: 'dont chuck it over your shoulder' (RN SJ 1924).

314 *I may as well be hanged for a sheep as a lamb*: a colloquial expression meaning that because the punishment for doing or saying two things is the same, one might as well commit the worse of them.

315 *wholly*: Shaw added this adverb in the proofs (SJ Proof 2).

not to gibe at my wife: Shaw directs La Trémouille to be 'gruff & grum here' (RN SJ 1924). To gibe is to sneer.

Who be old Gruff-and-Grum?: Shaw directs Joan: 'fun' (RN SJ n.d.).

Art afraid?: Shaw directs Joan: 'deep measured tone' (RN SJ n.d.).

not fighting: Shaw directs Charles to emphasize 'not' (RN SJ 1924).

quiet and sensible: Shaw originally wrote 'meek and timid' (SJ Folio).

316 *So if you are going to say 'Son of St Louis . . . victory'*: Shaw directs Charles to 'go up on' this line (RN SJ 1924). Louis IX (1214–70), also known as St Louis since he was canonized on 11 August 1297, led the Seventh Crusade to the Holy Land (1248–50) and died on another crusade in Tunisia.

spare your breath to cool your porridge: colloquial expression meaning 'be quiet' or 'don't bother saying what you have said or count on saying'.

Blethers!: Nonsense!

noddle: head.

holy oil has been poured on his hair: anointing a monarch during the coronation ceremony granted them the benediction of God.

Queen: Charles's queen consort was Marie of Anjou (1404–63).

317 *descending*: originally, the Dauphin was '*petulantly descending*' (SJ Proof 2) and he did not move away from Joan.

317 *Louis the Eleventh*: Louis XI (1423–83) continued his father's efforts to unify France following the Hundred Years War.

horrid boy . . . beast: Louis was known for his ugliness. Impatient to rule, he led a revolt against his father, known as the Praguerie, in 1440. Charles pardoned Louis and later sent him to live in exile.

and that is a miracle that will take some doing it seems: Shaw originally wrote 'and God only knows how I am to do it' (SJ Folio).

Anne: Shaw errs here. As noted earlier, Charles's wife is Marie of Anjou.

318 *Judas . . . betray me and Him*: one of the Twelve Apostles, Judas Iscariot (d. *c*.30 CE) betrayed Jesus.

gauntlet: a glove of armour.

319 *except . . . cursing*: originally, the Archbishop and La Trémouille also knelt (SJ Proof 2).

320 *pennon*: a long triangular flag.

bend sinister: in heraldry, a bend is a band that runs from the bearer's top right to the bottom left. A bend sinister is a band that runs from the bearer's left ('left' is *sinister* in Latin); it generally indicates bastardy.

Strumpet: harlot, whore.

wanton: disobedient or unmanageable, but also, in keeping with the misogyny of Dunois's curse of the wind as female, sexually promiscuous or unfaithful.

kingfisher: a small bird with colourful plumage and a long, pointed beak.

321 *snood*: a hood or hairband; the Virgin Mary is often depicted wearing a blue mantle or veil.

Hither: come.

rushes in in a blazing rage: originally this read: '*comes in quickly from the westward. She looks displeased*' (SJ Proof 2).

[cool and stern, pointing to his shield]: originally this read: '*stretching his baton towards the bar on his shield*' (SJ Proof 2).

322 *I say so*: originally, before Dunois says this, Shaw provided stage directions for him: '*not liking this*' (SJ Proof 2).

323 *I will never take a husband*: Shaw directs Joan to emphasize 'never' and to say the line with 'assertion' (RN SJ 1924).

breach of promise: the breaking of a legal promise to marry. The historical Joan was charged with such a breach.

My sword . . . church of St Catherine: Joan was said to have been directed by her voices to find her sword behind the altar of the church of St Catherine at Fierbois, in the Indre-et-Loire department, en route from Vaucouleurs to Chinon.

sally: a sudden rush to attack an enemy.

on this side: in the typescript, Shaw included a long discussion here between Dunois and Joan regarding the proper tactics and strategy for attacking the English fortifications at Orléans. Shaw cut this to sharpen the dialogue and to make Joan more assertive in her instructions (SJ Folio). Bryan Tyson discusses this emendation in *The Story of Shaw's Saint Joan* (Montreal: McGill-Queen's University Press, 1982), 32–3.

324 *I will pray*: Shaw directs Joan: 'eager' (RN SJ n.d.).

Seigneur: (Fr.) Lord.

326 *illuminated Book of Hours*: a Book of Hours is a devotional book 'containing prayers or offices appointed for certain hours of the day, days of the week' (*OED*). Many wealthy patrons commissioned these during the Middle Ages, beginning in the thirteenth century. As Warwick explains, illuminated in this sense means that the book is illustrated with any combination of decorative letters, borders, and drawings.

bonny: attractive; from the French *bonne*, meaning 'good'.

[poohpoohing]: dismissing or ridiculing.

But we are still being defeated: Shaw directs de Stogumber to emphasize 'still' and that he should not speak too quickly from 'I must say, my lord' to this speech (RN SJ 1924).

Jargeau, Meung, Beaugency ... Patay: all decisive victories for the French forces in the Loire campaign; they occurred in quick succession, from 10 to 18 June 1429.

butchered at Patay, and Sir John Talbot taken prisoner: Shaw notes that Talbot was the 1st Earl of Shrewsbury and was 'either 35 or 45 in 1428' and 'head of Ireland 1414–19'. Shaw describes him as 'pigheaded, pugnacious, violent, cruel'. He 'got the English defeated at Patay, where he was taken prisoner' and was 'compared to Herod by the Irish' (SJ Notes). Talbot's birth year is still uncertain; he died in 1453.

327 *serf*: a peasant who is tied to a feudal lord.

cassock: a priest's robe.

my pilgrimage to the Holy Land: Warwick made his pilgrimage in 1408, returning to England in 1410.

the Conqueror: William I (*c*.1028–87), also known as William the Conqueror. A Norman duke, William invaded and conquered England in 1066, becoming king of the country on Christmas Day of that year.

diocese: the religious jurisdiction of a bishop.

328 *a king's ransom*: a large sum of money.

that slut!: Shaw directs de Stogumber to 'spit it out' (RN SJ 1924).

Earl of Warwick: Shaw's research notes indicate that Warwick 'was 46 in 1428', was 'Pilgrim to Jerusalem & Knight errant', 'travelled across south & central Europe', was 'courtly, ambassador, diplo.', and 'took Henry VI to France in 1430 & superintended Joan's trial' (SJ Notes).

John de Stogumber: despite the biographical details provided, the character of John de Stogumber was Shaw's invention.

328 *Cardinal of Winchester*: Henry Beaufort (*c.*1374–1447), half-brother of Henry IV and uncle of Henry V, rose to considerable power, becoming Chancellor of Oxford University in 1397 and Chancellor of England in 1403; appointed bishop of Winchester in 1404, he was made a cardinal in 1426.

329 *Catholic court*: an international court governed by the Catholic Church.

330 *flower of courtesy*: epitome of chivalry. In Shakespeare's *Romeo and Juliet*, Juliet's nurse says Romeo 'is not the flower of courtesy, | but, I'll warrant him, gentle as a lamb' (II. v. 45–6).

Talbot is a mere fighting animal: Shaw's research notes include the quote 'Talbot our good dog' (SJ Notes).

Beelzebub: prince of the devils.

Sir William Glasdale: commander of the English forces, Glasdale insulted Joan when she demanded that he quit Orléans; shortly after, he fell from the walls and drowned in the Loire.

331 *he strikes at the Catholic Church*: Shaw directs Cauchon: 'climax' (RN SJ n.d.).

[fiercely]: the stage directions originally indicated '*overwhelming him*' (SJ Proof 2).

She is a heretic: Shaw directs Cauchon to yell: 'She is a heretic!!!' (RN SJ 1936).

332 *my first duty is to seek this girl's salvation*: Shaw's notes indicate that Cauchon was 'determined to seek her salvation' (SJ Notes).

the secular arm: the state or the civil power, as distinct from the Catholic Church.

333 *My lord … [he sits … submissive gesture]*: instead of speaking or being described this way, there were only stage directions for the chaplain: '*intimidated, makes an effort to speak, but can find no words, and sits down*' (SJ Proof 2).

In your language … English interests: this echoes Shaw's arguments in defence of Roger Casement during Casement's trial for treason. Shaw reasoned that he could not be a traitor to England because he was an Irishman.

I am sorry: I did not understand: Shaw directs Cauchon: 'amused & ironic, conciliatory' (RN SJ n.d.).

[resuming his seat, much relieved]: the stage directions originally read: '*to avoid an awkward silence*' (SJ Proof 2).

grow a very thick skin: become less sensitive.

334 *She sends letters to the king of England*: Joan sent her first letter to Henry V on 22 March 1429. Her correspondence was read at her fifth examination, on 1 March 1431 (Murray, 36–8).

A beggar on horseback!: proverb that continues 'will ride to hell'. It means that one who has recently accumulated wealth tends to be arrogant and irresponsible.

WcLeef: Wycliffe. See note to p. 268.

Arab camel driver: the prophet Muhammad.

Jerusalem: in the proofs, this appears as 'Byzantium' (SJ Proof), which is one of the former names of Istanbul, Turkey.

Pyrenees . . . damnation: the Muslim conquest of Spain began in 711. They advanced well into France until they were defeated by the Franks at the Battle of Tours in 732, after which they retreated to the other side of the Pyrenees, the mountain range that forms a natural border between Spain and France.

335 *Men go to the East . . . Saracen*: Shaw appears to allude here to T. E. Lawrence (1888–1935), also known as Lawrence of Arabia, who led the Arab forces against the Turkish army in the First World War. From 1922, Lawrence became a close friend of Shaw and Shaw's wife Charlotte, accepting their editorial suggestions for his book *The Seven Pillars of Wisdom* and changing his name to T. E. Shaw in 1927.

Englishmen heretics!!!: before this line, Shaw gave de Stogumber stage directions: '*fearfully taken aback*' (SJ Proof 2).

336 *liveried courtiers*: employees of the court who wear uniforms, or livery, to indicate their master.

337 *[conciliatory, dropping his polemical tone]*: originally, '*earnestly, dropping his debating tone*' (SJ Proof 2).

the pink of courtesy: like 'the flower of courtesy', this means chivalric, reverential; the line appears in Shakespeare's *Romeo and Juliet* when Mercutio says, 'I am the very pink of courtesy', to which Romeo responds, 'Pink for flower' (II. iv. 59–60).

338 *the woman is a rebel*: Shaw directs de Stogumber to emphasize 'rebel!!!' (RN SJ 1924).

Sancta simplicitas!: (Lat.) 'Holy simplicity!', an expression of astonishment at a person's naïvety. Here and throughout the play, Cauchon views de Stogumber as rather primitive.

339 *ambulatory*: a place for walking in, but more specifically the covered passage behind the altar of a cathedral or large church.

stations of the cross: a series of fourteen images depicting the Passion of Christ, beginning with Jesus's condemnation and ending with his burial in the tomb.

nave: the central part of a church that extends from the main entrance; it is where most of the congregation sits.

vestry: the room where the clergy dress.

Come, Joan!: before Dunois says this, Shaw originally provided him with stage directions: '*clapping her on the shoulder*' (SJ Proof 2).

just as you are in your food and drink, my little saint: Shaw directs Dunois that this is an 'affectionate afterthought' (RN SJ 1924).

340 *dug-outs*: retired officers recalled for temporary military service.

It is in the bells I hear my voices: Shaw's research notes indicate 'voices in the bells' (SJ Notes).

342 *my old sheep dog*: before Joan's next sentence, Shaw originally provided stage directions: '*They all laugh, except La Hire, who nods understandingly*' (SJ Proof 2).

I shall last only a year from the beginning: Shaw's research notes provide a quote from one source: 'I shall last but one year and no more' (SJ Notes).

343 *hubris*: excessive pride; in Greek tragedy, hubris is punished by the gods and leads to the hero's downfall.

344 *angelus*: in the Catholic faith, an angelus bell is traditionally rung in the evening to call people to pray.

strike while the iron is hot: act while circumstances are favourable.

flags: flagstones, which are flat and often used for floors and pathways.

I think that God . . . we conquered: Shaw directs Joan: 'in your rage, beam at him'. She is to change as he begins 'But I tell you as a soldier' (RN SJ 1924).

345 *Ah!*: before she utters this word, Shaw originally gave Joan stage directions: 'triumphantly' (SJ Proof 2).

If ifs . . . tinkers: the more classical form of this phrase is a rhyme: 'If ifs and ands were pots and pans, there'd be no work for tinkers' hands.' It is a response to a conditional expression of overconfidence. A tinker is an itinerant artisan who mends metal household utensils.

346 *Alexander*: king of Macedonia, Alexander the Great (356–323 BCE) led campaigns that conquered Egypt and the eastern Mediterranean, over-threw the Persian Empire, and advanced his forces as far as India.

Agincourt . . . Poitiers and Crecy: all three are important battles in the Hundred Years War won by the English. Agincourt (25 October 1415), Poitiers (19 September 1356), and Crécy (26 August 1346) were well before Dunois's time as a leader, meaning that he learned from their lessons through history.

Ouareek: Warwick.

Eh, laddie: Shaw directs Joan to 'drop the tone' here (RN SJ n.d.).

347 *The University of Paris*: founded *c.*1170, the University of Paris was supported by Rome and was a centre of orthodox Catholic teaching.

349 *the hate in yours*: Shaw directs Joan to emphasize 'hate' and to 'throw it at them' (RN SJ 1924).

350 *30th May 1431*: Joan's trial concluded on 29 May; she was burned on 30 May.

obtuse angle: greater than 90 but less than 180 degrees.

canons: clergymen generally attached to a cathedral.

The court is shielded . . . curtains: this originally read: '*To shield the court from the weather, screens have been placed behind the chairs, with a specially high one, decorated with the Bishop's armorial bearings, behind the judicial ones*' (SJ Proof 2).

Pious Peter . . . pickled pepper: the Page is light-heartedly mocking Cauchon. The phrase is adapted from a common nursery rhyme tongue-twister:

Peter Piper picked a peck of pickled peppers.
A peck of pickled peppers Peter Piper picked.
If Peter Piper picked a peck of pickled peppers,
Where's the peck of pickled peppers Peter Piper picked?

351 *John D'Estivet . . . Bayeux*: Jean d'Estivet was canon of the cathedrals of Bayeux and Beauvais, Cauchon being bishop of the latter.

vulpine: similar to a fox, that is, cunning.

captured: Joan was taken by the Burgundians on 23 May 1430, which was a little over a year earlier than the scene takes place.

three months: Joan was passed into Cauchon's hands by 3 January 1431, which was over four months earlier.

eleven weeks: Joan was interrogated on several occasions between 21 February and 24 March; the trial proper began around 25 March. The interrogation therefore started fourteen weeks earlier and the trial nine and a half weeks earlier.

352 *I hope not*: originally, 'I have given them no ground for any such intentions' (SJ Proof 2).

Men have dared: Shaw directs d'Estivet to emphasize 'dared' (RN SJ n.d.).

353 *I fear damnation*: Shaw directs Cauchon to emphasize 'fear', underlining it three times (RN SJ 1936).

354 *Canon de Courcelles*: Thomas de Courcelles (1400–69) was at the time the canon of Laon. He later became dean of the cathedral of Notre-Dame de Paris, and delivered the funeral oration for Charles VII in 1461, having become close to the monarch.

Some of the assessors . . . begin formally: this originally read: '*The assessors take their seats, each one bobbing his head perfunctorily to the Bishop before sitting down*' (SJ Proof 2).

in dudgeon: in indignation, resentment.

I am the culprit: Shaw directs the Inquisitor to emphasize 'I' (RN SJ 1924).

very great nonsense: Shaw directs Courcelles to play to this line (RN SJ 1924).

sixty-four articles cut down to twelve—: Shaw's research notes correctly indicate that seventy articles, not sixty-four, were reduced to twelve (SJ Notes).

355 *the blessed saints . . . spoke to her in French*: Shaw's research notes indicate 'Angels & Archangels & Saints speak French' (SJ Notes). In Joan's fifth examination, on 1 March 1431, when asked whether St Margaret spoke in English, Joan responded: 'Why should she speak English, when she is not on the English side?' (Murray, 40).

The Maid stole the Bishop of Senlis's horse: this was a point discussed in Joan's sixth examination, on 3 March 1431 (Murray, 51–2). Senlis is in the Oise department.

356 *dancings round fairy trees . . . magic wells*: Joan was asked about the Fairy Tree in her third examination, on 24 February 1431. She noted that people

came from all around to drink the spring that ran nearby to heal their ailments and that she and the other children decorated the tree and danced and sang around it (Murray, 20–1).

356 *LADVENU*: Martin Ladvenu, who was about 30 years old at the time, was appointed Joan's confessor.

Heresy begins: Shaw directs: 'Heresy begins' (RN SJ n.d.).

357 *yet they all began*: Shaw directs: 'yet they all began' (RN SJ n.d.).

Therefore . . . compassion: Shaw directs the Inquisitor that this line is 'not a close but a beginning' (RN SJ 1924).

our English friends are supported by no evidence: Shaw directs de Stogumber to play to this line (RN SJ 1924).

This girl: Shaw directs the Inquisitor to emphasize 'This' (RN SJ 1924).

358 *Innumerable lives*: Shaw directs the Inquisitor to emphasize 'Innumerable', underlining it thrice (RN SJ 1924).

unshriven: the state of not having confessed, and thus not being absolved from sin before death.

black death: the pandemic plague that struck Europe from 1347 to 1351, killing an estimated 25 million people.

359 *Moab and Ammon*: both children of incest, Moab was the son of Lot and his eldest daughter, while Ben-Ammi, more commonly known as Ammon, was the son of Lot and his youngest daughter. The followers of both Moab and Ammon were repeatedly in conflict with the Israelites.

the Bishop sent me some carp: Shaw's research notes indicate that Cauchon sent Joan carp (SJ Notes).

360 *silly people*: Shaw directs the others to remark 'Oh I say' (RN SJ 1924).

bled: Shaw notes that Warwick objected to her being bled (SJ Notes). To bleed someone refers to the now antiquated practice of draining their blood to rid one of evil or sickness and make them healthy again.

And why must I be chained by the feet: Shaw directs Joan to 'kick the chain' (RN SJ 1924).

361 *It is great nonsense*: Shaw directs the others to play to it when Joan speaks this line (RN SJ 1924).

I have warned you . . . pert answers: Shaw directs Cauchon to say this gently, not as a brutal admonishment (RN SJ 1924). On another occasion, he directs him to say it slowly and deeply (RN SJ n.d.).

I am weary of this argument: Shaw directs Joan to emphasize 'weary' (RN SJ 1924).

she should be put to the torture: Shaw's research notes indicate 'Courcelles wanted to torture her' (SJ Notes).

If you tear me . . . what is the use of it?: this was Joan's response under questioning on 2 May 1431 (Murray, 117). When the assessors met on 12 May, the majority, including Cauchon, did not recommend torture; Thomas de Courcelles was one of the two who did recommend it (Murray, 118).

362 *pleasure*: Shaw directs Courcelles to emphasize 'pleasure' (RN SJ 1924).

Thou art a rare noodle, Master: Shaw directs the others to 'Play to noodle' (RN SJ 1924). In a rehearsal for a later production, Shaw directs Joan to 'have a fleck of her old fun & fire' (RN SJ 1936). On another occasion, he directs her to 'laugh at him' (RN SJ n.d.). A noodle is a colloquial term for a fool or an idiot.

Nay: I am no shepherd lass: Shaw directs Joan to say this with 'offended pride' and on another occasion 'dont forget the vanity' (RN SJ n.d.).

that Burgundian soldier: Shaw's research notes indicate '£1000 + an annuity of £300 to the Burgundian soldier who captured her' (SJ Notes).

363 *Woman . . . heretics*: Shaw directs Cauchon to speak with 'despair in his voice' (RN SJ 1936).

364 *If I am not . . . may God keep me in it!*: this was Joan's response during her third examination, on 24 February 1431 (Murray, 18).

365 *I share the impatience*: Shaw directs d'Estivet to be 'very obsequious' (RN SJ n.d.), meaning obedient.

Do you think . . . clothes for him?: Shaw took Joan's response here from her fifth examination, on 1 March 1431: 'Do you think God has not the where-withal to clothe him?' (Murray, 42).

366 *Why, yes: what can be plainer commonsense?*: Shaw directs Joan: 'look at him, shew that you think him a fool' (RN SJ n.d.).

I was a soldier . . . with my brothers: Shaw's research notes state: 'She replied that she had assumed it because it seemed to her more suitable to wear man's clothing, being with men, than a woman's dress' (SJ Notes).

we are all trying to save you: Shaw directs Ladvenu to emphasize 'all' and that he should 'dig it more' (RN SJ 1924).

St Athanasius . . . damned: St Athanasius (c.293–373) was the bishop of Alexandria. The Athanasian Creed maintains that salvation requires adherence to the Catholic faith and belief in the Trinity.

367 *Woman: are you quite mad?*: Shaw directs Cauchon to add emphasis: 'QUITE' (RN SJ n.d.).

368 *a single promise*: Shaw directs Ladvenu to emphasize 'single' (RN SJ 1924).

meanwhile: the assessors were originally directed to be '*scandalized*' (SJ Proof 2).

369 *into his chair*: the stage directions originally continued: '*speechless with rage*' (SJ Proof 2).

370 *There!*: Shaw originally followed Joan's line with stage directions: '*She sits down in utter dejection*' (SJ Proof 2). Joan signed her recantation on 24 May 1431 (Murray, 130–2).

370 *the shepherd . . . just persons*: 'I say unto you, that likewise joy shall be in heaven over one sinner that repenteth, more than over ninety and nine just persons, which need no repentance' (Luke 15: 7).

My voices were right: Shaw directs Joan: 'My voices were <u>right</u>!!!' (RN SJ 1924). There was no such dramatic scene at her trial. On 29 May 1431, she was pronounced *in absentia* as lapsed because she had been found wearing a man's dress again. The authorities thereby declared her heretic and excommunicate. She was brought before them on 30 May and her death sentence was then pronounced (Murray, 139–41).

371 *the furnace . . . seven times*: believing that God would deliver them, Shadrach, Meshach, and Abednego refused to pray to King Nebuchadnezzar's gods and idols even when he threatened to burn them. Enraged, Nebuchadnezzar ordered that the furnace be heated seven times hotter than usual and had the three men cast into it. When he found them dancing in the fire with an angel, he called them out and decreed that anyone who offended their God would be killed (Daniel 3: 13–30).

372 *antiphonally*: singing alternately.

leprosy: an infectious disease of the skin tissue that can lead to deformation and erosion of a person's extremities. In Catholicism and other religions, it refers to a tainting influence that, like lepers, must be rejected and shunned for the health of the community.

division of the limbs: a reference to quartering, which is the cutting of a person's body into four parts.

sacrament of penance: a public ritual in which an excommunicated sinner is reconciled with and readmitted into the Catholic Church.

373 *We have proceeded . . . If the English*: Shaw directs the Inquisitor to emphasize 'We' and 'English' (RN SJ 1924).

375 *When the fire . . . save myself*: Shaw's research notes include the quote 'she begged me to descend as the fire was mounting' (SJ Notes).

376 *mystery*: in the typescript, Shaw originally wrote 'trade' and changed this to 'mystery' (SJ Folio).

377 *lancet window*: a narrow window with an arch.

settee: a long upholstered seat with a back and (usually) arms.

bed-clothes: the sheets and blankets that cover a bed.

valance: drapery that hangs from the bed's canopy.

Fouquet's Boccaccio: Jean Fouquet (*c*.1420–*c*.1481) was the pre-eminent French painter of the fifteenth century. He illustrated a French translation of *Des Cas des nobles hommes et femmes* (1458), which translates as *Stories of Noble Men and Women*, by Italian poet and scholar Giovanni Boccaccio (1313–75). As the date suggests, this is another of Shaw's errors in chronology as the book was published two years after the scene takes place.

watchman's rattle: a device that makes a loud sound; it is so named because watchmen (sentry guards on duty) would sound it to alert others of danger.

to justify: in the Catholic faith, to justify is to absolve or to declare someone free of confessed sin.

378 *a bee in your bonnet*: a colloquial expression meaning that the person is obsessed with some matter.

At this inquiry ... all men: Joan's retrial, which investigated the soundness of her first trial, took place from November 1455 to June 1456. On 7 July 1456, Joan was declared innocent and Cauchon was found guilty of convicting an innocent woman.

Is her rehabilitation complete?: Shaw directs: 'complete' (RN SJ n.d.).

379 *Charlemagne ... David*: Charlemagne (Charles the Great) (747–814), also known as Charles I, was crowned 'emperor of the Romans' by the Pope in 800, in direct imitation of the emperors of the Roman Empire, and is regarded as the first Holy Roman Emperor. Like Charlemagne, David, king of Israel, consolidated his empire through war.

I am but a dream that thourt dreaming: Shaw directs Joan to say this 'very distinct' (RN SJ n.d.).

380 *cinders of me?*: Joan originally followed this question with another: 'What has set you dreaming of me this night of all nights?' (SJ Proof 2).

381 *burned*: Shaw directs Joan: 'burnt' (RN SJ n.d.).

Your mother ... your salvation: during this exchange, Shaw directs Charles to tell Joan about her rehabilitation 'as a bit of good news' (RN SJ n.d.). The giant cross in Rouen, beside the church of Joan of Arc, is not on the exact spot where she was burned; the place of her burning is indicated by a sign nearby.

382 *[scrambling ... the bed]*: the original stage direction reads: '*chuckling*' (SJ Proof 2).

I am not dead: Shaw directs Dunois to emphasize 'I' (RN SJ 1924).

chaffering: to bargain or haggle.

383 *an improvised tune*: of the musical score that follows, Shaw wrote in the typescript that 'This key signature in D flat is wrong. It should be G flat. The mistake ran through several editions before I noticed & corrected it' (SJ Folio).

between Dunois and Joan: throughout this scene, Shaw directs the other characters to show 'surprise & interest in the soldier' (RN SJ 1936).

doggrel: a comic verse with an irregular rhythm.

straight from hell: Shaw has the Soldier emphasize 'hell' (RN SJ 1924).

384 *reproaching*: Shaw toyed with changing this to 'blaming' (SJ Proof).

You wont find it so bad, sir: for a depiction of hell that is similar to what the soldier describes, see Act III of Shaw's *Man and Superman*, also referred to as the 'Don Juan in Hell' scene.

chip: tease.

judy: slang for a woman.

385 *age*: changed from 'generation' (SJ Proof 3). The revision avoids Cauchon's line from reading like a rhyming couplet.

386 *Toulouse*: a major city in the south-west of France, Toulouse is the capital of the Haute-Garonne department.

howler: glaring blunder.

cocked up: to be placed in a defiant, boastful manner.

387 *Bishop of Orleans*: Stanislas-Arthur-Xavier Touchet (1848–1926) was appointed bishop of Orléans in 1894 and cardinal in 1922. He is known as 'Joan of Arc's Bishop' for having obtained her beatification by Pius X (1835–1914) on 11 April 1909, her canonization by Benedict XV (1854–1922) on 16 May 1920, and her proclamation as secondary patron saint of France by Pius XI (1857–1939) on 2 March 1922.

Venerable and Blessed: see note to p. 247.

A clerical-looking gentleman ... Mercy Seat: in the Lord Chamberlain's copy, the reader, George S. Street (1867–1936), marked this passage with a long blue line in the margin to indicate that he had an issue with it (SJ LC). In his report, Street noted that he thought that 'Catholics might take exception to the announcement of cannonization [*sic*]', but did not think that there was anything to censor. The next day, the Lord Chamberlain scribbled his response below the report: 'I do not think that there would be any reasonable ground for Catholic complaint, though there may of course be complaints. Passed for Licence' (LCP SJ). The Mercy Seat is the throne of God.

388 *Basilica Vaticana*: St Peter's Basilica in the Vatican.

[raising Joan]: originally, Joan raises herself a few lines later, turning to see the window after de Stogumber remarks the image of Winchester Cathedral (SJ Proof 2).

the statue in Winchester Cathedral: shortly after Joan's canonization, there was a campaign to raise funds for a statue of Joan in Winchester Cathedral. It was meant to make amends for the actions of Henry Beaufort, the Bishop of Winchester who helped to orchestrate Joan's trial, and as a declaration of friendship with the French people. Anglican authorities installed it in 1923.

the statue before Rheims Cathedral: in addition to a statue of Joan leading a charge on her horse just outside of Rheims Cathedral, there is a second, more subdued one of her inside, standing in repose on her sword with her eyes lowered. While the former was completed and installed in 1922, the latter was first exposed in 1902 and only offered to Rheims Cathedral following Joan's beatification in 1909.

389 *thou hast shewn that their hands are guiltless of the death of the soul*: Shaw originally wrote 'thou hast lifted the load of terror from them' (SJ Folio).

The heretic is always better dead: an earlier line was less emphatic: 'The heretic is still better dead' (SJ Proof 2).

The heretic is always ... Spare them: Shaw originally wrote: 'The vengeance of the judge might again be redeemed by the sacrifice of the priest' (SJ Folio).

The Oxford World's Classics Website

www.worldsclassics.co.uk

- Browse the full range of Oxford World's Classics online

- Sign up for our monthly e-alert to receive information on new titles

- Read extracts from the Introductions

- Listen to our editors and translators talk about the world's greatest literature with our Oxford World's Classics audio guides

- Join the conversation, follow us on Twitter at OWC_Oxford

- Teachers and lecturers can order inspection copies quickly and simply via our website

www.worldsclassics.co.uk

American Literature

British and Irish Literature

Children's Literature

Classics and Ancient Literature

Colonial Literature

Eastern Literature

European Literature

Gothic Literature

History

Medieval Literature

Oxford English Drama

Philosophy

Poetry

Politics

Religion

The Oxford Shakespeare

A complete list of Oxford World's Classics, including Authors in Context, Oxford English Drama, and the Oxford Shakespeare, is available in the UK from the Marketing Services Department, Oxford University Press, Great Clarendon Street, Oxford OX2 6DP, or visit the website at www.oup.com/uk/worldsclassics.

In the USA, visit www.oup.com/us/owc for a complete title list.

Oxford World's Classics are available from all good bookshops. In case of difficulty, customers in the UK should contact Oxford University Press Bookshop, 116 High Street, Oxford OX1 4BR.

Jane Austen	Emma
	Persuasion
	Pride and Prejudice
	Sense and Sensibility
Anne Brontë	The Tenant of Wildfell Hall
Charlotte Brontë	Jane Eyre
Emily Brontë	Wuthering Heights
Wilkie Collins	The Moonstone
	The Woman in White
Joseph Conrad	Heart of Darkness and Other Tales
	The Secret Agent
Charles Darwin	The Origin of Species
Charles Dickens	Bleak House
	David Copperfield
	Great Expectations
	Hard Times
George Eliot	Middlemarch
	The Mill on the Floss
Elizabeth Gaskell	Mary Barton
Thomas Hardy	Jude the Obscure
	Tess of the d'Urbervilles
Walter Scott	Ivanhoe
	Waverley
Mary Shelley	Frankenstein
Robert Louis Stevenson	Strange Case of Dr Jekyll and Mr Hyde and Other Tales
Bram Stoker	Dracula
W. M. Thackeray	Vanity Fair
Oscar Wilde	The Picture of Dorian Gray
Wordsworth and Coleridge	Lyrical Ballads